THE WORLD AROUND US

■ EASTERN ■ HEMISPHERE

The world around us is a fascinating place. There is much we can learn about the people who lived long ago. This death mask, for example, was found in the tomb of Tutankhamen, an ancient Egyptian king. He ruled his mighty kingdom more than 3,000 years ago, when he was only 9 years old.

JAMES A. BANKS   JEAN CRAVEN

BARRY K. BEYER   GLORIA LADSON-BILLINGS

GLORIA CONTRERAS   MARY A. McFARLAND

WALTER C. PARKER

MACMILLAN/McGRAW-HILL SCHOOL PUBLISHING COMPANY

NEW YORK   CHICAGO   COLUMBUS

PROGRAM AUTHORS

Dr. James A. Banks
Professor of Education and Director of
the Center for Multicultural Education
University of Washington
Seattle, Washington

Dr. Barry K. Beyer
Professor of Education and American Studies
George Mason University
Fairfax, Virginia

Dr. Gloria Contreras
Professor of Education and Director of
the Office of Multicultural Affairs
University of North Texas
Denton, Texas

Jean Craven
District Coordinator of Curriculum
Development
Albuquerque Public Schools
Albuquerque, New Mexico

Dr. Gloria Ladson-Billings
Assistant Professor of Education
University of Wisconsin
Madison, Wisconsin

Dr. Mary McFarland
Director of Staff Development and
Instructional Coordinator of
Social Studies, K-12
Parkway School District
Chesterfield, Missouri

Dr. Walter C. Parker
Associate Professor of Social
Studies Education and Director
of the Center for the Study of
Civic Intelligence
University of Washington
Seattle, Washington

CONTENT CONSULTANTS

Virginia Arnold
Adjunct Professor of Reading, Language Arts,
and Children's Literature
Virginia Commonwealth University
Richmond, Virginia

Yvonne Beamer
Resource Specialist
Native American Education Program
New York, New York

Joyce Buckner
Director of Elementary Education
Omaha Public Schools
Omaha, Nebraska

Sheila Clarke-Ekong
Director of Special Programming
James S. Coleman African Studies Center
University of California
Los Angeles, California

Walter Enloe
Director of Global Education
University of Minnesota
Minneapolis, Minnesota

Helen P. Gillotte
Associate Professor of English
San Francisco State University
Berkeley, California

Margaret Lippert
Literature Consultant
and Story Teller
North Bend, Washington

Narcita Medina
Reading Specialist
Middle School 135
New York, New York

Harlan Rimmerman
Director of Elementary Education
Kansas City Public Schools
Kansas City, Kansas

Joseph B. Rubin
Director of Reading and Language Arts
Fort Worth Independent School District
Fort Worth, Texas

Clifford E. Trafzer
Professor of Ethnic Studies and Director
of Native American Studies
University of California
Riverside, California

Nancy Winter
Former Member of the Executive Board of the
National Council for Geographic Education
Social Studies Consultant
Clark University
Worcester, Massachusetts

GRADE-LEVEL CONSULTANTS

Gail Hennessey
Sixth Grade Teacher
Harpursville Central School
Harpursville, New York

Helen Hicks-Wiley
Middle School Teacher
Lee Middle School
Fort Meyers, Florida

Tami Nauyokas
Middle School Teacher
Wylie Middle School
Wylie, Texas

Sister Barbara Neigh
Curriculum Director for Social Studies
San Francisco
Diocese of Pittsburgh
Bethel Park, Pennsylvania

James Verso
Sixth Grade Teacher
School 45
Buffalo, New York

Marjorie Zelner
Encinal Middle School
Atherton, California

TRADITIONS WRITERS

Virginia Arnold
Richmond, Virginia

Herbert M. Cole
Santa Barbara, California

Carrie Evento
Waterford, Connecticut

Eric Kimmel
Portland, Oregon

Diana Reische
Pelham, New York

Joseph B. Rubin
Fort Worth, Texas

Ruth Akamine Wassynger
Birmingham, Alabama

CONTRIBUTING WRITERS

Roberta Jackson
Alexandria, Virginia

Janet McHugh
New York, New York

ACKNOWLEDGMENTS

The publisher gratefully acknowledges permission to reprint the following copyrighted material: "Geography" from ELEANOR FARJEON'S POEMS FOR CHILDREN by Eleanor Farjeon. (J. B. Lippincott) Copyright © 1938, 1951 by Eleanor Farjeon. Renewed copyright © 1966 by Gervase Farjeon. Reprinted by permission of Harper and Row, Publishers, Inc. Quotation from "Hiroki's Hectic Life in Japan" by Clayton Jones in the CHRISTIAN SCIENCE MONITOR, 4/9/91. Other sources consulted: THE YELLOW WIND by David Grossman and Koteret Rashit. Translated by Haim Watzman, copyright © 1988 by Farrar, Straus & Giroux, Inc. "Africa" by Ilva Mackay. From POETS TO THE PEOPLE edited by Barry Feinberg. Copyright © 1974. First published by George Allen & Unwin Ltd. "Teen-Ager Demonstrates Poorest Can Succeed Through Education" by Fred Hiatt. From THE WASHINGTON POST, 9/6/88, ©1988.

Macmillan/McGraw-Hill School Division
10 Union Square East
New York, New York 10003

Printed in the United States of America
ISBN 0-02-146008-6
1 2 3 4 5 6 7 8 9 RRW 99 98 97 96 95 94 93 92

CONTENTS

USING YOUR TEXTBOOK   2

FIVE FUNDAMENTAL THEMES OF GEOGRAPHY   4

REVIEWING MAPS AND GLOBES   6
   Using Globes   6
   Using Maps   9
   Different Kinds of Maps   12

UNIT 1 Studying the Earth   16

CHAPTER 1 **LEARNING ABOUT EARTH'S GEOGRAPHY** 20
  LESSON 1 Discovering the Earth 21
  LESSON 2 Climates of the World 26
  LESSON 3 Earth's Resources 31
  BUILDING GEOGRAPHY SKILLS Understanding Latitude
   and Longitude 34
  CHAPTER 1 • Summary and Review 34

CHAPTER 2 **LEARNING ABOUT EARLY PEOPLE** 38
  LESSON 1 All People Have a Culture 39
  LESSON 2 How Early People Lived 43
  BUILDING CITIZENSHIP People Who Make a Difference
   Art on the Streets of Boston 47
  TRADITIONS Stone Paintings *By Virginia Arnold* 48
  LESSON 3 The Beginnings of Village Life 52
  LESSON 4 How Do We Know About the Past? 58
  BUILDING TIME SKILLS Reading Time Lines 61
  CHAPTER 2 • Summary and Review 62
  UNIT 1 REVIEW 64

UNIT 2 Four Early Civilizations   66

CHAPTER 3 **ANCIENT EGYPT** 70
  LESSON 1 The Geography of Ancient Egypt 71
  LESSON 2 The History of Ancient Egypt 76
  LESSON 3 Egyptian Civilization 83
  TRADITIONS Saving Abu Simbel *By Eric Kimmel* 88
  BUILDING GEOGRAPHY SKILLS Reading Historical Maps 92
  CHAPTER 3 • Summary and Review 94

CHAPTER 4   THE FERTILE CRESCENT   96
   LESSON 1   The Geography of the Fertile Crescent   97
   LESSON 2   Mesopotamian Civilization   100
   BUILDING CITIZENSHIP   People Who Make a Difference
     Protecting the Environment   107
   BUILDING THINKING SKILLS   Decision Making   108
   LESSON 3   The Birth of Judaism   110
   CHAPTER 4 · Summary and Review   116

CHAPTER 5   ANCIENT INDIA AND ANCIENT CHINA   118
   LESSON 1   The Indus River Valley   119
   LESSON 2   Ancient China   124
   BUILDING READING AND WRITING SKILLS   Writing a Summary   129
   CHAPTER 5 · Summary and Review   130
   UNIT 2 REVIEW   132

UNIT 3   Ancient Europe   134

CHAPTER 6   ANCIENT GREECE   138
   LESSON 1   The Geography of Ancient Greece   139
   LESSON 2   Greek City-States   144
   LESSON 3   The Birth of Democracy   150
   LESSON 4   The Legacy of Ancient Greece   154
   TRADITIONS   The Olympic Tradition *By Diana Reische*   161
   LESSON 5   The Spread of Greek Ideas   165
   BUILDING THINKING SKILLS   Asking Questions   168
   BUILDING CITIZENSHIP   Point/Counterpoint
     Should Britain Return the Elgin Marbles to Greece?   170
   CHAPTER 6 · Summary and Review   172

CHAPTER 7   ANCIENT ROME   174
   LESSON 1   The Geography of Ancient Rome   175
   BUILDING GEOGRAPHY SKILLS   Reading Contour Maps   178
   LESSON 2   The Roman Republic   180
   LESSON 3   The Roman Empire   186
   LESSON 4   The Legacy of Ancient Rome   190
   LESSON 5   The Birth of Christianity   194
   CHAPTER 7 · Summary and Review   200
   UNIT 3 REVIEW   202

UNIT 4 The Growth of Europe   204

CHAPTER 8 THE MIDDLE AGES   208
  LESSON 1 The Geography of Europe   209
  LESSON 2 Living in the Middle Ages   214
  LESSON 3 The Influence of the Church   219
  LESSON 4 A Time of Change   224
  BUILDING THINKING SKILLS Understanding Cause and Effect   230
  CHAPTER 8 · Summary and Review   232

CHAPTER 9 THE RENAISSANCE   234
  LESSON 1 The Art of the Renaissance   235
  LESSON 2 The Reformation   240
  BUILDING STUDY AND RESEARCH SKILLS Using the Library   244
  LESSON 3 Elizabethan England   246
  TRADITIONS A Theatrical Tradition *By Joseph B. Rubin*   250
  CHAPTER 9 · Summary and Review   254

CHAPTER 10 THE AGE OF EXPLORATION   256
  LESSON 1 Traders and Explorers   257
  BUILDING THINKING SKILLS Identifying Fact and Opinion   262
  LESSON 2 The Beginning of Modern Science   264
  BUILDING CITIZENSHIP People Who Make a Difference
    Learning About the Earth from Space   267
  CHAPTER 10 · Summary and Review   268
  UNIT 4 REVIEW   270

UNIT 5 Europe and North Asia in Modern Times   272

CHAPTER 11 TWO REVOLUTIONS CHANGE EUROPE   280
  LESSON 1 The Industrial Revolution   281
  BUILDING CITIZENSHIP Point/Counterpoint
    1820—Is Industrial Growth Good for England?   286
  LESSON 2 The French Revolution   288
  BUILDING STUDY AND RESEARCH SKILLS
    Using Primary and Secondary Sources   294
  CHAPTER 11 · Summary and Review   296

CHAPTER 12 **FROM RUSSIA TO THE COMMONWEALTH OF INDEPENDENT STATES** 298

LESSON 1 Geography: Russia and Its Neighbors 299
LESSON 2 The Growth of Russia 305
LESSON 3 The Russian Revolution 311
BUILDING GEOGRAPHY SKILLS Reading Distribution Maps 316
CHAPTER 12 • Summary and Review 318

CHAPTER 13 **THE TWENTIETH CENTURY** 320

LESSON 1 World War I 321
BUILDING THINKING SKILLS Determining Point of View 324
LESSON 2 World War II 326
TRADITIONS Living Memorials *By Eric Kimmel* 332
LESSON 3 Europe and North Asia Today 336
BUILDING CITIZENSHIP Point/Counterpoint
How Should Europe's Forests Be Protected? 344
CHAPTER 13 • Summary and Review 346
UNIT 5 REVIEW 348

UNIT 6 Middle East and North Africa 350

CHAPTER 14 **THE MIDDLE EAST AND NORTH AFRICA LONG AGO** 356

LESSON 1 Geography: Middle East and North Africa 357
BUILDING GEOGRAPHY SKILLS Using Maps at Different Scales 362
LESSON 2 The Beginnings of Islam 364
LESSON 3 Islamic Civilization 370
CHAPTER 14 • Summary and Review 376

CHAPTER 15 **THE MIDDLE EAST AND NORTH AFRICA TODAY** 378

LESSON 1 New Nations in the Middle East 379
BUILDING THINKING SKILLS Determining Accuracy 384
LESSON 2 Life Today: Middle East and North Africa 386
BUILDING CITIZENSHIP People Who Make a Difference
The School for Peace 393
TRADITIONS No-Rooz: A New Year's Celebration
By Diana Reische 394
CHAPTER 15 • Summary and Review 398
UNIT 6 REVIEW 400

UNIT 7   Africa South of the Sahara   402

CHAPTER 16   GREAT AFRICAN KINGDOMS   410

LESSON 1   Geography: Africa South of Sahara   411
LESSON 2   Africa's Ancient Kingdoms   418
LESSON 3   Kingdoms of the African Savanna   422
BUILDING GEOGRAPHY SKILLS   Understanding Map Projections   426
CHAPTER 16 · Summary and Review   428

CHAPTER 17   MODERN AFRICA   430

LESSON 1   The Age of Imperialism   431
BUILDING THINKING SKILLS   Drawing Conclusions   438
LESSON 2   Africa Today   440
BUILDING CITIZENSHIP   Point/Counterpoint
   1960—Should Colonialism Continue in Africa?   446
TRADITIONS   Kente: A Tradition in Cloth *By Herbert M. Cole*   448
CHAPTER 17 · Summary and Review   452
UNIT 7 REVIEW   454

UNIT 8   South Asia, China, Japan, and Korea   456

CHAPTER 18   SOUTH ASIA   462

LESSON 1   The Geography of South Asia   463
LESSON 2   Hinduism and Buddhism   468
LESSON 3   The Growth of India   474
BUILDING CITIZENSHIP   Point/Counterpoint
   Is Civil Disobedience a Good Way to Protest?   480
LESSON 4   South Asia Today   482
BUILDING STUDY AND RESEARCH SKILLS
   Comparing Circle, Line, and Bar Graphs   486
CHAPTER 18 · Summary and Review   488

CHAPTER 19   CHINA   490

LESSON 1   The Geography of China   491
BUILDING GEOGRAPHY SKILLS   Reading Time Zone Maps   496
LESSON 2   Chinese Civilization   498
TRADITIONS   Chinese Writing *By Ruth Akamine Wassynger*   507
LESSON 3   A Changing China   511
BUILDING THINKING SKILLS   Evaluating Information   516
LESSON 4   China Today   518
CHAPTER 19 · Summary and Review   522

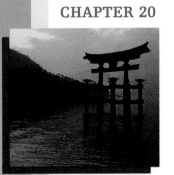

CHAPTER 20 JAPAN AND KOREA 524

LESSON 1 The Geography of Japan and Korea 525

BUILDING GEOGRAPHY SKILLS

Understanding Great-Circle Routes 528

LESSON 2 The History of Japan 530

LESSON 3 The History of Korea 536

LESSON 4 Japan and Korea Today 540

CHAPTER 20 • Summary and Review 544

UNIT 8 REVIEW 546

UNIT 9 Southeast Asia, Oceania, and Australia 548

CHAPTER 21 SOUTHEAST ASIA 554

LESSON 1 The Geography of Southeast Asia 555

LESSON 2 The History of Southeast Asia 559

LESSON 3 Southeast Asia Today 563

BUILDING THINKING SKILLS Using Information 566

CHAPTER 21 • Summary and Review 568

CHAPTER 22 AUSTRALIA AND OCEANIA 570

LESSON 1 The Geography of Australia and Oceania 571

BUILDING GEOGRAPHY SKILLS Reading Maps of the Ocean Floor 576

LESSON 2 The History of Australia and Oceania 578

TRADITIONS Walkabout *By Carrie Evento* 582

LESSON 3 Australia and Oceania Today 586

BUILDING THINKING SKILLS Decision Making 590

BUILDING CITIZENSHIP People Who Make a Difference

Bringing Good Health 591

CHAPTER 22 • Summary and Review 592

UNIT 9 REVIEW 594

CONCLUSION WORKING TOGETHER TOWARD A NEW CENTURY 596

BUILDING CITIZENSHIP You Can Make a Difference 602

ATLAS	604
DICTIONARY OF GEOGRAPHIC TERMS	618
GAZETTEER	620
BIOGRAPHICAL DICTIONARY	628
GLOSSARY	632
INDEX	642
CREDITS	650

Building Citizenship

PEOPLE WHO MAKE A DIFFERENCE

Art on the Streets of Boston / 47

Protecting the Environment / 107

Learning About the Earth from Space / 267

The School for Peace / 393

Bringing Good Health / 591

You Can Make a Difference / 602

POINT/COUNTERPOINT

Should Britain Return the Elgin Marbles to Greece? / 170

1820—Is Industrial Growth Good for England? / 286

How Should Europe's Forests Be Protected? / 344

1960—Should Colonialism Continue in Africa? / 446

Is Civil Disobedience a Good Way to Protest? / 480

Traditions

Stone Paintings, by Virginia Arnold / 48

Saving Abu Simbel, by Eric Kimmel / 88

The Olympic Tradition, by Diana Reische / 161

A Theatrical Tradition, by Joseph B. Rubin / 250

Living Memorials, by Eric Kimmel / 332

No-Rooz: A New Year's Celebration, by Diana Reische / 394

Kente: A Tradition in Cloth, by Herbert M. Cole / 448

Chinese Writing, by Ruth Akamine Wassynger / 507

Walkabout, by Carrie Evento / 582

Songs

"Scarborough Fair" / 227

"La Marseillaise" / 290

Building Skills

THINKING/READING

Decision Making / 108
Writing a Summary / 129
Asking Questions / 168
Understanding Cause and Effect / 230
Identifying Fact and Opinion / 262
Determining Point of View / 324
Determining Accuracy / 384
Drawing Conclusions / 438
Evaluating Information / 516
Using Information / 566
Decision Making / 590

GEOGRAPHY

Understanding Latitude and Longitude / 34
Reading Historical Maps / 92

Reading Contour Maps / 178
Reading Distribution Maps / 316
Using Maps at Different Scales / 362
Understanding Map Projections / 426
Reading Time Zone Maps / 496
Understanding Great-Circle Routes / 528
Reading Maps of the Ocean Floor / 576

STUDY/TIME

Reading Time Lines / 61
Using the Library / 244
Using Primary and Secondary Sources / 294
Comparing Circle, Line, and Bar Graphs / 486

Charts, Graphs, Diagrams, and Time Lines

History of Early People / 18
What Is Geography? / 22
Climate Zones / 27
Average Monthly Temperatures for Pikes Peak and Washington D.C. / 28
Cross Section of the United States / 29
Oil Production / 32
What Is Culture / 40
Catal Hüyük: A New Stone Age Village / 54
The Growth of Technology / 56
Reading Time Lines / 61
Reviewing Chapter 2 Time Line / 62
History of Four Early Civilizations / 68
Irrigation in Ancient Egypt / 75
Egypt's Three Crowns / 76
Building the Pyramids / 78

Hieroglyphics / 84
A Social Pyramid / 87
Periods in the History of Ancient Egypt / 92
Reviewing Chapter 3 Time Line / 94
How Cuneiform Developed / 103
Reviewing Chapter 4 Time Line / 116
Chinese Writing / 128
Reviewing Chapter 5 Time Line / 130
History of Ancient Europe / 136
A Greek Trireme / 141
Alphabets / 143
Ancient Athens / 147
The Gods of Mount Olympus / 155
The Greek Legacy / 160
Reviewing Chapter 6 Time Line / 172
A Roman Road / 192

The Influence of Latin / 193

Reviewing Chapter 7 Time Line / 200

History of the Growth of Europe / 206

Average Temperatures in Two European Cities / 212

Manor Life / 217

A Monastery / 220

A Day in the Life of a Monk / 220

Reviewing Chapter 8 Time Line / 232

Reviewing Chapter 9 Time Line / 254

Reviewing Chapter 10 Time Line / 268

Europe and North Asia in Modern Times / 274

Europe and North Asia / 276

Shoemaking Before and After the Industrial Revolution / 285

The Three Estates / 289

Reviewing Chapter 11 Time Line / 296

Reviewing Chapter 12 Time Line / 318

Reviewing Chapter 13 Time Line / 346

History of the Middle East and North Africa / 352

The Nations of the Middle East and North Africa / 354

Migrating Sand Dunes / 359

Reviewing Chapter 14 Time Line / 376

Oil Production / 388

Oil: A Valuable Resource / 389

Reviewing Chapter 15 Time Line / 398

History of Africa South of the Sahara / 404

Africa South of the Sahara / 406

African Wildlife / 417

Reviewing Chapter 16 Time Line / 428

Reviewing Chapter 17 Time Line / 452

History of South Asia, China, Japan, and Korea / 458

South Asia, China, Japan, and Korea / 460

Major World Religions / 487

India's Population, 1970–1990 / 487

Population of Five South Asian Nations / 487

Reviewing Chapter 18 Time Line / 488

The Pinyin System / 493

The Dynasties of China / 499

Building the Great Wall of China / 502

Reviewing Chapter 19 Time Line / 522

Comparing Four Economies, 1965–1990 / 541

Reviewing Chapter 20 Time Line / 544

World Population / 547

Population of China, 1950–1990 / 547

History of Southeast Asia, Australia, and Oceania / 550

The Nations of Southeast Asia, Australia, and Oceania / 552

Reviewing Chapter 21 Time Line / 568

The Making of an Atoll / 575

Geothermal Energy / 588

Reviewing Chapter 22 Time Line / 592

Maps

The World: Continent and Oceans / 7

Northern Hemisphere / 8

Southern Hemisphere / 8

Western Hemisphere / 8

Eastern Hemisphere / 8

France / 9

New Zealand / 10

New Zealand / 10

Kenya: National Parks / 11

Madagascar: Plant Life / 11

Middle East: Political / 12

Scandinavia: Landforms / 13

Central London / 14
India: Population / 15
Regions of the Eastern Hemisphere / 16
The World: Continents and Oceans / 23
The Great Lakes of North America / 24
The World: Vegetation / 25
The World: Climate / 27
Latitude and Altitude / 29
Ocean Currents / 30
Lines of Latitude / 34
Lines of Longitude / 34
Global Grid / 35
Reviewing Lines of Latitude / 37
Reviewing Lines of Longitude / 37
The Ice Age / 44
Reviewing Latitude and Longitude / 65
River Valley Civilizations / 66
Nile River Valley / 72
The Egyptian Empire / 81
Growth of Ancient Egypt / 93
The Fertile Crescent / 98
Sumer and Babylonia / 101
Beginnings of Judaism / 111
Indus River Valley / 120
Huang River Valley / 125
Reviewing Historical Maps / 133
Ancient Greece and the
    Roman Empire / 134
Aegean World / 140
Greek and Phoenician Colonies / 142
Persian Wars / 148
Empire of Alexander the Great / 167
Italy About 500 B.C. / 176
Sardinia: Contour Lines / 178
Naples and Vicinity / 179
Punic Wars / 184
Growth of the Roman Empire / 187
Spread of Christianity / 197

The Growth of Europe / 204
Europe: Elevation / 210
Europe: Climate / 213
Frankish Empire / 215
The First Crusade / 225
Religion in Europe, 1500s / 243
Voyages of Exploration / 260
Europe and North Asia / 272
Russia and Its Neighbors: Elevation / 300
Russia and Its Neighbors: Vegetation / 303
Growth of Russia, 1360–1917 / 309
World War II in Europe and
    North Africa / 313
Soviet Union: Population Density,
    1990 / 316
Soviet Union: Population Density,
    1990 / 317
The Cold War in Europe, 1948–1989 / 337
The Commonwealth of Independent
    States / 341
Europe and North Asia: Political / 342–343
Reviewing Distribution Maps / 349
The Middle East and North Africa / 350
Middle East and North Africa:
    Elevation / 358
Middle East and North Africa:
    Precipitation / 360
The World: Major Religions / 362
Middle East: Major Religions / 363
Islamic World, A.D. 750 / 369
Ottoman Empire A.D. 1672 / 380
Sea of Marmara / 381
Middle East and North Africa:
    Political / 387
Israel and the Disputed Territories / 391
Reviewing Maps at Different Scales / 401
Africa South of the Sahara / 402
Africa South of the Sahara: Elevation / 412
Africa: Vegetation / 415

Early African Kingdoms / 419

African Kingdoms, 400–1591 / 423

Equal-Area Projection / 426

Equal-Area Projection / 426

Mercator Projection / 427

Polar Projection / 427

Imperialism in Africa, 1914 / 436

Africa South of the Sahara: Political / 442

Growth of African Independence / 442

South Asia, China, Japan, and Korea / 456

South Asia: Elevation / 465

South Asia: Monsoons / 466

Spread of Hinduism and Buddhism, 500 B.C.–A.D. 600 / 473

Mogul Empire, 1707 / 475

South Asia: Political / 483

South Asia: Religion / 485

China's Three Regions / 492

China and Its Neighbors / 493

China and Its Neighbors: Vegetation / 494

The World: Time Zones / 497

The Great Wall / 503

China, 1368–1644 / 505

The Long March / 515

Japan and Korea / 526

Japan and Korea: Great-Circle Routes / 528

The World: Great-Circle Routes / 529

Northern Hemisphere: Great-Circle Route / 529

Imperial Japan, 1942 / 535

Korea's Three Kingdoms, A.D. 500 / 537

Japan and Korea: Population Density / 543

Southeast Asia, Oceania and Australia / 548

Southeast Asia: Elevation / 556

Khmer Empire, A.D. 1150 / 561

Southeast Asia: Political / 564

Australia and New Zealand / 572

Fin Island: Contour Lines / 577

World Cartogram: Gross National Product / 599

North America: Acid Rain / 600

The World: Political / 604

The World: Physical / 606

The 50 United States / 608

Europe and North Asia: Political / 610

Europe and North Asia: Physical / 611

South Asia: Political / 612

South Asia: Physical / 613

Africa: Political / 614

Africa: Physical / 615

Australia and New Zealand: Political / 616

Australia and New Zealand: Physical / 617

USING YOUR TEXTBOOK

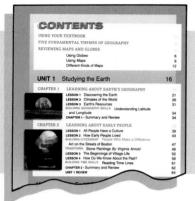

CONTENTS

USING YOUR TEXTBOOK
FIVE FUNDAMENTAL THEMES OF GEOGRAPHY
REVIEWING MAPS AND GLOBES
    Using Globes   6
    Using Maps   9
    Different Kinds of Maps   12

UNIT 1   Studying the Earth   16

CHAPTER 1 LEARNING ABOUT EARTH'S GEOGRAPHY
  LESSON 1 Discovering the Earth 21
  LESSON 2 Climates of the World 26
  LESSON 3 Earth's Resources 31
  BUILDING GEOGRAPHY SKILLS Understanding Latitude
    and Longitude 34
  CHAPTER 1 · Summary and Review 34

CHAPTER 2 LEARNING ABOUT EARLY PEOPLE
  LESSON 1 All People Have a Culture 39
  LESSON 2 How Early People Lived 43
  BUILDING CITIZENSHIP People Who Make a Difference
    Art on the Streets of Boston 47
  TRADITIONS Stone Paintings By Virginia Arnold 48
  LESSON 3 The Beginnings of Village Life 52
  LESSON 4 How Do We Know About the Past? 58
  BUILDING TIME SKILLS Reading Time Lines 61
  CHAPTER 2 · Summary and Review 62
  UNIT 1 REVIEW 64

TABLE OF CONTENTS
Lists all parts of your book and tells you where to find them

Your textbook contains many special features that will help you read, understand, and remember the people, geography, and history of the world.

REVIEWING MAPS & GLOBES

Using Globes

REVIEWING MAPS AND GLOBES
Reviews skills that will help you use the maps in your book

KENTE: A TRADITION IN CLOTH
by Herbert M. Cole

What can clothing tell us about a person and a culture? Look at the photograph to the left. It shows the current king of the Asante (ə sän' tē) people, who live in the West African nation of Ghana. The king's beautiful robe and gold jewelry suggest that he is very wealthy and highly respected. The multicolored robe the king is wearing is called a Kente (ken' tā) cloth.

Kente cloth was first woven by people in the ancient kingdoms of West Africa, which you read about in Chapter 16. The people of these kingdoms developed a style of weaving that lives on today. Their descendants, the Asante and the Ewe (ā' vā) of Ghana and Togo, have been making and wearing Kente cloth for centuries. The technique of weaving Kente cloth is passed down from generation to generation. Making and wearing Kente cloth are traditions that go back hundreds of years in West Africa. As you read this lesson, think about why Kente cloth is a source of pride to West Africans and of African ancestry all...

TRADITIONS
Lessons which give you a deeper understanding of the cultures of the regions you are studying

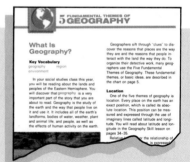

5 FUNDAMENTAL THEMES OF GEOGRAPHY

What Is Geography?

Key Vocabulary
geography region
environment

In your social studies class this year, you will be reading about the lands and peoples of the Eastern Hemisphere. You will discover that geography is a very important part of the story that you are about to read. Geography is the study of the earth and the way that people live on it and use it. It includes all of the earth's landforms, bodies of water, weather, plant and animal life, and people, as well as the effects of human activity on the earth.

Geographers sift through "clues" to discover the reasons that places are the way they are and the reasons that people interact with the land the way they do. To organize their detective work, many geographers use the Five Fundamental Themes of Geography. These fundamental themes, or basic ideas, are described in the chart on page 5.

Location
One of the five themes of geography is location. Every place on the earth has an exact position, which is called its absolute location. This position can be measured and expressed through the use of imaginary lines called latitude and longitude. You will read about latitude and longitude in the Geography Skill lesson on pages 34–35.
Relative ... for the relationship of ... is expressed ...

FIVE FUNDAMENTAL THEMES OF GEOGRAPHY
Introduces important themes of geography that will help you to compare, to contrast, and to understand the regions and people you will study

LESSON OPENER
Important vocabulary, people, and places introduced in the lesson

Lesson introduction

Asks you to think about what you already know from previous lessons or your own experience

Question you should keep in mind as you read the lesson

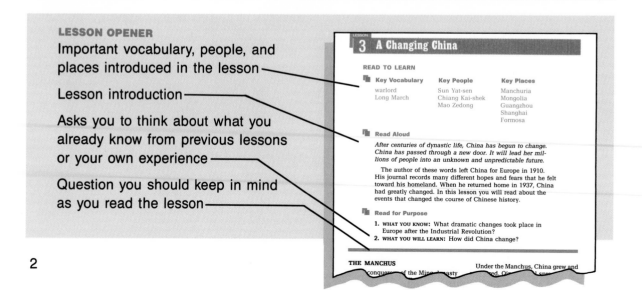

LESSON 3

A Changing China

READ TO LEARN

Key Vocabulary	Key People	Key Places
warlord	Sun Yat-sen	Manchuria
Long March	Chiang Kai-shek	Mongolia
	Mao Zedong	Guangzhou
		Shanghai
		Formosa

Read Aloud

After centuries of dynastic life, China has begun to change. China has passed through a new door. It will lead her millions of people into an unknown and unpredictable future.

The author of these words left China for Europe in 1910. His journal records many different hopes and fears that he felt toward his homeland. When he returned home in 1937, China had greatly changed. In this lesson you will read about the events that changed the course of Chinese history.

Read for Purpose

1. WHAT YOU KNOW: What dramatic changes took place in Europe after the Industrial Revolution?
2. WHAT YOU WILL LEARN: How did China change?

THE MANCHUS
... conquest of the Ming dynasty ...

Under the Manchus, China grew and ...

REFERENCE SECTION

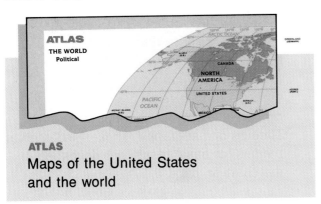

ATLAS
THE WORLD
Political

ATLAS
Maps of the United States
and the world

GAZETTEER

This Gazetteer is a geographical dictionary that will help you to pronounce and locate the places discussed in this book. Latitude and longitude are given for cities and some other places. The page number tells you where each place appears on a map.

GAZETTEER
Location and pronunciation
of Key Places discussed
in your book and page
where each is shown
on a map

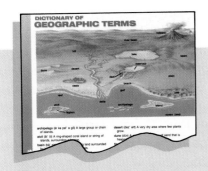

DICTIONARY OF GEOGRAPHIC TERMS

DICTIONARY OF GEOGRAPHIC TERMS
Definition and pronunciation
of major geographic features

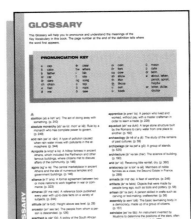

GLOSSARY

This Glossary will help you to pronounce and understand the meanings of the Key Vocabulary in this book. The page number at the end of the definition tells where the word first appears.

GLOSSARY
Definition and
pronunciation of all
Key Vocabulary and
page where each is
introduced

BIOGRAPHICAL DICTIONARY

This Biographical Dictionary will help you to pronounce and identify the Key People discussed in this book. The page number tells you where each person first appears in the text.

BIOGRAPHICAL DICTIONARY
Identification and
pronunciation of
all Key People
discussed in your
book and page
where each is
introduced

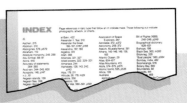

INDEX

INDEX
Alphabetical list of important
people, places, events, and
subjects in your book and
pages where information is
found

What Is Geography?

Key Vocabulary

geography   region
environment

In your social studies class this year, you will be reading about the lands and peoples of the Eastern Hemisphere. You will discover that geography is a very important part of the story that you are about to read. Geography is the study of the earth and the way that people live on it and use it. It includes all of the earth's landforms, bodies of water, weather, plant and animal life, and people, as well as the effects of human activity on the earth.

Geographers sift through "clues" to discover the reasons that places are the way they are and the reasons that people interact with the land the way they do. To organize their detective work, many geographers use the Five Fundamental Themes of Geography. These fundamental themes, or basic ideas, are described in the chart on page 5.

Location

One of the five themes of geography is location. Every place on the earth has an exact position, which is called its absolute location. This position can be measured and expressed through the use of imaginary lines called latitude and longitude. You will read about latitude and longitude in the Geography Skill lesson on pages 34–35.

Relative location, or the relationship of one place to other places, is expressed through words. For example, Algeria is closer to the equator than Russia is. This information helps to explain why Algeria is warmer year-round than Russia is.

Description of Place

Another theme of geography is description of place. This theme explains what a place is like by describing its physical and human characteristics. For example, the shape of a place's land, its climate, and animal life would be described along with how the people look and the kinds of buildings they live in. This theme also helps us to understand what a place is like by showing how it is similar to or different from other places.

5 FUNDAMENTAL THEMES OF GEOGRAPHY

THEME	
Location	• Where is a place located? What is it near? What direction is it from another place?
Description of Place	• What is a place like? What characteristics does it have?
Human-environment Interaction	• How are people's lives shaped by the place where they live? How has a place been shaped by human activity?
Movement	• How do people and things move from one place to another? Why do they make these movements?
Regions	• Why are some places similar to others? Why are some places thought of as "belonging" together?

Human-Environment Interaction

Another theme of geography is human-environment interaction. The environment is the surroundings in which people, plants, or animals live. This theme describes the relationship between people and their surroundings.

Think about how the environment helps to shape the way people earn a living. For example, many people in Japan earn their living by fishing. Japan is an island country whose surrounding waters are filled with fish. People, in turn, also affect the environment. For example, they may catch too many fish in an ocean area and thus endanger the fish that live there. The photo on page 4 shows how Indonesian farmers have affected their environment.

Movement

Another theme of geography is the movement of people, goods, and ideas around the world. In this book, for example, you will read about the large groups of people who moved to a fertile river valley in northern Africa thousands of years ago. They brought their ideas and traditions with them to their new home.

You will also read about how this area became a major center for trading goods and exchanging ideas.

Regions

Another theme of geography is regions. A region is an area with common physical or cultural features that set it apart from other areas. The size of regions can vary greatly. Think about the "regions" in your house or school. There are different areas for eating, sleeping, bathing, and studying. One example of a physical region is the huge desert that is part of the island continent of Australia. The language spoken in a place can set a cultural region apart. For example, people living in Switzerland speak French, German, or Italian, depending on the region of the country in which they live.

1. What is geography?
2. Use each of the Five Fundamental Themes of Geography to describe your community.
3. What are two of the common features that geographers use to divide the world into regions?

5

Using Globes

Key Vocabulary
continent
hemisphere
equator
prime meridian

In social studies this year, you will be learning about the lands and people of the Eastern Hemisphere. You will discover that maps and globes can often help you better understand what you read. Maps and globes are the "tools" you will use in your studies. They can help you answer questions about locations of countries and cities, oceans and rivers, mountains and deserts. They show the shapes and sizes of places on the earth. They can also help you make comparisons and determine distances and directions between places.

People long ago used maps and globes. The oldest known map was made about 2300 B.C. in a place called Babylonia. The earliest globes were made by the ancient Greeks about 1500 B.C. You will learn a great deal more about these ancient people later in this book.

Tools are helpful only if you know how to use them. In the following sections you will review some of the things you already know about maps and globes.

Look at your classroom globe. Globes are especially valuable tools for learning about the earth. Globes are models, or small copies, of the earth, and they provide very accurate information. Looking at a globe is a lot like looking at the earth from a point in outer space. On a globe, shapes and relative sizes are shown correctly. Directions and relative distances are also shown correctly.

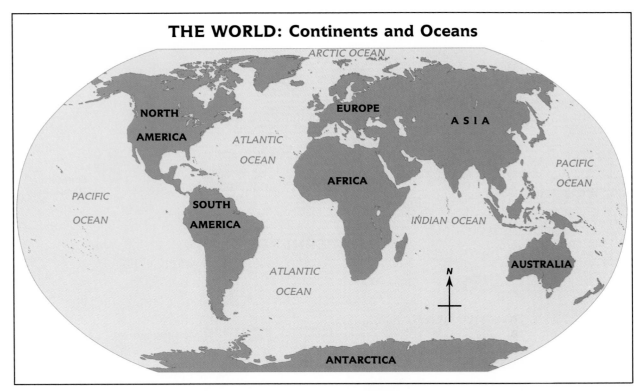

THE WORLD: Continents and Oceans

ARCTIC OCEAN

NORTH AMERICA

EUROPE

ASIA

ATLANTIC OCEAN

PACIFIC OCEAN

PACIFIC OCEAN

AFRICA

SOUTH AMERICA

INDIAN OCEAN

ATLANTIC OCEAN

AUSTRALIA

N

ANTARCTICA

Maps are drawings on flat surfaces of all or part of the earth. Thus maps have some advantages that globes do not. Maps can be folded or rolled. They can be carried and stored easily. A map can show the world so that it can be seen at once. On a globe, only half the world can be seen at a time. You will be using maps as you read this book.

Continents and Oceans

The surface of the earth is made up of land and water. Globes show the parts of the earth's surface that are land and the parts that are water. Large bodies of land are called continents. You may know that there are seven continents on the earth: North America, South America, Europe, Asia, Africa, Australia, and Antarctica. Find these continents on the map on this page.

As the map shows, the continents are separated, or nearly separated from one another by water. If you look carefully at

a globe, you will see that all the large bodies of water on the earth's surface are part of a single, large connected body of water. This body of water, which covers more than half the earth, is divided into smaller parts, called oceans. You may know that the earth has four oceans: the Atlantic, the Pacific, the Indian, and the Arctic. Find these oceans on the map above.

Hemispheres

Do you know what a hemisphere is? You may have noticed that this book is called *Eastern Hemisphere*. A sphere is a round object, such as the earth. *Hemi* is a Greek word that means "half." Thus, the word *hemisphere* means "half a sphere." Geographers use the term *hemisphere* to refer to half of the earth.

By turning a globe or moving around it, you can see that the earth can be divided into an almost endless number of hemispheres. In order to simplify, geographers divide the earth in two ways.

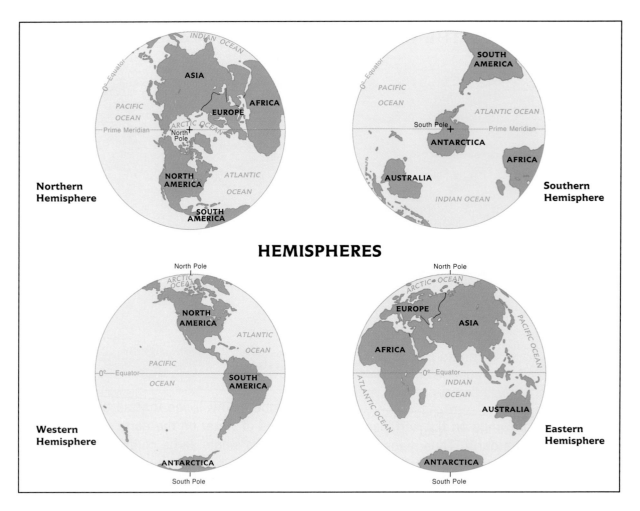

HEMISPHERES

One division is made along an imaginary line called the **equator**. The equator circles the earth halfway between the North Pole and the South Pole. The equator divides the earth into the Northern Hemisphere and the Southern Hemisphere. The Northern Hemisphere is the part of the earth you would see if you were looking at the earth from a point in space directly above the North Pole. The Southern Hemisphere is the part of the earth you would see if you were looking at it from a point in space directly above the South Pole.

The earth can also be divided into the Eastern Hemisphere and the Western Hemisphere. These hemispheres are separated by another imaginary circle around the earth. This circle is known as the **prime meridian**. You will learn about the prime meridian on pages 34–35.

One way in which you can identify the hemispheres is by learning the names of the continents they contain. As you can see from the maps of the hemispheres on this page, most of the earth's landmass is found in the Northern Hemisphere. Name the continents of the Eastern Hemisphere.

1. What is a continent? Name the continents that border the Atlantic Ocean.
2. What is a hemisphere?
3. What imaginary line separates the Northern and Southern hemispheres?
4. What imaginary line separates the Eastern and Western hemispheres?
5. How can using globes help you learn about the earth?

8

Using Maps

Key Vocabulary

cardinal directions
intermediate directions
scale
symbol
map key

While globes are the most accurate representations of the earth, maps are usually much more useful. Your book includes more than 100 maps. Some show the entire world, and others show only a part of the world.

In order to use maps effectively, you must know how to "read" them. Information on maps is presented in a special "language." The "language" of maps allows mapmakers to show a great deal of information in a small space. In this section you will learn to read the language of maps.

Directions

You already know that there are four **cardinal directions**—north, east, south, and west. North is the direction toward the North Pole. If you face north, south is directly behind you, east is to your right, and west is to your left. The letters *N*, *S*, *E*, and *W* are often used to stand for the cardinal directions.

There are also four **intermediate directions**. *Intermediate* means "between." The intermediate directions are the directions halfway between the cardinal directions. Northeast (*NE*), for example, is the intermediate direction halfway between north and east. The other intermediate directions are northwest (*NW*), southeast (*SE*), and southwest (*SW*).

Most maps are drawn so that north is toward the top of the map. Many maps have a north pointer that shows which

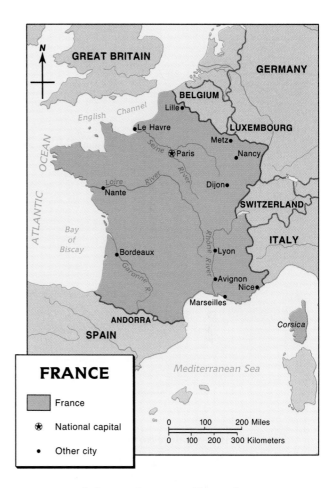

FRANCE

- France
- ⊛ National capital
- • Other city

way north is on the map. If you know where north is, you can easily find all the other directions. Look at the map of France on this page. In what direction is Nancy from Paris? As you can see from the map, Nancy lies east of Paris.

Scale

All maps are smaller than the part of the earth they show. For this reason, a short distance on a map stands for a much greater real distance on the earth.

The **scale**, or relative size, of a map will tell you how much smaller map distances are than real distances. The scale of a map can be shown in a few ways. On the maps in this book, scale is shown by lines, called line scales. Each map has two line scales, one for miles and the other for kilometers.

9

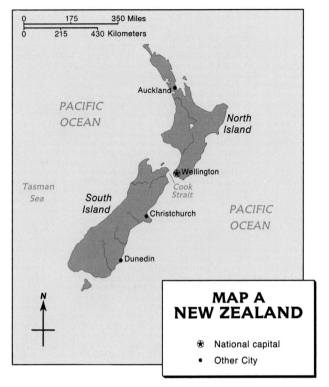

MAP A
NEW ZEALAND

⊛ National capital

• Other City

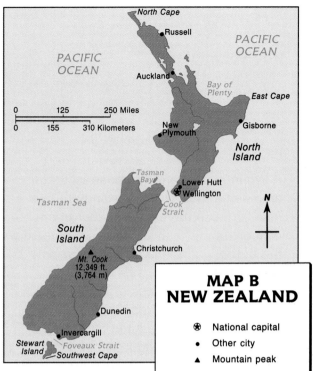

MAP B
NEW ZEALAND

⊛ National capital

• Other city

▲ Mountain peak

Find the line scales on **Map A** of New Zealand on this page. The top line shows how many miles on the earth are represented by one inch on the map. The bottom line shows how many kilometers on the earth are represented by two centimeters on the map. How many miles on the earth does one inch on the map represent? How many kilometers do two centimeters represent?

Suppose you want to know the distance between the cities of Auckland and Dunedin. Use a ruler to measure the map distance in inches between the two cities. Then, multiply the number of inches by 350 to find the real distance in miles. To get the number of kilometers between Auckland and Dunedin, multiply the number of centimeters by 215 to find the real distance in kilometers. What is the real distance between Auckland and Dunedin in miles? What is the distance in kilometers?

Now look at **Map B** on this page. It shows the same area shown on **Map A**. The shape of New Zealand is the same on both maps, but New Zealand appears larger on **Map B**. You know, of course, that New Zealand has not changed in size. What has changed is the scale of the map. One inch on **Map B** stands for a fewer number of miles than one inch stands for on **Map A**.

Use the line scale and a ruler to determine the distance between Auckland and Dunedin on **Map B** as you did on **Map A**. What is the distance in miles and in kilometers? If you measured and figured correctly, your answers will be the same as they were before.

The scale of **Map B** is larger than that of **Map A**. More details, that is, more information, can be shown on large-scale maps than on small-scale maps. What things shown on **Map B** are *not* shown on **Map A**?

Symbols

Information on maps can be shown by **symbols**. A symbol is anything that stands for something else. Common map symbols are dots, squares, circles, triangles, lines, letters, and numbers. Color is a special symbol on maps. It is often used to show differences in height above sea level, rainfall, weather patterns, and plant life. Different colors are often used to distinguish one state or country from another. Blue is a commonly used symbol for water.

Some symbols look like the things they stand for. Others suggest the things they stand for. For example, a tiny drawing of an airplane may be a symbol for an airport. A small drawing of a tree may be a symbol for a forest.

To find out what the symbols used on a map mean, you must look at the **map key**. The map key explains what each symbol stands for. It is important to check the map key on each map you use. A symbol that stands for one thing on one map may stand for a completely different thing on another map.

Look at the two maps on this page and check each map key. Use these maps to answer the following questions.

1. What are the cardinal and intermediate directions?
2. In what direction would you travel going from Nairobi to Mount Kenya? From Nairobi to Mount Kilimanjaro?
3. Do both maps on this page have the same scale?
4. What does the color purple stand for on the map of Madagascar? What does the color orange stand for on the same map?
5. What symbol is used to show cities?
6. Why do you think it is important to understand symbols on maps?

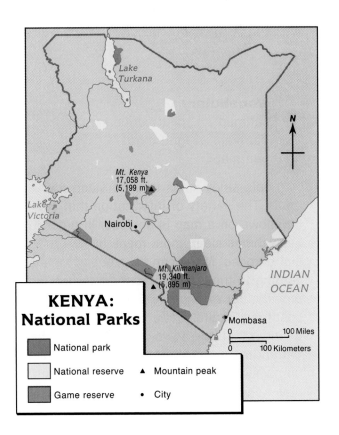

KENYA: National Parks

- National park
- National reserve
- Game reserve
- ▲ Mountain peak
- • City

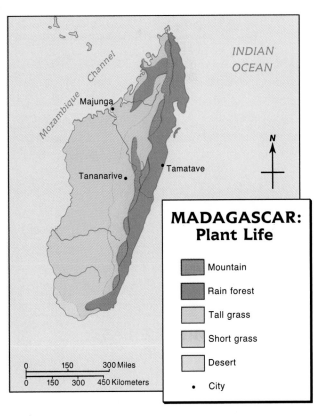

MADAGASCAR: Plant Life

- Mountain
- Rain forest
- Tall grass
- Short grass
- Desert
- • City

Different Kinds of Maps

Key Vocabulary

political map   distribution map
physical map   grid map
landform map

People study maps to understand the earth. The variety of information that can be shown on a map is endless. In order to keep things clear, most maps have a special purpose. Maps can be grouped according to the kind of information they provide. For example, political maps show countries, capitals, and other important political features. Physical maps show the natural features of the earth. For example, on physical maps you can find mountains, plains, lakes, rivers, and deserts.

Special-purpose maps provide information about particular subjects. The focus of a special-purpose map may be population, rainfall, language, or religion. No matter what you want to know about the world, there is sure to be a map for your purpose. As you read this book think about the purpose of each map.

Political Maps

This book has many different kinds of maps. In almost every unit you will find at least one political map. Political maps show political divisions such as countries and states. Political maps may also show capitals and other important cities.

The map on this page shows the countries of the Middle East. It is a political map. As you see, this map shows such

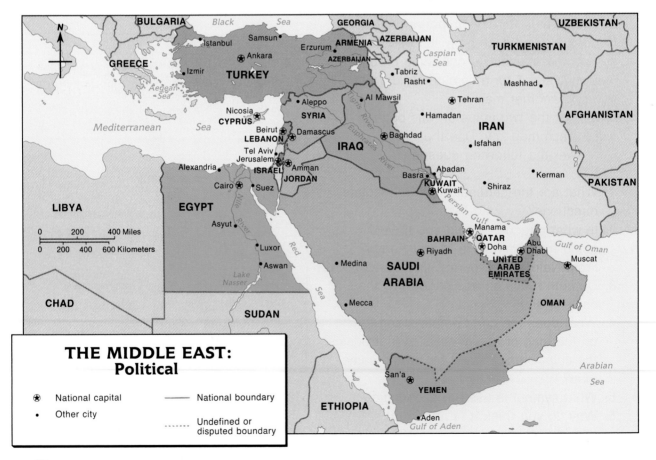

THE MIDDLE EAST:
Political

⊛   National capital   ——— National boundary
•   Other city
                   ········· Undefined or disputed boundary

political features as national boundaries, capitals, and other cities. Note that each country is shown in a special color. Also note that the land lying outside of the Middle East is shown in the same shade of tan. The map shows that some of the national boundaries are disputed, or uncertain. Use the map to identify the capital of Turkey. Name the countries that border Syria.

Physical Maps

Physical maps emphasize the natural features of the earth. The earth's physical features include continents, oceans, islands, lakes, rivers, mountains, plains, and deserts. Some physical maps also show some political features, such as national boundaries.

Landform maps are physical maps that show how the earth's surface varies from place to place. Landform maps use color to show the parts of the earth that are mountains, hills, plateaus, and plains. You may wish to use the Dictionary of Geographic Terms on pages 618–619 to help you picture some of these landforms. Some landform maps use shading to give a better idea of relief, or variation in height above sea level.

Look at the map of Scandinavia on this page. Check the key to see what colors are used to show mountains, hills, plateaus, and plains. Which country, Norway or Sweden, is more mountainous? What part of Finland is mostly plains? Which country has plateaus? How would you describe the landforms of Denmark?

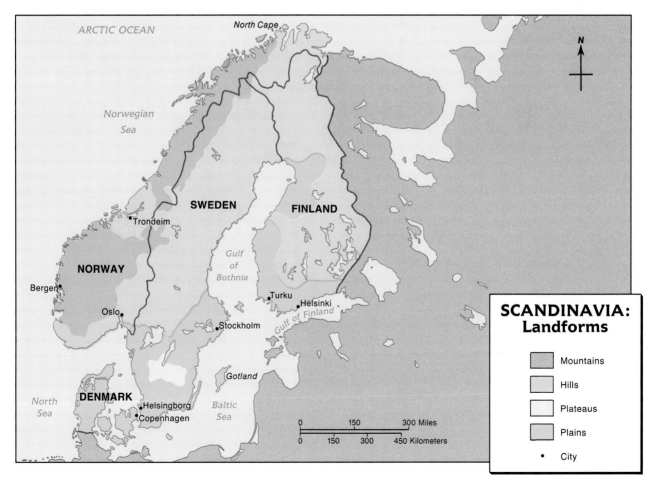

SCANDINAVIA: Landforms

- Mountains
- Hills
- Plateaus
- Plains
- City

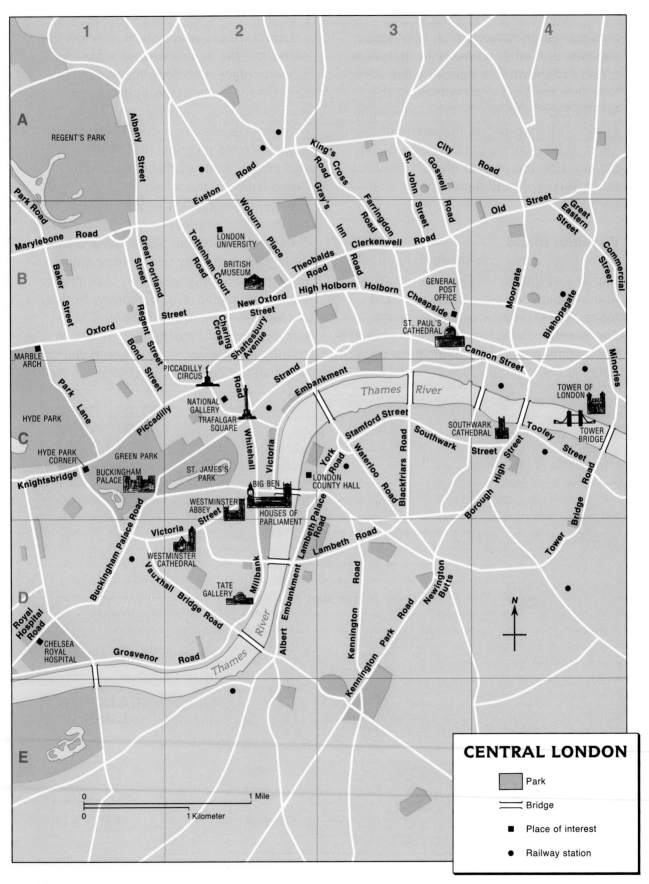

CENTRAL LONDON

■	Park
‖	Bridge
■	Place of interest
●	Railway station

Using a Grid Map

One kind of special purpose map is a city map. Imagine that you are about to take a trip to London, the capital city of England. Imagine that you have only a few days to spend in this important city. How will you be able to find your way around London?

Those who have made the journey to London before suggest that you pick up a good city map. As the map on the opposite page shows, London's streets dart off in many directions. If you do not want to get lost, you will need to use this city map carefully.

City maps are special-purpose maps because they have a unique purpose: they help people find their way around a city. A good city map is also a grid map. For example, the map of London shows the central part of the city. This map has a number–letter grid that makes it easy to find places. Each square on the map can be identified by its letter and number. For example, St. Paul's Cathedral is found in square B–3. Find this place of interest on the map. Give the number and letter of the square in which Buckingham Palace is shown on the map.

Distribution Maps

Some maps show how such things as population, rainfall, language, and religion are distributed in parts of the world. Such maps are called distribution maps.

The map on this page shows the distribution of population in India. Different colors are used to show the parts of India where there are few people per square mile (or square kilometer) and where there are many people per square mile (or square kilometer). Look at the map key. It shows different population categories. What color shows areas where there are more than 500 people per square mile.

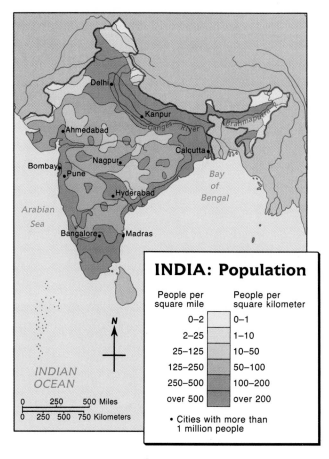

INDIA: Population

People per square mile	People per square kilometer
0–2	0–1
2–25	1–10
25–125	10–50
125–250	50–100
250–500	100–200
over 500	over 200

• Cities with more than 1 million people

What parts of India have more than 500 people per square mile (200 people per square kilometer)? What part or parts of India have two or fewer people per square mile (one or fewer people per square kilometer)?

1. What are some of the things commonly shown on political maps?
2. What are some of the things commonly shown on physical maps?
3. What is a distribution map? Explain how distribution is shown on the map on this page.
4. What is a grid map?
5. In what grid on the map on page 14 are the following sites located? St. Paul's Cathedral; General Post Office; London University; St. James Park; Parliament; Victoria Street.
6. How can a grid map help you find your way around a city?

15

North Pole

ARCTIC   OCEAN

ATLANTIC OCEAN

Arctic Circle

75°N

60°N

Sea of Okho

EUROPE AND NORTH ASIA

Black Sea

Caspian Sea

Mediterranean Sea

NORTH AFRICA AND THE MIDDLE EAST

Persian Gulf

Red Sea

SOUTH ASIA, CHINA, JAPAN, AND KOREA

AFRICA SOUTH OF THE SAHARA

Arabian Sea

Bay of Bengal

15°N

South China Sea

SOUTHEAST ASIA, OCEANIA, AND AUSTRALIA

0° Equator

INDIAN   OCEAN

45°E

60°E   15°S

75°E   90°E   105°E

Tropic of Capricorn

30°S

45°S

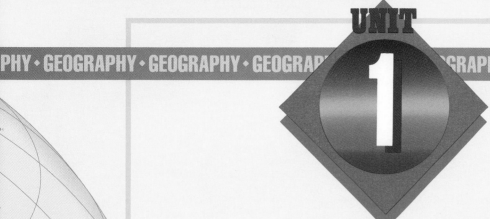

UNIT 1

STUDYING THE EARTH

WHERE WE ARE

You are about to begin an adventure that will take you through the world around us. This journey will take you to the other side of the earth. As the map shows, you will be looking at the lands of the Eastern Hemisphere. You know that the Eastern Hemisphere is made up of the continents of Africa, Asia, Australia, and Europe.

Look closely at the map. As you can see, the Eastern Hemisphere is divided into five regions. What is the name of each region? You will learn that the people of each region have developed their own special way of life. You will also learn that people everywhere have a great deal in common.

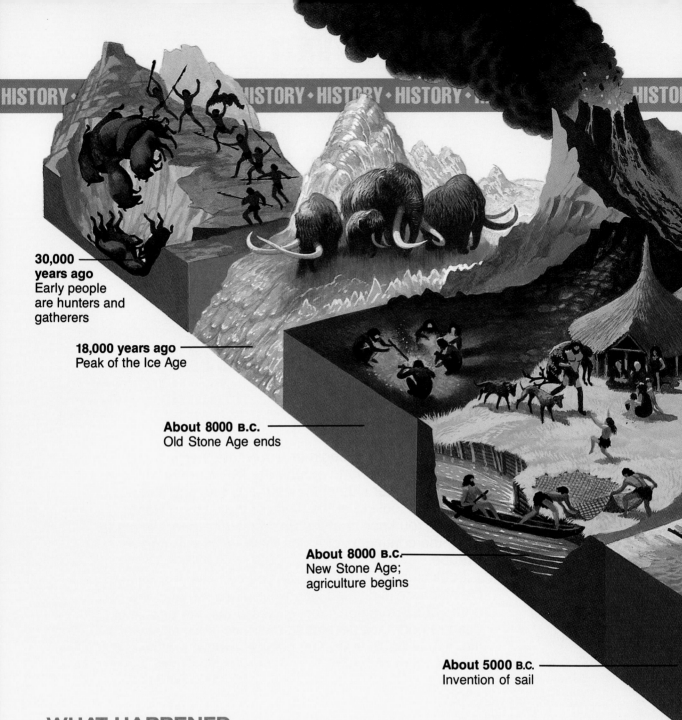

30,000 years ago
Early people are hunters and gatherers

18,000 years ago
Peak of the Ice Age

About 8000 B.C.
Old Stone Age ends

About 8000 B.C.
New Stone Age; agriculture begins

About 5000 B.C.
Invention of sail

About 4000 B.C.
Invention of wheel and plow

WHAT HAPPENED

Long before there were written records, people were making important contributions. Before there were towns and cities, people lived in small groups and worked together to meet their basic needs. As the time line shows, early people learned how to use fire and make tools. Gradually, they learned to grow food and tame animals. In some places, they began to live in villages, to trade, and to learn new skills.

CHAPTER 1

LEARNING ABOUT
EARTH'S GEOGRAPHY

FOCUS

Islands and peninsulas, continents and capes,
Dromedaries, cassowaries, elephants and apes,
Rivers, lakes and waterfalls, whirlpools and the sea,
Valley-beds and mountain-tops—are all Geography!

The capitals of Europe with so many curious names,
The North Pole and the South Pole and Vesuvius in flames,
Rice-fields, ice-fields, cotton-fields, fields of maize and tea,
The Equator and the Hemispheres—are all Geography!

Eleanor Farjeon

1 Discovering the Earth

▪ Key Vocabulary

geography   vegetation
environment   gazetteer

▪ Read Aloud

The tiny pea, pretty and blue, was the earth. I put up my thumb and shut one eye, and my thumb blotted out the planet Earth. I didn't feel like a giant. I felt very, very small.

These are the words of the astronaut Neil Armstrong. He looked at the earth from space on the *Apollo XI* flight in 1969. Have you ever wondered what it would be like to see the earth from space? What would it look like?

▪ Read for Purpose

1. **WHAT YOU KNOW:** How does your community compare with others?
2. **WHAT YOU WILL LEARN:** What is the geography of the earth?

THE STUDY OF GEOGRAPHY

When Neil Armstrong looked down from space, he had a special view of the earth's geography. You have already read in the Five Fundamental Themes of Geography about the different ways scientists study the earth. In fact the word *geography* comes from two Greek words, *ge*, meaning "earth," and *graphein*, meaning "to write." Looking down from space is just one way to study geography.

Clearly, there is much to learn about a topic as vast as the earth's geography. One way to begin is to investigate the variety of places on the earth. Through time, people have settled all over the world. Why did they settle where they did? How does where people live affect their lives? How have people affected the places where they live?

A WORLD OF ENVIRONMENTS

The world looks beautiful and colorful from space because geography varies greatly from place to place. As you have read, the earth has many different environments. An environment is made up of all the surroundings of a place. An environment includes the land and the water. It includes weather

21

patterns and all the plants and animals that live in a place. It also includes the things people have done to change a place.

People live in many different environments. They live in deserts, on mountains, on small islands, and in forests. They live along winding rivers or near great oceans. Wherever people live, they develop special connections with their environment. They learn how to live in or change their environment to suit their needs.

Do you know why people originally settled in your area? What were their reasons? Were they attracted by the good soil, a natural harbor, a wide river? If you live in Pittsburgh, Pennsylvania, you know that the city was originally settled because of its special

People live in different **environments**. Living by a river or a mountain affects the way people work and travel.

CHART SKILL: Can you describe the geography of your community? Use the chart to describe it.

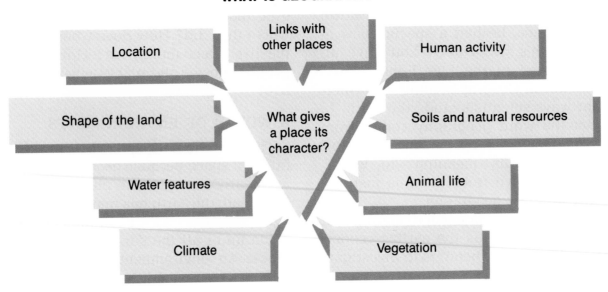

WHAT IS GEOGRAPHY?

- Location
- Links with other places
- Human activity
- Shape of the land
- What gives a place its character?
- Soils and natural resources
- Water features
- Animal life
- Climate
- Vegetation

geographic features. Pittsburgh lies between two rivers, the Monongahela and the Allegheny. These rivers unite at Pittsburgh to form the great Ohio River, which can take travelers and goods deep into the heart of America.

DIFFERENT LANDFORMS

Did you know that only 30 percent of the earth's surface is covered by land? The bodies of land on the earth's surface range in size from huge continents to small islands.

What is the land like in your community? Is it flat? Does your community lie among hills? Are there mountains in the distance? Answers will vary depending on where you live. However, by answering these questions you will be describing many different types of landforms.

Turn to the Dictionary of Geographic Terms on page 618. You will find the meanings of all the landforms you will read about in this book. You already have studied most of them. Are there any landforms shown in the dictionary that you do not know? For example, do you know what an isthmus (is′ məs) is? Find the definition in your Dictionary of Geographic Terms. Then find an isthmus on the map on pages 604–605 of the Atlas.

BODIES OF WATER

The map below shows that water covers more than 70 percent of the earth's surface. Most of the water on the earth is one large body of water that flows around the world.

Bodies of water also lie within the continents and other landmasses. The

MAP SKILL: Which of the continents is the largest? Which is the smallest? Are the oceans all about the same size?

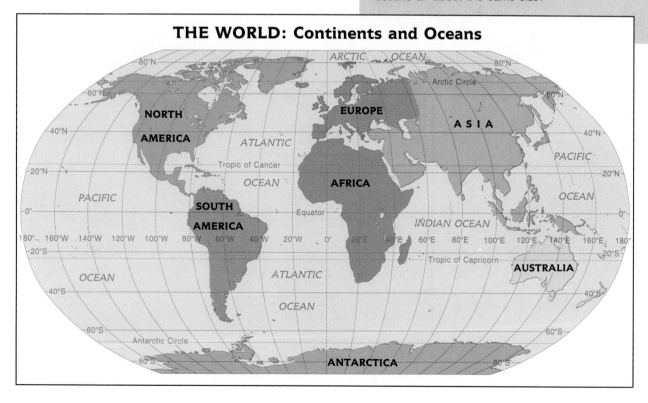

THE WORLD: Continents and Oceans

23

largest of these bodies of water are the seas. Rivers and lakes are other bodies of water found within landmasses. Great river systems crisscross the continents. They collect runoff water from rains and melting snows and carry this water into the oceans. A lake is a body of water completely surrounded by land. Lakes come in all shapes and sizes. Both rivers and lakes supply fresh water and food.

EARTH'S VEGETATION

The study of the earth's geography also includes the study of the many kinds of plants that grow here. Each environment has its own unique plant life. The natural plant life of a region is called its vegetation (vej ə tā' shən). Vegetation groupings vary from mountain forests to desert shrubs.

The map on page 25 shows the wealth of vegetation across the earth. What kind of vegetation exists in your region? What kinds of vegetation are found along the equator? Can you imagine what life would be like in a region that has little or no vegetation?

LEARNING FROM A GAZETTEER

This book has a special section that will help you answer such questions. It

The Great Lakes, shown in this photograph taken from space, are the world's largest group of freshwater lakes. In what continent are they located?

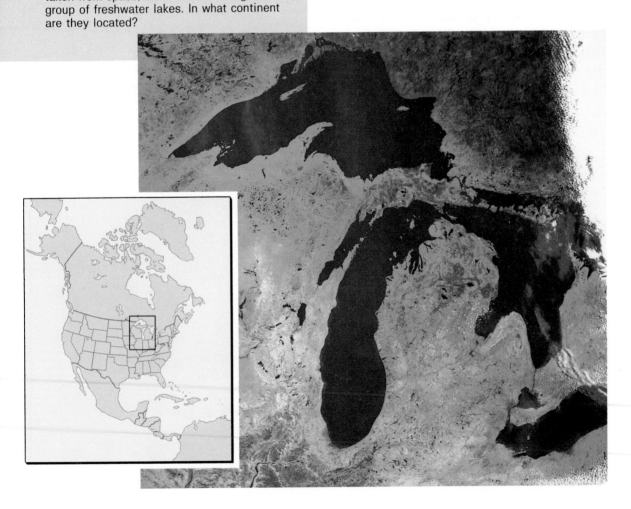

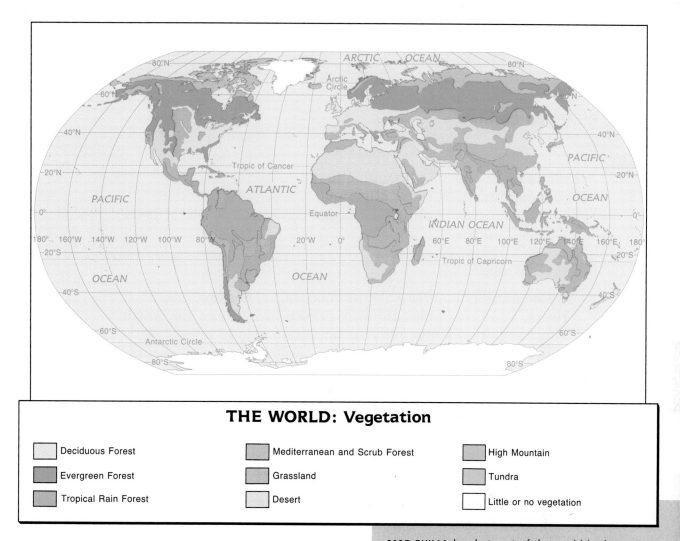

THE WORLD: Vegetation

▢	Deciduous Forest	▢	Mediterranean and Scrub Forest	▢	High Mountain
▢	Evergreen Forest	▢	Grassland	▢	Tundra
▢	Tropical Rain Forest	▢	Desert	▢	Little or no vegetation

MAP SKILL: In what part of the world is the vegetation mainly tundra? How many kinds of vegetation are found on the continent of Antarctica?

is the Gazetteer (gaz ə tēr′), which begins on page 620. A gazetteer is a list of countries, states, cities, mountains, deserts, rivers, lakes, and other places of geographical significance. The gazetteer tells you a little about these places and gives their exact locations.

As you study the many parts of the world this year, use the gazetteer often. It will help you identify and locate the places you read about.

You will find that an understanding of geography is very useful. The world is a huge place—filled with different environments, different people, different ideas. What better way is there to

begin to understand the world than to study its geography?

Check Your Reading

1. What are environments?
2. What is an isthmus? Name one isthmus.
3. **GEOGRAPHY SKILL:** What is the difference between an ocean and a sea?
4. **THINKING SKILL:** What are the physical features of your environment?

2 Climates of the World

READ TO LEARN

Key Vocabulary

climate
precipitation
latitude
tropical climate

temperate climate
polar climate
altitude
current

Read Aloud

Geographic features such as mountains, deserts, oceans, rivers, and lakes affect the way people live around the world. Weather patterns also play an important role in our lives. How does weather affect the way people live in your part of the world?

Read for Purpose

1. **WHAT YOU KNOW:** What yearly weather pattern does your community have?
2. **WHAT YOU WILL LEARN:** What is climate?

MANY DIFFERENT CLIMATES

Imagine that you are visiting the Sahara of Africa. This great desert has endless waves of sand. Its shimmering heat can climb to 136°F. (58°C) during the day, but at night the temperature can drop below 50°F. (10°C). There is almost no water. Only about 1 inch (2.5 cm) of rain falls here all year!

Now imagine that you are a scientist working in Antarctica near the South Pole. Your laboratory is surrounded by great plains of ice. In fact, Antarctica is a continent almost completely covered by a giant sheet of ice! But what is the weather like? It is not unusual for temperatures here to dip to −100°F. (−73°C) below zero!

These are just two examples of the many kinds of climates, or weather patterns, that are found around the world. Climate is a description of the pattern of weather that an area has over a long period of time. Moisture that falls in the form of rain or snow, or precipitation (pri sip ə tā′ shən), and temperature are factors used to describe climate. Although most climates are not as extreme as the climates of the Sahara and Antarctica, climate is always a very important part of the environment.

Look at the map on the top of the next page. It shows the variety of the earth's climates and briefly describes what is special about each one.

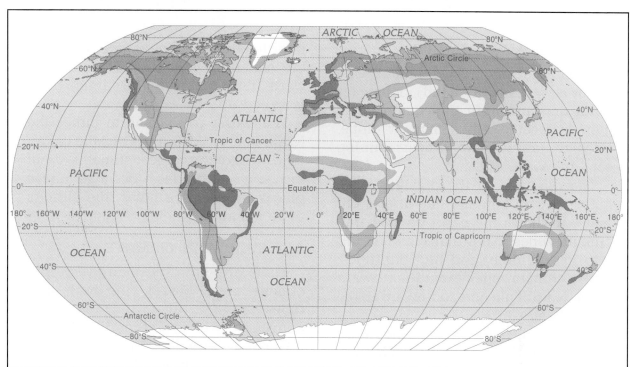

THE WORLD: Climate

- ☐ Ice cap
- ☐ Very cold winter, cold summer, dry
- ☐ Very cold winter, cool summer, wet
- ☐ Highlands, temperature and precipitation vary with elevation
- ☐ Semi-dry, temperature varies with latitude
- ☐ Cold winter, hot or warm summer, wet
- ☐ Mild winter, cool summer, wet
- ☐ Mild or warm winter, hot summer, wet
- ☐ Mild, wet winter; hot, dry summer
- ☐ Dry, temperature varies with latitude
- ☐ Warm all year, wet with one dry season
- ☐ Warm and wet all year

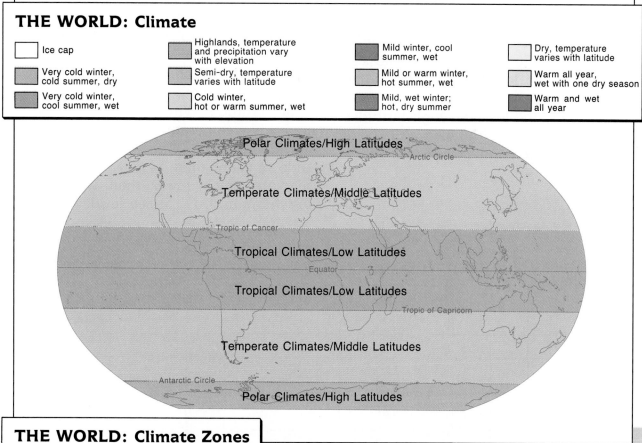

THE WORLD: Climate Zones

MAP SKILL: How many types of climate are found in the United States? In which climate zone are they located?

27

LATITUDE AND CLIMATE

Several factors affect climate. One factor is latitude (lat′ ə tüd), or how far north or south from the equator a region is located. On a map or globe, lines of latitude are drawn running east and west.

The diagram on the previous page helps explain how latitude affects climate. It shows the earth divided into climate zones. Note that climates fall into low, middle, and high latitudes. These climate zones extend northward to the North Pole and southward to the South Pole.

In general, the nearer a place is to the equator, the warmer it is. The hottest climates are in the low latitudes. Note that the low latitudes reach from the Tropic of Cancer to the Tropic of Capricorn. For this reason, the climates of the low latitudes are called tropical climates.

Between the low and high latitudes are the middle latitudes. Much of North America and Europe lies in the middle latitudes. The middle latitudes are generally cold in the winter and warm in the summer. The climate there is called a temperate climate.

The closer a place is to either the North Pole or the South Pole, the colder it is. Most of the coldest climates are in the high latitudes. Because these places lie near the poles, the climate there is called a polar climate.

ALTITUDE AND CLIMATE

There are, however, many very cold climate areas outside the high latitudes. Altitude (al′ tə tüd), or height above sea level, is a second factor that influences climate. In general, the higher the altitude of a place, the cooler the temperatures usually are.

Look at the graph below and the map on the next page. As you see from the map, both Washington, D.C., and Pikes Peak, Colorado, are at about the same latitude. Why are their average monthly temperatures so different? Temperatures on Pikes Peak, at an altitude of more than 14,000 feet (4,270 m), are much lower than those in Washington, D.C., at sea level.

GRAPH SKILL: What is the difference in average temperature between Pikes Peak and Washington, D.C., in July?

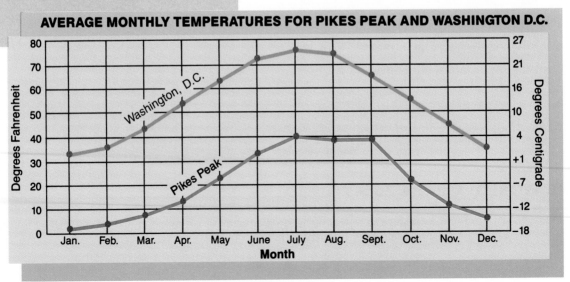

AVERAGE MONTHLY TEMPERATURES FOR PIKES PEAK AND WASHINGTON D.C.

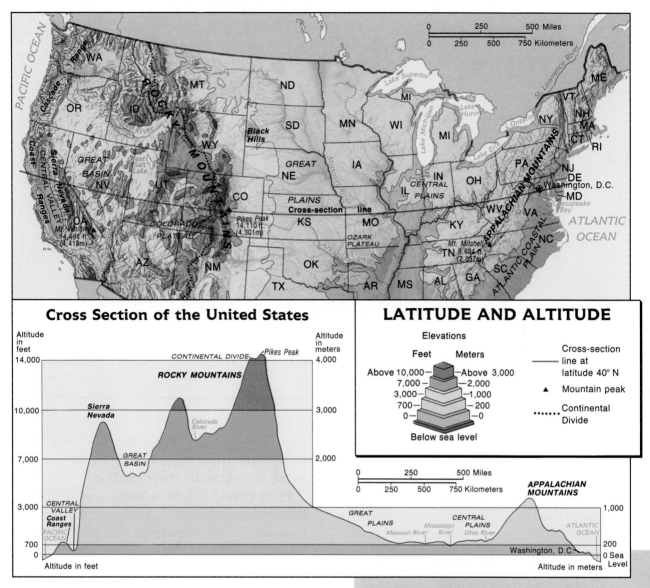

Cross Section of the United States

LATITUDE AND ALTITUDE

Elevations

Feet   Meters

Feet	Meters
Above 10,000	Above 3,000
7,000	2,000
3,000	1,000
700	200
0	0

Below sea level

⎯⎯⎯ Cross-section line at latitude 40° N

▲ Mountain peak

······ Continental Divide

MAP SKILL: What part of the United States has the highest **altitude**? What parts have the lowest altitude?

CURRENTS AND CLIMATE

There is another reason why climates vary. Look at the map on page 30. As you can see, Europe lies farther north than much of North America. You might expect Europe to have a cooler climate than North America. In fact, the climate of the British Isles is warmer than Newfoundland. The answer to this puzzle is found in the Atlantic Ocean.

The Atlantic Ocean, like all oceans, has **currents**. Currents are like rivers or streams flowing through the oceans. Cold currents flow from the polar regions toward the equator. Warm currents flow from the equator toward the poles.

Look again at the map on the next page. Do warm or cold ocean currents flow toward Europe? Why should this make a difference? It makes a difference because warm currents heat the

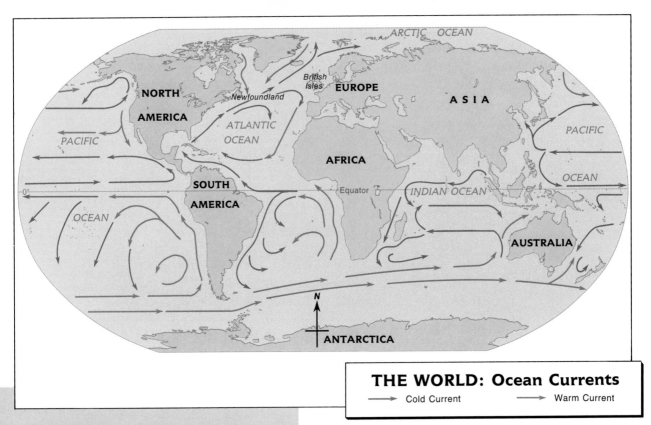

THE WORLD: Ocean Currents

——▶ Cold Current   ——▶ Warm Current

MAP SKILL: Does a warm or cold **current** move toward Europe from North America? Do cold currents flow in the Indian Ocean?

air above them and cause warmer temperatures. The British Isles, so near the flow of a warm ocean current, has a milder climate than Newfoundland.

CLIMATE'S INFLUENCE

Climate has an important effect on plant and animal life and on human activities in different regions. The world supply of food and other products depend on climate. Some crops, such as bananas and rubber, can grow only in tropical areas where there are no frosts.

Climate also influences animal life. In order to survive, animals must adapt to their environment. In polar climates, animal life consists of animals, such as penguins, that are able to survive in extreme cold. In very dry

regions, camels are able to survive partly because they can store up a reserve of water in their bodies.

How does climate affect human life? People have lived in every climate on the earth—the very cold and dry to the very hot and wet. As you read about the many world regions in this book, you will be introduced to the ways people have met the challenge of survival in different climates.

Check Your Reading

1. Are temperatures warmer in low latitudes or high latitudes? Why?
2. Why are temperatures generally lower at higher altitudes?
3. **GEOGRAPHY SKILL:** How do ocean currents affect climate?
4. **THINKING SKILL:** How does the climate of your region change from month to month?

30

3 Earth's Resources

READ TO LEARN

Key Vocabulary

natural resource   renewable resource
mineral   nonrenewable resource

Read Aloud

Think for a moment of all the things we must have to survive. We must have air to breathe, water to drink, and food to eat. We must have clothing and shelter for warmth and protection. Many environments provide a wealth of resources that help us meet our needs. Like the earth's landforms and climates, resources vary greatly from one location to another.

Read for Purpose

1. **WHAT YOU KNOW:** How do you treat the earth?
2. **WHAT YOU WILL LEARN:** Why are resources important?

NATURAL RESOURCES

What are resources? A resource can be almost anything as long as it is helpful to people. That's what makes something a resource—its usefulness.

Many things that are part of nature are useful. For example, water, air, soil, sunlight, and wild animals are natural resources. People tend to take natural resources for granted. But these resources make it possible for life to exist on the earth.

Can you think how you would survive without water? Water is used for drinking, cooking, and washing. Without water, farmers could not grow food. People also use water as a means of transportation.

Like landforms and climate, natural resources greatly affect how the people of an area live. Natural resources are not spread evenly across the earth. Some areas are rich in them and others are not. What problems might exist in a region that does not have a rich supply of natural resources?

USING MINERALS

Some of the most important natural resources are minerals (min′ ər əls). Minerals are natural substances that are reached by mining, or digging into the earth. Minerals can be divided into two groups: metals and nonmetals. Most metallic minerals are hard and shiny.

To realize how important minerals are, you only have to look around. Think of the things you use each day.

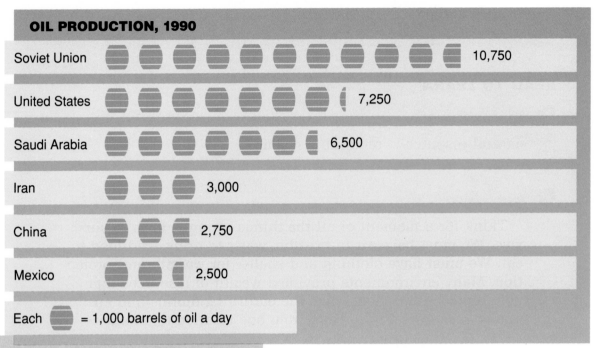

OIL PRODUCTION, 1990

Country	Barrels
Soviet Union	10,750
United States	7,250
Saudi Arabia	6,500
Iran	3,000
China	2,750
Mexico	2,500

Each = 1,000 barrels of oil a day

GRAPH SKILL: How much oil does the United States produce in five days? Is this more than Saudi Arabia produces in ten days?

You can probably see in your classroom many products made from metallic minerals. Your desk may be made partly of iron. Coins are made of nickel or copper.

What about nonmetallic minerals? The salt you use to flavor your food is a nonmetallic mineral. At one time, salt was even used to make window glass. The cement used to make sidewalks is also a mixture of many nonmetallic minerals.

Like most natural resources, minerals are not spread evenly around the world. An area of the world may be very rich in some resources and poor or lacking in others. South Africa, for example, has some of the largest reserves of gold and uranium. However, it has very little natural gas and oil. Saudi Arabia, on the other hand, lacks most metallic minerals but has large deposits of oil beneath the desert sands.

PRESERVING EARTH'S RESOURCES

It is important to realize that all resources are very valuable. Some resources are renewable resources, or resources that can replace or rebuild themselves. If used correctly, renewable resources will always be available. Most living resources such as plants and animals are renewable. Sunlight, wind, air, soil, and water are also renewable resources. Although renewable resources can be replaced, they must be used wisely. Water, for example, can become dirty and unusable.

In modern times, the uses of and need for natural resources have grown greatly. Many important resources are nonrenewable resources, or resources that can never be renewed or replaced. Metals are nonrenewable resources. Once a nonrenewable resource is gone, it is gone forever.

Meeting today's energy needs demands vast quantities of precious

Some natural resources can be renewed. On this field in Belgium, trees have been planted to provide a new forest for the future.

nonrenewable resources. In order to make and provide power for goods such as cars and computers, great amounts of natural resources are needed. You can see why people must carefully plan how these resources are used—especially if the needs of future generations are to be met.

PEOPLE AND THE EARTH

People are an important factor in the world's resources. Every person is different, with his or her own skills. In this book you will explore the many different groups of people across the globe. You will also learn about the special connections between people and world geography.

The map on pages 16–17 in the Unit Opener shows the regions of the Eastern Hemisphere you will study in this book. The geography of these regions includes almost every kind of landform, vegetation, climate, and natural resource. Discovering how the people of these regions have, over thousands of years, dealt with the geography of their lands is a fascinating story. It is the story you will learn about in the chapters that follow.

 Check Your Reading

1. What are natural resources?
2. Explain how renewable resources and nonrenewable resources are different.
3. **GEOGRAPHY SKILL:** What are some of the ways you can preserve the world's resources?
4. **THINKING SKILL:** Classify the resources mentioned in this lesson into two groups. Label each group.

33

Understanding Latitude and Longitude

Key Vocabulary

latitude	prime meridian
longitude	meridian
degree	grid
parallel	

You have read in the Five Fundamental Themes of Geography that one way to determine absolute location is with imaginary lines called latitude and longitude. Lines of latitude run east and west, and lines of longitude run north and south.

Latitude and Longitude

Although lines of latitude run east and west, they measure the distance, in degrees, north and south of the equator. A degree is a unit of measurement that describes the distance between lines of latitude and lines of longitude. The symbol for degrees is °.

The equator is the starting line for measuring latitude. Notice on **Map A** that the line marking the equator is labeled 0°, meaning zero degrees latitude. The line above the equator is marked 30°N, or 30 degrees north; the line below the equator is marked 30°S, or 30 degrees south. There are 90 degrees of latitude between the equator and each of the poles.

Lines of latitude are also known as parallels. Parallels are lines that run in the same direction and are always the same distance apart.

Map B shows lines of longitude, which run north and south. Lines of longitude

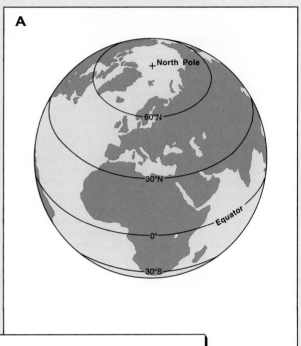

A

LINES OF LATITUDE

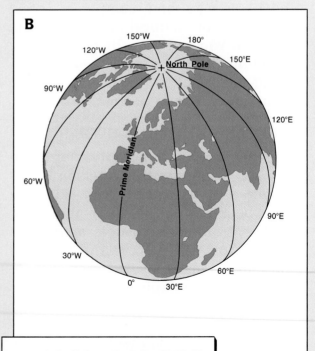

B

LINES OF LONGITUDE

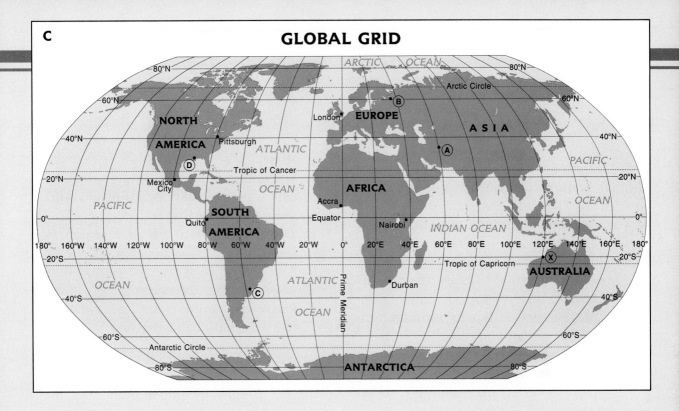

C **GLOBAL GRID**

measure distance in degrees east and west of the prime meridian. Find the prime meridian on **Map B**.

Notice that it is marked 0°, meaning zero degrees longitude. All the lines east and west of the prime meridian are called meridians.

A Global Grid

Why is understanding latitude and longitude useful? Notice on **Map C** that the parallels and meridians cross each other and form a grid. This grid makes it possible to pinpoint exact locations.

Suppose that you want to give the correct latitude and longitude of Pittsburgh. To find its exact location, first note the place where the equator and the prime meridian cross. Then, move your finger north along the prime meridian away from the equator to the line of latitude, or parallel, on which Pittsburgh falls. As you see, it is marked 40°N. In other words, Pittsburgh is located 40 degrees north of the equator.

Now you must find Pittsburgh's correct line of longitude, or meridian. To find this measure, remember that you are counting its distance from the prime meridian. Move your finger west from the prime meridian, along 40°N until you reach Pittsburgh. You will note that 80°W is the correct measure. Thus, Pittsburgh's correct location is 40°N, 80°W.

Reviewing the Skill

Use **Map C** to answer these questions.
1. How do lines of latitude and lines of longitude help you to read a map?
2. Is the line marked 60°S a parallel or a meridian? Why?
3. What two cities on the map fall on the same line of latitude? What two cities are on the same line of longitude?
4. The location of Buenos Aires is 35°S, 60°W. What letter on the map shows this location?
5. Give the latitude and longitude of the places marked *A*, *B*, and *X*.

CHAPTER 1 • SUMMARY AND REVIEW

IDEAS TO REMEMBER

■ Geography is the study of the earth and its features and how people affect the earth. The earth has many different environments that help shape the way people live.

■ Climate consists of patterns of weather over a long period of time. The climate of a particular region is highly influenced by such things as latitude, altitude, and ocean currents.

■ Natural resources are an essential part of the earth and should be preserved. Some resources are renewable; other resources are nonrenewable.

REVIEWING VOCABULARY

altitude	mineral
current	natural resource
environment	precipitation
geography	renewable resource
latitude	vegetation

Number a sheet of paper from 1 to 10. Beside each number write the word or term from the above list that best completes each sentence.

1. The _____ of a place includes land, water, climate, plants, animals, buildings, and all of its other surroundings.
2. The _____ of a place will tell you how high above sea level it is.
3. The study of the earth and its features and how people affect the earth is called _____.
4. A _____ is a natural substance that is reached by digging into the earth.
5. The _____ of a place indicates how far north or south it is from the equator.
6. _____ is moisture in the form of rain or snow.
7. Something found in nature, such as soil, water, vegetation, and even a wild animal is called a _____.
8. The natural plant life of a region is called its _____.
9. A _____ is like a river or stream that flows through the ocean.
10. Plants and animals are _____ because they can replace themselves.

REVIEWING FACTS

Number a sheet of paper from 1 to 10. Write whether the following statements are true or false. If the statement is false, rewrite it to make it true.

1. Geography includes the study of the effects that people have on the earth.
2. Natural resources are evenly distributed throughout the earth.
3. Natural resources such as altitude and ocean currents have little effect on how people live.
4. The altitude of a place has little influence on its climate.
5. The hottest climates are found in the high latitudes.
6. Currents in the Atlantic Ocean make Europe's climate colder than it would otherwise be.
7. Minerals are natural substances that are reached by digging into the earth.
8. Water covers more than 70 percent of the earth.
9. The low latitudes tend to have very cool climates.
10. Weather is the climate of a region over a long period of time.

✏ WRITING ABOUT MAIN IDEAS

1. **Writing a Letter:** Think about the ways in which people have influenced and changed the environment in your community. Write a letter to your local newspaper that explains why you support or oppose these changes.

2. **Writing a Story:** Every community had its first settlers. Think for a moment of the chief geographic features in your community. Do you live near a special body of water? Do you live in fertile farming country? Write a story telling why you think early settlers might have chosen to build your community. In your story, explain what it was about the geography of your community that may have attracted the first settlers.

3. **Writing About Perspectives:** Imagine that you work for a travel magazine. Write an advertisement describing several things in your environment that might be of interest to visitors.

BUILDING SKILLS: UNDERSTANDING LATITUDE AND LONGITUDE

Use the maps on this page to answer the following questions.

1. Describe lines of latitude and lines of longitude.
2. What is the first line of latitude shown north of the equator? What line of latitude is shown south of the equator?
3. What lines of longitude are shown closest to the Prime Meridian?
4. Why is it helpful to use lines of latitude and longitude on a map?

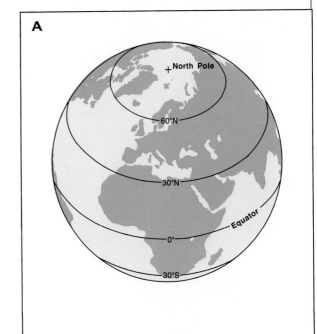

A

LINES OF LATITUDE

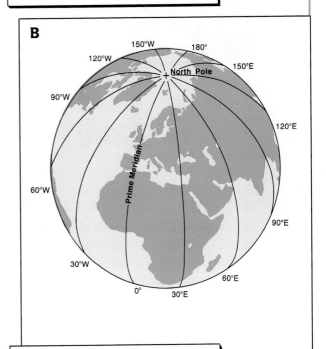

B

LINES OF LONGITUDE

CHAPTER 2

LEARNING ABOUT EARLY PEOPLE

FOCUS

How many years have passed and gone since human feet last trod on this floor? You feel it could have been yesterday. Other feelings follow . . . suspense and the thought that you are about to add another page to history. . . .

Have you ever wondered what it would be like to be the first person to find an ancient ruin? The writer of the above words spent 20 years looking for one of the world's oldest villages. In this chapter you will begin a journey into the world of the earth's early people.

1 All People Have a Culture

READnbspTO LEARN

Key Vocabulary

culture   government
custom   religion
society   legacy
values

Read Aloud

What do you know about people who lived long ago? As you read this book, you will learn about many different groups of people. Some of these people lived thousands of years ago. Others lived only a few hundred years in the past. You also will learn about people living in the world today who live differently than you do.

Read for Purpose

1. **WHAT YOU KNOW:** What helps you stay active and healthy?
2. **WHAT YOU WILL LEARN:** What do people all around the world have in common?

MEETING BASIC NEEDS

All over the earth, people have the same basic needs. Everyone needs food, clothing, and shelter. People need these things just to stay alive. By living and working together, people are able to meet these needs.

As you read this book, you will find that each group of people meets its basic needs in different ways. You will also learn that as people work together they develop a special way of life. The way of life belonging to a group of people is called its **culture** (kul′ chər). A group's culture includes all the ways that its people live, think, believe, and feel. All people have a culture. Cul-tures develop as groups of people work together to meet basic needs.

All people have the same basic needs. But different cultures meet their needs in many different ways. For example, everyone must have food. What people eat, however, often depends on the **customs** (kus′ təms) of their culture. Customs are social habits or ways of living in a group. It is customary in some cultures to eat a lot of beef and chicken. In other cultures, it is a custom never to eat meat.

People also need shelter. The kinds of shelter people build is another part of culture. Homes vary for different

WHAT IS CULTURE?

The governments we organize	The tools we use	The arts and recreation we develop
The clothes we wear		The religion we believe in
The shelters we live in	**What gives a society its character?**	The values we accept
The things we make		The customs and traditions we follow
The foods we eat	The language we speak	The knowledge we share

CHART SKILL: Use the chart to describe some features of your culture.

reasons. They often vary from climate to climate, for example. In warm areas many people build open, airy homes. In some tropical rain forests, houses are built on stilts high above the ground. This protects them from rising rivers and helps to catch breezes.

The way people dress is also part of their culture. In a hot and humid climate people wear light clothing. It might be just a strip of cloth wrapped around the body. How might clothing be different for people living in a cold climate?

LIVING AND WORKING TOGETHER

The ways people develop to live and work together form another part of their culture. For example, people developed language to communicate with one another. Today more than 3,000 languages are used by the cultures throughout the world. Without languages, how would important ideas and skills be passed from parents to their children?

All over the earth, people are organized into social groups. In many cultures, the main social group is the family. Clubs and teams are other social groups.

A group of people bound together by the same culture is called a society (sə sī' ə tē). Societies vary in the things that they make and the ways that they make them. The people in one society might make only a few kinds of goods, such as wooden bowls or clay pots. To make them, they use simple tools like a knife and a wood-fired oven.

Cooperation is an important value in American society. Working for a fire department or taking part in a town meeting are two ways in which people cooperate.

People in another society might make many complex goods like automobiles and airplanes. To make such goods, they must use highly complex tools, like machines and computers.

VALUES AND CULTURE

People of all societies have always felt the need to find the answers to basic questions in life. How should people act toward one another? What is right and what is wrong? What is the purpose of life?

The way people answer such questions often depends on their values (val′ ūz). Values are the beliefs, or ideals, that guide the way people live. Values are an important part of every culture. A culture's values reflect what its people believe is important. In the United States, for example, most people believe that they should deal with one another as equals. In some other cultures, people believe that one person or group stands above the rest.

Such values affect how people are governed. Government (guv′ ərn mənt), or the established form of ruling, is another part of culture. In the United

41

States, the belief in equality helped form a government in which the people elect leaders in free elections.

Values are also a part of religion (ri lij′ ən). Religion is a belief in God or gods. Members of a religion have a common way to worship their God or gods. The beliefs of a religion help its members answer questions about life's mysteries.

Thousands of religions have emerged over time. Some religions, such as Judaism and Christianity, teach that there is one God. Others teach that there are many gods. Some religions are widespread and are shared by many different societies.

Many Japanese couples wear traditional clothes when they get married. Do Americans wear special clothes at their weddings?

THE LEGACY OF DIFFERENT CULTURES

As you read this book, you will learn about many world cultures. You will discover that, whenever and wherever people have lived, their basic needs are always the same. You will learn, however, that cultures also differ in important ways.

Each culture is built upon a legacy (leg′ ə sē) from the past. A culture's legacy is made up of traditions that have developed over many years. A legacy is handed down, from one generation to the next. While you explore many new regions of the earth, try to discover what is unique about them. What are their legacies? What are their achievements? How have they contributed to world history and caused today's world to be a better place?

You will discover that the people of the earth speak many different languages and have many different values. You will learn that there are many different systems of government and religion. You will also learn about societies that have built upon the legacies of even earlier people. Read on. You are about to start an adventure that will take you far into the past. In the next lesson you will be learning about the world's earliest people!

 Check Your Reading

1. What are basic needs?
2. How does the chart on page 40 help you understand how cultures around the world differ?
3. Why are values important? How do they affect society?
4. **THINKING SKILL:** Look at the picture at the left. What does it tell you about Japanese culture?

2 How Early People Lived

READ TO LEARN

Key Vocabulary

Ice Age
glacier
Old Stone Age
nomad

Read Aloud

To learn about the world's first cultures, we must go far back in time. The earth known by the earliest people was a very different place than it is today. Both the earth's surface and climate have changed. Such changes have greatly affected the growth of culture.

Read for Purpose

1. **WHAT YOU KNOW:** Why do people often work together?
2. **WHAT YOU WILL LEARN:** What were the achievements of the world's earliest people?

THE EARTH AND EARLY PEOPLE

Long ago, the earth had long cold periods. This time, known as the Ice Age, lasted millions of years. During the Ice Age, glaciers (glā′ shərs), or great sheets of ice, covered parts of the earth. The glaciers moved slowly but powerfully, like rolling mountains of ice. They moved south from the Arctic regions and covered large areas of Europe, Asia, and North America. At the peak of the Ice Age, glaciers covered almost one fourth of the earth, as the map on the next page shows.

It was during the Ice Age that people began to live together in small groups.

Although they lived long ago, we know many things about them. They left behind traces of their campsites, artwork, and tools. From these things, we have learned about their cultures.

This first stage of human life is called the Old Stone Age. The Old Stone Age began about 2 million years ago and ended only 10,000 years ago. It got its name from the fact that Old Stone Age people made their tools from stone. People discovered how to use fire for warmth and cooking during the Old Stone Age. This was a time when people were learning how to work together. As you will learn, it was an exciting time of great change.

43

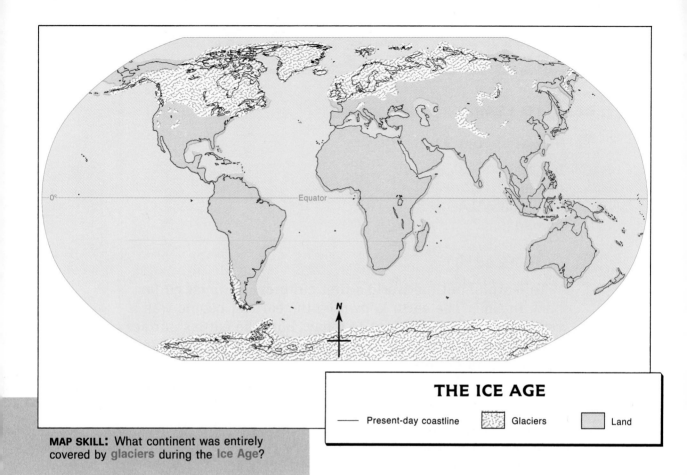

THE ICE AGE

—— Present-day coastline   ░ Glaciers   ▢ Land

MAP SKILL: What continent was entirely covered by glaciers during the Ice Age?

A STORY OF THE OLD STONE AGE

Imagine that you have gone back in time to the Old Stone Age, more than 12,000 years ago. The world was a very different place.

One day a boy named Gam was just waking up. The gray light of dawn was beginning to lighten his shelter. During the night the fire had died out in the hearth, so Gam drew his deerskin tightly around him for warmth. Sitting up, Gam could see that the other members of his group were still sleeping. His group consisted of family members and close relatives. All 24 of them were there.

Before long the campsite was stirring as everyone rolled up their deer-skins and began relighting the fires. But Gam did not move. It was too cold to get up. Perhaps if he just lay still . . . but another day of hunting and food gathering was about to begin.

Gam recalled reaching this campsite several days earlier. His people were following a deer herd that was on the move. Like other Old Stone Age groups, Gam's people were **nomads** (nō′ mads), traveling from place to place in search of food. They had no permanent homes or villages. They made temporary homes in caves or tents.

Gam's people were nomads because their lives centered on hunting and gathering. This way of life kept Old Stone Age people on the move. When the animals left their area or the food supply ran short, the people moved on.

44

It was clear to Gam why his people constantly followed deer herds. Deer filled many of their needs. Deer flesh provided them with food. Deer hides gave them skins needed to make clothing and tents. Even deer bones and antlers had many uses. They were carved into needles and other tools.

Deer herds were not the only animals Gam's people hunted. During the Old Stone Age, people also followed herds of bison, wild horses, and mammoths. In those days the shaggy mammoths were one of the world's largest animals. Mammoths stood up to 14 feet (4 m) tall.

HUNTING AND GATHERING

People of the Old Stone Age were skillful hunters. In order to catch a wild animal, Gam's people had to work together. Sometimes they would disguise themselves as deer and close in on a herd. Together, they would surround an animal and charge at it with their weapons. Sometimes early hunters killed animals by chasing them over a cliff, as shown on the time line in the Unit Opener on pages 18–19.

The earliest hunters used stones and sticks for weapons. Later hunters learned to use flint, or a stone that could be chipped to make a sharp cutting edge. Using flint, early hunters made many kinds of tools. These included knives and spearpoints for hunting, scrapers for cleaning animal skins, and axes to cut up meat.

The hunters of Gam's time also made spear-throwers. A spear-thrower helped hunters to throw weapons very far. Spear-throwers were often beautifully carved, as shown on this page.

While some of Gam's people were hunters, others were skillful food gath-

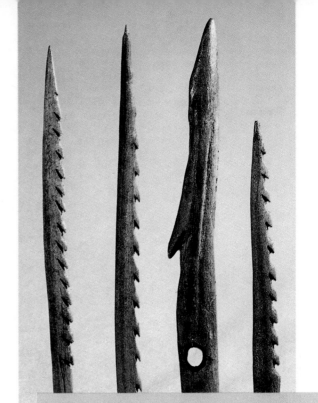

People of the Old Stone Age needed weapons to survive. They carved the harpoons, spear-throwers, and spear handle shown here.

erers. Early people could not always depend on a good hunt. Thus, it was important to find other sources of food.

Gam's people knew that the earth provided many kinds of foods. The gatherers of his group knew which plants were the best to eat. Some plants, they knew, were poisonous. Others were good to eat. They often picked berries, pine nuts, and fruits. Sometimes Gam helped the gatherers dig into the earth in search of roots. Early people used digging sticks, carved out of branches, to make the job easier.

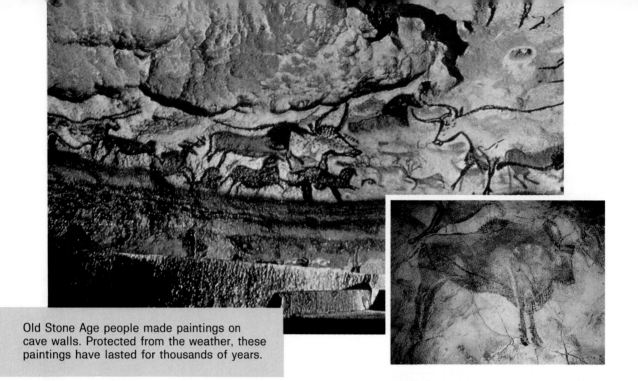

Old Stone Age people made paintings on cave walls. Protected from the weather, these paintings have lasted for thousands of years.

THE BEGINNING OF CULTURE

Early people, like the members of Gam's group, developed their own special cultures. An important part of that culture grew from the ways people met their basic needs for food, clothing, and shelter. At the same time, people also developed unique languages and religious beliefs.

The development of language had a major effect on the growth of culture. Through the use of language, people could share ideas about religion, values, customs, and skills. Thus, a group's culture could be learned and spread more quickly.

The religious beliefs of Old Stone Age people were tied to their environment. Other beliefs were tied to important parts of their daily life like hunting and gathering. Such beliefs may have led early people to paint pictures on the walls of the caves in which they lived. They painted pictures of the animals they hunted. These paintings probably had religious meaning for

early people. You will read more about these cave paintings in the Traditions lesson on pages 48–51.

What were the achievements of people who lived during the Old Stone Age? You have learned that it was a time when people struggled to meet the needs of daily living. Remember that early people developed the first languages and religious beliefs. They worked together and learned important skills. These accomplishments mark the beginning of culture.

 Check Your Reading

1. How did people live during the Old Stone Age?
2. What tools did early people have? What were they made of?
3. **GEOGRAPHY SKILL:** Which continents were most affected by the Ice Age? Explain your answer.
4. **THINKING SKILL:** What could have been the consequences if the Ice Age had never ended? What would the earth be like?

ART ON THE STREETS OF BOSTON

Art is an important part of culture. As you have read, people have created art since earliest times. Even the people of the Old Stone Age drew pictures of the animals they hunted. Art continues to be a central part of modern culture. Today Bob Guillemin, better known as Sidewalk Sam, uses colorful chalk to create wonderful designs. He kneels for long hours on concrete to bring great art out where people can see and enjoy it.

Sidewalk Sam is a screever, or pavement artist. He has special permission from the City of Boston to draw his chalk pictures on city sidewalks. The city appreciates the way Sam and his work brighten the streets and involve the people.

It takes Sam all day to chalk a giant copy of a famous painting on the sidewalk. Sam uses the sidewalk because he believes that beautiful things should be a part of our everyday lives, not saved for trips to a museum. You might find Sam working in front of a bank, near a store, or on a busy corner. But one thing is certain, you will always find him working where there are lots of people.

Sam likes to watch the reactions of people to his work as it takes shape. People see all the steps that it takes to make a portrait or draw a landscape. This way great art becomes understandable.

As he works, he talks with the people who stop to watch. Strangers will stand and talk together about the painting and

its progress. People start to smile as they see what Sam is doing. He and his work add a feeling of warmth and friendliness to the city streets.

How long does Guillemin's artwork last? Most of his creations begin to wear away in a week. Sometimes a sudden rain washes away a picture before he even finishes it. But in the words of Sidewalk Sam:

It's the process that's important. It's enough for me just to have people enjoy it while I was doing it.

47

STONE PAINTING

by Virginia Arnold

Compare the cave paintings on page 46 to the sidewalk painting on page 47. The cave paintings were painted thousands of years ago. The sidewalk painting was painted very recently. Both paintings are, of course, examples of art, a tradition that has been important for a very long time to people all over the world.

A tradition is a custom or belief that has been handed down from generation to generation. Traditions are an important part of culture. Like the cave paintings, they may be very old and help remind people of the past. But traditions may also help people express beliefs and feelings about the present. Like artists today, the artists of long ago painted because they wanted to communicate something about their lives. As you read, think about what life may have been like for people who lived long ago and painted on stone.

ANCIENT ARTISTS

At the edge of a high cliff, a man squatted under an overhanging ledge of rock. Far down below he could see herds of animals moving like waves across the plain. Elephants, giraffes, ostriches, and gazelles could be seen through the bright sunlight.

The man picked up a rock that he had shaped into a sharp point. Reaching up as high as he could, he began to scratch the shape of a giraffe into the stone wall. First he made the outline of the giraffe's small head and its two slender horns. Then he made the giraffe's long, thin neck and the rest of its body. When the outline was finished, the man took a wooden bowl in which he had crushed red berries and iron dust. Adding animal fat and water, he stirred the mixture into a reddish paint. With a thin brush made from animal hair, he traced the paint over the giraffe outline scratched into the stone wall. Finally he added nine large spots and a squiggly tail.

THE TASSILI PLATEAU

We will never really know who painted the giraffe or why the painting was made. But we do know that this painting still exists today. It can be seen on the Tassili (tas sēl' ē) Plateau in Algeria, a country in Africa. Some of the most

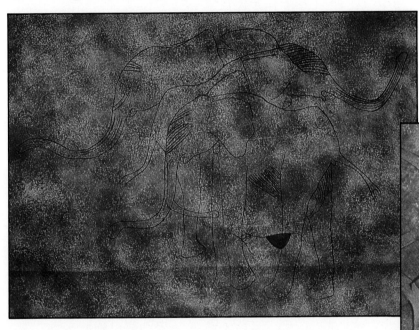

beautiful stone paintings anywhere in the world are found in this place. There are over 15,000 paintings. They tell us much about the lives of the people who lived in this region as long as 8,000 years ago.

What did these early artists paint? Most of the paintings are of animals. There are paintings of rabbits, elephants, giraffes, rhinoceroses, and other animals still found in many parts of Africa today. Paintings of other kinds of animals that are extinct, or no longer alive, were also made.

There are many paintings of people. These paintings tell us much about the lives of the people in Tassili. Some paintings show hunting or the gathering of food. Many show scenes of village life, such as people herding cows, riding horses, and taking part in ceremonies that included music and dance.

There are so many paintings at Tassili that in some places several have been painted one on top of another. Different generations of artists used the same walls and caves over thousands of years. In most cases, the artists used animal-hair brushes or their own fingers to apply paint to the stone walls. Sometimes hollow animal bones were used to blow paint onto the walls.

PAINTINGS AS HISTORY

The stone paintings at Tassili tell us much about the history of the region. Today the Sahara, where Tassili is located, is one of the driest places on earth. Few trees and even fewer animals live there. The rabbits, elephants, and other animals in the Tassili paintings could not have survived in the environment of Tassili today. But 8,000 years ago the environment was different. Scientific evidence as well as the Tassili paintings show that the Sahara was once a region of grassy plains and flowing rivers. Many kinds of plants and animals made the region ideal for people who depended on hunting and gathering wild foods.

About 2,000 years ago the environment of the Tassili Plateau began to get drier. The subjects painted by Tassili artists also began to change. Fewer animals were painted. Instead of horses, camels, which are better suited to a dry climate, began to appear. The paintings from this period appear to be less skillful. As the environment changed, people moved away and there were probably fewer skilled artists. Those who did remain in the harsher environment would have had less time for painting.

STONE PAINTING AROUND THE WORLD

Stone paintings are also found in many other places around the world. In 1940 a group of young boys in southwestern France were looking for a lost dog. They came upon the opening of a large cave and went inside. The boys discovered beautiful paintings on the walls. Deer, wild horses, and other animals had been painted in black, red, brown, and yellow. Made by artists over 15,000 years ago, these are among the most impressive stone paintings in the world. Today this famous cave is called Lascaux (la skō'). Other well-known stone paintings have been found in Australia, France, Spain, and the southwestern United States.

UNDERSTANDING ANCIENT ART

No one truly knows how the artists at Tassili and other ancient sites chose the subjects that they painted. Some experts think that a hunter may have believed he would have magical powers over any animal he painted. Thus, a hunter who painted elephants may have thought he had greater power to kill elephants. Some of the paintings also may have had religious meanings. Today the walls of houses of worship are sometimes covered with religious paintings. Perhaps some of the painted areas at Tassili were places in which religious ceremonies took place.

We may not understand the meanings of the stone paintings at Tassili. But it is easy to appreciate their beauty. The artists at Tassili probably painted for some of the same reasons that people enjoy painting and looking at art today. The tradition of painting allows artists to communicate thoughts, emotions, beliefs, and ways of life both to people of their own time and to people of the future.

Why do you think that the tradition of painting goes so far back in time all over the world?

3 The Beginnings of Village Life

READ TO LEARN

Key Vocabulary

New Stone Age
civilization
domesticate
cultivate

specialize
artisan
technology

Key Places

Catal Hüyük

Read Aloud

The culture of the world's earliest people centered on hunting and gathering. This way of life lasted for thousands of years. By 10,000 years ago, or about 8000 B.C., people began to live differently. Read on. A new age was about to begin.

Read for Purpose

1. **WHAT YOU KNOW:** Was hunting and gathering a hard way of life?
2. **WHAT YOU WILL LEARN:** How did farming change the way of life of early people?

THE END OF TWO AGES

Both the Ice Age and the Old Stone Age came to an end about 8000 B.C. By that time the earth's climate had greatly changed. For millions of years the earth had been a cold, icy place. Then, gradually, the earth's climate became warmer and caused the great glaciers to melt. The glaciers carved the land as they melted, creating plains and lakes. In the Northern Hemisphere, vast areas of land that had been under ice were uncovered.

The warming of the earth caused a major turning point, or important change, in human life—the birth of farming. Due to the milder climate, plant and animal life prospered. The food supply grew larger, making it possible for people to spend more time in one place and farm the land. The birth of farming marked the end of the Old Stone Age. The period that followed lasted about 5,000 years and is called the New Stone Age.

THE NEW STONE AGE

The New Stone Age began around 8000 B.C. This marked the beginning of civilizations (siv ə lə zā′ shənz). A civilization is a culture that has developed systems of government, religion, and learning. For the first time, people learned that they could tame, or domesticate (də mes′ ti kāt), some of

Discoveries made during the New Stone Age are part of life today. People **domesticate** animals and **cultivate** crops all over the world.

the animals that roamed the land. By domesticating such animals as goats, sheep, and cattle, people would always be provided with meat, milk, and hides.

As time passed, people learned to use animals in other ways. Horses and cattle were trained to carry heavy loads. Dogs were used to hunt smaller animals.

THE FIRST VILLAGES

The domestication of animals also encouraged farming. Instead of spending their time hunting and gathering, people began to stay in one place. Since they did not have to move so often, they could build more permanent shelters. They also learned how to **cultivate** (kul′ tə vāt), or prepare and use land for raising crops.

Through these twin developments— domesticating animals and cultivating the land—people could depend on a steady food supply. As a result, they began to settle down and live together in villages.

The types of housing found in a village depended on the materials that the surrounding environment provided. Where wood was plentiful it became a basic building material. A village near a forest might have houses built of strong wooden posts. In regions lacking forests, people made building blocks out of earth and clay.

Village life allowed people to spend time on other needs and learn new skills. People of the New Stone Age often built their villages along rivers. This way they would always have plenty of water. People also began to build boats to use in the rivers.

53

CATAL HÜYÜK:
A NEW STONE AGE VILLAGE

Artisans

Herding

Cultivation

DIAGRAM SKILL: The New Stone Age people of Catal Hüyük built an impressive village. It grew into a center of farming, trade, and religion. What activities are shown in this diagram?

LIVING IN CATAL HÜYÜK

Imagine that you have gone back in time 8,000 years to the New Stone Age. You are in the land that is the present-day country of Turkey. A large village called Catal Hüyük (chä′ təl hü′ ük) is flourishing. Imagine that you are standing outside the village of Catal Hüyük. All the houses are built right next to each other with no room in between for streets. To walk around this village, you must walk across its rooftops!

You enter the village by climbing a ladder. From the rooftops, Catal Hüyük looks like a maze of courtyards and houses. Look at the illustration on page 54. To enter a house, you must go through an opening in the roof and climb down a ladder.

It takes a few seconds for your eyes to adjust to the dimness of the interior. The only light comes from the small openings near the roof. The grandmother of the house invites you to the courtyard where she demonstrates her weaving skills on a great loom. The people of Catal Hüyük spin wool into thread. They use looms to make thread into colorful cloth.

The grandmother has been making a special blanket for a shrine. A shrine is a place where people worship their God or gods and goddesses. In Catal Hüyük, a shrine's decorations set it off as something different. Bright wall paintings show both human and animal figures. Clay statues of the village gods and goddesses line the walls of the shrine.

SPECIALIZATION

The people of Catal Hüyük, like those of other New Stone Age villages, have begun to specialize (spesh′ ə līz). This means that people are trained to do a particular kind of work. Now that

The ruins of Catal Hüyük were covered by sand for thousands of years and not discovered again until 1958. Scientists have found over 1,000 houses here, in which about 6,000 people once lived.

THE GROWTH OF TECHNOLOGY

	Bone tools Flint tools Spear-throwers	10,000 B.C.
	Baskets for storage	9000 B.C.
	Herding animals Cultivating crops Villages	8000 B.C.
	Metal working Pottery Catal Hüyük	7000 B.C.
	Specialization Artisans Irrigation	6000 B.C.
	Sail	5000 B.C.
	Plow Wheel Using Bronze Writing	4000 B.C.
	Cities Armies War chariots	3000 B.C.
	Codes of law Using Iron Alphabet	2000 B.C.

CHART SKILL: Technology has developed gradually. How long did people of ancient times make baskets before making pottery? Was the sail or the wheel invented first?

it is no longer necessary for everyone to hunt and gather food, people have learned unique skills. Some people in Catal Hüyük, for example, specialize as weavers and provide the villagers with clothing. Other people work as farmers and provide food. Specialization was a great turning point for early civilizations. Society had never before been so complex.

During your visit, you also meet an artisan (är′ tə zən), or craftsworker. Some artisans in Catal Hüyük work with obsidian. Obsidian is a volcanic glass taken from the nearby volcano. One artisan is chipping off flakes from a piece of obsidian to make a knife. Obsidian knives are highly prized because they are among the sharpest made. Such goods play a large part in making Catal Hüyük a busy place—traders come here from villages many miles away.

THE GROWTH OF TECHNOLOGY

Technology (tek nol′ ə jē) greatly advanced during the New Stone Age. Technology is the use of skills and tools that serve human needs. Look at the chart on this page showing the growth of technology. You can see that as time passed, people learned new and better ways to meet their basic needs.

For example, the farmers of the New Stone Age needed storage containers for food. At first, they met their needs by weaving baskets from wild grasses. By 7000 B.C., however, people were creating ways of forming clay into bowls and pots, called pottery.

It was no easy task to make good pottery. The right clay had to be found. Sticks and stones had to be removed.

Technology has continued to advance as people's needs change. What new technology is shown in this photograph?

After the objects were shaped, they had to have just the right amount of baking to make them strong. Early people must have tried and failed and tried again many times before they made good pottery. It may not seem like an important achievement, but think about how you would cook and eat without pottery.

What other technological steps did early people take? The chart also shows that early people invented the sail and the wheel. How do you think these inventions improved technology?

As you read the chapters that follow, you will see many other signs of technological growth. You will meet flourishing civilizations with busy cities and active governments. A new age was about to begin.

 Check Your Reading

1. What twin developments helped increase the food supply?
2. Why did specialization develop?
3. Describe technology. How did it change?
4. **THINKING SKILL:** Compare and contrast the culture of the Old Stone Age with New Stone Age culture. How were they different or similar?

4 How Do We Know About the Past?

READ TO LEARN

Key Vocabulary

history   archaeology
prehistory   primary sources
artifacts   secondary sources

Read Aloud

Have you ever wondered what the region where you live was like 50 years ago, 100 years ago, or even 5,000 years ago? What existed then? Did it look very much the same? Did people live nearby?

How do people today know what it was like to live during the Ice Age or in a New Stone Age village like Catal Hüyük? For that matter, how do we know about life and events that took place in the more recent past?

Read for Purpose

1. **WHAT YOU KNOW:** Have you ever thought about what it would have been like to live long ago?
2. **WHAT YOU WILL LEARN:** Where does our knowledge of the past come from?

HISTORY AND PREHISTORY

History is the record of what has happened in the past. We learn about history from written and oral records. People who write about the past are called historians. When you read the work of historians, you learn about what happened in the past.

The people of both the Old Stone Age and New Stone Age left no written records. They had no system of writing and therefore could not write about themselves. This period of time before writing began is called prehistory.

If prehistoric people left behind no record of their lives, how do we know so much about them? To learn about people who lived before writing began you must study the objects they left behind. Objects that were made by people long ago are called artifacts (är′ tə fakts). Tools, pottery, and even cave paintings are artifacts.

THE SCIENCE OF ARCHAEOLOGY

To gather facts about prehistoric people often means digging into the earth for artifacts. The study of the remains of past cultures is called archaeology (ar kē ol′ ə jē). Archaeologists dig into the earth to find evidence, such as artifacts, of past life. They also study what the artifacts tell about the people who made them.

Although the story of Gam and his people that you read in Lesson 2 did not really happen, it is based on facts we have learned from artifacts. Archaeologists have found flint tools, spear-throwers, and other weapons in some Old Stone Age campsites. From these, archaeologists can conclude that the people of the time were hunters. From all the deer bones they have found near long-buried campsites, archaeologists also know that deer were central to the life of many Old Stone Age people.

The village of Catal Hüyük that you read about in Lesson 3 is real. Its buried ruins were discovered in the 1950s and to this day archaeologists are digging through them. Archaeologists can rebuild the housing of early people because foundations still stand.

Archaeologists have learned that the villagers made pottery because they have found thousands of pieces. What do you think an archaeologist might conclude about having found over 40 shrines in Catal Hüyük? As you can guess, it was a religious center.

THE HISTORIAN'S CRAFT

All over the world people today keep written records about many things. Business organizations preserve records of their activities. Governments store information about their citizens. Town and religious groups keep accurate records of births, marriages, and deaths. Today the job of keeping records has been made easier. We have

Archaeologists work in teams. Every inch of soil must be examined. When an artifact is found, its location is carefully marked. Each artifact is a clue to the past.

invented computers that can store huge amounts of information. But written records are kept, too.

Historians call such records as these primary sources. Primary sources are first-hand accounts of an event. Documents and official records are examples of primary sources. Letters, diaries, and even belongings of the people who took part in past events are other examples. Primary sources help historians understand what people thought about the events in their lives. Belongings and other artifacts can help explain what materials a culture used.

59

The scrapbook these students are making is a primary source. Historians of the future may use it to learn about us.

Part of the historian's job is gathering facts. Historians must find as many facts as possible about the events they want to discuss. It is also part of the historian's job to explain the meaning of the facts. Historians try to explain how the pieces go together. In this way, they record the story of history. But all parts of the story must be supported with evidence.

The conclusions historians make about the past are usually not first-hand accounts. Historians of prehistory, for example, write about events that occurred long ago. They did not see the events for themselves.

This is why historians' writings are called secondary sources. Secondary sources are writings about past events that are based on information from primary sources. Like primary sources, secondary sources help explain the past. This textbook, for example, is a secondary source.

MAKING HISTORY

Looking at the past is not only a job for historians. In some ways, you are a historian. You use primary and secondary sources every day. You read newspapers and books. Even the photographs you take record events. Have you ever kept a scrapbook? A scrapbook can also tell the history of something—a family, for example, or a baseball season. As the photograph on this page shows, these students are making a scrapbook. Perhaps historians of the future will use it to answer questions about the late 1900s. What do you think they may want to know about us?

History affects the lives of all people. Thus, records are kept to preserve memories of events. It is important not to forget the past. Learning about how people have acted in the past may help us prepare for the future.

Check Your Reading

1. What is prehistory? How is it different from history?
2. How are artifacts useful?
3. What are primary sources? Name four examples.
4. **THINKING SKILL:** Find out about the history of your family. What primary or secondary sources can you use?

Reading Time Lines

Key Vocabulary

time line

Time lines are an important part of this book. You can find time lines in both the Unit Openers and Chapter Summaries. Using them will help you understand when events took place. A time line is useful because it shows the order in which many events occurred and how much time passed between events.

Understanding B.C. and A.D.

Look at the time line. The earliest dates are on the left. As you move toward the right, the dates are more recent.

Today most people use a system that divides time into B.C. and A.D. The events you have been reading about in this chapter happened before Jesus Christ was born. For this reason, those dates are followed by the letters *B.C.*, meaning "before Christ." As you have read, the New Stone Age began about 8000 B.C., or 8,000 years before Christ was born.

To read B.C. dates, you need to remember one important rule. The *higher* the number, the *earlier* the time in history. For example, the New Stone Age ended about 4000 B.C., or 2,000 years before the earliest alphabets were used in 2000 B.C.

The letters *A.D.* stand for *anno Domini*, a Latin phrase meaning "in the year of the Lord." An event that took place in A.D. 150 happened 150 years after Christ was born.

Reading A.D. dates is easy because we do it all the time. The *higher* the number the more *recent* the time in history. For example, A.D. 1993 is more recent than A.D. 1920.

Reviewing the Skill

1. How do time lines help you to find out when events took place?
2. Which event on the time line is the earliest?
3. Did the New Stone Age end before or after the birth of Jesus? How can you tell?
4. Do you think time lines are a good way to show past events? Why or why not?

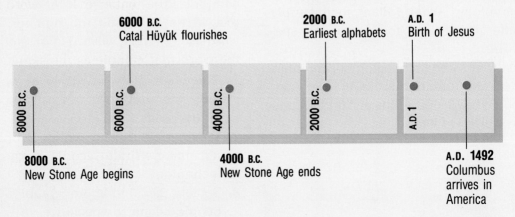

6000 B.C.
Catal Hüyük flourishes

2000 B.C.
Earliest alphabets

A.D. 1
Birth of Jesus

8000 B.C. 6000 B.C. 4000 B.C. 2000 B.C. A.D. 1

8000 B.C.
New Stone Age begins

4000 B.C.
New Stone Age ends

A.D. 1492
Columbus arrives in America

IMPORTANT EVENTS

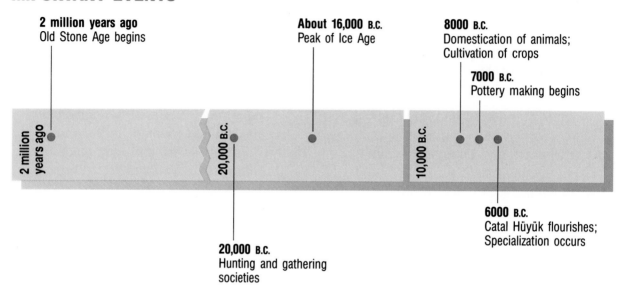

2 million years ago
Old Stone Age begins

About 16,000 B.C.
Peak of Ice Age

8000 B.C.
Domestication of animals;
Cultivation of crops

7000 B.C.
Pottery making begins

2 million years ago

20,000 B.C.

10,000 B.C.

20,000 B.C.
Hunting and gathering
societies

6000 B.C.
Catal Hüyük flourishes;
Specialization occurs

IDEAS TO REMEMBER

■ Although the customs and values of a culture vary, all people have the same basic needs for food, clothing, and shelter.

■ During the Old Stone Age people were hunters and gatherers and lived in small groups.

■ The New Stone Age marked the beginning of civilization and the growth of technology. An abundant food supply made it possible for people to specialize.

■ Historians and archaeologists are interested in finding out about the past. Their knowledge helps us understand the world we live in.

REVIEWING VOCABULARY

archaeology	prehistory
civilization	society
culture	specialize
glacier	technology
legacy	value

Number a sheet of paper from 1 to 10. Decide whether the underlined word in each of the following statements correctly completes the sentence. If the word is correct, write **C** beside the number. If the word is incorrect, write **I** and then write the word that completes the sentence.

1. The wheel, the spear-thrower, and pottery are examples of advances in <u>archaeology</u>.
2. The period during which people did not make written records is known as <u>technology</u>.
3. Society became more complex when people began to <u>specialize</u>.

4. Thanks to the science of <u>technology</u>, we have learned a great deal about the people of ancient times.

5. <u>Prehistory</u> includes a people's beliefs and ways of doing things.

6. The traditions that people hand down to later generations are their <u>legacy</u>.

7. During the Old Stone Age, a huge mass of ice, called a <u>glacier</u>, covered large parts of the earth.

8. A <u>civilization</u> is a culture that has developed systems of government, religion, and learning.

9. One American <u>value</u> is religious freedom for all.

10. The people of Catal Hüyük, who were bound together by their common culture, are an example of a <u>legacy</u>.

REVIEWING FACTS

1. What are the three basic needs of people everywhere?

2. Why are values important?

3. Name two ways in which the deer herds filled the basic needs of people during the Old Stone Age.

4. Why did the people of the Old Stone Age live as nomads?

5. How did the end of the Ice Age affect the growth of society?

6. What two major benefits did the domestication of animals bring to New Stone Age people?

7. How did the village of Catal Hüyük become a center of trade?

8. Describe specialization.

9. How do archaeologists learn about people who lived long ago?

10. Describe the work of the historian.

✎ WRITING ABOUT MAIN IDEAS

1. **Writing a Paragraph:** Look at the chart on page 40. Write a paragraph defining what a culture is. Give two examples of American culture in your paragraph.

2. **Writing a Research Report:** Think about life during the Old Stone Age and during the New Stone Age. Write a report comparing the two periods. Discuss **a.** methods of obtaining food, **b.** types of shelter, and **c.** technology.

3. **Writing About Perspectives:** Imagine that you have gone back in time to live in the New Stone Age. Using the diagram of Catal Hüyük on page 54, write a story about your daily life there—the people you see, the work you do, and the way your family lives.

BUILDING SKILLS: READING TIME LINES

Look at the time line on the left page. Note how it is constructed. Use the information from the chart on page 56 to construct a new time line. Add the following events to their correct place on your time line:

8000 B.C.	Bow and arrow developed
7500 B.C.	Arctic hunters settle Pacific Northwest
5800 B.C.	Wooden bowls made in Catal Hüyük
5500 B.C.	Villagers at Catal Hüyük build shrines

REVIEWING VOCABULARY

altitude	legacy
archaeology	natural resource
civilization	renewable resource
environment	technology
geography	vegetation

Number a sheet of paper from 1 to 10. Beside each number write the word or term from the above list that best matches the definition.

1. The skills and tools used to serve human needs
2. The study of the earth, including its land, water, weather, and plants
3. The traditions that people hand down from one generation to the next
4. The scientific study of the remains of past cultures
5. A culture that has developed systems of government, religion, and learning
6. The surroundings of a place—land, weather, plants, and animals
7. A thing in nature, such as a plant or an animal, that can replace itself
8. The natural plant life of a region
9. The height of land above sea level
10. Any raw material that comes to us from nature

✐ WRITING ABOUT THE UNIT

1. **Writing an Explanation:** Look at the places listed below. Which of the choices in each list probably has a colder climate? Explain why.
   a. A village in the Alps or Paris, France?
   b. Argentina in the middle latitudes or Mexico in the low latitudes?

2. **Writing a Speech:** Imagine that you are running for a state office. Write a speech telling people why it is important to save our natural resources.
3. **Writing a List:** List three ways Old Stone Age people *used* their environment. List three ways the people of the New Stone Age *changed* their environment.
4. **Writing About Perspectives:** Write a letter to a pen pal who lives in a far-away country. Describe what you think are the three most interesting geographical features in your community. Be sure to tell why you think these features are so interesting.

ACTIVITIES

1. **Recording the Weather:** Keep a record of the weather in your community for a month. Put that information on a chart. You may wish to illustrate the chart with photographs or drawings showing the weather of certain days. Then, write a description of the weather.
2. **Making a Poster:** Read a book on archaeology. Make a poster that explains what you have learned.
3. **Working Together on Conservation Research:** Choose a partner and conduct research on ways of conserving energy. Then, write a group report on your findings and recommend two methods your community could try. Develop a plan to encourage people to try your methods to save energy.
4. **Making a Time Line:** With your class, begin a time line of world history. As you read each chapter, you can add new dates and facts.

GLOBAL GRID

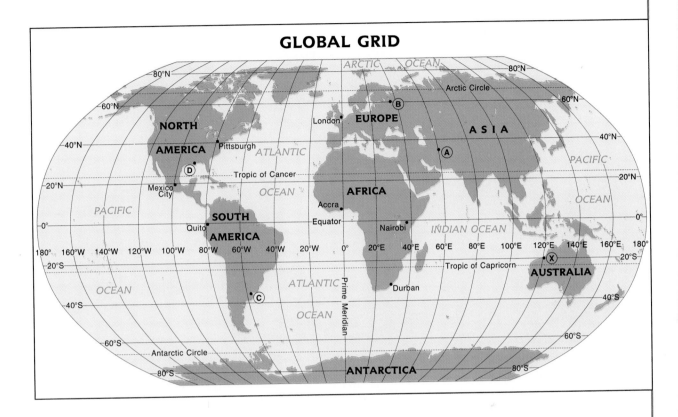

BUILDING SKILLS:
UNDERSTANDING LATITUDE AND LONGITUDE

Use the map above to answer the following questions.

1. Describe a global grid.
2. Locate Pittsburgh on the map. What is its latitude?
3. What is the latitude of point **X**?
4. Which point is farther from the equator: **A** or **D**?
5. What city is at about 55°N latitude? What is the same city's longitude?
6. 0° latitude is also known as the _____.
7. What point in Europe lies on the same line of longitude as Nairobi?
8. How might understanding latitude and longitude help sailors?

LINKING PAST, PRESENT, AND FUTURE

Imagine that archaeologists 2,000 years from now are looking at artifacts from your community to learn about twentieth-century American culture. Choose three things that you think would tell them most about our culture today. Explain your choices.

+North Pole

75°N

60°N

Arctic Circle

Mediterranean Sea

Black Sea

Caspian Sea

Euphrates River

Tigris River

NILE VALLEY

TIGRIS-EUPHRATES VALLEY

Red Sea

Persian Gulf

Nile River

Indus River

INDUS VALLEY

Huang River

HUANG VALLEY

Yellow Sea

Arabian Sea

15°N

0° Equator

INDIAN OCEAN

45°E

60°E

15°S

75°E

90°E

105°E

Tropic of Capricorn

30°S

45°S

66

UNIT 2

FOUR EARLY CIVILIZATIONS

WHERE WE ARE

As the map shows, in Unit 2 you will be looking at four ancient civilizations of the Eastern Hemisphere. One is found on the African continent and the other three lie on the continent of Asia. It is no coincidence that they are all located in river valleys. Rivers were key to the survival and growth of the world's early people.

In this unit you will learn how these four river valleys became the scenes of tremendous growth. Though people began to move into these lands at about the same time, each society grew in different ways and developed its own special culture. In these four river valleys farmers lived and built the world's first cities and kingdoms.

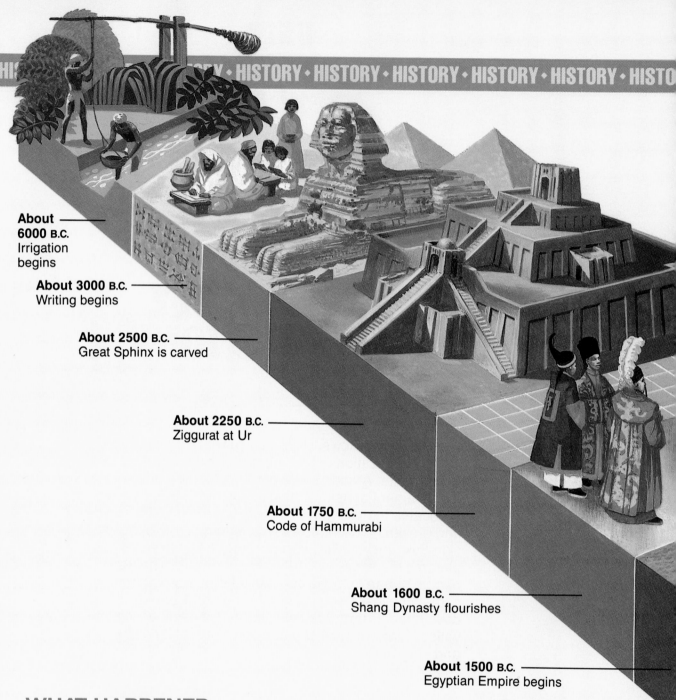

About 6000 B.C.
Irrigation begins

About 3000 B.C.
Writing begins

About 2500 B.C.
Great Sphinx is carved

About 2250 B.C.
Ziggurat at Ur

About 1750 B.C.
Code of Hammurabi

About 1600 B.C.
Shang Dynasty flourishes

About 1500 B.C.
Egyptian Empire begins

1504-1482 B.C.
Rule of Hatshepsut

About 1290 B.C.
The Ten Commandments

WHAT HAPPENED

The societies that flourished in the river valleys of Africa and Asia lasted for thousands of years. People worked together and set up the world's first governments. The time line shows that they invented useful tools and developed new ways of farming and building. Although some advances took hundreds of years, their influence was great. Read on. You will learn more about the legacy of these ancient people.

68

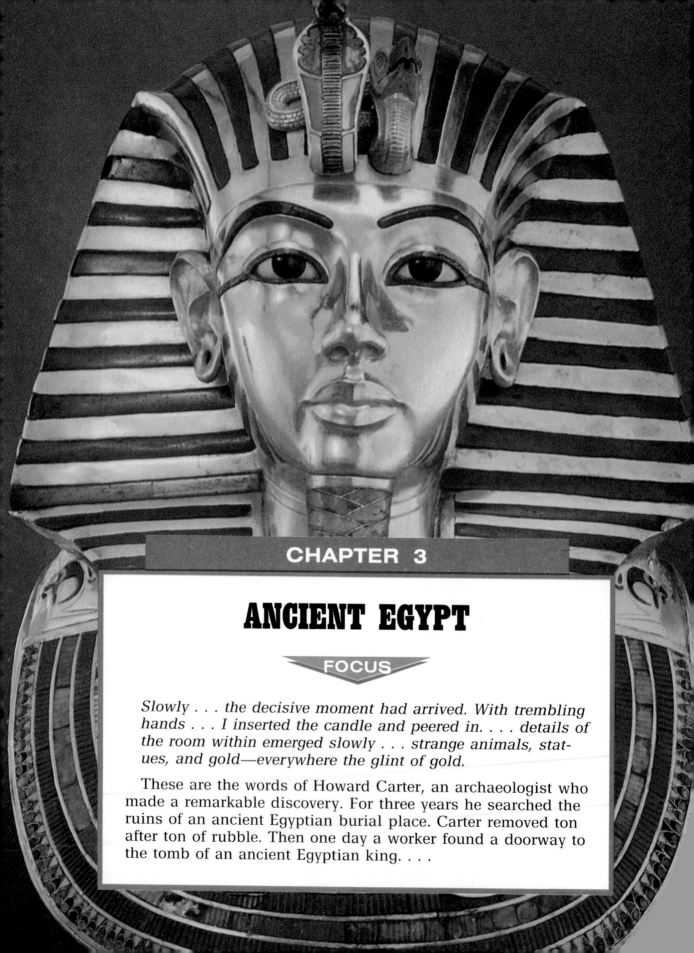

CHAPTER 3

ANCIENT EGYPT

FOCUS

Slowly . . . the decisive moment had arrived. With trembling hands . . . I inserted the candle and peered in. . . . details of the room within emerged slowly . . . strange animals, statues, and gold—everywhere the glint of gold.

These are the words of Howard Carter, an archaeologist who made a remarkable discovery. For three years he searched the ruins of an ancient Egyptian burial place. Carter removed ton after ton of rubble. Then one day a worker found a doorway to the tomb of an ancient Egyptian king. . . .

READ TO LEARN

Key Vocabulary

silt
delta
economy
irrigation

Key Places

Nile River Valley
Upper Egypt
Lower Egypt

Read Aloud

Hail to thee, O Nile, that flows from the earth and . . . keeps Egypt alive! . . . When the Nile rises, then the land is in celebration, then every belly is in joy, every backbone takes on laughter, and every tooth is exposed.

So begins the *Hymn to the Nile*, written over 3,000 years ago by an Egyptian poet. It celebrates the influence of the mighty Nile River—a river that flowed from the heart of Africa through the world's first nation.

Read for Purpose

1. **WHAT YOU KNOW:** Why did early people think a river valley was a good place to live?
2. **WHAT YOU WILL LEARN:** How did the geography of the Nile River Valley help the ancient Egyptians?

THE NILE RIVER VALLEY

In order to understand the history of ancient Egypt, you must first understand Egypt's geography. It will help explain why the early Egyptians knew their river was important.

Ancient Egypt flourished for nearly 3,000 years in the Nile River Valley of Africa. Find the Nile River Valley on the map on the next page.

People began to move into the Nile River Valley after 10,000 B.C., during the New Stone Age. By 4500 B.C., many small villages dotted the Valley. Ancient people were drawn to the Nile River Valley because it was a small ribbon of fertile land in the North African desert. Land that is good for farming is called fertile. The Nile River Valley owes its fertility to the great river that flows through it.

The Nile River is the longest river in the world. It flows north from the mountains of East Africa to empty into the Mediterranean Sea. In ancient times, as it is today, the Nile River was an important part of life in Egypt. Egypt is a large country, but most of it

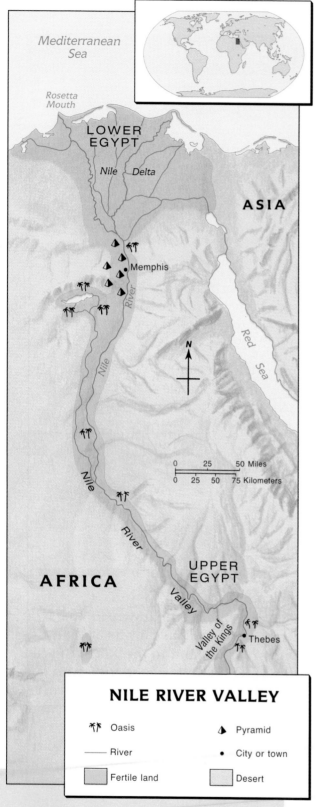

NILE RIVER VALLEY

⋀⋀ Oasis	⬗ Pyramid
—— River	• City or town
▨ Fertile land	☐ Desert

MAP SKILL: Is Lower Egypt in southern or northern Egypt? Into what body of water does the Nile River flow?

is a sandy desert. Without the Nile River, which brings valuable moisture to the dry land, all of Egypt would be desert.

There is something else you should understand about ancient Egypt. Look again at the map. You can see that in ancient times Egypt was divided into **Upper Egypt** and **Lower Egypt**. It may seem confusing to see Upper Egypt to the south, and Lower Egypt to the north. The reason for this is that the Nile River flows from south to north. Therefore upstream, or south, means Upper Egypt, and downstream, or north, means Lower Egypt.

THE OVERFLOW OF THE NILE

The Nile River brought life to the desert in a very important way. Year after year, the Nile River overflowed its banks every summer. The floods followed the rainy season of East Africa, where the Nile River has its source. Thus the ancient Egyptians knew when the yearly floods would arrive.

In fact, the people of ancient Egypt looked forward to the summer floods. How could this be so? Floods often wash away important minerals needed for farming. The overflow of the Nile, however, was unique.

The Nile flood waters carried silt. Silt is made up of clay and bits of black soil and rock. It has minerals that make soil rich and therefore good for farming.

On its way north from East Africa, the rushing Nile picked up silt. In Egypt, as the flood waters spread out and soaked deep into the earth, silt was left behind on the ground. Over thousands of years the silt that was left behind built up a ribbon of rich, fertile soil running through the desert.

In some places the ribbon of fertile land was very narrow. In parts of Upper Egypt, for example, it was only 1 mile (1.6 km) wide. The rest of the land was desert. But in Lower Egypt, more land was good for farming. In some places the fertile strip was more than 100 miles (160 km) wide.

THE NILE DELTA

Where the Nile River emptied into the Mediterranean Sea, the silt created a **delta** (del′ tə). A delta is land made by deposits of silt, sand, and small stones at the mouth of a river. It is a triangle-shaped area of marshy land.

Ancient Egyptians compared their land to the lotus flower. The delta, or Lower Egypt, was the spreading blossom. Upper Egypt was the long thin stalk that fed the blossom. Look at the shape of Egypt in the photograph taken from space shown below. Do you understand what the ancient Egyptians meant?

The satellite photo at left shows the Nile River Valley. On the right is a lotus flower. Compare the two shapes.

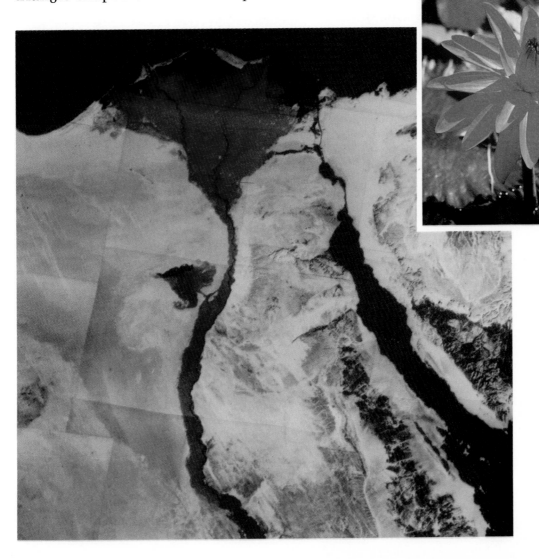

AN ECONOMY BASED ON FARMING

Farming was the basis for the economy (i kon' ə mē) of ancient Egypt. The economy of a country is its use of workers and resources to produce goods. Ancient Egypt's economy was based largely on crops of wheat and other grains.

The Nile River Valley was the richest farming land in the ancient world. Farming there, however, took careful planning. Egyptian farmers worked together and planned their work around the seasonal flooding. They planted their crops in October, after the flood waters were gone. One farmer used a wooden plow led by a pair of oxen. This helped break up the soil and prepare it for planting. Another farmer would follow the plow and throw seeds. Later, pigs and goats were let loose to trample the seeds into the soil. Finally, other farmers smoothed the ground with wooden rakes.

The crops were harvested in the spring. In earliest times, the ancient Egyptians used tools made of flint to cut the wheat. By 2800 B.C. the Egyptians had learned to make stronger tools from bronze. People worked together in the fields with their bronze tools. Everyone was needed to gather the crops before the floods came.

IRRIGATION

One of the greatest accomplishments of early people was the development of

Ancient Egyptian art shows many scenes of daily life. The economy of ancient Egypt was based on farming. What else could an archaeologist conclude about daily life in the Nile Valley from these artifacts?

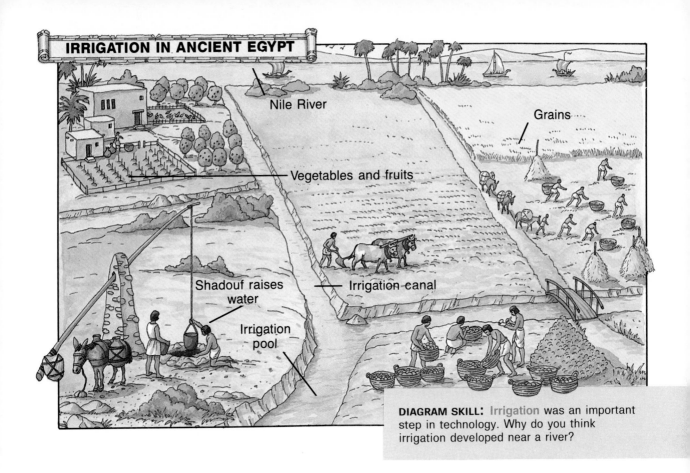

IRRIGATION IN ANCIENT EGYPT

Nile River

Grains

Vegetables and fruits

Shadouf raises water

Irrigation canal

Irrigation pool

DIAGRAM SKILL: Irrigation was an important step in technology. Why do you think irrigation developed near a river?

irrigation (ir ə gā′ shən). Irrigation is the watering of dry land by means of streams, canals, or pipes. Irrigation helps farmers grow more crops, thus building a stronger farm economy.

The ancient Egyptians learned very early how to irrigate their fields. By 6000 B.C. they were making storage pools to catch some of the Nile's overflow. In this way they could store water for their crops. They could also bring water to land that was not reached by the Nile's overflow.

The ancient Egyptians had easy ways of moving water across the dry land. The water might be carried to the fields in skin bags or it could be channeled through canals. Dams were built to trap and store some of the floodwaters. By irrigating dry lands, ancient Egyptians were able to increase their food supply.

UNITED VILLAGES

Throughout Egyptian history, the Nile River helped unite the villages along its banks. The need to build canals and dams for irrigation made it essential for the people of each village to cooperate. Farming, however, was only one way people were brought together by the Nile River. In the next lesson you will learn how the world's first nation emerged along the banks of the Nile River.

Check Your Reading

1. Where is the Nile River Valley?
2. Why did the Nile River have a delta at its mouth?
3. GEOGRAPHY SKILL: How did the Nile's overflow affect Egypt's soil?
4. THINKING SKILL: Use the diagram above to describe farming in Egypt.

2 The History of Ancient Egypt

READ TO LEARN

Key Vocabulary

pharaoh
pyramid
empire

Key People

Menes
Khufu
Hatshepsut
Howard Carter
Tutankhamen

Key Places

Memphis
Thebes
Kush
Valley of the Kings

Read Aloud

The nation that was born along the banks of the Nile River was led by powerful rulers. During this time the people of the Nile River Valley prospered under a strong government. The stage was set for many wondrous achievements.

Read for Purpose

1. **WHAT YOU KNOW:** How can we learn from the history of early people?
2. **WHAT YOU WILL LEARN:** What important events led to the rise of ancient Egypt?

UNITING LOWER AND UPPER EGYPT

At one time Lower and Upper Egypt were two different kingdoms. A vast desert lay between them. Each was ruled by a different king and each king wore a different crown. The king of Upper Egypt wore a white crown. The king of Lower Egypt wore a red crown.

In 3100 B.C., **Menes** (mē′ nēz), a king of Upper Egypt, changed the course of Egyptian history. Menes swept into Lower Egypt and united the two kingdoms. From that time on, the kings of ancient Egypt wore a double crown. The crowns were written in Egyptian writing like this:

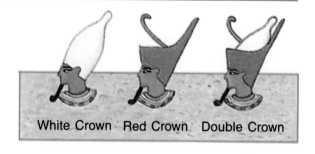

White Crown   Red Crown   Double Crown

Menes built the city of **Memphis** (mem′ fis) for his capital. Memphis was located where the "stalk" of Upper Egypt meets the "blossom" of Lower Egypt. There Menes built a great palace. After that, Egypt's supreme ruler was always called **pharaoh** (fâr′ ō), which means "great palace."

To the people of ancient Egypt, a pharaoh was more than a king. Every

76

pharaoh was also worshiped as a god. Therefore, the people believed that they owed loyalty to the pharaohs.

GOVERNMENT UNDER THE PHARAOHS

Ancient Egypt was one of the first societies to have an organized government. The pharaohs divided Egypt into about 40 regions and named a governor to rule each one. Each governor was responsible to the pharaoh and had to obey the pharaoh's commands.

The pharaohs had total power over the lives of their people. They made the laws that the people had to follow. Since the pharaohs owned all of Egypt's land, the people had to pay rent and taxes. Farmers, for example, had to give three fifths of their crops and some of their livestock to the pharaohs in payment for using the land. They also had to spend a few months each year working on building projects ordered by the pharaohs.

THE AGE OF PYRAMIDS

Even today, more than 5,000 years after Menes united Egypt, people marvel at the accomplishments of ancient Egypt. It was during this time that the Egyptians built huge pyramids (pir′ ə mids). The pyramids were used as tombs in which the pharaohs were buried. The amazing size of these structures explains why this time is sometimes called the "Age of Pyramids." Even today, the pyramids are among the world's greatest marvels.

People have always wondered how the ancient Egyptians were able to build the pyramids. How did they move the huge stone blocks to the building site? How could they raise heavy stones to such heights? The illustration on pages 78–79 shows the methods these workers used.

The largest pyramid, called the Great Pyramid, was ordered built by Pharaoh Khufu (kü′ fü) sometime around 2600 B.C.

For thousands of years, the pyramids have reminded us that a great ancient society once flourished in the Nile River Valley.

UNDER CONSTRUCTION

BUILDING THE PYRAMIDS

INSIDE THE PYRAMID

Casing

Air shaft

King's chamber

Air shaft

Queen's chamber

Grand Gallery

Air shaft

Underground room

Guarding the pyramids was the Great Sphinx. It has the head of a human with the body of a lion. Its lion's body stood for the great power of the pharaoh.

The Great Pyramid stands almost 500 feet (150 m) tall, the height of a 48-story building. The Greek historian Herodotus (hə rod' ə təs) wrote about the pyramids in 450 B.C. He tells us that the building of Khufu's pyramid used 100,000 workers and took 20 years.

Near the Great Pyramid lies the famous Sphinx. This strange statue looks like a crouching lion with a human head! Historians believe that the statue's face was carved to look like one of Khufu's children. The Sphinx was the largest head of stone in the world until modern times, when Americans carved the faces of four presidents into Mount Rushmore, in South Dakota.

LEARNING FROM AN INVASION

The powerful leadership of the pharaohs during the "Age of Pyramids" helped Egypt grow stronger and larger. This time, however, was only the first 500 years of early Egyptian history. You can see by looking at the time line in the Chapter Summary on page 94 that pharaohs ruled Egypt for over 2,000 years.

In the middle of the long stretch of ancient Egyptian history, however, an event occurred that inspired the following words:

The wrongdoer is everywhere. . . . The Nile is in flood, yet none ploweth . . . it is grief that walketh through the land . . . the storehouse is bare.

These sorrowful words were written around 1800 B.C., a time when Egypt was overrun by an invading army. A powerful group of nomads called the Hyksos (hik' sos) had settled earlier near Egypt's borders. The Hyksos used weapons and technology unknown to the Egyptians—horse-drawn chariots, swords, and metal armor. The Egyptians were not able to protect their borders against such weapons, and the powerful Hyksos gradually conquered, or took over, Egypt.

While the Hyksos ruled Egypt, the Egyptians learned important military skills from them. They also learned to ride horses and became expert charioteers. Finally, around 1574 B.C., the Egyptians put their new skills to use and drove the Hyksos out of Egypt.

BUILDING AN EMPIRE

During the next 500 years, ancient Egypt reached the peak of its power. After the Hyksos were pushed out, the pharaohs used Egypt's new military strength to conquer other countries. They placed the lands they conquered under Egyptian rule and created an empire (em' pīr). An empire is a group of lands and people under one government. Look at the map of the Egyptian Empire on this page. What other lands did Egypt rule? In the years that followed, Thebes (thēbz) became the glorious capital city of a great empire.

Trade was extensive during the time of the empire. During the rule of Hatshepsut (hat' shəp sut), the first woman ruler known to history, Egypt traded with many faraway places. As a result, Hatshepsut greatly enriched Egypt's wealth. She was known to send peaceful trading expeditions to East Africa and Asia. Egyptian traders returned with ivory, gold, and spices. The temples she ordered built at Thebes are among the greatest surviving buildings of ancient Egypt.

By about 1100 B.C., however, ancient Egypt had passed its time of greatness. After a long and wonderous existence, the government of Egypt grew weak. Sadly for the Egyptians, their neighbors grew stronger. Libyans from the western desert invaded and the "Sea Peoples" of Mediterranean islands attacked the Nile Delta. Finally, powerful rulers from Kush took over Egypt's southern lands. Egypt was forced to live under foreign rule.

THE VALLEY OF THE KINGS

How is it possible that so much is known today about the history of ancient Egypt? Until recent times, little was known about the pyramid builders and their way of life. However, about 200 years ago, archaeologists began to make many discoveries. Great pyramids have been opened and the passages inside them have been explored. Through these discoveries many questions have been answered about ancient Egypt.

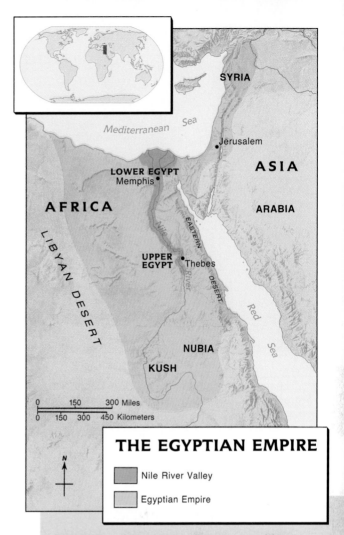

THE EGYPTIAN EMPIRE

Nile River Valley

Egyptian Empire

MAP SKILL: What lands were conquered by the ancient Egyptians? The powerful Egyptian empire was built by mighty pharaohs such as Hatshepsut, shown below.

81

The walls inside King Tut's tomb were decorated with paintings of his family and friends. To the right, you can see Howard Carter cleaning King Tut's golden mask.

The Valley of the Kings was the site of one such discovery. The valley received its name because many pharaohs and other rulers of the kingdom were buried there. The tombs are a maze of hallways and rooms cut into the cliffs. To protect the tombs, entrances were tightly sealed or kept secret.

The Valley of the Kings was a great curiosity to archaeologists. What pharaohs were buried there? What could be found inside? After years of research and exploration, an archaeologist named Howard Carter made an impressive discovery. In 1922, Carter found the tomb of the pharaoh Tutankhamen (tù tängk ä' mən). King Tut, as Tutankhamen is often called, was only nine years old when he began his rule. It lasted until his death, at 19, in 1352 B.C.

The contents of King Tut's tomb were dazzling. There were four rooms filled with golden objects, fine vases, precious jewelry, dried flowers, and furniture. Tutankhamen was found in a separate room, lying in a gold coffin. Imagine how Carter felt to be entering rooms that had been closed for 3,000 years! What he found inside showed how rich and mighty the ancient Egyptian Empire was.

Check Your Reading

1. Did ancient Egypt have a strong or a weak government? Explain your answer.
2. Describe the role of the pharaohs.
3. **GEOGRAPHY SKILL:** How were Lower and Upper Egypt united?
4. **THINKING SKILL:** Compare and contrast a pharaoh with a king.

3 Egyptian Civilization

READ TO LEARN

■ Key Vocabulary

hieroglyphics   Rosetta Stone
papyrus   slavery
scribe

■ Read Aloud

The ancient Egyptians made a lasting mark on the world. While the Egyptians prospered, their neighbors called Egyptian lands *Misr*. This word means "place of civilization and many people."

■ Read for Purpose

1. **WHAT YOU KNOW:** How was ancient Egypt different from other early societies you have read about?
2. **WHAT YOU WILL LEARN:** How did the development of a system of writing change life for the people of Egypt?

A NEW CIVILIZATION

The developments in ancient Egypt were numerous. You have already learned about its farming economy and government under the pharaohs. In this lesson you will read about many other developments. A system of writing emerged. Ideas about religion grew more complex. Jobs became more specialized and villages grew into cities.

The Egyptian culture achieved a level of civilization far beyond that of New Stone Age societies. The Egyptians developed systems of government, religion, and learning that were much more complex than those of earlier cultures. We know much about this special culture because the Egyptians left behind written records.

A SYSTEM OF WRITING

Imagine how different life would be without writing! Writing is so much a part of our lives today that it is not easy to imagine a world without it. Writing was one of the greatest developments in ancient history. Without it, Egyptian civilization would have been very different. Without it, we would not know as much about these ancient people.

The early Egyptians wrote with pictures and signs. The earliest examples of Egyptian writing date from about 3000 B.C. We call their system of writing **hieroglyphics** (hī ər ə glif′ iks). Hieroglyphs are the pictures, or signs, of ancient Egyptian writing.

Look at the chart on the next page. Do you recognize some of the hiero-

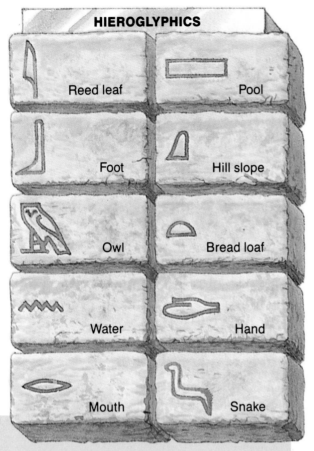

HIEROGLYPHICS

Reed leaf

Pool

Foot

Hill slope

Owl

Bread loaf

Water

Hand

Mouth

Snake

CHART SKILL: Egyptian hieroglyphics are fun to read. Which of the hieroglyphs look most like the things they stand for?

glyphs? Each hieroglyph is a picture of something that was familiar to the ancient Egyptians. It was the custom in ancient Egypt to carve the story of a person's life on the walls of his or her tomb. Pharaohs often had a record of the events of their time carved on buildings. You will read about several of these buildings in the Traditions lesson on pages 88–91.

Most Egyptian written records, however, were on papyrus (pə pī' rəs). Papyrus was a paper made from reeds that grew in the Nile Delta. To make paper, layers of the papyrus reed were pasted together and flattened. By join-

ing sheets of papyrus together, the ancient Egyptians made scrolls, or long rolls of paper. They used a long sharp reed for a pen, and dipped it into an ink made of soot. Papyrus is one of the earliest forms of paper known.

BECOMING A SCRIBE

Although ancient Egypt had a system of writing, not everyone knew how to write. People who received training to write hieroglyphics were called scribes (skrībz). It was a scribe's job to write and keep records. Scribes were important to an efficient government. They kept records of taxes and the activities of the pharaohs.

The ancient Egyptians had a great respect for writing and learning. A scribe was thought to be a special person and was treated as such. A scribe began his schooling as a boy. Girls were not allowed to go to school in ancient Egypt.

One Egyptian father's advice to his son around 2000 B.C. was, "Understand that I am putting you in school for your own good. A scribe never knows poverty, and from his childhood is treated with respect." However, boys who became scribes were also advised to "love writing, hate dancing, and not to set their hearts on playing."

THE ROSETTA STONE

For thousands of years after ancient Egypt's existence, no one could read the hieroglyphs of this ancient civilization. The language was long-forgotten and the writings of ancient Egypt were a mysterious secret.

In 1799, however, an important key to the mystery was found. It centered on the discovery of a large black stone that was found in Rosetta, near the

Nile Delta. The Rosetta Stone was special because it had carvings in three languages: hieroglyphics, late Egyptian, and Greek. Working from the Greek, which many people could read, scholars finally learned the meaning of hieroglyphics. Thus they gained a key to ancient writings and, more importantly, a knowledge of the past written by people who had lived it.

RELIGION IN ANCIENT EGYPT

The ancient Egyptians produced a large body of written literature. From their writings we know that religion was very important in Egyptian society. Many writings are prayers and ideas about religion.

These writings show that the people of ancient Egypt believed in many gods. Egyptians worshiped animals such as cats and crocodiles. They believed that the gods could turn themselves into birds or other animals or into human form. For example, Thoth, the god of learning, was often shown as a man with the head of a bird.

One of the most important gods of the ancient Egyptians was Osiris (ō sī' ris), god of the Nile. According to legend, Osiris was killed by an evil god who often ruined the crops. Osiris's body was found near the Nile by the beautiful Isis (ī' sis), goddess of the moon. Isis, according to the legend, brought Osiris back to life.

To the ancient Egyptians, Osiris's return to life was like the yearly overflow of the Nile. Each year the Nile River Valley once again became a ribbon of green in a harsh desert. The people believed that when the Nile was low, Osiris was dead. When he was brought back to life by Isis, the waters of the Nile rose again.

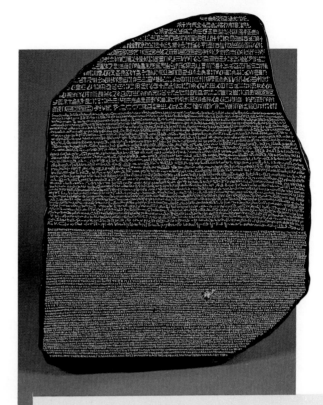

The Rosetta Stone contains the same message in three languages: from the top, hieroglyphics, late Egyptian, and Greek.

Osiris is the figure seated below. Behind him is his wife Isis. Thoth, who was their protector, had the head of an ibis.

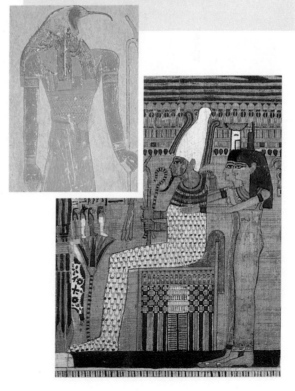

85

LIFE AFTER DEATH

Ancient Egyptians also believed in life after death. According to their religion, death was another part of life. It was thought that the dead went to a place called the "Next World"—a land filled with comfort and happiness.

The early Egyptians believed that for the pharaohs to enjoy life in the "Next World" they needed their earthly bodies. Therefore, a pharaoh's body was preserved with oils and salts and linen wrappings. A body treated in this way was called a mummy. Archaeologists have found many well-preserved mummies. The dry Egyptian air as well as the process used to treat the bodies before their burial helped to preserve them for thousands of years.

Ideas about the "Next World" led ancient Egyptians to believe that the dead would need clothing and food. Thus Tutankhamen, like other pharaohs, was buried with his personal belongings. The "Next World," however, was not a place only for the rich. Even the poorest Egyptians could make the journey. They, too, were buried with belongings that would help them in the "Next World."

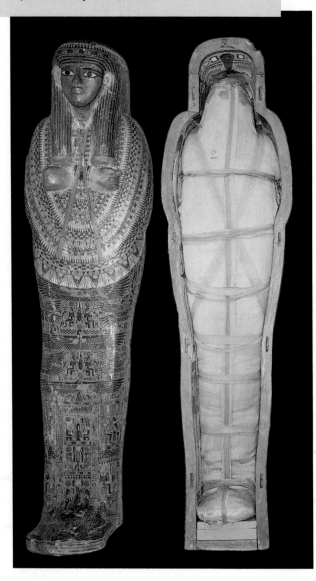

An artist drew on the lid of this mummy case to show what the person looked like. Inside, the body is tightly bound in linen and preserved by oils and salts.

A SOCIAL PYRAMID

The writings of ancient Egypt have also helped us to understand the organization of early Egyptian society. One important part of this society was slavery. Slavery is the practice of one person owning another. After 1500 B.C., slavery became common in Egypt. This was the time when Egyptian soldiers were conquering other lands. They brought back people from these lands to work as slaves in Egypt. Many enslaved people worked in the gold mines of Nubia. Others worked as servants in the households of the ruling classes.

Look at the diagram on the next page to see that the organization of Egyptian society resembled a pyramid. Slaves were at the base of the pyramid. At the very top of the pyramid was the pharaoh.

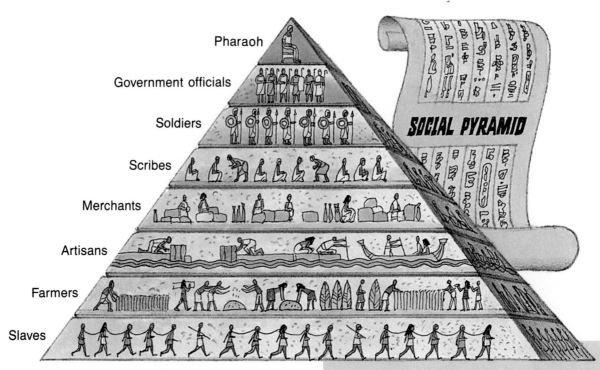

SOCIAL PYRAMID

Pharaoh
Government officials
Soldiers
Scribes
Merchants
Artisans
Farmers
Slaves

DIAGRAM SKILL: Were scribes more important than merchants in Egypt? How can you tell?

Women were found on all levels of the social pyramid. Compared to other ancient civilizations you will study, women in ancient Egypt had some power. During the time of the Egyptian Empire, women had the right to buy and sell property. In fact, this was a right very few women had in ancient times. This was a right that many women in our own country did not have until the 1800s.

THE LEGACY OF ANCIENT EGYPT

Imagine that it were up to you to tell the world about the ancient Egyptians. What would you include in your account? Remember that ancient Egypt left the world a rich legacy of treasures. You may visit the pyramids today or go to a museum to see the contents of the pharaohs' tombs.

Over 3,000 years have passed since ancient Egyptian civilization flour-ished in the Nile River Valley. Many of the monuments its people built still survive. However, the ancient Egyptians were more than great builders. Their civilization was made up of priests, government officials, artisans, farmers, and scientists. The heights they reached mark a period of great civilization.

Check Your Reading

1. What system of writing started in ancient Egypt?
2. What were some religious beliefs of the early Egyptians?
3. How was ancient Egyptian society organized?
4. **THINKING SKILL:** What items may ancient Egyptians have wanted to take with them to the afterlife? Classify the items into groups.

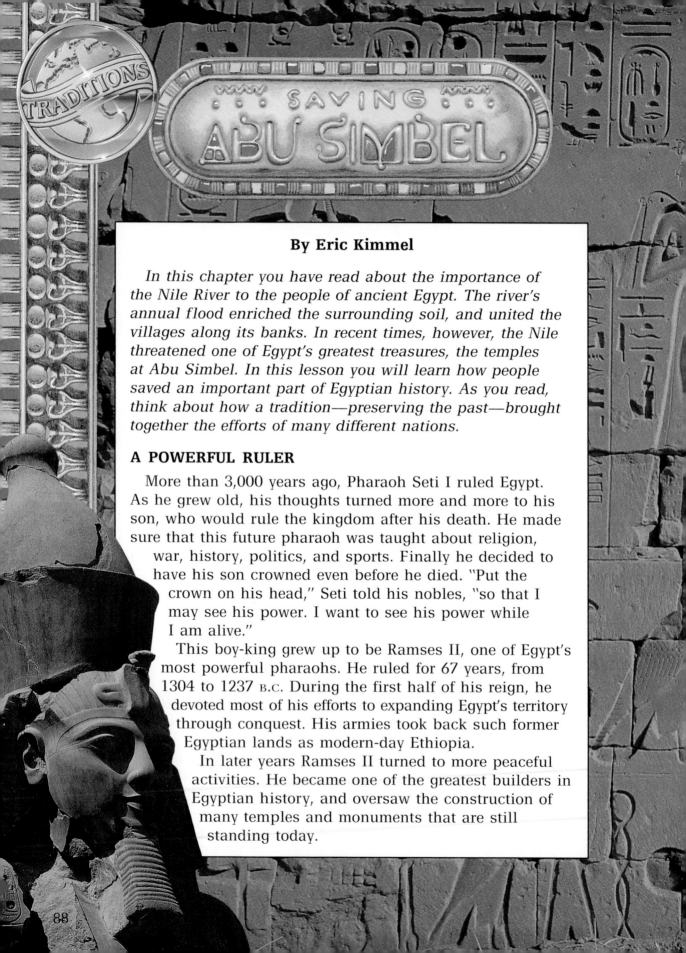

SAVING ABU SIMBEL

By Eric Kimmel

In this chapter you have read about the importance of the Nile River to the people of ancient Egypt. The river's annual flood enriched the surrounding soil, and united the villages along its banks. In recent times, however, the Nile threatened one of Egypt's greatest treasures, the temples at Abu Simbel. In this lesson you will learn how people saved an important part of Egyptian history. As you read, think about how a tradition—preserving the past—brought together the efforts of many different nations.

A POWERFUL RULER

More than 3,000 years ago, Pharaoh Seti I ruled Egypt. As he grew old, his thoughts turned more and more to his son, who would rule the kingdom after his death. He made sure that this future pharaoh was taught about religion, war, history, politics, and sports. Finally he decided to have his son crowned even before he died. "Put the crown on his head," Seti told his nobles, "so that I may see his power. I want to see his power while I am alive."

This boy-king grew up to be Ramses II, one of Egypt's most powerful pharaohs. He ruled for 67 years, from 1304 to 1237 B.C. During the first half of his reign, he devoted most of his efforts to expanding Egypt's territory through conquest. His armies took back such former Egyptian lands as modern-day Ethiopia.

In later years Ramses II turned to more peaceful activities. He became one of the greatest builders in Egyptian history, and oversaw the construction of many temples and monuments that are still standing today.

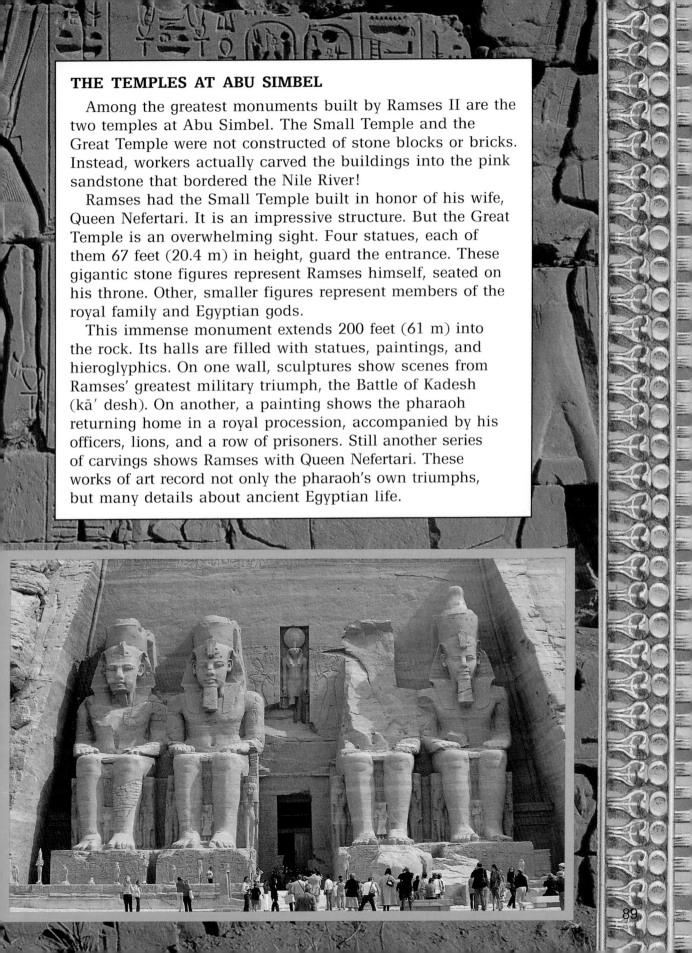

THE TEMPLES AT ABU SIMBEL

Among the greatest monuments built by Ramses II are the two temples at Abu Simbel. The Small Temple and the Great Temple were not constructed of stone blocks or bricks. Instead, workers actually carved the buildings into the pink sandstone that bordered the Nile River!

Ramses had the Small Temple built in honor of his wife, Queen Nefertari. It is an impressive structure. But the Great Temple is an overwhelming sight. Four statues, each of them 67 feet (20.4 m) in height, guard the entrance. These gigantic stone figures represent Ramses himself, seated on his throne. Other, smaller figures represent members of the royal family and Egyptian gods.

This immense monument extends 200 feet (61 m) into the rock. Its halls are filled with statues, paintings, and hieroglyphics. On one wall, sculptures show scenes from Ramses' greatest military triumph, the Battle of Kadesh (kā' desh). On another, a painting shows the pharaoh returning home in a royal procession, accompanied by his officers, lions, and a row of prisoners. Still another series of carvings shows Ramses with Queen Nefertari. These works of art record not only the pharaoh's own triumphs, but many details about ancient Egyptian life.

THE ASWAN HIGH DAM

The magnificent temples at Abu Simbel stood undisturbed for 3,000 years. Then, in 1960, Egypt began construction of the Aswan High Dam. The completed dam would supply electrical power to many Egyptian villages. It would also help to provide irrigation and flood control throughout the entire Nile Valley.

However, during the course of the construction of the dam, a new lake was created. Today Lake Nasser extends

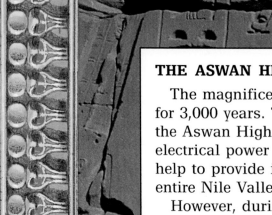

up the Nile for about 300 miles (483 km). But even before the dam was finished, the rising waters of this new lake began threatening some of Egypt's most important monuments. Among them was Abu Simbel.

SAVING THE TEMPLES

Egypt searched for a way to save these treasures. The government soon realized that the job was much too enormous for any single country, so the Egyptians appealed to the United Nations for help. You already have read about how the Nile River once helped to unite the villages along its banks. In 1964 the Nile united many nations throughout the world to save Abu Simbel. These nations contributed money, equipment, and technical skills.

How could the temples be saved? Architects and engineers from all over the world submitted their ideas. It was finally decided that the best plan would be to cut the temples into pieces and reassemble them above the level of the water. Work began in the spring of 1964. A temporary dam was constructed to protect the temples from Lake Nasser's waters. The rock above the temples was removed. Then, using power saws and handsaws, workers cut the actual temples into huge sandstone blocks.

Each block was reinforced with steel rods. Giant cranes then raised each 20-ton (18.1-metric t) block to an area of high ground overlooking the river. The process was a triumph of engineering. Not a single block cracked during its upward journey.

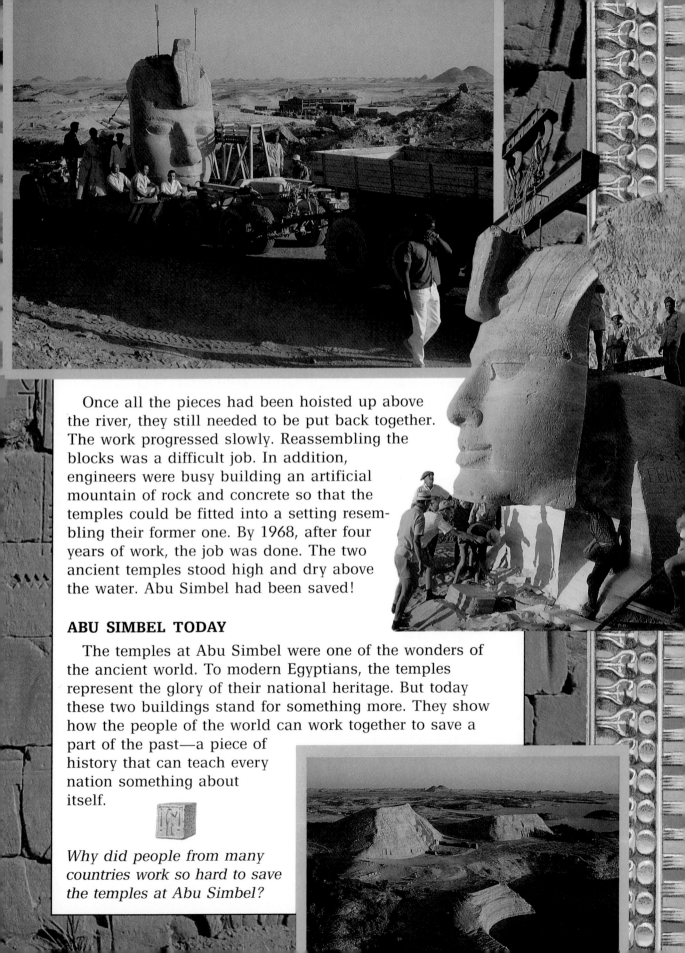

Once all the pieces had been hoisted up above the river, they still needed to be put back together. The work progressed slowly. Reassembling the blocks was a difficult job. In addition, engineers were busy building an artificial mountain of rock and concrete so that the temples could be fitted into a setting resembling their former one. By 1968, after four years of work, the job was done. The two ancient temples stood high and dry above the water. Abu Simbel had been saved!

ABU SIMBEL TODAY

The temples at Abu Simbel were one of the wonders of the ancient world. To modern Egyptians, the temples represent the glory of their national heritage. But today these two buildings stand for something more. They show how the people of the world can work together to save a part of the past—a piece of history that can teach every nation something about itself.

Why did people from many countries work so hard to save the temples at Abu Simbel?

Reading Historical Maps

Key Vocabulary
historical map
boundary
cataract

As you read about the history of ancient Egypt, you probably found it helpful to refer to the maps within the chapter. These maps show you the lands that made up Egypt at two different times in the past. The map on page 72, the "Nile River Valley," shows the lands of Egypt at its earliest, prehistoric time. The map on page 81, the "Egyptian Empire," shows how much land the Egyptians conquered. As you have read, this was the time when Egyptian civilization reached its peak.

How the World Was
In this book you will come across many historical maps such as those you have used in Chapter 3. Historical maps show you something about *how the world was* in the past. For example, they show how an empire was shaped, the route of an invasion, or the places where important battles were fought. All historical maps show something about the past.

The map on the next page is also a historical map. It combines the information from the two maps in your text with other information. This map shows how ancient Egypt grew and how its boundaries changed through time. As you may know, a boundary is an imaginary line dividing one country from another. As Egypt extended its boundaries, it changed in size

and shape. This map will help you to understand what was meant by *Egypt* at different times in the past.

In order to use the map, you will want to refer to the chart below. The chart shows how the history of ancient Egypt is divided into different periods. Suppose you want to know what lands were part of Egypt during the Age of Pyramids. The chart shows that the Age of Pyramids was a period of Egyptian history called the Old Kingdom. If you look at the map key, you will find the symbol for the boundary of the Old Kingdom. During the Old Kingdom, Egypt included the area lying inside this line on the map.

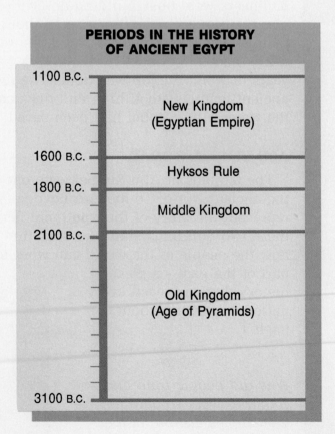

PERIODS IN THE HISTORY OF ANCIENT EGYPT

1100 B.C.	New Kingdom (Egyptian Empire)
1600 B.C.	Hyksos Rule
1800 B.C.	Middle Kingdom
2100 B.C.	
	Old Kingdom (Age of Pyramids)
3100 B.C.	

What Does the Map Say?

You can see from the map that during the time of the Old Kingdom, Egypt extended both east and west of the Nile River. You can also see that it did not expand to the south. This was not an accident. As the map on this page shows, the first cataract (kat′ ə rakt) on the Nile marked the southernmost limit of both predynastic and Old Kingdom Egypt. A cataract is a waterfall or churning rapids in a river. The Egyptians could sail up and down the Nile from the Mediterranean Sea to the first cataract. But they could not sail beyond the first cataract. In fact, the first cataract served as the southern boundary of Egypt for nearly 1,000 years.

Learning from Historical Maps

The map shows that the Egyptians of the New Kingdom conquered land as far south as the fifth cataract. As their technology improved, the ancient Egyptians began to expand the reach of their empire. Clearly, they had learned that they could haul their boats over land around the first cataract. They could then sail deeper into the African continent until they reached the second cataract.

If you study the map carefully, you will discover how ancient Egypt grew during its 3,000-year history. You can compare the areas it occupied at different times.

Reviewing the Skill

Use the map above to answer the following questions.

1. What is a historical map?
2. In what directions did Egypt expand after the Old Kingdom?

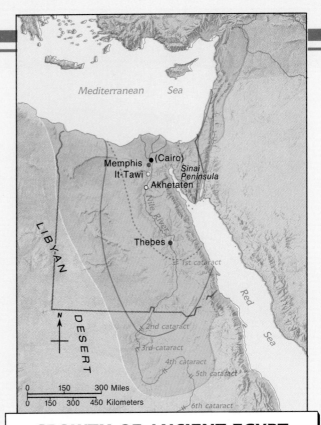

GROWTH OF ANCIENT EGYPT

New Kingdom	○ New Kingdom capital
—— Middle Kingdom boundary	● New Kingdom and Middle Kingdom capital
------ Old Kingdom boundary	◎ Middle Kingdom capital
∥ Cataract	● Old Kingdom capital
—— Boundary of modern Egypt	● Capital of modern Egypt

3. What bodies of water limited the growth of Egypt to the north and east?
4. During what period did the Sinai Peninsula become part of Egypt?
5. What city served as a capital of Egypt during both the Middle Kingdom and the New Kingdom?
6. What regions named on the map became part of Egypt during the New Kingdom?
7. During what period did ancient Egypt reach its maximum size?
8. Do you think historical maps are a good way to show past events? Why or why not?

93

IMPORTANT EVENTS

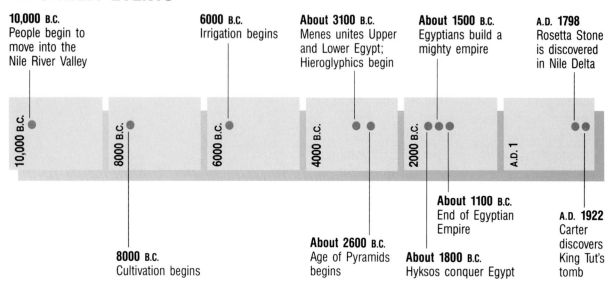

10,000 B.C.
People begin to move into the Nile River Valley

6000 B.C.
Irrigation begins

About 3100 B.C.
Menes unites Upper and Lower Egypt; Hieroglyphics begin

About 1500 B.C.
Egyptians build a mighty empire

A.D. 1798
Rosetta Stone is discovered in Nile Delta

10,000 B.C. — 8000 B.C. — 6000 B.C. — 4000 B.C. — 2000 B.C. — A.D. 1

8000 B.C.
Cultivation begins

About 2600 B.C.
Age of Pyramids begins

About 1800 B.C.
Hyksos conquer Egypt

About 1100 B.C.
End of Egyptian Empire

A.D. 1922
Carter discovers King Tut's tomb

PEOPLE TO KNOW

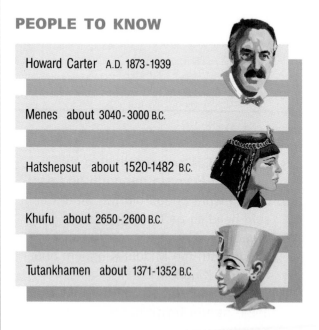

Howard Carter A.D. 1873-1939

Menes about 3040-3000 B.C.

Hatshepsut about 1520-1482 B.C.

Khufu about 2650-2600 B.C.

Tutankhamen about 1371-1352 B.C.

IDEAS TO REMEMBER

■ The people of the Nile River Valley prospered in their environment. The development of irrigation enabled them to build an economy that was based on farming.

■ The ancient Egyptians were led by a strong government. Their rulers were called pharaohs. Under their leadership, great pyramids were built and one of the world's first empires was established.

■ Ancient Egypt was one of the world's great ancient civilizations. The growth of hieroglyphics, religion, and cities caused it to become a remarkable place.

REVIEWING VOCABULARY

delta	papyrus
economy	pharaoh
empire	pyramid
hieroglyphics	Rosetta Stone
irrigation	scribe

Number a sheet of paper from 1 to 10. Beside each number write the word or term from the above list that best matches each definition.

1. A form of writing developed by the ancient Egyptians
2. The supreme ruler in ancient Egypt
3. A method of supplying water to dry land
4. One of the few members of Egyptian society who could write
5. A paper made from reeds that grew in the Nile Delta
6. The use of workers and resources to produce goods
7. A triangular piece of land found at the mouth of rivers
8. A large black object with carvings in three languages that provided the key to ancient writings
9. A group of lands and people ruled by one government
10. A huge structure used as a tomb for ancient Egyptian pharaohs

REVIEWING FACTS

1. In what region of Egypt does Upper Egypt lie? Lower Egypt?
2. What was the main economic activity of ancient Egypt?
3. Why was the flooding of the Nile important to ancient Egypt's economy?
4. What powerful group of nomads conquered Egypt around 1800 B.C.?
5. What three languages appear on the Rosetta Stone? How did this help scholars discover the meaning of the Egyptian hieroglyphics?

WRITING ABOUT MAIN IDEAS

1. **Writing a Pamphlet:** Look at the diagrams on pages 78–79. Write a pamphlet for a museum explaining how the Egyptians built the giant pyramids without modern technology. What points should your pamphlet discuss?
2. **Writing a List:** List five things about ancient Egypt that mark it as an important civilization.
3. **Writing About Perspectives:** Reread the paragraphs on pages 86–87 about the social pyramid in ancient Egypt. Then choose one group and write a paragraph describing what their life might have been like.

BUILDING SKILLS: READING HISTORICAL MAPS

Use the map on page 81 to answer the following questions.

1. What is the map about?
2. According to the map key, what color shows the Nile River Valley?
3. What lands became part of the Egyptian Empire?
4. What is the distance between Memphis and Thebes?
5. What does the locator map show? Give one reason why locator maps help you "read" a historical map.

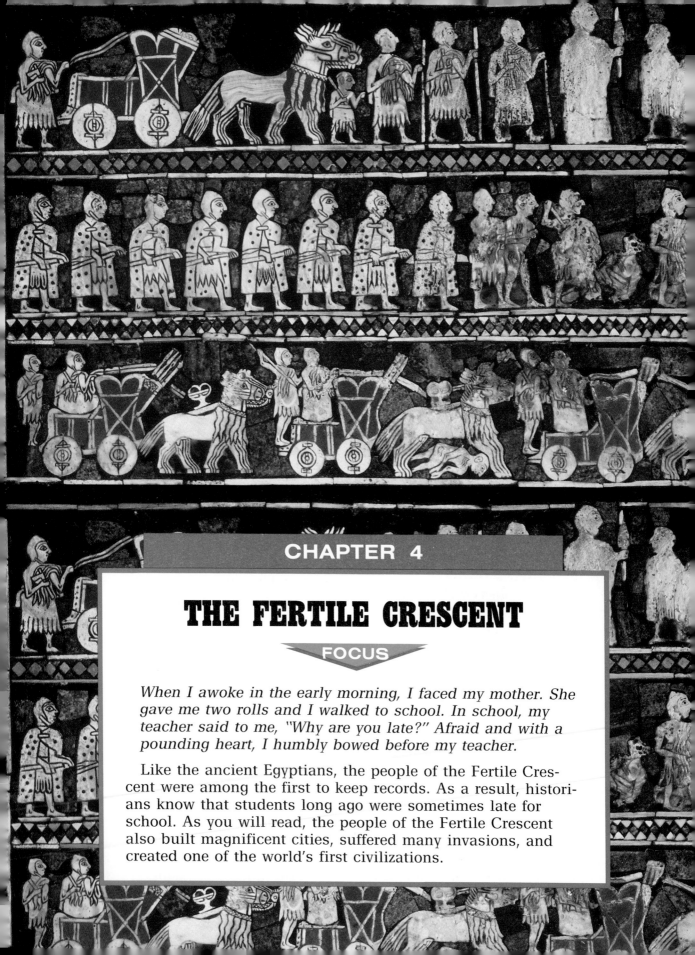

CHAPTER 4

THE FERTILE CRESCENT

FOCUS

When I awoke in the early morning, I faced my mother. She gave me two rolls and I walked to school. In school, my teacher said to me, "Why are you late?" Afraid and with a pounding heart, I humbly bowed before my teacher.

Like the ancient Egyptians, the people of the Fertile Crescent were among the first to keep records. As a result, historians know that students long ago were sometimes late for school. As you will read, the people of the Fertile Crescent also built magnificent cities, suffered many invasions, and created one of the world's first civilizations.

1 The Geography of the Fertile Crescent

READ TO LEARN

Key Vocabulary

drought
famine
surplus
barter

Key Places

Fertile Crescent
Mesopotamia

Read Aloud

It is an odd and astonishing fact that civilizations emerged in two separate places at the same time. Between 3500 and 3000 B.C., as Egypt was beginning to prosper under the first pharaohs, another great civilization arose. It arose in a harsh environment that challenged the presence of human life.

Read for Purpose

1. **WHAT YOU KNOW:** How did the geography of the Nile River Valley affect the growth of ancient Egypt?
2. **WHAT YOU WILL LEARN:** How did the people of the Fertile Crescent meet the challenge of a harsh environment?

THE FERTILE CRESCENT

In a region known as the Middle East, there is a strip of rich, well-watered land called the Fertile Crescent. As you can see on the map on the next page, it begins along the eastern shore of the Mediterranean Sea. Note how the Fertile Crescent arches northward and then curves down to the Persian Gulf. It is called a crescent because it is shaped like a quarter moon. It is called fertile because its soil can be made to produce a good food supply.

In Chapter 3 you learned that early people found the Nile River Valley a good place to farm. Around the same time, people were drawn to a river valley in the heart of the Fertile Crescent. The Greeks called this river valley "Mesopotamia" (mes ə pə tā′ mē ə), meaning "land between two rivers." Like the Nile River Valley in Egypt, the "land between two rivers" became one of the earliest centers of civilization.

The two rivers that flow across the Mesopotamian plains are called the Tigris and the Euphrates. Find these rivers on the map on page 98. As the map shows, the rivers flow so much in the same southeastwardly direction that they are often called the "twin rivers." Into what body of water do they finally flow?

97

A CHALLENGING ENVIRONMENT

In many ways, Mesopotamia was similar to the Nile River Valley. For example, in the spring and early summer, melting snows from the northern mountains caused the rivers to overflow. Unlike the floods of the Nile, however, the floods of the Tigris and Euphrates were not predictable. In some years, the rivers never rose above their banks. In other times, savage floods destroyed villages and took many lives. Sometimes the floods even caused the rivers to change their courses!

In addition to flooding, Mesopotamia suffered dangerous summer **droughts** (drouts). A drought is a long period of dry weather. Droughts can turn fertile soil to dust, shrivel crops, and cause widespread lack of food, or **famine** (fam' in).

With so many obstacles in the way of successful farming, you may be wondering why people continued to live in Mesopotamia. Moreover, with the risk of drought and famine, how did civilization emerge on the "land between two rivers"?

TAMING THE RIVERS

Do you remember how the overflow of the Nile brought Egyptian lands precious silt and increased its fertility? The soil of Mesopotamia was also improved by silt deposits. As the waters of the mighty Tigris and Euphrates rivers drained, silt was left upon the land. Fertile soil meant that farming was possible. But successful farming requires more than good soil.

The climate of Mesopotamia was exceptionally dry. With little rainfall all year long, farmers had to work hard to find ways to provide water for their crops. As in Egypt, Mesopotamian farmers learned to irrigate their fields. Irrigation involved a great network of canals and dikes, which helped trap the waters of the Tigris and Euphrates rivers.

The effects of irrigation in Mesopotamia were tremendous. By 3000 B.C. farmers were producing a **surplus**, or extra supply, of food. They grew grains, such as wheat and barley, and vegetables and fruits. This had a profound effect on Mesopotamia's growth.

As the food surplus became more reliable, not everyone was needed to work in the fields. Thus some people were free to develop other skills and work at new jobs. During the height

THE FERTILE CRESCENT

- Fertile Crescent
- Mesopotamia

MAP SKILL: Did Mesopotamia reach the banks of the Mediterranean Sea? Was the Fertile Crescent larger than Mesopotamia?

of Mesopotamian civilization, people worked as potters, metalworkers, boat builders, scribes, jewelers, and carpenters. Such specialization, made possible by a food surplus, enabled the region to develop many popular items of trade.

The beautiful gold helmet, dagger, and sheath show why Mesopotamian goods were highly prized trade articles.

MESOPOTAMIA'S LIVELY TRADE

Trade was at the heart of life in Mesopotamia. A farmer might trade his surplus grain for a piece of pottery. Sheep raisers might trade wool fleece for woven wool blankets. This trade of one kind of product for another without the use of money is called barter.

Merchants, or people who buy and sell products, became rich by trading in more distant places. They sent boats overflowing with grain up the rivers toward the mountains in the north. There a merchant might barter his grain for lumber and stone that Mesopotamia lacked. Merchants also bartered their goods to get gold and copper that the mountain villagers dug from their hillsides.

Merchants brought the metals back to their villages where artisans worked them into tools, weapons, and jewelry. You can see from the photographs on this page that the artisans of Mesopotamia had mastered the art of metalworking.

The harsh environment of the Fertile Crescent did not hold back its people. The great strides the Mesopotamians made in farming and trade were only the beginning. As you will learn, the Fertile Crescent became the home of societies whose legacies have left a lasting impression.

Check Your Reading

1. How did the Fertile Crescent get its name?
2. What causes a famine?
3. GEOGRAPHY SKILL: What were the effects of irrigation on Mesopotamia?
4. THINKING SKILL: What might have happened in Mesopotamia if farmers had not produced a surplus?

2 Mesopotamian Civilization

READ TO LEARN

Key Vocabulary	Key People	Key Places
city-state	Hammurabi	Sumer
ziggurat		Babylon
cuneiform		
Code of Hammurabi		

Read Aloud

The father begins by asking his son, "Where did you go when you should have been in school?"
"I did not go anywhere."
"If you did not go anywhere, why do you idle about? Go to school, open your school bag, recite your assignment, and do your work. . . . Don't stand about in the public square or wander around the street. . . . Be humble and show fear before your teacher. When you show terror, your teacher will like you."

The passage above was written more than 4,000 years ago by a Mesopotamian scribe. Apparently, the young student had missed a day of school without his father's permission. Such ancient writings help bring the past to life.

Read for Purpose

1. **WHAT YOU KNOW:** Based on what you have read so far, how would you define a civilization?
2. **WHAT YOU WILL LEARN:** How was the civilization of Mesopotamia different from that of Egypt?

MYSTERIOUS ORIGINS

Ancient writings have brought the ancient world closer to us. Such writings show that people today have some things in common with those who lived 4,000 years ago. As you read this lesson you will learn more about the people of Mesopotamia and how greatly they contributed to the first stages of civilization as we know it today.

Among the earliest groups in the Fertile Crescent to make important contributions were the Sumerians. The Sumerians moved into the region around 4000 B.C. Although their origins are a mystery, one thing is certain;

for many years people who followed the Sumerians in the Fertile Crescent would build upon their legacy. But who were the Sumerians?

No one knows exactly where the Sumerians came from. A Sumerian legend says that their origins cannot be found on a map. According to legend, the first Sumerian was a fisherman named Oannes (ō a′ nəs). Oannes swam up the Persian Gulf, bringing with him the gifts of civilization.

Where do you think the Sumerians came from? Some historians think they may have wandered from the east, from what is now Iran or perhaps from India. Or did they come from the mountains of Asia Minor? Find Iran, India, and Asia Minor in the Atlas on pages 612 and 613. What route might the Sumerians have taken from these places to reach Mesopotamia?

Wherever the Sumerians came from, they were probably nomads before they settled down to farm the plains of lower Mesopotamia. Their land became known as Sumer (sü′ mər). Find Sumer on the map on this page.

SUMERIAN CITY-STATES

By 3000 B.C. the villages of Sumer had grown into lively cities of more than 10,000 people. Compared to modern cities, this may not seem like a lot of people. In their time, however, these were the largest cities in the world.

Each Sumerian city was the center of an independent city-state. A city-state is a self-governing city and the lands surrounding it. At Sumer's height in 2500 B.C., it had 12 bustling city-states. Everyone who lived there spoke the same language, shared customs and religious beliefs, and worked together to meet basic needs.

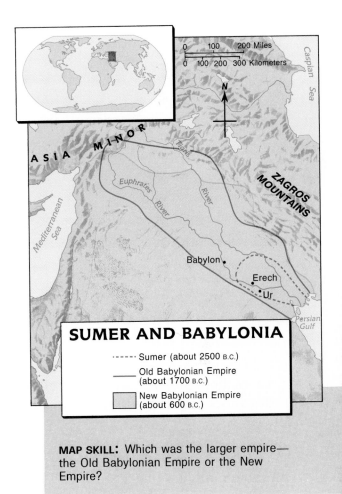

SUMER AND BABYLONIA

- - - - - Sumer (about 2500 B.C.)

———— Old Babylonian Empire (about 1700 B.C.)

New Babylonian Empire (about 600 B.C.)

MAP SKILL: Which was the larger empire—the Old Babylonian Empire or the New Empire?

In spite of the harmony within each city-state, Sumer was not a united nation. You remember that ancient Egypt was ruled by a pharaoh who had power over all the people of the Nile River Valley. Sumer did not have a central government. Each city-state was like a separate nation with its own ruler. This often created conflict between the city-states. Wars over land and water rights were common. For many years Ur fought Erech, for example, to gain control of the lower Euphrates River.

TEMPLES TO THE GODS

Unlike the Egyptian pharaohs, the rulers of the Sumerian city-states were not worshiped as gods. The people reserved their worship for the special

The Sumerians believed this ziggurat at Nippur was the home of Enlil, the storm god. At right is a Sumerian carving that may show a husband and wife.

gods and goddesses who were believed to protect their city and crops. One visitor described the buildings that the Sumerians used for worship.

> In the middle of the city there is a tower . . . upon which is raised a second tower, and on that a third, and so on up to eight. . . . On the topmost tower there is a spacious temple, and inside a couch of unusual size. . . . They declare that their god comes down and sleeps upon the couch.

The Sumerians built these temples to honor the gods and goddesses they worshiped. These temples, called **ziggurats** (zig' ŭ ratz), were easily the most important buildings in the city-states. They were also the tallest buildings, towering over the countryside. Sumerians believed that the great height of the ziggurats brought each city-state nearer to the gods. Each ziggurat was intended to be a "bond between heaven and earth."

Look at the photograph of the famous ziggurat on this page. A narrow, rugged stairway leads up to the top. It was believed that the gods and god-

desses used these steps to descend to the earth from the heavens.

In ancient times the mud brick ziggurat was brightly decorated with colorful designs and pictures of sacred animals. Today, as the photograph shows, the ziggurat is in ruins. But historians know such decorations existed because Sumerians wrote descriptions of them.

SUMERIAN WRITING

As you recall, the Egyptians developed a system of writing called hieroglyphics. About the same time, around 3000 B.C., the Sumerians invented their own system of writing called **cuneiform** (kū nē' ə fôrm). Writing began in Sumer as a way to keep accounts of business deals. For example, a merchant needed a record of the number of bushels of grain he was trading for a load of lumber.

Sumerian scribes wrote on clay tablets using a pointed instrument made of reed called a stylus. Pressing the edge of the stylus against a tablet of soft clay, the scribe produced wedge shapes. This explains why Sumerian writing came to be called cuneiform, which means "wedge-shaped." The chart on this page shows some examples of words written in cuneiform.

In all early civilizations writing was regarded as magical. To be able to write a name was thought to give the writer magical power over the person or thing named. As in ancient Egypt, scribes were treated as special people.

Sumerian scribes left behind thousands of clay tablets. Many of the tablets record business deals. Many others, however, tell us about the Sumerians' values and religious practices. Even the passage you read on page 100 was taken from ancient Sumerian tablets.

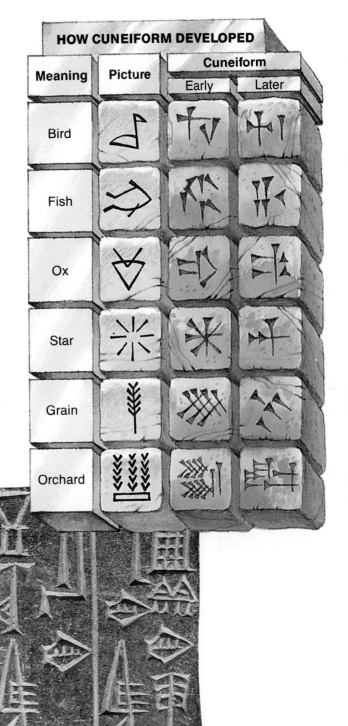

HOW CUNEIFORM DEVELOPED

Meaning	Picture	Cuneiform	
		Early	Later
Bird			
Fish			
Ox			
Star			
Grain			
Orchard			

CHART SKILL: Use the chart to tell how the cuneiform symbols changed. Is early or later cuneiform carved on this stone?

THE BABYLONIANS

Woe is me, my house is a ruined stable, I am a herdsman whose cows have been scattered. . . . I am an exile from the city that has found no rest; I am a stranger in a strange land.

These words were written by a Sumerian scribe around 2,000 B.C. What had happened to cause him to write such mournful lines? Around that time many different groups of people were on the move through the Fertile Crescent. The arrival of new groups brought a wave of warfare.

The first conquerors moved into the city of Babylon (bab′ ə lon), a little upstream from Sumer. The Babylonians had been nomads, but they quickly adopted the ways of the Sumerians. They irrigated fields, built ziggurats, and wrote cuneiform. By 1700 B.C. the Babylonians conquered all of Sumer and Mesopotamia, spreading their civilization over a large area. The Babylonians built an empire that, over a long period of time, covered the lands of the Fertile Crescent.

The Babylonians built a magnificent palace known as the Hanging Gardens of Babylon. People came from faraway places to see the palace and called it one of the "Seven Wonders of the World." Built in the sixth century B.C., the Hanging Gardens of Babylon was made up of many levels of gardens and palace rooms. Colorful plants and flowers hung over the edges. It must have been a sight to see.

This is an artist's idea of how the famous Hanging Gardens of Babylon may have looked. Why do you think these gardens were called one of the world's Seven Wonders?

AN IMPORTANT CODE OF LAWS

Historians have learned that the Babylonians were the first people to write down their laws. One of the greatest lawgivers of ancient history was the mighty Babylonian ruler Hammurabi (hä mǜ rä′ bē). Hammurabi recorded a system of laws around 1780 B.C. His purpose, he declared, was:

to cause justice to prevail in the land, to destroy the wicked and the evil, to prevent the strong from oppressing the weak . . . and to further the welfare of the people.

Hammurabi's system of laws, called the Code of Hammurabi, was the world's first effort to record laws. Hammurabi's code had 282 laws. Arranged under headings such as trade, family, work, and property, it took 3,600 lines of cuneiform to write them all down.

If you could read its cuneiform writing, you would discover that the punishments of the Code of Hammurabi were very harsh. Hammurabi believed that anyone who injured another person should receive the same injury in return. The code states, for example, that if a man put out the eye of another, the man's eye should be put out. Thus Hammurabi's laws are sometimes called an "eye for an eye justice."

Hammurabi's laws were carved on a great stone column, which was placed in the center of town. On top of the column sat Shamash (sha′ mash), the god of the sun and justice. Look at the photograph of the Code of Hammurabi on this page. Shamash is shown handing the laws to Hammurabi. What do you think this image meant to the people of Mesopotamia? Do you think it caused people to obey laws? Why?

THE CODE OF HAMMURABI

*I*f a son has struck his father, they shall cut off his hand.

If a man has destroyed the eye of another, they shall destroy his eye.

If he has broken the bone of a man, they shall break his bone.

If a man stole either an ox or a sheep. . .or a pig or a goat, if it belonged to the temple or if it belonged to the state, he shall pay thirtyfold. If it belonged to another man, he shall make good tenfold. If the thief cannot pay, he shall be put to death.

If a man was too lazy to make the dike of his field strong. . .and a break has opened up in his dike and he has let the water ravage the farmland, the man whose dike was opened shall make good the grain that he let get destroyed.

I, Hammurabi, the perfect king. . . I rooted out the enemy above and below; I made an end of war; I promoted the welfare of the land; . . .The great gods called me, so I became a righteous shepherd of people. . . .

A written code of laws like the Code of Hammurabi helped leaders govern an empire that had many different groups of people.

How do these examples of Babylonian art help historians understand the power of the Babylonian Empire?

THE LEGACY OF MESOPOTAMIA

It is important to remember that the people of Mesopotamia lived in a harsh environment. Remembering this, it is easy to appreciate the great ad-vances made by the people of Mesopotamia. The Sumerian and Babylonian legacies to the world are known to us because their scribes kept accurate records. As you know, the Code of Hammurabi helps us understand that the Babylonians had a strong central government. This surely enabled them to build one of the world's first great empires. In time, later societies would create similar codes of law to help govern an ever-changing world.

 Check Your Reading

1. What is a city-state?
2. Describe Sumerian civilization.
3. Why do you think the Code of Hammurabi is considered a major contribution to civilization?
4. **THINKING SKILL:** Compare and contrast hieroglyphic and cuneiform writing. Use the charts on pages 84 and 103.

PROTECTING THE ENVIRONMENT

The people of Mesopotamia knew that the Tigris and Euphrates rivers were a valuable source of life. As you have read, civilization flourished in the "land between the rivers." Even the laws of the Code of Hammurabi warned:

If a man fails to honor the rivers, he shall not gain the life from them.

In modern times, people have often failed to remember just how important the environment is. There is, however, a senior citizen in Levittown, Pennsylvania, who reminds us of the great value of nature. His name is Ray Proffitt and he is a one-man environmental hero. When Ray sees people who pollute, or dirty the environment, he does not look away.

Ray Proffitt has lived a full, active life. Though he is a retired air force test pilot and stockbroker, he refuses to "slow down" and is determined to make a difference in his community. Ray works hard to help protect the Delaware River. As you see from the photograph on this page, he uses a special amphibious (am fib′ ē əs) car. An amphibious car can ride on land and float on water.

Steering his amphibious car up and down the Delaware River, Ray is constantly on the lookout for polluters. He has spotted many families dumping trash into the river from their boats. Other times, Ray has witnessed illegal dumping on the riverside lands. Often, however, he only finds evidence of the crime—trash.

Whenever Ray finds evidence of criminal activity against the environment, he records everything he sees in his notebook. Like a detective he takes photographs and studies the evidence. He is often able to trace the trash he finds to the people who left it behind.

Do the polluters listen to Ray? Not always. But Ray has a reputation for winning when he takes polluters to court. The evidence that Ray gathers against polluters is so vast and accurate that the courts usually declare polluters "guilty." As you can imagine, guilty polluters are often ordered to pay large amounts of money in fines. The money is then used to help clean up the environment.

Ray Proffitt's war against polluters in the Delaware River is just beginning. Ray figures he still has a long way to go.

This battle is not over. I'll clean up this whole area. You haven't seen anything yet.

107

Decision Making

Do you like to go shopping? Perhaps you have a favorite record or book store. If you like to shop, you already know a lot about decision making. Decision making means *choosing*. Making a decision means choosing one out of many alternatives, or options. In this lesson you will learn how to make better decisions.

Trying the Skill

Read the following story to identify how one decision was made a long time ago.

Henry Rawlinson once found a monument carved high on a cliff. He wanted to study the writing on it.

Rawlinson considered several ways to reach the monument. He could climb the smooth cliff. He could look at the monument through a telescope from the base of the cliff. Or he could lower himself down from the top of the cliff.

Climbing was risky, Rawlinson thought. Although he could get close enough to copy the cuneiform, he might easily fall. Using the telescope was not risky at all. However, some of the writing would be hidden from view. By suspending himself from the top of the cliff in a strong harness he could reduce the risk of falling. He could also get close enough to make actual paper casts of the cuneiform.

Rawlinson finally chose the third alternative. The casts came out perfectly, so that he was able to understand the writing. At last, the secrets of the Middle East would be uncovered.

1. What was Rawlinson's goal?
2. What alternatives did he consider?

HELPING YOURSELF

The steps on the left help people make good decisions. The example on the right shows how Rawlinson may have made his decision.

One Way to Make a Decision	Example
1. Identify and define the goals you wish to achieve.	Rawlinson's goal was to understand cuneiform.
2. Identify all the possible alternatives, or options, by which you can reach your goal.	He identified three ways to accomplish his goal. He could climb the cliff, he could look at the monument through a telescope, or he could lower himself down the cliff and make paper casts.
3. Consider long range results as well as immediate results for each alternative.	Rawlinson considered the likely outcomes of each alternative. For instance, he realized that climbing the cliff would probably have resulted in an accident or, even worse, in his death.
4. Evaluate each alternative by determining whether the results and costs would be beneficial or harmful to you and others involved.	After figuring out the result of each alternative, Rawlinson decided that making paper casts would be the most helpful—and least costly—to himself and others.
5. Choose the best alternative.	Rawlinson's choice was the best. By safely making accurate copies, he was able to understand the cuneiform.

Applying the Skill

Now apply what you have learned to identify the decision-making process in the following story.

I want my son to be respected in Babylon. I could have him trained to be an architect, a physician, or a scribe. Each would suit my purpose. But my son is not a leader and cannot build. The Code of Hammurabi demands the death of any architect whose building falls and kills someone. The code also punishes a physician by cutting off his fingers if a patient dies after surgery. Physicians are well paid but they cannot work without hands!

I think it would be best to send my son to school to learn to write. Although school will be expensive, scribes are highly respected and their lives are rarely in danger. So—a scribe he will be!

1. What was the father's goal?
   a. having a respected son
   b. getting rich quickly
   c. having his son get married
2. Which alternative below was not considered by the father for his son?
   a. farming
   b. becoming a doctor
   c. designing buildings
3. What did the father think might happen to his son if he became an architect?

Reviewing the Skill

1. What is another word for alternatives?
2. Name some steps a person could take in order to make a good decision.
3. When making a decision, why is it important to consider as many alternatives as possible?

READ TO LEARN

Read Aloud

I am the first and I am the last; besides me there is no god. . . . Is there a God besides me? I know not any.

Thus the sacred writings of the ancient Hebrews proclaim their belief in one God. From such writings you can learn about the events that led to the emergence of a unique religious tradition.

Read for Purpose

1. **WHAT YOU KNOW:** What were the religious beliefs of the societies you have already read about?
2. **WHAT YOU WILL LEARN:** How was the religion of the ancient Hebrews different from others?

THE ANCIENT HEBREWS

Much of what we know about the ancient Hebrews comes to us from their sacred writings in the Bible. The Bible tells us that the earliest Hebrews were shepherds who lived in Mesopotamia. In the Bible you can read about many heroic men and women who guided the ancient Hebrews.

As you read about the ancient Hebrews, you should know that one of the world's great religions developed among them. This religion, called Judaism (jü′ dē iz əm), is followed today by more than 17 million people, known as Jews.

THE ORIGINS OF JUDAISM

Around the time Hammurabi ruled Mesopotamia, Abraham became a great Hebrew leader. He also lived in Mesopotamia. According to the Bible, God said to Abraham:

Go from your country and your father's house to the land that I will show you. And I will make of you a great nation. . . . So Abraham took his wife Sarah . . . and all their possessions which they had gathered, and all members of their household; and they set forth.

This was a difficult journey for the Hebrews. They wandered for many

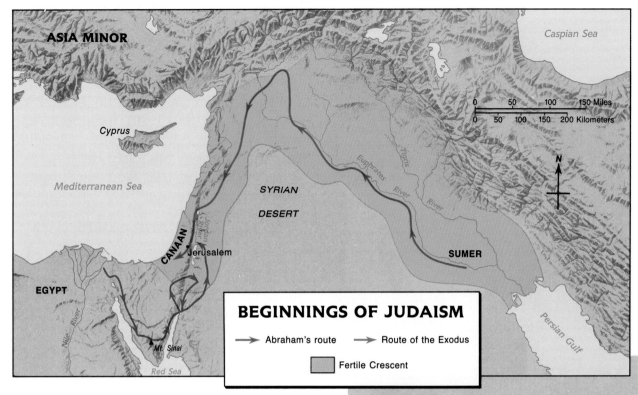

ASIA MINOR

Caspian Sea

Cyprus

Mediterranean Sea

SYRIAN

DESERT

CANAAN

Jerusalem

SUMER

EGYPT

Nile River

Mt. Sinai

Red Sea

Euphrates River

Tigris River

Persian Gulf

0   50   100   150 Miles
0   50   100   150   200 Kilometers

N

BEGINNINGS OF JUDAISM

→ Abraham's route   → Route of the Exodus

Fertile Crescent

MAP SKILL: According to this map, what river did Abraham follow on his journey from southern Mesopotamia?

months across the Fertile Crescent. The Bible says that when the Hebrews reached Canaan (kāʹ nən), God said to Abraham, "To your descendants I will give this land." Thus Canaan became the new home of the ancient Hebrews. Canaan is located in the western part of the Fertile Crescent between the Jordan River and the Mediterranean Sea. You can find it on the map above.

CAPTIVITY IN EGYPT

According to the Bible, the Hebrews lived in Canaan until a famine struck. The famine forced them to move to Egypt for food. The lives of the Hebrews, however, were not happy among the ancient Egyptians. The Hebrews were made slaves there. You can read in the Bible that:

The Egyptians made the Hebrews serve with rigor. And they made their lives bitter with hard bondage . . . .

The Hebrews lived in slavery for more than 400 years before a leader named Moses arose among them in Egypt. Although Moses was a Hebrew, he had been raised in the pharoah's palace. The Bible explains that as a baby Moses had been saved from death by a daughter of the pharoah. Later, "When Moses had grown up, he went out to his people the Hebrews and looked on their burdens."

One day Moses saw a Hebrew slave being beaten. In anger, Moses killed the Egyptian overseer who was doing the beating. As a result, Moses had to flee for safety to the wilderness. The Bible records that God appeared to Moses while he was in the wilderness. There God commanded Moses to free the Hebrews from slavery and to lead

111

Moses holds the tablets on which the **Ten Commandments** were written. This code of laws contains values that have influenced many religions and governments.

them to Canaan, a "land flowing with milk and honey."

Obeying God's command, Moses led the Hebrews out of captivity in Egypt. Following their escape, the Hebrews wandered in the desert for about 40 years. Their journey finally ended when the Hebrews reached the boundaries of the land that God had promised them in Canaan.

THE TEN COMMANDMENTS

During the Hebrews' long desert wanderings, they developed their most important laws. The most significant ones emerged while the Hebrews were living near **Mount Sinai**. There, according to the Bible, God gave Moses the laws that became known as the **Ten Commandments**.

The Ten Commandments are one important foundation of Hebrew law governing religious belief and behavior. They have also had a great influ-

THE TEN COMMANDMENTS

I am the Lord Thy God. Thou shalt have no other gods before me.	Thou shalt not kill.
Thou shalt not make unto thee any graven image, or any likeness of any thing that is in heaven above	Thou shalt not commit adultery.
Thou shalt not take the name of the Lord thy God in vain	Thou shalt not steal.
Remember the sabbath day, to keep it holy	Thou shalt not bear false witness against thy neighbor.
Honor thy father and thy mother.	Thou shalt not covet thy neighbor's house . . . nor anything that is thy neighbor's.

ence on other religions. The commandments forbid lying, stealing, and murder. They urge people to obey their parents and respect neighbors' property. The Hebrews believed that if they obeyed the Commandments and other Hebrew laws they would receive God's blessing and protection.

THE IDEA OF ONE GOD

The first of the Ten Commandments was unusual for its time: "You shall have no other gods before me." As you have read, the Egyptians and the Mesopotamians worshiped many gods. Belief in many gods is called polytheism (pol′ ē thē iz əm). Polytheism was common among people throughout the world. According to their belief, the gods had many roles and varied in importance. The Hebrew religion was different.

The Hebrews practiced monotheism (mon′ ə thē iz əm), or belief in one God. They were the first group of people to believe in one God. The monotheism of the ancient Hebrews set them apart from other ancient peoples of the Fertile Crescent.

The Hebrews believed that God was an all-important being. The God of Abraham and Moses was a God of peace. Moreover, the Hebrews believed that God was a just God. He wanted the Hebrews to follow His laws and share them with the world.

THE WISDOM OF SOLOMON

Some books contain the writings of Hebrew teachers and rulers such as Solomon. Nearly 3,000 years ago Solomon, a young prince, became king of his people, now organized into the kingdom of Israel. The name Solomon means "peace" in the Hebrew language. While Solomon was king, Israel was at peace with its neighbors. In addition to being known as a powerful

Solomon governed from the ancient city of Jerusalem. Today, Jerusalem is the capital of Israel and is a great religious center.

ruler, Solomon had a reputation for wisdom.

Solomon grew up in **Jerusalem**, a big, busy city that his father, King David, had conquered for Israel. Solomon liked to read and write poetry. He also liked music. Even when he was young Solomon wanted to learn everything there was to learn. When he became king Solomon made knowledge important in his court.

Solomon's teachers used short sayings to pass along ideas quickly. Many of these sayings, called proverbs, are in the Bible. According to the Bible, Solomon "spake three thousand prov-erbs: and his songs were a thousand and five." You can read some of Solomon's famous proverbs in the chart on this page.

King Solomon became famous for his wisdom. One day two women came before him. The women were fighting over a baby. Each one said the baby was hers. Solomon thought for a moment and then ordered a soldier to cut the baby in half!

One woman did not resist. The other pleaded with Solomon to let the first woman have the baby. Solomon pointed to the second woman. "Give her the living baby," he ordered. "She is the mother." Solomon wisely knew that the *real* mother would rather give her baby up to the false mother than let the baby die.

PROVERBS OF SOLOMON

"*W*isdom is the principal thing; therefore get wisdom."

"One who is slow to anger has great understanding, but one who has a hasty temper exalts folly.

"Wisdom lives in the mind of a person of understanding, but it is not known in the hearts of fools."

"A soft answer turns away wrath, but a harsh word stirs up anger."

"Bread gained by lies is sweet, but afterward the mouth is full of gravel."

Studying the Bible's wisdom, such as these proverbs, is an important part of Judaism. In the bar mitzvah ceremony on the right, a boy becomes an adult in the Jewish religion.

The ancient writings of **Judaism**, called the Torah, make up the first five books of the Bible. Today the Bible is the most widely read book in the world.

THE LEGACY OF THE ANCIENT HEBREWS

The religious beliefs and traditions of Israel have influenced many societies for thousands of years. Monotheism, for example, came to be the belief of millions of people throughout the world.

Israel was also responsible for some of the world's most treasured writings. For many centuries its beliefs were carried down by word of mouth. Then, in about 1000 B.C., the beliefs began to be written down. Many of these writings are collected in the Bible from which you have learned about Abraham and Moses.

Throughout their long history the Jews have held on to their religious beliefs and traditions. The world is fortunate to have the rich writings that preserve their legacy. As you study this book, you will see that many of the world's societies have built upon the wisdom of ancient Israel.

Check Your Reading

1. Why did Moses lead the Hebrews out of Egypt?
2. What are the Ten Commandments?
3. Describe the difference between polytheism and monotheism.
4. **THINKING SKILL:** What alternatives might the Hebrews have considered before deciding to move to Egypt?

115

IMPORTANT EVENTS

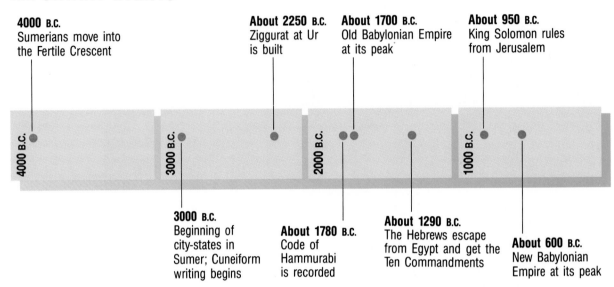

4000 B.C.
Sumerians move into
the Fertile Crescent

About 2250 B.C.
Ziggurat at Ur
is built

About 1700 B.C.
Old Babylonian Empire
at its peak

About 950 B.C.
King Solomon rules
from Jerusalem

4000 B.C.

3000 B.C.

2000 B.C.

1000 B.C.

3000 B.C.
Beginning of
city-states in
Sumer; Cuneiform
writing begins

About 1780 B.C.
Code of
Hammurabi
is recorded

About 1290 B.C.
The Hebrews escape
from Egypt and get the
Ten Commandments

About 600 B.C.
New Babylonian
Empire at its peak

PEOPLE TO KNOW

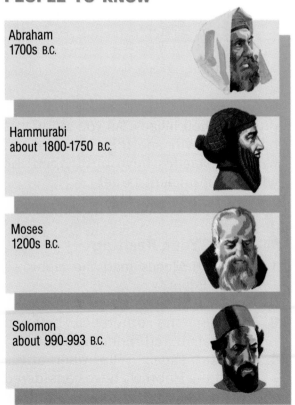

Abraham
1700s B.C.

Hammurabi
about 1800-1750 B.C.

Moses
1200s B.C.

Solomon
about 990-993 B.C.

IDEAS TO REMEMBER

■ Early people settled in the "land between the rivers," or Mesopotamia.
Floods and droughts often made farming difficult, but the development of irrigation allowed civilization to grow.

■ Civilization in the Fertile Crescent first
emerged among the Sumerians. The
Sumerians built great temples called
ziggurats to honor their gods and goddesses. They also developed one of the
world's earliest systems of writing,
called cuneiform. The Babylonians
built upon the Sumerian legacy.

■ Judaism, one of the world's great religions, developed among the ancient
Hebrews. Their traditions and religious
beliefs have influenced many different
cultures for thousands of years.

REVIEWING VOCABULARY

city-state   monotheism
cuneiform   polytheism
drought   surplus
famine   Ten Commandments
Judaism   ziggurat

Number a sheet of paper from 1 to 10. Beside each number write the word or term from the above list that best completes the sentence.

1. The belief in many gods is called ____.

2. When farmers produce more food than people need, that extra food is called a ____.

3. A self-governing political unit made up of a city and surrounding lands was called a ____.

4. The system of "wedge-shaped" writing is called ____.

5. ____ is the belief in one God.

6. ____ is the religion of the Hebrews.

7. A long period of dry weather is called a ____.

8. A Mesopotamian temple honoring a god or goddess is a ____.

9. A lack of food, often leading to mass starvation, is a ____.

10. Laws governing Hebrew religion are the ____.

REVIEWING FACTS

1. What was the name of the strip of rich land, shaped like a quarter moon, that became the site of several important civilizations in the Middle East?

2. This Greek word means "land between two rivers."

3. What was the name of the first important civilization to appear between the Tigris and Euphrates rivers?

4. What group of people conquered Mesopotamia and brought an end to Sumerian civilization?

5. What was the name of the first written system of laws?

WRITING ABOUT MAIN IDEAS

1. **Writing an Explanation:** Look at the photo on page 105. Write two or three sentences that would explain why the Code of Hammurabi is regarded as an important step forward in civilization.

2. **Writing About Perspectives:** Suppose that you are a historian writing about ancient civilizations. Write a comparison of the governments and rulers of ancient Egypt and Sumer. How were they similar? How were they different?

BUILDING SKILLS: DECISION MAKING

Read the following account. Then make a decision based on the given information.

You are Hammurabi, the great Babylonian king. Your people often argue over land and water rights. Should you develop a code of laws?

1. What goal do you hope to achieve?

2. What alternatives did you consider?

3. What might be the consequences of these alternatives?

4. Which alternative will you choose?

5. Do you think you made a "good" decision? Explain.

CHAPTER 5

ANCIENT INDIA AND ANCIENT CHINA

FOCUS

For thousands of years these lands developed at their own speed in their own way, so that, to us, civilization there seems a world apart.

The historian who wrote these words understood that ancient India and ancient China had separate, unique histories. In this chapter you will read about the origins of these two mighty world cultures. They both have a magnificent past.

1 The Indus River Valley

READ TO LEARN

Key Vocabulary

subcontinent
tributary
citadel
migration

Key Places

Indus River Valley   Mohenjo-Daro
Himalayas   Harappa
Hindu Kush

Read Aloud

In the 1870s, when a railroad was being built across Asia, workers came upon the ruins of an ancient city. They found streets and homes carefully laid out in straight lines. The city had been a glorious place to live, that was easy to see. But now the city was quiet and little remained.

The workers began to use the stone remains of this once great city to build the railroad. Streets were torn up. Houses were taken apart. The stones were used to build a bridge that would carry the railroad across the Indus River. Very little would remain, however, of the ancient city they had found.

Read for Purpose

1. **WHAT YOU KNOW:** How do archaeologists learn about ancient civilizations?
2. **WHAT YOU WILL LEARN:** What have we learned from the artifacts left behind by the people of the Indus River Valley?

GEOGRAPHY OF THE INDUS RIVER VALLEY

If you were to journey eastward from the Fertile Crescent, you would eventually come to the Indian peninsula. This peninsula is so large that it is called a subcontinent. A subcontinent is a large landmass that is connected to a continent. Find the Indian subcontinent in the Atlas on page 612. The Indian subcontinent extends south from Asia into the Indian Ocean.

In the country known today as Pakistan, you will find the Indus River Valley. In ancient times this was the location of an important civilization. Look at the map of the Indus River Valley on the next page. In the north the Indus River Valley is wedged between some of the world's highest mountain peaks. The massive walls of the great Himalayas (him ə lā′ əz) and the Hindu Kush (hin′ dü kush) mountains form the borders for this river valley.

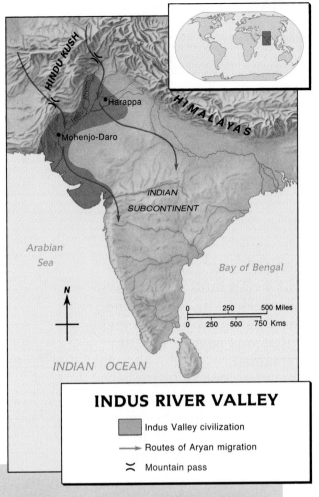

INDUS RIVER VALLEY

- Indus Valley civilization
- → Routes of Aryan migration
- ⋊ Mountain pass

MAP SKILL: What bodies of water surround the Indian subcontinent?

tains. Each year the river overflows its banks and covers the valley floor with new soil rich in minerals.

A FARMING ECONOMY

The yearly flooding of the Indus River provides plenty of water for productive farming. By about 4000 B.C., people began farming along the banks of the Indus River. During the next 1,000 years, many villages grew up along the Indus and its tributaries (trib′ yə ter ēz). Tributaries are the small rivers and streams that flow into a large river. Find the tributaries of the Indus River on the map on this page.

By 3000 B.C. the villagers of the Indus River Valley had learned how to irrigate their fields in order to make farming more productive. Farming became the most important part of the economy. Farmers grew dates, melons, and other fruits. They also grew crops of wheat, barley, and rice. The farmers of the Indus River Valley were the first people in the world to grow cotton.

AN ANCIENT CIVILIZATION

The railroad workers who stumbled upon the ruins you read about on page 119 told archaeologists about their discovery. Even though the workers damaged the ruins of one city, archaeologists searched the region and found ruins of more than 100 ancient villages. An ancient civilization had been discovered!

Among the ruins of the many villages were the ruins of what had been two thriving cities—Mohenjo-Daro (mō hen′ jō där′ ō) and Harappa (hə rap′ ə). Find Mohenjo-Daro and Harappa on the map on this page. Both of these cities are significant because, by 2300 B.C., they each had a popula-

High in the Himalayas and the Hindu Kush, warm spring weather causes the winter snowfall to melt. Small mountain streams swell and rush to join the larger streams and rivers that wind their way into the valley. These large streams and rivers come together to form the Indus River. The Indus River flows southward to empty into the Arabian Sea.

The plains of the Indus River Valley are among the most fertile in the world. The rich soil, like that of the Nile River Valley and the Fertile Crescent, is the gift of flooding river waters. The Indus River carries silt down from the mountion of more than 40,000 people. Even the largest Sumerian cities had only 10,000 people.

Among the artifacts found in the cities of the Indus River Valley were hundreds of decorated bowls and vases. It was an exciting surprise for archaeologists to realize that some of the pottery found there was made in Mesopotamia and other regions far to the west. What do you think this told archaeologists about Indus civilization?

Clearly, the Indus people were busy traders. Examples of jewelry, cloth, razors, mirrors, toys, and fishhooks have been unearthed and are believed to have been popular items of trade. The quality of these artifacts tells us that the artisans of the Indus River Valley were highly skilled.

LEARNING FROM STONE

In addition to these items, archaeologists also unearthed over 2,000 stone seals. These seals show drawings of animals and a form of writing. You can see some of the seals that were found in Harappa on this page. Unfortunately, scholars have not yet been able to read this ancient writing. Nonetheless, why do you think archaeologists were excited to find such ancient writings?

You remember that the growth of writing was one of the greatest achievements of early people. The emergence of writing in ancient Egypt and ancient Sumer greatly changed the way that people lived. It took many years for scholars to learn how to read hieroglyphics and cuneiform. It may take many more years before scholars can read the writing of Indus people. Imagine the stories the stone seals might tell!

These ancient Indian seals show animals that lived in the Indus River Valley. Such seals have been found in faraway Mesopotamia.

The seals, however, do give some useful clues about life in the Indus River Valley. For example, you can learn something about the religion of the Indus people by taking a close look at the seals. As you see, the seals show many different kinds of animals. The animal drawings have led scholars to conclude that the Indus people worshiped certain animals. What animals are found on the seals? Wouldn't it be wonderful if you could read the writing, too?

VISIT MOHENJO-DARO

Are the streets in your community perfectly straight? Do they run north to

121

Mohenjo-Daro was once among the largest cities in the world. It was a complex center of civilization. But even simple artifacts like the toy, above, have been unearthed in its ruins by archaeologists.

south and east to west, forming a pattern of squares, or blocks? If they do, then someone probably planned it that way. More than 4,500 years ago some people in the Indus River Valley also planned a city that way.

Imagine that you have gone back in time. Perhaps you are a trader from the Fertile Crescent and have come to Mohenjo-Daro to exchange goods. The city is impressive, overflowing with houses, shops, and many public buildings—all built of perfectly matched bricks. Buildings face paved streets and form row after row of square blocks. Houses have indoor plumbing and are connected to underground sewers. That's something new for a city built more than 4,500 years ago!

In the center of the city you come across a massive citadel (sit′ əd əl). A citadel is a walled-in area, like a fortress. People can go there for protection if invaders attack. The citadel of Mohenjo-Daro stands higher than most Sumerian ziggurats and is the center of both government and religion.

If you actually visit Mohenjo-Daro today, you will find a city in ruins. The ruins are evidence of the skillfulness and organization of one of the world's great ancient civilizations.

THE FALL OF THE INDUS PEOPLE

By 1500 B.C. Mohenjo-Daro, Harappa, and many of the villages throughout the Indus River Valley had been mysteriously abandoned. Historians are not certain why this happened. Did overpowering floods wash away whole villages? Did the soil lose its fertility and make it impossible to farm? Did famine and drought cause the people of the valley to flee into other regions?

This photograph shows what Mohenjo-Daro looks like today. It is located in the present-day country of Pakistan.

Archaeologists and historians do not know the answers to these questions. However, they do know that a group of people swept into the Indus River Valley in about 1500 B.C. An ancient Indian legend tells of a great migration (mī grā' shən), or movement, by a large group of people who admired the civilization of the Indus River Valley. You remember that in ancient times migrations were common. Early people, such as Gam's people during the Old Stone Age, migrated in order to find food.

The people who migrated into the Indus River Valley called themselves Aryans (er' ē əns), which means "noble ones." They came from Asia's interior and made their way across the Hindu Kush by crossing its few mountain passes.

It is not clear that the Aryan migration caused the fall of the Indus people. It is possible that the Aryans arrived after the main Indus cities had already emptied. Although you will read more about the Aryans and the Indian subcontinent in Chapter 18, the fate of the Indus people remains unknown. Perhaps you will be the archaeologist who, one day, will solve the mystery.

Check Your Reading

1. What mountains form the northern borders of the Indus River Valley?
2. Why do historians think the Indus River Valley was the site of an ancient civilization?
3. **GEOGRAPHY SKILL:** Based on what you have learned about Mohenjo-Daro, draw a map of the city.
4. **THINKING SKILL:** What alternatives might the railroad workers have considered when deciding what to do with the ruins of the Indus city?

123

2 Ancient China

READ TO LEARN

Key Vocabulary

plateau
dynasty
ancestor
oracle

Key Places

Huang River Valley
Anyang

Read Aloud

Civilization in the land known as China began more than 3,000 years ago. As you know, there were civilizations in other parts of the world before China. However, these earlier civilizations did not survive into modern times. The Chinese civilization is special because it exists even today. It is the oldest continuous civilization in the history of the world.

Read for Purpose

1. **WHAT YOU KNOW:** What river valley civilizations have you studied?
2. **WHAT YOU WILL LEARN:** How do we know that China has a rich and ancient past?

GEOGRAPHY OF THE HUANG RIVER VALLEY

Some of the oldest signs of life left behind by early people are found in China. By 4000 B.C. farming communities had grown up throughout the Huang (hwäng) River Valley. It was along the banks of the Huang [Hwang] River that civilization was born in China.

The mighty Huang River begins its long journey to the sea in the vast plateau (pla tō′) of Tibet. A plateau is an area of flat land raised above the surrounding land. The Huang winds its way across the vast North China Plain and finally empties into the Yellow Sea.

The Huang and its tributaries brought both joy and sadness to the people of the North China Plain. The rivers became known as "China's Sorrow." In their ordinary floodings, fertile deposits of silt were left behind. About every 25 years, however, terrible flooding occurred. River waters rushed over the surrounding land. These terrible floods washed crops away, causing famines lasting many seasons and bringing "sorrow" to China's villagers.

MAP SKILL: The lands of the Shang dynasty covered a vast region. The photograph above shows part of the Huang River. What other river flowed through its lands?

THE SHANG DYNASTY

The farming villages of the Huang River Valley, like the other river valley civilizations you have studied, grew into towns and cities. Then, in about 1700 B.C., a powerful family called the Shang united the valley. They began a legacy of family rule that lasted until the twentieth century.

The Shang founded, or set up, a **dynasty** (dī′ nəs tē). A dynasty is a line of rulers who belong to the same family and pass control from one generation to the next. The Shang dynasty lasted nearly 600 years, from about 1700 B.C. until 1122 B.C.

Sometime after 1600 B.C., the Shang built a great city called **Anyang** (än′ yäng). Anyang rose on one of the Huang's many tributaries. Like the great cities of Egypt, Anyang was the political and cultural center of ancient China.

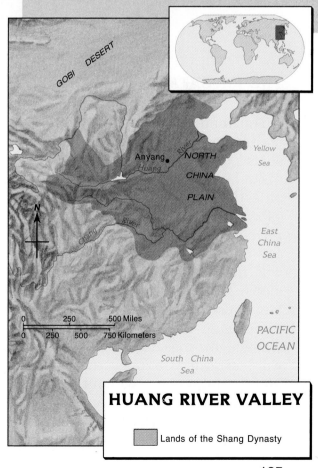

HUANG RIVER VALLEY

Lands of the Shang Dynasty

125

It is important for members of families to work together. The members of this ancient Chinese family are cleaning silk cocoons.

THE IMPORTANCE OF THE FAMILY

The family was also an important governing unit in ancient China. A person's position in a family determined his or her role in life. The elderly, or the oldest members of the family, were especially respected and had a lot of influence. The young had almost no say in family affairs. The oldest man was in charge of the family's possessions. He also had final approval of any important family matters. The oldest woman had power over all other women in the household. Children were expected to obey their parents and grandparents without question. One of the most important values in Chinese society was respect for one's parents.

In ancient China, the family was closely linked to religion. The spirits of family ancestors (an' ses tərs), or the people from whom one is descended, were very special. Spirits of dead ancestors were thought to have the powers to bring good luck or disaster to living members of the family. The Chinese did not think their ancestors were mighty gods. They believed the spirits of their ancestors were more like helpful or troublesome neighbors. Every family paid respect to its ancestors and made small shrines in their honor.

ORACLE BONES

About 100 years ago on the North China Plain, farmers began to plow land that had not been cultivated "as long as they could remember." In these fields the farmers found strange bones. Even more strange were the marks and writing on them. The bones were also oddly cracked.

At first the farmers thought the bones were those of ancient dragons, a popular animal of Chinese legends. Later, some of the bones were given to archaeologists for study. These scholars knew that the bones did not come from dragons but from the shoulder blades of pigs and oxen. Moreover, scholars also realized that the markings on the bones were clearly a form of writing—the earliest trace of writing in East Asia.

This is how writing on the oracle bones began. It worked this way. Suppose that a Shang king wanted to know if a drought were about to strike the land. He had his scribe write the following question on a bone: "Is there a drought coming?" Then, the king gave the bone to an oracle (ôr′ ə kəl). Oracles are special priests who are believed to receive messages from the gods. In order to receive the answer, the oracle applied heat to the bone until it cracked. Then he "read" the cracks and interpreted what he believed to be the gods' answer to the king's question.

The king was not the only one to consult these oracle bones. Many of the Shang people used them to ask the gods their own questions. If you had lived in ancient China, what kinds of questions might you have liked to ask?

CHINESE WRITING

Like the writings of the ancient Egyptians and the Sumerians, the writings of the ancient Chinese tell us about a rich history. Like hieroglyph-

ics, the earliest examples of Chinese writing show pictures of objects. Modern Chinese writing developed from the system of picture writing used in China 3,500 years ago.

The Chinese language does not have an alphabet. As you know, there are 26

In addition to oracle bones, the scribes of ancient China decorated special bowls with writing. You can see a detail of Chinese writing below.

The scribes of ancient China developed thousands of different characters.

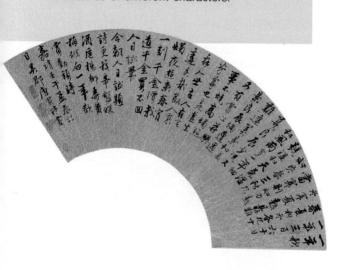

THE LEGACY OF ANCIENT CHINA

The Huang River Valley is today part of a vast modern nation. Much of present-day Chinese culture traces its origin back to the Shang dynasty. Even today, remembering the past has a special significance in China. The Chinese believe that the events of long ago should be used as models or guides for the present. "Those who ignore the mistakes of the past are doomed to repeat them," one Chinese philosopher said. In Chapter 19, you will learn more about the history of China.

letters in the English alphabet. In Chinese writing, many different characters, or signs, are used. Some characters stand for complete words, others stand for only parts of words.

If you wanted to learn to write in ancient China, you had to learn 3,000 different characters! Modern Chinese writing has about 50,000 characters! You will read more about modern Chinese writing in the Traditions lesson on pages 507–510.

 Check Your Reading

1. What are ancestors?
2. How does Chinese writing differ from our writing?
3. **GEOGRAPHY SKILL:** Why is the Huang River known as "China's Sorrow"?
4. **THINKING SKILL:** How was the Huang civilization similar to the Indus civilization? How was it different?

Writing a Summary

Key Vocabulary

summary

topic sentence

This book overflows with information. On every page and in every paragraph you will find many facts. Sometimes it is a challenge to remember all the interesting things that you are reading about.

What Is a Summary?

A good way to help you to remember what you have read is to write a short summary. A summary briefly states the main ideas contained in a piece of writing. Writing a summary helps you to sort out the most important information.

To prepare for writing a summary, look for the topic sentences, or the sentences that contain the main ideas. First, read through the entire selection and write down the topic sentences. Often a topic sentence is the first sentence in a paragraph. However, it may also be in the middle or at the end of a paragraph. Notice that the rest of the sentences give supporting details.

When you write a short summary, you will be concerned only with main ideas. In a longer summary, you might want to include some important details.

Summarizing the Lesson

To write a summary of Lesson 2 on ancient China, first read through the whole lesson. It will help to pay close attention to the bold headings within the lesson. Headings help you to figure out what each section is about. Headings also provide an outline of the main ideas of the lesson.

For example, the first heading in Lesson 2 tells you that one of the main ideas in your summary will have to do with the geography of the Huang River Valley. You can find it on page 124. Write down the most important ideas in each section.

As you read each section, ask yourself these questions: "What is the main idea of this paragraph? Which are supporting details?" When you have finished, write a summary using your own words.

Reviewing the Skill

Read the paragraph below. Then write a summary in two or three sentences.

The ancient Chinese had a legend about how the world was created. It told of Pan Ku, the first man. He emerged from an egg. The top half of the egg became the sky. The lower half became the earth. Pan Ku lived for 18,000 years. When he died, his head became the sun and moon. His blood became the rivers and oceans. His sweat became the rain; his breath the wind. His voice became the wind; his hair the forests. And Pan Ku's fleas were the ancestors of the first humans.

IMPORTANT EVENTS

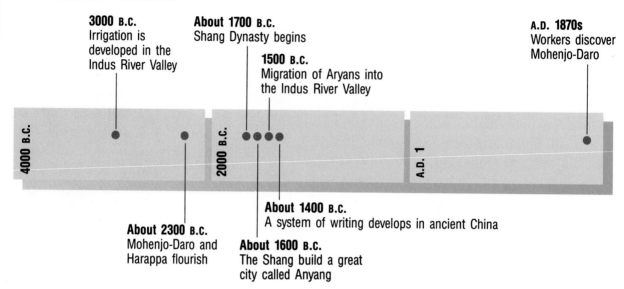

3000 B.C.
Irrigation is developed in the Indus River Valley

About 1700 B.C.
Shang Dynasty begins

1500 B.C.
Migration of Aryans into the Indus River Valley

A.D. 1870s
Workers discover Mohenjo-Daro

4000 B.C.

2000 B.C.

A.D. 1

About 2300 B.C.
Mohenjo-Daro and Harappa flourish

About 1600 B.C.
The Shang build a great city called Anyang

About 1400 B.C.
A system of writing develops in ancient China

IDEAS TO REMEMBER

■ Civilization also flourished in the Indus River Valley. The Indus people were busy traders and highly skilled artisans. The cities of Mohenjo-Daro and Harappa were among the most "modern" cities in ancient times.

■ Chinese civilization was born along the Huang River. China is the oldest continuous civilization in the world. In about 1700 B.C. the Shang family united the people of the Huang River Valley and founded a dynasty that lasted nearly 600 years.

REVIEWING VOCABULARY

citadel   subcontinent
dynasty   tributary
migration

Number a sheet of paper from 1 to 5. Beside each number write the word from the above list that best matches the definition.

1. An area surrounded by massive walls, used to protect people during an attack
2. A small river or stream that flows into a main river
3. A large land mass that resembles a peninsula
4. A line of rulers who pass their power from one generation to the next within the same family
5. The movement of a large group of people from one place to another

REVIEWING FACTS

1. What three bodies of water surround the Indian subcontinent?
2. How was the civilization of the Indus River Valley discovered?
3. In what present-day nation was most of the Indus River Valley civilization located?
4. Which two mountain ranges mark the northern boundary of the Indus River Valley?
5. What were the names of the two major Indus River Valley cities?
6. Name three ways in which the large cities of the ancient Indus River Valley civilization were "ahead of their time."
7. What group of invaders destroyed the civilization of the Indus River Valley around 1500 B.C.?
8. In what region did the first civilization appear in China? What does its name mean in English?
9. What was the first major dynasty to unite large areas of China? When did this occur?
10. Name two ways in which the Chinese way of writing is different from English.

◀◁▶WRITING ABOUT MAIN IDEAS

1. **Writing and Explanation:** Look at the route of the Aryans on the map on page 120. What reasons could explain their migration?
2. **Writing a Paragraph of Contrast:** Look at the photograph of the Chinese scroll on page 128. Then, in a short paragraph, compare and contrast ancient Chinese writing with Egyptian hieroglyphics.
3. **Writing a Letter:** Imagine that you are one of the first archaeologists to explore the ruins of the cities of the Indus River Valley. In a letter to a friend, describe the artifacts you have found. In a separate paragraph, describe what these artifacts reveal about the Indus people.
4. **Writing About Perspectives:** For a travel magazine, write a short paragraph explaining what important contributions Chinese civilization has made to world history.

BUILDING SKILLS: WRITING A SUMMARY

Write a summary of the following paragraph. Your summary should be only one sentence.

High in the Himalayas and the Hindu Kush, warm spring weather causes the winter snowfall to melt. Small mountain streams swell and rush to join the larger streams and rivers that wind down into lower lands. These large streams and rivers come together to form the Indus River. The Indus River rushes south. It flows through the green, fertile lands of the Indus Valley. It passes the remains of ancient cities. It also flows through large, overflowing, modern cities until, finally, it empties into the Arabian Sea.

REVIEWING VOCABULARY

economy   monotheism
empire   plateau
irrigation   polytheism
Judaism   surplus
migration   tributary

Number a sheet of paper from 1 to 10. Beside each number write the word from the above list that matches the definition.

1. The way a country uses its workers and resources to produce goods and services
2. The amount that is left over after a need is satisfied
3. Belief in many gods
4. The religion of the Hebrews
5. A large area of flat land that is raised high above the surrounding land
6. The movement of a large group of people from one place to another
7. Belief in one God
8. A small river or stream that flows into a main river
9. A method of supplying water to dry land
10. A group of lands and people ruled by one government

WRITING ABOUT THE UNIT

1. **Writing an Explanation:** Although they existed at roughly the same time, the civilizations of Egypt and ancient China knew almost nothing about each other. Write a paragraph explaining why you think this was so. Consider the means of communication and forms of travel that existed then.

2. **Writing a Comparison:** In a short paragraph, compare the Hebrew religion with the religions of the Egyptians and the Sumerians. How are they similar?

3. **Writing About Perspectives:** Reread the section on page 84 about being a scribe in ancient Egypt. Pretend you are a scribe. Write a paragraph describing what you like or do not like about being a scribe.

ACTIVITIES

1. **Making a Chart:** Work as a group to make a chart on the four ancient civilizations you have studied in this unit. Use your chart to compare their environments, types of government, economies, religious beliefs, and writing.

2. **Making a Model:** Use clay or papier-mâché to make a model of a river valley. Show that you understand what a delta is and what irrigation is by including them in your model.

3. **Giving an Oral Report:** Select one of the famous people from Unit 2. Use the library to find out more information about the person. You can look through special reference books such as encyclopedias. You can also use a biography of the person's life. Report your findings to the class.

4. **Working Together to Research the Pyramids:** As a group, use the library to research how the pyramids were built. Some members of the group can write the step-by-step directions, beginning with cutting the stone blocks. Other group members can make drawings to be included with the directions.

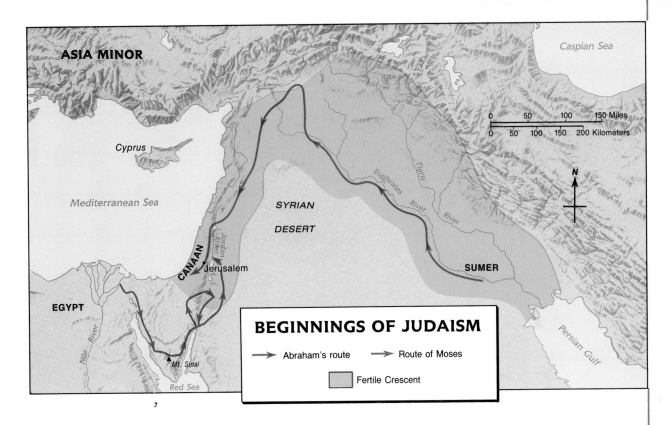

BEGINNINGS OF JUDAISM

→ Abraham's route → Route of Moses

Fertile Crescent

BUILDING SKILLS:
READING HISTORICAL MAPS

Use the map above to answer the following questions.

1. What are historical maps?
2. What bodies of water lay near the lands of the Fertile Crescent?
3. Describe Abraham's journey.

4. Identify the part of Egypt where the Hebrews lived before the Exodus.
5. Describe the route taken by Moses. Identify the land areas the route seems to have crossed.
6. Give three reasons why this map is a historical map. What can it also tell you about the region's geography?

 **LINKING PAST, PRESENT, AND FUTURE**

You have read that the invention of writing was of greatest importance in the growth of early civilizations. Is writing still important today? How has the growth of modern technology affected writing today? Do you think books and magazines will still be read in the next century? Explain your answers in two or three short paragraphs.

North Pole

ARCTIC
OCEAN

Arctic Circle

60°N

ATLANTIC
OCEAN

45°N

North
Sea

Bay of
Biscay

ROMAN EMPIRE

30°N

Tropic of Cancer

Rome

Danube
River

Black Sea

Caspian Sea

Tigris River

ANCIENT
GREECE

Athens

Mediterranean Sea

Euphrates River

30°W

Persian Gulf

15°W

Nile River

Red Sea

15°N

INDIAN

OCEAN

0°

15°E

Equator

60°E

45°E

0°

15°S

Tropic of Capricorn

134

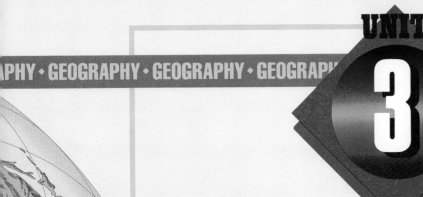

ANCIENT EUROPE

WHERE WE ARE

The civilizations of Greece and Rome prospered along the shores of the Mediterranean Sea. As the map shows, ancient Greece was located in the eastern part of this sea. From the city of Athens, Greek civilization developed an amazing legacy.

As the Greeks founded cities throughout the Mediterranean Sea, they spread their ideas far beyond their homeland. For example, the Greeks were an important influence upon the people of ancient Rome. You will learn that the Romans were fearsome conquerers and skilled empire-builders. They took up Greek culture and extended it to three continents.

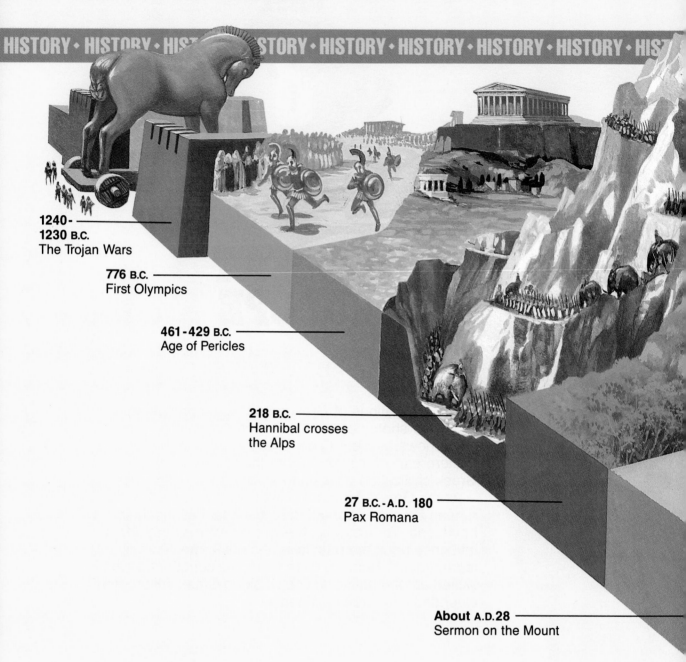

1240-
1230 B.C.
The Trojan Wars

776 B.C.
First Olympics

461-429 B.C.
Age of Pericles

218 B.C.
Hannibal crosses
the Alps

27 B.C.-A.D. **180**
Pax Romana

About A.D. **28**
Sermon on the Mount

A.D. 312-337
Rule of Constantine

WHAT HAPPENED

As the time line shows, world
civilization owes much to the ancient
Greeks and the ancient Romans. The Greeks
made amazing achievements in art and literature.
The Romans also contributed greatly to the growth
of civilization. You will learn how they governed one
of the world's largest empires.

136

CHAPTER 6

ANCIENT GREECE

FOCUS

Fix your eyes on the greatness of Athens as you have it now before you day by day . . . and when you feel her greatness, remember that it was won by men with courage, with knowledge of their duty. . . . For you now it remains to rival what they have done.

These words were written nearly 2,400 years ago. They celebrate the glory of ancient Greece. In this chapter you will read that the remarkable people of this ancient civilization introduced valuable ideas that shaped the course of history.

1 The Geography of Ancient Greece

READbold TO LEARN

▣ Key Vocabulary

peninsula
colony

Key Places

Attica   Rhodes
Peloponnesus   Phoenicia
Crete

▣ Read Aloud

The four ancient civilizations that you have studied so far were societies tied to mighty rivers. By 2000 B.C. a new civilization had appeared in a land with no great rivers. Instead, ancient Greece owed its life to the broad seas that surrounded it.

▣ Read for Purpose

1. **WHAT YOU KNOW:** What do the civilizations you already have read about have in common?
2. **WHAT YOU WILL LEARN:** Why was the sea important to the early Greeks?

THE AEGEAN WORLD

The civilization that you will read about in this chapter grew up in a region known as the "Aegean (i jē′ ən) World." The Aegean is a sea lying north of the eastern end of the great Mediterranean Sea. This was the site of ancient Greece. Its lands were very different from the river valleys of the civilizations you have read about.

The "Aegean World" includes the shores of two continents—Europe and Asia. As you will learn, the history of Greece was influenced by this fact. Its history was also shaped by the fact that the "Aegean World" is made up of countless **peninsulas** (pə nin′ sə ləz) and islands. A peninsula is land that is surrounded by water on three sides. **Attica** and the hilly **Peloponnesus** (pel ə pə nē′ səs) are major peninsulas. **Crete** and **Rhodes** are the largest of the Aegean islands. There are, however, hundreds of Aegean islands.

A RUGGED PLACE

I am at home in sunny Greece . . . a rugged place, but a good nurse of men; for my part I cannot think of a sweeter place to look at.

These words are taken from an ancient poem that is about 3,000 years old. According to the poet, the lands of Greece are a "rugged place." Indeed, chains of mountains extend into every

139

part of ancient Greece. The highest peak is the towering, snow-capped Mt. Olympus. Find Mt. Olympus on the map on this page.

Greece does not have much fertile farmland. Narrow valleys make up most of its lands. These valleys are watered by small mountain streams, not large rivers. As a result, farming in ancient Greece differed from farming in the river valley civilizations. Greek lands did not provide a surplus of grains and other important crops. Early Greek farmers learned to cultivate crops, such as olive trees and grapes, which could thrive in a mountainous environment.

The Greeks also raised sheep and goats. Such animals can feed along the rocky hillsides. The sheep were shorn for their wool and some were raised for meat. Goats also provided meat as well as milk for drinking and making cheese.

THE IMPORTANCE OF THE SEA

The early Greeks imagined the world as encircled by the mighty river of ocean, and held that all life derived [began] from it.

Understanding the geography of Greece makes it easy to understand why these words were written. But the

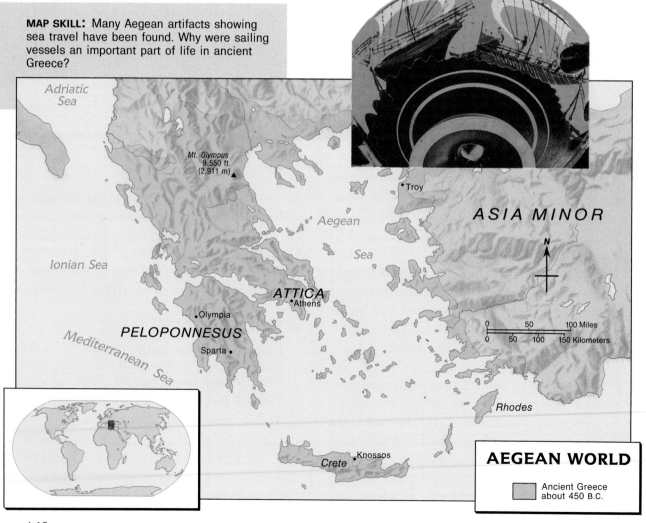

MAP SKILL: Many Aegean artifacts showing sea travel have been found. Why were sailing vessels an important part of life in ancient Greece?

Adriatic Sea

Mt. Olympus
9,550 ft.
(2,911 m) ▲

Troy

Aegean

ASIA MINOR

Sea

Ionian Sea

N

ATTICA
Athens

Olympia

PELOPONNESUS

Mediterranean Sea

Sparta

0   50   100 Miles
0 50 100 150 Kilometers

Rhodes

Knossos
Crete

AEGEAN WORLD

Ancient Greece
about 450 B.C.

ancient Greeks were more than fascinated by the sea. They depended on it. In the first place, good farmland was scarce so the Greeks had to look to the sea for food. In the second place, sea travel was easier than travel on rugged land.

Sea travel gradually linked ancient Greece to other societies. The Greek islands were like steppingstones across the Aegean Sea. Even in small ships, Greek sailors could go from one island to another and have contact with the older, richer civilizations in Asia and Africa.

By 800 B.C. the Greeks had become accomplished sailors. Their major sailing vessel, a trireme (trī′ rēm), was powered by three banks of oarsmen. Greek ships grew in number and became larger and faster. Look at the diagram of a Greek trireme below.

Triremes enabled the early Greeks to sail far and wide. Greek merchants traveled all around the Mediterranean Sea. Triremes sailed to the Black Sea for fish, to Cyprus for timber, to the Nile Delta for grains, and to the Italian peninsula for meat. In exchange for these goods, Greece traded grapes, wine, olives, olive oil, wool, pottery, tiles, marble, and works of art.

MEDITERRANEAN COLONIES

The Greeks were not the only seafaring traders in the Mediterranean Sea in ancient times. The people of Phoenicia (fə nish′ ə) also had learned the advantages of sea travel. The Phoenicians had become great sailors because their

DIAGRAM SKILL: These drawings show a trireme from the side and from above. How was the trireme powered?

A GREEK TRIREME

Cross View

Side View

Top View

homeland also stretched along Mediterranean shores.

Find Phoenicia on the map on this page. As you see, it lies north of the land of the ancient Hebrews. Both the Greeks and the Phoenicians sailed in search of goods that their lands could not supply.

The Greeks and the Phoenicians sent groups of their people to settle in new lands. Such a settlement, or colony, helped trade. Greek and Phoenician colonies were set up throughout the Mediterranean region. Look at the map on this page. By 750 B.C. there were colonies in Asia Minor, along the shores of the Black Sea, in North Africa, along the Italian and Iberian peninsulas, and on many Mediterranean islands. Often the Greeks and Phoenicians competed for control of useful places. For example, why do you think the Greeks may have wanted control of the mouth of the Black Sea?

THE EXCHANGE OF IDEAS

You read in previous chapters that when different cultures meet they often borrow ideas from one another. You may recall that the Egyptians learned from their invaders, the Hyksos, how to make their army stronger. From their contact with Phoenician culture, the ancient Greeks learned a system of writing.

MAP SKILL: The Greeks and Phoenicians competed for colonies. What bodies of water and major islands lay between Greece and Phoenicia? Who dominated the Black Sea?

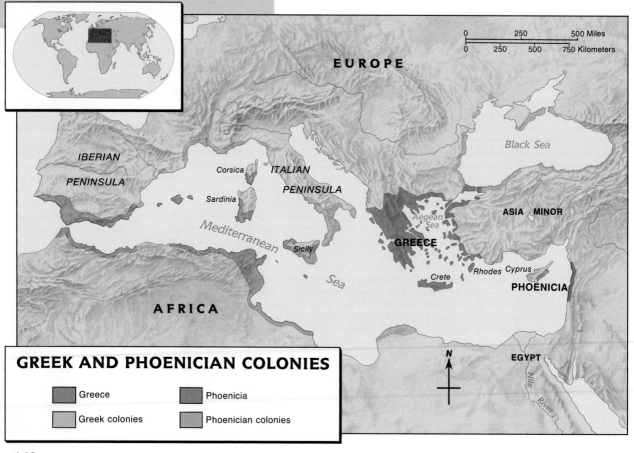

GREEK AND PHOENICIAN COLONIES

Greece
Greek colonies
Phoenicia
Phoenician colonies

The Phoenicians developed a unique alphabet around 900 B.C. During their travels, the Phoenicians needed a way to keep a record of the goods they bought and sold. Cuneiform, with its 600 symbols, took up too much space on a tablet or papyrus. Thus, the Phoenicians invented a new alphabet with just 22 symbols.

The Phoenician alphabet was carried to trading centers all over the Mediterranean Sea. As the chart on this page shows, the Greeks borrowed many Phoenician symbols. You can also see that the modern alphabet we use has its origins in the Phoenician and Greek alphabets. In fact, the word *alphabet* comes from the first two letters of the Phoenician alphabet, *aleph* and *beth*.

Can you imagine how important the invention of the alphabet was? Unlike hieroglyphics and cuneiform, the Phoenician way of writing was a simple system. Many more people could learn how to use the letters and spell words. As a result, more was written and ideas began to spread quickly.

THE FIRST STEP

The sea was to the ancient Greeks what the Nile River was to the ancient Egyptians. As the early Greeks learned how to take advantage of their environment, they prospered.

As you have read, ancient Greece was a rugged place. Its land was not good for farming, and wide seas surrounded it. From faraway colonies, however, the Greeks were able to obtain the food their land could not supply. Sea travel also became a way in which important new ideas could be exchanged. Read on. In the next lesson you will see that this was only the be-

ALPHABETS

Phoenician	Greek	Latin	Modern

CHART SKILL: What modern letters are missing from the list? How would you write your name using the Greek alphabet?

ginning of the "Aegean World." Soon a great civilization would emerge.

Check Your Reading

1. What lands and bodies of water make up the "Aegean World"?
2. Why did the Greeks turn to the sea to meet their needs?
3. **GEOGRAPHY SKILL:** Why was the exchange of ideas between the Greeks and Phoenicians possible?
4. **THINKING SKILL:** Predict how the development of modern civilization would have been different without the early exchange of new ideas.

2 Greek City-States

READn TO LEARN

READ TO LEARN

Key Vocabulary
polis
helot
agora
Acropolis

Key People
Herodotus

Key Places
Sparta
Athens
Thermopylae
Marathon

Read Aloud

As ancient Greece grew, it soon was dominated by two powerful communities. In this lesson, you will learn that these communities were fiercely independent and had different ideas about almost everything. The rivalry between these two communities, however, helped to inspire the growth of the world's most famous civilization.

Read for Purpose

1. **WHAT YOU KNOW:** How did the Sumerian city-states differ from each other?
2. **WHAT YOU WILL LEARN:** How did Sparta and Athens differ?

THE POLIS

By 750 B.C. Greece was made up of more than 200 city-states. Like the city-states that grew up in Sumer 1,000 years before, the Greek city-states were independent. The Greeks called each city-state a polis (po′ ləs).

As in Sumer, the Greek polis was made up of a city as well as the lands around it. Each polis had its own government. All the people who lived in the polis had to obey its laws and its leaders.

Greek city-states grew up all over the "Aegean World." They were found on the coasts of Greece, Asia Minor, and on the Aegean islands. Of all the city-states, however, Sparta and Athens became the most powerful.

SPARTA

Sparta was located on the southern tip of the Peloponessus. A writer from a city-state that was conquered by Sparta wrote, "Other states admired Sparta for its power, but none wished to be like it." Sparta was a military, or warlike, city-state. It had little trade with other city-states and did not set up colonies. Instead, Sparta gained wealth by conquering city-states around it.

The Spartans were cruel to the people they conquered. Conquered people were forced to become slaves called **helots**. Helots had to farm the land and honor the Spartan polis. Even though there were many more helots than Spartans on the Peloponnesus, the Spartans had absolute power.

But the helots often rebelled against their Spartan masters. Thus, in order to keep control over the Peloponnesus, the Spartans had to build and maintain a strong army. The Spartans also adopted a harsh code of laws designed to protect themselves from the large helot population.

LIFE IN SPARTA

Life in Sparta was harsh. From birth to death, everything was controlled by the military government. The government wanted only the "best" people in Spartan society. Thus, a group of warriors examined each baby. If the child was judged to be strong, it was allowed to live. If the child was considered weak, its parents were ordered to put the child on a mountainside to die.

Spartan boys were only seven when they began their military training. They joined a troop of boys their own age and marched off to military camp. With their troop, they learned to use spears and swords. They learned to obey orders without question. Everything was done to make the boys strong. They did not wear clothing or shoes. Their beds were piles of straw. They ate plain food.

Spartan girls also led hardy lives. Unlike girls in other Greek city-states, Spartan girls wrestled and played sports. They were trained to defend their polis. As adults, they ran family estates while their husbands served the polis. Spartan women had many rights, but were not allowed to vote.

Like their brothers, girls in Sparta took part in sports. This Spartan statue is called "The Running Girl."

The Spartans became famous for their bravery and harsh way of life. Even today a person who leads a simple, stern life is called "Spartan." Once a Spartan was asked why his city did not have a wall. He replied: "Every Spartan is a brick in the wall of Sparta." What do you think he meant?

ATHENS

O bright and violet-crowned and famed in song, bulwark of Greece, famous Athens, divine city!

It is not hard to imagine how the author of these words felt about Athens. At the time they were written in 500 B.C., life in the Athenian polis was very different from life in Sparta.

Athens is on the peninsula of Attica. It used its location near the sea to grow as a center of trade. Artisans from all over the Aegean flocked to Athens to practice their crafts. As a result of their long history of sea travel, Athenians were the most skillful sailors.

The Athenian polis became an exciting and vital place where new ideas were welcome. Rather than the strict, military ways of Sparta, freedom was cherished in Athens. The Athenians believed that life was empty unless people tried to gain new knowledge and lived freely.

LIFE IN ATHENS

Imagine that you have gone back in time to the Athenian polis. You are standing in the agora (ag′ ə rə), or central marketplace of the city. The agora is overflowing with activity, and it takes a moment to get your bearings. Is it possible that there is any place on the earth as busy as the Athenian agora?

Shops, temples, and government buildings surround the agora. Young men who are students stand in the shadows of these great buildings and wait for their teachers. Small children explore the fruit stands with their parents. Merchants have come from all over the "Aegean World"—and farther —to gather in the agora and sell their goods.

Tables are piled high with vegetables, bread, fish, and cheese. Beautifully painted pottery is for sale, and even toys can be bought. Merchants from Asia and North Africa sell colorful cloth, fine jewelry, and sweet perfumes. The agora is truly a lively place.

Explore the agora. Wander around the tables and along the edges of the market. Then, begin to follow some of the roads that lead away from the agora. One road climbs uphill. You wonder where it leads. . . .

THE ACROPOLIS

As you continue climbing the uphill road from the agora, you come upon a remarkable site. The people of Athens built one of the world's most magnificent landmarks of civilization. Called the Acropolis (ə krop′ ə lis), it was a hill-top fortress. *Acropolis* is a Greek word meaning "high city."

Look at the diagram on the next page showing how the Acropolis may have looked in ancient times. Note how it rises above the agora and all of Athens. As you see, the Acropolis was made up of many buildings. The citizens of Athens met in this "high city" to discuss the affairs of their community.

Like the pyramids and ziggurats of earlier societies, the Acropolis also had a special, religious purpose. The largest building on the Acropolis was the Parthenon. The Parthenon was a temple dedicated to Athena, the Greek goddess of wisdom who was believed to be the protector of Athens. Built in the fifth century B.C., it has been called one of the world's most beautiful buildings. You can read about some of the Parthenon's famous carvings in the Point/Counterpoint on pages 170–171.

THE PERSIAN WARS

Though Sparta and Athens differed greatly, an invasion caused them to unite temporarily. As you will learn, Athens would show even more strength than Sparta.

Go tell the Spartans, thou that passeth by, that here, obedient to her laws, we lie.

Parthenon

Acropolis

ANCIENT
ATHENS

Agora

DIAGRAM SKILL: Towering over Athens, the Acropolis was the site of religious and political activity. As the diagram shows, the Parthenon stands at the hill's crest. What activities are taking place in the agora?

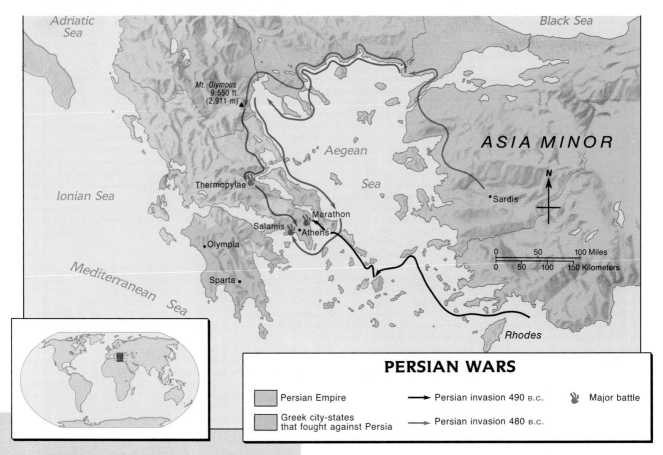

PERSIAN WARS

Persian Empire
Greek city-states that fought against Persia
→ Persian invasion 490 B.C.
→ Persian invasion 480 B.C.
✋ Major battle

MAP SKILL: Use the map to name the battle fought by Greeks and Persians on the sea.

These sad lines mark the site at Thermopylae (thər mop′ ə lē) where hundreds of Spartan soldiers were killed. A great empire had risen that was far more powerful than Sparta. The empire tried to conquer ancient Greece—twice. Both times it was not Sparta, but peaceful Athens, that forced the conquerers back.

In Chapter 4 you read about the growth of civilization in the Fertile Crescent. After 550 B.C. the Persians rose there and built a vast empire. The Persian Empire stretched from the Indus River in the east to the Greek colonies of Asia Minor in the west.

We know a lot about the Persians because of a Greek historian named Herodotus (hə rod′ ə təs). Herodotus wrote a history of the wars fought by the Greeks with the Persians and is called the "Father of History." Herodotus wrote that in 490 B.C., 25,000 Persian soldiers landed on the plains of Marathon. Marathon is only about 25 miles (40 km) from Athens. There, only 10,000 Athenians stood waiting, shoulder to shoulder. Singing as they charged, the Athenians forced the Persians back into the Bay of Marathon.

Ten years later the Persians returned. This time, however, it was the Spartans who were waiting for them at Thermopylae. According to Herodotus, "the ground ran red with Spartan blood" at Thermopylae.

Four times the Spartans drove the enemy off . . . and withdrew into the

The large picture shows how the Parthenon looked when it was built. Its colors have faded, but even its ruins are impressive.

narrow neck of the pass. . . . Here they resisted to the last, with their swords, if they had them, and if not, with their hands and teeth, until the Persians finally overwhelmed them.

The mighty Spartans, whose ways had been so warlike, were defeated.

The Athenians were amazed. Something had to be done to hold back the invading Persians. Then, the great Athenian fleet lured the Persian fleet into the narrow straits by the island of Salamis. Once again, the skillful Athenians won a stunning victory over the Persians.

THE GLORY OF ATHENS

After the Persian Wars, Athens became the leader of Greece. In addition to its success at warfare, its ideas about government and culture contin- ued to grow. Herodotus understood Athens' mighty influence when he wrote:

In a word I claim that our city as a whole is an education to Greece.

Check Your Reading

1. What is a polis?
2. Why was rebellion a constant threat in Sparta? How did the Spartans respond to this threat?
3. **GEOGRAPHY SKILL:** Describe the routes taken by the Persians to attack Greece in 480 B.C.
4. **THINKING SKILL:** Compare and contrast life in Athens and Sparta.

149

3 The Birth of Democracy

READ TO LEARN

Key Vocabulary

monarchy   democracy
tyranny   assembly
oligarchy

Key People

Pericles

Read Aloud

Our ship of state, which recent storms have threatened to destroy, has come safely to harbor at last.

The writer of these words lived in the "Century of Athens." From about 500 to 400 B.C. the Athenian polis was the political and cultural center in the "Aegean World."

Read for Purpose

1. **WHAT YOU KNOW:** How does government affect your life?
2. **WHAT YOU WILL LEARN:** How did the ancient Greeks build the world's first democracy?

BUILDING A JUST GOVERNMENT

The people of most Greek city-states worked hard to build just, or wise and fair, governments. Government was an important part of the life of each polis. Athenians, for example, tried out ideas from many systems of government.

In earliest times Athens was governed by a monarchy (mon' ər kē). *Monarchy* is a Greek word meaning "rule by one." A monarchy is a system of government ruled by a king or queen. Its ruler is called a monarch. The powerful Egyptian pharaohs you read about were monarchs.

Unlike ancient Egypt, monarchy did not last long in Athens. Soldiers often handpicked a new leader and put him in power. This leader would often be forced to obey the soldiers' wishes in order to remain in power. This system of government was called a tyranny (tir' ə nē). Athenians believed that tyranny was unjust and oppressive. Its ruler, a tyrant, could never represent anyone but himself and the soldiers who gave him power.

By 800 B.C. Athenians had built a new government called an oligarchy (ol' ə gär kē). An oligarchy is a government that is ruled by a few people—usually by members of rich, powerful families. According to one Athenian:

Oligarchy is a government resting on the value of property, in which the

150

rich have power and the poor have none.

Many Athenians agreed that oligarchy was not a fair system. But how could they improve it?

WHAT IS DEMOCRACY?

Of all the city-states, the citizens of Athens had achieved the greatest freedoms. A government run by the people, in which citizens make their own laws, is called a democracy. *Democracy* is a Greek word meaning "power of the people." Athens was the world's first democracy.

The basic lawmaking body in any democracy is an assembly, or group of citizens. In the United States the lawmaking body is called Congress. The Athenian Assembly was made up of male citizens over the age of 18. Any member of the Assembly could speak up for or against any law. He could bring before the Assembly any topic that seemed important.

On four days of each month, old and young men could be seen climbing a hill near the Acropolis to attend the meeting of the Assembly. Some men would wander up from the agora. Others would come from their meetings in the Parthenon.

THE AGE OF PERICLES

Ours is a democracy because power is in the hands not of a minority but of the whole people. . . . Here each individual is interested not only in his own affairs but in the affairs of the state as well. . . . We do not say that a man who takes no interest in politics is a man who minds his own business; we say that he has no business here at all.

These are the words spoken by Pericles near the end of his rule in 431 B.C. Under Pericles' leadership democ-

Pericles was one of the greatest Athenians. He ordered the construction of the Parthenon and many other buildings on the Acropolis.

Our jury system in the United States has its roots in the Athens of Pericles. Every citizen today has a duty to serve on a jury.

racy had become the foundation of government in ancient Greece.

Pericles was only 20 when he went to the Assembly for the first time. In 461 B.C. the Assembly elected Pericles one of Athens' ten generals. Year after year, he was reelected and was able to spread his love of democracy. One of history's greatest leaders, Pericles dominated the life of ancient Greece for 32 years. Thus, this period is known to present-day historians as the Age of Pericles.

During this time, Pericles passed laws to strengthen democracy. For example, Pericles invited all male citizens to serve on juries. A jury is a group of citizens that helps decide a case brought to trial. Athenian juries were large, ranging from 101 to 501 jurors each. Juries in modern democracies usually have fewer than 15 jurors. Pericles arranged for jury members to be paid, so that the poor could serve as easily as the rich. Everyone's opinion was important.

The right to a trial by jury was a great contribution to democracy. You may remember that punishments were quick and harsh in other societies. The Code of Hammurabi was important as one of the world's earliest body of laws. But it lacked the fairness found in Athenian democracy.

NOT "JUSTICE FOR ALL"

This was only the beginning of the democratic form of government. Though democracy in ancient Greece was a great step forward, you must remember that it was very different from modern democracies. Democracy in Athens did not give freedom to everyone.

As you know, democracy in the United States is set up to give every person equal rights. Democracy under Pericles, however, did not mean "justice for all." As you have read, only male citizens were allowed to vote and take part in the Assembly. Although women were citizens, they were not allowed to vote.

Slaves made up the other half of Athens' population during the Age of Pericles. They, too, had no role in government. Slavery was a common practice in ancient times. It was accepted as a fact of life. Thus, even in its most democratic period, only 25 percent of the population had a real voice in the Athenian government. And they were all male citizens.

American **democracy** has roots in Athens. Greek ideas inspired the writers of the United States Constitution.

THE LEGACY OF ATHENIAN DEMOCRACY

We form a government not to enslave, but to set a country free, and today's Athenians shall make room for the honest to live.

These words were written by James Madison, our country's fourth president, who is called the "Father" of our Constitution. The legacy of Athenian democracy left a lasting impression. It greatly influenced the birth of our own American democracy. Democracy as a form of government is one of the greatest legacies ever given to the world. Many modern governments, including our own, have looked to the impressive Greek example.

In this lesson you have read how Athenian democracy was organized. As you read the next lesson, think about how democracy encouraged the growth of Greek civilization.

Check Your Reading

1. What is democracy?
2. In what ways could an Athenian take part in government?
3. What were the democratic features of Athenian government?
4. **THINKING SKILL:** How does American democracy differ from the democracy that grew under Pericles?

4 The Legacy of Ancient Greece

READ TO LEARN

Key Vocabulary

myth   comedy
epic   philosophy
tragedy

Key People

Homer   Socrates
Aeschylus   Plato
Aristophanes

Read Aloud

"Future worlds will wonder at us, as the present age wonders at us now." Pericles made this prediction over 2,400 years ago. Time has proved that he was right. Even today the world marvels at the legacy of Greek civilization. Ancient Greece was a place of dazzling achievements.

Read for Purpose

1. **WHAT YOU KNOW:** What does it mean to say that a civilization has left a rich legacy?
2. **WHAT YOU WILL LEARN:** What was the legacy of ancient Greece?

ANCIENT GREEK RELIGION

You read in Lesson 2 that the Acropolis was dedicated to the goddess Athena. The Athenians believed that Athena was their special protector. But they also worshiped other goddesses. The ancient Greeks were polytheists and thus believed in many gods and goddesses.

The Greeks developed a rich set of myths, or stories about their gods and goddesses. According to the Greek myths, the gods and goddesses controlled different parts of the universe. For example, Zeus, the ruler of the gods, was in charge of the weather. The ancient Greeks believed that when it thundered, Zeus was at work.

The ancient Greeks also believed that the gods and goddesses were not very different from humans. They were just like any other family. Zeus was the father, and his wife, Hera, was the mother. There were many children and relatives. As the chart on the next page shows, each god and goddess had a special role.

What did the ancient Greeks believe was the basic difference between the gods and humans? Most gods and goddesses were stronger than humans. The main difference was mortality, or death. Humans died, but gods never died. Humans lived temporary lives, but the gods lived forever.

THE GODS AND GODDESSES OF ANCIENT GREECE

ZEUS
Ruler of the gods

HERA
Queen of the gods

HESTIA
Goddess of the home

POSEIDON
God of the sea

DEMETER
Goddess of agriculture

HEPHAESTUS
God of fire

ARES
God of war

ATHENA
Goddess of wisdom

APHRODITE
Goddess of love

APOLLO
God of music

ARTEMIS
Goddess of the moon

HERMES
Messenger of the gods

CHART SKILL: The **myths** of the ancient Greeks tell us about many of their gods and goddesses. What was the role of Poseidon?

HOMER'S EPICS

About 3,000 years ago, a blind poet named **Homer** roamed the "Aegean World." Homer believed he had a special purpose. He wished to tell his people the myths of celebrated gods and goddesses. Homer wrote that "the glorious lessons of the gods are not to be cast aside."

Because few Greeks during Homer's time knew how to read or write, people relied on the spoken word to pass on knowledge to their children. Homer wrote long, beautiful poems called **epics**. His epics were so detailed and full of adventures that they took many evenings to tell!

Homer's two great epic poems, *The Iliad* and *The Odyssey*, both tell of events connected with the long war between the Greeks and the Trojans. These epics are among the oldest

155

THE ILIAD

Odysseus devised the means by which we would take Troy at last. He made us build a great wooden horse. We built it and left it upon the plain of Troy and the Trojans wondered at it greatly. And Odysseus had counselled [*advised*] us to bring our ships down to the water and to burn our stores [*supplies*] and make it seem in every way that we were going to depart from Troy in weariness. This we did and the Trojans saw the great host sail away from before their city. But they did not know that a company of the best of our warriors was within the hollow wooden horse. . . .

We had left a spy hidden between the beach and the city. Now when the wooden horse had been brought within the walls and night had fallen, the spy lighted a great fire that was a signal to the ships that had sailed away. They returned with the host before the day broke. Then we who were within the wooden horse broke through the boards and came out on the city with our spears and swords in our hands. . . . The warriors from the ship crossed the wall where it was broken down, and we swept through the streets and came to the citadel [*fort*] of the king. Thus we took Troy and all its treasures. . . .

Today, we use the expression "a Trojan horse" to describe something that may seem good, but is really harmful.

works of literature. No one knows who finally wrote them down, but they were the same stories Homer told long ago. These epics are a vivid record of life in ancient Greece. You can read an interesting part of *The Iliad* above.

THE OLYMPIC GAMES

Just as we read Homer's epics even today, we also value another "gift" to modern times from the Greeks. Did you know that the Olympic Games have their roots in ancient history? The lighting of the Olympic flame, the oath of loyalty to Olympic ideals, and the release of doves as a symbol of freedom began with Greek festivals.

The tradition of the games originated as a festival to Zeus in 776 B.C. In the green valley of Olympia, a young cook called Coroebus (kor ō′ bəs) of Elis won the 200-yard dash. Although historians date the Olympic Games from this first recorded contest, they probably stretch even farther back in history.

Olympic competition was the glory of ancient Greece. Every four years, athletes from all over the "Aegean World" came to compete in the Olympic Games. Victory in an Olympic event brought the winner a crown of olive leaves. It also brought glory to the victor's polis.

Though many women athletes compete for their countries in the modern

156

The Olympic games are held every four years. In 1992 the Winter Olympics were hosted by Albertville, France.

Olympic Games, women could not compete in ancient times. Women were not even allowed to watch the games! But, according to Greek law, women could win Olympic events. How was that possible?

Women could win the chariot races because the horse's owner was considered the winner. A Spartan woman, who owned the winning horse, won the Olympic chariot race in 392 B.C. You will read more about the Olympic Games in the Traditions lesson that begins on page 161.

THEATER BEGINS

Theater also had its beginnings in ancient Greece. Like the Olympic Games, theater grew out of important religious festivals. Each spring thousands of Greeks gathered to honor Dionysus (dī ə nī′ səs), the god of pleasure. As many as 20,000 people met at an outdoor theater carved into the slope of the Acropolis. Sitting close together on steep rows of stone seats, they watched a festival of plays.

As it is today, the theater in ancient Greece was a magical place. For an entire week, people returned every morning to their seats on the slopes of the Acropolis. They wondered who had written the best play. Would it be sad or funny? Like the Olympic champions, the best writer received special honors.

157

TRAGEDY AND COMEDY

Theaters were carved into hillsides all over the "Aegean World." Though the festival was held in Athens, every Greek polis had a theater and developed plays. Many of these theaters are still in use, as the photograph below shows.

One of the most famous writers of Greek plays was Aeschylus (es′ kə ləs). He was well known because he won first prize in the festival 13 times in a row. Aeschylus loved Athens and wrote plays to honor it. He had fought with his countrymen against the Persians on the plains of Marathon and later in the battle at Salamis.

His experiences in war caused him to write plays called tragedies. A trag-

Ancient Greek plays still attract large crowds. The actors above are performing in New York City. Below, an audience in Athens' ancient theater watches a play first seen there more than 2,500 years ago.

edy is a play in which life is treated seriously and usually has a sad ending. Aeschylus is known as the "father of tragedy." Tragedies were performed only in the morning at the festivals. Perhaps the audience liked to get the sad plays behind them.

Comedies, or plays that are funny and usually have happy endings, were performed late in the day. One of the most famous writers of comedy was Aristophanes (ar is tof' ə nēz). His comedies were loud, happy events. Aristophanes liked it when the crowds at his comedies talked and roamed around the theater. Sometimes they would shout at the actors. A comedy in ancient Greece was always full of jokes. Comedies were also written to make fun of famous people.

Did you hear that Aeschylus was a savage-creating, stubborn-pulling fellow, uncurbed, unfettered, uncontrolled of speech, and downright ridiculous!

As you see in these lines, Aristophanes even made fun of Aeschylus, the "father of tragedy."

THE LOVE OF WISDOM

Like theater, philosophy is part of the Greek legacy. *Philosophy* is a Greek word meaning "love of wisdom." Through philosophy the Greeks searched for answers about their role in the universe. The Athenians loved ideas as much as they loved freedom.

Athens' most famous philosopher was a special man named Socrates (sok' rə tēz). Socrates was well known in Athens because he dared to raise questions about Athenian values. He believed that it was important to examine laws, social customs, and even religious values. His motto was "Know thyself." What do you think he meant?

159

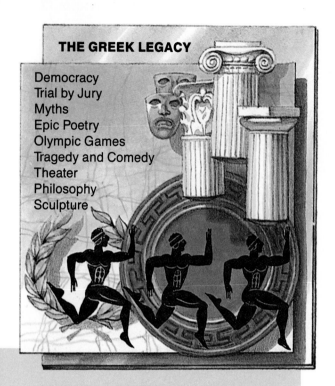

THE GREEK LEGACY

Democracy
Trial by Jury
Myths
Epic Poetry
Olympic Games
Tragedy and Comedy
Theater
Philosophy
Sculpture

CHART SKILL: Which Greek contribution is most important to our government? Which is most important to sports today?

Many Athenians were angry that Socrates doubted the "glory of Athens." As a result, in 399 B.C. Socrates was accused by the government of "forming an idea of revolt" among Athens' young people. A jury decided that Socrates was guilty and sentenced him to death. But guilty of what? Is it wrong to ask questions? Later, when Socrates sat talking with his friends, his jailer brought him a cup of hemlock to drink. This poisonous drink quickly killed Athens' first philosopher.

One of those present at Socrates' death was his brilliant student Plato. To Plato, Socrates was "the wisest and most just and best Athenian." So Plato carried on the work of his teacher by gathering together the ideas of Socrates and writing them down. He also founded the world's first university, known as the Academy. Plato's Acad-

emy lasted long after his death—in fact, for 900 years. As you can imagine, Greek ideas spread from Plato's Academy to distant lands in Europe, Asia, and Africa. Even in the United States today, students study the teachings of Plato and the other Greek philosophers.

A UNIFYING FORCE

As you have read, ancient Greece was made up of many different city-states. Each polis had its own ruler and system of government. Remember that warlike Sparta and democratic Athens were very different in many ways. You have read, however, that democratic Athens triumphed and became the center of the "Aegean World." In Athens, a magnificent culture blossomed and spread to every Greek polis.

In this lesson you have learned that ancient Greece developed a rich legacy. The "Aegean World" was united by this common heritage. Ancient Greek religion, literature, theater, and philosophy affected every polis. The people of ancient Greece were bound together by their common culture. As you read later chapters, search for the influence of ancient Greece in other societies.

Check Your Reading

1. Why were myths and epics important to the ancient Greeks?
2. What contributions were made by the Greeks to literature and theater?
3. What ideas and practices of the ancient Greeks do you think we should continue to use today? Explain your answer.
4. **THINKING SKILL:** Classify all the people mentioned in this lesson into three groups. Label each.

THE OLYMPIC TRADITION

by Diana Reische

Have you ever watched the Olympic Games on television? If so, you have seen one of the world's oldest sports traditions. As you read in Lesson 4, the first recorded Olympic Games were held in 776 B.C., nearly 3,000 years ago. The Games were held every four years until A.D. 393. Then, there were no Olympic Games until they were started again in 1896.

Today, the Olympics are more popular than ever. There are two versions of the modern Olympic Games: the Summer Olympics and the Winter Olympics. Thousands of people attend these games and millions more watch them on television. In this lesson you will learn more about how the Olympic Games have changed over time. As you read, think about how the tradition of the Olympics has helped people of the world to build bridges of understanding.

AN OLYMPIC CHAMPION

Mark Spitz of the United States crouched over the starting block. He was about to compete in a 100-meter (109-yd)

swimming race, one of the most exciting events in the Summer Olympics. His muscles tightened as he waited for the starting gun to fire. When the shot rang out, Spitz dove like lightning into the pool. While his legs churned the water behind him, Spitz's arms leapt like rockets out of the pool and plunged back down again. Two minutes later, Mark Spitz had set a new world's record and had won his first gold medal of the 1972 Summer Olympics. Before the 1972 games were finished, he had won seven gold medals. Mark Spitz was a true Olympic champion.

THE ANCIENT OLYMPIC GAMES

How did the Olympic Games begin in ancient Greece? They were first held at a place called Olympia, in a grove of olive trees where people worshiped the Greek gods. Olympia had long been a place to which officials from warring city-states came to settle disputes. In their spare time between discussions about peace and war, the officials took part in running races. Before long, skilled athletes were sent to represent their city-states, and the Olympic Games grew out of these competitions.

In the earliest Olympics, there was only one event. It was a running race called the *stade* (stod), which was similar in length to today's 200-meter (220-yd) dash. In ancient Greece all the athletes were men. Women were not allowed to compete or even to watch the Games. Over time, more races and other events were added. For example, in about 520 B.C. a race was added to the Games in which the runners wore many pounds of armor.

There was great glory for winners of Olympic events. As soon as an event was over, messengers would fan out to all the city-states of Greece to announce who had won. At Olympia a winner received only a wreath, or crown of leaves and flowers. But a winner also received instant fame. At home he became an immediate hero. When one Olympic champion arrived home, he was greeted by a parade of 300 chariots. Sometimes, a part of a city-state's surrounding wall would be knocked down so that an Olympic champion could enter the town in a new way. City-states were very proud of their Olympic champions.

By 400 B.C. the Olympic Games had become a festival of sports, religious ceremonies, and entertainment. But as the ancient Olympics became more popular, they began to change. City-states started paying athletes to compete, and the bribing of judges became common. At the same time, Greek civilization and Greek traditions were weakening. As you will read in the next chapter, Roman civilization was becoming more powerful.

These changes brought an end to the ancient Olympic Games. The Games were not to be held for another 1,500 years until they were started again not far from their original Greek home.

THE MODERN OLYMPIC GAMES

A horseback rider galloped into a stadium in Athens, the capital of modern Greece. The year was 1896. It was the first modern Olympic Games. The man on horseback brought an update to the Greek king sitting in his royal box.

Athletes in the longest Olympic race, called the marathon, were about to enter the stadium, and a Greek runner had just taken the lead. The news that a Greek was in the lead spread through the crowd. When a thin, exhausted runner appeared through the stadium's marble entrance, the crowd roared its approval. The runner, Spiridon Loues (spi rē′ don lü ēz′), had just become Greece's first modern Olympic legend.

Athletes from 13 countries competed at Athens in the Olympic Games of 1896. Watching with pride was a Frenchman named Baron Pierre de Coubertin (pyer də kü ber tan′). Believing that sports should be an important part of education, Coubertin had formed the International Olympic Committee in 1894. Today this committee still organizes the Games and chooses where they will be held. Because of his role in getting the games started once again, Coubertin has been called the "father of the modern Olympic Games."

THE SPORTS TRADITION

There are many differences between the modern and ancient Olympic Games. Unlike the ancient Games, women compete in the modern Olympics. In 1924 the International Olympic Committee added a Winter Olympics, which includes cold-weather sports such as ice-skating, skiing, and ice hockey. The modern Games include team sports such as basketball and hockey. In the ancient Games only individual sports were included.

Regardless of changes, the ancient Greek tradition still shapes many aspects of the modern Olympic Games. As in the ancient Games, an Olympic flame still burns from the opening to the close of the Games. Modern events that originated in the ancient Olympics include the javelin (*spear*) throw, running races, and boxing. At the opening ceremonies of the modern Olympics, the athletes of every nation enter the stadium in alphabetical order according to country name. But there's one exception. As a reminder of where the Olympics began, the athletes from Greece lead the way into the stadium at the opening of every modern Olympic Games.

The spirit of the ancient Olympics still survives. The Olympics are a time when many countries try to put aside their disputes and send their best athletes to compete in peace. Many countries honor the Olympic spirit by issuing stamps showing Olympic events. Although the Games have changed, the tradition of peaceful competition and friendship between athletes from different parts of the world lives on.

Why do you think the Olympics have remained such a popular sports tradition for so long?

5 The Spread of Greek Ideas

READ TO LEARN

Key People

Thucydides   Alexander the Great
Philip II   Aristotle

Key Places

Macedonia
Alexandria

Read Aloud

Fellow Citizens, why are you driving us out of our city? Why do you want to kill us? We have never done you any harm. We have shared with you splendid festivals; we have danced with you and gone to school with you and fought in the army with you, braving together the dangers of sea and land in defense of our common safety and freedom.

These sorrowful words were written by an Athenian as the other Greek city-states united against Athens. The wars that followed not only meant the end of the Athenian polis, but of all Greek city-states. You will learn, however, that the Greek legacy could not die.

Read for Purpose

1. **WHAT YOU KNOW:** What was the Greek legacy?
2. **WHAT YOU WILL LEARN:** Why did Greek culture survive?

THE PELOPONNESIAN WARS

This was the greatest event . . . in my opinion, in Greek history; at once most glorious to the victors and most calamitous [harmful] to the conquered. The Athenians were beaten at all points and altogether; their sufferings in every way were great. They were totally destroyed—their fleet, their army, everything—and few out of many returned home.

These words described Athens' final battle. They were written by the Greek historian Thucydides (thü sid′ ə dēz) in 404 B.C. In 437 B.C. Sparta and the other Peloponnesian city-states had united against Athens. They were jealous of Athens' riches and influence.

For 27 years, the Athenians held back their fellow Greeks. At first the Athenian fleet easily triumphed on the seas. But year by year their fleet was ruined and Athens had no more strength to fight. The Athenian polis was destroyed. In 404 B.C. the exhausted Athenians lost their army, their power, and their democracy. But, you will learn, the legacy of Greek civilization was not defeated.

165

ALEXANDER THE GREAT

After 27 years of war, not only Athens lay weakened. All of the "Aegean World" was open to invasion. Suddenly, a new empire called Macedonia (mas ə dō′ nē ə) conquered Greek lands.

The Macedonians had long admired Greek culture. Few loved it as much as the Macedonian king Philip II and his son Alexander. Alexander the Great, as the son was later called, learned about Greek ways from a special teacher. When Alexander was a boy he had been taught by Aristotle (ar′ is tot əl), a wise, famous philosopher from Athens. Aristotle taught Alexander to love philosophy and Greek ways.

When Alexander was 20 in 336 B.C., he was crowned king. His greatest wish was to spread the Greek legacy. Alexander quickly proved that he was one of the most talented generals of all time.

Alexander never lost a battle and was never forced to retreat. As you see from the map on the next page, Alexander's conquests built a massive empire. What lands fell under Alexander's rule? You have already read about earlier empires that occupied these lands. None, however, was as vast as Alexander's empire.

BLEND OF EAST AND WEST

Alexander's most lasting achievement was to spread Greek culture. As you can see from the map on the next page, Alexander's armies marched across Persia into the Indian subcontinent. Thousands of Greek government officials, merchants, and artisans followed and settled these eastern lands. In the lands he conquered, Alexander built cities modeled on the Greek polis. As many as 70 cities named Alexandria were set up across the empire.

Alexander encouraged the blend of Greek culture with the cultures of the ancient Middle East. For example, he began to worship Persian as well as Greek gods and goddesses. He also adopted Persian customs and dress. Although Alexander thought of himself as Greek, he gained support from different cultures by adopting their ways.

Alexander the Great is one of history's greatest generals. This mosaic, or design made up of many pieces of colored stone and glass, shows Alexander in battle.

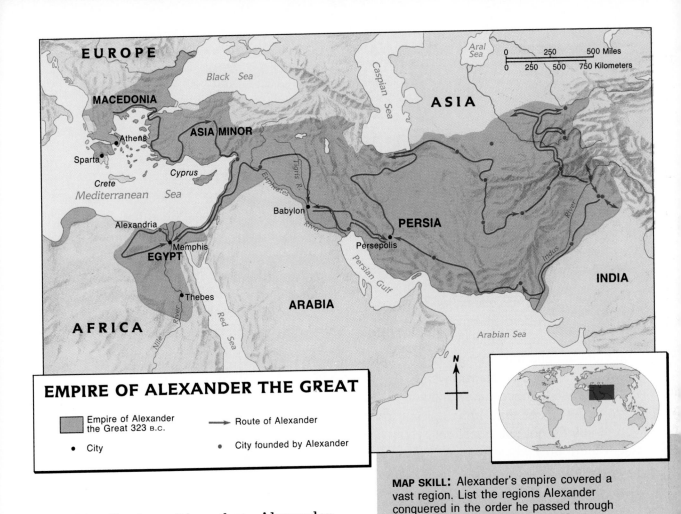

EMPIRE OF ALEXANDER THE GREAT

Empire of Alexander
the Great 323 B.C.

→ Route of Alexander

• City

• City founded by Alexander

MAP SKILL: Alexander's empire covered a vast region. List the regions Alexander conquered in the order he passed through them. Where did his journey end?

Of all the cities that Alexander founded, one grew to become truly remarkable. Called Alexandria like the other cities he built, this one was in the Nile Delta. The Egyptian Alexandria attracted scholars, sailors, and merchants. It had the world's first museums and libraries. One library is said to have contained more than 500,000 scrolls of papyrus.

THE GREEK HERITAGE

You have read a lot of history in this chapter. You have learned that Greek civilization built lasting legacies. The ancient Greeks cherished the growth of art and ideas and built the world's first democracy.

In this lesson you learned how Alexander the Great spread the ways of the Greeks throughout the ancient Middle East. As you continue to read this book, look for signs of the Greek legacy. You are bound to find them.

Check Your Reading

1. Why did the Peloponnesian city-states unite against Athens?
2. Why do you think Alexander the Great admired Greek civilization?
3. **GEOGRAPHY SKILL:** What ancient lands were part of Alexander's empire?
4. **THINKING SKILL:** What do you think would have happened if Alexander had not spread Greek ideas?

Asking Questions

Your teacher has just explained how to do your history report. Then she asks, "Are there any questions?"

Have you ever thought that your questions were not good enough to ask? It is very important to realize that asking questions is a key part of learning. Do not ever be afraid to ask questions. Of course, it is sometimes hard to know *what to ask*.

How do you know what to ask? Asking questions means thinking of what to ask in order to find out what you want to know. By asking good questions you can learn about things that are important to you. If you do not ask questions, you might learn only what someone else wants you to know.

Trying the Skill

One legacy of the Greeks is the skill of asking good questions. Socrates, Plato, and Aristotle asked questions to guide their search for knowledge. In this chapter you read that the Peloponnesian War brought about the end of the Greek city-states. List three questions you could ask to better understand this topic.

• What did you do to come up with your questions?

HELPING YOURSELF

The steps on the left will help you to ask questions on any topic. The example on the right shows how these steps can can help you learn more about the Peloponnesian War.

One Way to Ask Good Questions	Example
1. Identify and clarify the topic or subject that you want to examine.	The topic is the Peloponnesian War. To clarify the topic you might ask yourself, "What was the Peloponnesian War about?"
2. Try to come up with questions you could ask about the topic. Use question starters like *who, what, when, where, how* and *why* to invent good questions.	Ask *who* was jealous, *what* they were jealous about, and *how* their jealousy led to war. Use other words that start questions, such as *where* and *why* to help you invent more questions.
3. Determine whether each of your questions focuses in on the topic or whether it goes beyond the topic.	The question "Who was jealous?" helps focus in on the topic of the Peloponnesian War. A question such as "How did the war affect the future of Athens?" broadens the topic to include the impact of the war on Athens.
4. Review your questions. Then decide what they will help you learn about the topic.	The questions above might help you learn about the causes and effects of the Peloponnesian War.
5. Choose those questions that will help you to learn what you want to know. Add other questions that focus on what you want to know.	To accomplish your goal you should choose questions that deal with cause and effect. A new question might be, "What events triggered the conflict between Athens and Sparta?"

Applying the Skill

In this chapter you also read about Alexander the Great.

1. Which of the following questions would help you learn about the importance of Alexander the Great in world history?
   a. What lands made up Alexander's empire?
   b. Where and when did he live?
   c. How many cities did he name after himself?
2. What are three questions you can ask to learn more about Alexander's role in history?
3. Are your questions "good" questions? How do you know?

Reviewing the Skill

1. What does it mean to ask good questions?
2. What are some steps that could help you to ask good questions?
3. Why is it important to come up with your own questions?

169

Should Britain Return the Elgin Marbles to Greece?

For more than 2,400 years the Parthenon has stood on the crest of the Acropolis. Rising over modern Athens, Greece, the Parthenon was the ancient temple to the goddess Athena. Though the Parthenon is in ruins today, millions come to marvel at what remains of this stately and beautiful building.

In London, England, meanwhile, art lovers from all over the world flock to the British Museum. At this famous museum, people can view the exhibit of marble sculptures that were once part of the Parthenon. For these visitors, the art of ancient Greece comes to life at close range.

The Elgin Marbles, as they are known, form one of the British Museum's most important collections. The marbles from the Parthenon arrived in Britain in the early 1800s. At that time Greece was under Turkish rule. The Earl of Elgin, the British ambassador to Turkey, received permission to remove "some stones" from the Parthenon. Under Elgin's direction 83 marble statues became part of the collection of the British Museum.

When Greece regained its independence in 1830 its leaders asked Britain to return the Elgin Marbles. The British government refused. In 1983 the Greek government once again asked that the sculptures be returned. Once again, the British refused.

What do you think? Should the Elgin Marbles be returned to Greece? Or should they remain in Britain?

POINT

A Symbol of Our Heritage

The viewpoint of Greece was written by its minister of culture. These remarks were published in an Athenian newspaper.

Lord Elgin had no right to remove the marbles from the Acropolis. They are the property of the Greek people. More importantly, the marbles are a major part of the Parthenon. Do not compare them with other museum artifacts. They are not simple objects that were carved long ago by a remote people in a remote place. The Parthenon marbles are among the world's greatest pieces of art. Their value is unimaginable.

Historians of art agree that the Parthenon is a unique example of Greek art. In the center of Athens, the ruins attract thousands of foreign visitors each year. What are they coming for? The Acropolis was the center of the world's greatest ancient civilization. Yet those who visit modern Athens find a Parthenon without its sculptures. "Where are the sculptures?" they ask. "Are they ruined? Are they bits of dust on the Acropolis?"

● Why does the Greek minister of culture think that the Elgin Marbles should be returned to Greece?

COUNTERPOINT

An International Treasure

David Wilson, director of the British Museum, defended the position of the British Museum in a London newspaper.

Lord Elgin received the legal title to the Parthenon marbles nearly two centuries ago. They have been preserved and protected in the British Museum ever since. Openly displayed for the enjoyment of the general public, the Elgin Marbles are the "crowning jewels" of our collection of ancient art.

There are quite a few people who think that returning the marbles would be a nice gesture for the British to make. It really is a much more difficult problem, however. It would lead to the destruction of the British Museum.

The British Museum receives a lot of different materials for its collections. There will not be an increase in our collections if we started returning our treasures to anyone who thought they had a claim to them. The museum also has to think of the many visitors who come from faraway countries to view the magnificent marbles.

● Why does the director of the British Museum think that the Elgin Marbles should remain in Britain?

UNDERSTANDING THE POINT/COUNTERPOINT

1. Who do you think makes a stronger argument about whether Britain should return the Elgin Marbles to Greece?
2. If you were a tourist in Greece visiting the Parthenon, how do you think you would feel about the Elgin Marbles?
3. Can you suggest a compromise that might be acceptable to both the Greek minister of culture and the British Museum director?

IMPORTANT EVENTS

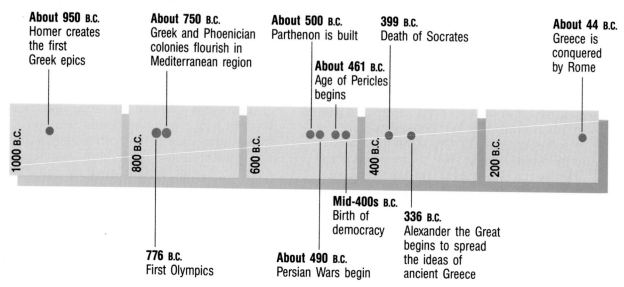

About 950 B.C.
Homer creates
the first
Greek epics

About 750 B.C.
Greek and Phoenician
colonies flourish in
Mediterranean region

About 500 B.C.
Parthenon is built

399 B.C.
Death of Socrates

About 44 B.C.
Greece is
conquered
by Rome

About 461 B.C.
Age of Pericles
begins

1000 B.C.

800 B.C.

600 B.C.

400 B.C.

200 B.C.

776 B.C.
First Olympics

Mid-400s B.C.
Birth of
democracy

336 B.C.
Alexander the Great
begins to spread
the ideas of
ancient Greece

About 490 B.C.
Persian Wars begin

PEOPLE TO KNOW

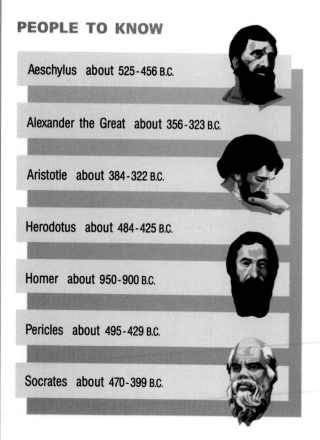

Aeschylus about 525-456 B.C.

Alexander the Great about 356-323 B.C.

Aristotle about 384-322 B.C.

Herodotus about 484-425 B.C.

Homer about 950-900 B.C.

Pericles about 495-429 B.C.

Socrates about 470-399 B.C.

IDEAS TO REMEMBER

- Surrounded by the sea, the ancient Greeks became expert sailors. They set up colonies throughout the Mediterranean region.
- Ancient Greece was dominated by two city-states—Athens and Sparta.
- Athens was the world's first democracy. Under the leadership of Pericles, democracy became the foundation of the government of ancient Greece.
- Ancient Greece left a rich cultural heritage in art, mythology, literature, theater, and philosophy.
- Alexander the Great encouraged the spread of Greek culture throughout his vast empire.

REVIEWING VOCABULARY

Acropolis	myth
assembly	peninsula
democracy	philosophy
epic	polis
monarchy	tragedy

Number a sheet of paper from 1 to 10. Beside each number write the word or term from the above list that matches the statement or definition.

1. Because power was in the hands of a king or queen, this form of government was rejected by the ancient Greeks.
2. Made up of a city and all the land surrounding it, this type of political organization was typical of ancient Greece.
3. Sometimes called the birthplace of Western Civilization, this hill was the center of ancient Athens.
4. These are plays in which life is treated seriously and usually end sadly.
5. The ancient Greeks listened for hours to these long poems that told of the adventures of their gods and heroes.
6. The United States House of Representatives is an example of this lawmaking body, which is basic to all world democracies.
7. The relationship between the gods and human beings is one of the things explained in this type of story.
8. This search for truth—one of the great achievements of the ancient Greeks— is concerned with basic questions of life and man's place in the universe.
9. The ancient Greeks were the first to practice this form of government.
10. This term describes land that is surrounded by water on three sides.

REVIEWING FACTS

1. Although Sparta was as powerful as its rival Athens, it contributed little to Greek civilization. Why?
2. How did the gods of ancient Greece differ from the gods of other civilizations you have studied?
3. List two ways in which the ancient Greek polis was different from American cities.
4. Given a choice between an oligarchy and a monarchy, a person fighting for democracy might choose an oligarchy. Why?
5. Describe the Greek legacy. What were its most important achievements?

WRITING ABOUT MAIN IDEAS

1. **Writing an Article:** Write an article explaining how the Greek and Phoenician alphabets helped the spread of ideas. Why was the alphabet superior to hieroglyphics and cuneiform?
2. **Writing About Perspectives:** Imagine that you are a woman who lives in ancient Athens. Write a pamphlet explaining why you think women should be allowed to participate in the Athenian democracy.

BUILDING SKILLS: ASKING QUESTIONS

One legacy of the Greeks is the skill of asking good questions. List at least five questions you could ask about the legacies of ancient Greece. Then choose those questions that will help you learn more about what you want to know about the topic.

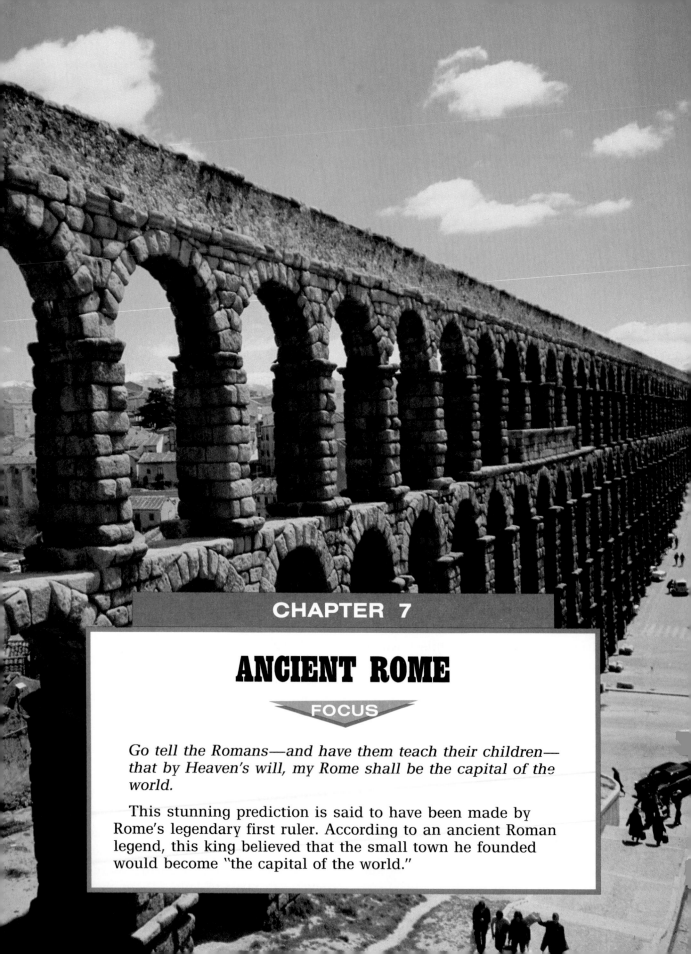

CHAPTER 7

ANCIENT ROME

FOCUS

*Go tell the Romans—and have them teach their children—
that by Heaven's will, my Rome shall be the capital of the
world.*

This stunning prediction is said to have been made by
Rome's legendary first ruler. According to an ancient Roman
legend, this king believed that the small town he founded
would become "the capital of the world."

1 The Geography of Ancient Rome

READING TO LEARN

Key Vocabulary

basin

Key Places

Rome   Appennines
Sicily   Gaul
Alps

Read Aloud

While the mighty Athenians were creating a democracy in the "Aegean World," an important new city was growing nearby. To the west of Athens, on the Italian peninsula, lay the city of Rome. Its greatness caused one ancient writer to proclaim, "The city of Rome, a name glorious and famous in the mouths of men."

In this lesson you will read about the geographic setting of ancient Rome. Rome grew to become the heart of an important new civilization.

Read for Purpose

1. **WHAT YOU KNOW:** How did the Mediterranean Sea affect the growth of Greek civilization?
2. **WHAT YOU WILL LEARN:** What are the chief geographic features of the Italian peninsula?

THE ITALIAN PENINSULA

Italy is a long, boot-shaped peninsula in southern Europe. The geography of the Italian peninsula was important to the success of ancient Rome. The peninsula stretches into the Mediterranean Sea and seems ready to kick the nearby island of Sicily. The lands of ancient Greece lie to the east of Italy. To the west of Italy stretches the southern coast of western Europe. To the south you can find the coast of northern Africa.

The Italian peninsula is near the midpoint of the Mediterranean, dividing the sea into an eastern and a western half. Rome itself is located midway between the Italian peninsula's southern tip and the peninsula's northern, mountainous boundary.

Italy's land is mountainous but not as rugged as the land of Greece. Unlike the early Greeks, the early Romans did not have to become a seafaring people. Instead, they could grow a surplus of food on their rich farmland.

NATURAL REGIONS

The Italian peninsula has four natural regions. The first region is made up of the majestic **Alps** in the north. The snowcapped peaks of the Alps separate the peninsula from the rest of Europe. There are, however, passes through the Alps that enabled migrating groups to reach the peninsula.

The second region includes a lower mountain range called the **Apennines** (ap′ ə nīnz). These mountains extend the length of the peninsula and continue on into Sicily. In the north the Apennines hug the western coast, then cross the peninsula and follow the eastern coast to the south.

The third region is made up of the wide, flat lands of the Po Basin south of the Alps. A **basin** is an area of land drained by a river and its tributaries. As the map on this page shows, the Po River and its tributaries flow through the Po Basin. Basins are also surrounded by higher lands. Note that the Po Basin is found between two major mountain ranges.

The fourth natural region of the Italian peninsula is the long, narrow plain extending along its western coast. This fertile plain attracted Italy's earliest people. This was the region where they built their farming villages.

THE EARLY ROMANS

Who were the first farmers of ancient Italy? As the map on this page shows,

MAP SKILL: What three large islands are close to the Italian peninsula?

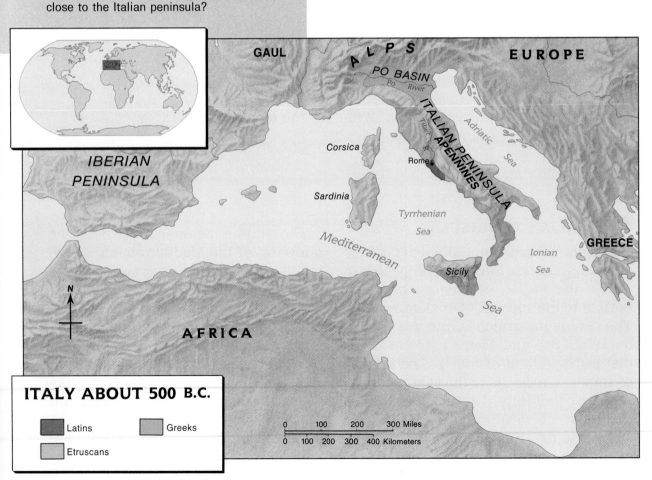

ITALY ABOUT 500 B.C.

- Latins
- Greeks
- Etruscans

three different groups of early people lived on the peninsula. Each group had an important contribution to make.

The people who lived in early Rome were Latins. The Latins migrated from central Europe around 1000 B.C. They settled on a cluster of seven hills near the Tiber River. The Latins built villages and farmed the fertile fields near the Tiber River.

But the Latins were not alone. Between 750 and 600 B.C., settlers from Greece established many colonies on the peninsula's southern coast. The busy Greek colonies brought the early Latins into close contact with Greek civilization. The Latins greatly admired the ways of the Greeks.

A third group of people, called the Etruscans, had been living north of the Tiber River since about 900 B.C. For nearly 500 years the Etruscans dominated most of the Italian peninsula from the Po Basin to the Tiber River.

Historians have never been sure where the Etruscans came from. Many think they came from Asia Minor. Other historians think the Etruscans migrated south from Gaul, or the land that is modern-day France. It is known for certain, though, that by 600 B.C. the Etruscans had crossed the Tiber River and conquered the Latins. Thus, as you see, the early history of Rome is tied to three different groups of people.

THE GROWTH OF ROME

As you have read, the geography of ancient Rome was important to its success. The fertile coastal plain of the Italian peninsula attracted people from afar. Latins, Etruscans, and Greeks each played roles in Rome's early history. Read on. In the next lesson you will read how the people of the

These Etruscan sculptures were found in northern Italy and are evidence of the Etruscans' highly advanced culture.

Italian peninsula were united under a single government.

Check Your Reading

1. Where is the Italian peninsula?
2. What three groups settled the Italian peninsula?
3. **GEOGRAPHY SKILL:** Where did the early Romans come from? What reasons might they have had for settling on the Italian peninsula?
4. **THINKING SKILL:** Sequence the different groups that settled in ancient Rome.

Reading Contour Maps

Key Vocabulary

contour map   altitude
contour line   relief

The geography of the Italian peninsula includes a great variety of landforms, ranging from flat plains to rugged mountains. Cartographers, or people who make maps, can show differences in the height of the land in several ways.

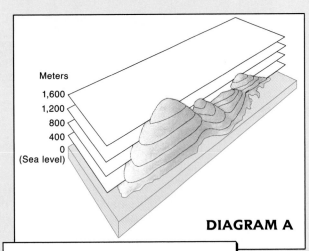

DIAGRAM A

SARDINIA: Contour Lines

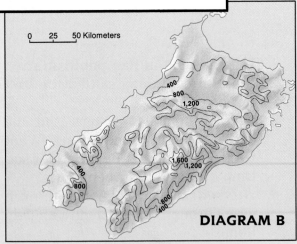

DIAGRAM B

What are Contour Maps?

The elevation and features of a place can be shown by contour maps. *Contour* means "shape." Contour maps provide detailed information about the earth's surface. They help us picture the shape of the land.

Contour maps outline landforms with lines or different colors showing different elevations. A contour line on a map connects areas of the same elevation. As you know, elevation is height above sea level. It is measured vertically, or straight up. You may have noticed from the many maps you have used in this book that elevation is given in either feet or meters. Another word for elevation is altitude. Altitude refers to height above sea level.

Using the Diagrams

Diagram A on this page will help you understand contour lines. It shows Sardinia, the island off the coast of Italy. This diagram illustrates how the island can be separated, or cut, into layers by horizontal sheets intersecting the land. Note the elevation of each sheet. Imagine that you can push the sheets completely through the model, line them up directly above one another, and trace the outline of each "cut" on the sheet below it. If you took each outline in turn, positioned it correctly over a piece of paper, you would have a simple contour map of Sardinia as shown in Diagram B.

If you compare Diagram A with Diagram B, you will see that the contour lines reflect the shape of the land. The closed, somewhat circular contour lines on Diagram B show the varied elevation of Sardinia.

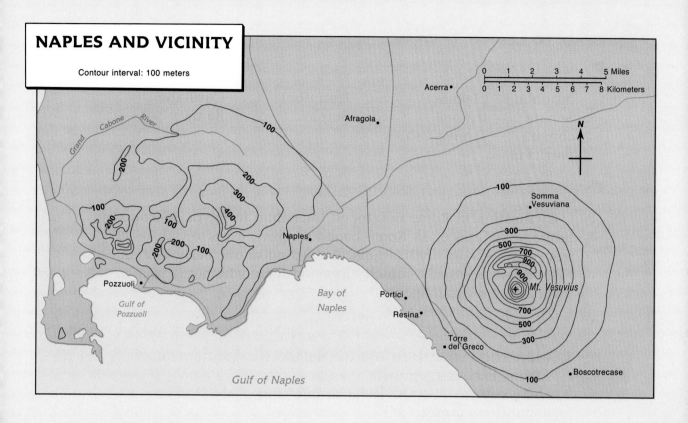

NAPLES AND VICINITY

Contour interval: 100 meters

Grand Cabone River

Acerra

Afragola

Pozzuoli

Gulf of Pozzuoli

Naples

Bay of Naples

Portici

Resina

Torre del Greco

Somma Vesuviana

Mt. Vesuvius

Boscotrecase

Gulf of Naples

0 1 2 3 4 5 Miles

0 1 2 3 4 5 6 7 8 Kilometers

N

Contour Maps Show Relief

Contour maps also show the **relief** of a region. Relief is variation in elevation. Relief is a description of the roughness of the land. Flat or nearly level areas with little variation in elevation have low relief. Plains and plateaus are landforms of low relief. Rugged areas with great variation in elevation have high relief. A mountainous region, for example, is an area that has high relief.

Relief is shown by the pattern and spacing of contour lines. For example, contour lines drawn far apart mean that the land slopes gently. A steep slope, on the other hand, is shown by lines drawn very close together. As the map on this page shows, the region around Naples has both low and high relief.

When using contour maps, it is a good idea to first check the contour interval. The contour intervals are differences in elevation between contour lines. As you become skilled in reading contour maps, you will begin to be able to picture the shape of the land.

Reviewing the Skill

Use the map on this page to answer the following questions.

1. What are contour maps?
2. What is the contour interval of the map shown on this page?
3. According to the map, Torre del Grecco lies how many meters below Mount Vesuvius?
4. How do contour maps help you picture the elevation of the land?

179

2 The Roman Republic

READ TO LEARN

Key Vocabulary

republic   plebeian
Senate   tribune
consul   Twelve Tables
patrician

Key People

Hannibal
Scipio

Key Places

Carthage
Zama

Read Aloud

Civilization in Rome developed later than in Egypt, Mesopotamia, and Greece. As Rome began to grow, it borrowed freely from these earlier civilizations. According to one early Roman, "The Romans eagerly copied any good idea, whether it was from a friend or an enemy."

Read for Purpose

1. **WHAT YOU KNOW:** How did the democratic government of Athens encourage growth?
2. **WHAT YOU WILL LEARN:** What events caused the Roman Republic to grow?

THE LEGENDARY BEGINNING

The early Romans had a legend about their beginnings. They believed that twin brothers named Romulus (rom' yə ləs) and Remus (rē' məs) founded their city. According to the legend, Romulus and Remus were born to the princess of a small city on the Italian peninsula. The twins' cruel uncle wanted to rule the city, so he placed the infants in a basket in the Tiber River. Left to drown, the twins floated down the river until the basket drifted ashore.

According to the legend:

As the helpless infants lay crying, a kindly she-wolf came by and, taking pity on them, carried them back to her lair [den], where she tended them as if they were her own cubs. . . . The two royal babies . . . grew up tall and strong, and were adopted by a shepherd and his wife. . . . Born with a natural gift of leadership, they placed themselves at the head of a band of young shepherds, and after a time drove their uncle from the throne which he had seized. . . .

Romulus and Remus built a city on the site where they had washed ashore. The city was called Rome, after Romulus, its first king. This was the legendary beginning of Rome. Read on. A new civilization was beginning to grow.

This model of ancient Rome shows how the city grew from its legendary beginnings. By A.D. 300 Rome was the largest city in the world, with more than 1 million people.

THE BIRTH OF A REPUBLIC

Like ancient Greece, Rome was ruled by kings in its early years. Between about 600 and 509 B.C., seven different kings governed the Romans. The seventh king, an Etruscan, was so cruel that the Romans rose up against him.

In 509 B.C. Rome set up a republic. A republic is a government in which citizens have the right to choose their leaders. The word *republic* comes from the Latin phrase *res publica*, which means "public things."

For the Romans, a republic was not a democracy. You may remember that in ancient Greece, all male citizens could vote and participate in the Assembly. But in the Roman Republic, only male citizens with money and property could vote. In addition, the more wealth a citizen had, the greater was his power.

Like the Athenian Assembly, the Romans had a lawmaking council which they called the Senate. Senators elected two people to serve as consuls, who shared power equally over all of Rome. The consuls also commanded Rome's army. By shouting "Veto!" one consul could stop the actions of the other. *Veto* is a Latin word meaning "I forbid."

PATRICIANS AND PLEBEIANS

As you have read, all people did not share the same rights in the Roman Republic. The Senate was made up of members of rich, powerful families, called patricians (pə trish' ənz). There were only about 200 patrician families in Rome, and they had all the power. In the early Republic, only patricians were allowed to become senators.

Most people in Rome were plebeians (pli bē' ənz). Plebeians were farmers,

181

artisans, and merchants. Though plebeians were free citizens, they could not participate in government.

Not long after the Roman Republic was founded in 509 B.C., the plebeians demanded more rights. In 494 B.C. thousands of unhappy plebeians marched out of Rome. They threatened to build their own city unless they got more rights. Their actions frightened the patricians, who were afraid of losing the labor of the plebeians. Rome could not run without its farmers, artisans, and merchants.

The plebeians proved that they were important citizens and deserved equal rights. Their walkout led to the creation of tribunes. Tribunes were officials who were elected to protect plebeian interests. Ten tribunes held office and were elected each year by the plebeians.

THE TWELVE TABLES

From 494 to 287 B.C., the plebeians protested many times. Each time, they won new rights. Among the greatest of victories for the plebeians was the creation of a written law code.

From its earliest history, Roman law had rested on custom. Because laws were unwritten, patrician officials could act unfairly. You may remember that the Code of Hammurabi was written on a column of stone. Anyone who could read was free to study the laws. Thus, people of Babylonian times always knew what the law was.

In 451 B.C. a special group of patrician and plebeian officials were given the job of writing down Roman laws. The laws were carved on 12 bronze tablets, or tables, and placed on the walls of public buildings. The Twelve Tables became the foundation of Roman law. Even Roman schoolboys had to memorize the Twelve Tables.

Roman tribunes, like all Romans, were bound to obey the laws listed on the Twelve Tables. This painting shows the Roman government in action—a trial by jury.

Any male citizen, no matter how poor he was or where he came from, could serve in Rome's mighty army.

ROME BEGINS TO EXPAND

By 264 B.C. the Roman Republic ruled all of the Italian peninsula south of the Po Basin. But the Romans were not the only power in the Mediterranean region.

By this time, there were three important centers of power in the Mediterranean region. One was Rome, which was the center of a growing republic. The second was Alexandria, in Egypt, which had been built by Alexander the Great. The third was Carthage, located on the northern coast of Africa.

Carthage had first been built as a Phoenician colony. By the third century B.C., however, Carthage was a rich trading center. Like Rome, Carthage had the advantage of a location in the middle of the Mediterranean region.

183

WAR WITH CARTHAGE

As the map on this page shows, both Carthage and Rome had claims on Sicily. In 264 B.C., Carthage and Rome went to war for control of Sicily. This began a period of harsh struggle known as the Punic Wars. *Punic* comes from the Latin word for Phoenicia.

Rome won the first battles of the Punic Wars. Victory brought it control of the islands of Sicily, Sardinia, and Corsica. Victory also earned Rome the hatred of the Carthaginians. Their defeated general vowed to get revenge and gave his son, Hannibal, the duty to stop the rise of Rome.

HANNIBAL CROSSES THE ALPS

In 218 B.C., when Hannibal was 29 years old, he built an army of 60,000 soldiers and 60 elephants. Hannibal had decided that it was time to fulfill his father's wish for revenge.

You can follow the route of Hannibal's army on the map on this page. As you can see, Hannibal led his soldiers on a long trek from Spain across Gaul and up the dizzying heights of the Alps. The heights, cold, and fierce blizzards caused the deaths of more than half his men and most of the elephants. But why do you think Hannibal wanted to enter the lands of the Roman Republic from the north? What other route might he have taken?

MAP SKILL: What mountain ranges did Hannibal and his troops have to cross in order to reach Rome?

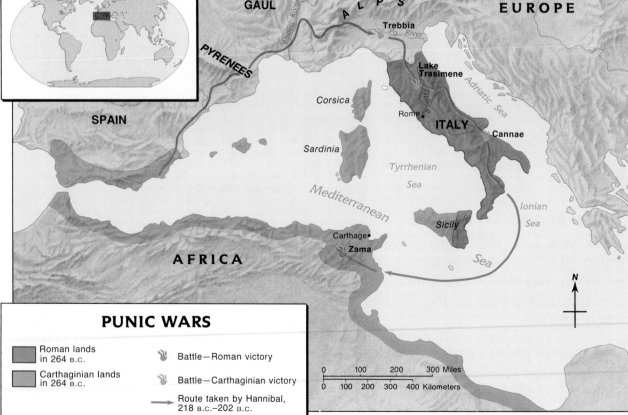

PUNIC WARS

Roman lands in 264 B.C.

Carthaginian lands in 264 B.C.

Battle—Roman victory

Battle—Carthaginian victory

Route taken by Hannibal, 218 B.C.–202 B.C.

0   100   200   300 Miles
0   100   200   300   400 Kilometers

When Hannibal's army reached the Po Basin south of the Alps, the Romans were indeed surprised. But the Romans still believed they did not have much to fear. One Roman writer said of the Carthaginians:

They are mere shadows of men, half-dead with hunger, cold, filth and . . . bruised on the rocks and cliffs. . . . Their weapons are shattered and broken, their horses are weak and lame.

Although Hannibal had fewer soldiers than the Romans, his army won three battles against Rome. With each battle, Rome was closer to defeat. In 202 B.C., however, a shrewd Roman general named Scipio led his fleets across the Mediterranean to attack Carthage. Hannibal was at last forced to leave Roman lands and rush home to the rescue. But the mighty Hannibal, unbeaten on European soil, was badly defeated by Scipio at the Battle of Zama.

THE GLORY OF ROME

Zama was a battle that truly changed the course of history. Had Hannibal been the victor, Carthage and not Rome would probably have become the greatest empire in the world. But because Rome was victorious, Roman laws and government began to spread throughout the Mediterranean region. As one Roman historian wrote after the Battle of Zama:

Areas geographically remote, shores divided by the sea, now merge in allegiance to a single government.

But Rome was only beginning to grow. Foreign treasures poured into the city of Rome as it conquered many new lands. Soon Rome would be the center of a new empire. Read on. What

Hannibal's crossing of the Alps was difficult—especially with elephants. The way was narrow and rough. It took him five months to reach the Italian peninsula.

kind of empire would the Romans build? You are about to read how Rome became the "capital of the world."

Check Your Reading

1. Describe the patricians and plebeians of the Roman Republic.
2. What is a republic?
3. GEOGRAPHY SKILL: What bodies of water were crossed by Hannibal on his journey to Rome?
4. THINKING SKILL: What would have been the consequence if Hannibal had won the Battle of Zama?

3 The Roman Empire

READ TO LEARN

Key Vocabulary

territory
dictator
civil war
Pax Romana

Key People

Julius Caesar
Cleopatra
Octavian

Read Aloud

Remember, Romans, your task is to rule nations and your genius shall be to lead men into peace; to be generous to the conquered and to stand firm against the proud.

With these words, a Roman poet described the future that Romans firmly believed was theirs. Soon, they would create the greatest empire the world had ever known.

Read for Purpose

1. **WHAT YOU KNOW:** What other empires have you studied?
2. **WHAT YOU WILL LEARN:** How did Rome's government and rulers help create a vast empire?

BUILDING AN EMPIRE

You read in Lesson 2 that Rome's victory over Carthage caused the republic to expand. As the map on the next page shows, Rome continued to grow after the Punic Wars. Rome grew from a small republic into an empire that stretched across parts of three continents. New territories, or large areas of land, were added as Roman armies marched throughout the Mediterranean region. According to the map, when did the empire reach its greatest extent?

The strong Roman government made this growth possible. Rome divided its new territories into separate states.

Each state was ruled by a Roman governor who collected taxes and sent the money back to Rome. Roman government allowed the people of the added territories to keep their own customs. Do you think this was a wise decision?

JULIUS CAESAR

In addition to a strong and well-organized government, Rome had powerful generals. One of the most famous leaders in world history was the Roman patrician Julius Caesar (jül′ yəs sē′ zər). Caesar was born in 100 B.C. and rose to become a popular general. His troops were almost always outnumbered, yet they followed him

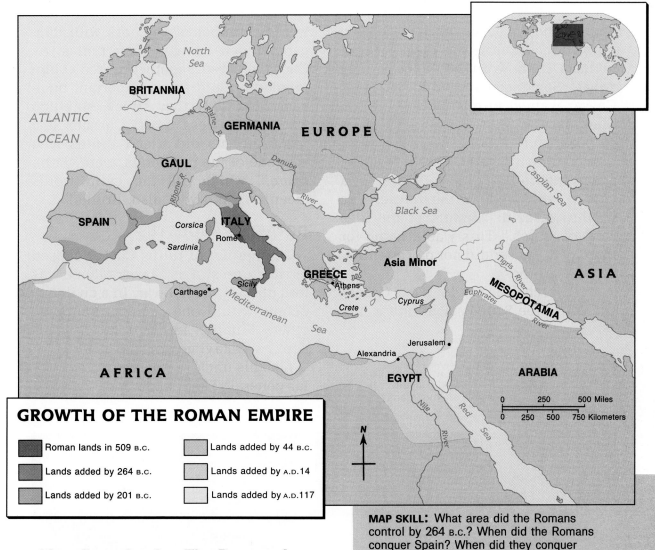

GROWTH OF THE ROMAN EMPIRE

- Roman lands in 509 B.C.
- Lands added by 264 B.C.
- Lands added by 201 B.C.
- Lands added by 44 B.C.
- Lands added by A.D. 14
- Lands added by A.D. 117

MAP SKILL: What area did the Romans control by 264 B.C.? When did the Romans conquer Spain? When did they conquer Mesopotamia?

with a fierce loyalty. The Romans believed that men who were ordinary soldiers in other battles had unbeatable courage under Caesar.

In the middle of the first century B.C., Caesar's army marched swiftly through Gaul and conquered lands in the Middle East and North Africa. According to legend, while Caesar was in Egypt a large rug was brought into his tent. Rolled up inside was Egypt's 21-year-old queen, Cleopatra.

Cleopatra had herself smuggled into Caesar's tent because she was at war with her brother, the pharaoh. With Caesar's help, Cleopatra defeated her brother and became the ruler of Egypt.

But Rome soon brought that ancient civilization under its mighty influence.

When Caesar returned to Rome in 46 B.C., he had the support of the entire Roman army and the citizens of the empire. Because of his victories, the Senate made him the dictator of Rome. A dictator is a ruler who has absolute power and authority.

THE IDES OF MARCH

As dictator, Caesar took power away from the Senate. Many senators grew

187

angry when Caesar began wearing purple robes. Purple was the color said to have been worn by Rome's early kings. Some senators believed that Caesar wanted to make himself king. They decided that Caesar had to be stopped.

According to legend, Caesar received a warning from an old soothsayer, or a person who predicts the future. The soothsayer said: "Beware of the ides (īdz) of March." This was a name for March 15. Caesar did not pay attention to the warning.

On March 15 in 44 B.C., Caesar walked to the Senate. Waiting for him were a number of senators with daggers hidden beneath their tunics. As Caesar entered, senators rushed at him pretending to discuss important business. Suddenly they struck, stabbing Caesar countless times. Caesar's last words, to his old friend Brutus who was one of the murderers, were "*Et tu, Brute!*" which are the Latin words meaning "And you, also, Brutus!"

OCTAVIAN AUGUSTUS

The murder of Julius Caesar caused terrible unrest. For 17 years Rome was torn apart by a civil war. In a civil war, people within one country fight each other. Finally, in 27 B.C., Caesar's nephew Octavian won the civil war.

Like his uncle, Octavian was a popular general. The Senate gave Octavian

The death of Julius Caesar would cause a civil war. This painting shows his murderers rushing away triumphantly.

Octavian Augustus said, "All roads lead to Rome." Even the ruins of ancient Rome command admiration today.

the title of *Augustus*, which is a Latin word meaning "grand" or "honored one." *Augustus* was also a word used to describe the gods. Thus, with this new title, Octavian Augustus became a powerful godlike emperor in the minds of the Romans.

Octavian Augustus ruled the Roman Empire for 41 years. Near the end of his life he announced, "I found Rome a city of bricks and left it a city of marble." In addition to massive building projects, Octavian brought peace and good government to Rome. He carefully chose people to fill government jobs and made sure that the territories of the empire had fair governors.

THE *PAX ROMANA*

Octavian's rule marked the beginning of the *Pax* (paks) *Romana*. *Pax* is the Latin word for "peace." The *Pax Romana* lasted for about 200 years. During the time of the "Roman Peace," the empire reached its greatest extent.

Such growth caused trade to flourish. One ancient traveler wrote that there was an "endless flow of goods." Describing Rome during the *Pax Romana* he wrote:

Anyone who wants to behold all these goods must either journey through the whole world to see them or else come to this city [Rome]. . . . Whatever can not be seen here must not exist.

In this lesson you have read about the growth of the Roman Empire. Read on. In the next lesson you will learn about the rich legacy of ancient Rome.

Check Your Reading

1. How did Rome rule its territories?
2. Why was Caesar called a dictator?
3. **GEOGRAPHY SKILL:** What lands were added to Rome by A.D. 117?
4. **THINKING SKILL:** List three questions you could ask to learn the most about the *Pax Romana*.

4 The Legacy of Ancient Rome

READ TO LEARN

Key Vocabulary

architecture forum
Colosseum aqueduct
gladiator Romance language

Key People

Virgil

Read Aloud

From its center on the Italian peninsula, the Roman Empire reached in every direction. Millions of people looked upon Rome as the center of the world. Even today, more than 1,500 years after the height of its power, signs of Roman influence are still evident. Ancient Rome left the world a rich legacy.

Read for Purpose

1. **WHAT YOU KNOW:** What was the legacy of ancient Greek civilization?
2. **WHAT YOU WILL LEARN:** What were the achievements of the ancient Romans?

ARCHITECTURE

The Romans were among the greatest builders in the ancient world. They borrowed many ideas about art and architecture (är′ kə tek chər), or the science of building, from earlier civilizations. But the Romans also greatly expanded the understanding of architecture. From the Greeks and the Etruscans, for example, the Romans learned how to use columns and arches in buildings. The Romans improved on the arch by inventing the dome, or a roof formed by rounded arches.

The Romans also introduced new building materials, such as concrete. They made concrete by mixing lime and soil that would harden when dry. The use of concrete enabled Roman architects to build huge structures.

THE COLOSSEUM

Imagine that you have gone back in time. One early morning in A.D. 80, you are among the 50,000 Romans pouring into the new sports arena called the Colosseum. To celebrate its opening, chariot races will be held there every day for 100 days.

The Colosseum is an amazing building. Nothing ever built anywhere before compares to it. Even the pyramids of Egypt are dwarfed by the Roman Colosseum. It can even be filled with water for mock naval battles.

Special schools trained gladiators for combat. Only the best came to the Colosseum, which still stands as an impressive reminder of the past.

The shows in the Colosseum start early in the morning and last all day. But the shows here are not like the day-long theater festivals of ancient Greece. These Roman spectacles are usually bloody events.

Read what one Roman wrote about his visit to the Colosseum:

> I stopped in at a midday show, expecting fun, wit, and some relaxation . . . it was just the opposite. . . . In the morning men are thrown to the lions and the bears. The outcome is death; the fight is waged with sword and fire.

Not only lions and bears, but elephants and giraffes were also herded into the giant Colosseum. Sometimes gladiators fought these animals or one another. The word *gladiator* comes from the Latin word *gladius*, or sword. Most gladiators were slaves, prisoners of war, or condemned criminals. Gladiators were always expected to die in the Colosseum. These bloody events were considered entertainment.

A CITY OF MONUMENTS

The Colosseum was only one of many massive buildings in Rome. Ancient Rome was filled with such buildings. According to one historian, "Rome became the most spectacular

191

tourist attraction of the ancient world." Visitors came from faraway territories to see its 10,000 statues, 700 public pools, 500 fountains, and 37 monumental gates.

At the center of the city was the forum. Like the agoras in the city-states of ancient Greece, the Roman forum was the central marketplace. Architects designed magnificent public buildings to surround the forum.

After seeing Rome, many visitors went home and copied its splendor. They, too, surrounded themselves with domed buildings and fountains.

ROMAN ROADS AND AQUEDUCTS

Another important achievement of the ancient Romans was a network of roads. To link every part of the empire with Rome, miles and miles of roads were built. From about A. D. 100 to 150, the network of roads stretched from one end of the empire to the other.

Romans designed roads to last forever. They were built of heavy blocks that were set in layers of crushed stones and pebbles. In fact, Roman roads were still in use as recently as 100 years ago. Their stone foundations can be seen in parts of Europe today.

In addition to roads, Roman architects built another long-lasting network. Because Roman cities had grown into the largest and most populated in the world, water was sometimes scarce. Thus, the Romans had to find ways of bringing water into the cities.

The solution was to supply water from distant wells or natural springs. The Romans built stone structures, called aqueducts (ak′ wə dukts), to carry water. Aqueducts tunneled through mountains and crossed deep valleys. More than 200 aqueducts were built by the Romans. Many can still be seen today, as shown in the Chapter Opener on page 174.

DIAGRAM SKILL: Sturdy roads linked Rome with the rest of its empire. What materials were used to build Roman roads?

Flat paving stones

Curbstones

Drainage ditch

Top of road is curved to drain water

Flat slabs in mortar

Pebbles

Concrete and gravel

A ROMAN ROAD

THE IMPORTANCE OF THE LATIN LANGUAGE

As the Roman Empire expanded, the Latin language reached all parts of the empire. Latin is the basis for the modern languages of French, Spanish, Portuguese, Italian, and Romanian. These Latin-based languages are called the Romance languages. As the chart on this page shows, many words in the Romance languages are alike. What else can you learn from the chart?

The chart shows that even the English language has gained words from Latin. In fact, most European languages use the original Latin alphabet. You may remember that the Greeks borrowed their alphabet from the Phoenicians. The Greek alphabet was then borrowed and changed by the Romans.

Though most people in ancient Rome did not know how to read or write, Rome developed an important body of literature. The Roman poet Virgil greatly admired Homer's epics. Emperor Octavian paid Virgil a large sum of money to write an epic about Rome's beginnings. Virgil spent ten years writing an important work called the *Aeneid* (i nē' id). The *Aeneid* traces the beginnings of Rome far back before Romulus and Remus to the heroes of the Trojan War.

The following lines are from the *Aeneid*. What do you think Octavian would have thought about them?

> *Rome is glorious . . . as long as rivers shall run down to the sea, or shadows touch the mountain slopes, or stars gaze downward, so long shall your honor, your name, your praises last.*

As you can imagine, Octavian would have liked such praise for Rome.

THE INFLUENCE OF LATIN

Latin	liber	schola
French	livre	école
Italian	libro	scuola
Spanish	libro	escuela
Portuguese	livro	escola

English	book	school

CHART SKILL: The chart shows the similarity among the Romance languages. What English word is like the Latin word for *book*?

THE GIFTS OF ROME

Civilization reached new heights in the days of ancient Rome. From simple beginnings the Romans had developed a powerful empire.

In this lesson you have read about the legacy of ancient Rome. The gifts of Rome were truly the result of an advanced civilization. Think for a moment of the earlier civilizations you have studied. Even the mighty Greeks did not expand as far or rule as long as the Romans.

Check Your Reading

1. What are Romance languages? Why and how are they alike?
2. Do you think that the aqueduct was a useful invention? Why?
3. **GEOGRAPHY SKILL:** How do you think the Roman roads helped the growth of civilization?
4. **THINKING SKILL:** Compare and contrast the legacies of ancient Rome and ancient Greece.

5 The Birth of Christianity

Key Vocabulary

New Testament
Christianity
apostle
bishop
pope

Key People

Jesus
Paul
Peter
Constantine

Key Places

Palestine
Bethlehem
Nazareth

Read Aloud

Fear not; for, behold, I bring you good news of a great joy . . . for to you is born in the city of David a Savior, who is Christ the Lord. And this will be a sign for you; you will find the babe wrapped in swaddling clothes, lying in a manger.

These words, taken from the writings of an important new religion, announce the birth of a child. Though its conditions were humble and far away from the center of the Roman Empire, this child's birth would lead to important changes.

Read for Purpose

1. **WHAT YOU KNOW:** Why is religion an important part of culture?
2. **WHAT YOU WILL LEARN:** What are the teachings of the religion known as Christianity?

THE LAND OF PALESTINE

According to the Bible, during the rule of Caesar Augustus the leaders of the Roman Empire wanted to know its total population. They made it law for everyone to be counted.

Now it came to pass in those days that a decree [law] went forth from Augustus that all the people of the world were to be counted.

Obeying the decree, people journeyed to large towns in the empire where Roman officials could count them. In **Palestine**, a Jewish couple named Mary and Joseph traveled to the city of **Bethlehem**. Palestine was the land of the ancient Hebrews. You may recall that in earlier times it was known as Canaan. Now, however, it was called Palestine and was ruled by Rome. Most of the people who lived in Palestine were Jews. Like other Jews, Mary and Joseph had to be counted.

The Jewish people were very different from their Roman conquerers. As you read in Chapter 4, they were monotheists, believing in one God. The Romans, on the other hand, were like the ancient Greeks and believed in many gods.

JESUS OF NAZARETH

While visiting Bethlehem, Mary's son, Jesus, was born. Though the exact year of his birth is not known, historians think it was about 6 B.C.

Much of our knowledge of Jesus's life comes to us from the New Testament of the Bible. The New Testament tells the story of early Christianity. Christianity is the religion founded by Jesus and based on his teachings.

According to the New Testament, Jesus grew up in the Palestinian town called Nazareth and was raised under the laws of Judaism. As a boy he studied Judaism's sacred writings and loved to talk with his teachers about its laws. According to the New Testament:

Jesus's parents went to Jerusalem every year at the . . . Passover [Jewish feast remembering the escape of the Jews from Egypt]. *And when he was twelve years old, they went up to Jerusalem as was their custom. After three days they found Jesus in the temple, sitting among the teachers, both listening to them, and asking them questions. And all who heard him were amazed at his understanding and his answers.*

This painting shows Jesus as a small child in his father's workshop.

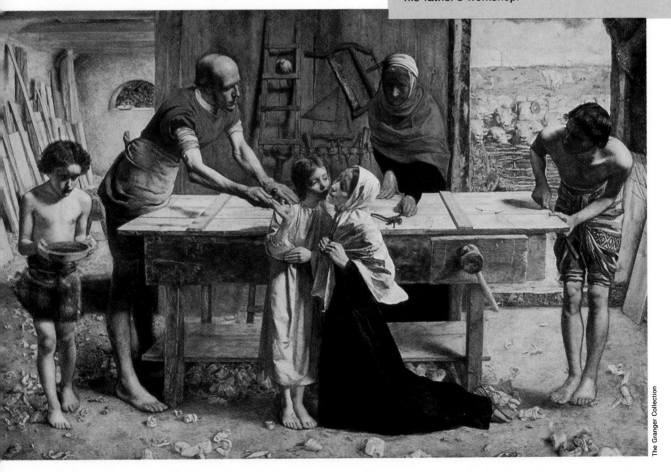

The Granger Collection

When Jesus was about 30 years old, he began a period of teaching that lasted approximately three years. He traveled from village to village in Palestine, telling people his ideas. Huge crowds of both men and women gathered to hear him speak. Jesus's closest followers were a group of 12 men called the **apostles** (ə pos' əlz), who went everywhere with him. Many of the apostles would help organize the Christian Church after Jesus's death.

THE TEACHINGS OF JESUS

Jesus's teachings were rooted in Judaism. Like other Jewish teachers, he taught that there was one God. Jesus urged people to obey the commandments handed down from Moses. According to the New Testament, a learned man asked Jesus, "Master, which is the greatest commandment in the Law [the Ten Commandments]?" Jesus replied:

> *Thou shalt love the Lord thy God with thy whole heart and with thy whole soul and with thy whole mind. And the second is like it. Thou shalt love thy neighbor as thyself.*

In his teachings, Jesus stressed love for God and love for other people. According to the New Testament, Jesus gave an important sermon, or speech, to a crowd that had gathered one day on a hillside. Jesus's teachings from this occasion are known as the Sermon on the Mount. Read part of what Jesus told the crowd in the chart below.

The Granger Collection

Jesus's Sermon on the Mount is an important part of the New Testament.

SERMON ON THE MOUNT

Blessed are the poor in spirit, for theirs is the kingdom of heaven. Blessed are they that mourn, for they shall be comforted. Blessed are the meek, for they shall inherit the earth. . . . But I say to you . . . to him who strikes you on the right cheek, *offer the other also, and from him who takes away your coat, let him have your cloak also. Give to him that asks of you. . . . as you wish that men would do to you, do so to them. . . .*

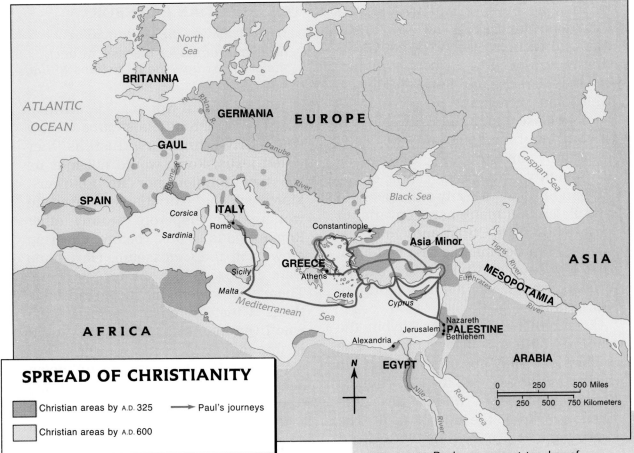

SPREAD OF CHRISTIANITY

- ■ Christian areas by A.D. 325 → Paul's journeys
- □ Christian areas by A.D. 600

MAP SKILL: Paul was a great teacher of Christianity. As the map shows, his journeys took him to many places. What islands did he pass through on his journeys?

The teachings of Jesus won him many followers. But his teachings brought him enemies, too. The large crowds Jesus attracted worried both Roman and Jewish officials. The Roman government in Palestine was afraid that Jesus was organizing a revolt against Rome. Some people thought Jesus wanted to be king because his teachings described the coming of God's Kingdom.

In about A. D. 30, Jesus was arrested and taken to the Roman governor. On the day of his arrest, Jesus was condemned to die. He was executed according to Roman custom by crucifixion, or being nailed to a cross. The followers of Jesus believe that he rose from the dead on the next Sunday.

THE SPREAD OF CHRISTIANITY

After these events, the followers of Jesus set out to spread his teachings. They spread out across the Roman Empire and formed small groups of Christians. Together, the apostles set up the first Christian churches.

A person who was very successful at spreading the teachings of Jesus, however, was Paul. Paul had never known Jesus but felt strongly about his teachings. As the map on this page shows, Paul traveled far and wide in order to share what he called "the good news."

On his long journeys, Paul wrote letters that make up part of the New Testament. In them, he declared that Christianity was open to all people including Jews, Greeks, and Romans. He also welcomed women and people from all social classes, including slaves.

Both Paul and the apostle Peter eventually brought the message of Christianity to the very center of the Roman Empire—the city of Rome. Paul and Peter won many new converts, or new believers, to Christianity in Rome. There, Peter became the first bishop of that new church. A bishop is a church official who leads a large group of Christians.

Eventually, every major city in the empire would have its own bishop. The bishop in Rome, however, became the most important of these officials. Later, Christians would give the Bishop of Rome the title of pope. The word *pope* comes from the Latin word *papa*, meaning "father."

THE CHRISTIAN EMPEROR

If the Tiber overflows, if there is drought, famine, or disease, at once the cry goes up—the Christians to the lions!

These frightful words are a record of how the Roman officials came to deal with early Christians. Just as they killed Jesus, Rome would not tolerate the new religion nor its followers. Moreover, the Christians refused to worship the emperors or any other Roman gods. Thus, before cheering crowds in the Colosseum, Christians were forced to go out on the field. There, lions were let loose to attack them. Great numbers of Christians who lived in ancient Rome were killed in this manner.

In A. D. 312, however, an unknown general named Constantine became the emperor of Rome. A Christian bishop wrote that Constantine favored Christianity. The bishop wrote about an event that he claimed had happened to Constantine. He wrote that one night Jesus appeared to Constantine in a dream. Jesus told him to make a cross and carry it into battle.

This is how a museum in Italy displays the remains of what once was a towering statue of Constantine.

The next morning, Constantine ordered artisans to build a cross, the symbol of Christianity, and to paint a cross on his soldiers' shields. As a result, the bishop wrote, Constantine's army won a mighty victory and Constantine was made emperor of Rome. You can look at the great arch that was built to celebrate Constantine's victories in the Unit Opener on page 137.

As a result of these victories, an important event occurred in A. D. 313. The recently crowned emperor Constantine gratefully announced the end to the killing of Christians in the empire. Constantine also gave "both to the Christians and to all people freedom to follow the religion they choose." As for himself, Constantine became a Christian. This was an important turning point for the history of Christianity. In A. D. 395, Christianity became the official religion of the Roman Empire.

Today, Christianity is one of the world's major religions. These young people are preparing to become adult members of their church.

THE FALL OF ROME

Christianity continued to flourish after the death of Constantine, but the Roman Empire gradually lost its lands and wealth. Invaders from the north began to conquer the empire. These people from central Europe used mountain passes through the Alps and even Roman roads to invade the Italian peninsula. Finally, in A. D. 476, the city of Rome fell to invaders.

But the glory of Rome was not forgotten. A modern English historian has written:

Into the Roman Empire, all life of the ancient world was gathered. Out of it, all the life of the modern world arose.

As you have read, the history of ancient Rome is the story of how a small republic grew into a vast empire. Stretching across parts of three continents, it gained the riches and legacies of earlier civilizations.

Life would be very different without the unifying power of the Roman Empire. But civilization in Europe would continue to grow in exciting new directions. In the next chapter you will learn how Europe faced its new challenges.

Check Your Reading

1. Why is the New Testament important to Christians?
2. What do the teachings of Judaism and Christianity have in common?
3. Why do you think the Romans feared the growth of Christianity?
4. **THINKING SKILL:** What goal did Constantine achieve with his decision to let Christians practice their religion?

IMPORTANT EVENTS

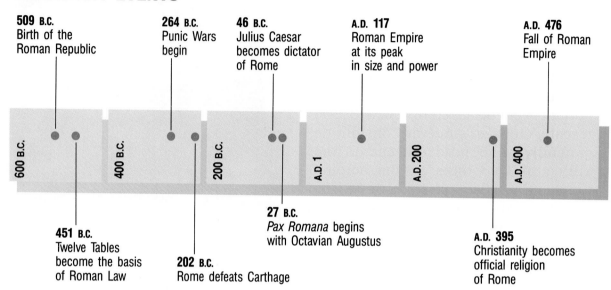

509 B.C.
Birth of the
Roman Republic

264 B.C.
Punic Wars
begin

46 B.C.
Julius Caesar
becomes dictator
of Rome

A.D. 117
Roman Empire
at its peak
in size and power

A.D. 476
Fall of Roman
Empire

600 B.C. | 400 B.C. | 200 B.C. | A.D. 1 | A.D. 200 | A.D. 400

451 B.C.
Twelve Tables
become the basis
of Roman Law

202 B.C.
Rome defeats Carthage

27 B.C.
Pax Romana begins
with Octavian Augustus

A.D. 395
Christianity becomes
official religion
of Rome

PEOPLE TO KNOW

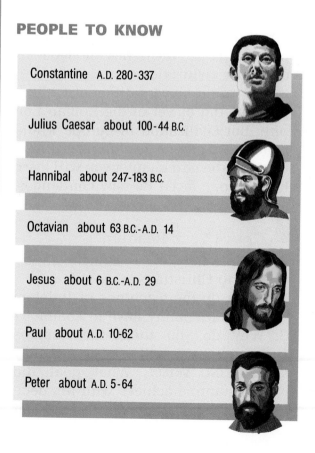

Constantine   A.D. 280-337

Julius Caesar   about 100-44 B.C.

Hannibal   about 247-183 B.C.

Octavian   about 63 B.C.-A.D. 14

Jesus   about 6 B.C.-A.D. 29

Paul   about A.D. 10-62

Peter   about A.D. 5-64

IDEAS TO REMEMBER

- Ancient Rome developed on the Italian peninsula. The peninsula was the home of three different early groups—the Etruscans, Latins, and Greek colonists.
- Rome set up the world's first republic in 509 B.C. The Twelve Tables were the basis of Roman law.
- Ancient Rome grew into a vast empire. Octavian's rule marked the beginning of the *Pax Romana* which lasted for about 200 years.
- Ancient Rome left a rich cultural legacy. Rome itself was known to be a city of monuments.
- A new religion called Christianity was born in Palestine. Based on the teachings of Jesus, Christianity had it roots in Judaism and belief in one God.

REVIEWING VOCABULARY

architecture   Pax Romana
basin   plebeian
Christianity   pope
dictator   republic
patrician   Romance language

Number a sheet of paper from 1 to 10. Beside each number write the word or term from the list above that best completes each sentence.

1. A ____ is a form of government in which citizens choose their leaders.
2. ____ means "Roman Peace" and refers to a period of peace and prosperity that lasted almost 200 years.
3. French, Italian, and Spanish are called ____ because they all grew from Latin.
4. A ____ is a geographical term referring to a region that is drained by a river and its tributaries.
5. Because they were not wealthy, the ____ had few rights in the early days of the Roman Republic.
6. Only after he became a ____, or absolute ruler, was Caesar able to take power away from the Senate.
7. The dome and the arch were two important Roman contributions to ____, or the science of building.
8. ____ were members of wealthy families who had total control of the Senate during the early Roman Republic.
9. From its humble beginnings in Palestine, ____ grew to become one of the world's chief religions.
10. Christians gave the Bishop of Rome the special title of ____.

REVIEWING FACTS

1. How did the early Romans come into contact with Greek civilization?
2. List three advantages Rome gained by defeating Carthage.
3. Name two results of the murder of Julius Caesar.
4. Give two reasons why the emperor Octavian adopted the name "Augustus."
5. List three ways in which Jesus's ideas spread throughout the Roman Empire.

WRITING ABOUT MAIN IDEAS

1. **Writing a Letter:** Imagine that you are a Roman citizen. Write a letter to a pen pal who lives in another part of the empire. Write about three things that unite the distant parts of the Roman Empire. Then, describe the city of Rome.
2. **Writing About Perspectives:** Write a short paragraph explaining some of the reasons for the conflict that existed between Christianity and the Roman Empire.

BUILDING SKILLS: READING CONTOUR MAPS

Use the contour map on page 179 to answer the following questions.

1. What are contour lines? What is the contour interval on this map?
2. What does the contour map show? How does it show it?
3. What is the highest elevation shown? What is the lowest?
4. Who might find a contour map useful? Why?

REVIEWING VOCABULARY

assembly	philosophy
dictator	plebeian
democracy	polis
monarchy	republic
peninsula	tragedy

Number a sheet of paper from 1 to 10. Beside each number write the word or term from the above list that best matches the statement or definition.

1. Because they were not rich, this group had few rights in Rome's early days.
2. A kind of play in which life is treated seriously and usually ends very sadly.
3. The United States House of Representatives is an example of this lawmaking body, which is basic to all world democracies.
4. The ancient Greeks were the first to practice this form of government which allowed everyone to join in the lawmaking process.
5. An absolute ruler who holds all authority and power in government.
6. This form of government, in which citizens choose their own leaders, prospered in ancient Rome.
7. The study of ideas and the search for truth was first developed by the ancient Greeks.
8. Because it places all power in the hands of a king or queen, this form of government was rejected by the ancient Greeks.
9. Made up of a city and the surrounding land, this type of political unit was typical in the "Aegean World."
10. A special kind of landform that is surrounded by water on three sides.

WRITING ABOUT THE UNIT

1. **Writing a List:** Rome spread its mighty civilization throughout Europe and the Mediterranean region. Write a list of sentences that describe some key characteristics of Roman civilization.
2. **Writing About Perspectives:** Reread the section on pages 190-191 about the Colosseum and gladiators. Write a paragraph describing how you would feel if you were watching one of these spectacles.

ACTIVITIES

1. **Developing a Strategy:** Imagine that you are Hannibal, the great Carthaginian general. You are trying to decide how to attack Rome. Draw a map of the area and then write a strategy that you will use in your attack. Draw the route of your attack on the map. Show alternate routes in a different color.
2. **Working Together to Prepare a Report:** As a group make a list of several important ancient Greeks or Romans to study. Divide into small groups and have each group research one person from the list. Decide what you would like to learn about each person.

    Then use encyclopedias, biographical dictionaries, and biographies to gather information. One member of the group can make a time line of the person's life. Other members can write a report. Then one member can present it to the class. Staple the reports together to form a book titled "Who's Who in the Ancient World" for your classroom library.

THE QUALITIES OF HANNIBAL

The Roman historian Livy wrote the following account about Hannibal in about 20 B.C.

*U*pon his first arrival in Spain, Hannibal became the center of attention in the whole army. . . . They saw the same energetic expression and features in Hannibal as were characteristic in his father. But very quickly the similarity to his father was not an important factor in winning approval. Never were such high abilities for obeying and commanding— very different qualities—combined to such a degree in a single person as in Hannibal. It was not easy to decide whether the army or the general [Hannibal's father] loved him best. It was under the loyal son [Hannibal] that the soldiers showed great confidence and daring. He seemed completely fearless in undertaking dangerous routes; he was cautious in following them. . . .

BUILDING SKILLS: ASKING QUESTIONS

Use the account above to answer the following questions.

1. What are two questions that Livy was trying to answer about Hannibal? Why do you think these questions would have interested Livy?

2. What are two facts you already know about Hannibal?

3. Which of these questions would help you learn the most about Hannibal?
   a. When was he born?
   b. How did he feel about his soldiers?
   c. When did he first arrive in Spain?

4. What are two questions you could ask to learn more about Hannibal?

LINKING PAST, PRESENT, AND FUTURE

You have learned about two great civilizations, Greece and Rome, from the standpoint of a person living in the twentieth century. How do you think future historians will view our civilization? List the pluses and minuses that they are likely to write about us. Do you think historians of the future will talk about the "fall" of American civilization in the same way that we talk about the fall of Rome? Why or why not?

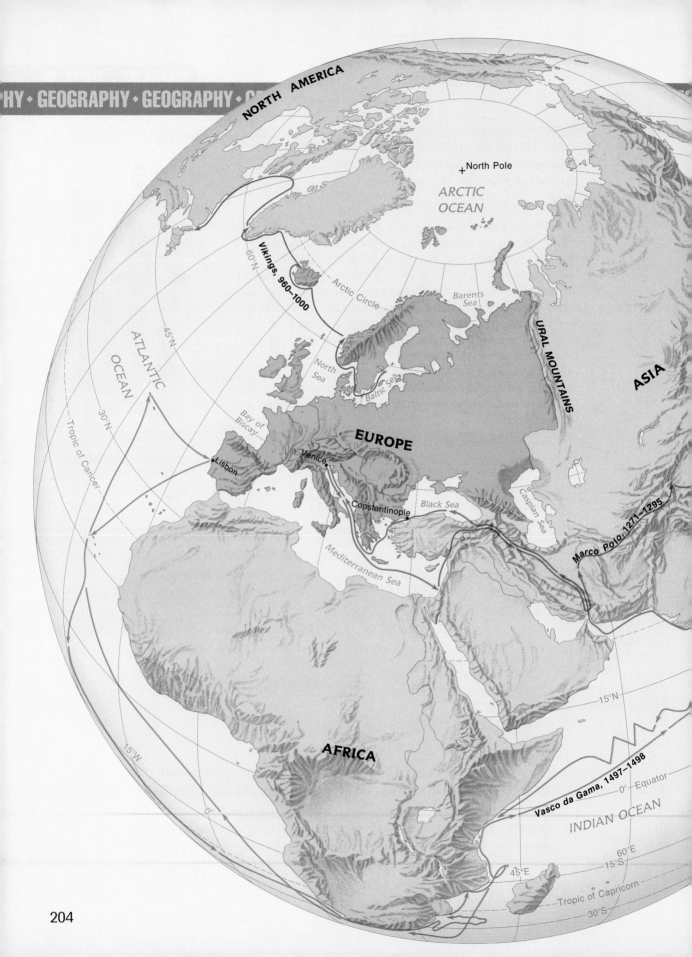

North Pole

ARCTIC
OCEAN

60°N

Vikings, 960–1000

Arctic Circle

Barents
Sea

URAL MOUNTAINS

ASIA

ATLANTIC
OCEAN

45°N

North
Sea

30°N

Baltic Sea

EUROPE

Tropic of Cancer

Bay of
Biscay

Lisbon

Venice

Constantinople

Black Sea

Caspian Sea

Marco Polo, 1271–1295

Mediterranean Sea

15°N

15°W

AFRICA

Vasco da Gama, 1497–1498

0°

0° Equator

INDIAN OCEAN

60°E

45°E

15°S

Tropic of Capricorn

30°S

204

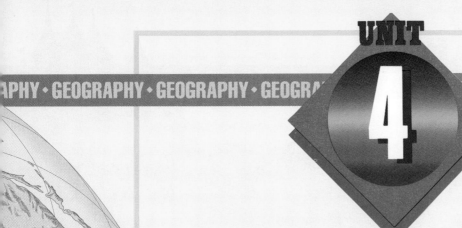

UNIT 4

THE GROWTH OF EUROPE

WHERE WE ARE

As the map shows, in Unit 4 you will continue your adventure through the world around us. Find the continent of Europe on the map. Note that this great land stretches from the Atlantic Ocean to the Ural Mountains. Building upon the rich legacies of ancient Greece and ancient Rome, Europe was the scene of amazing activity.

Look closely at the map. Note that three long journeys led Europeans far beyond their homeland. You will learn that each of these journeys was very important. As they reached out to the rest of the world, European civilization was undergoing many changes.

Khanbalik

205

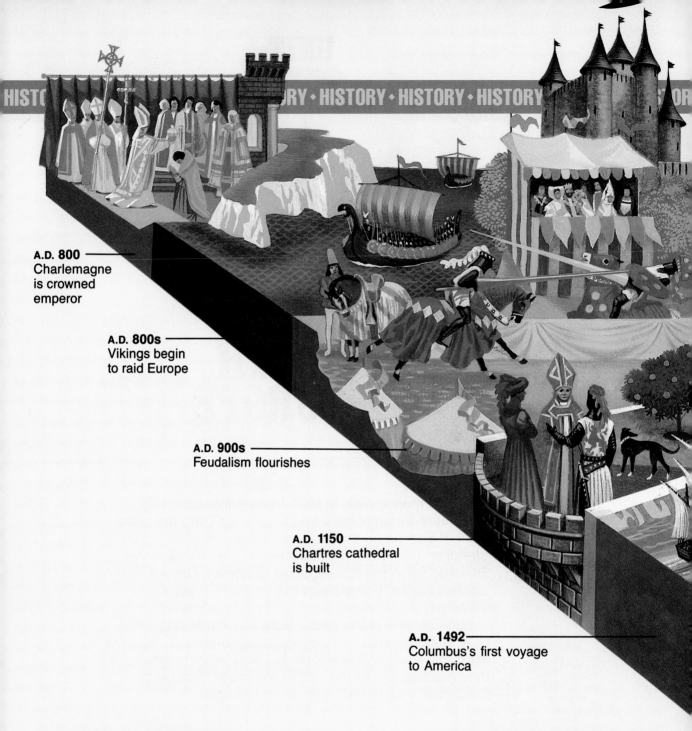

A.D. 800
Charlemagne
is crowned
emperor

A.D. 800s
Vikings begin
to raid Europe

A.D. 900s
Feudalism flourishes

A.D. 1150
Chartres cathedral
is built

A.D. 1492
Columbus's first voyage
to America

WHAT HAPPENED

The fall of the Roman Empire
in A.D. 476 marked the end of ancient
times. Gradually, a new kind of European
civilization took shape. As the time line shows,
many important events changed the course of
European history. In this unit you will read about
these events and the many men and women who
led Europe during a period of great change.

A.D. 1517
Luther leads the
Reformation

A.D. 1609
Galileo proves the
heliocentric theory

206

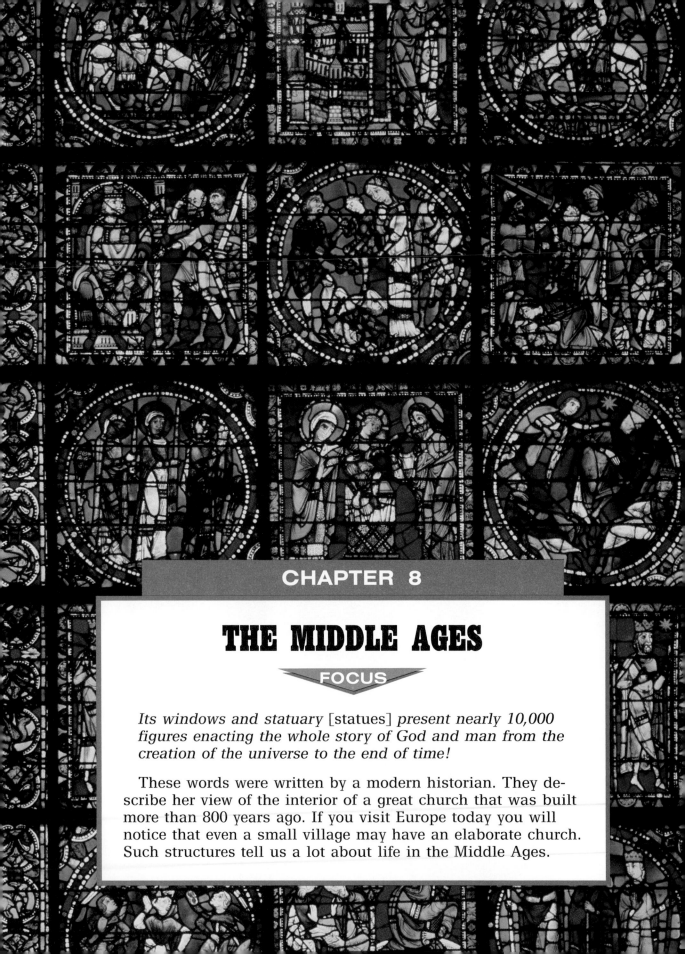

CHAPTER 8

THE MIDDLE AGES

FOCUS

Its windows and statuary [statues] present nearly 10,000 figures enacting the whole story of God and man from the creation of the universe to the end of time!

These words were written by a modern historian. They describe her view of the interior of a great church that was built more than 800 years ago. If you visit Europe today you will notice that even a small village may have an elaborate church. Such structures tell us a lot about life in the Middle Ages.

1 The Geography of Europe

READ TO LEARN

Key Vocabulary

Gulf Stream
North Atlantic
Drift

Key Places

Eurasia
Ural Mountains
Caucasus Mountains
Jutland Peninsula
Scandinavian Peninsula
Kola Peninsula
Carpathian Mountains

Iceland
British Isles
Pyrenees
Alps

Read Aloud

You are about to start a journey that will take you across the continent of Europe. In this lesson you will explore the varied geography of a region that today includes more than 30 countries. Later in this chapter you will also travel through nearly 1,000 years of history.

Read for Purpose

1. **WHAT YOU KNOW:** Where is the continent of Europe?
2. **WHAT YOU WILL LEARN:** What are Europe's main geographic features?

THE CONTINENT OF EUROPE

As you know, Europe is one of the seven continents. Did you know that it is also part of a large landmass called Eurasia? Eurasia includes the continents of Europe and Asia. The Ural Mountains and the Caucasus Mountains are the boundaries between these two continents. Only about one fifth of the Eurasian landmass, however, is Europe. The European part of Eurasia is a continent of great diversity. In this lesson you will read about Europe's chief landforms and bodies of water.

Europe is the second-smallest continent, yet it has a population larger than any other continent except Asia. Although it is small, Europe is a land of many nations. The countries of Europe range in size from Russia, the largest country in the world, to Vatican City, the smallest. Yet there are more world powers in Europe than on any other continent.

A LAND OF CONTRASTS

What is the physical geography of Europe? Europe has regions of low-

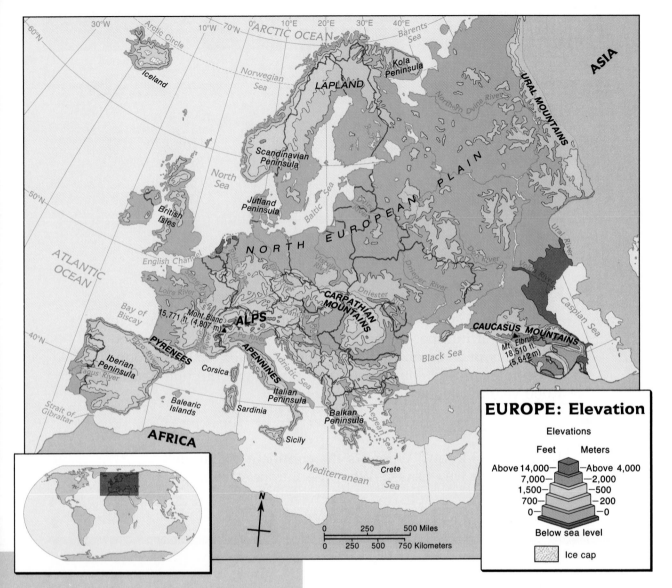

EUROPE: Elevation

Elevations

Feet — Meters

Above 14,000	Above 4,000
7,000	2,000
1,500	500
700	200
0	0

Below sea level

Ice cap

MAP SKILL: Mountain ranges cross Europe. Which range is higher, the Alps or Pyrenees?

lying plains, high plateaus, and towering mountains. Some countries are islands, others are landlocked nations. Many have at least one border on a sea or ocean. No part of the continent, however, is more than a few hundred miles from the sea.

You have already learned about some parts of Europe. In Chapters 6 and 7 you read about civilizations that grew up on the Balkan, Italian, and Iberian peninsulas. These peninsulas are Europe's southernmost lands and stretch into the Mediterranean Sea.

Important peninsulas are found in northern Europe, too. As the map above shows, the Jutland Peninsula divides the North Sea from the Baltic Sea. Farther north lie the Scandinavian and Kola peninsulas. How many other peninsulas can you find? Is it any wonder that Europe is often called "a peninsula of peninsulas"?

The Danube River flows from Central Europe to the Black Sea. Since ancient times, it has been an important transportation route.

Europe includes many islands, too. In the north are Iceland and the British Isles. Many small islands dot the Baltic Sea. Find these islands on the map on page 210. What are the largest islands of the Mediterranean Sea?

EUROPE'S LANDFORMS

Some of the world's most fertile farmland is found on the huge plain that sweeps across Europe. Called the North European Plain, it extends from the Atlantic Ocean in the west all the way to the Ural Mountains in the east.

Many mountain ranges form the southern boundary of the North European Plain. Find the Pyrenees, the Alps, and the Carpathian Mountains on the map on the opposite page. The highest mountain peaks in Europe are found in these mountain ranges.

You may remember that Hannibal crossed the treacherous Alps in order to invade the Roman Empire in the third century B.C. The Alps are also world-famous for their beauty. The Alps are a region of majestic snow-covered mountains and deep valleys, of broad glaciers and long, narrow lakes. The words *alps* and *alpine* are often used to describe other mountain ranges in the world.

EUROPE'S CHIEF RIVERS

Many of Europe's great rivers have their sources in the Alps, the Pyrenees, and the Carpathians. Europe has many navigable rivers. A navigable river is deep and wide enough so that large ships and boats can travel on it. Navigable rivers serve as natural highways for transporting goods and people.

Study the map on page 210 and name some of Europe's chief rivers. As you can see, Europe's longest river is the Volga. It flows across the North European Plain to the Caspian Sea. The Danube, Europe's second-longest river, winds from highlands in western Europe through the Carpathians to the Black Sea in the east. The Rhine and the Rhone, for example, also have their sources in the Alps. Do they flow into the same body of water?

Each of these rivers flows in a different direction to a different sea. The Rhine flows north and west into the North Sea. After the Rhone River starts in the Alps, it forms Lake Geneva, the largest of the Alpine lakes. Then it flows south to the Mediterranean Sea.

MANY CLIMATES

You have already learned that the southern regions of Europe, those areas bordering the Mediterranean Sea, have a mild climate. But even in the north—for example, in the British Isles—the climate is also quite mild.

To understand why, think back to what you learned about climate and ocean currents in Chapter 1. Warm climate can result from the effect of ocean currents on temperature. Remember that warm currents in the oceans heat the air above them. Winds carry the temperate, or mild, air to the lands they blow across.

The climate of northwestern Europe is mild because of warm ocean currents flowing toward it. The Gulf Stream flows north and east through the Atlantic Ocean from the warm waters of the Gulf of Mexico. The Gulf Stream joins the North Atlantic Drift. The North Atlantic Drift flows near the British Isles. Westerly winds carry the temperate air to the British Isles and other parts of western Europe. Thus, temperatures are higher than they would normally be in these latitudes.

Not all of Europe has a mild climate, however. Scandinavia, especially north of the Arctic Circle, and eastern Europe have very cold temperatures. Look at the graph showing the average monthly temperatures for two large European cities. Are their average monthly temperatures similar?

As the graph shows, temperatures in Warsaw, Poland, are a lot cooler than temperatures in London, England. How do you explain this? Remember that eastern Europe does not benefit from the North Atlantic Drift. Thus, inland countries such as Poland tend to have cooler climates.

THE STAGE IS SET

Europe's rich geographic features encouraged the growth of European civilization. Its navigable rivers and mild climate attracted groups of energetic and daring people. Building upon

GRAPH SKILL: Using the graph, tell which city has a milder winter.

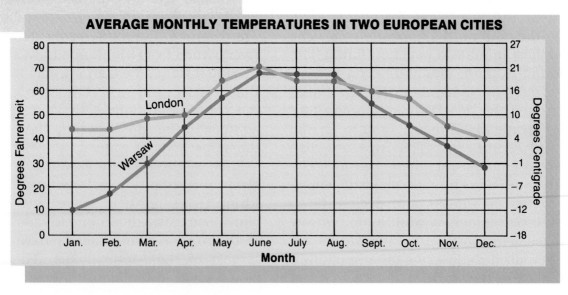

AVERAGE MONTHLY TEMPERATURES IN TWO EUROPEAN CITIES

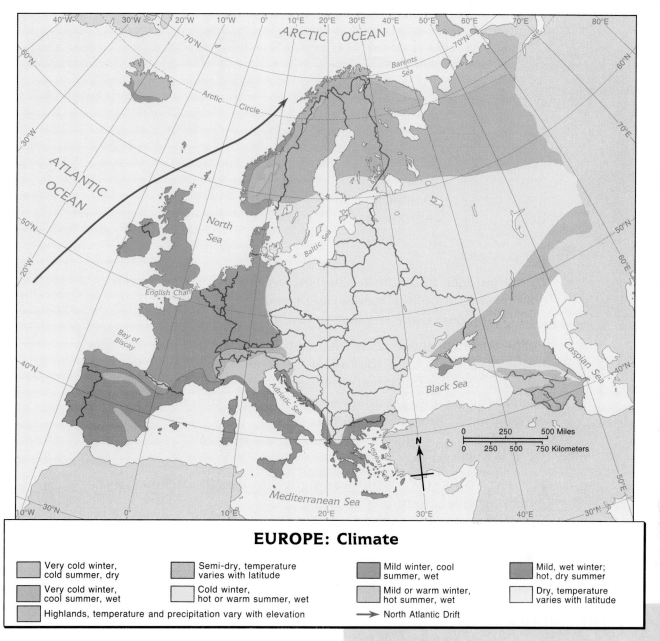

EUROPE: Climate

Very cold winter, cold summer, dry	Semi-dry, temperature varies with latitude
Very cold winter, cool summer, wet	Cold winter, hot or warm summer, wet
Highlands, temperature and precipitation vary with elevation	North Atlantic Drift
Mild winter, cool summer, wet	Mild, wet winter; hot, dry summer
Mild or warm winter, hot summer, wet	Dry, temperature varies with latitude

MAP SKILL: Europe has a wide range of climates. Which countries are affected by the North Atlantic Drift?

the legacy of earlier European civilizations, these people would flourish on the European continent.

Check Your Reading

1. Why is Europe called "a peninsula of peninsulas"?
2. What are Europe's chief mountain ranges and rivers?

3. **GEOGRAPHY SKILL:** Why does London, England, have milder winters than most east European cities?
4. **THINKING SKILL:** Look at the picture at the top of page 211. What does it tell you about the geography of Central Europe?

2 Living in the Middle Ages

READ TO LEARN

Key Vocabulary

Middle Ages	vassal
feudalism	serf
lord	manor
fief	knight

Key People

Charlemagne

Read Aloud

In the villages and country houses, in the fields and in the countryside, on every road—death, sorrow, slaughter, fires, and crying. All Gaul smoked in one great funeral pyre.

The writer of these sorrowful words tells us what it was like to live in Europe after the fall of the Roman Empire in the fifth century. The Roman government and army no longer existed to protect the people. Invaders swept in like a sudden storm, leaving lands and homes in ruins.

Read for Purpose

1. **WHAT YOU KNOW:** What was daily life like in ancient Greece and ancient Rome?
2. **WHAT YOU WILL LEARN:** How did people live during the Middle Ages?

THE MIDDLE AGES BEGIN

As you know, the first civilizations of Europe were those of ancient Greece and ancient Rome. You may remember that these civilizations lost their importance by the third and fourth centuries A. D. By the end of the fifth century, however, Europeans were already beginning to rebuild.

This period of time is known to historians as the Middle Ages. The Middle Ages began around A.D. 500 and lasted for about 1,000 years. The time line in the Unit Opener on pages 206–207 shows some key events of the Middle Ages.

A GREAT EMPEROR

In the sixth century a group of people known as the Franks began to establish a powerful kingdom in Europe. The Franks had lived on the North European Plain for centuries. Year by year, the Franks conquered neighboring people and extended their power.

214

By the late 700s a large part of Europe was under their control.

Charlemagne (shär′ lə mān), or Charles the Great, was one of the Franks' greatest rulers. In fact, people of Charlemagne's time called him "the greatest man of all those living." Charlemagne ruled from 768 to 814. During his 46-year rule, he led more than 50 major military campaigns and nearly doubled the size of his kingdom. In doing so, he united a great variety of European people under the same government.

The height of Charlemagne's power came on Christmas Day in the year 800. On that day Pope Leo III placed a jeweled crown on Charlemagne's head and declared him emperor. This was an important turning point in European history. For the first time since the end of the Roman Empire, Europe had an all-powerful emperor.

Charlemagne governed his empire from a castle at Aachen (ä′ kən). Find Aachen on the map of the Frankish Empire on this page. For his court in Aachen, Charlemagne invited Europe's best scholars. There was a music teacher from Italy, a poet from Spain, and many others. Charlemagne's court became an important center of learning. If you were to visit Aachen today, you would find the church that Charlemagne built in the center of a modern city.

THE MIGHTY VIKINGS

"From the rage of the Northmen, O Lord, save us!" This prayer was said in Christian churches after Charlemagne's death in 814. The Franks were being attacked by northern raiders.

The Northmen, also called Vikings, were skillful sailors and fierce warriors

MAP SKILL: One scribe wrote that the great "Charlemagne had a king's face," and "could command his armies to conquer with a nod." Did Charlemagne conquer Spain or Italy?

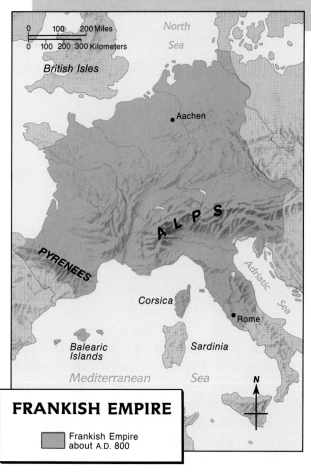

FRANKISH EMPIRE

Frankish Empire about A.D. 800

215

Archaeologists have found evidence of Viking ships and armor throughout northern Europe. Vikings terrorized Europe for many years.

were sleeping. With amazing speed, they attacked churches and homes and killed many people. Then the Vikings sailed away, preparing to strike elsewhere.

For 250 years Europe was terrorized by such raids. By the middle of the eleventh century, however, the Vikings began to settle down. They became traders instead of raiders. Some Vikings became brave explorers. As you may recall, the Vikings reached North America about 500 years before Christopher Columbus.

FEUDALISM

The Vikings left Europe a legacy of fear. No community felt safe unless guarded by soldiers. Peasants could not work in their fields without protection. During this time of unrest, a new way of organizing and governing society arose. This system was called feudalism (fūd′ əl iz əm).

To help restore order, kings granted large pieces of land to important nobles, or lords, in exchange for their loyalty. This gift of land was called a fief (fēf). In return for the fief, the lord promised to fight and to provide other services for the king. However, the lord was not able to do all this by himself.

In return for a promise to fight when needed, a lord would grant parts of his fief to less powerful nobles, or vassals. Vassals had to fight in the lord's army when called.

Most people during the Middle Ages were not lords and vassals. By far, the largest number of people were serfs who lived and worked on the land belonging to the nobles. Serfs were not free, but they were not quite slaves either. Unlike the slaves of ancient Egypt and ancient Greece, serfs could not be

from Scandinavia. From their home ports, the Vikings could easily reach the British Isles and mainland Europe.

The Vikings were daring raiders whose methods were speed and surprise. The Vikings slipped into villages when it was dark and people

216

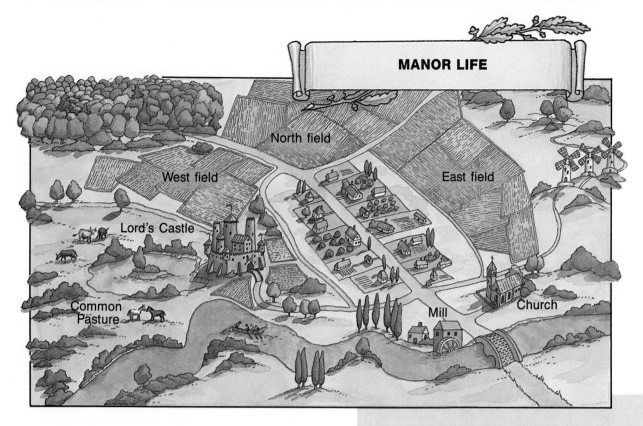

MANOR LIFE

North field

West field

East field

Lord's Castle

Common Pasture

Mill

Church

bought, sold, or traded to another lord. Yet serfs "belonged" to the land and could not leave it without the lord's permission. Not even a wedding could take place without the lord's approval!

In return for the lord's protection and the use of the lord's land, serfs had to pay a great price. For example, serfs might have to work three days a week for the lord, tilling his fields, repairing his buildings, or running his mill. Women often worked in the noble's house, spinning or weaving.

MANOR LIFE

For most Europeans, life during the Middle Ages was based on the manor. A manor was a large farming estate where nobles and serfs lived and worked. A manor was a self-sufficient economic unit. Almost everything needed was either grown or made on the manor. There were few towns or cities in Europe at this time.

Clothing, for example, was made from the wool of sheep raised on the manor. Blacksmiths made tools and weapons. Other skilled workers, such as masons and carpenters, lived and worked on the manor. You can find the mill where grain was turned to flour in the diagram on this page. What jobs would you have wanted if you lived on a manor?

THE MAKING OF A KNIGHT

As you have read, feudalism became the common way of life in the Middle Ages because there was a constant threat of attack. Thus, the lord of a manor always had to be prepared for war. A lord never knew when his help would be needed by his king or by another lord.

Knights practiced their skills against each other in contests called tournaments.

From childhood, male children of nobles were trained to become **knights**. Knights were trained soldiers and specialists in war. They gave military service to a king or lord in return for the right to hold land.

Beginning their training at the age of seven, young knights were called pages. Pages grew up in a great lord's castle, where they acted as a kind of servant and messenger.

When a page was 14 years old, he became a squire. Each squire served one knight, taking care of his horse and polishing his armor. The squire was taught how to ride a horse and how to use a sword and lance. Squires were on call at all hours and followed knights into battle.

If a squire served well, he was made a knight when he was 20 years old. Kneeling before his lord, the new knight promised his loyalty and agreed to fight when needed.

A HARSH LIFE

The years from 500 to 1000 were harsh for Europeans. Change came slowly. The system of feudalism did not encourage growth.

In this lesson you have read about the way people lived under feudalism. You learned that the riches of the feudal lords and vassals came from the hard work of the serfs. Even knights owed their lords a willingness to risk their lives in battle.

There is more to tell about the Middle Ages, however. In the next lesson you will read about the importance of religion in daily life.

Check Your Reading

1. Why did feudalism develop?
2. How was a fief ruled and protected?
3. How were the lives of serfs and knights different?
4. **THINKING SKILL:** Classify the different people living on a manor into groups. Label each group.

3 The Influence of the Church

Key Vocabulary

monastery
convent
monk
nun
saint
cathedral

Key People

Benedict
Francis of Assisi

Key Places

Chartres

Read Aloud

Each one has his own gift from God, the one in this way, the other in that. . . . The heart of the Church lies in the heart of its servants. The greatest gift is to have a willingness to serve.

According to this Christian writer of the Middle Ages, God has given everyone a special gift, or talent. In this lesson you will read about the influence of the Christian religion in the Middle Ages. Along with feudalism, Christianity was one of the strongest forces in daily life.

Read for Purpose

1. **WHAT YOU KNOW:** Who were the first Christians?
2. **WHAT YOU WILL LEARN:** What were the contributions of the Christian Church during the Middle Ages?

MONASTERIES

"Blessed are the poor, for they shall inherit the Kingdom of Heaven." These words were spoken by Jesus of Nazareth on a hillside in Palestine almost 2,000 years ago. During the Middle Ages the impact of Jesus's message inspired thousands of men and women to leave their families and enter special religious communities. There they could live simple religious lives. These communities were called monasteries and convents.

Hundreds of monasteries and convents were set up across Europe. Religious men called monks lived and worshiped God together in monasteries. Religious women called nuns lived and worshiped in convents.

Like a manor, a monastery or a convent was a self-sufficient economic unit. These communities had everything people needed. There were houses, workshops, barns, and fields for raising crops. At the heart of a monastery, however, was the church.

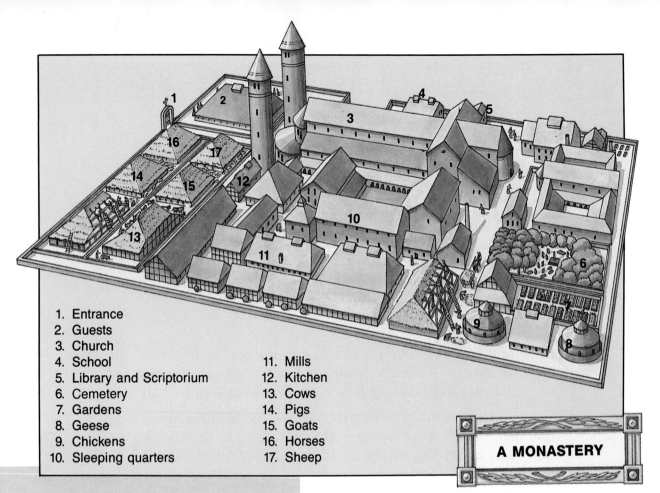

1. Entrance
2. Guests
3. Church
4. School
5. Library and Scriptorium
6. Cemetery
7. Gardens
8. Geese
9. Chickens
10. Sleeping quarters
11. Mills
12. Kitchen
13. Cows
14. Pigs
15. Goats
16. Horses
17. Sheep

A MONASTERY

DIAGRAM SKILL: The monastery was a self-sufficient community. Within it monks led a life governed by strict rules. Which activities differed from those on a manor?

A DAY IN THE LIFE OF A MONK

TIME	DUTIES
Midnight	Rise for morning prayers
1 A.M.	Attend church service
2 A.M.	Return to bed
7 A.M.	Rise for church service
8 A.M.	Wash
9 A.M.	Morning prayers
10 A.M.	Monastery meetings
11 A.M.	Work. No talking allowed.
Noon	Attend church service
3 P.M.	Dinner. No talking allowed.
4 P.M.	Work. No talking allowed.
6 P.M.	Attend church service
8 P.M.	To bed until midnight

MONASTIC LIFE

Daily life in many monasteries followed strict rules that had been set down in the sixth century by a monk named Benedict. For example, "Laziness is the great enemy of the soul," Benedict wrote. "Therefore, monks should always be kept busy, either in manual labor or holy reading."

Think what it might have been like to live in a monastery during the Middle Ages. It was not uncommon for parents to give one or two of their children to a monastery or convent. There, a son or daughter would be raised and go to school. They might live in the monastery or convent all their lives.

Monasteries were the most important places of learning during the Middle Ages. Therefore, every monastery needed a library. The library included Bibles and other texts related to the religious life of the community. The library also kept records of the deeds and the documents needed for running the monastery. Key to the life of the library, however, was the room directly below it.

Beneath the library of most monasteries was a room called the scriptorium (skrip tōr′ ē əm), or "copying workroom." During the Middle Ages, the only way to reproduce books was to copy them by hand. Thus, if you were a scribe, you might be found leaning over a desk and carefully copying ancient manuscripts, letter by letter. Books were borrowed by one monastery from another in order to make copies.

Without the efforts of the scribes of the Middle Ages, the world would know very little about the legacy of ancient Greece and ancient Rome. While copying texts, these scribes were making a very important contribution to civilization.

THE ART OF THE CHURCH SCRIBES

It was drawn by an angel while the monks slept, for it is certain that no human hand can draw out of the letter X such loveliness.

These are the words of the historian who found the drawing shown on this page. It shows the first letter of the first word of the New Testament, the part of the Bible that tells about the early Christians. The letter was not "drawn by an angel" but by an Irish scribe in the ninth century. Imagine how he must have loved the text to fill a page with just one letter. It looks as though he was also having some fun when he drew this page.

Church scribes worked long hours in a monastery room called the scriptorium. Irish monks produced this page from the Book of Kells, shown below.

221

In addition to illustrating Bible stories, scribes drew scenes showing events in the lives of Christian saints, as shown below. Saints were men and women thought to be especially holy. The Christian Church of the Middle Ages began the tradition of honoring such people after their deaths.

The good deeds of saints became popular subjects for illustration. The life of Saint Francis of Assisi, for example, was well known. Saint Francis was one of the most widely loved saints of the Middle Ages. He was born in Assisi, Italy, in about 1181 and died in 1226. Known for his joyful love of all living things, his life inspired countless numbers of people to follow his example. Even today there are more than 64,000 men and women called "Franciscans." Franciscans strive to live simple lives and share the legacy of their founder's teachings.

THE AGE OF FAITH

Because religion was so important to people during this period, the Middle Ages are also known as the Age of Faith. Remember that earlier civilizations built great structures that served special religious purposes. The Egyptians built pyramids, the Sumerians built ziggurats, and the Greeks and Romans built temples.

The people of the Age of Faith built elaborate churches called cathedrals (kə thē′ drəlz). Between 1000 and 1300, more than 500 cathedrals were built. Their towers rose high above shops and homes. In a time when most people did not know how to read and write, cathedrals served an important purpose.

Some historians have called cathedrals "Bibles for the poor." Colorful stained-glass windows were lessons in Christian history. Windows showed stories from both the Old and New Testaments of the Bible, as well as illustrating the lives of important saints.

Monks cultivated the land near their monasteries. Can you find the saint in this painting? The monk who painted it drew a symbolic ring around the saint's head.

A **cathedral** was a source of pride to all the people of the city that had built it. Chartres, like other cathedrals, overflows with stained glass and dramatic sculptures.

You can see the lessons of one colorful window in the Chapter Opener on page 208. Dramatic sculptures also expressed the ideas of the Church.

The cathedral shown on this page is located at **Chartres** (shär′ trə) in France. Chartres Cathedral is one of the world's most magnificent buildings. It took thousands of artisans more than 100 years to build. Like an encyclopedia, the cathedral overflows with Christian teachings about life and death. Look at the pictures above. As you can see, Chartres was built with tremendous love and faith. The sculptures on the right represent three of the 12 Apostles of the Church.

In this lesson you have read about the mighty influence of the Christian Church during the Middle Ages. In the next lesson you will read more about its far-reaching influence.

Check Your Reading

1. What is a monastery?
2. List two achievements of the Christian Church during the Middle Ages.
3. Why are the Middle Ages also called the Age of Faith?
4. **THINKING SKILL:** Compare and contrast daily life on a manor to that in a monastery.

223

4 A Time of Change

READ TO LEARN

Key Vocabulary

pilgrimage
Crusade
commerce
guild
apprentice
journeyman
charter
Magna Carta

Key People

King John

Key Places

Holy Land
Venice
Genoa

Read Aloud

"It is as though the very world had shaken herself and cast off her old age," wrote a French monk in 1100. What had happened to cause these words to be written? After centuries of feudalism, Europe was on the brink of new life.

Read for Purpose

1. **WHAT YOU KNOW:** Was Europe in the Middle Ages united by a strong government?
2. **WHAT YOU WILL LEARN:** How did the economy of Europe change during the late Middle Ages?

THE CRUSADES

As you know, Christianity was the main religion in Europe during the Middle Ages. During this time, however, another great religion was growing in the Middle East. Its followers were called Muslims (muz' limz), which means "faithful" in Arabic.

In the seventh century, Muslim rulers conquered Palestine—a land known to Christians as the Holy Land. For Christians the Holy Land was special because it was the birthplace of Christianity. This region was also holy for Jews and Muslims. Every year many European Christians, rich and poor, made a pilgrimage (pil' grə mij) to the Holy Land. A pilgrimage is a journey that a person makes to a holy place for a religious purpose.

At first the Muslims allowed the Christians to make their pilgrimages to Palestine. However, around the year 1000, the Seljuk Turks came to power in the Muslim lands. They killed thousands of Christians who made pilgrimages to the Holy Land.

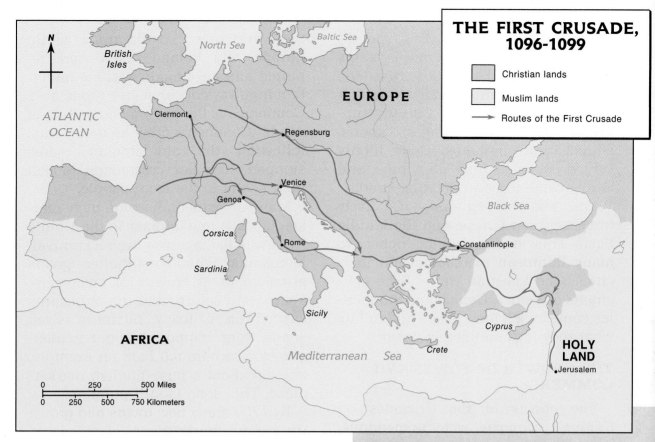

THE FIRST CRUSADE, 1096-1099

Christian lands

Muslim lands

→ Routes of the First Crusade

North Sea · Baltic Sea · British Isles · EUROPE · ATLANTIC OCEAN · Clermont · Regensburg · Venice · Black Sea · Genoa · Corsica · Rome · Constantinople · Sardinia · AFRICA · Sicily · Cyprus · Crete · Mediterranean Sea · HOLY LAND · Jerusalem

0   250   500 Miles
0   250   500   750 Kilometers

MAP SKILL: The First Crusade caused many people to travel incredible distances. What cities were along the main pilgrimage routes? What city was the destination?

As you can imagine, this angered Christian leaders. In 1095 Pope Urban II addressed a huge gathering of Christians in Clermont, France.

> I speak to those present, I send word to those not here . . . go forth against the Turks in a battle worthy to be undertaken now and to be finished in victory!

According to Robert the Monk, who was in the crowd:

> When Pope Urban had said this and much more of the same sort, all who were present were moved to cry out with one accord, "It is the will of God! It is the will of God!"

Thus began the first of many fierce Crusades, or holy wars. For the next 200 years, waves of crusaders—kings, queens, lords, knights, monks, nuns, and serfs—set out to recapture the Holy Land.

LESSONS OF THE CRUSADES

The Crusades were a great failure for the Church. In the first place, the crusaders did not recapture the Holy Land. In the second place, many innocent people, both Christians and Muslims, died as a result of the "holy wars." One eyewitness who traveled to Jerusalem with the First Crusade reported that "at the Temple of Solomon men rode in blood up to their knees."

The Crusades played a major role in causing Europe to "cast off her old age" and become open to new ideas. To reach the Holy Land, the crusaders had to travel great distances, as the map on this page shows.

The Italian cities of Venice (ven′ is) and Genoa (jen′ ō ə) sent trading ships to the Holy Land with the crusaders. These ships returned with foods that Europeans soon wanted a steady supply of—sugar, rice, oranges, lemons, pepper, and cinnamon. Other highly valued goods such as silks, rugs, and jewels came to be in great demand.

This was the beginning of a lively trade between Europe and the Middle East. This trade brought riches to many European merchants and their cities. One Venetian wrote: "The merchants of Venice, Genoa, and other cities come to sell their goods and to buy what they lack and sorely desire."

THE GROWTH OF TOWNS AND COMMERCE

The effects of the Crusades on Europe's economy were tremendous. As Europe's trade with other parts of the world grew, so did trade within Europe. Old Roman roads were repaired and once again became important highways of commerce (kom′ ərs). Commerce is the buying and selling of goods. Commerce grew as merchants, following the old Roman roads, stopped at major crossroads to sell their goods to the local people.

Many crossroads became busy marketplaces. A marketplace in the Middle Ages was like a fair or even a carnival. Merchants with sought-after goods attracted great crowds of customers. Tents were set up, and the merchants carried on a lively business. Even songs were composed about marketplaces. *Scarborough Fair,* for example, tells us about a busy English marketplace. This song is still popular.

By 1200 many new towns had grown up around marketplaces. Artisans as well as merchants flocked to the towns to make and sell their goods. Peasants from nearby manors were also drawn to towns, bringing their surplus crops and livestock to sell.

After the Crusades, many serfs abandoned the hard work of the manor for life in towns. This painting shows the busy commerce of a town marketplace.

Detail from *The Fight Between Carnival and Lent,* 1559, Pieter Brueghel, Kunsthistorisches Museum, Vienna.

Scarborough Fair

English Folk Song

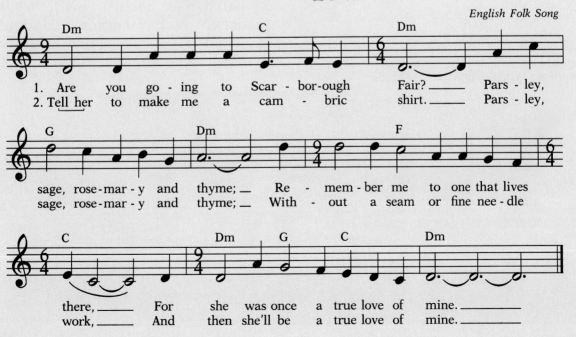

1. Are you go-ing to Scar-bor-ough Fair? Pars-ley,
2. Tell her to make me a cam-bric shirt. Pars-ley,

sage, rose-mar-y and thyme; Re-mem-ber me to one that lives
sage, rose-mar-y and thyme; With-out a seam or fine nee-dle

there, For she was once a true love of mine.
work, And then she'll be a true love of mine.

227

THE GROWTH OF GUILDS

As towns grew larger, groups called guilds were formed to control trade. A guild was an organization of people who performed the same craft. At first, only the richer merchants joined together in guilds. However, by 1300 artisans also were organized in guilds. Guilds were formed for bakers, metalworkers, weavers, shoemakers, candlemakers, and many others.

The guild system had its own set of rules and opened its doors only to proven masters of the trade. How did someone master a trade? Parents paid a fee to a master to take their child in as an apprentice (ə pren' tis). An apprentice lived in the master's home and worked in his shop, which might be in the same building. Apprentices worked for 3 to 12 years without pay.

At the end of his training period, an apprentice became a journeyman and was paid for his work. *Journeyman* comes from an old French word meaning "day." A journeyman was a skilled worker who put in a day's work for pay.

Journeymen were not guild members and could not open their own shops.

According to guild rules, a journeyman had to work at least three years under a master. As the final step, a journeyman had to make an item—whether it was a sword, a shoe, or a candle. The quality of the item, however, had to be considered a "master piece." Only then could a journeyman become a master, enter the guild, and open his own shop.

THE GREAT CHARTER

From about the time of the First Crusade, many Europeans began to think that kings, queens, and popes had too much power. As towns and guilds grew, people wanted more rights and freedoms.

In 1199 a greedy, cruel king began to rule in England. King John forced his people to give huge sums of money to help pay for his costly way of life. Anyone who could not pay was thrown into prison without trial by jury.

By 1215 the lords of England were prepared to act against King John's injustice, or lack of fairness. The lords drew up a charter listing their demands and presented it to the king. As

A bakers' guild would buy flour for all its members. The guild also set the prices that members would charge for their goods.

The Granger Collection

The Granger Collection

you can imagine, King John treated the charter with scorn and refused to grant the rights named in it. He changed his mind, however, when he saw that his great army of knights supported the charter.

This statement of rights is called the Magna Carta (mag′ nə kär′ tə), which means "great charter" in Latin. The Magna Carta is a very important document. It established the idea that the king must live by the law. Although the rights it granted were mostly enjoyed by nobles, common people soon claimed and received the same rights.

THE LEGACY OF THE MIDDLE AGES

In the years following the Crusades, civilization in Europe reached new heights. Town life and commerce flourished across the continent. Europe changed from a feudal society without much trading activity into a bustling civilization with flourishing towns.

As you continue to study European civilization, you will learn that it went through many more changes. The ideas of the Magna Carta, for example, spread throughout Europe. You will discover how its legacy affected the course of history. Look for its presence in the chapters that follow.

THE MAGNA CARTA

*W*e have granted to all free men of our kingdom for us and our heirs forever all the liberties written below. . .

- A free man shall not be fined for a small offense. . .
- No sheriff, or anyone else, shall take horses or wagons of anyone without permission. . .
- Neither we nor our sheriffs will take the wood of another for our castles without permission. . .
- No freeman shall be taken, or imprisoned, or banished, or in anyway injured, except by the law of the land. . .
- To no one will we sell, to no one will we deny or delay, rights or justice. . .
- All merchants shall be safe and secure in going out from England, as well as by land as by water, for buying and selling. . .
- All men of our kingdom, as well clergy [priests] as laymen [freemen] shall observe these laws. . .

The lords of England forced King John to sign the Magna Carta. The "great charter" was a turning point in the growth of democracy. Of its many points, which one is still very important today?

Check Your Reading

1. What were guilds? How did people become members?
2. Why did commerce grow after the Crusades?
3. **GEOGRAPHY SKILL:** Why did Venice flourish after the Crusades?
4. **THINKING SKILL:** What are three questions you could ask to find out facts about the Crusades?

Understanding Cause and Effect

Key Vocabulary

cause

effect

When you understand why something happened you have a better chance of predicting what will happen next. Something that makes something else happen is a **cause**. What happens as a result of a cause is called an **effect**.

Finding cause and effect connections is important in solving problems in your own life. For example, if the grade you earn on a history test is not what you expected, ask questions to find the cause. When you ask *why*, you might find out that you did not study enough.

Learning about causes and effects can help you understand why certain events in history happened. Read on to find out how you can use this skill to better understand the information in this book.

Trying the Skill

What cause-and-effect connection is being described in the following paragraph?

When the invading Crusaders captured an Arab city, they not only killed the men, but enslaved the women and children. So the Muslims who survived began preaching the idea of *jihad*, or holy war. Soon, the sultan promised to send an army to defend Islam against the Crusaders.

1. What effects are described here?
2. What causes are described?
3. How do you know?

230

HELPING YOURSELF

The steps on the left will help you identify the causes and effects of an event. The example on the right shows one way to apply these steps to the paragraph you read on page 230.

One Way to Identify Cause and Effect	Example
1. Recall the definition of cause and effect.	Remember, a cause is something that makes something else happen. What happens is called the effect.
2. Recall the word clues for causes and effects.	Word clues include: • words that signal causes, such as *as a result of*, *since*, *because* • words that signal effects, such as *so*, *therefore*, *as a result*
3. Search each sentence for these word clues.	Search the paragraph to see if you find any clues. Did you find the word *so* in the second sentence?
4. If you cannot find any word clues, arrange the events in the order in which they occurred. Then try to find any connections among them. Ask yourself, "What did one event have to do with another?"	The Crusades came *before* the sultan sent an army.
5. State the causes and effects you find. An effect can have more than one cause. A cause can bring about several effects.	Raising an Islamic army was an effect of the Crusades.

Applying the Skill

Now use what you have learned about cause and effect to analyze the events described below.

Because merchants attracted great crowds, towns grew around marketplaces. Townspeople bought charters from the nearby lords. Since the charters freed the towns from any ties to the manor, many serfs fled to the towns. As a result, the feudal system began breaking down.

1. Which came first?
   a. The feudal system broke down.
   b. Many serfs fled to towns.
   c. Townspeople bought charters.
2. Which of the following events was both a cause and an effect?
   a. Serfs fled to the towns.
   b. Merchants attracted large crowds.
   c. Townspeople bought charters from nearby lords.
3. What was the main cause for the breakdown of the feudal system?

Reviewing the Skill

1. What are some words that signal causes? What are some words that signal effects?
2. Name some steps you could use to find causes and effects in a paragraph.
3. Where else in this class or outside of school would it be useful to find cause-and-effect connections?

IMPORTANT EVENTS

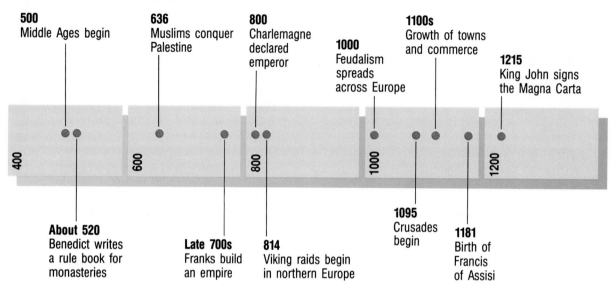

500
Middle Ages begin

636
Muslims conquer Palestine

800
Charlemagne declared emperor

1000
Feudalism spreads across Europe

1100s
Growth of towns and commerce

1215
King John signs the Magna Carta

400   600   800   1000   1200

About 520
Benedict writes a rule book for monasteries

Late 700s
Franks build an empire

814
Viking raids begin in northern Europe

1095
Crusades begin

1181
Birth of Francis of Assisi

PEOPLE TO KNOW

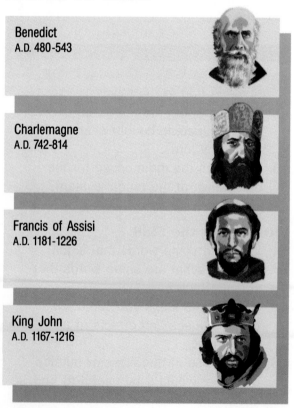

Benedict
A.D. 480-543

Charlemagne
A.D. 742-814

Francis of Assisi
A.D. 1181-1226

King John
A.D. 1167-1216

IDEAS TO REMEMBER

■ Europe is part of a large landmass called Eurasia. Europe itself extends from the Ural Mountains to the Atlantic Ocean.

■ The Middle Ages began about A.D. 500. During this time, most people were serfs and lived on large manors. Charlemagne and the Vikings left their mark on Europe during this period.

■ Because of the importance given to religion, the Middle Ages has also been called the Age of Faith. Thousands of men and women entered monasteries and convents.

■ During the Crusades, trade started between Europe and the Middle East. As a result, towns grew up around market places and European civilization spread.

REVIEWING VOCABULARY

cathedral	manor
commerce	Middle Ages
Crusades	monastery
feudalism	pilgrimage
Magna Carta	serf

Number a sheet of paper from 1 to 10. Beside each number write the word or term from the above list that best matches the statement or definition.

1. A type of church architecture that emerged around A.D. 1000.
2. One reason why this type of social organization emerged was the fear and unrest caused by the Vikings.
3. Most Europeans were members of this social group during the Middle Ages.
4. Bitterly opposed by King John of England, this was one of the first documents to limit the powers of a ruler.
5. This historical period began after the end of the Roman Empire in the 400s.
6. Because of the work of its scribes, this religious community contributed to the growth of learning in Europe.
7. Despite failure to achieve its goal of recapturing the Holy Land, this movement helped increase trade and brought new ideas to Europe.
8. Reflecting religious faith, this journey to a holy place was very popular among Christians of the Middle Ages.
9. In a time when there were few towns or cities, this self-sufficient community of nobles, serfs, and skilled workers was able to provide for its own needs.
10. The growth of towns was one factor in the growth of this economic activity.

REVIEWING FACTS

1. Why is Europe sometimes called a "peninsula of peninsulas?"
2. Why does Western Europe have mild winters?
3. What was the life of a serf like?
4. How did the Crusades affect commerce?
5. How was the Magna Carta different from the United States Constitution?

◖◖═▶ WRITING ABOUT MAIN IDEAS

1. **Writing Sentences:** The terms in the word pairs below are related to each other in some way. For each pair, write a sentence to explain how they are related: **a.** Europe, peninsula; **b.** monastery, manor; **c.** Crusades, urban growth.
2. **Writing About Perspectives:** Imagine that you live in England during the time of King John. Write a paragraph explaining how the Magna Carta might change your life.

BUILDING SKILLS: UNDERSTANDING CAUSE AND EFFECT

Read the paragraph below. Then answer the questions.

The Vikings were fierce raiders and terrorized much of Europe. Communities had to be guarded by soldiers. Peasants needed protection to work in their fields. During this time, feudalism developed.

1. What causes and effects are described in the paragraph?
2. What was the main cause of the development of feudalism?

CHAPTER 9

THE RENAISSANCE

FOCUS

Have I reached too far? Look at how high off the ground I am. And I am in agony . . . . my beard curls up; my head leans tightly over; my brush endlessly dripping onto my face has coated it with a multicolored layer of paint.

Yet even as paint dripped into his eyes, this young painter never lost sight of his grand design. On the ceiling and walls of a great church in Rome, he painted breathtaking scenes. In this chapter you will read about a great revival of art and ideas.

The Art of the Renaissance

READ TO LEARN

Key Vocabulary

Renaissance
classics
patron

Key People

Petrarch
Lorenzo de'Medici
Michelangelo
Leonardo da Vinci

Key Places

Florence

Read Aloud

Do not forget the ancient Greeks and Romans. Add a little every day and gather things in. . . . The ancient books are welcome friends . . . that encourage you, take care of you, and teach you the world's secrets. . . .

The Italian thinker named Petrarch (pē′ trärk) believed that the writings of the ancient Greeks and Romans could teach the "world's secrets." Living in Italy in the 1300s, he wondered what a person could learn from the past. Such curiosity became common in Petrarch's time and helped to start a new, exciting time of growth.

Read for Purpose

1. **WHAT YOU KNOW:** Why is the study of history useful?
2. **WHAT YOU WILL LEARN:** How did the Renaissance affect European culture?

THE RENAISSANCE BEGINS

Like other great changes in history, Europe's new age did not replace the Middle Ages overnight. Nor did the change take place at the same time everywhere in Europe. Remember that after the Crusades, Europe began to change. Trade increased greatly and towns began to grow. You may recall that the Italian seaports of Venice and Genoa flourished as a result of the growth of commerce.

This change was the background for the Renaissance (ren ə säns′), which began in Italy in about 1350. *Renaissance* is a French word meaning "rebirth." Lasting until about 1600, the Renaissance was a dazzling time.

GREEK AND LATIN REVIVED

Why was this time called the Renaissance? What was being reborn? Like Petrarch, many people who lived in the 1300s hoped to bring back to life the great culture of ancient civilizations. Renaissance thinkers believed that, since the fall of Rome in 476, the people of Europe had "lived in darkness." Even the beautiful cathedrals throughout Europe were thought to be ugly. Admiring only Greek and Roman art, Petrarch called the Middle Ages "the Dark Ages."

During the Renaissance there was a great wave of new interest in the classics (klas' iks), or the literature of ancient Greece and Rome. Petrarch believed that the classics were superior to, or better than, anything written since the fall of Rome. He traveled from monastery to monastery in search of the classics. You may recall that during the Middle Ages monasteries were centers of learning and had libraries. Often, the conditions of these libraries shocked Petrarch. At one monastery library he found that only the walls remained standing. Petrarch searched through the piles of rotting books. Surely, he thought, an ancient Greek or Roman text could be found.

PATRONS SUPPORT THE RENAISSANCE

Many Italian artists were also influenced by the revival of Greek and Latin. They, too, wanted to restore the rich culture of ancient Europe. To do this they began to copy the art of the ancient Greeks and Romans. Yet, in striving to bring the past back to life, the artists of the Renaissance also created something very new.

Renaissance artists had the support of the families who ran the rich cities of northern Italy. Many of these families became patrons of the arts. *Patron* comes from the Latin word for "father." A patron is a person who supports, or assists, another person by the use of his or her money and influence. The most influential of all Renaissance patrons was a man named Lorenzo de'Medici (lô ren' zō də med' i chē).

Lorenzo the Magnificent, as he was also called, brought the most talented artists to his palace in Florence, Italy. Artists under his patronage made some of the world's most beautiful art. Florence became known as the "dynamo of the Renaissance."

The citizens of Florence were proud of their city and compared it to ancient Athens.

Michelangelo was a painter, poet, musician, architect, and sculptor. In works like the *Pietà* his goal was "liberating [freeing] the figure from the marble that imprisons it."

MICHELANGELO

Lorenzo de'Medici's favorite artist was Michelangelo (mī kəl an' je lō). You saw a photograph of his paintings in the Sistine Chapel in the Chapter Opener. But Michelangelo was also the greatest sculptor of the Renaissance. Like the Greek sculptures that inspired him, Michelangelo created art that seemed to be living. About Michelangelo's sculpture, de'Medici wrote:

Each act, each limb, each bone is given life and, lo, man's body is raised breathing, alive, in wax or clay or stone.

When he was only 23, Michelangelo made a statue called the *Pietà*. *Pietà* is an Italian word meaning "pity." This statue shows Mary holding the body of Jesus after his death by crucifixion. One writer, who saw it when it was shown for the first time in about 1540, wrote the following words:

It would be impossible for any craftsman or sculptor, no matter how brilliant, ever to surpass the grace or design of this work or to try to cut and polish the marble with the skill that Michelangelo displayed.

Looking at the photograph of the *Pietà*, it is easy to wonder how a block of marble could be turned into a piece of art.

LEONARDO DA VINCI

During Michelangelo's time, another towering artist was at work. "I wish to work miracles," Leonardo da Vinci (lē ə när′ dō də vin′ chē) wrote when he was very young. As a boy, Leonardo was apprenticed to a famous master painter in Florence. As an apprentice he quickly showed tremendous ability. In fact, Leonardo's master was so overwhelmed by the beauty of Leonardo's early work that he threw down his own paintbrush. The master vowed never to paint again, knowing he could never match the great talent of his young apprentice.

Leonardo da Vinci was one of the most important Renaissance painters. He was also a man of many new ideas. For example, he wrote in his notebook:

Cut the bat open, study it carefully, and on this model build the flying machine.

The machine that Leonardo imagined had huge, batlike wings. Below the wings, he imagined a person standing on a wooden frame and pedaling furiously. By means of ropes and pulleys, the pedals would make the wings flap. Though such a machine could not fly, Leonardo's idea was far ahead of its time.

As his notebooks show, Leonardo was fascinated with science. He left behind more than 5,000 notebook pages. In addition to unique inventions, he drew objects with lifelike details. To find out more about the human body, he made careful drawings of the structure of muscles and bones. Perhaps this explains why the

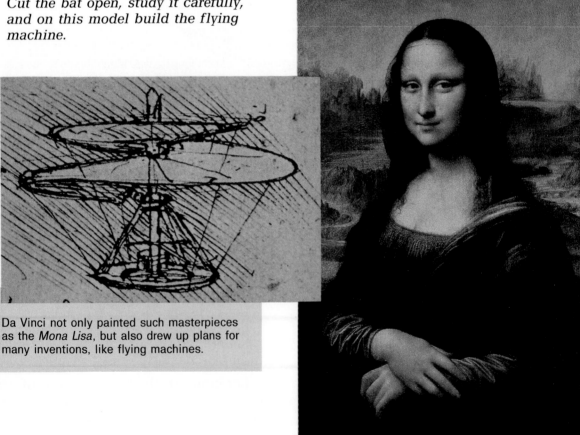

Da Vinci not only painted such masterpieces as the *Mona Lisa*, but also drew up plans for many inventions, like flying machines.

The church of St. Peter's in Rome is one of the greatest buildings of the Renaissance. Michelangelo spent 18 years designing it, but the dome was completed after his death.

Mona Lisa, his painting of a young woman from Florence, looks so real. One historian of art wrote that the *Mona Lisa* "seems to glow with a gentle, human light from within."

THE SPREAD OF THE RENAISSANCE

As you have read, the Renaissance blossomed first in Italy, where rich patrons supported the arts. The *Pietà*, for example, can be viewed today in Saint Peter's cathedral shown above. In fact, the towering dome of Saint Peter's was designed by Michelangelo.

The Renaissance was a time of great artistic creativity. Its artists created some of the world's most beautiful works of art. But Michelangelo and Leonardo da Vinci were only two examples of many Renaissance artists. Italian workshops were overflowing with artists from all over the continent. Similarly, Petrarch was only one Renaissance thinker. In the next lesson you will read how the ideas of another Renaissance thinker caused a new religious movement to begin.

Check Your Reading

1. Who was Petrarch? How did he encourage the spread of ideas?
2. How did patrons support the growth of Renaissance culture?
3. What other name could you give the "Renaissance"?
4. **THINKING SKILL:** In what ways was the Renaissance similar to the Age of Pericles in ancient Greece?

239

2 The Reformation

READ TO LEARN

Key Vocabulary

Reformation
Roman Catholic
Protestant

Key People

Martin Luther
Johann Gutenberg

Key Places

Wittenberg
Trent

Read Aloud

Luther was like a man climbing in the darkness a winding staircase in the steeple of an ancient cathedral. In the blackness he reached out to steady himself, and his hand laid hold of a rope. He was startled to hear the clanging of a bell.

According to this historian, Martin Luther was "startled to hear the clanging of a bell." All his life, Martin Luther wished only to lead the quiet life of a monk. He never thought that he would help start a movement that would change the course of European history.

Read for Purpose

1. **WHAT YOU KNOW:** How did the Renaissance encourage freedom of thought?
2. **WHAT YOU WILL LEARN:** What was the Reformation?

THE NEED FOR REFORM

Martin Luther was born in a small German village in 1483. Most of his life was spent as a monk and teacher of religion in Wittenberg, Germany. But Martin Luther began a movement that changed his life and the course of European history.

The movement Luther started is now called the Reformation. The Reformation was a time when many reformers, like Luther, began to question the power of the Roman Catholic Church. The Roman Catholic Church is the name for the Christian organization that is headed by the pope. You may recall that during the Middle Ages, the Church was extremely powerful. Remember, for example, that Charlemagne was crowned by the pope. What had happened to make Martin Luther question the religion he had believed in and loved all his life?

Luther was outraged by some new Church practices. For example, as a way of raising money, the Church had begun to sell indulgences. Indulgences were pardons from the pope for certain mistakes. If you did something that

This painting is a symbolic picture of Luther and his supporters. The **Reformation** began when Luther posted his 95 statements.

was against Church teachings, for instance, you could pay some money and receive forgiveness. Luther did not believe that people could "buy their way into Heaven." Instead, Luther thought that each person must "be faithful to deserve happiness after death."

"HERE I STAND"

The Reformation began in 1517 when Luther nailed a list of 95 statements on the door of a church in Wittenberg. The statements were protests against many Church practices, including indulgences. The list began, "Out of love and zeal for truth and the desire to bring it to light . . ."

Luther took no steps to spread his ideas among the people of Germany. He was only inviting Church leaders to explain and defend some Church practices. But news of Luther's protests spread quickly. Forced to defend his statements, Luther expanded his attack against the Church. He claimed,

for example, that a person's own conscience, or feeling of what is right, was more important than what the pope said was right.

Pope Leo X became alarmed by the popularity of the "wild boar," as he called Luther. The pope threatened to expel Luther from the Church unless he took back his protests. But Luther declared:

I cannot act against my conscience. . . . On this I take my stand. I cannot do otherwise. God help me. Here I stand. Amen.

PRINTING SPREADS LUTHER'S IDEAS

The ideas of the Reformation spread very quickly. In order to understand how, you need to learn about an important invention.

You read in Chapter 8 that the only way to reproduce books during the

Middle Ages was to copy them by hand. In the 1300s people experimented with printing books from wood blocks. They carved a page on the block, which was then inked and pressed on paper. Both of these methods, however, made books very expensive and very rare.

The inventive Johann Gutenberg (yō′ hän güt′ ən bûrg) changed all this. In about 1450 he developed a printing press that could make books cheaply and quickly. Gutenberg's printing press used small pieces of metal, or movable type. Each piece had a single letter from the alphabet. The metal pieces could be placed in trays to form lines of print. Whole pages could be assembled quickly. What might take a scribe many days to copy, Gutenberg's incredible press could produce in moments!

Printing soon became an important business. The increase in the number of books made it possible for information to spread rapidly.

Once one page was printed over and over again, the letters could be moved around. This movable type was then reassembled into another page, and another and another. There were perhaps a total of 100,000 books—all hand-copied, of course—in Europe before the invention of Gutenberg's printing press. By 1500 there were 9 million books in Europe. As you can see, the invention of the printing press was a great turning point. It might be compared to the impact of television and the computer in modern times.

THE REFORMATION CHANGES EUROPE

Now you can understand how the news of Martin Luther's attack on the Church spread across Europe. Only days after Luther nailed his protest on the church door in Wittenberg, printing presses rolled out hundreds of copies of his message. The new printing technology helped Luther gain many followers. According to a Church official who visited Germany in 1521:

Nine tenths of the people are shouting "Luther!" And the others are shouting "Down with Rome!"

Martin Luther was not alone. After he left the Roman Catholic Church in 1520, millions of people followed his example. Because these Christians *protested* against many Roman Catholic teachings, they became known as Protestants.

The Roman Catholic Church also changed as a result of the Reformation. In 1545 a new pope announced, "We know that for many years there has been much to be regarded with horror." With that statement, the Roman Catholic Church admitted that it needed re-

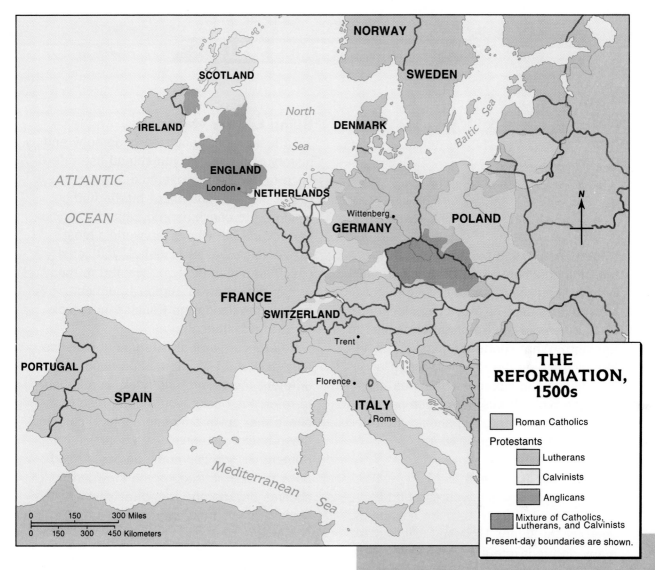

THE
REFORMATION,
1500s

☐ Roman Catholics

Protestants

☐ Lutherans

☐ Calvinists

☐ Anglicans

☐ Mixture of Catholics,
Lutherans, and Calvinists

Present-day boundaries are shown.

MAP SKILL: Different religions became strong in parts of Europe. Which religion was most widespread?

form. The Church organized a council in the city of Trent, Italy. The Council of Trent struggled for many years to define Church teachings more clearly.

A DIFFERENT EUROPE

In this lesson you have read how the courage of one Renaissance thinker caused tremendous change. You have read that Martin Luther took a stand against some Church practices because he did not believe they were correct. As a result, the Protestant movement began to grow, and the Roman Catholic Church began to reform.

Check Your Reading

1. What was the Reformation?
2. How did printing affect the spread of the Reformation?
3. **GEOGRAPHY SKILL:** Use the map above to name Protestant nations.
4. **THINKING SKILL:** Why did Martin Luther decide to "take a stand"? What was his goal? What alternatives might he have considered? What were possible outcomes of each alternative?

243

Using the Library

Key Vocabulary

reference   almanac

dictionary   atlas

encyclopedia

As you study the people and events that helped shape world history, you may want to learn more about certain things. What did Lorenzo de'Medici's palace look like? When did the Reformation spread to England? What sports did people play in Florence during the Renaissance? How did Johann Gutenberg get the idea for movable type? If this book does not answer your questions, you should go to the library and search for answers.

Search for Answers

For many questions, you can find a quick answer in the reference section of your school library. Here you will find many different reference books, or books that are sources of information. Four useful types of reference books are dictionaries, encyclopedias, almanacs, and atlases. These reference books will give you many different kinds of useful information.

A dictionary gives the meanings of words and tells how to pronounce them. An encyclopedia has articles about many subjects, including important people, places, and events. An almanac is a book published every year with up-to-date facts on many subjects. There are also specialized reference books such as historical atlases that show where and when events happened.

Using Library Materials

To learn more about the geography and history of the world, you should use reference materials. For example, a good way to get more details about Martin Luther would be to check an encyclopedia. If you had to find out where the world's most active volcanoes are located, you could check an almanac. If you wanted to study a map that showed Europe's political boundaries during the Renaissance, look for it in a historical atlas.

Reference materials are useful because they pack a lot of information about many different things into one book. In addition to reference books, your library also has books that cover only one subject. Finding those books also involves a search. Sometimes you can come across a good book by looking through the crowded shelves of a library. It is often faster, however, if you use the card catalog or computer.

Title or Author

There is something you should know about looking for a library book. All you really need to know is the title or author's name. If you know the title or author of a book, simply look it up in the card catalog or computer. If your library has the book, it will be listed.

As you may know, a card catalog is a listing of all the books in a library. Each book gets its own card. In fact, there are three different cards for each book. One is a title card, one is an author card, and one is a subject card. The first line on each card gives the title, the author, or the subject of the book. And all the cards

244

are arranged in alphabetical order in the drawers of the card catalog cabinets.

Cards in a card catalog list the author's last name first, followed by a comma and the first name. The cards also tell the name of the book's publisher as well as the place and date of publication. The most important information on a card is the *call number*. This number tells you on which shelf to look for the book.

Subject Only

But what if you do not know the title or author's name? What if, for example, all you know is that you have to write a book report about the Reformation? You have already used the encyclopedia to gather some general facts. Now you want more details.

The solution to this problem is simple. Simply use the card catalog or computer and look under the name of the subject— Reformation. Looking at the subject name is a good way to see how many books the library has on a topic.

Reviewing the Skill

1. What is a reference book?
2. What kind of information is found in almanacs?
3. What reference book would you look at to find out where Florence is located?
4. Where could you get information about Martin Luther's followers?
5. Why is it important for you to be able to use the library?

3 Elizabethan England

READ TO LEARN

Key Vocabulary

armada
Parliament
Bill of Rights
absolute
   monarchy
constitutional
   monarchy

Key People

Elizabeth I
Francis Drake
William Shakespeare

Key Places

English Channel
London

Read Aloud

I only desire that my name be recorded in a line or two, which shall briefly express my name, the years of my reign [rule], the reformation of religion under it, and my preservation of peace and culture.

Elizabeth I spoke these words near the end of her remarkable reign as queen of England. Elizabeth was one of the world's greatest leaders. Under her rule, England became a country of tremendous power and influence.

Read for Purpose

1. **WHAT YOU KNOW:** How did the Renaissance affect the growth of European culture?
2. **WHAT YOU WILL LEARN:** What is the legacy of Elizabethan England?

THE SPANISH ARMADA

Queen **Elizabeth I** was one of Europe's greatest monarchs. She ruled England for 45 years, from 1558 to 1603. During her reign, England faced one of its most terrifying invaders.

My loving people . . . let tyrants fear! . . . I know I have the body of a weak and feeble woman but I have the heart and courage of a king, and a king of England too, and think foul scorn that . . . any prince of Europe should dare to invade the borders of my realm.

These were the very words shouted by Elizabeth to her troops in August 1588. On this day the Spanish **Armada** was somewhere off the English coast. An armada is a fleet of warships. Everyone knew that the enemy Spanish Armada had come to invade England. But would the armada succeed?

246

When the Spanish Armada entered the English Channel, it met Elizabeth's fleet of warships. Led by Francis Drake, the English set fire to some of their own ships. Winds and currents carried the burning ships into the closed ranks of the Armada. To avoid the blazing hazards, the Spanish broke up their tight formation.

Now the smaller, faster English ships with their better guns began pounding the giant Spanish ships. As guns boomed and masts split, a furious storm came up and scattered the damaged Armada. The Spanish de-cided to give up their invasion and sail home. However, more storms wrecked many of their ships. Only half the mighty Armada made it back to Spain. And Elizabethan England entered its height of power and influence. Elizabeth herself was a product of the Renaissance. Not many rulers before or since could boast the ability to speak English, French, Italian, Latin, and Greek.

Queen Elizabeth I was a shrewd and popular ruler. She turned down offers of marriage from nobles and foreign kings. She did not want to share her power with a husband.

ELIZABETH'S LONDON

In England the Renaissance was most visible in London, England's capital city. London became one of Europe's largest cities in the late 1500s. There were probably more than 200,000 Londoners celebrating Francis Drake's victory over the Spanish Armada.

Elizabeth's London hummed with activity. The city walls had been built in the Middle Ages and enclosed an area of only one square mile. Within that square mile, houses were so close together that neighbors could reach out their second-story windows and shake hands across the narrow streets.

Because the streets were so clogged with crowds and food carts, the fastest way through the city was the Thames River. Boatmen waited along each bank of the Thames to offer rides, as taxi drivers do today. The ride along the river was usually faster, but sometimes a bit dirty. Garbage was known to fall on travelers on the Thames, especially as they passed under London Bridge. People who liked to take risks might order the boatman to take a chance and shoot under the bridge. Less daring riders would remember the old English proverb:

London Bridge was made for wise men to walk over and fools to go under.

Nowhere in England could one see a greater variety of people than in London. Observing the activity of daily life in London was William Shakespeare (shāk' spêr), a man who became a masterful writer. Shakespeare was the greatest Elizabethan writer. He wrote both poetry and plays. Even Queen Elizabeth loved to go to the theater to watch his plays. You will read more about Shakespeare in the Traditions lesson on pages 250–253. Have you ever seen any of his plays?

THE ENGLISH BILL OF RIGHTS

Elizabeth's England was very different from the city-states you have studied. It was even very different from its own European neighbors in its own time. As England's power and culture grew, it also developed a strong, central government.

You may recall that in Chapter 8 you read that the Magna Carta stopped King John from making unfair laws. The Magna Carta was a great and important document because it gave rights to more people. Even under Elizabeth's strong leadership, Parliament, or the governing body that makes the

The Tower of London was originally built to protect the king. Under Elizabeth, it was a jail for important prisoners.

country's laws, built upon the legacy of the Magna Carta.

After Elizabeth's death in 1603, many different conflicts emerged between England's new monarchs and Parliament. You know, for example, that some religious tensions drove the Pilgrims from England in 1608.

In 1689 Parliament wrote the **Bill of Rights**. This document was a giant step for freedom. No other European country had limited the power of their monarchs as clearly as the English. Before the Bill of Rights, England was an **absolute monarchy**, or was ruled by a monarch with complete power to govern. After 1689 England became a **constitutional monarchy**, or a government whose ruler was bound by the laws of a constitution. No monarch could change the laws without the agreement of Parliament.

You can read part of the English Bill of Rights in the chart on this page. You may recognize these same liberties as belonging to Americans, too. When the United States Constitution was adopted 100 years later, such liberties were included in its own Bill of Rights.

THE LEGACY OF ELIZABETHAN ENGLAND

In this chapter you have read about the Renaissance. You have read that after the Middle Ages Europe began to change. Starting in Italy, a great revival of learning and the arts took place. You have read that, beginning in Martin Luther's Germany, a religious reformation began. Finally, in this lesson you have learned about the Renaissance in Elizabethan England and how the English people gained more power and individual freedoms.

THE ENGLISH BILL OF RIGHTS

*T*he lords. . .being now assembled in a full and free representation of this nation. . . for the defense of their ancient rights and liberties, declare:

- The king does not have the right to end laws without the consent of Parliament. . .
- The king does not have the right to collect money without the consent of Parliament. . .
- All people have the right to petition the king. . .
- There can be no army during a time of peace without the consent of Parliament. . .
- The election of members of Parliament ought to be free. . . .
- The freedom of speech and debates in Parliament should not be questioned in any court. . .
- Bails, fines, and punishments should be fair and just. . .
- Parliament should meet often to amend, strengthen, and preserve the law. . .

How did the English **Bill of Rights** lessen the power of the monarchy?

Check Your Reading

1. What is an absolute monarchy?
2. List two examples of the legacy of Elizabethan England.
3. How is a constitutional monarchy different from any other form of government you have studied?
4. **THINKING SKILL:** What do you think could have been the consequences if England had been defeated by the Spanish Armada?

A Theatrical Tradition

by Joseph Rubin

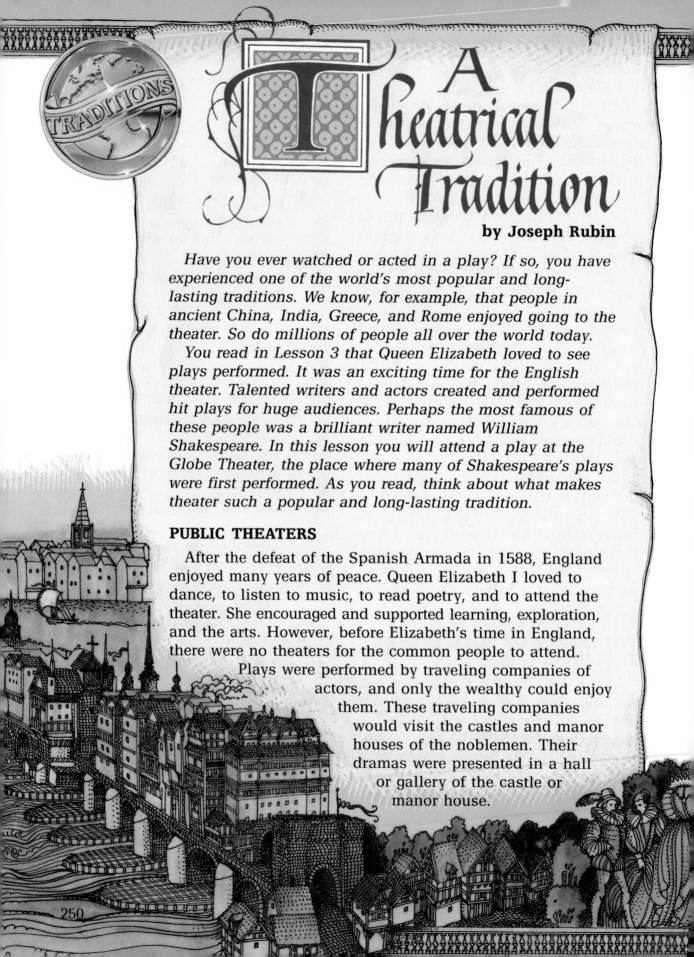

Have you ever watched or acted in a play? If so, you have experienced one of the world's most popular and long-lasting traditions. We know, for example, that people in ancient China, India, Greece, and Rome enjoyed going to the theater. So do millions of people all over the world today.

You read in Lesson 3 that Queen Elizabeth loved to see plays performed. It was an exciting time for the English theater. Talented writers and actors created and performed hit plays for huge audiences. Perhaps the most famous of these people was a brilliant writer named William Shakespeare. In this lesson you will attend a play at the Globe Theater, the place where many of Shakespeare's plays were first performed. As you read, think about what makes theater such a popular and long-lasting tradition.

PUBLIC THEATERS

After the defeat of the Spanish Armada in 1588, England enjoyed many years of peace. Queen Elizabeth I loved to dance, to listen to music, to read poetry, and to attend the theater. She encouraged and supported learning, exploration, and the arts. However, before Elizabeth's time in England, there were no theaters for the common people to attend. Plays were performed by traveling companies of actors, and only the wealthy could enjoy them. These traveling companies would visit the castles and manor houses of the noblemen. Their dramas were presented in a hall or gallery of the castle or manor house.

In 1576 the first public theater in London was built. It was called the Theater. It became so popular that soon many more public theaters were built. They had names like the Curtain, the Swan, and the Rose. In 1599 the Globe Theater was built. Because many of Shakespeare's plays were first performed there, the Globe became the most famous public theater of all. There are no surviving drawings of the Globe Theater. However, by studying the designs of other public theaters of that time, historians have developed a good idea of what the Globe looked like.

A VISIT TO THE GLOBE THEATER

Imagine that you have a time machine and have traveled back to Elizabethan England. You are in London and the year is 1600. It is an exciting day because you have been invited to attend a play at the famous Globe Theater. You will be a guest of the Lord Chamberlain. He is the main supporter of William Shakespeare's acting company, which is called Lord Chamberlain's Men. Your excitement mounts as you see a crowd of people walking over the London Bridge to attend the play. It is a fine day. The sun is shining brightly and there is not a cloud in sight.

As you approach the theater you can see that it is round and made entirely of wood, except for the roof, which is of straw. The flag flying on the roof tells you that today you will see one of Shakespeare's most famous plays, *Romeo and Juliet*. You can hardly wait.

William Shakespeare

251

When you enter the theater you realize that most of it is not covered. The roof covers the stage and extends over the "galleries," but in the center is a large uncovered area that has no seats. The central area is becoming filled with people. Lord Chamberlain tells you that the central area without seats is called the "pit," and that the people standing there are called "groundlings." They have this name because they stand on the ground to watch the play. If it rained they would get soaked.

Off to one side of the pit, you notice people selling snacks just like in theaters today. You go to buy something to eat. There is no popcorn, so you settle for a bag of hazelnuts. You certainly are glad to have this snack because it is almost 2 o'clock in the afternoon and you are hungry. Lord Chamberlain explains that all the plays in the public theaters take place during the day. Daylight is necessary for the show to go on. Candles or torches are too dangerous in a theater built of wood and straw.

When the play finally begins, it seems very different from plays you have seen. The main stage has no curtain to raise, and there is no scenery. The actors come and go in colorful costumes, reciting their lines while musicians play in an area above them. It is very hard for you to understand the words the actors are speaking. It is English but many words sound different. The actors speak in a singsong manner that takes a little while to get used to.

Lord Chamberlain whispers to you that Shakespeare wants his plays to be enjoyed by everyone. Shakespeare's plays are funny and exciting. Some of his plots are farfetched because the people in his audience like make-believe stories.

After a little while the language of the play becomes easier to understand. You realize that *Romeo and Juliet* is about the love between a young man and a young woman whose families are fighting each other. In one scene the actor playing Juliet asks, "O Romeo, Romeo! Wherefore art thou Romeo?" You understand that "art thou" means "are you."

The story may remind you of a musical called *West Side Story*. It can be seen today on TV. One big difference, though, is that in *Romeo and Juliet* all the parts are played by men or boys. Even the female roles are played by male actors. In Elizabethan England women were not allowed to

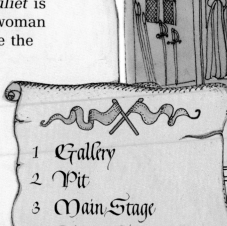

1 Gallery
2 Pit
3 Main Stage
4 Upper Stage
5 Wardrobe and Storage

perform on a public stage. It may seem strange to you that women were not permitted to be actors in a country ruled by a woman.

A LIVING TRADITION

People from all levels of London society attended plays at the Globe Theater. They went to the theater to relax, to be entertained, and to forget about their own lives for a while. These are some of the same reasons that people enjoy going to the theater or to the movies today. Traditions such as the theater link us across the centuries to people of long ago.

Why do you think that theater has become a tradition in many different parts of the world?

IMPORTANT EVENTS

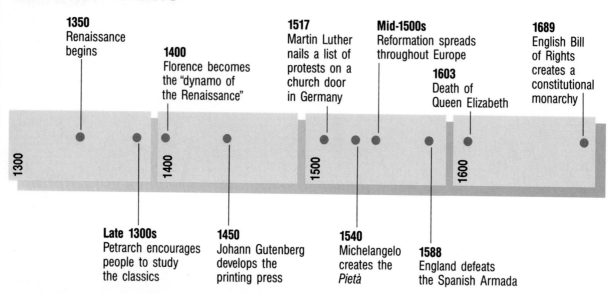

1350
Renaissance begins

Late 1300s
Petrarch encourages people to study the classics

1400
Florence becomes the "dynamo of the Renaissance"

1450
Johann Gutenberg develops the printing press

1517
Martin Luther nails a list of protests on a church door in Germany

1540
Michelangelo creates the *Pietà*

Mid-1500s
Reformation spreads throughout Europe

1603
Death of Queen Elizabeth

1588
England defeats the Spanish Armada

1689
English Bill of Rights creates a constitutional monarchy

1300 · 1400 · 1500 · 1600

PEOPLE TO KNOW

Queen Elizabeth A.D. 1533-1603

Johann Gutenberg A.D. 1400-1468

Leonardo da Vinci A.D. 1452-1519

Lorenzo de'Medici A.D. 1449-1492

Martin Luther A.D. 1483-1546

Michelangelo A.D. 1475-1564

William Shakespeare A.D. 1564-1616

IDEAS TO REMEMBER

- The Renaissance was a period in which people hoped to bring back the great cultures of ancient civilizations. There was a renewed interest in the classics and great support of the arts.
- The creation of the printing press allowed the ideas of the Reformation to spread quickly. The number of books in Europe increased by millions.
- Under the rule of Queen Elizabeth I, England experienced its own Renaissance. After her death, the English Bill of Rights turned England into a constitutional monarchy.

REVIEWING VOCABULARY

absolute monarchy	Parliament
armada	Protestant
Bill of Rights	Reformation
classics	Renaissance
constitutional monarchy	Roman Catholic

Number a sheet of paper from 1 to 10. Beside each number write the word or term from the above list that best matches the statement or definition.

1. Many of the liberties expressed in this English document were included in the U. S. Constitution 100 years later.
2. This was Europe's only major religion until about A.D. 1500.
3. Despite its great size and power, this fleet of Spanish warships was defeated by the quicker English ships.
4. The discovery of these ancient works encouraged a renewed interest in learning among Europeans.
5. The name given to members of this movement because they protested certain practices of the Roman Catholic Church.
6. In this form of government all power was held by a king or queen.
7. This term refers to a cultural and artistic movement in Europe that marked the end of the Middle Ages.
8. This type of government is headed by a monarch, but with limited powers.
9. When Martin Luther nailed his 95 statements to a church door, he set in motion this movement against the Catholic Church.
10. This English law-making body limited the powers of kings.

REVIEWING FACTS

1. List three things that contributed to the birth and spread of the Renaissance.
2. Who were two of Italy's chief artists during the Renaissance?
3. What part of Europe became Protestant and which remained Roman Catholic?
4. Describe the English Renaissance.
5. Name two effects that the Reformation had on the Roman Catholic Church.

◖▭▷ WRITING ABOUT MAIN IDEAS

1. **Writing a Paragraph:** Write a paragraph explaining why the following statement is false: "Luther's goal from the very beginning was to lead a Reformation and to change Europe."
2. **Writing About Perspectives:** Imagine that you are a reporter for a newspaper in Spain or England in 1588. Write a feature story telling about the defeat of the Spanish Armada from your side. Use the library to gather more information if necessary.

BUILDING SKILLS: USING THE LIBRARY

Imagine that you are one of the famous people you have studied in this chapter. You will be interviewed by one of your classmates. Prepare for your interview by using library resources. Take notes from such references as encyclopedias and biographical dictionaries. Use the card catalog to locate biographies and history books. Try to guess which questions will be asked. Prepare your answers.

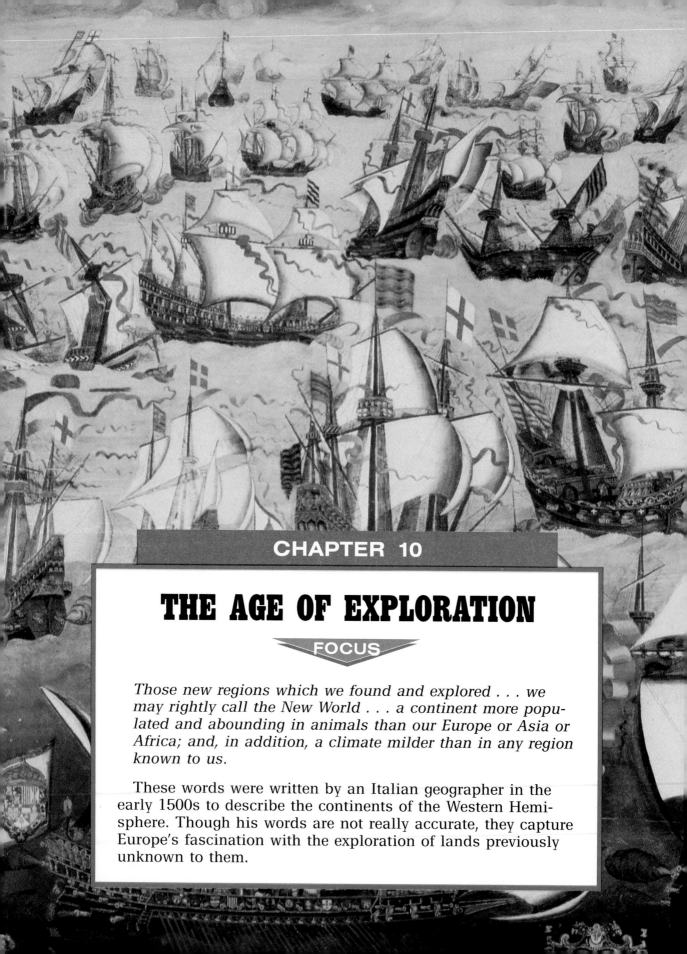

CHAPTER 10

THE AGE OF EXPLORATION

▼ FOCUS ▼

*Those new regions which we found and explored . . . we
may rightly call the New World . . . a continent more populated and abounding in animals than our Europe or Asia or
Africa; and, in addition, a climate milder than in any region
known to us.*

These words were written by an Italian geographer in the
early 1500s to describe the continents of the Western Hemisphere. Though his words are not really accurate, they capture
Europe's fascination with the exploration of lands previously
unknown to them.

1 Traders and Explorers

READ TO LEARN

Key Vocabulary
astronomy
compass
caravel

Key People
Marco Polo
Kublai Khan
Henry the Navigator
Bartholomeu Dias
Vasco da Gama
Christopher Columbus

Key Places
Khanbalik
Calicut

Read Aloud

As you know, the Vikings were the first Europeans to make voyages of exploration. About 500 years later, southern Europeans began to reach out to other parts of the world. In fact, these new explorers of the Renaissance learned that the world was a much larger place than anyone had ever imagined.

Read for Purpose

1. **WHAT YOU KNOW:** Who were the first Europeans to reach North America?
2. **WHAT YOU WILL LEARN:** Why did the Europeans want new sea routes?

THE TRAVELS OF MARCO POLO

You may remember that during the Middle Ages, the people of Europe did not know much about the rest of the world. Most of Africa and Asia, and the great civilizations that flourished there, were unknown to Europeans. The Europeans of this time did not even know that North and South America existed. Though Europeans began to trade with the Middle East and North Africa, they knew little about the people who lived there.

One European, however, did much to change the view his people had of far-away places. This Italian merchant, named Marco Polo, made a remarkable journey. Marco Polo was only 17 years old when he left Venice in 1271. He spent nearly 25 years traveling deeper and deeper into Asia until he reached a city called Khanbalik (kän bə lēk'). Khanbalik was a city in China that was unknown to Europeans. You can follow Marco Polo's route on the map in the Unit Opener on pages 204–205.

Marco Polo spent many years in China, living with its great leader, the Kublai Khan (kū' blī kän'). The Kublai

Marco Polo's account of his trip to China was greeted with disbelief when he returned to Italy. This painting shows the Polo brothers in the Persian Gulf.

Khan liked the young Marco Polo and gave him important work to do. Polo learned the language and customs of China, and the Khan sent him to look after important business in distant parts of the Chinese empire.

When Marco Polo finally returned to Venice in 1292, he wrote a book about his travels. It began with these words:

Royal Princes, Emperors and Kings, Dukes, Counts, Knights, and People of all degrees who desire to get knowledge of the many races of people and of the diversities of the many regions of the World, take this Book and cause it to be read to you. For ye shall find all kinds of wonderful things!

Marco Polo's book amazed European readers. They could not imagine that Marco Polo really had traveled to a land with "mountains higher than birds could fly" and a land that had "black stones that would burn." What could Marco Polo possibly be describing? Europeans did not know about the incredible Himalayas or about burning coal. Most Europeans had never traveled beyond their hometowns.

Marco Polo's exciting stories helped to make people interested in lands unknown to them. As the stories were told, people dreamed of exploring such lands.

THE NEED FOR NEW TRADE ROUTES

In the years of the Renaissance that followed Marco Polo's death, Europeans began to reach out to other parts of the world. Many countries established trading relationships with faraway countries in Asia and Africa. As commerce grew, Europeans began to enjoy many special, exotic goods. From the "Indies," or the lands of south Asia, came spices, silk, fine cottons, precious stones, tea, costly woods, and many other goods. Europeans found that Africa was rich in precious stones, ivory, and gold.

The routes over which these goods were carried were long and difficult. Land routes lay across deserts and

258

mountains. Goods shipped from the Indies by sea had to be reloaded in ports either in the Persian Gulf or the Red Sea. From there they went by land to the shores of the Mediterranean Sea, where the goods were again placed on boats and shipped to Europe. Products from the Indies were not only carried great distances but also handled by many people. No wonder such products were very costly by the time they arrived in Europe.

HENRY THE NAVIGATOR

It is easy to understand why European merchants wanted to find a cheaper way of transporting goods from the Indies. Prince Henry of Portugal, or Henry the Navigator as he was called, was determined to find a better, cheaper route.

Henry was convinced that there was an all-water route from Europe to the Indies. He believed it was possible for ships to travel south along the west coast of Africa, around the southern tip of Africa, and into the Indian Ocean. Then, he was sure, they could sail east to the Indies.

To help achieve his goal, Henry the Navigator founded a school for sailors in 1418. The best maps of the time were gathered together. Sea captains and mapmakers from all over Europe were brought together. Sailors studied geography and astronomy. Astronomy is the study of the planets, stars, and other heavenly bodies. Sailors used their knowledge of astronomy to navigate the seas.

LANDMARKS IN TECHNOLOGY

Important new landmarks in technology were used and developed at Prince Henry's school. For example,

Though called "the Navigator," Henry stayed in Portugal waiting for news of voyages.

the Portuguese learned from Arabs how to use sailing instruments, such as the compass. Have you ever used a compass? It was perhaps the most important instrument of navigation. The compass, as you may know, shows the direction of the magnetic north. Thus, it could be used to set a ship on course in bad, cloudy weather.

Another landmark in technology was the caravel (kar' ə vel). The caravel was a sailing vessel better suited for rough seas and long voyages. For centuries sailors tried to never lose sight of land. If they did, they knew their ships could be crushed by the swift currents and violent storms of the oceans. Sailors on a caravel could dare the rough seas because its massive size and triangular sails helped it to glide safely through ocean storms.

VOYAGES THAT CHANGED THE WORLD

Year by year Henry the Navigator sent out caravels to explore the west coast of Africa. And little by little, these vessels sailed farther south into unknown waters. Europeans had never sailed along Africa's coast.

Prince Henry did not live to see the day when his sailors rounded the southern tip of Africa. In 1487 a fleet of three ships, under the command of **Bartholomeu Dias** (bär tü lü mā′ ü dē′ əs), set out from Portugal. On this voyage Dias steered his fleet around Africa's southernmost tip, calling it the "Cape of Storms." It was later renamed "Cape of Good Hope."

Ten years later a fleet of four ships, commanded by **Vasco da Gama**, sailed into the harbor of **Calicut**. Calicut was a port in India. As the map on this page shows, Da Gama brought his fleet through the Atlantic Ocean, around the Cape of Good Hope, and across the Indian Ocean to India. There his fleet was loaded with spices and other goods, and then sailed back to Europe. Europeans, at last, had found an all-water route to the Indies that Henry the Navigator had dreamed of.

MAP SKILL: European ships sailed east and west, searching for a route to Asia. Which explorer first reached India?

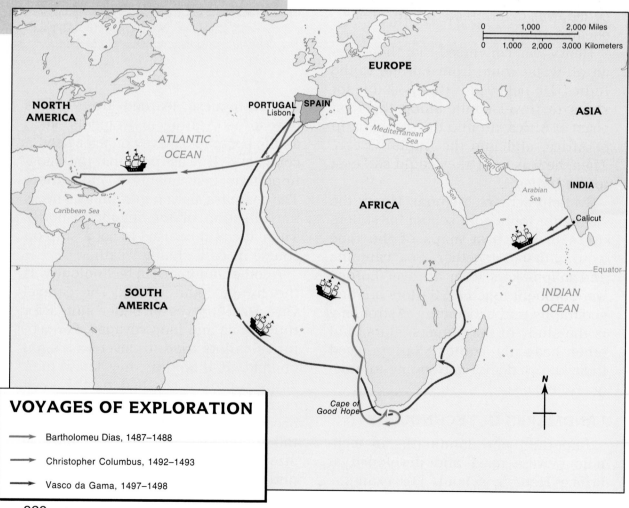

VOYAGES OF EXPLORATION

→ Bartholomeu Dias, 1487–1488

→ Christopher Columbus, 1492–1493

→ Vasco da Gama, 1497–1498

Five years before Da Gama's voyage, an Italian seaman named Christopher Columbus began the first of four breakthrough voyages. Columbus thought that there had to be a faster route. He believed that "one could sail west to reach the Indies of the East." The Portuguese, Columbus believed, had been wasting their time.

Departing from Spain, Columbus's fleet of three ships set sail in 1492. Unlike all previous voyages made by the Portuguese, Columbus steered his small fleet westward, out across "the Green Sea of Darkness." About two months later, his fleet at last caught sight of land. As you may know, Columbus was convinced that they had reached India. But after his fourth voyage in 1502, Columbus wrote, "I have come to believe that this is a mighty continent which was before unknown."

A LARGER WORLD

Most of the world as we know it today was unknown to Europeans when the Renaissance began. Known

Information gathered on Columbus's voyages helped mapmakers chart new maps. On this old map even wind currents are shown.

only through a few travelers' reports such as those of Marco Polo, the world was very small. As trade increased, however, Europeans began to show a greater interest in the lands beyond their borders. In the fifteenth century, new technology made more ambitious exploration possible. Each voyage out into the unknown world seemed to make the world a larger place.

Check Your Reading

1. What is astronomy?
2. What role did Henry the Navigator play in Portuguese exploration?
3. **GEOGRAPHY SKILL:** How did the growth of new technology help expand knowledge of geography?
4. **THINKING SKILL:** List the events discussed in this lesson in the order in which they happened.

Identifying Fact and Opinion

Key Vocabulary

fact

opinion

Do you know which football team in your neighborhood is the best? How do you know this? Separating **facts** from **opinions** can help you determine what to believe about each team.

A fact is a statement that can be proven true. An opinion is a personal view or belief. It cannot be proven true. Sometimes we believe something to be true even though there is no evidence to support it. Take the question of the best football team. Does winning the League championship support the opinion that one team is the best? What other evidence is needed to support that opinion?

Trying the Skill

Which of the following statements about caravels are facts? Which are opinions? Which opinions are based on facts?

The caravel was faster than other ships, and better fitted for maneuvering. Caravels had a square stern, and a foremast that leaned far forward, giving the ship a jaunty look. A caravel's holds—the space below the deck—were large, and its forward section had openings for cannons. It was a serious ship—a cargo carrier with teeth.

1. What facts and opinions did you find?
2. Which opinions were supported by facts?
3. How did you identify the facts?

HELPING YOURSELF

The steps on the left present one way to separate facts from opinions. The example on the right shows how these steps can be used to find facts and opinions in the paragraph on page 262.

One Way to Identify Facts and Opinions	Example
1. Recall the meaning of a fact and an opinion.	A fact is a statement that can be proven true. An opinion is a personal belief.
2. Recall clues that signal facts and opinions:	• *Fact Clue*: specific information that can be checked. • *Opinion Clue*: Key words such as *probably,* or adjectives such as *the best.*
3. Examine the statements carefully to find clues to facts or opinions.	You could check old records to see what a caravel looked like and how it was built. The words *faster*, *better*, and *serious* are expressions of opinion.
4. Tell whether each statement is a fact or an opinion.	The statement that the caravel's fore-mast leans forward can be checked. It is a fact. The statement that the ship had a "jaunty look" is an opinion. To the writer, it looked "jaunty." Does the fact that the caravel's sides had openings for cannons support the opinion that it was a "serious ship"?

Applying the Skill

When Christopher Columbus told Queen Isabella that "one could sail west to reach the Indies of the East," he had to support his opinion with facts. Below are some statements he might have made. Which of the statements are facts? Which are opinions? Explain your answers.

1. The earth ought to be a globe to match the globe of the heavens.
2. The gradual disappearance of a ship as it sails out to sea shows that the earth curves downward from the place of observation. Therefore, I believe the earth is round.
3. The earth's shadow as it falls on the moon during a partial eclipse is always part of a dark circle. A shadow is the image of the object, therefore the earth is round.

Reviewing the Skill

1. What is a fact? What is an opinion?
2. What are some steps you could take to identify a fact and an opinion?
3. Why is it important to identify facts and opinions?

2 The Beginning of Modern Science

READ TO LEARN

Key Vocabulary

geocentric theory
heliocentric theory
telescope
gravity

Key People

Copernicus
Galileo
Isaac Newton

Read Aloud

During the Age of Exploration, daring European explorers sailed into uncharted seas and overcame some of the world's great geographic barriers. At the same time, daring European thinkers were entering into another uncharted area. They were gaining a greater knowledge of science. These explorers were opening up new ways of understanding the world.

Read for Purpose

1. **WHAT YOU KNOW:** How did the Age of Exploration change the world?
2. **WHAT YOU WILL LEARN:** How did the ideas of three scientists change the world?

COPERNICUS AND THE SUN

Copernicus (kə pûr′ ni kəs) had a unique and dangerous idea. The Polish astronomer believed that the earth revolved, or moved in a circle, around the sun. From his rooms atop a high tower in Poland, Copernicus had a clear view of the heavens. He could study stars and planets as they seemed to move across the night sky. But could he ever publish his ideas when he knew that they would not be accepted? In about 1535, Copernicus wrote:

What I know, the public disapproves. And what it approves, I know to be in error. This is my conflict.

During the early 1500s, scientists believed that the earth was the center of the universe. This earth-centered view of the universe is called the geocentric (jē ō sen′ trik) theory. The geocentric theory was first developed by the ancient Greeks but was later adopted by the Christian Church. They thought that the earth stood still and that the sun, stars, and planets all moved around it. According to the geocentric theory, seven "planets"—the moon, the sun, Mercury, Venus, Mars, Jupiter, and Saturn—revolved around Earth. But this theory was wrong.

The Granger Collection

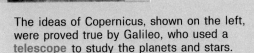

The ideas of Copernicus, shown on the left, were proved true by Galileo, who used a telescope to study the planets and stars.

Copernicus's observations caused him to question the geocentric theory. He concluded that the earth was not the unmoving center of the universe. Copernicus thought instead that the sun was the center. This idea is known as the heliocentric (hē lē ō sen′ trik) theory. According to the heliocentric theory, the earth and the other planets moved in orbits around the sun. The heliocentric theory would not be accepted until more than 100 years after the death of Copernicus. Yet his ideas marked the beginning of modern science.

GALILEO'S TELESCOPE

As Copernicus had expected, his discovery was condemned by the Church. But an Italian scientist named Galileo (gal ə lā′ ō) was convinced that Copernicus was correct.

In 1609 Galileo developed a way to prove the truth of the heliocentric theory. He learned about a Dutch invention called the telescope (tel′ ə skōp). The telescope is an instrument that makes faraway objects appear closer. Galileo built his own telescope and made it even more powerful. It made objects appear 30 times closer and 1,000 times larger than normal. Through his telescope, Galileo studied the movements of the planets and the stars. What he saw was proof of the heliocentric theory.

Isaac Newton found that great ideas can occur even while one is sitting under an apple tree on a fine sunny day.

NEWTON AND THE LAWS OF GRAVITY

On Christmas Day in 1642, the year Galileo died, Isaac Newton was born. During his lifetime, this English mathematician and scientist would offer the final proof that the planets revolve around the sun. Newton asked:

If Earth and the planets are all in motion, what keeps them from flying out in all directions? And what keeps people from falling off a moving Earth?

According to legend, Newton found his answer when he was sitting beneath an apple tree in 1675. Suddenly, an apple fell from a high branch and bounced off his head. Newton concluded that there was a force called gravity at work. Gravity is a force that causes objects to be pulled toward the center of the earth, like the apple was pulled to the ground.

In 1687 Newton published his belief that the "law of gravity" causes the planets to circle the sun. He wrote, however, that his discovery was based upon the legacies of greater thinkers:

If I have been able to see farther than others, it is because I have stood on the shoulders of giants.

THE LEGACY OF THE NEW SCIENCE

Newton and the other scientists of his time developed what is now called the "scientific method." This method of thinking holds that no idea should be accepted as true unless it is thoroughly tested.

Scientists like Copernicus, Galileo, and Newton were the courageous pioneers of modern science. They refused to be tied to old ideas. Instead, they dared to question old knowledge and demand proof for it. If the old answers were not provable, they looked for new answers that were. You will learn in later chapters that their legacy helped give birth to modern science.

Check Your Reading

1. What is gravity?
2. Why was Copernicus afraid to publish his ideas?
3. What are the geocentric and heliocentric theories?
4. **THINKING SKILL:** How did the work of Galileo and Newton affect the ideas of Copernicus?

LEARNING ABOUT THE EARTH FROM SPACE

In every age throughout time, explorers have left their homelands in search of adventure or great fortune. Sometimes they were successful. Sometimes they were not. As one modern explorer noted:

Explorers of every age have returned greatly changed by their journies. They come home with a new and different way of looking at the world.

The most popular explorers these days are the American astronauts and the Soviet cosmonauts. Indeed, many of these brave modern explorers have come back to the earth with very strong feelings about the world they live in. In 1969 astronaut Rusty Schweickart flew in space aboard *Apollo 9*. From his viewpoint near the moon he thought that the earth looked very small and fragile.

In 1985 Rusty helped start the Association of Space Explorers, a club for those whose flights in space gave them a certain vision. That vision is the hope to have the nations of the world work together on projects on the earth and in space.

The Association of Space Explorers has members from 16 nations. Although they were all trained in either the American or Soviet space programs, members try to share their experiences. From space, they say, the earth is very small.

From up in space, you don't see the barriers of color and religion and politics that divide the world. You know that if you could get everyone in the world up there, they would feel differently.

The space explorers think that all the people of the earth should be working to protect the health of our planet.

Is the Association of Space Explorers making a difference? The members believe they are. They have chosen various ways to share their space experiences. Former astronaut Alan Bean, for example, is an artist who paints the sights he saw from his Apollo mission in space. Other American and Soviet space explorers travel together on speaking tours. The Association publishes books, has traveling exhibits, and puts together research on future space projects.

Rusty Schweickart and the other space explorers want young people to think of the future with hope and excitement. They think that the young men and women of the earth have the potential to do great things . . . if they work together.

IMPORTANT EVENTS

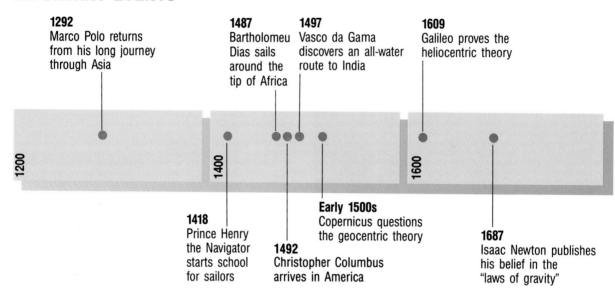

1292
Marco Polo returns from his long journey through Asia

1487
Bartholomeu Dias sails around the tip of Africa

1497
Vasco da Gama discovers an all-water route to India

1609
Galileo proves the heliocentric theory

1200

1400

1600

1418
Prince Henry the Navigator starts school for sailors

1492
Christopher Columbus arrives in America

Early 1500s
Copernicus questions the geocentric theory

1687
Isaac Newton publishes his belief in the "laws of gravity"

PEOPLE TO KNOW

Christopher Columbus A.D. 1446-1506

Copernicus A.D. 1473-1543

Vasco da Gama A.D. 1469-1524

Galileo A.D. 1563-1642

Henry the Navigator A.D. 1394-1460

Isaac Newton A.D. 1642-1727

Marco Polo A.D. 1254-1324

IDEAS TO REMEMBER

■ Marco Polo's stories of his voyage to China excited all of Europe. Europeans began to reach out to all parts of the world. The study of astronomy, and the development of the compass and the caravel helped sailors to make major journeys throughout the world.

■ Copernicus was the first of the early modern scientists to make important new discoveries. Like Copernicus, Galileo and Newton were also pioneers who believed that no idea should be accepted as true unless thoroughly tested.

REVIEWING VOCABULARY

astronomy	gravity
caravel	heliocentric
geocentric	theory
theory	

Number a sheet of paper from 1 to 5. Beside each number write the word or term from the above list that best completes each sentence.

1. _____ is the belief that the sun, planets, and stars all revolve around the earth.
2. Because of its large size and special sails, the _____ enabled Europeans to explore more of the earth.
3. _____ is the force that pulls all things toward the earth's center.
4. Copernicus developed and believed in the _____ to explain the movements of the sun, stars, and planets.
5. Sailors used _____, the study of heavenly bodies, to navigate in uncharted waters.

REVIEWING FACTS

1. Name three results of Marco Polo's journey to China.
2. Who was the first European to sail around the southern tip of Africa?
3. What is the scientific method? How did the scientific method lead to the growth of new ideas?
4. How did Isaac Newton's "falling apple" experience lead to his discovery of the law of gravity?
5. Why did European merchants want to find an all-water route to the Indies? What effect did overland transport have on the price of goods?

WRITING ABOUT MAIN IDEAS

1. **Writing a Journal Entry:** Many people believed that Columbus's expedition was doomed to sail off "the edge of the world." Imagine you are a sailor on Columbus's first voyage. You have not seen land for weeks. Write an entry in your journal describing your feelings and experiences.
2. **Using a Dictionary:** The word *telescope,* an invention that you read about in this chapter, is made up of the Greek terms *tele* and *skopein.* Using an unabridged dictionary, write the English meaning of the two words. Then do the same for the following words: television, telegraph, telephone, telepathy, and telekinesis.
3. **Writing a Paragraph:** One writer has called America "the accidental nation discovered in the search for spices." Write a paragraph describing what you think this writer meant.
4. **Writing About Perspectives:** For centuries Europeans believed that the sun, stars, and planets revolved around the earth. Write a paragraph describing how Copernicus's theory changed people's view of their place in the universe.

BUILDING SKILLS: IDENTIFYING FACT AND OPINION

On a sheet of paper, list three statements from this chapter that are facts and three statements that are opinions. Exchange papers with a partner. Have your partner label the statements that are facts and underline words that signal opinions.

UNIT 4 - REVIEW

REVIEWING VOCABULARY

Each of the following statements contains an underlined vocabulary word. Number a sheet of paper from 1 to 10. Beside each number write whether the following statements are true or false. If the statement is true, write "true". If it is false, write "false" and rewrite the sentence using the vocabulary word correctly.

1. The Magna Carta was a French document that increased the powers of the king of France over the nobility.
2. The geocentric theory, created by Copernicus, claimed that the sun was at the center of the universe.
3. The Renaissance was a period of artistic and cultural growth that began in Italy and moved northward.
4. Under feudalism, lords were required to provide protection to serfs in exchange for their labor.
5. The Roman Catholic Church defined its teachings at the Council of Trent.
6. Protestants were Christians who protested against Martin Luther's 95 statements.
7. The Crusades were holy wars carried out by the Vikings against the Christian rulers of northern Europe.
8. The Middle Ages lasted about 500 years from the beginning of the Crusades to the time of Queen Elizabeth I of England.
9. Parliament was a law-making body that helped transform England into a constitutional monarchy.
10. The Reformation did much to increase the power of the pope and the unity of the Christian religion.

WRITING ABOUT THE UNIT

1. **Writing Paragraphs:** Petrarch and other Renaissance thinkers believed that the Middle Ages was a period of backwardness. Write two paragraphs agreeing or disagreeing with this idea.
2. **Writing an Owner's Manual:** Write a manual describing how a compass works. Include suggestions as to when a compass would be useful.
3. **Writing an Explanation:** Explain what Isaac Newton meant when he said, "I stand on the shoulders of giants."
4. **Writing About Perspectives:** Imagine that you are traveling through Europe in a "time machine." On your trip through the past, write five postcards to your friends in the twentieth century. Which five events from Europe's past would you choose to write about? Why?

ACTIVITIES

1. **Reading a Map:** Look at the map of the Frankish Empire on page 215. Which part of Europe was not ruled by Charlemagne? How do you know? Find the present-day political map of Europe in your Atlas on page 610. Which present-day European countries did Charlemagne's empire include?
2. **Presenting a Television Report:** Imagine that you could go back in time to actually witness one of the events described in this unit. Write an "on the scene" report for the evening news.
3. **Working Together on Letters:** Work with a partner to write and answer a letter from Marco Polo or Copernicus.

270

LONDON IN THE TWELFTH CENTURY

The following account was written by William Fitz-Stephen who lived in London during the 1100s.

*A*mong the noble cities of the world that fame celebrates, the City of London, of the Kingdom of the English, is one seat that pours out its fame more widely, sends to farther lands its wealth and trade, lifts its head higher than the rest. It is happy in the healthiness of its air, in the Christian religion, in the strength of its defenses, the nature of its site, the honor of its citizens, the modesty of its women, pleasant in sports, fruitful of noble men. . . .

In the holidays, all the summer the youths are exercised in leaping, dancing, shooting, wrestling, casting the stone, and practicing their shields. . . . Every youth is full of pleasure and every Londoner is joyous.

BUILDING SKILLS: IDENTIFYING FACT AND OPINION

Use the account above to answer the following questions.

1. What is a fact? How does a fact differ from an opinion?
2. What are two facts you can find in Fitz-Stephen's account?
3. What are two opinions you can find in the account?
4. Which opinions were supported by facts? How can you tell?
5. Summarize Fitz-Stephen's view of London in the twelfth century.
6. Why is it important to identify facts and opinions?

 **LINKING PAST, PRESENT, AND FUTURE**

Periods such as the Middle Ages were not named by the people who lived in them, but by those who came after them. For example, you read that historians have also called the Middle Ages the "Dark Ages" or the "Age of Faith." What name do you think people living 100 years from now will give to the age in which we are living? Give reasons to support your answer.

NORTH AMERICA

+ North Pole

ARCTIC
OCEAN

Arctic Circle

ICELAND

Barents
Sea

60°N

SWEDEN

UNITED
KINGDOM

NORWAY

FINLAND

RUSSIA

IRELAND

North
Sea

DENMARK

ESTONIA

LATVIA

ATLANTIC

OCEAN

45°N

NETHERLANDS
BELGIUM
LUXEMBOURG

GERMANY

Baltic
Sea

LITHUANIA

(RUSSIA)

BYELARUS

KAZAKHSTAN

Bay of
Biscay

SWITZERLAND

POLAND

FRANCE

AUSTRIA

CZECHOSLOVAKIA

UKRAINE

KYRGYZSTAN

PORTUGAL

Tropic of Cancer

30°N

SPAIN

ITALY

HUNGARY

YUGOSLAVIA

ROMANIA

MOLDOVA

UZBEKISTAN

TAJIKISTAN

ALBANIA

BULGARIA

Black Sea

GEORGIA

Caspian Sea

GREECE

ARMENIA

TURKMENISTAN

30°W

Mediterranean Sea

AZERBAIJAN

INDIAN

15°W

15°N

OCEAN

0°

AFRICA

60°E

Equator

45°E

0°

Tropic of Capricorn

15°S

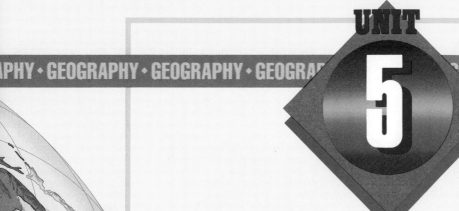

UNIT

5

EUROPE AND NORTH ASIA IN MODERN TIMES

WHERE WE ARE

In Unit 5 you will read about modern Europe and Russia and its neighbors in North Asia. As the map shows, the lands of this huge region stretch from the Atlantic Ocean in the west all the way to the Pacific Ocean in the east.

You have already read a great deal about the history and geography of Europe. This unit will give you a chance to meet the people who live in Europe today. You will also read about Russia, its land, and its people. Read on. The adventure through the world around us continues.

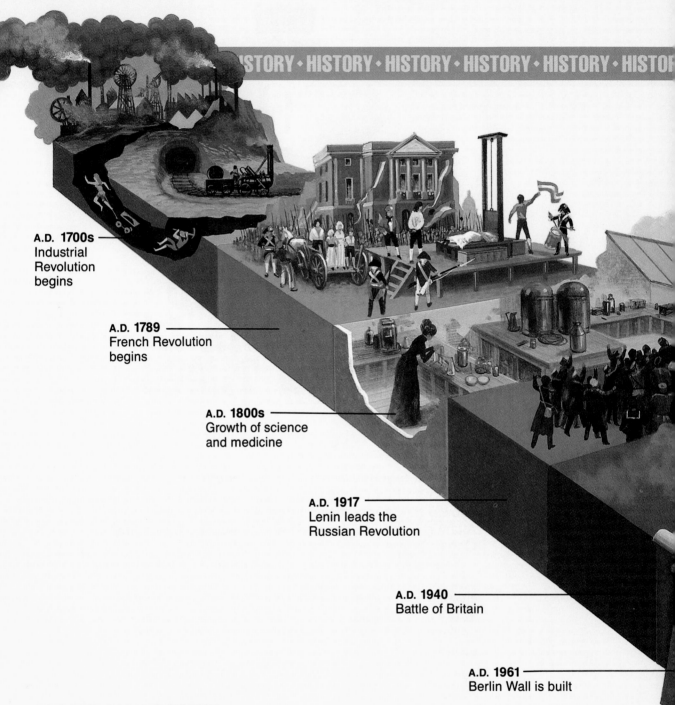

A.D. 1700s
Industrial
Revolution
begins

A.D. 1789
French Revolution
begins

A.D. 1800s
Growth of science
and medicine

A.D. 1917
Lenin leads the
Russian Revolution

A.D. 1940
Battle of Britain

A.D. 1961
Berlin Wall is built

WHAT HAPPENED

New ways of thinking about
technology and government have changed
the world around us. In this unit you will read
about the growth of amazing new technology. You
will also learn about a new system of government that
changed the lives of millions of people in Russia. As the
time line shows, you will discover that modern times have
brought both destruction and cooperation.

A.D. 1989-1991
The Cold War comes
to an end

EUROPE AND
NORTH ASIA

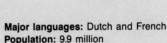

ALBANIA

Capital ★
Tiranë

Major language: Albanian
Population: 3.3 million
Area: 11,100 sq mi; 28,750 sq km
Leading export: minerals

BELGIUM

Capital ★
Brussels

Major languages: Dutch and French
Population: 9.9 million
Area: 11,779 sq mi; 30,510 sq km
Leading exports: machinery, and
iron and steel products

ANDORRA

Capital ★
Andorra la Vella

Major languages: Catalan, French,
and Spanish
Population: 53,000
Area: 174 sq mi; 450 sq km
Leading export: stamps

BULGARIA

Capital ★
Sofia

Major languages: Bulgarian and
Turkish
Population: 9.0 million
Area: 42,822 sq mi; 110,910 sq km
Leading export: machinery

ARMENIA

Capital ★
Yerevan

Major language: Armenian
Population: 3.3 million
Area: 11,490 sq mi; 29,800 sq km

BYELARUS

Capital ★
Minsk

Major languages: Byelarusian and
Russian
Population: 10.3 million
Area: 80,134 sq mi; 207,600 sq km

AUSTRIA

Capital ★
Vienna

Major language: German
Population: 7.7 million
Area: 32,375 sq mi; 83,850 sq km
Leading exports: iron and steel
products, and machinery

CZECHOSLOVAKIA

Capital ★
Prague

Major languages: Czech
and Slovak
Population: 15.7 million
Area: 49,365 sq mi; 127,870 sq km
Leading export: machinery

AZERBAIJAN

Capital ★
Baku

Major languages: Azerbaijani, Russian,
and Armenian
Population: 7.1 million
Area: 33,430 sq mi; 86,600 sq km

DENMARK

Capital ★
Copenhagen

Major language: Danish
Population: 5.1 million
Area: 16,629 sq mi; 43,070 sq km
Leading exports: food and machinery

ESTONIA

Capital ★
Tallinn

Major languages: Estonian and Russian
Population: 1.6 million
Area: 17,413 sq mi; 45,100 sq km

HUNGARY

Capital ★
Budapest

Major language: Hungarian
Population: 10.4 million
Area: 35,919 sq mi; 93,030 sq km
Leading export: machinery

FINLAND

Capital ★
Helsinki

Major languages: Finnish and Swedish
Population: 5.0 million
Area: 130,128 sq mi; 337,030 sq km
Leading exports: paper and machinery

ICELAND

Capital ★
Reykjavik

Major language: Icelandic
Population: 0.3 million
Area: 39,768 sq mi; 103,000 sq km
Leading export: fish

FRANCE

Capital ★
Paris

Major language: French
Population: 56.7 million
Area: 211,209 sq mi; 547,030 sq km
Leading exports: machinery and manufactured goods

IRELAND

Capital ★
Dublin

Major languages: English and Irish
Population: 3.5 million
Area: 27,135 sq mi; 70,820 sq km
Leading exports: machinery and food

GEORGIA

Capital ★
Tbilisi

Major languages: Georgian and Russian
Population: 5.5 million
Area: 26,900 sq mi; 69,700 sq km

ITALY

Capital ★
Rome

Major language: Italian
Population: 57.7 million
Area: 116,305 sq mi; 301,230 sq km
Leading exports: machinery and manufactured goods

GERMANY

Capital ★
Berlin

Major language: German
Population: 79.5 million
Area: 95,977 sq mi; 248,580 sq km
Leading exports: machinery and manufactured goods

KAZAKHSTAN

Capital ★
Alma-Ata

Major languages: Kazakh and Russian
Population: 16.7 million
Area: 1,049,155 sq mi; 2,717,300 sq km

GREECE

Capital ★
Athens

Major language: Greek
Population: 10.1 million
Area: 50,942 sq mi; 131,940 sq km
Leading exports: fruits and vegetables, and textiles

KYRGYZSTAN

Capital ★
Bishkek

Major languages: Kyrgyz, Russian, and Uzbek
Population: 4.4 million
Area: 76,640 sq mi; 198,500 sq km

LATVIA

Capital ★
Riga

Major languages: Latvian and
    Russian
Population: 2.7 million
Area: 24,595 sq mi; 63,700 sq km

MONACO

Capital ★
Monaco

Major languages: French and
    Monégasque
Population: 30,000
Area: 0.7 sq mi; 1.9 sq km
Leading export: stamps

LIECHTENSTEIN

Capital ★
Vaduz

Major language: German
Population: 30,000
Area: 62 sq mi; 160 sq km
Leading export: stamps

NETHERLANDS

Capital ★
Amsterdam

Major language: Dutch
Population: 15.0 million
Area: 14,405 sq mi; 37,310 sq km
Leading exports: machinery, chemicals,
    and manufactured goods

LITHUANIA

Capital ★
Vilnius

Major languages: Lithuanian and
    Russian
Population: 3.7 million
Area: 25,170 sq mi; 65,200 sq km

NORWAY

Capital ★
Oslo

Major language: Norwegian
Population: 4.3 million
Area: 125,182 sq mi; 324,220 sq km
Leading exports: oil and natural gas

LUXEMBOURG

Capital ★
Luxembourg

Major languages: Letzeburgesch,
    German, and French
Population: 0.4 million
Area: 998 sq mi; 2,586 sq km
Leading exports: iron and steel
    products

POLAND

Capital ★
Warsaw

Major language: Polish
Population: 38.2 million
Area: 120,726 sq mi; 312,680 sq km
Leading export: machinery

MALTA

Capital ★
Valletta

Major languages: Maltese and English
Population: 0.4 million
Area: 123 sq mi; 320 sq km
Leading exports: machinery
    and clothing

PORTUGAL

Capital ★
Lisbon

Major language: Portuguese
Population: 10.4 million
Area: 35,552 sq mi; 92,080 sq km
Leading exports: machinery,
    manufactured goods, and timber

MOLDOVA

Capital ★
Kishinev

Major languages: Moldovan, Ukrainian,
    and Russian
Population: 4.4 million
Area: 13,000 sq mi; 33,700 sq km

ROMANIA

Capital ★
Bucharest

Major language: Romanian
Population: 23.4 million
Area: 91,699 sq mi; 237,500 sq km
Leading export: machinery

RUSSIA

Capital ★
Moscow

Major language: Russian
Population: 148.0 million
Area: 6,592,813 sq mi; 17,075,000 sq km

SAN MARINO

Capital ★
San Marino

Major language: Italian
Population: 23,000
Area: 23 sq mi; 60 sq km
Leading export: stamps

SPAIN

Capital ★
Madrid

Major languages: Spanish and
Catalan
Population: 39.0 million
Area: 194,884 sq mi; 504,750 sq km
Leading exports: iron and steel
products, and manufactured goods

SWEDEN

Capital ★
Stockholm

Major language: Swedish
Population: 8.6 million
Area: 173,730 sq mi; 449,960 sq km
Leading export: machinery

SWITZERLAND

Capital ★
Bern

Major languages: German, French,
Italian, and Romansch
Population: 6.8 million
Area: 15,942 sq mi; 41,290 sq km
Leading exports: machinery and
chemicals

TAJIKISTAN

Capital ★
Dushanbe

Major languages: Tajik and Russian
Population: 5.3 million
Area: 55,240 sq mi; 143,100 sq km

TURKMENISTAN

Capital ★
Ashkhabad

Major languages: Turkmen and
Russian
Population: 3.6 million
Area: 186,400 sq mi; 488,100 sq km

UKRAINE

Capital ★
Kiev

Major languages: Ukrainian and
Russian
Population: 51.8 million
Area: 231,990 sq mi; 445,000 sq km

UNITED KINGDOM

Capital ★
London

Major language: English
Population: 57.5 million
Area: 94,525 sq mi; 244,820 sq km
Leading exports: machinery and
manufactured goods

UZBEKISTAN

Capital ★
Tashkent

Major languages: Uzbek and
Russian
Population: 20.3 million
Area: 172,741 sq mi; 447,400 sq km

VATICAN CITY

Capital ★
Vatican City

Major languages: Italian and Latin
Population: 750
Area: 0.17 sq mi; 0.44 sq km

YUGOSLAVIA

Capital ★
Belgrade

Major languages: Serbo-Croatian,
Slovene, and Macedonian
Population: 23.9 million
Area: 98,765 sq mi; 255,800 sq km
Leading exports: machinery and
manufactured goods

CHAPTER 11

TWO REVOLUTIONS CHANGE EUROPE

FOCUS

*Would you realize what revolution is, call it Progress;
and would you realize what Progress is, call it Tomorrow.*

When Victor Hugo wrote these words in 1830, great changes had been exploding across Europe for 100 years. Many of the most important changes began in England and France. As you read this chapter, think about Hugo's words. Do you agree with him that the changes taking place were "progress"?

1 The Industrial Revolution

READ TO LEARN

 Key Vocabulary

revolution
Industrial Revolution
textile

factory
middle class
working class

Key People

John Kay
James Hargreaves
James Watt

 **Read Aloud**

In 1700 England was neither the largest country nor the smallest. But a few, simple new inventions led the way to a time of incredible change. Many small villages were about to become large industrial centers.

 Read for Purpose

1. **WHAT YOU KNOW:** What was England like under Elizabeth I?
2. **WHAT YOU WILL LEARN:** How did the Industrial Revolution change England?

WHAT IS A REVOLUTION?

A revolution is often described as a great change that affects how people think and live, and how leaders govern. You know that the American Revolution caused the birth of a new government. The revolution you will read about in this lesson was different.

During the early 1700s, most people in England made their living by farming. Although some people worked at making special goods in small shops, most goods were made by people in their homes. By the mid-1700s, however, a great change in the way goods were made was taking place. Called the Industrial Revolution, this change affected millions of people in England. Moreover, the Industrial Revolution swept from England to other countries.

THE TEXTILE INDUSTRY

How did it all begin? In the middle of the 1700s, England was ripe for the growth of industry. The country had a good food supply and a large work force. The revolution first emerged in the textile, or cloth, industry.

Textile production was one of England's largest industries in the 1700s. England had long been one of the world's leading sheep-raising countries. Raw wool and wool cloth had been England's major trade goods as far back as the Middle Ages. Textiles were produced from cotton by women working in their homes.

Working by hand at their spinning wheels and weaving looms, workers could not keep up with the demand for cloth. Textile merchants knew that they

281

could make more money if they found a way to speed up the work of spinning and weaving.

NEW TECHNOLOGY

By 1800 new technology had totally transformed the textile industry. The first invention came in 1733, when a watchmaker named John Kay made a shuttle that moved back and forth on wheels. The flying shuttle, as it was called, was not much more than a boat-shaped piece of wood to which yarn was attached. Yet it allowed a weaver to work twice as fast.

Now weavers were working so quickly that spinners could not keep up. A prize was offered to anyone who could make a better spinning machine. The prize went to a creative worker named James Hargreaves.

In 1764 Hargreaves invented a new spinning wheel. He called it the "spinning jenny" in honor of his wife. This simple machine allowed one spinner to work six or eight threads at a time instead of just one. Later models could spin as many as 80 threads at once.

The first spinning machines were small enough to use in the home. But later models were too large and costly to keep at home. Thus, rich merchants set up many large machines in buildings called factories. The first textile factories were powered by water mills. But these factories, too, had drawbacks. Not only did a factory have to be built next to a river, but all power failed if there was a drought, or when the water was frozen.

THE STEAM ENGINE

The steam engine was the most important invention of the Industrial Revolution. At last people had a way of

The Industrial Revolution turned England into the world's major producer of colorful textiles.

The Granger Collection

changing heat energy into a kind of power that was not dependent on wind or water. The earliest steam engines were built in the early 1700s. These early machines, however, lacked power. In 1763 a Scottish inventor named James Watt greatly improved the early steam engines.

Watt's steam engine burned coal. Burning coal provided energy by turning water into steam. The steam pushed against certain parts of the machine and made them move. By 1800 almost 500 steam engines were huffing and puffing in England's textile factories.

Watt's improvements made the steam engine much more practical for use in industry. For the first time in history, people had a source of power that could be used anywhere.

CHILD LABOR

Because steam engines burned coal, more and more people were needed to work in the coal mines. Coal mining was probably the most difficult job in the 1700s.

Although animals were used to hoist the mined coal up the shafts, children also worked in the pits. Boys and girls, some as young as six years old, dragged cartloads of coal through dark, cramped tunnels. One young worker named Betty Harris left a record of her working conditions. It is hard to imagine such terrible conditions.

I have a belt round my waist, . . . and I go on my hands and feet. The road is very steep. . . . There are six women and about six boys and girls in the pit I work in. The pit is very wet . . . and the water always floods in. . . . My clothes are wet all day long.

Young children worked long hours on machines like the spinning jenny and dragged coal through dark mine shafts.

A CHANGING WAY OF LIFE

The growth of industry changed the way people lived. Towns with factories quickly grew into cities and important social changes took place. In the first place, many families who lived in the countryside moved to industrial centers for work. The biggest social change, however, was the growing importance of the middle class. The middle class was made up of business people. Some of these people owned factories, mines, railroads, and banks.

The growth of industry dramatically changed transportation. Trains and steamships allowed people to travel long distances more quickly.

The new middle class greatly changed the social structure of England. In the past, rich landowners were in the top position in English society. Now, some factory owners and merchants had more money and, often, more power than the landowners.

The growth of factories also led to a huge working class. The people of the working class lived near the factories. Many of these people were poor and lived in crowded conditions. One person wrote:

> The dwellings of the working class in the back alleys are woeful [sad]. . . . The amount of room used by many families is miserably small; most have only one room for the whole family.

PLUSES AND MINUSES

The Industrial Revolution brought a great deal of hardship to many people, but it also led to many improvements. For example, new farming technology made it possible for fewer farmers to grow more food. As you will read, revolutionary changes in transportation also took place.

The new steam-powered Liverpool-Manchester Railroad opened in 1830. People were terrified by the noise and

SHOEMAKING BEFORE AND AFTER THE INDUSTRIAL REVOLUTION

How shoes are made	Before Industrialization	After Industrialization
1. cut out uppers	One shoemaker, working without machinery, makes one pair of shoes a day. 	Six factory workers, working together, with machinery make 36 pairs of shoes a day. 
2. sew back and front		
3. attach sole		
4. add heel		
5. add insides		
6. add holes for laces		

CHART SKILL: The new technology spread from textiles to other industries. How did factories affect the shoe industry?

clatter of the "iron horse," but it was an immediate success. Thousands of passengers traveled between Liverpool and Manchester every day on a dozen separate trains. In 1850, only 20 years after the first railroad, England's chief cities were linked together. You can read more about what people thought the pluses and minuses of the Industrial Revolution were in the Point/Counterpoint on pages 286–287.

Were people better or worse off as a result of the Industrial Revolution? Historians do not agree. Because England was the first country to industrialize, social problems were the worst there. But, as you have read, England was also the birthplace of many new inventions that improved lives.

The Industrial Revolution spread to other European countries and to the United States. In the next lesson you will read about another revolution that was taking place in France.

Check Your Reading

1. What English industry was first revolutionized in the 1700s?
2. How did factories change the way people lived and worked?
3. **GEOGRAPHY SKILL:** Why was England suited for industrial growth?
4. **THINKING SKILL:** How did the spinning jenny lead to the growth of England's textile industry?

1820—Is Industrial Growth Good for England?

The Industrial Revolution began in England in the 1700s. As you have read, many things favored England's industrial growth. For example, the island nation had many natural resources such as coal, as well as navigable rivers and seaports. England's population nearly doubled between 1700 and 1800. This growing number of people provided a market for goods and a source of labor.

By the mid-1700s England had changed from a farming society into the world's chief industrial power. Towns seemed to turn into large, and often filthy, industrial centers overnight. New factories were built across the countryside. People moved from place to place, in search of jobs. Old jobs disappeared and new ones were created.

By the early 1800s many people wondered if they were really better off than they had been before the Industrial Revolution.

POINT ☆\☞

For the Good of All

A factory owner in Manchester named Eliot Bakerman wrote about the advantages of industrial growth.

> In this otherwise dull place, industry and trade have found fertile soil. Steam-power has been introduced and successfully applied to all forms of machinery. Rivers are now used to produce power for the factories. They are crossed with dozens of bridges bearing roads and railroads.
>
> Industry has raised the prosperity of all the places it touches. It has even extended its benefits to the surrounding neighborhoods. The planted acres through which we passed were once only wasteland. They would have remained that way if the growth of population around the factories had not opened a new market for food.
>
> Thus we have outlived the senseless charge that machines take work away from laborers and bread from the poor. Work in every branch of industry has increased by the introduction of machinery into it. Every new factory creates a fresh demand for labor.

Why did Eliot Bakerman think that industrial growth was good for England?

COUNTERPOINT ☜\☆

The Burden of Factory Labor

A London reporter named William Bentley wrote about the problems created by industrial growth.

> Julia Simms has worked in a cloth factory since the age of six. She is today a young woman of 16, yet she has had no childhood. This is the way of industry. This is the way of poor Julia who, from five in the morning till nine at night, has removed spindles from the spinning jenny. This poor girl in Lancashire was given nothing but a bit of 40 minutes to eat at noon. As far as breakfast and drinking, she got it as she could. And Julia has had no schooling. But work, work, work. This is the progress that industry has brought England.
>
> A factory is a miserable place for children, and England's factories are filled with children. This is a crime against us. It is not only the child who is enslaved by industry. Many men and women are enslaved. But why must the burden of factory labor fall on a child's back? If this is the way of industry, let industry find another land to spoil.

Why did William Bentley think that industrial growth was not good for England?

UNDERSTANDING THE POINT/COUNTERPOINT

1. Who do you think made a stronger argument about the growth of industry?
2. How do you think that an English farmer would have felt about this issue?
3. Can you think of a compromise that might have been acceptable to both Eliot Bakerman and William Bentley? Explain your answer.

2 The French Revolution

READ TO LEARN

Key Vocabulary

divine right
estates
aristocracy

Key People

Louis XVI
Marie Antoinette
Napoleon Bonaparte

Read Aloud

"Here and today begins a new age in the history of the world." That is how one person described the French Revolution. Beginning in 1789, it was a time of sweeping change, hope, and bloodshed. It would symbolize a new age for millions of people.

Read for Purpose

1. **WHAT YOU KNOW:** What caused the American Revolution?
2. **WHAT YOU WILL LEARN:** How did revolution change France?

ABSOLUTE MONARCHY

While the Industrial Revolution was spreading across Europe, another revolution was starting. The people of France had been governed by absolute monarchs for more than 800 years. You may recall that with the Magna Carta and the Bill of Rights, the English turned their government into a constitutional monarchy. But no changes had taken place in France. Why did millions of French people want to change what they had lived with for so long?

King Louis XVI had governed France since 1774. Louis and all the French kings before him believed that they ruled by divine right. Divine right meant that the monarch's authority to rule came from God and could not be questioned.

Many French people did not believe that their monarchs had a divine right to govern. Such people wanted to limit their ruler's power, and set up a constitutional monarchy. Some people in France wanted to do away with the monarchy altogether.

FRENCH SOCIETY BEFORE THE REVOLUTION

Since the Middle Ages, the people of France had been divided into three large social classes, or estates. The priests of the Roman Catholic Church formed the First Estate. The Church held about 15 percent of all the land in France and was incredibly rich. French priests paid no direct taxes to the government. Instead, they paid a "free gift" of about 2 percent of their earnings.

The aristocracy, or the members of noble families, made up the Second Estate. You may recall that ancient Rome had a similar group of people called the patricians. Like the patricians, the French aristocracy held all the important jobs in government. Although they made up less than 2 percent of the French population, the aristocracy owned more than 25 percent of the land. For centuries, this Second Estate enjoyed the privilege of paying no taxes at all.

The seeds of revolution lay among the people of the Third Estate. As the graph on this page shows, about 98 percent of France's population belonged to the Third Estate. This vast majority of people were the middle and working classes. They were merchants, butchers, weavers, farmers, servants, and all common people of French society. Though there was a wide range among the people of this group, they were all bound to the Third Estate and had no voice in government. They were powerless. As one priest, sympathetic to the cause of the Third Estate, wrote:

What is the Third Estate? Everything. What has it been up to now in the political order? Nothing. What does it demand? To become something.

A NEED FOR CHANGE

In the spring of 1789, the French government ran out of money. One reason was that Louis XVI had supported the Americans in their revolution against Great Britain. He and the monarchs before him had spent money unwisely. For example, they had borrowed huge sums of money to build the world's most splendid palace, called Versailles (ver sī′). The French monarchs lived there in extreme luxury.

GRAPH SKILL: The Third Estate often met to discuss how they could gain their rights. Do you think land was equally distributed among the three estates?

THE THREE ESTATES

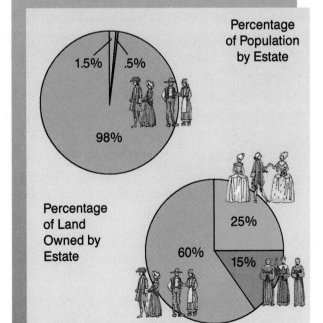

Percentage of Population by Estate

1.5%   .5%

98%

Percentage of Land Owned by Estate

60%   15%   25%

| First Estate | Second Estate | Third Estate |

National Anthem of France

La Marseillaise

Refrain   *Rouget de Lisle*

To arms, ___ to arms, ye brave! Th'a - veng - ing sword un -

sheathed! March on, march on!

all hearts re - solved on vic - to - ry or death.

Louis XVI decided to tax the wealthy Second Estate in order to solve his money problems. But the aristocracy refused to pay, insisting that:

All public financial burdens should be borne [carried] by the Third Estate.

The people of the Third Estate saw their chance. They established a governing body called the National Assembly. As far as the people of the Third Estate were concerned, the National Assembly had the right to pass new laws and reforms.

STORMING THE BASTILLE

Rumors raced across France that Louis XVI was planning to crush the National Assembly. On the morning of July 14, 1789, angry mobs gathered in the streets of Paris. They marched to an old fortress called the Bastille (bas tēl'). Built in the Middle Ages, the Bastille served as a jail for the king's enemies. Twenty thousand pounds of gunpowder were also stored there.

After many tense hours of waiting, the aristocratic commander of the Bastille gave the order to fire upon the crowd. Cannons began to thunder into the mass of people.

Not far away from the Bastille, another commander was pleading with his fellow soldiers.

Brave guards, can't you hear the cannons? The villains are murdering our brothers, our parents, our wives, and our children who are gathered unarmed around the Bastille. Will you allow them to be massacred? Will you not march on the Bastille?

Moved by these words, 60 soldiers rushed to the Bastille, dragging their cannons with them. Faced with this unexpected firepower, the Bastille was forced to surrender.

The storming of the Bastille was important for many reasons. In the first place, it forced Louis XVI to recognize the power of the National Assembly. Secondly, it became a great symbolic act of revolution and independence in the minds of the French people. Ever since 1789, France has celebrated July 14, Bastille Day, as a national holiday, similar to the American July 4th. You can read part of France's national anthem on the left page. It was composed during the French Revolution.

"LIBERTY! EQUALITY! FRATERNITY!"

The motto "Liberty! Equality! Fraternity [brotherhood]!" could be heard throughout France after the fall of the Bastille. Three weeks later, the National Assembly wrote a revolutionary document called the Declaration of the Rights of Man and of the Citizen. This document is like the American Declaration of Independence. It stated that good government is based on the ideas of liberty, equality, and fraternity. It also stated that government should protect the rights of its citizens. This seems only natural to people of the United States today.

The Declaration of the Rights of Man did not end monarchy in France. It did, however, turn France into a constitutional monarchy. Now an elected assembly held lawmaking power. The king was given the power to enforce laws, but the monarchy had lost its absolute power.

Louis XVI was forced to approve the Declaration. Then, in June 1791, Louis and his family tried to escape from France. Just as they neared the French border, however, a postmaster recognized the king from his portrait on

The Granger Collection

During the Reign of Terror, Queen Marie Antoinette was accused of plotting with Austria against France. She was executed in October 1793.

Paris angry mobs filled the streets. They attacked Versailles and threw Louis and his queen, Marie Antoinette, into prison. Hundreds of nobles and Church officials were also jailed.

A tall killing machine called a guillotine (gil′ ə tēn) was built in one of Paris's great open squares. Each day, as crowds watched and jeered, wagonloads of people rumbled down the cobblestone streets toward the guillotine. In January 1793, the guillotine's blade fell on King Louis XVI. Nine months later, Marie Antoinette was also killed by the guillotine.

A period known as the Reign of Terror had begun all over France. Its early victims were mainly people of the aristocracy. But, eventually, even members of the revolution were killed. During the Reign of Terror, at least 3,000 people died by the guillotine in Paris. Some historians believe as many as 40,000 were killed altogether. Eighty percent were peasants and merchants—the common people of the Third Estate for whom the Revolution was started.

NAPOLEON BONAPARTE

"Great men are meteors destined to burn up the earth." So said the French dictator Napoleon Bonaparte. Born in 1769, Napoleon was a young army captain of 24 when the Reign of Terror began. By the end of the terror in 1794, Napoleon was the youngest general in France. In 1799 he took over the government and changed the course of French history.

Napoleon knew that he could take as much power as he wanted. On December 2, 1804, dressed in a splendid robe of purple velvet, Napoleon walked down the long aisle of Notre Dame Cathedral in Paris. The pope waited to

some paper money. The royal family was returned to Paris under guard. As a result of this attempted escape, Louis XVI was considered to be a traitor.

THE REIGN OF TERROR

In the summer of 1792, France ended the monarchy and became a republic. Violent protests against the former king spread throughout the country. In

In 1804 Napoleon became "Emperor of the French." After crowning himself, Napoleon crowned his wife Josephine.

present him with a glittering crown. As thousands watched, the new emperor took the crown from the pope's hands and placed it on his own head.

A DIFFERENT FRANCE

Why did the people of France, who had suffered for many years under an absolute monarch, accept a new absolute ruler? At his coronation, Napoleon became Emperor Napoleon I. The French Revolution was dead. In its place stood the beginnings of an empire. But Napoleon did not try to return France to the days of Louis XVI. He kept many of the changes that had come with the Revolution.

Napoleon wanted to expand the French Empire throughout Europe. His army was one of the largest and best trained in the world. With Napoleon in charge, the army won many battles against the Belgians, Dutch, Germans, and Italians. By 1812 Napoleon ruled most of the western part of Europe. Napoleon's empire would crumble, however, in 1815. France would once again struggle to build a republic.

Check Your Reading

1. How was French society organized before the Revolution?
2. What caused unrest in France in 1789?
3. How did the National Assembly change French government?
4. **THINKING SKILL:** State one opinion mentioned on page 292 and explain how you know it is an opinion.

Using Primary and Secondary Sources

Key Vocabulary

primary source
secondary source

How do we know what Marie Antoinette wore on the day she was executed? How do we know what Napoleon said after he crowned himself in 1804? How do we know what anyone said about anything?

As you have read this book you may have noticed many quotations from famous and nonfamous people. These sections are always in italics and are set off from the text just a little bit. Pay close attention to these sections. As one historian wrote:

A quotation from the past is very likely some kind of truth. Or it is some kind of lie. In either case, it is from the horse's mouth.

Using Primary Sources

The quotations you are reading in this book are one of two kinds of sources. Many of them are primary sources, or first-hand accounts. Accounts written by people actually involved in an event are primary sources. Primary sources on the Industrial and French revolutions, for example, include newspapers of the time, as well as diaries, letters, and songs. Other primary sources are official documents such as business contracts, treaties, and wills. The Declaration of the Rights of Man is a primary source.

Nonwritten material can be primary sources, too. Cannons, clothes, and even toys from the time of the French Revolution are primary sources. They show how people fought, dressed, and played. Photographs, tape recordings, and films of events from the recent past are also important primary sources.

Historians always examine primary sources carefully. A primary source may give an accurate picture of an event. However, it may also give an untrue one. An aristocrat from the Second Estate would more than likely disapprove of the way the Bastille was attacked. But a revolutionary from the Third Estate might say it was a wonderful moment in history. Both are primary sources, but they give differing versions of events.

When historians read primary sources, they ask questions that will help them understand the point of view of the source. With a letter about the storming of the Bastille, they would ask: Who wrote the letter? To whom was the letter written? Why? Did the writer actually *see* the events described *first-hand*?

Using Secondary Sources

When you want to learn about the past, you often use secondary sources. This book is a secondary source. A biography of Marie Antoinette and a history of Napoleon's wars are also examples of secondary sources. Encyclopedias, atlases, and art books are also secondary sources.

Why are secondary sources useful? In the first place, they help you summarize information. Think of what your social studies class would be like without textbooks. You would have to spend a lot of time reading official documents and studying many letters, diaries, newspapers, and other primary sources to learn about events in history.

Comparing Sources

The following accounts are about Napoleon Bonaparte. They represent both primary and secondary sources. Read each account carefully. Decide whether you are reading a primary or secondary source.

Napoleon dictated his letters and reports with great ease. He never wrote anything with his own hand. His handwriting was awful. He could barely read himself. And his spelling was very poor. . . .

Those who wrote from the man's dictation made a shorthand for themselves in order that their pens might travel as fast as Napoleon's thoughts. . . . He never repeated anything that he had already said, even if it had not been heard. . . . This was very hard on Napoleon's poor secretary. This I know quite well because I was his secretary.

Those that served under the celebrated Napoleon are known to believe that their master was a remarkable leader. He could dazzle and captivate those in his command. He inspired confidence by his ability to understand problems and make quick decisions.

It is said that Napoleon once declared that his mind was like a chest of drawers which he could open and close at will. It is said that Napoleon could tuck away any subject and then pull it forth—subjects pulled with all the necessary details.

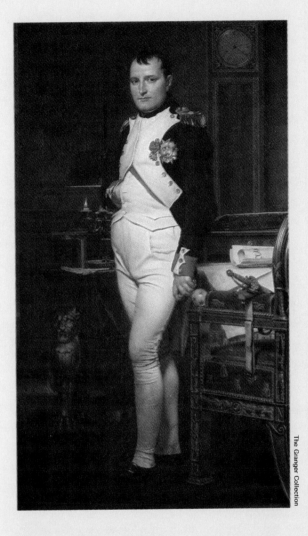

Reviewing the Skill

Use the sources on this page to answer the following questions.

1. How is a secondary source different from a primary source?
2. Which account is a primary source? How can you tell?
3. What are two things that you learned about Napoleon from the first account? From the second account?
4. List two advantages in using a primary source to describe the past. List two disadvantages.

IMPORTANT EVENTS

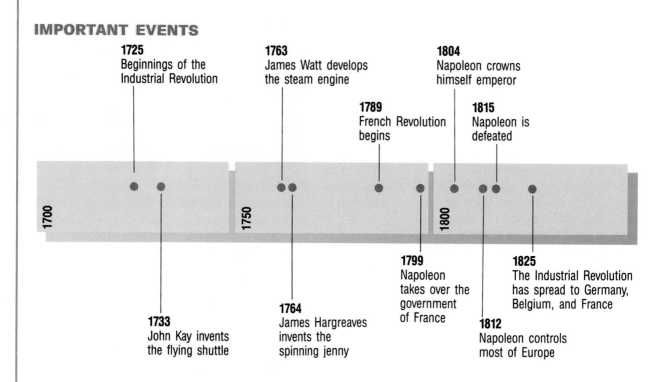

1725
Beginnings of the
Industrial Revolution

1763
James Watt develops
the steam engine

1804
Napoleon crowns
himself emperor

1789
French Revolution
begins

1815
Napoleon is
defeated

1700

1750

1800

1799
Napoleon
takes over the
government
of France

1825
The Industrial Revolution
has spread to Germany,
Belgium, and France

1733
John Kay invents
the flying shuttle

1764
James Hargreaves
invents the
spinning jenny

1812
Napoleon controls
most of Europe

PEOPLE TO KNOW

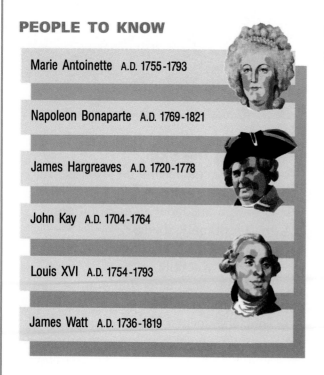

Marie Antoinette A.D. 1755-1793

Napoleon Bonaparte A.D. 1769-1821

James Hargreaves A.D. 1720-1778

John Kay A.D. 1704-1764

Louis XVI A.D. 1754-1793

James Watt A.D. 1736-1819

IDEAS TO REMEMBER

■ The Industrial Revolution began in England during the 1700s. This period provided the world with incredible new inventions. Factories and railroads spread throughout England. It was just the beginning.

■ A lack of equality between the three estates helped cause the French Revolution. Revolution ended many years of monarchy and began waves of freedom but also violence. Napoleon Bonaparte became the emperor of France after the French Revolution.

REVIEWING VOCABULARY

divine right   middle class
Industrial   textile
  Revolution   working class

Number a sheet of paper from 1 to 5. Beside each number, write the word or term from the above list that best completes the sentence.

1. The _____ was a poor class of people created by the growth of factories.
2. In England, changes in the _____ industry led to the rise of factories.
3. For centuries French kings believed that they had a _____ to govern.
4. The _____ brought great changes in the way people worked, the hours they worked, and working conditions.
5. The _____ was made up of business people who owned factories, mines, railroads, and banks.

REVIEWING FACTS

1. How did inventions such as the flying shuttle, spinning jenny, and steam engine contribute to the growth of the Industrial Revolution?
2. Which of the three French estates was the largest? Describe its role in the early stages of the French Revolution.
3. How did factories help to create a working class and a middle class?
4. List four important causes and effects of the Industrial Revolution.
5. Which one of the following terms does not belong? Why?: National Assembly, Third Estate, middle class, aristocracy, First Estate, working class.

WRITING ABOUT MAIN IDEAS

1. **Writing a Descriptive Paragraph:** Although the American and French revolutions shared many of the same ideals and goals, the French revolution turned out to be bloodier and less successful than the American. Write a descriptive paragraph about the results of the French Revolution. Describe how society was structured before the revolution and the changes that took place as the revolution unfolded.
2. **Writing a Paragraph:** Think back to Chapter 2 when you read about the growth of technology during the New Stone Age. Write a paragraph explaining why the Industrial Revolution has been called the greatest social change since the invention of farming.
3. **Writing About Perspectives:** Imagine that you are an American living during the French Revolution. You are disturbed by reports about the Reign of Terror. Write a letter to the French ambassador to the United States voicing your concerns.

BUILDING SKILLS: USING PRIMARY AND SECONDARY SOURCES

1. What is a primary source?
2. What is a secondary source?
3. Give three examples of primary and secondary sources.
4. Write a paragraph explaining why both types of sources are important.

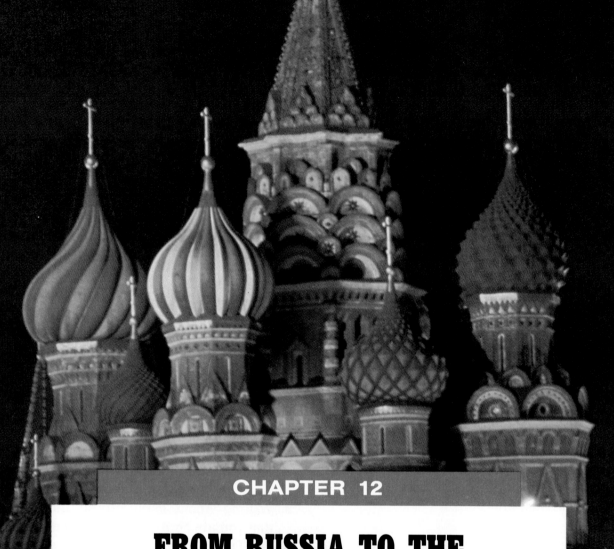

CHAPTER 12

FROM RUSSIA TO THE COMMONWEALTH OF INDEPENDENT STATES

FOCUS

Wretched and abundant,
Oppressed and powerful,
Weak and mighty,
Mother Russia!

A Russian poet used these powerful words to describe his country more than 100 years ago. They can still be used about the nation today. In this chapter you will study the geography and history of Russia and its neighbors. These are lands of great beauty and contrasts.

1 Geography: Russia and Its Neighbors

READ TO LEARN

Key Vocabulary

strait	taiga
tundra	steppe
permafrost	

Key Places

Russia	St. Petersburg
Siberia	Moscow
Bering Strait	Vladivostok

Read Aloud

There is no land so beautiful as ours. . . . The endless forests and valleys . . . wonderland of riches.

This is how one Russian writer describes his country. Russia is the largest country in the world. In fact, it is larger than the continent of Europe. Russia and its neighbors are lands of great beauty and diversity.

Read for Purpose

1. **WHAT YOU KNOW:** What mountain range divides Europe and Asia?
2. **WHAT YOU WILL LEARN:** What are the important geographic features of Russia and its neighbors?

ACROSS TWO CONTINENTS

For many years Russia and its neighbors were republics in a country called the Soviet Union. In 1991 the Soviet Union broke apart into 15 independent countries. Soon Russia and 10 of these other countries joined together to form the Commonwealth of Independent States. A commonwealth is a group of independent countries that work together to help one another.

Today, the land of the Commonwealth of Independent States stretches from the European plains of Ukraine across Asia to the Pacific coast of Russia. The four former Soviet republics that did not join the commonwealth are Georgia, Latvia, Lithuania, and Estonia. Georgia is located in Asia near the Caspian Sea. The other countries are located in Europe.

NATURAL BOUNDARIES

Russia is such a large country that it lies on both the continents of Asia and Europe. The Ural Mountains divide these two continents. The northern part of Russia that lies between the Ural Mountains and the Pacific Ocean is a region called Siberia.

Bodies of water form many of the boundaries of Russia. The northern

299

RUSSIA AND ITS NEIGHBORS:
Elevation

Elevations

Feet	Meters
Above 14,000	Above 4,000
7,000	2,000
1,500	500
700	200
0	0

Below sea level

+++ Trans-Siberian Railroad

MAP SKILL: The Ural Mountains form a natural boundary between Europe and Asia. How high are these mountains?

boundary of Russia is the Arctic Ocean. In the west, Russia has boundaries on the Barents Sea, the Baltic Sea, the Black Sea, and the Caspian Sea. As you will learn, these bodies of water have played an important part in the history of Russia.

The Black Sea is connected to the Mediterranean Sea. You may recall that the ancient Greeks had colonies along the Black Sea. Today the busy port cities of Odessa and Sevastopol are found on the Black Sea. The Caspian Sea is interesting because it is the world's largest inland body of water. Lake Michigan could fit into the Caspian Sea almost seven times. Look at the map above. Although it is called a sea, the Caspian Sea is really a lake. Which seas hug the eastern coast of Russia?

NEIGHBORS

Did you know that Russia and the United States are neighbors? As you see from the map, Russia's easternmost point reaches into the Bering Strait. A strait is a narrow waterway connecting two larger bodies of water. The Bering Strait connects the Bering Sea and the Arctic Ocean. The state of

Alaska is on the other side of the Bering Strait. In fact, only 56 miles (90 km) lie between our two countries.

THE TRANS-SIBERIAN RAILROAD

If you ever visit Russia, you may want to ride the Trans-Siberian Railroad. *Trans* is a word meaning "across." As you can see from the map on the left page, the Trans-Siberian Railroad goes all the way across Russia. How long does such an incredibly long journey take? Boarding near the Baltic Sea, you could begin a ten-day journey that would take you southeast to the Sea of Japan. According to one recent traveler, this railroad journey is a real adventure.

> As the train chugged . . . deeper into the Asian landmass, I wondered if our travels would ever end. . . . We crept through thick and unimaginably dense and dark forests. . . . At one moment we were awake, and the next we were stirred by the brilliance of the light: vast openness, grasslands stretching without end. . . . Winds rattled our

> train which, compared to the size of the continent it was now moving upon, had become a mere toy object. . . . and day after day my daughter's joy carried us east, her face pressed against the glass in wonder.

A RAILROAD JOURNEY

Imagine that you are setting out on a journey across Russia. Such a trip will provide a view of many different environments. Beginning in St. Petersburg, by the Baltic Sea, you climb aboard a railroad car that will be your home for ten days. After picking up passengers and supplies in Moscow, the railroad travels along the Volga River. You may recall having learned that the Volga River is the longest river in Europe and flows into the Caspian Sea.

Your adventure across Russia will next take you through the Ural Mountains. You know that this mountain range forms the boundary between

The Trans-Siberian Railroad is the world's longest railroad. It takes ten days for this train to cross Russia.

Europe and Asia. As your train moves eastward, you journey through the "vast openness" of the Siberian plains. You will also cross many Siberian rivers. Unlike the rivers of European Russia, most of the rivers of Siberia are of little use for transportation. Most of them flow into the Arctic Ocean, which is frozen most of the year.

You will be interested to know that your journey takes you along Lake Baikal (bī käl'), the world's deepest lake. Before 1916 there was no track around the lake. Rail cars had to be ferried 50 miles (80 km) across the lake during the summer months. From January to May, Lake Baikal freezes over. So, in winter, tracks were laid on the ice and horses pulled the cars across the lake one car at a time.

Your final destination is a city called Vladivostok (vlad ə vos' tok), on the Sea of Japan. After ten days aboard a cramped train, you may wish to continue your visit through Russia by some other means of transportation. If you decide to travel by air, you could be back in St. Petersburg, where you began, in just seven hours.

CLIMATE AND VEGETATION

Russia is famous for its long, bitter winters. But in fact, you will experience many different climates on your journey across Russia. Almost every kind of climate except a tropical climate is found there.

Like the United States and Canada, most of Russia is in the middle latitudes. As you know, the middle latitudes generally have temperate, or mild, climates. You know that climate has an effect on vegetation. In Russia and its neighboring countries, the influence of climate on plant life is clearly seen. As the map on page 303

The Volga River is one of many rivers crossed by the Trans-Siberian Railroad. Like most Russian rivers, it freezes over during the winter months.

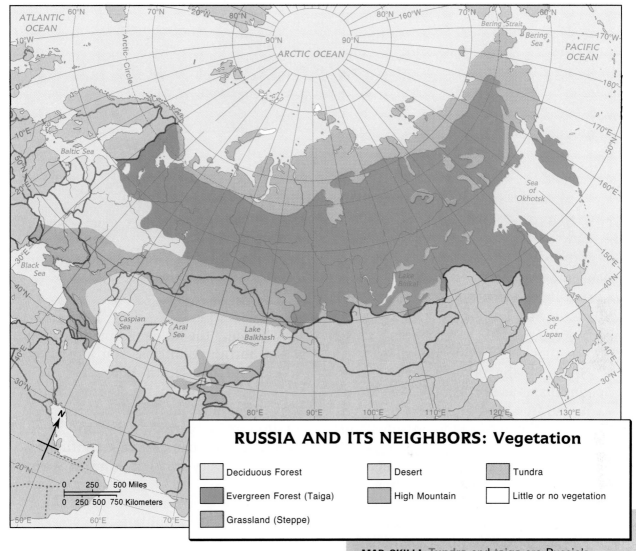

RUSSIA AND ITS NEIGHBORS: Vegetation

- Deciduous Forest
- Evergreen Forest (Taiga)
- Grassland (Steppe)
- Desert
- High Mountain
- Tundra
- Little or no vegetation

0   250   500 Miles
0   250 500 750 Kilometers

MAP SKILL: Tundra and taiga are Russia's largest vegetation regions. What area of the country has many deciduous forests?

shows, seven different vegetation regions stretch across Russia and its neighbors.

In the far north is the treeless tundra (tun′ drə). The tundra stretches along the Arctic Ocean from the Barents Sea to the Bering Sea. Winter in the tundra lasts from October to June, making it impossible for much vegetation to grow there. As a result, only mosses and low bushes survive in the tundra. Just a few feet below the surface, the earth remains frozen all year. This permanently frozen earth is called the permafrost. Summers are too cool and short for the permafrost to thaw out.

TAIGA AND STEPPE

Like the traveler on the Trans-Siberian Railroad, you would be amazed by the thick forests all along your route. A broad belt of forest, called the taiga (tī′ gə), stretches from the Baltic Sea to the Pacific Ocean. The taiga is made up of many kinds of evergreen trees.

303

The diverse geography of Russia and its neighbors ranges from these tall mountains to this fertile **steppe**.

An evergreen forest has green leaves or needles throughout the year.

South of the taiga region in European Russia is another forested region. You can find a deciduous (di sij' ü əs) forest on the map on the previous page. Deciduous trees shed their leaves each year. Today, much of the region is without trees because it has been cleared for farming.

South of the deciduous forest and taiga lies a grassland region called the **steppe** (step). Like the Great Plains of North America, the steppe is a rich farming region. Great silt deposits on the steppe have developed into a very rich black soil. The farms of the steppe region are among the most productive in the world.

A LAND OF CONTRASTS

You have read that Russia and its neighbors formed the Soviet Union until 1991. With the collapse of the Soviet Union, Russia and ten of its neighbors established the Commonwealth of Independent States.

In this lesson, you have taken a journey through the lands of Russia and its neighboring countries. You have traveled from the North European Plain through Siberia to the Bering Strait. You have read that the climate and vegetation are as varied as the landscape. Stretching across two vast continents, Russia is very much a land of many contrasts.

There is a lot more to learn about Russia and its neighbors. As you can imagine, this region has a rich and fascinating history. As you read on, you will learn about the long history of the people who live there.

 Check Your Reading

1. On which two continents is Russia located?
2. Which vegetation regions lie near the Trans-Siberian Railroad?
3. **GEOGRAPHY SKILL:** How is the geography of the United States similar to that of Russia?
4. **THINKING SKILL:** What are three questions you could ask to learn more about Siberia's geography?

304

2 The Growth of Russia

READ TO LEARN

Key Vocabulary

oppression
Golden Horde
tsar
abolition

Key People

Rurik
Batu Khan
Ivan the Great
Peter the Great
Catherine the Great
Alexander II

Key Places

Novgorod
Kiev
Moscow
St. Petersburg

Read Aloud

Russia has a long history. In this lesson you will read about Russia's early history. You will read about many of the rulers who led Russia as it slowly developed into one of the world's most powerful nations.

Read for Purpose

1. **WHAT YOU KNOW:** What is the geography of Russia?
2. **WHAT YOU WILL LEARN:** How did Russian rulers guide their country to greatness?

LAND OF THE RUS

In Lesson 1 you read that in 1991 Russia became an independent country. But Russia has a long, rich history that spans hundreds of years. The Russians are part of a large ethnic group called the Slavs. In ancient times the Slavs lived in Central Europe, near the Carpathian Mountains. By the tenth century, however, the Slavs had broken into different groups.

The Russians, called the East Slavs, were farmers. They lived in log cabins and cultivated small patches cleared in the steppe. The East Slavs did not always live peacefully. The earliest written record of Russian history tells of a quarrel in the village of Novgorod (nov′ gə rod). According to this record, the people of Novgorod invited the Vikings to rule them and bring order to their land. They wrote:

Our whole land is great and rich, but there is no order in it. Come to rule and reign over us.

Headed by Rurik, the Vikings arrived in 862 and began to govern the region around Novgorod, which became known as the "land of the Rus." *Rus* was a word used by the East Slavs to describe their Viking rulers. From this word came the name of the country, *Russia*.

Batu Khan led the Golden Horde across the lands of Russia. He brought with him the riches and ideas of Central Asia.

Oppression in Russia began long ago. The Russian people were first oppressed by the Mongols. The Mongols were from Central Asia. In 1227, Batu Khan, a cousin of Marco Polo's famous friend Kublai Khan, led more than 200,000 Mongol troops into Russia. The Mongols destroyed one Russian town after another. They made Russia part of the Mongol Empire that was ruled by the Golden Horde— *golden* because of their great wealth and *horde* from the Mongol word meaning "camp."

Batu Khan forced the surviving Russian princes to pledge allegiance to the Golden Horde and to pay heavy taxes. From time to time, the Mongols left their camps near the Caspian Sea and brutally crushed uprisings against their rule. Countless numbers of people were killed. But the Golden Horde did not really want the trouble of governing a vast new region. They were chiefly interested in collecting taxes.

THE RISE OF MOSCOW

People today hear and read a lot about a city called Moscow. You may know that Moscow is the capital city of Russia. Like our capital, Washington, D.C., Moscow is one of the most important cities in the world. When the Golden Horde ruled Russia, however, Moscow was only a small village and not very important.

The princes of Moscow believed that the location of their city destined them for greatness. Moscow lies near the sources of the Volga, Dnieper (nē′ pər), and Don rivers. If the princes of Moscow could gain control of these rivers, they could control nearly all of Russia and force the Golden Horde back into Central Asia.

Many historians, of course, doubt that the Slavs of Novgorod really invited the fierce Vikings to rule them. You may recall having read in Chapter 8 that the Vikings terrorized communities near the North and Baltic seas. Novgorod lies near the Baltic Sea and could easily have been a target for the Vikings. The descendants of Rurik ruled Russia from the city of Kiev (kē′ ef) for over 700 years. Today Kiev is the capital of the country of Ukraine.

THE GOLDEN HORDE

As you read in the Chapter Opener, the words *wretched* and *oppressed* were used to describe Russia. What does it mean to say that people are "oppressed"? Oppression (ə presh′ ən) is the act of governing unjustly.

In 1480 Moscow finally freed itself from Mongol oppression. Ivan the Great, a prince from Moscow, refused to pay taxes to the Mongols. Rising to the challenge, the outraged Mongols darted to the banks of the Don River. The Russian army stood on the opposite bank. The two armies glowered at each other, neither daring to cross the river. Finally, without shooting a single arrow, the Mongols retreated, or turned around, and marched back home. After this bloodless face-off, Russia was free of the terrible Mongol oppression.

PETER THE GREAT

Russia was not free of oppression, however. After the rise of Moscow, its grand prince came to be called tsar (zär). *Tsar* is a Russian word meaning "Caesar." Russian rulers continued to bear the title of *tsar* until 1917. Like the French monarchs before the French Revolution, the tsars believed that they ruled Russia by divine right. They were absolute monarchs whose word was law.

Russia under the tsars was not a democracy. But some tsars did help turn Russia into a modern nation. Peter the Great, for example, is considered to be one of the greatest of all the Russian tsars.

Peter came to the throne in 1682 at the age of ten. One of his first acts as a young king was to travel outside of Russia. He spent 15 months in the Netherlands and England, visiting factories, workshops, and shipyards. New ideas and new technology were changing the rest of Europe. Peter wanted to learn as much as possible about the new technology so that he could improve the economy of his country.

Peter's travels in Western Europe convinced him that Russia was very backward in its social and technical development. He decided that his people should learn all they could from their neighbors to the west. He vowed to westernize Russia, or adopt the culture and technology of the Western Europeans. He announced that he would lead his people "toward a new day, which shall be better than this."

To accomplish this end, Tsar Peter decided to "open a window to the West." In 1703 he ordered a brand-new port city to be built on the Baltic Sea, facing Western Europe. He called the

The Cathedral of St. Basil was built after the defeat of the Mongols. Its colorful onion domes are a famous Moscow sight today.

Peter the Great ordered the builders of his capital to make its streets "as wide and lovely as the boulevards of Paris."

new city **St. Petersburg**, in honor of his own patron saint. Nine years later it was finished and was one of Europe's most beautiful cities. Peter made St. Petersburg Russia's capital. From 1924 until 1991, St. Petersburg, Russia's second-largest city, was called Leningrad, after a more recent Russian leader.

CATHERINE THE GREAT

There was another tsar who changed Russia. This tsar also earned the title "the Great." **Catherine the Great** was not even a Russian. She was a German princess who had married Peter's weak and unpopular grandson. But the strong-willed Catherine worked hard to learn all she could about Russia— its language, its customs, and the workings of its government.

Catherine's husband became tsar in 1762, but his reign lasted only six months. With the help of palace guards, the clever Catherine overthrew him and later poisoned him. That same year she had herself proclaimed empress of Russia.

Like Peter the Great, Catherine wanted to westernize Russia. She too tried to bring the Industrial Revolution to Russia. She even built a great museum called the Hermitage to showcase paintings by European artists.

Catherine's greatest contribution to Russia was her conquest of new lands. She herself announced that her chief aim was to gain warm-water ports for Russia. Why do you think this was a concern for Catherine? By 1770 Catherine the Great had captured a sizable territory bordering the Black Sea. This enabled Russian ships to sail to the Mediterranean Sea. Catherine also gained huge territories by splitting up Poland with Prussia and Austria.

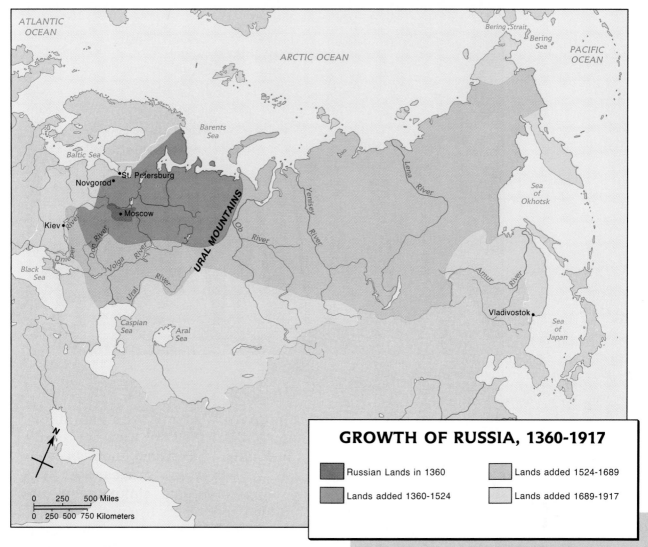

GROWTH OF RUSSIA, 1360-1917

▮ Russian Lands in 1360   ▮ Lands added 1524-1689

▮ Lands added 1360-1524   ▯ Lands added 1689-1917

MAP SKILL: It took hundreds of years for Russia to reach its present size. Between what years did Russia reach the Sea of Japan?

MOST RUSSIANS WERE SERFS

In Chapter 8 you read about feudalism in the Middle Ages. You read that serfs lived on manors and were bound to their masters. As commerce grew, however, feudal ties broke down and the serfs fled to the towns or became freemen. Serfdom continued in Russia, however, long after it had disappeared in Western Europe.

More than half of the people in Catherine's Russia were serfs. She allowed landowners to move serfs from farm to farm, sometimes even breaking up families. Many serfs were sold, and their status was comparable to that of slaves. To make matters worse, rulers such as Catherine did not understand the misery of serfdom.

By 1855 there were more than 40 million serfs in Russia, every one of them enslaved. According to one Russian reformer, the majority of serfs lived miserably. He wrote:

A bitter struggle was going on to help the serfs . . . to give them medical help, to raise them from their darkness and misery.

When Catherine visited the countryside, she saw well-dressed people who pretended to be serfs. The real serfs were hidden.

In 1855 Alexander II became tsar. The most important of Alexander's actions was the abolition (ab ə lish′ ən) of, or doing away with, serfdom in 1861. You know that the United States abolished slavery during the Civil War. As in America, however, freedom for the serfs did not necessarily improve living conditions. The Russian serfs had to pay high taxes and were charged huge sums of money for tiny strips of farmland. As a result, former serfs, now called peasants, worked about as hard as before without much more to eat or better clothes to wear.

THE SEEDS OF REVOLUTION

By 1900 the masses of people who had been freed were little better off than they had been in 1861. More than 80 percent of the Russian population were peasants. Most lived in miserable conditions. The serfs who had migrated to the cities to work in newly developing industries soon became unhappy with low wages and bad working conditions. Unions were forbidden and workers began to dream of revolution—a revolution that would bring equality to all the Russian people. Read on. In the next lesson you will discover how the Russians struggled to make that dream come true.

Check Your Reading

1. What contributions to Russian history were made by Peter the Great and Catherine the Great?
2. Why did many Russians want to change their government?
3. **GEOGRAPHY SKILL:** By what year had Russia expanded to the Arctic?
4. **THINKING SKILL:** Sequence five of the most important events in the growth of Russia.

3 The Russian Revolution

READ TO LEARN

Key Vocabulary
socialism
communism
totalitarian
collective farm

Key People
Lenin
Karl Marx
Joseph Stalin

Read Aloud

"Whatever I try, nothing succeeds. I am out of luck." These were the words of Nicholas II, Russia's last tsar, as he watched his government collapse. Tsarist Russia had indeed run out of luck, after 300 years of rule. A mighty revolution was about to transform Russia into the Soviet Union.

Read for Purpose

1. **WHAT YOU KNOW:** Why did many Russians want a revolution to change their country?
2. **WHAT YOU WILL LEARN:** How did government and daily life in Russia change after the revolution?

LENIN AND A NEW IDEA OF GOVERNMENT

There is no other man who is absorbed by the revolution 24 hours a day, who has no thoughts but thoughts of revolution, and even in his sleep dreams of revolution.

These words describe a man who called himself Lenin. Lenin worked tirelessly for revolution in Russia. He was arrested, sent to Siberia, and even forced to live outside Russia for 17 years. When he returned to Russia in 1917, Lenin led his people to a victorious revolt against the tsar.

Why did Lenin feel so strongly about the need for revolution? It began when he was a student. Lenin supported the teachings of a German philosopher named Karl Marx. Marx believed that throughout history, all societies had suffered from a struggle between different economic classes.

Freeman and slave, patrician and plebeian, lord and serf, guild master and journeyman.

What was the key to ending this oppression? Marx said that class struggle was between those who owned property and those who did not. His solution was to abolish private ownership of property. Instead of individuals owning land, banks, factories, and

Karl Marx developed a new philosophy called socialism. The Russian Revolution was built upon many of Marx's ideas.

other businesses, he believed such property should be owned and controlled by all the people.

This idea of government was exciting to Lenin. Russia was a vast country. Why not allow every member of society to share in its wealth? he thought. Called socialism, this system of government and economy attracted many followers in Europe in the late 1800s. Marx said that there had always been a struggle between people who owned property and those who did not. He believed socialism would end that struggle and bring freedom and equality to all people. Lenin wanted to bring socialism to Russia. Like Marx, Lenin believed that socialism could end all poverty in the world.

"DOWN WITH THE TSAR!"

It was bitterly cold in St. Petersburg on the morning of February 25, 1917. As the sun rose over the frozen parks, thousands of women huddled in the doorways of the city's bakeries, waiting as they waited every morning, for bread.

Then came the news. There was no bread. The bakers could not bake without flour, and there were no trains to bring flour to the city. Russia had been at war with Germany for nearly three years, and the country's railroads were under enormous strain. Every train was needed to carry soldiers, not flour.

During past shortages, the women of St. Petersburg had quietly returned home without their bread. This time they refused to leave. Instead, they stayed on the icy streets, shouting, "We want bread! We want bread!" They gathered on trolley tracks, stopping traffic. They forced passengers off streetcars and even turned a few streetcars over. Some women began throwing rocks through shop windows and the windows of government buildings.

The women did not consider themselves to be revolutionaries. They were just tired—tired of waiting for bread that never came, tired of their children going hungry, tired of seeing their husbands, brothers, and sons march off to die in the endless war.

Within hours, the women were joined by thousands of workers from nearby factories. By early afternoon, massive crowds had gathered along St. Petersburg's main street. The demonstrators shouted and sang. Many even dared to hold up banners proclaiming: "Down with the Tsar!" The Russian Revolution had begun.

BIRTH OF THE SOVIET UNION

History will not forgive us if we do not seize power now.

As you can tell from this remark made by Lenin in 1917, he knew that the time for revolution had come. Using the slogan "Peace! Land! Bread!" Lenin captured the hopes of thousands of oppressed and hungry Russians. By November 1917, Lenin's followers took over government buildings and arrested the leaders of the tsar's government. Lenin declared himself head of the Russian government. "Comrades!" Lenin cried, "We shall now build a socialist order!"

What was this new socialist order? Lenin called it **communism**. *Communism* means "the common ownership of land and industry by a people as a group." This idea came from the writings of Karl Marx. Marx used the word *communism* to describe the economic system that would exist after workers had seized power. Lenin, for example, ordered all farmland to be divided among the peasants. His government took over all major industries. From now on, workers' councils were to run the factories—not the wealthy families who had owned the factories when the tsars were in power.

Lenin's slogan of "Peace! Land! Bread!" captured the support of millions of Russians. He organized the world's first **Communist** government in 1917.

The new leaders of Russia's Communist government demanded dramatic change. In 1922 they gave Russia a new name—the Union of Soviet Socialist Republics, or the Soviet Union. Eventually, the Soviet Union was made up of 14 other republics as well as Russia. The people of this nation had little freedom.

A TOTALITARIAN COUNTRY

After Lenin's death in 1924, St. Petersburg was renamed Leningrad, in honor of the great hero of the Russian Revolution. Joseph Stalin headed the new Communist government. Stalin was one of history's cruelest leaders. Under Stalin's rule, the Soviet Union became a totalitarian country. In a totalitarian country, a dictator or a small group of people control every part of the lives of its citizens.

Like Peter the Great, Stalin wanted to modernize his country. Stalin wrote that his goal was to:

> . . . transform our land from an agricultural [farming] country to an industrial giant.

To reach his goal, Stalin began a series of "five-year plans." Under these plans, the government told farms and factories what to produce and how much to produce. Always it was "more, more, more."

Stalin was even more brutal when it came to reforming the Soviet Union's 25 million small farms. In 1928, he

Joseph Stalin forced millions of Soviet people to work on collective farms. The food they grew was owned by the government.

Lenin's picture looked down on meetings of the Communist party in Moscow. You had to be a member of the party in order to get a good job in the Soviet Union.

announced that all family farms would be abolished. They would be replaced by collective farms, or large farms worked by hundreds of families. The government expected that these collective farms, with the help of modern technology, would produce more food with fewer workers.

Life in Stalin's totalitarian country was often worse than life under the tsars. Managers of factories and collective farms who failed to produce the expected amount were killed. People were arrested for practicing their religion or for simple remarks overheard by police informers. Even the director of the Moscow Zoo was arrested because his monkeys got a deadly disease.

A HEAVY PRICE FOR CHANGE

In this lesson you have read about the Russian Revolution and the first years of the Soviet Union. The Russian Revolution did not bring real freedoms. Lenin's government established the Communist party, which limited free-

dom. The cruel dictatorship of Joseph Stalin created a totalitarian country and caused people to live in fear. But the Soviet Union would continue to change.

In the next chapter you will study how the Soviet Union played a major role in world history during the twentieth century. You will also learn how this totalitarian nation finally collapsed, bringing democracy and freedom to this land at last.

Check Your Reading

1. Name one of the most important causes of the Russian Revolution.
2. Describe the political systems you have studied in this lesson.
3. How did Stalin try to modernize the Soviet Union?
4. **THINKING SKILL:** Compare and contrast totalitarian government and democratic government.

315

BUILDING SKILLS
GEOGRAPHY SKILLS

Reading Distribution Maps

Key Vocabulary
distribution map
population density

What if you need to find your way in Siberia? Perhaps you are interested in knowing where the Ural Mountains are located. Maybe you are wondering where gold is mined along the Amur River. These questions and concerns can be answered by looking at the right maps. Because people use maps for many different kinds of reasons, there are many different kinds of maps.

Distribution Maps

Simple maps show only land and water. More complex maps may show countries, cities, roads, and even railroads. Maps that show things not having a single location or things that are not places, such as population, climate, vegetation, rainfall, and temperature, are called distribution maps. Distribution maps are special-purpose maps. They usually show how one particular feature is spread over an area.

Look at the map on page 303. It shows the distribution of vegetation in Russia and its neighboring countries. Different colors represent different kinds of vegetation. For example, you can see that the vegetation in Siberia is mostly tundra and evergreen forest. How many different vegetation categories are shown? Which category is the most widespread? What color on the map represents the least widespread category?

Distribution maps such as this vegetation map are helpful for finding out specific information. If you were interested in locating farm land, for example, you could look at this map to see where the steppe region is located. What kind of distribution map would you look at if you wanted to see which areas of a country receive the most rainfall?

Population Density

Not all distribution maps show distribution by color-keyed areas as the map on page 303 does. Look at **Map A** below. It shows the distribution of people in the Soviet Union in 1990 by small red dots. How many people does each dot stand for? As the map shows, each dot represents 100,000 people. Maps such as this one are called population density maps. *Population* means "total number of people." *Density* means "number of units in a certain space." The units here are people.

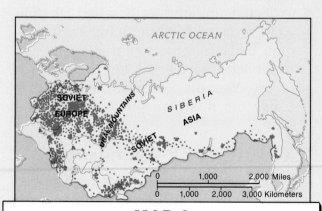

MAP A
SOVIET UNION:
Population Density, 1990
Each dot represents 100,000 people

MAP B
SOVIET UNION:
Population
Density, 1990

• Cities with more than
  1 million people

	People per square mile	People per square kilometer
	0–2	0–1
	2–25	1–10
	25–125	10–50
	125–250	50–100
	250–500	100–200
	over 500	over 200

It is important to understand that the more people who live in a given space, the greater the population density. On **Map A**, areas where there are many dots indicate that many people live there. Areas of high population density are shown by dots close together. In places where few people live, the dots are shown far apart.

Map B gives more specific information than **Map A** does. For example, **Map B** shows that more than 500 people per square mile live in the city of Moscow. What is the population density of the city of Minsk? Is the population more dense in Alma-Ata or in Leningrad?

Reviewing the Skill
Use the map on this page to answer the following questions.
1. What is the purpose of a map that shows distribution? What kind of distribution is shown on **Map B**?
2. How many categories of distribution are shown on **Map B**?
3. What color is used to show 0–2 people per square mile (0–1 people per sq km)? What does the color red represent on the map?
4. What population density is the most widespread in **Map B**?
5. How are distribution maps useful? Who would use these maps?

317

IMPORTANT EVENTS

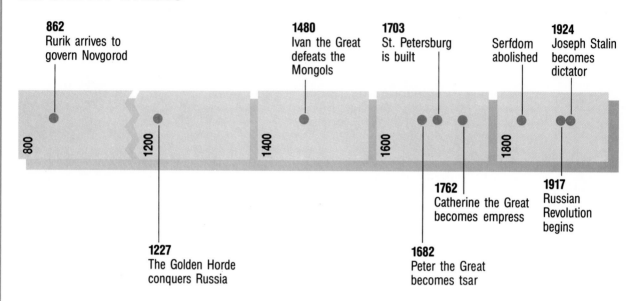

862
Rurik arrives to govern Novgorod

1480
Ivan the Great defeats the Mongols

1703
St. Petersburg is built

Serfdom abolished

1924
Joseph Stalin becomes dictator

800

1200

1400

1600

1800

1227
The Golden Horde conquers Russia

1762
Catherine the Great becomes empress

1917
Russian Revolution begins

1682
Peter the Great becomes tsar

PEOPLE TO KNOW

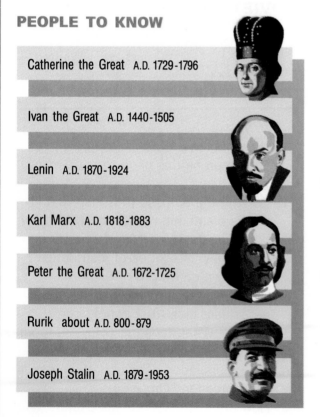

Catherine the Great A.D. 1729-1796

Ivan the Great A.D. 1440-1505

Lenin A.D. 1870-1924

Karl Marx A.D. 1818-1883

Peter the Great A.D. 1672-1725

Rurik about A.D. 800-879

Joseph Stalin A.D. 1879-1953

IDEAS TO REMEMBER

■ In 1991 the government of the Soviet Union collapsed and the 15 Soviet republics became independent countries. These countries, the largest of which is Russia, stretch from Europe through Asia to the Pacific Ocean. These are lands of great geographic diversity.

■ Many rulers led Russia to greatness. Rurik, the legendary Viking, Ivan the Great, and Peter the Great are just a few. Most Russians were serfs, however, until they were freed by Alexander II.

■ With the cry "Peace! Land! Bread!" Lenin led the Russian Revolution and set up the world's first Communist nation. After Lenin's death, Joseph Stalin turned the Soviet Union into a totalitarian country.

REVIEWING VOCABULARY

Each of the following statements contains an underlined vocabulary word. Number a sheet of paper from 1 to 5. Beside each number write whether the following statements are true or false. If the statement is true, write "true." If the statement is false, write "false" and rewrite the sentence using the vocabulary word correctly.

1. People under a <u>totalitarian</u> form of government enjoy many of the same freedoms as people in a democracy.
2. Because of its severe climate, little vegetation is found in the <u>tundra</u>.
3. A <u>strait</u> is a narrow land bridge connecting two larger land masses.
4. Under <u>communism</u> individuals are allowed to own their own land.
5. The <u>steppe</u> is a region that is very good for farming.

REVIEWING FACTS

1. Why did Peter the Great want to westernize Russia? How did he hope to accomplish this?
2. Name three different vegetation regions that exist in Russia. Explain what is special about each of these vegetation regions.
3. Why did Tsar Alexander II's abolition of serfdom in 1861 not improve the lives of former serfs? How did this contribute to the Russian Revolution?
4. List two important ideas that Lenin borrowed from Karl Marx. How did Lenin use these ideas to overthrow the tsar? Describe the revolution that followed.
5. What two important Russian cities were controlled by the Vikings and their descendants? In what modern countries are these cities located?

WRITING ABOUT MAIN IDEAS

1. **Writing a Summary:** Lenin promised that communism would end poverty and oppression in Russia. Write a summary of the historical events that followed Lenin. Did Lenin's promise come true?
2. **Writing a Paragraph:** Write a paragraph describing three of the important political changes that have come to Russia since 1900.
3. **Writing About Perspectives:** Imagine that you were one of the women who protested for bread during 1917, starting the Russian Revolution. Explain your feelings and what changes you think should be made in your country.

BUILDING SKILLS: READING DISTRIBUTION MAPS

Use the map on page 317 to answer the following questions.

1. Why is this map a distribution map? List three other things a distribution map might show.
2. What part of the world does the map show?
3. What information does the map give? How is the information given?
4. Locate another distribution map in your book. List the page number, the type of information given, and how it is shown.

CHAPTER 13

THE TWENTIETH CENTURY

FOCUS

Big Ben up there tells England's standard time. As it ticks through the twentieth century, may it toll [ring] for peace, prosperity, and harmony among all the nations of Europe.

As Winston Churchill said these hopeful words to the members of the British Parliament, a war was raging across Europe. Churchill's courage led his nation through difficult times. In this chapter you will read about modern Europe.

1 World War I

READ TO LEARN

Key Vocabulary
nationalism
alliance

Key People
Franz Ferdinand

Read Aloud

"The lights are going out all over Europe. We shall not see them lit again in our lifetime." With these sad words, a British leader described the events of 1914. Europe stood on the brink of a terrible war.

Read for Purpose

1. **WHAT YOU KNOW:** How did the Industrial and French revolutions change Europe?
2. **WHAT YOU WILL LEARN:** How did nationalism lead to World War I?

WHAT HAD GONE WRONG?

During the 1800s many Europeans worked to unify their lands. Before the French Revolution, many "countries" were simply groups of small states. Such states often shared a common language, religion, and many cultural traditions.

You will remember that the French dictator Napoleon tried to conquer and unite all Europe under his rule. As a result, strong feelings of nationalism (nash′ ə nə liz əm) grew throughout Europe. Nationalism is a feeling of loyalty and devotion to one's country, language, and culture. The regions that spoke German, for example, did not want to become "French" under Napoleon. Due to such nationalistic feelings, many nations were born.

Nationalism also caused some nations to start "territory wars." Sometimes a region might be made up of people with many different backgrounds. For example, French, German, and Belgian families may have lived side by side in one small region for generations. Nationalism, however, could end friendships.

NEW ALLIANCES

Fearful of attack by rivals, many European nations joined together in an alliance (ə lī′ əns). An alliance is a formal agreement between two or more nations to work together in war or commerce. If an alliance member is attacked by a rival nation, for example, other members of the alliance will come to its defense.

321

By the early 1900s, two rival alliances angrily faced each other in Europe. The nations of Germany, Austria-Hungary, and Italy formed the alliance known as the Central Powers. Britain, France, and Russia made up the Allied forces. One observer said that the rivalry between the members of these two alliances made Europe like a powder keg, needing only a small spark to set it off.

THE ROAD TO WAR

The spark was struck in a small country called Serbia, on the Balkan peninsula. The Serbs had strong feelings of nationalism and led territory wars against their more powerful neighbors. The Serbs believed, for example, that some lands within Austria-Hungary belonged to them. This created a difficult problem.

On June 28, 1914, Archduke Franz Ferdinand, heir to the throne of Austria-Hungary, visited Serbia. Only an hour after his arrival, however, both he and his wife were killed by a Serbian nationalist. By August the world was at war. Known today as World War I, this war stretched on for four agonizing years.

TRENCH WARFARE

The men slept in mud, washed in mud, ate mud, and dreamed mud.

This is how one soldier described his war years when he finally got back home to Britain. Soldiers from both alliances dug trenches, or deep ditches, for protection. The muddy trenches were their terrible homes during the war. Look at the photograph on the opposite page. You can see for yourself how terrible the trenches were.

After three years of such warfare, neither alliance was winning. Many people wondered if the war would ever end. After the Russian Revolution in 1917, many Europeans thought that the Central Powers would win. Lenin, the new Russian leader, had signed a peace treaty with Germany. As a result, Germany and Austria-Hungary no longer had to fight in the east. They could send more troops to the trenches in the west. But the year 1917 brought another important change.

The United States entered the war on the side of the Allies in April 1917. By the summer of 1918, 200,000 American soldiers arrived in Europe each month. These soldiers helped the Allies win

A Serbian nationalist fired the shots that killed Archduke Franz Ferdinand and his wife. This action plunged Europe into a long and devasting war.

These soldiers had to spend many weeks in the same trench. How do photographs help historians understand the past?

important victories and forced the Central Powers to surrender in November 1918.

THE TREATY OF VERSAILLES

In January 1919, 27 nations met at the Palace of Versailles near Paris to work out a peace treaty. Some of the Allies wanted to punish the Central Powers, especially Germany, for the war. These leaders wanted to make sure that Germany would be too weak ever to start another war.

As a result, the Treaty of Versailles called for Germany to lose 13 percent of its lands, and forbade it to make weapons. Under the treaty, Germany was also ordered to pay a huge amount of money to the Allies.

"THE WAR TO END ALL WARS"

As World War I was breaking out, some people called it "The War to End All Wars." By the time it ended, a whole generation of men had been killed. Europeans believed there would never again be such a terrible war. But only 20 years would pass before another war would explode.

Check Your Reading

1. What is nationalism? How can it become dangerous?
2. Why was the war in Europe a "world war"?
3. **GEOGRAPHY SKILL:** Why did many people think the Central Powers would win in 1917?
4. **THINKING SKILL:** What are three questions you could ask to learn more about World War I?

Determining Point of View

Key Vocabulary

point of view

Have you ever read *The Adventures of Robin Hood*? If you have, were you glad when Robin and his followers stole from the rich and gave to the poor? Whenever you have strong reactions to a story, you should ask yourself, "From whose point of view has the story been told?"

Identifying how an author feels about a subject is the same thing as recognizing **point of view**. Point of view is the position of the author who presents a subject or topic. It is important to try to identify an author's point of view to help determine the accuracy of what he or she has to say. Have you ever considered the events in *Robin Hood* from the point of view of the people who were robbed?

Trying the Skill

Below are two reports of the debate in Germany over the Treaty of Versailles. Read both reports and then determine the point of view of the first report.

Report A

If the will of our enemies becomes law, we meet for the last time as Germans. We must hold together. We are of one flesh and one blood, and he who tries to separate us cuts with a murderous knife into the live flesh of the German people. I would prefer utter ruin to a disgraceful peace. The treaty will not unite Germans, it will divide them.

Report B

We are done with fighting; we want peace. We watch in horror what war has caused. With a shudder we turn our heads away from these long years of murder. The people are without clothing, shoes, and bread. Must the people go on starving? Sign the treaty! Then I believe there will be bread.

1. What is the point of view expressed in **Report A**?
2. How do you know?

HELPING YOURSELF

The steps on the left will help you recognize a point of view in any description. The example on the right shows one way to apply these steps to **Report A**.

One Way to Determine Point of View	Example
1. Identify the subject or topic.	The topic is the signing by the Germans of the Treaty of Versailles.
2. Identify statements of fact.	There are no facts.
3. Identify statements of opinion.	The author says he prefers ruin to a disgraceful peace. The word *prefer* is a clue that someone is about to give an opinion. The word *disgraceful* is also an expression of opinion. Notice, however, that the author supports his view with the fact that under the treaty Germany would be divided.
4. Identify words or phrases that suggest how or what the author feels or believes about the subject.	The powerful image of the treaty cutting into living flesh suggests that the author feels it would destroy Germany.
5. Identify parts of the topic that the author does not include but probably could have.	The author does not mention that by September 1918 the Germans were in a hopeless position. In November they asked for an armistice, or cease-fire.
6. Describe the view or position expressed by the author.	The author's point of view is that the treaty would destroy Germany. The author seems ready to give up his life in order to preserve the German nation.

Applying the Skill

Reread **Report B**. What point of view does it express?

1. Which two of the following sentences in **Report B** are statements of fact?
   a. We want peace.
   b. I believe there will be bread.
   c. The people are without shoes.
2. What is one fact the author omitted in order to make his point more convincing?
   a. According to the terms of the treaty, Germany had to pay for the damages it caused.
   b. Millions of people died in World War I.
   c. The treaty established the League of Nations.
3. What is the point of view of the author of **Report B**?

Reviewing the Skill

1. What is a person's point of view?
2. What are some steps you could take to help you recognize point of view?
3. When is it important to try to recognize point of view in a statement?

2 World War II

READ TO LEARN

Key Vocabulary

depression
blitzkrieg
Holocaust
concentration camp

Key People

Adolf Hitler
Joseph Stalin
Winston Churchill
Franklin Roosevelt
Anne Frank

Read Aloud

We shall defend our island, whatever the cost may be. We shall fight on the beaches. . . . We shall fight in the fields and in the streets. . . . We shall never surrender!

In June 1940 Prime Minister Winston Churchill of Britain proclaimed this rallying cry to the British people. Once again, the nations of Europe were swept up in war. And soon it would sweep across the world, bringing with it widespread death and destruction.

Read for Purpose

1. **WHAT YOU KNOW:** How did nationalism cause World War I?
2. **WHAT YOU WILL LEARN:** What events led to the fall of Nazism?

DEPRESSION IN GERMANY

No country suffered greater economic troubles after the First World War than did Germany. Beginning in 1929, a worldwide depression, or slowdown of business, caused terrible poverty. Factories ground to a halt. Banks closed. By 1932 nearly 40 percent of Germany's work force was unemployed, or without jobs.

The Germans blamed the Treaty of Versailles for their troubles. They said that Germany's economic problems were caused by the loss of European territories and overseas colonies taken away by the treaty. Germany would never end its terrible depression, they said, until it regained its military strength. Moreover, many Germans wrongfully blamed the depression on German Jews.

HITLER AND THE NAZIS

In 1933 a dictator came to power in Germany. His name was Adolf Hitler and he promised the Germans that he would free their country "from the death sentence of Versailles." Hitler

326

Hitler spoke before huge rallies. His followers raised their arms and shouted *"Sieg Heil!"* meaning "Hail Victory!"

led a political party named the National Socialists, or the Nazis. Under Hitler's leadership in Berlin, Nazi Germany would terrorize the people of Europe for many years.

Hitler told the unhappy Germans that they were a "master race" meant to rule other nations. In 1935 the Nazi government passed laws against its own Jewish citizens. Jews were no longer allowed to call themselves Germans. They were not allowed to write books, to act on stage or in films, to teach, to work in hospitals or banks, or to sell books. All Jews were required to wear a yellow Star of David.

THE AXIS POWERS

"Today Europe, tomorrow the world!" Hitler's words stirred millions of Germans. Promising to bring his "master race" to glory, Hitler created a powerful alliance called the Axis. Its members were Germany, Italy, and faraway but mighty Japan.

By 1939 the Axis was on the move in Europe. By the spring, Hitler had taken over the countries of Austria and Czechoslovakia. Hitler's next move would be against Poland. Both Britain and France declared that they would help to defend Poland. They tried to get the Soviet Union to join them. Instead the Soviet leader, Joseph Stalin, signed a treaty of friendship with Hitler. In return for half of Poland, Stalin agreed not to stop Hitler's invasion.

THE INVASION OF POLAND

The sirens wail, the bombers skim the rooftops, their shadows glide across the road, and in the streets the people run, and clutch their heads.

A young Polish boy recorded these words as the Germans invaded his city. In the early hours of September 1, 1939, waves of German planes roared over Poland. Squadrons of German dive bombers destroyed Polish towns and airfields. In less than 48 hours, the Germans wiped out the Polish air force. At the same time, German tanks and trucks crossed the Polish border, carrying an army of more than 1 million men. Long columns of German

Airplanes were an essential part of warfare during the Second World War.

The Granger Collection

tanks rolled swiftly across the flat Polish lands, destroying everything in their path.

In less than a month, Poland was conquered. Nazi armies occupied the western half. As agreed, the Soviet Union occupied the eastern half. Meanwhile, Britain and France prepared for war against Germany.

THE "LIGHTNING WAR"

The Germans called their sudden, massive attack on Poland blitzkrieg (blits' krēg), or "lightning war." The fast-moving weapons of modern war— the armored tank and the dive bomber —were central to this new kind of warfare. The German blitzkrieg struck again in the spring of 1940. Nazi forces conquered Norway, Denmark, Belgium, and the Netherlands. By June even France had fallen into the hands of the Nazis.

In all of Europe, only one country still held out against Hitler. That country was Great Britain. In August 1940 Hitler turned his blitzkrieg against London, the British capital. Night and day, British and German air forces battled for control of the skies over London. As you read at the beginning of this lesson, the British Prime Minister Winston Churchill declared that his people would never give in to the Nazis. Despite fire-filled nights, the British fought on. Can you find the Battle of Britain on the Unit Opener time line on pages 274–275?

HOW THE NAZIS LOST

The chance of a total victory for Germany was lost during the summer of 1941. Hitler broke his friendship treaty with Stalin and ordered a blitzkrieg against the Soviet Union. By late

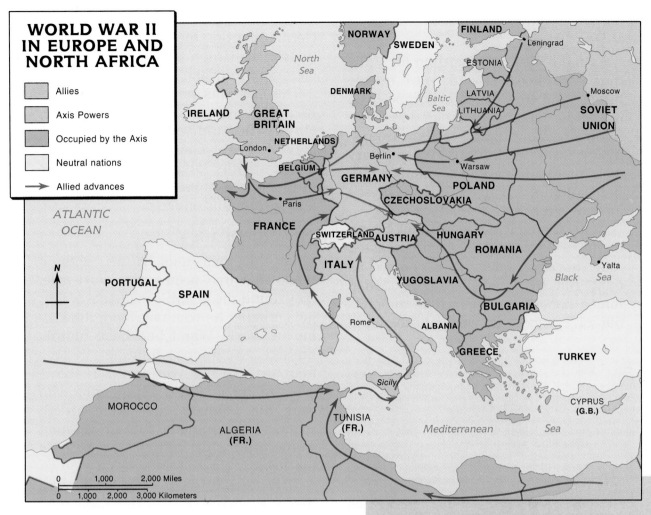

WORLD WAR II IN EUROPE AND NORTH AFRICA

Allies

Axis Powers

Occupied by the Axis

Neutral nations

→ Allied advances

November, Nazi troops were close to conquering Moscow and Leningrad. Like the people of Britain, however, the people of the Soviet Union refused to surrender. As the map on this page shows, Hitler's forces could not break the Soviet line of defense and were pushed back by Stalin's troops.

It was also a great blow to the Axis when, in December 1941, the United States entered the war on the side of the Allies. Japan made a surprise attack on an American naval base in Pearl Harbor, Hawaii. Within two hours, Japanese bombers destroyed 19 ships in America's fleet, 200 planes, and killed more than 2,000 American citizens. The next day, the United States declared war on Japan. Soon after, the other Axis powers, Germany and Italy, declared war on the United States.

Within months the United States, led by President Franklin Roosevelt, was shipping much-needed soldiers and supplies to help fight against the Axis powers. American industrial strength revived the Allied push against Hitler. After a long struggle, Allied troops finally defeated Nazi troops in northern Africa. Slowly, the Allies moved up the Italian peninsula and freed Italy.

329

D-DAY

As the Allies were battling for Italy, they also began to plan to invade France and free Western Europe from the Nazis. The Allies gathered together a force of more than 2 million troops, along with mountains of military equipment and supplies. Another million soldiers stood ready to give sea and air support to the attack.

Code-named D-day, the attack began on June 6, 1944. Hitler had boasted that "no army on earth can drive us out." But by November 1944, Allied forces had driven their Axis enemies out of France and were approaching

Germany from the west. Meanwhile, the Soviet Union was driving toward Germany from the east.

The end was near for Hitler's Germany. Knowing that defeat was close, Hitler killed himself. A week later, on May 7, 1945, Germany surrendered. Three months later, the United States dropped two atomic bombs on Japan and it, too, surrendered.

THE HOLOCAUST

As the victorious Allies entered lands that had been under Nazi rule, they found the horrible evidence of Hitler's cruelty. As you have read, the killing in World War I had been mainly limited to troops fighting in the trenches. During World War II, however, many civilians, or people who were not soldiers, also were killed. Hitler's government turned against whole groups of civilians—especially the Jews.

This terrible destruction of human life is known today as the Holocaust (hol' ə kost). It comes from a Greek word meaning "destruction of an entirety, a whole."

As countries fell under Hitler's power, the Holocaust spread throughout Europe. No country under Hitler's power was spared. Jewish families were in the greatest danger. Nazi police stormed into their homes and arrested whole families, simply because they were Jews.

A young Jewish girl named Anne Frank was arrested with her family in the Netherlands in 1944. Before she was taken away, however, she hid her diary in a secret place. You can read some of her courageous words on the next page. Anne Frank and most of her family were killed.

Winston Churchill, Franklin Roosevelt, and Joseph Stalin—the leaders of the Allied countries—met in Yalta to make plans for defeating Germany.

*W*hoever is happy will make others happy too. He who has courage and faith will never perish in unhappiness.

My father said: "All children must look after their own upbringing." Parents can only give them good advice or put them on the right paths, but the final forming of a person's character lies in their own hands. . . .

It is really a wonder that I have not lost all my ideals [beliefs], because they seem so absurd and impossible to carry out. Yet I keep them, because in spite of everything I still believe that people are really good at heart. . . .

I think that it will all come right, that this cruelty will end, and that peace and calm will return again. In the meantime, I must hold onto my ideals, for perhaps the time will come when I shall be able to carry them out.

Anne Frank was one of the 6 million Jews killed in **concentration camps** during the **Holocaust**. Her courage, however, lives on in the diary she kept.

Jewish families like Anne Frank's were taken to horrible prisons called **concentration camps**. The Nazis built more than 30 concentration camps across Europe. These prisons were also called death camps. By the end of the war, about 6 million Jews had been tortured and murdered by the Nazis in concentration camps.

Jews were not the only victims of the Holocaust. Another 8 million prisoners died in the Nazi concentration camps. This included many Poles, Russians, Czechs, and Gypsies.

THE COST OF WAR

Europe was devastated by World War II. Having begun in 1939, the war lasted for six terrible years. The scale of its destruction was staggering. Cities lay in ruins. No fewer than 16 million soldiers lost their lives. The number of civilians who died was even greater. Half of Europe's Jewish population was murdered. One third of the population of Poland was wiped out. Now Europe faced the challenge of rebuilding itself on its ruins.

 Check Your Reading

1. How did World War II end?
2. Why is the term "Holocaust" used to describe the loss of human life during World War II?
3. **GEOGRAPHY SKILL:** Why were Britain and the Soviet Union a greater challenge for Hitler to conquer?
4. **THINKING SKILL:** Compare and contrast the two world wars.

331

LIVING MEMORIALS

by Eric Kimmel

As you have read in this chapter, the twentieth century witnessed two of the most terrible conflicts in history. World War I and World War II cost the lives of millions of people and led to the destruction of countless towns and cities. In many cultures, including our own, it is a tradition to honor those who gave their lives in war. People may remember the dead with a monument, a special prayer, or with a holiday set aside in their honor. In this lesson you will learn about some of these special traditions of remembering—and honoring—the tragic victims of war.

THE TOMB OF THE UNKNOWNS

One such memorial is the Tomb of the Unknowns, located in Arlington National Cemetery near Washington, D.C. (By "unknowns," we mean soldiers whose identities aren't known.) This simple stone monument honors the United States citizens who died in World War I, World War II, the Korean War, and the Vietnam War. One soldier from each of these conflicts is buried within the tomb, and the monument bears this inscription: "Here rests in honored glory an American soldier known but to God."

Special ceremonies are held at this monument on May 30 of every year—Memorial Day. The flag flies at half-mast. Flowers are placed on the tomb. At the same time, people all over the United States take time to honor the men and women who gave their lives in war.

MEMORIAL DAY

Although the dead of World War I and World War II are honored on Memorial Day, the holiday itself goes back to the 1860s. It was first celebrated in Georgia, shortly after the end of the Civil War.

The founder of the holiday, Elizabeth Rutherford Ellis, worked as a volunteer in a Southern military hospital during the war. She took care of the sick and the dying and tended the graves of both Southern and Northern soldiers. After the war ended, she worked to establish Confederate Memorial Day as a holiday throughout the South.

Memorial Day became a national holiday soon after. In 1867 Mary Cunningham Logan visited the South. She saw that the soldiers' graves were decorated with flags and magnolia blossoms. Impressed by this custom, she discussed it with her husband, who was a general in the Union army. General John Logan urged the United States Congress to establish a national holiday. Decoration Day (later renamed Memorial Day) was first celebrated on May 30, 1868.

KHATYN

Another memorial honors the victims of Khatyn (kä tin′). This small village was located in Byelarus (byel ə rüs′), a country which was then part of the Soviet Union. During World War II, Nazi soldiers burned the village to the ground, killing all but 2 of the 149 inhabitants. Khatyn was never rebuilt. Instead, the site has become a monument to the 205,000 Byelarusians who perished during the war.

At one end of the memorial, a large sculpture and an inscribed stone slab commemorate the villagers who were killed by the Germans. The Khatyn Memorial also includes 26 columns called obelisks (ob' ə lisks). Grouped along a white marble walkway, the obelisks mark the spots where the 26 huts in the village once stood. A black bell on top of each obelisk rings every 30 seconds, reminding visitors of the terrible toll the war took on Byelarus.

The memorial includes a note of hope. A black marble slab stands at one end, lit by an eternal flame. Three birch branches grow out of the slab, and beyond it is a forest of young trees, symbolizing the way a hopeful future can rise out of suffering.

YAD VASHEM

Jerusalem's Yad Vashem commemorates destruction on even a larger scale—the Holocaust. The marble floor at Yad Vashem is inscribed with the names of the Nazi concentration camps, which you read about in the last lesson. The ashes of Jews who were killed at these camps are buried here. An eternal flame represents the promise that they will be remembered forever.

Yad Vashem is more than a monument. It is a library, a museum, and a research center for the study of the Holocaust. In this way Yad Vashem is a living memorial, ensuring that the truth about these terrible events will never be falsified or forgotten.

Like the people of the United States, Israelis observe their own "memorial day." On the twenty-seventh day of the Hebrew month Adar, sirens sound across the country. Traffic comes to a halt. All activity stops. For two minutes the entire country falls silent, and at Yad Vashem large crowds gather. They, too, are carrying out a promise to remember.

HIROSHIMA'S PEACE PARK

In the city of Hiroshima, Japan, a park stands in the middle of the city. This is the spot on which the first atomic bomb was dropped. The Peace Park honors the memory of the dead, and warns the world of the horrors of nuclear war.

The Peace Park contains many individual monuments. One of the most powerful monuments honors Sadako Sasaki, who was two years old when the bomb fell. Sadako survived the explosion unharmed. Ten years later, however, she developed leukemia, an illness that often strikes people who have been exposed to nuclear radiation.

According to an old Japanese tradition, a sick person may be able to get well by folding 1,000 sheets of paper into birds called cranes. Sadako decided to try. She had folded 964 paper cranes before her illness finally killed her.

Sadako's friends folded the rest of the cranes for her. Then they built a monument in the Peace Park to honor her and all the children who perished as a result of the bomb. A statue on the monument shows Sadako standing on

the mountain of paradise, holding a golden crane in her arms. Beneath her are chains of paper cranes sent from all over the world. At the base of the monument, an inscription expresses the hope of all the monuments you have just read about: "This is our cry, this is our prayer: peace in the world."

How does remembering tragedies of the past help give people hope for the future?

335

3 Europe and North Asia Today

READ TO LEARN

Key Vocabulary

United Nations
Iron Curtain
Cold War
NATO
Warsaw Pact
glasnost
European Community

Key People

Lech Walesa
Mikhail Gorbachev
Boris Yeltsin

Key Places

Latvia
Estonia
Lithuania

Read Aloud

Once again Berlin has become a symbol, but now it has become a symbol of hope. What had once stood for tyranny and tragedy has come tumbling down, and the world watches to see where freedom will ring again.

Willy Brandt fought back tears as he spoke these words in the autumn of 1989. Brandt, who had been mayor of Berlin when the Berlin Wall was built in 1961, now watched joyfully as citizens from East Germany and West Germany joined together to bring down the hated wall. In this lesson you will read how this wall came to divide this region and how it finally came tumbling down.

Read for Purpose

1. **WHAT YOU KNOW:** How did World War II divide the nations of the world?
2. **WHAT YOU WILL LEARN:** In which ways are the countries of Europe and North Asia becoming more dependent on one another?

THE UNITED NATIONS

In February 1945 Franklin Roosevelt, Winston Churchill, and Joseph Stalin met in a town on the Black Sea called Yalta. These world leaders had grown tired of seeing their people suffer through another world war. Just months away from victory in World War II, they declared:

We express our determination that our nations shall work together in war and in the peace that will follow.

After the war, representatives from 51 nations met in San Francisco, California, to carry out this declaration. They formed an organization called the United Nations. Its purpose was "to save succeeding generations from the scourge [punishment] of war." The United Nations was to serve as a "town meeting" for the world. Countries now could discuss world problems rather than go to war over them.

THE SPREAD OF COMMUNISM

After World War II, however, much of Europe and North Asia remained in turmoil. The leaders of the Soviet Union were determined to spread their political system of communism to countries in Eastern Europe. At Yalta, Stalin had promised to allow free elections in Poland and other parts of Europe "as soon as possible." By July 1945, however, Stalin made it clear that he would not keep this promise.

A freely elected government in any of these Eastern European countries would be anti-Soviet, and that we could not allow.

By 1948, Soviet-backed communist governments ruled the countries of Poland, Bulgaria, Romania, Hungary, and Czechoslovakia. Look at the map on this page to locate these countries.

This region was now divided into two political regions: a mostly democratic Western Europe and a communist Eastern Europe and North Asia. Winston Churchill described this division as an "Iron Curtain."

From Stettin in the Baltic [Sea] to Trieste in the Adriatic [Sea], an iron curtain has descended across the continent. Behind that line lie all the capitals of the ancient states of Central and Eastern Europe. . . .

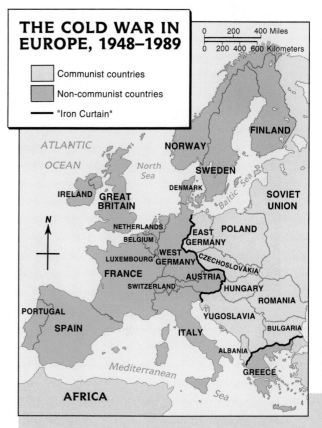

THE COLD WAR IN EUROPE, 1948–1989

☐ Communist countries
■ Non-communist countries
— "Iron Curtain"

MAP SKILL: During the Cold War, were most communist countries located in Eastern or Western Europe?

In 1961 East Germany, with the help of the Soviet Union, built a massive concrete wall that cut through the heart of the German city of Berlin. The purpose of the Berlin Wall was to keep people who lived in communist East Germany from escaping into democratic West Germany. Still, hundreds of East Germans risked their lives trying to climb over or to tunnel under the wall.

THE COLD WAR

The concrete and barbed wire of the Berlin Wall became a symbol of the Cold War. The term *Cold War* describes the tense war of words and ideas that developed between the United States and Western Europe on the one hand and the Soviet Union and

337

In the 1980s the Solidarity movement, led by Lech Walesa (*right*), challenged the communist government in Poland.

Eastern Europe on the other after 1945. Relations between the United States and the Soviet Union were especially icy during this time. These two powerful nations engaged in a struggle that sometimes brought them to the brink of nuclear war.

During the Cold War, leaders in Western Europe and North America feared that the Soviet Union would try to bring more countries under communist control. Therefore, in 1949 the United States, Canada, and ten Western European countries formed the North Atlantic Treaty Organization, or NATO. NATO members declared that an attack against one member country would be considered an attack against them all.

The Soviet Union responded by forming its own alliance with seven Eastern European nations. In an agreement called the Warsaw Pact, the eight member nations also pledged to support one another in case of war.

UPRISINGS AGAINST COMMUNISM

For nearly 50 years after World War II, Soviet-controlled communist governments ruled the Warsaw Pact countries with an iron hand. During that time, people who spoke out against their governments were imprisoned and sometimes killed.

But even in this atmosphere of fear and uncertainty, many Eastern Europeans held onto their visions of democracy. For example, in Hungary protests against the Soviet-controlled government turned into a revolution in 1956. Angry Hungarians stormed through the streets demanding free elections. But the Soviet Union responded by sending in tanks and soldiers, brutally crushing the Hungarian Revolution.

In Poland in 1970, a shipyard worker named Lech Walesa (lek vä len′ sə) helped to lead a strike by Polish workers. They protested the communist government's decision to increase food

338

prices. Fifty workers were shot to death by Polish troops. But Walesa and his fellow workers did not allow their hopes for a democratic Poland to die.

Ten years later, in 1980, Walesa led workers on another strike for better wages. Now they also wanted the government to recognize their union, called Solidarity. *Solidarity* means "unity." This time, the Polish government agreed to the union's demands. This strike marked the first time that Eastern Europeans had successfully challenged a Soviet-backed government.

CHANGES IN THE SOVIET UNION

Another encouraging event was the rise to power of Mikhail Gorbachev (myik el′ gôr′ bə chôf), who became head of the Soviet Union in 1985.

Gorbachev set out to reform the Soviet government and economy. He astonished people around the world when he called for a reduction in Soviet nuclear weapons and reform of the nation's weakening communist economy.

More suprising still was Gorbachev's new policy of glasnost (glas′ nōst), or "openness." Glasnost made it possible for the people of Eastern Europe and the Soviet Union to speak freely and to practice their religions openly, without fear of arrest. Gorbachev declared, "Let every nation in Eastern Europe decide for itself what course it will follow."

UPHEAVAL IN THE EAST

The spirit of glasnost spread throughout the countries of Eastern Europe. More and more people joined in the chorus of voices criticizing their communist governments. The democracy movement that began as a trickle in Poland soon flooded the entire Warsaw Pact. In the fall of 1989, hundreds of thousands of East Germans gathered in city squares to demand

As the spirit of glasnost and reform spread, the Cold War began to end. In 1991 President Bush and President Gorbachev signed a treaty to limit nuclear weapons.

Among the dramatic changes that came to Europe and North Asia were the fall of the Berlin Wall (*below*) and the triumph of Boris Yeltsin (*above*) and democracy in the Soviet Union.

symbol of the Cold War—came tumbling down. These breathtaking events paved the way for the reunification of East Germany and West Germany and for more changes in Eastern Europe.

Following the collapse of the East German government, other Soviet-backed governments gave in to their people's demands for democratic changes. In 1989 alone, the people of East Germany, Poland, Hungary, Czechoslovakia, and Romania all overthrew their communist governments. In 1990, 20 years after he led his first revolt against Poland's communist government, Lech Walesa was elected president of his country.

THE SOVIET UNION COLLAPSES

In 1991 the reforms that Gorbachev had started began to break the Soviet Union apart. The republics of Latvia, Estonia, and Lithuania became independent countries. The election of Boris Yeltsin as president of Russia marked the birth of democracy in this Soviet republic. Newspapers began to print criticisms of the communist government and economy.

changes in their government. Thousands more fled to West Germany.

These events strained the East German government to its limit. Then, on the night of November 9, 1989, gates in the Berlin Wall swung open. Soon after, the Berlin Wall—the terrifying

In the summer of 1991, a group of communist leaders attempted to overthrow Gorbachev and roll back the democratic changes. Their effort failed, and the changes came faster and faster. Before long, all of the republics declared their independence and the Soviet government collapsed. On December 25, 1991, Mikhail Gorbachev resigned. After nearly 70 years, the Soviet flag was lowered over Moscow for the last time.

In place of the Soviet Union, there are now 15 independent countries. As you read in Chapter 12, 11 of the former republics joined together in the Commonwealth of Independent States. Look at the map on this page to see the members of this commonwealth.

CHANGES AND CHALLENGES

In spite of these sweeping changes in parts of Europe and North Asia, the region faced many serious problems. There were shortages of food and many other goods. Many people lost their jobs. Germans and other Western Europeans sometimes resented the thousands of immigrants from the East who came to their countries in search of a better life. In Yugoslavia, nationalist disputes led to a terrible civil war in 1991 that broke the country apart and left thousands dead or homeless.

MAP SKILL: The Soviet Union split into 15 independent countries in 1991. Which of these are not part of the Commonwealth of Independent States?

COMMONWEALTH OF INDEPENDENT STATES: Political

⊛ National capital   • Other city

☐ Members of the Commonwealth

☐ Former Soviet Republics not part of the Commonwealth

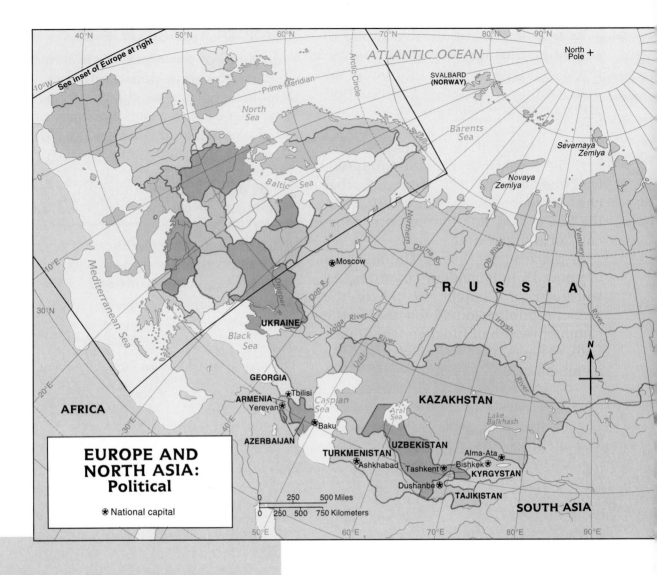

EUROPE AND NORTH ASIA: Political

⊛ National capital

0   250   500 Miles
0 250 500 750 Kilometers

MAP SKILL: Which countries of Europe and North Asia border the Black Sea?

THE EUROPEAN COMMUNITY

With the end of the Cold War, a once-divided region has become increasingly united. Countries of Europe and North Asia are developing new ways to cooperate with one another.

Plans for a new Europe have been developed by a powerful group of 12 Western European countries called the European Community, or EC. The goal of the EC is to work together for the benefit of all of Europe.

EC countries agreed to begin operating as a single economic unit, starting in 1993. Before 1993, for example, truck drivers transporting compact-disc players from the Netherlands to Portugal needed to carry 2 pounds (1 k) of documents in order to pass through four border crossings. Now they need only one piece of paper to transport the product from the Netherlands, through Belgium, France, and Spain, and on to Portugal. The EC is also working to help the countries in Eastern Europe and North Asia to reform their economies.

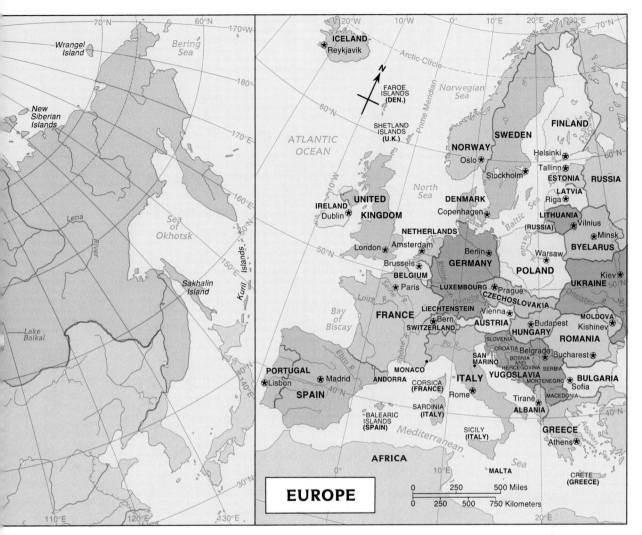

EUROPE

| 0 | 250 | 500 Miles |
| 0 | 250 | 500 | 750 Kilometers |

TOWARD A NEW CENTURY

The 1900s have been a stormy century for Europe and North Asia. Two world wars spread suffering across these lands. A Cold War raised fears of nuclear destruction. The Soviet Union forced communist governments on the countries of Eastern Europe. Today, new democratic governments are struggling to bring freedom and equality to their people. The words of a Czechoslovakian folk song echo the longing of many people in this region:

May peace be with this land.
Let hate, envy, fear, and conflict pass.
May they pass, may they pass.

Check Your Reading

1. Why were Europe and North Asia divided into two alliances after World War II?
2. In what way was the Berlin Wall a powerful symbol of the Cold War?
3. **GEOGRAPHY SKILL:** How is the European Community changing the way in which European countries interact with one another?
4. **THINKING SKILL:** Reread Winston Churchill's quote on page 337. What was his point of view about events in Europe? How can you tell?

How Should Europe's Forests Be Protected?

Europe was once covered with forests. We have a duty to treat Europe's last forests with care.

The German chancellor made this statement in 1988. Germany is a highly industrialized and densely populated country. As in other European nations, there is widespread concern about the loss of valuable forests. Scientists think that acid rain is causing the damage to Europe's forests.

As you may know, acid rain is formed by the reaction of the water vapor in clouds with pollutants. The pollutants are gases discharged into the air by factory smokestacks. The gases are formed by the burning of coal, oil, and natural gas. The gases form strong acids with water. A strong acid is found in the battery of a car, for example. Examples of weak acids are lemon juice and vinegar. But imagine how house plants would react if they were sprinkled with vinegar!

Acid rain is an important issue in the modern world. But what should be done about it? In Germany, for example, a great debate is taking place. People argue over how to help the forests. Some people argue that enough has been done.

POINT ☆ 👉

Prevent Damage at all Costs

A supporter of strict measures against industry, Volker Hoffmann, wrote the following in a popular German magazine.

The forest is more than a playground for humans. The forest is a home to many kinds of animals and plants. Indeed, a forest can provide a peaceful setting and a place for recreation. The German people love their forests. Many may not know that they are killing the forests—a forest that gives the raw materials to build housing developments. What, may I ask, shall we build our homes with when there are no more forests?

Pollution is out of control. We have lost so much as a result of acid rain. In the fall of 1988, some 15,000 square miles (37,000 sq km) suffered damage in varying degrees. This area is more than half of the total forestland. The damage affects large regions. It is time we come up with strict protective measures in order to prevent more damage.

● Why does Volker Hoffmann think that Europe's forests should be protected from acid rain?

COUNTERPOINT 👈 ☆

Industry Comes First

Ignaz Langer is a German who does not support "strict measures" to protect forests.

During a debate in our legislature all political parties expressed concern about the condition of the forests. Many speakers have supported strict measures to protect the environment of our country. Many have argued that our northern industrial centers spill pollutants into the air. Criminal industries will be brought to justice but, indeed, we have been equipped with protective technology for many years. Yet the loss of trees grows at an astonishing rate.

We must not act too quickly. Unless more protective technology is invented, we Germans can do little. There are already laws governing large industrial furnaces. These laws carefully regulate pollution. Finally, for a nation whose economy is built itself upon industry it is unimaginable that some would threaten this progress.

● Why does Ignaz Langer think that Europe's forests should not be protected?

UNDERSTANDING THE POINT/COUNTERPOINT

1. Who do you think makes a stronger argument about whether Europe's forests should be protected?
2. How do you think a person living in one of Germany's neighboring countries would feel about this issue?
3. Can you think of a compromise that might be acceptable to both Volker Hoffmann and Ignaz Langer? Explain your answer.

IMPORTANT EVENTS

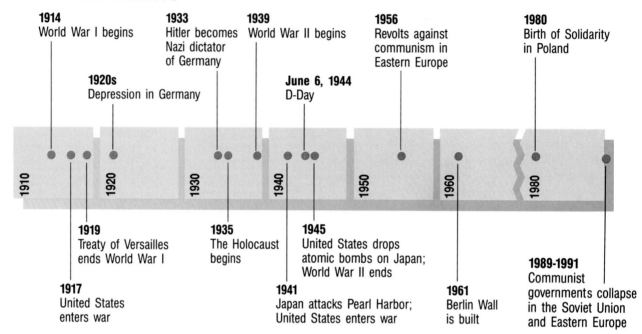

1914
World War I begins

1920s
Depression in Germany

1933
Hitler becomes
Nazi dictator
of Germany

1939
World War II begins

June 6, 1944
D-Day

1956
Revolts against
communism in
Eastern Europe

1980
Birth of Solidarity
in Poland

1910 1920 1930 1940 1950 1960 1980

1919
Treaty of Versailles
ends World War I

1917
United States
enters war

1935
The Holocaust
begins

1945
United States drops
atomic bombs on Japan;
World War II ends

1941
Japan attacks Pearl Harbor;
United States enters war

1961
Berlin Wall
is built

1989-1991
Communist
governments collapse
in the Soviet Union
and Eastern Europe

PEOPLE TO KNOW

Winston Churchill   A.D. 1874-1965

Franz Ferdinand   A.D. 1863-1914

Franklin Roosevelt   A.D. 1882-1945

Joseph Stalin   A.D. 1879-1953

Anne Frank   A.D. 1929-1945

Adolf Hitler   A.D. 1889-1945

Mikhail Gorbachev   A.D. 1931-

IDEAS TO REMEMBER

- Strong feelings of nationalism and new alliances helped cause World War I. The Treaty of Versailles ended the war and redrew many boundaries.
- Germany suffered a terrible depression after World War I and Adolf Hitler became dictator. Forming an alliance with Italy and Japan, Hitler brought the world to war.
- Following World War II an "iron curtain" divided Europe between communist and non-communist countries. Beginning in 1989, communist governments collapsed in the countries of Eastern Europe and in the Soviet Union. This ushered in a new era of democracy in Europe.

REVIEWING VOCABULARY

alliance
blitzkrieg
Cold War
concentration
  camp
depression

Holocaust
nationalism
NATO
United Nations
Warsaw Pact

Number a sheet of paper from 1 to 10. Beside each number, write the word or term from the above list that best matches the statement or definition.

1. A term used to describe the murder of millions of European Jews by the Nazis during World War II.
2. This "war of ideas" between the Soviet Union and the Western democracies lasted more than 40 years.
3. The Allies and the Axis Powers of World War II are examples of this type of military union.
4. A severe business slowdown in which factories and businesses close and millions of people lose their jobs.
5. This military alliance was formed after World War II to protect Western Europe from Communist expansion.
6. Hitler used this type of sudden, massive warfare to defeat countries.
7. This intense feeling for one's country helped cause World War I.
8. Millions of innocent people were murdered in these during World War II.
9. This alliance among the Soviet-controlled nations of Eastern Europe was formed during the Cold War.
10. This organization of nations was formed in response to the terrible bloodshed of World War II.

REVIEWING FACTS

1. Name two problems in Europe that helped bring about World War I.
2. What important change occurred in 1917 that helped bring an end to World War I?
3. List two ways in which the Treaty of Versailles helped bring about World War II.
4. How did Hitler justify Germany's rule over other nations?
5. What was the main reason for creating the United Nations?

WRITING ABOUT MAIN IDEAS

1. **Writing an Explanation:** Hitler's invasion of the Soviet Union is widely regarded as his greatest blunder, the one event that cost Germany the war. Write a paragraph explaining why this was so.
2. **Writing About Perspectives:** Write a paragraph expressing your opinion about whether the term *Cold War* was a good description of the tensions between East and West after World War II.

BUILDING SKILLS: DETERMINING POINT OF VIEW

1. In your own words define the term "point of view."
2. List two ways you might determine an author's point of view.
3. Reread the quotation about the Berlin Wall on page 336. What is Willy Brandt's point of view? How do you know?
4. Why is it important to determine an author's point of view?

REVIEWING VOCABULARY

communism   Industrial Revolution
depression   nationalism
divine right

Number a sheet of paper from 1 to 5. Beside each number, write the word or term from the above list that matches the statement or definition.

1. Although this feeling was "love of country," it also created fear and hatred of other countries.
2. This transformation brought sweeping changes in the way people lived, worked, and saw themselves.
3. Although it proclaims equality and the common ownership of land and factories, this system of government does not allow private ownership.
4. The kings of France and other nations used this idea to justify their often harsh rule.
5. This type of severe economic slowdown helped bring Hitler to power.

WRITING ABOUT THE UNIT

1. **Writing an Article:** Imagine that you are living in the late 1700s. Write a magazine article describing ways in which your life has been influenced by the Industrial Revolution.
2. **Writing a Paragraph:** You read that World War I was called "the war to end all wars"; yet only 20 years later another world war broke out that was far more destructive than the first. Write a paragraph to explain why it was more destructive and how advances in technology contributed to the devastation.

3. **Writing a Report:** Choose one European nation to write about. Find and read current magazines or newspaper articles on the country you have selected. Organize the different articles by topic. Topics could include government, economy, environment, culture, or relations with the United States. Write a brief report about the nation's current affairs.
4. **Writing About Perspectives:** Imagine that you are a Russian citizen who was involved in the sweeping changes that came during the summer of 1991. Write a letter to the leaders of your government explaining what changes you think should be made in the Russian government and economy.

ACTIVITIES

1. **Using a Map Scale:** Turn to the map on page 343. How far is Kiev from the European cities of Berlin, Paris, and Helsinki? How far is Sicily from the coast of Africa? About how many kilometers long is Italy?
2. **Writing a Summary:** Find a recent newspaper or magazine article about Russia. Write a summary of the article by stating the main idea and briefly describing the most important details. Present your summary.
3. **Working Together on a Time Line:** Work as a group to review the important events covered in this unit. Make a time line by arranging the events and their dates in order. Find other dates in the library to put on the time line. Add illustrations and pictures on the time line.

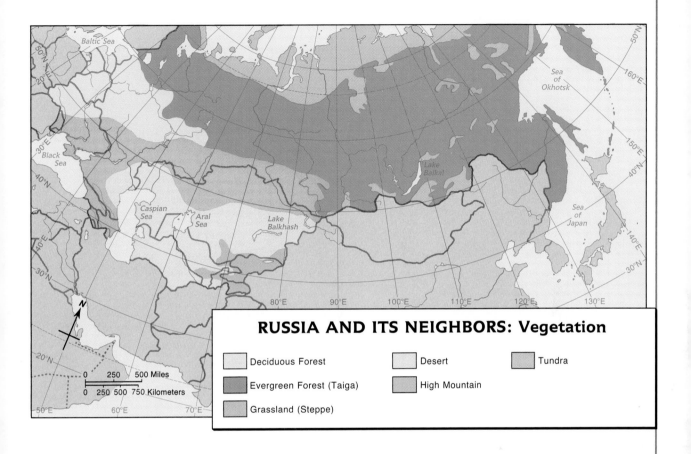

RUSSIA AND ITS NEIGHBORS: Vegetation

- Deciduous Forest
- Evergreen Forest (Taiga)
- Grassland (Steppe)
- Desert
- High Mountain
- Tundra

BUILDING SKILLS: READING DISTRIBUTION MAPS

Use the map above to answer the following questions.

1. What is a distribution map?
2. How many vegetation zones appear on this map? Which type of vegetation is the most widespread?
3. What can you conclude about the bits of tundra mixed with taiga?
4. Describe the probable climate of the region near the Barents Sea.
5. Describe the probable climate of the region near the Caspian Sea.
6. How do distribution maps help you understand a region "at a glance?"

LINKING PAST, PRESENT, AND FUTURE

During the twentieth century, Europe and North Asia have been witness to two world wars and a Cold War. The end of the Cold War has brought peace as well as a new set of problems. What do you think will happen in this region in the years ahead?

349

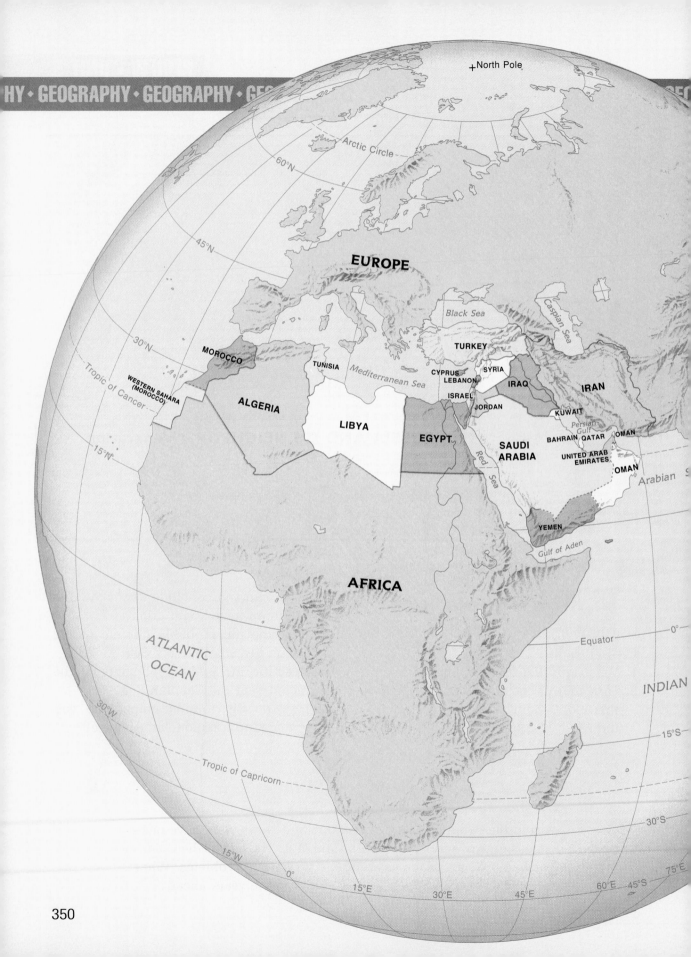

+North Pole

Arctic Circle

60°N

45°N

EUROPE

Black Sea

Caspian Sea

30°N

MOROCCO

TUNISIA

Mediterranean Sea

TURKEY

CYPRUS

SYRIA

IRAQ

IRAN

WESTERN SAHARA
(MOROCCO)

LEBANON

ISRAEL

KUWAIT

ALGERIA

JORDAN

Persian
Gulf

OMAN

LIBYA

EGYPT

SAUDI
ARABIA

BAHRAIN QATAR

UNITED ARAB
EMIRATES

OMAN

Tropic of Cancer

15°N

Red Sea

Arabian S

YEMEN

Gulf of Aden

AFRICA

ATLANTIC
OCEAN

Equator

0°

INDIAN

30°W

15°S

Tropic of Capricorn

30°S

15°W

0°

15°E

30°E

45°E

60°E

45°S

75°E

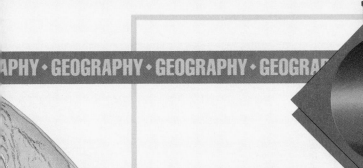

UNIT
6

ASIA

OCEAN

90°E

MIDDLE EAST
AND
NORTH AFRICA

WHERE WE ARE

As the map shows, the Middle East and North Africa lie at a crossroads where three continents meet. The countries of this region are among the hottest and driest in the world. Although much of the Middle East and North Africa is dry, there are also fertile plains and high mountains.

For thousands of years, farming and herding have been the chief occupations of the people of the Middle East and North Africa. Commerce and trade have long been important in this region. Today, many countries are becoming industrialized. The discovery of oil, for example, has brought new wealth and new power to this historic region.

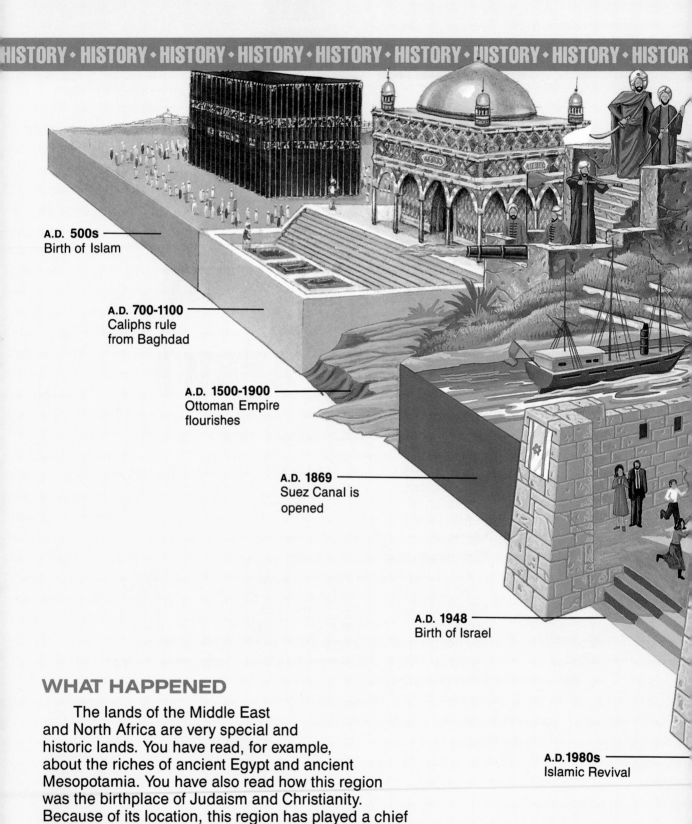

A.D. 500s
Birth of Islam

A.D. 700-1100
Caliphs rule
from Baghdad

A.D. 1500-1900
Ottoman Empire
flourishes

A.D. 1869
Suez Canal is
opened

A.D. 1948
Birth of Israel

A.D. 1980s
Islamic Revival

WHAT HAPPENED

The lands of the Middle East
and North Africa are very special and
historic lands. You have read, for example,
about the riches of ancient Egypt and ancient
Mesopotamia. You have also read how this region
was the birthplace of Judaism and Christianity.
Because of its location, this region has played a chief
role in the history of trade. As the time line shows, people
and ideas, as well as goods, have moved through this region.

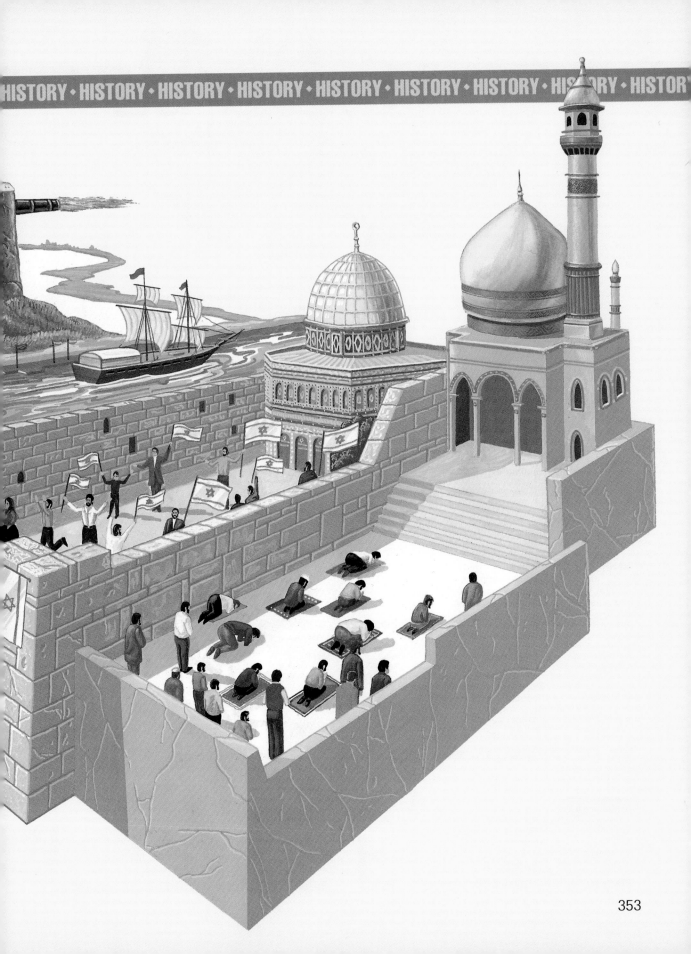

MIDDLE EAST AND NORTH AFRICA

IRAN

Capital ★
Tehran

Major languages: Farsi, Azarbaijani, and Kurdish
Population: 58.6 million
Area: 636,294 sq mi; 1,648,000 sq km
Leading export: oil

ALGERIA

Capital ★
Algiers

Major languages: Arabic, Berber and French
Population: 26.0 million
Area: 919,592 sq mi; 2,381,740 sq km
Leading exports: oil and natural gas

IRAQ

Capital ★
Baghdad

Major languages: Arabic and Kurdish
Population: 17.1 million
Area: 167,923 sq mi; 434,920 sq km
Leading export: oil

BAHRAIN

Capital ★
Manama

Major language: Arabic
Population: 0.5 million
Area: 239 sq mi; 620 sq km
Leading export: oil

ISRAEL

Capital ★
Jerusalem

Major languages: Hebrew and Arabic
Population: 4.9 million
Area: 8,091 sq mi; 20,770 sq km
Leading exports: diamonds and machinery

CYPRUS

Capital ★
Nicosia

Major languages: Greek and Turkish
Population: 0.7 million
Area: 3,571 sq mi; 9,250 sq km
Leading exports: clothing, fruit, and potatoes

JORDAN

Capital ★
Amman

Major language: Arabic
Population: 3.4 million
Area: 35,475 sq mi; 91,880 sq km
Leading exports: phosphates and chemicals

EGYPT

Capital ★
Cairo

Major language: Arabic
Population: 54.5 million
Area: 386,661 sq mi; 1,001,450 sq km
Leading export: oil

KUWAIT

Capital ★
Kuwait

Major language: Arabic
Population: 1.4 million
Area: 6,880 sq mi; 17,820 sq km
Leading export: oil

LEBANON

Capital ★
Beirut

Major languages: Arabic and French
Population: 3.4 million
Area: 4,015 sq mi; 10,400 sq km
Leading exports: jewelry, clothing, and metal products

SYRIA

Capital ★
Damascus

Major languages: Arabic and Kurdish
Population: 12.8 million
Area: 71,498 sq mi; 185,180 sq km
Leading exports: oil and textile

LIBYA

Capital ★
Tripoli

Major language: Arabic
Population: 4.4 million
Area: 679,360 sq mi; 1,759,540 sq km
Leading export: oil

TUNISIA

Capital ★
Tunis

Major languages: Arabic and French
Population: 8.4 million
Area: 63,170 sq mi; 163,610 sq km
Leading export: oil

MOROCCO

Capital ★
Rabat

Major languages: Arabic, Berber, and French
Population: 26.2 million
Area: 172,413 sq mi; 446,550 sq km
Leading exports: food and phosphates

TURKEY

Capital ★
Ankara

Major languages: Turkish and Kurdish
Population: 58.5 million
Area: 301,383 sq mi; 780,580 sq km
Leading exports: textiles and food

OMAN

Capital ★
Muscat

Major language: Arabic
Population: 1.6 million
Area: 82,013 sq mi; 212,460 sq km
Leading export: oil

UNITED ARAB EMIRATES

Capital ★
Abu Dhabi

Major language: Arabic
Population: 2.4 million
Area: 32,278 sq mi; 83,600 sq km
Leading export: oil

QATAR

Capital ★
Doha

Major languages: Arabic and English
Population: 0.5 million
Area: 4,247 sq mi; 11,000 sq km
Leading export: oil

YEMEN

Capital ★
San'a

Major language: Arabic
Population: 10.1 million
Area: 203,850 sq mi; 527,970 sq km
Leading exports: oil and coffee

SAUDI ARABIA

Capital ★
Riyadh

Major language: Arabic
Population: 15.5 million
Area: 829,997 sq mi; 2,149,690 sq km
Leading export: oil

355

CHAPTER 14

THE MIDDLE EAST AND NORTH AFRICA LONG AGO

FOCUS

Our history was born in the desert. It was among the desert nomads that our religion, our culture, and our knowledge of the world began.

This is how William Said (sī′ ēd), an Arab historian, has described the desert people of Arabia. To understand the people of the Middle East and North Africa, he says, you must study their desert beginnings. Said also wrote that his people "make up a region of many nations and many different dreams."

1 Geography: Middle East and North Africa

Key Vocabulary

desert
erosion
arid
caravan

Key Places

Arabian peninsula
Anatolia
Dead Sea
Sahara

Read Aloud

You have learned that the Middle East and North Africa were home to some of the world's earliest civilizations. Although much of this region is desert, these early cultures thrived in the fertile river valleys and coastal areas. Today, the people of this region are finding new ways to meet the challenges of their environment.

Read for Purpose

1. **WHAT YOU KNOW:** How did irrigation encourage the growth of civilization in the Nile River Valley?
2. **WHAT YOU WILL LEARN:** What are the geographic features of the Middle East and North Africa?

A HISTORICAL REGION

The Middle East includes the part of southwest Asia that stretches from Turkey to Iran. When Europeans began trading with Asia, they called this region the Middle East because it lay between their homes and the more distant eastern lands of India, China, and Japan. Today North Africa is often considered part of the Middle East because it has strong cultural ties to the Middle Eastern countries.

You have already read a great deal about the early history of this region. In Unit 2, for example, you read about the early civilizations which flourished in the Nile and Tigris-Euphrates river valleys. In Unit 3 you read how the ancient Greeks established many colonies on the coast of North Africa and exchanged goods and ideas with the Phoenicians. Later you read how the Romans built an empire that included not only large parts of Europe, but also most of the Middle East and North Africa. Finally you may recall that the Europeans of the Middle Ages developed a trading relationship with their neighbors far across the Mediterranean Sea.

357

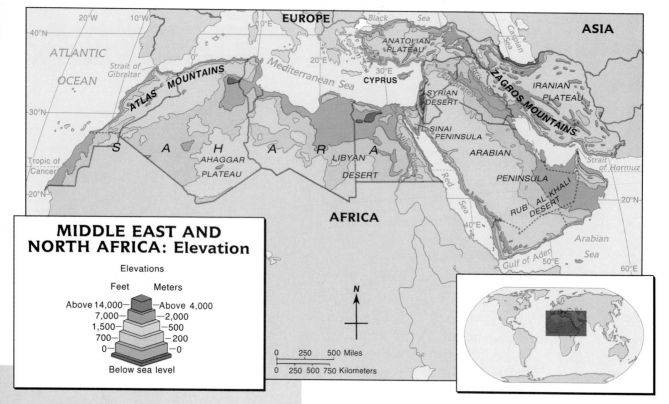

MIDDLE EAST AND NORTH AFRICA: Elevation

Elevations

Feet	Meters
Above 14,000—	—Above 4,000
7,000—	—2,000
1,500—	—500
700—	—200
0—	—0

Below sea level

N

0   250   500 Miles
0 250 500 750 Kilometers

MAP SKILL: You have read about Asia Minor in many chapters. What is the name of its vast plateau?

MAJOR LANDFORMS

Two large peninsulas make up a great part of the Middle East. The larger peninsula is called the Arabian peninsula. It is separated from Africa by the Red Sea, and from the rest of Asia by the Persian Gulf.

The peninsula of Asia Minor extends west into the Aegean Sea. You may recall having read in Chapter 2 that the Stone Age village, Catal Hüyük, was located in Asia Minor. This peninsula is also called Anatolia (an ə tō′ lē ə). As the map on this page shows, much of Anatolia is a vast plateau.

REGION OF EXTREMES

The geography of the Middle East and North Africa is a good study in

extremes. For example, you can find extreme differences in elevation. The Dead Sea, located between Israel and Jordan, is the lowest point on the earth. Use the map on this page to identify the highest points in the Middle East and North Africa.

Nowhere are the extremes of the Middle East and North Africa more apparent than in its deserts. A desert is a place where almost no rain falls. Deserts get less than 10 inches (25 cm) of rain a year. Every continent except Antarctica and Europe has large deserts. People often think of deserts as vast seas of sand dunes. Dunes, as you may know, are mounds and ridges heaped up by the wind.

Deserts cover large areas of the Middle East and North Africa. The largest desert is the Sahara, which extends over much of North Africa. The term

Sahara comes from the Arabic word for "wilderness." You may have a picture in your mind of the Sahara as one vast stretch of sand dunes. In addition to sand dunes, though, the Sahara is made up of flat, rocky plateaus. Bare stretches of sand and rock extend as far as the eyes can see.

WINDS CAUSE EROSION

We traveled through the Sahara for hours without seeing a living thing, neither tree nor bird nor animal nor man. We camped wherever the darkness found us.

As this explorer recorded, living things do not survive easily in the desert. Though there is some plant life, vegetation is usually sparse. Without plants to hold the soil, winds shape the desert by a process called erosion. Erosion is a gradual wearing away of land by wind, glaciers, running water, or waves. Erosion occurs in deserts as windblown sands strike the bottom of rocks and dunes with stinging force. They undercut boulders and gouge caves and hollows in the ground. Winds not only erode loose rock, they carry it from one place to another.

As the diagram on this page shows, winds also cause sand dunes to migrate. Grains of sand are blown up a slope, tumble over the crest, and then roll down the steep slope that lies away from the wind. In this manner, migrating dunes have caused the Sahara to spread.

AN ARID CLIMATE

As you have read, no part of the Sahara receives more than 10 inches (25 cm) of rain a year and at least half of it gets less than 5 inches (12 cm). Some areas of the dry Sahara may

DIAGRAM SKILL: Erosion is caused by wind, glaciers, and water. How do winds affect the spread of deserts?

MIGRATING SAND DUNES

Direction of wind

Stationary dune

Migrating dune

receive no rain at all for many years and then have a violent downpour. Though water may be needed badly, intense rains can also cause erosion. Entire fields have been known to simply wash away and disappear in terrible rainstorms.

As you can see from the map on this page, both the Middle East and North Africa have arid climates. A climate that receives little rainfall is called arid. Notice that the Mediterranean coastal lands have a wetter climate than most other areas of the region. As the map shows, the whole northern part of the Middle East receives more precipitation than the rest of the region. The Arabian peninsula and North Africa, however, have the most arid climates in the world.

Despite its harshness, you should know that arid lands are not lifeless. It is one of the wonders of nature that plants and animals have managed to adapt themselves to temperatures that sometimes reach 120°F. (48°C)—the hottest in the world. These plants and animals have one thing in common: they are able to survive on very little water. Plants with deep roots are able to find water deep beneath the ground.

THE DESERT ANIMAL

One desert animal that you are probably familiar with is the camel. The camel is especially suited for desert living. It can go for days without drinking, can carry heavy loads, and can exist on sparse vegetation.

As you may know, camels are a major means of transportation in desert lands. Special saddles fit over

MAP SKILL: The Middle East and North Africa have arid climates. Name two of the driest areas in the region.

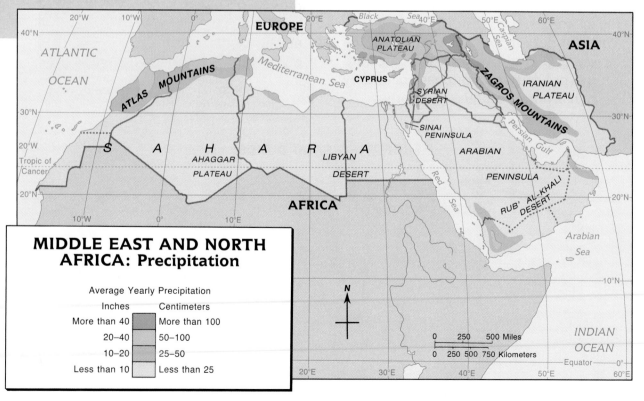

MIDDLE EAST AND NORTH AFRICA: Precipitation

Average Yearly Precipitation

Inches	Centimeters
More than 40	More than 100
20–40	50–100
10–20	25–50
Less than 10	Less than 25

their humps, making it possible for camels to carry a rider and great loads of goods across the desert.

Even today, people sometimes cross the vast "seas of sand" by a caravan of camels. A caravan is a group of people traveling together. As one African trader recorded, when people are traveling across the desert, it is important to stay together.

A desert storm blinds every man. A lazy trader who has let his camel lag behind is as doomed as the eager one who had wandered ahead.

FARMING AND IRRIGATION

Although much of this region is desert, most people live in fertile areas along rivers or near the coast. Here, where the geography and climate are less severe, they have built large cities and developed agriculture.

Look at the map on page 360 to see the areas where plentiful rain allows for farming. In the drier areas of the Middle East and North Africa, irrigation is essential to wide-scale farming. You may recall how ancient Egyptians developed a system of irrigation to trap the overflow of the Nile. Today, a huge dam along the Nile helps control the flow of the river so that farmers have water year round. Because of new methods of irrigation, crops such as wheat, cotton, olives, and oranges thrive in the arid areas of the Middle East and North Africa.

MEETING THE CHALLENGE

The people of the Middle East and North Africa have met the challenge of living in an arid environment. Though high temperatures and a lack of water are common throughout this region, people have nonetheless prospered.

Camels can travel across vast "seas of sand." Yet even a camel enjoys an occasional ride across the desert.

Beginning in ancient times, the Middle East and North Africa has been the scene of historic activity. You read in previous chapters about two important religions—Judaism and Christianity—that were born in the Middle East. In the next lesson you will read about another major religion that emerged "out of the sands and hearts of the desert Arabia." Read on. A new adventure is about to begin.

Check Your Reading

1. What are two important geographic features of the Middle East and North Africa?
2. How does wind cause erosion?
3. **GEOGRAPHY SKILL:** Does Asia Minor or the Arabian peninsula receive more precipitation?
4. **THINKING SKILL:** What are three questions you could ask to find out more about the Sahara?

Using Maps at Different Scales

Key Vocabulary

small-scale map
large-scale map

Sometimes you need a map that shows general information about a particular subject. Suppose you want to know about the major world religions. For example, you know that there are many religions in Asia. But you want to know if a particular religion that has its roots in South Asia also appears in Africa. A small-scale map, such as **Map A**, would be helpful.

Small-scale Maps

Map A will help you understand what the term *small-scale map* means. On **Map A** a very small unit of measure, one inch, stands for 4,000 miles. Small-scale maps are maps on which one inch stands for vast distances of many hundreds or thousands of miles, and on which two centimeters stand for hundreds or thousands of kilometers. Small-scale maps generally show the entire earth or large parts of it in a fairly *small* space.

Because of their size, small-scale maps can show information only in a general way. Small-scale maps cannot give detailed information.

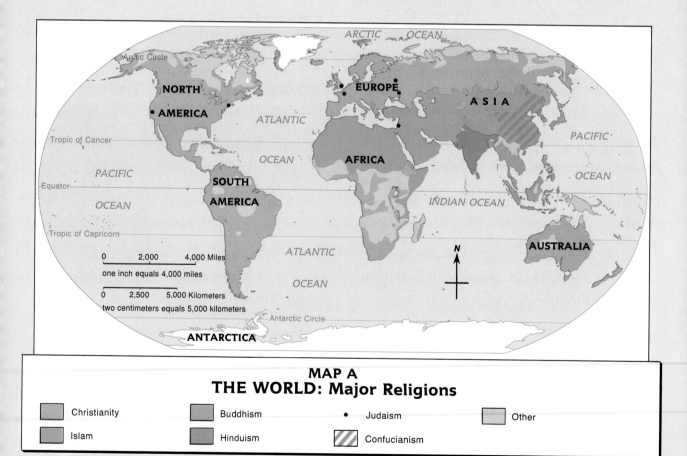

MAP A
THE WORLD: Major Religions

- Christianity
- Islam
- Buddhism
- Hinduism
- Judaism
- Confucianism
- Other

Studying a small-scale map can be very useful. It can show you how climate, vegetation, religion, or almost anything is distributed over a large area. For example, Christianity is one of the world's major religions that has many different branches. A small-scale map could be used to show how these branches are distributed worldwide. A small-scale map showing the different branches of Christianity as well as those of the other major religions would be confusing. As you can imagine, such a map would be very difficult to read.

Map A shows the main religions practiced by the majority of the people in different parts of the world. It shows, for example, that Christianity is the major religion of the United States. This does not mean, however, that no other religions are practiced there.

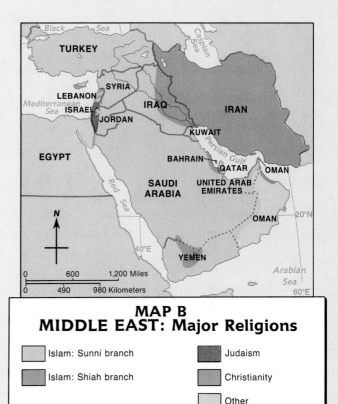

MAP B
MIDDLE EAST: Major Religions

Islam: Sunni branch

Islam: Shiah branch

Judaism

Christianity

Other

Large-scale Maps

For more detailed information about the distribution of religions, you need a large-scale map. On large-scale maps, one inch or two centimeters stand for far lesser distances than they do on small-scale maps. Large-scale maps generally show small parts of the earth in a fairly *large* space.

Map B on this page is a large-scale map. Large-scale maps can show details not possible on small-scale maps. What are the major religions of the Middle East? As this map shows Islam, Judaism, and Christianity are practiced in the Middle East. It also shows the areas where each of the two main branches of Islam is practiced. What are the two branches of Islam shown on **Map B**?

Reviewing the Skill

1. What are the differences between small-scale maps and large-scale maps? Explain.
2. How many miles does one inch stand for on **Map B**? How many kilometers do two centimeters stand for?
3. What is the major religion of India? In what countries is the Shiah branch of Islam the major religion? In what country is Judaism the major religion?
4. In what countries of the Middle East is Christianity a significant religion?
5. The majority of the people in Cyprus practice one or the other of two religions. What are these two religions?
6. How can using maps at different scales be helpful?

2 The Beginnings of Islam

READal READ TO LEARN

Key Vocabulary

Islam   Kaaba
oasis   Koran
sheik

Key People

Muhammad
Charles Martel

Key Places

Mecca
Medina

Read Aloud

In the seventh century, one of the world's great religions was born in the desert of the Arabian peninsula. An Arab merchant announced that he had heard the voice of God and had been commanded to start a new religion. Like Judaism and Christianity before, this new "Arabian faith" called for the worship of a single, mighty God.

Read for Purpose

1. **WHAT YOU KNOW:** Where is the Arabian peninsula?
2. **WHAT YOU WILL LEARN:** How did Islam unite the people of the Middle East and North Africa?

THE ARABS

You will recall having read that Judaism and Christianity have their roots in the Middle East. In about A.D. 600, a new religion called Islam was founded among the Arab people. Today Islam is a major world religion. Its roots, too, are in the Middle East and North Africa.

At the time of Islam's birth, most people in the Arabian peninsula were Bedouins (bed' ü inz). *Bedouin* is an Arabic word meaning "desert dweller." The Bedouin people were desert nomads, tending herds of sheep, goats, and camels as they moved from place to place. They slept in tents made from the hides of camels and drank camel milk. Mounted on camels, Bedouins traveled between widely scattered oases (ō ā' sēz), or well-watered places in the desert. As you can imagine, an oasis was a busy place.

By A.D. 500 one oasis, called Mecca, had grown into a town. In fact, Mecca was the largest of many oases on the western coast of Arabia. The most prosperous people living in Mecca were merchants because their oasis was located on an active caravan route. Travelers to Mecca brought both goods and ideas from the surrounding lands of the Middle East and North Africa. Arab merchants also made the long caravan journey to other lands such as Egypt and Palestine.

The deserts of the Middle East and North Africa are dotted with oases. Linked by caravan routes, many oases have become important centers of trade.

Though commerce prospered in Mecca and other Arabian towns, the people of Arabia were not united. Each town or nomadic group had its own sheik (shēk), or leader. During much of the year, Bedouin sheiks led raids on one another's camps and caravans. Sheiks who were town dwellers also attacked other towns as well as Bedouin caravans.

MUHAMMAD

About five centuries after the death of Jesus, a new religious leader was born among the Arabs. Like Jesus, Muhammad (mü ham′ əd) changed the course of history. Historians have gathered many facts about Muham-

mad's life. They believe Muhammad was born in about A.D. 570 in Mecca. As a young man, Muhammad took part in the caravan trade, which surely brought him into contact with many different groups of people. Like other caravan merchants, Muhammad traveled to Palestine and Syria. On such trips Muhammad met many Jews and Christians.

Muhammad developed a great interest in the religion of his people. During this time, the Arabs of the Middle East were polytheists and worshiped many gods. The one thing that united the

Today, followers of Islam come from all over the world to pray and study near the Kaaba in Mecca.

people of the Arabian peninsula was their yearly pilgrimage to the Kaaba (kä′ bə), a sacred building in Mecca. In the Kaaba the Arabs worshiped the images of many different gods and goddesses.

Muhammad came to believe that it was wrong to worship the images of many gods. Muhammad thought that there was only one God. Every year Muhammad went to a mountain cave to pray alone, sometimes for many nights. In about A.D. 610, Muhammad's life was changed during one of his visits. According to one Islamic writer:

Muhammad went forth until, when he was midway on the mountain, he heard a voice from heaven saying, "O Muhammad! Thou art the messenger of God."

According to Islamic belief, Muhammad heard a voice tell him that there was only one God—for which the Arabic word is *Allah*—and that he, Muhammad, was Allah's messenger.

A NEW RELIGION

By A.D. 613 Muhammad began to teach the people of Mecca about the idea of one God. At first he had little success. Many Meccans thought that his revolutionary ideas were bad for business. They feared that Mecca would lose its position as a pilgrimage center if people accepted Muhammad's beliefs. Some of his followers were stoned to death in the streets. Others fled into the deserts.

Facing persecution, or harsh punishments, for his beliefs, Muhammad decided to leave Mecca. In 622 he fled to the town of Medina, taking a small group of followers with him. This escape became known as the *Hegira* (hi jī′ rə), the Arabic word for "flight."

The Hegira marked a turning point for Muhammad. In Medina he attracted many devoted followers. He also won great political influence. It was in Medina that Muhammad's new religion became known as *Islam*, which means "surrender to God." Believers in Islam became known as *Muslims* (muz' limz), or "followers of Islam." On the Muslim calendar, the year of the Hegira became the year 1, the first year of the Islamic era.

From Medina, Muhammad led raids against Meccan caravans. Later his armies completely defeated the Meccans. Such victories impressed the Bedouins. Within ten years most of them had accepted Islam as their faith. In 630 Muhammad and 10,000 followers entered Mecca in triumph. Muhammad went to the Kaaba and declared, "Truth has come and falsehood has vanished." Mecca became a holy city for all Muslims.

THE KORAN

Like other religions, Islam has special writings that are considered sacred. While Muhammad lived, his followers had listened to his prayers and teachings. They believed that these teachings were the word of God spoken through Muhammad.

Muslims who knew how to read and write, wrote these words on scraps of paper and even on palm leaves. Soon after Muhammad's death in 632, these teachings were gathered into a book. This book is the Koran. Believed by Muslims to be the very word of God, the Koran is the most important book in the Islamic religion.

THE TEACHINGS OF ISLAM

The Koran sets down the basic beliefs of Islam. The first is the belief that " . . . there is no God but Allah. And Muhammad is His messenger." Thus, followers of Islam, like those of Judaism and Christianity, practice monotheism, or the belief in one God. In

fact, according to the Koran, Muslims worship the same God as the Jews and Christians.

We believe in God, and in that which has been sent down on Abraham . . . and that which was given to Moses and Jesus.

The Koran teaches that Muhammad is the last in the line of prophets, some of whom were Abraham, Moses, and Jesus. A prophet is a person who delivers a message believed to be from God. According to the Koran, Muslims believe that these prophets brought a more complete understanding of God.

Arabic writing decorates many Islamic paintings, as in this Hegira scene. According to Islamic tradition, to discourage the worship of images, Muhammad's face is never shown.

367

1. **Faith**
   According to the Koran, Muslims are expected to make a statement of faith: "I believe there is no god but God, and Muhammad is His Prophet."

2. **Prayer**
   Muslims rise at dawn to the sound of a man calling them to prayer. They wash their hands and arms up to their elbows, their feet up to their ankles. They use water if it is available, but Bedouins may wash themselves with sand. Muslims are required to pray five times daily. Each time, they remove their shoes, turn to face the holy city of Mecca, kneel and bow on the ground, and recite special prayers.

3. **Alms**
   Muhammad strictly commanded his followers to give part of their wealth as alms to the needy.

4. **Fasting**
   Special laws about how, what, and when to eat are obeyed. For example, Muslims cannot eat or drink between sunrise and sunset during the month of Ramadan. At such times, families can sit down together for a meal only after sunset.

5. **Pilgrimage**
   Muslims are expected to make a pilgrimage to Mecca at least once in their lifetime. For many, this involves a difficult journey across deserts, mountains, and seas.

The Five Pillars of Islam are the duties required of every Muslim. They form an important part of the **Koran**.

The Koran also teaches that every believer must carry out five duties. These duties are known as the *Five Pillars of Islam*. You can read more about these duties in the box on this page. As you will see, to be a Muslim is both simple and very demanding.

THE SPREAD OF ISLAM

By means both peaceful and militant, Islam spread to nearby lands with incredible speed. All of the Middle East and North Africa soon became part of the Muslim World.

As the map on page 369 shows, a battle took place in Tours, deep in the heart of Europe. There the Muslims were defeated by a powerful Frank named **Charles Martel**. One day Charles Martel would have a grandson known as Charlemagne, whom you read about in Chapter 8. But even as Charlemagne ruled central Europe, the Muslims ruled the Iberian peninsula and all of North Africa and the Middle East. In fact, they came to control more territory than the Romans, and all in one century!

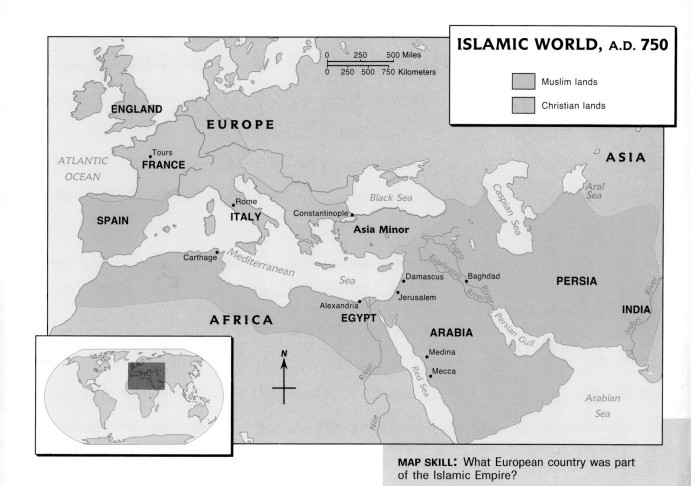

ISLAMIC WORLD, A.D. 750

Muslim lands

Christian lands

MAP SKILL: What European country was part of the Islamic Empire?

AN ISLAMIC EMPIRE

Know that every Muslim is the brother of every other Muslim. All of you are equal.

As Islam spread, Muslim society changed. Muhammad had taught that all Muslims were equal in the eyes of Allah. However, as Arab armies conquered new lands, people who were not Arabs began to accept Islam. Jews and Christians were the only other people allowed to practice their religions. As monotheists, or believers in one God, Jews and Christians had the respect of the Muslim conquerers.

The building of an Islamic empire changed the Middle East and North Africa. Suddenly this vast region was opened to the ideas of Islam. Unlike the Roman Empire that had spread out across the region a few centuries earlier, the power of Islam would never die. Even today, the legacy of the Koran's teachings flourish throughout the world.

Check Your Reading

1. What does "Islam" mean?
2. How did Islam unite the people of the Middle East and North Africa?
3. **GEOGRAPHY SKILL:** Name four lands shown on the map above that became Muslim.
4. **THINKING SKILL:** Compare and contrast the Five Pillars of Islam with the Ten Commandments.

3 Islamic Civilization

READ TO LEARN

Key Vocabulary   **Key People**   **Key Places**

caliph   Avicenna   Baghdad
astrolabe
mosque

Read Aloud

I have no power to act without Allah. I am here to warn, and to bring good gifts to those who believe.

As Muhammad spoke these words, his armies were bringing the message of Islam far beyond the deserts of Arabia. As Islam spread, Arab civilization reached new heights in the Middle East and North Africa.

Read for Purpose

1. **WHAT YOU KNOW:** How did Islam spread throughout the Middle East and North Africa?
2. **WHAT YOU WILL LEARN:** What is the legacy of Islamic civilization?

AN ISLAMIC EMPIRE

In Lesson 2 you read about the beginnings of Islam. You will recall that Muhammad became a powerful religious leader. In fact, in Muhammad's last years he was a political leader as well as a religious leader. After Muhammad's death in A.D. 632, the leaders who followed him were called caliphs (kā′ lifs), meaning "successors to the prophet." Like Muhammad, caliphs had both political and religious authority and were thus very powerful. Under their leadership, a unique civilization was established and spread throughout the Middle East and North Africa.

For about 400 years, from A.D. 700 to 1100, Islamic civilization flourished throughout the Middle East and North Africa. In the year 1000, for example, people in the cities of the Muslim world lived more comfortably than the people of Europe. One Muslim city was especially splendid. On the banks of the Tigris River, Muslims built the city of Baghdad (bag′ dad). Baghdad became Islam's cultural center.

THE ROUND CITY

Picture three round walls, one inside the other, encircling a perfectly round city. This was Baghdad. At the very center of the inner circle was the famous green dome of the caliph's palace. Four broad avenues ran into the heart of circular Baghdad, carving the city into four equal quarters. Everything in this round city seemed to revolve around the caliph's palace.

Under the green dome was a grand throne room. There the caliph awaited his visitors behind a colorful curtain. Standing behind the caliph's throne, however, stood a soldier with a sword always drawn and sharpened. Thus, a visitor who displeased the caliph in any way could be beheaded on the spot.

THE RICHES OF TRADE

Between the middle wall and the palace lay Baghdad's main business district. Along the four major avenues, merchants sold Arabian perfumes, Syrian glassware, Chinese silk, and Indian silver. There were also swords from Russia, leather goods from Spain, and gold from Africa.

By the year 1000, more than 100,000 people lived in this magnificent city. Baghdad's riches were the result of its location. Caravan routes from India and China passed through Baghdad. Ships from Arabia and India came to the city, too. They sailed from the Persian Gulf up the Tigris River.

THE SPREAD OF IDEAS

Do you remember having read about the active exchange of ideas between the ancient Greeks and Phoenicians in Chapter 6? The result, you may recall, was the birth of the alphabet you use today. In the same way that the Greeks built upon Phoenician ideas, the Muslims built upon the legacies of the many groups they met.

Like all Muslims, **caliphs** were expected to make at least one pilgrimage to Mecca during their lifetime.

For example, Muslim scholars were inspired by the ancient Greeks—especially by ideas of Socrates and Aristotle. Manuscripts from many different lands were gathered and brought back to Baghdad's House of Wisdom, a huge library where scholars translated Greek books into Arabic. After mastering many Greek sources, Muslim thinkers and scientists went on to make their own discoveries and inventions.

Like civilization under Alexander the Great, many groups contributed to Islamic culture. You may recall that Alexander's empire covered a large area of the Middle East. Under the caliphs, the teachings of Islam and the Arabic language united the people of the Middle East.

First used by the ancient Greeks, the astrolabe was rediscovered and improved by Muslim astronomers.

ISLAMIC SCIENCE

Active trade and the exchange of ideas encouraged growth in the field of science. The Muslims became great astronomers, for example. They built observatories, or buildings for watching and studying stars and planets.

The Muslims also used different kinds of instruments to study the heavens. One of these instruments was the astrolabe (as′ trə lāb). An astrolabe is an instrument used to figure out the positions of the stars. Muslim sea captains and caravan leaders found the astrolabe to be useful in guiding them across the seas and deserts.

With remarkable accuracy, Muslim geographers also charted many seas and deserts. Many geographers drew maps that today seem more like works of art than guides through the wilderness. Look at the circular map on page 373, for example. Muslim geographers made maps that showed they knew the earth was round.

Mathematics is another area in which the Muslims led the way. You may know that the Muslims also invented algebra, called *al-jabr* in Arabic. They also added the symbol for zero to the system of numbers they had borrowed from India. As they conquered other lands, the Muslims spread the idea of their new number system. The Arabic numbers we use today are based on that system.

By A.D. 1000 the Muslims also had the most advanced medical knowledge in the world. Their understanding of disease was far better than that of Christian Europe. They built hospitals and medical libraries where doctors could work. Avicenna (av ə sen′ ə), a Persian philosopher, wrote an encyclopedia of medical knowledge. This was translated into Latin and used in European medical schools until the 1700s.

Europe owes a great deal to the achievements of Islamic civilization. Islamic learning spread to Europe through Muslim Spain and through southern Italy as a result of the Crusades. You will recall that the Crusades caused European commerce to grow. By 1100 European scholars were being introduced to Islamic learning. Moreover, countless ancient Greek and ancient Roman books, later called the classics, had been preserved by Muslim scribes. You may recall having read in Chapter 9 that these historic books led to the growth of the European Renaissance.

ISLAMIC LITERATURE

The contribution by Islam to science, mathematics, and medicine can be appreciated by many people. But many Muslims consider poetry to be their greatest art and legacy. The thousands of poems created during Islam's golden age were meant to be sung and recited in Arabic. Poems were written on various topics, such as love, the beauty of nature, and devotion to Islam. To the Muslims, however, the most precious book was the Koran—the source of Islamic civilization.

Maps made by Muslim geographers are also works of art. City maps showed amazing detail and thus give useful information to modern historians.

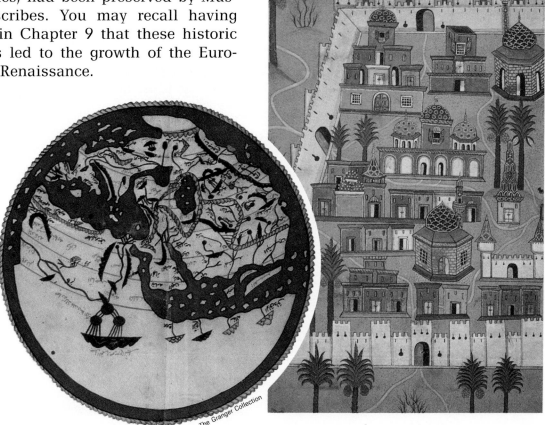

The Granger Collection

Islamic writers produced a great variety of literature. Muslim writers filled hundreds of books on history, geography, law, philosophy, and religion. In Islamic folk tales, stories are told with wonderful imagination. In some tales, for example, heroes used a flying carpet to travel magically from place to place. A collection of folk tales known as *The Arabian Nights* is one of the most famous Muslim books. It includes the tale of "Ali Baba and the Forty Thieves." You can read part of this tale on this page.

The Arabian Nights has made readers happy for many years. You can read more about Ali Baba in your school library.

DOME OF THE ROCK

Like its literature, Muslim architecture is part of the legacy of Islamic civilization. Throughout their empire, the Muslims built places of worship called **mosques** (mosks). One of the greatest mosques, called al-Aqsa, still stands in Jerusalem, a city that is sacred to Jews, Christians, and Muslims.

In 691 the caliph Omar ordered the construction of a building in Jerusalem over the rock from which Muhammad was believed to have "ascended into paradise" or risen to heaven. This beautiful building, located next to al-Aqsa, became known as the Dome of the Rock because of its golden dome.

Below the dome, framed by a circle of marble, is the sacred rock. Muslim

THE ARABIAN NIGHTS

*M*any years ago in Persia, there lived a poor woodcutter named Ali Baba. One day as he was chopping wood, he heard the clatter of galloping hoofs in the distance and saw a great cloud of dust drawing near. Curious to find out the cause of the commotion, he climbed into a tall tree.

Ali Baba was terrified. As the dust cleared, forty fierce-looking thieves with swords in the their belts stood beneath him. The robbers hoisted their heavy sacks from their horses, dragging them to a huge boulder at the bottom of a hill. Suddenly their captain faced a great boulder and with a loud voice cried, "Open, Sesame!"

Ali Baba was astonished to notice that, at the mention of this word—the name of a cereal commonly eaten in Persia—the rock rolled aside. The entire band of robbers filed in. In a few moments they emerged, carrying their now empty sacks, and the captain cried, "Close, Sesame!" The rock at once shut behind them.

As soon as the thieves had mounted their horses and ridden off, Ali Baba climbed down from the tree and went up to the mysterious rock. He marveled at the magic that had forced the boulder to move aside.

"Open, Sesame!" Ali Baba cried. After a moment, the boulder rolled aside.

worshipers cannot walk on it. Worshipers spread their prayer rugs at the very edge of the walled-off rock and kneel to pray. As always, they face Mecca—the birthplace of Islam.

The Dome of the Rock marks the place where, according to Islam, Muhammad is said to have risen to heaven.

THE LEGACY OF ISLAM

As you have read, Islam is one of the world's major religions. Even today millions of Muslims, wherever they may live, face Mecca to pray.

The Middle East and North Africa is united by the legacy of Islamic civilization. Under the caliphs, the region entered a remarkable age. Religion, learning, science, literature, and architecture prospered. In the next chapter you will read how the legacy of Islam continues to influence the people of the Middle East and North Africa.

Check Your Reading

1. Who were the caliphs? Why were they considered to be important?
2. What are two important achievements of Islamic civilization?
3. GEOGRAPHY SKILL: Relate the geography of the Middle East and North Africa to the use of the astrolabe.
4. THINKING SKILL: Classify Muslim contributions into different fields.

375

IMPORTANT EVENTS

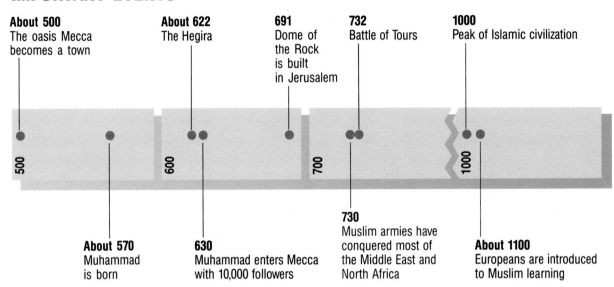

About 500
The oasis Mecca becomes a town

About 622
The Hegira

691
Dome of the Rock is built in Jerusalem

732
Battle of Tours

1000
Peak of Islamic civilization

500

600

700

1000

About 570
Muhammad is born

630
Muhammad enters Mecca with 10,000 followers

730
Muslim armies have conquered most of the Middle East and North Africa

About 1100
Europeans are introduced to Muslim learning

PEOPLE TO KNOW

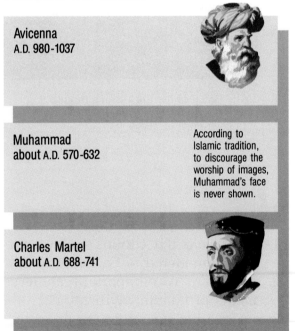

Avicenna
A.D. 980-1037

Muhammad
about A.D. 570-632

According to Islamic tradition, to discourage the worship of images, Muhammad's face is never shown.

Charles Martel
about A.D. 688-741

IDEAS TO REMEMBER

■ The Middle East is well known for its deserts, but most people live along the fertile river valleys and in land where rainfall is more plentiful.

■ Muhammad founded one of the world's great religions. Called Islam, it was spread across the Middle East and North Africa.

■ Under the leadership of the caliphs, Islamic civilization was established. Great contributions were made in astronomy, medicine, mathematics, and literature.

REVIEWING VOCABULARY

arid	Islam
caliphs	Koran
caravan	mosque
desert	oasis
erosion	sheik

Number a sheet of paper from 1 to 10. Beside each number write the word or term from the above list that best completes each sentence.

1. A _____ can still be seen carrying goods, often on the backs of camels, across the Middle East.
2. A _____, or local leader, spent much of his time launching raids against other towns or caravans.
3. Written down soon after Muhammad's death, the _____ contains the very words of God according to Muslim belief.
4. Because they were "successors to the Prophet," _____ had great political and religious authority.
5. A _____ is a dry region with little vegetation or rainfall that covers much of the Middle East.
6. Because it is well-watered, an _____ is among the few places where cities could grow in the Middle East.
7. _____ is a word that is used to describe regions that receive little rain.
8. Founded by Muhammad, _____ means "surrender to God" and is the dominant religion of the Middle East.
9. Wind and running water contribute to _____, or the wearing away of land by natural forces.
10. A Muslim place of worship is called a _____.

REVIEWING FACTS

1. Why is irrigation important to the countries of the Middle East?
2. How does Islam regard the "prophets" of Judaism and Christianity, such as Moses and Jesus?
3. Why is North Africa considered to be part of the Middle East?
4. How did the learning of ancient Greece spread to the Middle East? How did Islamic learning spread to Europe?
5. Discuss two ideas from the Koran that may have contributed to the rapid spread of Islam.

◄═►WRITING ABOUT MAIN IDEAS

1. **Writing a Pamphlet About Mecca:** Imagine that you are a travel agent. Write a pamphlet about Mecca describing why it is an interesting place to visit.
2. **Writing About Perspectives:** Imagine that you are traveling in a caravan through the Sahara. Describe what you see on a postcard to a friend.

BUILDING SKILLS: USING MAPS AT DIFFERENT SCALES

1. What is meant by the term *scale?*
2. What does a small-scale map show? What does a large-scale map show?
3. Which kind of map can show the most information? Why is this possible? Explain.
4. Why is it important to know how to use maps at different scales?

CHAPTER 15

THE MIDDLE EAST AND NORTH AFRICA TODAY

▼ FOCUS

From the towers of this great mosque, cries called men and women to prayer and to battle. From the gentle gardens below, an empire spread forth in three directions.

The empire that "spread forth in three directions" would have a lasting effect on the future of the Middle East and North Africa. As you will read in this chapter, modern times have brought many changes to this exciting region.

1 New Nations in the Middle East

READ TO LEARN

Key Vocabulary
sultan
shah
Zionist

Key People
Mustafa Kemal Atatürk
Reza Shah
Ayatollah Khomeini
Golda Meir

Key Places
Istanbul

Read Aloud

We only want that which is given naturally to all peoples of the world, to be masters of our own fate, not of others. . . .

These words were written in 1947 by a Jewish leader named Golda Meir (me êr'). The time had come, she believed, for Jews to claim their ancient legacy—a homeland in the Middle East. But the Jewish people were not alone. New Arab nations were also rising to reclaim their own ancient legacies.

Read for Purpose

1. **WHAT YOU KNOW:** What is nationalism?
2. **WHAT YOU WILL LEARN:** How did nationalism affect the growth of nations in the Middle East and North Africa?

THE OTTOMAN EMPIRE

The people of the Middle East began to reclaim their ancient legacies after World War I. You may recall having read about nationalism in Chapter 13. Remember that fierce loyalties caused many nations to organize into alliances and led the world to war in 1914. When World War I was over, nationalism also swept the Middle East and gave birth to many new nations.

In order to understand how new nations developed in the region, it is important to learn something about the Ottoman Empire. From the 1400s to the end of the First World War, the Ottoman Empire ruled most of the Middle East and North Africa. The Ottomans were not Arabs. They were Turks who had adopted Islam. In fact, the Ottomans felt so strongly about their new religion that they called themselves the "Swords of God."

The Ottomans ruled from a city where the continents of Asia and Europe meet. Called Istanbul (is tan bül'), it is located in present-day Turkey. In ancient times, Istanbul had been the site of a Greek colony. Later it became one of the largest cities in the Roman Empire. When Constantine became emperor in A.D. 324, the city was named Constantinople. In the 1400s, the Ottomans renamed this city Istanbul.

From Istanbul, the Ottomans fought to enlarge their influence. At its peak in 1683, the Ottoman Empire controlled many different lands, including Turkey, Syria, Palestine, Arabia, and Egypt. As the map on this page shows, the Ottomans even controlled most of the Balkan peninsula on the European continent. For nearly 600 years the sultans, or Turkish rulers, forced the people of these lands to pay heavy taxes and obey Muslim laws.

THE END OF AN EMPIRE

You read in Chapter 11 about the Industrial Revolution. You will recall how dramatically it changed England and then spread throughout the rest of Europe. The Industrial Revolution, however, made little impact on the Ottoman Empire. The sultans made few efforts to build factories or to keep up with other European advances.

World War I "blew apart the sultan's closed doors." The sultan allied his empire with the Central Powers—Germany and Austria-Hungary. When the Central Powers were defeated, the Ottoman Empire was forced to give up huge amounts of land. By 1919 Turkey was all that remained of the Ottoman Empire. The rest of the empire was divided up by Britain, France, and Italy.

MAP SKILL: The Ottomans extended their empire across three continents. Which islands did the empire include?

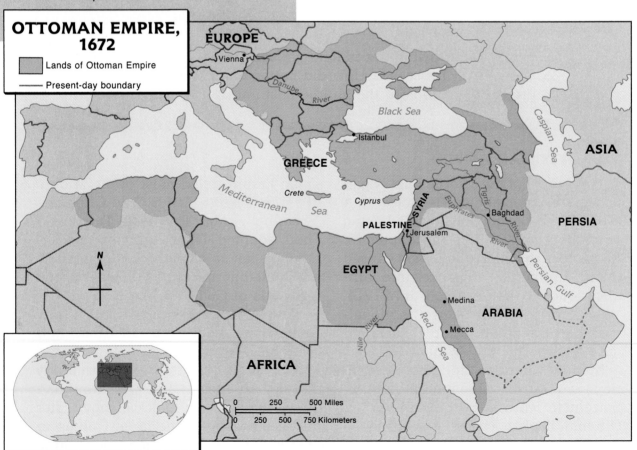

OTTOMAN EMPIRE, 1672

Lands of Ottoman Empire

Present-day boundary

EUROPE
Vienna
Danube River
Black Sea
Istanbul
Caspian Sea
ASIA
GREECE
Mediterranean Sea
Crete
Cyprus
SYRIA
Euphrates
Tigris River
Baghdad
PERSIA
PALESTINE
Jerusalem
EGYPT
Persian Gulf
N
Medina
ARABIA
Nile River
Red Sea
Mecca
AFRICA

0   250   500 Miles
0   250   500   750 Kilometers

A NEW REPUBLIC IN ASIA MINOR

Nationalism in the Middle East had its beginnings in Asia Minor. In 1919 soldiers from neighboring Greece invaded Istanbul and threatened to conquer what remained of the Ottoman Empire. The sultan, weak and corrupt, was powerless to stop them. Many Turks believed that their country's only hope for survival lay in the overthrow of the sultan.

In 1923 Mustafa Kemal Atatürk and other nationalists established the Republic of Turkey, the first republic in the Middle East. As its new president, Atatürk set out to make Turkey a modern nation. He gave women equal political rights, including the right to vote and the right to hold political office.

Atatürk also believed that the future of his country lay in the education of its young people. Under the sultans, few people had received an education.

Atatürk pushed for economic growth, which the sultans had frowned upon. He built railroads and factories in many parts of the country. By the time of Atatürk's death in 1938, Turkey was a modern nation.

THE BIRTH OF IRAN

Nationalism also developed in Iran after World War I. Iran is the modern name of a land that had been known for hundreds of centuries as Persia. In ancient times Persia was a rich kingdom that lay between Mesopotamia and the Indus River Valley. You read about the Persian Empire in Chapter 6. Remember how the Greeks and the Persians clashed at Marathon and Salamis in the 500s B.C. For the people who live in Iran today, Persia's historic legacy is a source of pride.

381

Although the Persians adopted Islam in the eighth century and were very much a part of Islamic civilization, they never came under the control of the Ottomans. However, both Britain and Russia established strong ties there in the 1800s. By the early 1900s, Persia was virtually a colony shared by Britain and Russia.

Nationalism swept across Persia after World War I. In 1921 a Persian army general named Reza Khan (ri zä' kän') started a struggle to free his people from European control. With the support of his people, Reza Khan seized control of Persia and forced the British and Russians to leave.

In 1925 Reza Khan proclaimed himself shah, or monarch, of Persia. Reza Shah, as he was now called, also declared that the new nation would be called Iran. The shah worked to modernize Iran by building schools, railroads, and factories, and by giving women more rights. In 1941, the shah's son, Muhammad Reza, became leader of Iran and continued these reforms.

Many Muslims began to speak out against the new shah's reforms. The shah responded by ruthlessly punishing anyone who opposed him. In 1979 Muslim religious leaders, led by Ayatollah Khomeini (ä yə tō' lə kō mā' nē), took control of Iran's government and ruled by Islamic law.

THE BIRTH OF ISRAEL

One of the lands that had been a part of the Ottoman Empire was Palestine. As you read in Chapter 4, Palestine was the ancient homeland of the Jewish people. For many years Jewish kings ruled from Jerusalem. Twice the Jewish kingdom was destroyed, once by the Babylonians in 586 B.C., and again by the Romans in A.D. 70. Each time, many Jews fled Palestine and migrated to other countries.

The Jewish people faced centuries of persecution. Still, they had kept their beliefs and traditions. For many Jews, though, these traditions were not enough. They wanted a homeland, a place where Jewish laws and traditions would also be the laws of their nation. Jewish nationalists were known as Zionists (zī' ə nists). *Zion* is a biblical term used to describe Jerusalem.

One young Zionist was named Golda Meir. In 1921 she left her home in Milwaukee, Wisconsin, to join other new settlers of Palestine. Later, when a Jewish nation was finally established, Meir would become one of its most important leaders. This is what she wrote about her move to Palestine.

The step in my life I'm most proud and happy about was my decision to come to Palestine when I did.

In 1979 the Ayatollah Khomeini took control of Iran's government from the shah.

Golda Meir was one of Israel's early **Zionist** settlers. After Israel gained its freedom in May 1948, its people began to celebrate the birth of their nation every spring.

Largely as a result of the Zionist movement, the number of Jews living in Palestine increased from 85,000 in 1914 to 445,000 in 1939. In 1948 the Jewish people saw their dream come true. A new Jewish nation, called Israel, was founded in Palestine.

The founding of Israel did not come peacefully. Israelis and their Arab neighbors battled for control of territory. Thousands of Arabs called Palestinians, who had lived for hundreds of years on the land that became Israel, took refuge in Arab countries. Others remained in the new nation of Israel.

NEW NATIONS

Israel, like Turkey and Iran, sprang to life in order to reclaim its historic legacy. You have read that when the Ottoman Empire collapsed after World War I, Muslims and Jews in the Middle East began to build their own nations. North African Muslims could only watch. Their governments still were ruled by Europeans. But, as you will read in the next lesson, independence would also come to North Africa.

 Check Your Reading

1. What was the Ottoman Empire?
2. How did the end of the Ottoman Empire lead to the growth of nationalism in the Middle East?
3. **GEOGRAPHY SKILL:** What did Turkish, Persian, and Zionist nationalism have in common?
4. **THINKING SKILL:** Describe Jewish goals from a Zionist point of view.

383

Determining Accuracy

Imagine that you are being given your choice of a computer for your birthday. First, you have to decide which computer has all the features that you want. Books about computers fill the shelves of your library. But many of the sources say different things. Before you can rely on any of the information, you need to be sure it is accurate, or true. When you are deciding if information is accurate, you are evaluating it.

One step in deciding if information is accurate is to determine the believability, or **credibility**, of its source. Deciding if a source should be believed is the same thing as determining its credibility.

Trying the Skill

In Chapter 15, Lesson 1, you read about the spread of nationalism in Asia Minor. As you know, the lands of the old Ottoman Empire were taken over by the Allies after World War I. Suppose you want to know more about how the people of Turkey lived under the Allied government. Were the Allies kind rulers? Were the Turks better off under the foreign rulers?

Imagine that you have done a lot of research to answer these questions. But you must *evaluate the accuracy* of the information you find. For example, imagine that you have read the diary of a Turkish soldier. You want to determine the accuracy of the following statement: "The Turkish press was censored [tightly controlled] by the Allied rulers."

1. Is this statement accurate?
2. How did you go about determining its accuracy?

HELPING YOURSELF

The steps on the left can help you determine the accuracy of information. The example on the right show how these steps can be used to determine the accuracy of the statement on page 384.

One Way to Determine the Accuracy of Information	Example
1. Identify the source of the information.	The source is a Turkish soldier.
2. Determine the credibility, or believability, of the source by asking the following questions. • Is the author or speaker an expert or well-informed on the topic? • Does the author or speaker have anything to gain by giving inaccurate information?	The source is a diary belonging to a Turkish soldier. Because the source was intended to be private, the author is probably describing his true feelings. But you have no way of knowing his reputation for accuracy.
3. Ask yourself: Is the information current?	This question does not apply here, but is asked when statistical data is given.
4. Compare the information with similar information in other sources.	The library has an autobiography of a Turkish journalist. The journalist confirmed the censorship policies of the Allied armies. You might also check a book on the history of Turkey. Here, too, you find that the Turkish press was censored after World War I.

Applying the Skill

Apply what you have learned to determine the accuracy of this statement: "George Washington was one of Gamal Nasser's heroes."

1. Which of the following sentences restates the statement above?
- **a.** Nasser thought Washington was someone to be admired.
- **b.** George Washington is a character in one of Nasser's favorite novels.
- **c.** Washington and Nasser were friends.

2. Suppose you read the above statement in a history textbook as well as in a popular magazine. In which source would you be more likely to find an accurate statement? Why?

3. What are two other credible sources you might check to determine whether the statement is accurate? How will you determine the credibility of these additional sources?

Reviewing the Skill

1. What is another word for accuracy?

2. Name some steps you could follow to determine the accuracy of information.

3. When is it important to check the accuracy of information?

Life Today: Middle East and North Africa

READ TO LEARN

Key Vocabulary

protectorate
export
import
OPEC
refugee
terrorism
intifada

Key People

Gamal Abdel Nasser
Saddam Hussein

Key Places

Persian Gulf

Read Aloud

Clouds and the smoke from oil-well fires blocked the sun so that at 2:00 P.M. cars had to turn on their headlights.

With these words reporter Donatella Lorch described war-torn Kuwait in March 1991. In this lesson you will read about these terrible fires and the war that caused them.

Read for Purpose

1. WHAT YOU KNOW: What happened to the Ottoman Empire after World War I?
2. WHAT YOU WILL LEARN: What are some of the reasons for the continued conflict in the Middle East and North Africa?

NEW NATIONS IN NORTH AFRICA

In the last lesson you read that Turkish sultans of the Ottoman Empire ruled North Africa beginning in the 1400s. By the 1800s, the empire started losing control of its lands to European powers. France took control of Algeria in 1830 and of Tunisia in 1881. Britain occupied Egypt beginning in 1882.

During World War I, European nations increased their control over the countries in North Africa. Egypt became a **protectorate** (prə tek′ tər it) of Britain in 1914. A protectorate is a weak country that is controlled and protected by a stronger country. But many people in Egypt resisted this change in power. They were tired of being ruled by foreigners. One saying summarized their nationalist feelings: "In the land of Egypt, what is good belongs to others."

In 1922 the people of Egypt won the right to hold free elections. But for the next 30 years Egypt's king continued to work closely with the British.

In 1952 a group of young Arab nationalists overthrew the king and

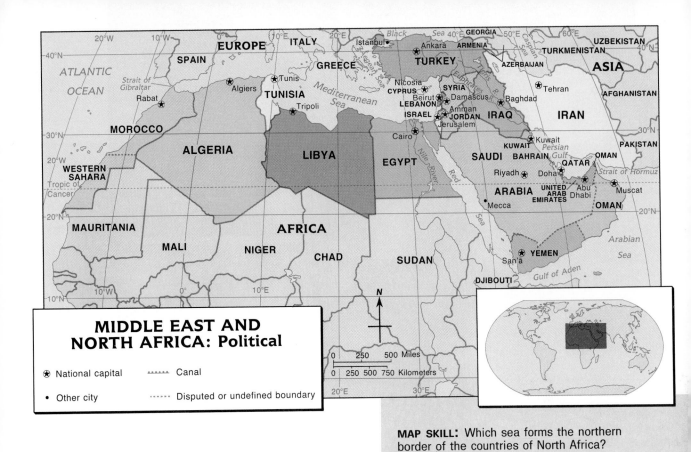

MIDDLE EAST AND NORTH AFRICA: Political

★ National capital
• Other city
.... Canal
...... Disputed or undefined boundary

MAP SKILL: Which sea forms the northern border of the countries of North Africa?

established a republic. Their leader, Gamal Abdel Nasser, became Egypt's first president. A year later, he encouraged his fellow North Africans to fight for independence.

> *Can we ignore that there is an Arab World with which we are tied? How can we ignore our common heritage? We have the right to be free and united.*

Nasser's stirring words excited Egypt's African neighbors. Soon, the people of Morocco, Algeria, and Tunisia followed Egypt's example of fighting colonial rule. You can find these nations on the map on this page.

OIL UNDERGROUND

While nationalism spread from the Middle East through North Africa, the whole region's economy was taking a new direction. When people think of the Middle East and North Africa, they often think of oil. That is because much of the world's oil is located under the land and off the shores of this region.

People in the Middle East and North Africa have known about the oil in their region for thousands of years. In ancient Egypt, people used a solid form of oil called pitch to coat the mummies of pharaohs. Workers in Babylon used the oil by-product we call asphalt to create the legendary Hanging Gardens. The ancient Romans gave a name to this sticky substance that oozed out of the earth. They called it petroleum (pə trō′ lē əm), which means "rock oil" in Latin.

387

GRAPH SKILL: These workers in Saudi Arabia use computers to help turn crude oil into oil products. Which region produces the largest percentage of the world's oil?

WORLD OIL PRODUCTION

- Africa South of the Sahara 4%
- Southern and Eastern Asia 7%
- Latin America 9%
- United States and Canada 17%
- Europe and North Asia 25%
- Middle East and North Africa 37%
- Australia and New Zealand 1%

A VALUABLE RESOURCE

In Chapter 11 you read about the Industrial Revolution that swept through Europe and the United States in the 1800s. By the middle of the 1800s, people began to use oil to grease the mighty machines that drove the Industrial Revolution. With the invention of gasoline-powered engines, oil became one of the world's most valuable resources. One reason that oil became so valuable is that people use it in many ways, as the diagram on page 389 shows. A second reason is that oil, unlike resources such as wood or fish, is a nonrenewable resource. Once it has been used, it cannot be replaced.

In the early 1900s, American and European oil companies began searching the world for new sources of oil. Soon, these companies found vast oil deposits in the Middle East and North Africa. In 1908 they struck oil in Iran.

Twenty years later they discovered huge oil reserves under the deserts of Saudi Arabia.

The oil-producing countries of the Middle East and North Africa had few factories or machines that needed fuel. They also did not have the technology that was needed to drill their own wells, so they often rented drilling rights to foreign oil companies.

Almost overnight, oil became the chief export of the Middle East and North Africa. Exports are goods that are sold by one country to another. These oil exports brought tremendous wealth to the rulers of oil-producing countries. They began to order imports such as machinery, automobiles, and grain from countries all over the world.

Imports are goods that a country buys for itself from other countries. These rulers also used their new wealth to develop better education and transportation systems for their countries.

OIL POWER

For almost 50 years, the rulers of the region's oil-producing nations allowed foreign companies to control their oil industries. But as Arab nationalism swept through the Middle East and North Africa in the 1950s, this situation began to change.

In 1960, these oil-producing nations joined together to form the Organization of Petroleum Exporting Countries, or OPEC. One leader from Saudi Arabia explained why OPEC was formed.

The colonial era is gone forever. We are master of our own affairs, and we shall decide how and to whom our oil is exported.

Since the 1970s, OPEC members have worked to control the amount of oil that their countries produce. This has helped cause oil prices to rise. For example, Saudi Arabia received only 22 cents for a barrel of oil in 1948. In 1992 a barrel sold for $19.

WAR IN THE PERSIAN GULF

In the summer of 1990, tension mounted between two members of OPEC. Iraq accused its neighbor, Kuwait, of cheating on the rules that OPEC had set for oil production. According to Iraq's president, Saddam Hussein (hü sān'), Kuwait was producing too much oil and causing the price to drop.

In the early morning hours of August 2, 1990, Iraqi troops invaded Kuwait. The Kuwaiti armed forces proved no match for the Iraqi army, the strongest

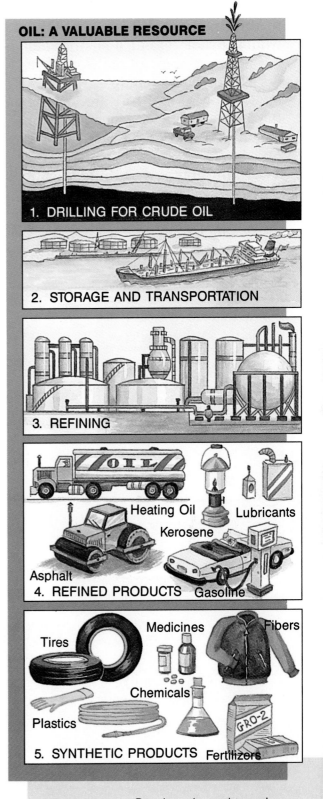

OIL: A VALUABLE RESOURCE

1. DRILLING FOR CRUDE OIL

2. STORAGE AND TRANSPORTATION

3. REFINING

4. REFINED PRODUCTS
Heating Oil · Lubricants · Kerosene · Asphalt · Gasoline

5. SYNTHETIC PRODUCTS
Tires · Medicines · Fibers · Chemicals · Plastics · Fertilizers

DIAGRAM SKILL: Petroleum is used to make many products. Which synthetic products are made from petroluem?

389

in the Arab world. The fact that Iraq would invade its much smaller neighbor alarmed many of the world's leaders. Also, as the map on page 387 shows Kuwait and Iraq are located on the **Persian Gulf**, a waterway through which over half of the world's oil supply flows.

Within hours the United Nations condemned Iraq's invasion of Kuwait and called for the Iraqi army to withdraw. The United States formed an alliance with Arab and European nations to oppose Iraq's invasion. By the end of August, soldiers representing this alliance began pouring into Saudi Arabia.

On the moonless night of January 15 1991, allied jets flew over Kuwait and Iraq and began bombing Iraq's army. Three weeks later, allied troops marched into Kuwait and Iraq. Just four days later, Saddam Hussein called on his army to retreat from Kuwait. The retreating Iraqi army set hundreds of Kuwait's oil wells on fire, spreading dark clouds of smoke across the Middle East. The brief war left much of two countries—Iraq and Kuwait—in ruins. But the war, called "Operation Desert Storm" in the U.S., succeeded in freeing Kuwait.

ISRAELIS AND PALESTINIANS

The people of the Middle East and North Africa also have felt the effects of another conflict that has been simmering for years. In Lesson 1 you read about the founding of Israel in Palestine in 1948. For hundreds of years Jews had faced persecution around the world. Now they were building a nation in their ancient homeland.

Soldiers from the United States (*right*) and other countries drove Saddam Hussein's army from Kuwait. Retreating Iraqi troops set fire to Kuwait's oil wells.

390

However, the land that became Israel was also claimed by Palestinians. Efforts by the United Nations to divide Palestine into two homelands—one for Jews and one for Palestinians—failed. In 1948, Israel was attacked by its Arab neighbors. During this war, the armies of Israel, Egypt, and Jordan divided up the land that had been set aside for Palestinians. Thousands of Palestinians became refugees, or people who flee their homeland in search of safety. Many of these refugees fled to the neighboring Arab countries. Others remained in the area that was now controlled by the young nation of Israel.

Relations between Palestinians and Israelis became increasingly bitter. Palestinians created the Palestine Liberation Organization, or PLO, which wanted to replace Israel with an independent country of Palestine. To achieve this goal, the PLO sometimes used terrorism, or acts of violence against innocent people.

In 1967, for the third time in 20 years, Arab nations placed armies along Israel's borders. But Israel struck first, sending a massive air-and-land attack against its neighbors. During the Six Day War, Israel quickly gained control over lands known as the Sinai Peninsula, the Gaza Strip, the Golan Heights, and the West Bank. Look at the map on this page to see these lands.

Again, Palestinians found themselves at the center of an Arab-Israeli conflict. More than 1 million Palestinians lived in the territories that now were occupied by Israel. Arab countries demanded that the lands be returned to them. But many Israelis felt that they could not give up these lands without a promise of peace. Golda Meir, who became prime minister of Israel in 1969, expressed the feelings of many Israelis.

This nation, this Jewish people, this state of Israel has exactly the same right to defend itself as any other people in the world. We pray that we will never again have to send our sons into battle. We pray that our Arab neighbors will finally realize that peace is as necessary for them as for us.

MAP SKILL: Which land did Israel occupy in 1967 and return to Egypt between 1975 and 1982?

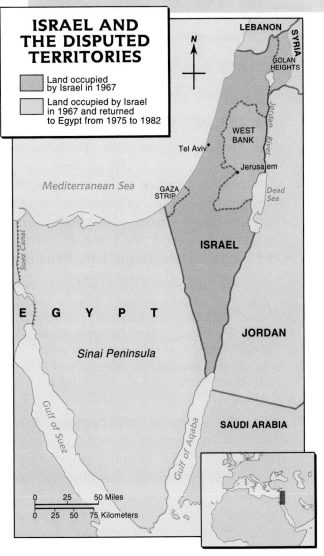

ISRAEL AND THE DISPUTED TERRITORIES

Land occupied by Israel in 1967

Land occupied by Israel in 1967 and returned to Egypt from 1975 to 1982

LEBANON
SYRIA
GOLAN HEIGHTS
Jordan River
WEST BANK
Tel Aviv
Jerusalem
Mediterranean Sea
GAZA STRIP
Dead Sea
Suez Canal
ISRAEL
E G Y P T
Sinai Peninsula
JORDAN
Gulf of Suez
Gulf of Aqaba
SAUDI ARABIA

0   25   50 Miles
0   25   50   75 Kilometers

In 1991 Israelis, Palestinians, and other Arab representatives began discussions to bring peace to their region.

THE INTIFADA

As time went on, life became increasingly difficult for the Palestinians who lived in these occupied territories. They could not vote, yet they had to pay taxes to the government of Israel. Many Palestinians lived in refugee camps under harsh conditions. One Palestinian described life in a refugee camp.

> Life in the camp is bad. After a few years you have nothing left but fear and poverty. . . . You become like a dead person: you do not want anything and you do not hope. Even the children there are old. They are born with fear.

These conditions only increased Palestinians' bitterness toward Israel. In December 1987, violent demonstrations broke out in the occupied territories. This rebellion against Israel is known as the intifada (in tē fa′ də), which means "uprising" in Arabic.

Many Palestinian teenagers took to the streets, waving Palestinian flags and throwing stones at Israeli soldiers. The soldiers sometimes responded with gunfire. By the early 1990s, more than 25 Israelis and 950 Palestinians had been killed in the occupied territories.

Despite the violence that has flared in this region in recent years, some signs of hope have appeared. Egypt and Israel signed a peace treaty in 1978. In 1988 the PLO moved away from terrorism and agreed to recognize Israel's right to exist. In 1991 Israelis, Palestinians, and other Arab representatives met for the first time to discuss their region's problems.

AN UNCERTAIN FUTURE

Today the Middle East and North Africa face an uncertain future. The Persian Gulf war and the tensions between Israel and its neighbors have troubled this region. As you have read, these conflicts have deep roots in the history of the region. But while the roots of conflict run deep, so does the desire for peace. It remains to be seen how this region, so rich in history and resources will resolve its future.

Check Your Reading

1. Which forces helped to bring an end to colonial rule in North Africa?
2. What are some reasons for the conflicts that have flared up in the Middle East?
3. **GEOGRAPHY SKILL:** Why is the Persian Gulf considered so important by the industrial nations of the world?
4. **THINKING SKILL:** What could you do to determine the accuracy of the Palestinian's statement on this page.

392

The School for Peace

Neve Shalom/Wahat Al Salam

Neve Shalom/Wahat Al Salam

Abdel El-Salam Najjar and his friends were at a beach in Israel when a young woman approached them. "Maybe I dreamed it," she said, "or I am crazy. But I think I heard both the Hebrew and Arabic languages being spoken here."

Abdel smiled and replied, "It was no dream. And you are not crazy. We are from Neve Shalom/Wahat al Salam (NS/WAS)." *Neve Shalom* means "oasis of peace" in Hebrew. *Wahat al Salam* means "oasis of peace" in Arabic.

Conflict between the Jews and Arabs of Israel has been going on for the 40-year history of the nation. But NS/WAS is a ray of hope in this gloomy picture. This tiny community in the hills outside Tel Aviv in Israel was created to prove that the peoples of the Middle East could live together in peace. Both Jewish and Palestinian families live in the settlement.

The community is proof that peace is possible. But they have done more than prove that people can live together peacefully. The people of NS/WAS have started a school to help change the attitudes of Jews and Arabs toward one another. They call it the School for Peace.

In Israel Jews and Arabs are taught in separate Arabic or Hebrew schools. Young people of the two cultures usually do not mix and are not friendly. The School for Peace invites small groups of high school students to 3-day workshops. Here Jewish and Arab students gather to learn more about each other. They are surprised to learn how alike they really are. How do you think this makes them feel?

The idea behind the School for Peace is to build some understanding between the young Jews and Arabs who will be tomorrow's leaders. Nearly 1,000 students attend workshops each year. If these young people can learn to talk to one another about their differences now, perhaps there is hope for a peaceful future.

No-Rooz:
A New Year's Celebration

by Diana Reische

In the last lesson you read about how Reza Shah brought public schools, railroads, and industry to Iran. During his reign he introduced many kinds of modern technology to this ancient nation. Like most nations, however, Iran's culture remains a mixture of new and old. For example, when Iranian families celebrate the new year, they celebrate a holiday with roots that go back at least 3,500 years. In this lesson you will read about the tradition of No-Rooz, the Iranian New Year. As you read, think about why new year's celebrations are important to many cultures.

THE NEW YEAR AND THE CHANGING SEASONS

In Iran snow still covers the ground in early March. Yet indoors, people begin planting seeds in small earthen pots. Why? They are getting ready for No-Rooz—the biggest, oldest holiday in Iran. No matter which religion they practice, all Iranians celebrate No-Rooz. This holiday, which is older than either Islam or Christianity, is probably the oldest new year's celebration anywhere in the world.

Iran's new year begins on the first day of the month the Iranians call Farvardeen (fär vär dēn'). On this day, which is called the vernal equinox (vûr' nəl ē' kwə noks), day and night are of exactly the same length. And from here on in, the long, dark winter nights will grow shorter and shorter. Thus, No-Rooz marks not only the start of the new year, but also the end of winter and the beginning of spring.

394

Because No-Rooz is based on
the sun's movements, it does not happen
at the same time every year. The vernal equinox
most frequently falls on the date the United States
calendar calls March 21. However, the hour changes from
year to year. To allow people to plan ahead, Iranian calendars list the hour, minute, and second of No-Rooz.

PREPARING FOR NO-ROOZ

The No-Rooz holiday is much more than a single day. It also includes weeks of preparation and the first 13 days of the new year. During these holiday weeks, Iranian families around the world follow customs handed down from their ancestors in ancient Persia.

Fifteen days before No-Rooz, families plant pots of wheat or barley. While these fast-growing seeds are sprouting, spring cleaning gets underway. Every corner of the home gets dusted, washed, and scrubbed during this "house-shaking." As in many cultures, Iranians like to think of the new year as a "clean start."

As part of that clean start, everyone needs at least one new piece of clothing. Children usually get a whole new outfit for No-Rooz. While people shop for clothes, they also buy gifts for their family and friends. For a month before the new year, stores and bazaars stock up on jewelry, clothes, flowers, and special foods.

On the eve of the last Wednesday of the old year, Iranian families gather outdoors for a special ceremony. First they light small bonfires. Each person in the family jumps across the fire and says, "My yellowness [*sickness*] to you, your redness [*health*] to me." Jumping over the fire represents leaving the sorrows of the old year behind.

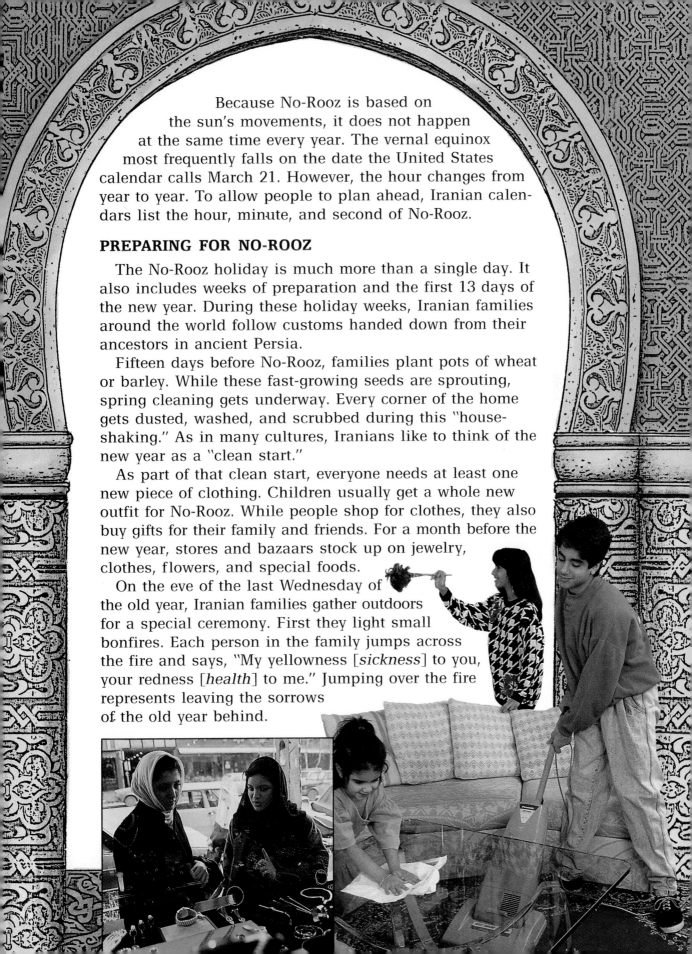

THE EVE OF NO-ROOZ

Finally the high point of the holiday arrives—the evening before No-Rooz. If you were lucky enough to be invited to an Iranian home on No-Rooz eve, you would smell chicken roasting. You would be offered honey-flavored desserts and candy. On the floor you would notice a clean cloth covered with seven special foods—the "Seven *S*'s."

The custom of the "Seven *S*'s," or *Haft-Sean* (häft sā' än), is thousands of years old. The Persian name for each of these seven foods begins with the letter *s*. Each one is said to bring happiness, luck, or good fortune in the coming year. You can see these seven foods on the chart on this page.

Other items are also placed on the cloth. There is usually a bowl of hard-boiled eggs, since eggs symbolize new life. And in Muslim homes, the Koran sits on the cloth. The family will read aloud from this holy book during the course of the evening.

Haft-Sean: the Seven *S*'s			
sabzee	säb' zē	fast-growing green plants	
seer	sêr	garlic	
samanoo	sä' mä nü	green wheat pudding	
serkeh	sâr' kyə	vinegar	
sumac	sü' mac	an herb	
seeb	sēb	an apple	
senjed	sen' jed	dates	

THE MOMENT OF NO-ROOZ

The next day, when the family gathers around the cloth shortly before the moment of No-Rooz, each person holds a mirror and a flickering candle. Looking into the mirror in the candlelight, everyone sees a bright future. The candle must burn all the way down. Blowing it out is believed to bring bad luck.

Legend says that whatever a person is doing at the moment of No-Rooz will shape his or her luck during the coming year. Some people hold money in their hands to bring good fortune. Children pop candy into their mouths as the moment approaches.

At the exact second the new year arrives, bells begin ringing outside, and in some places cannons boom. Each child in the family kisses the hands of the older people.

The older family members kiss the young ones on the face. Amid much laughter and good wishes, people hand out gifts. Relatives and friends drop by during the rest of the day, bringing flowers, almonds, colored eggs, and jewelry.

THE NEXT THIRTEEN DAYS

For the next 12 days, Iranians visit family and friends to exchange gifts and greetings. Many also go to sporting events, concerts, movies, and other holiday entertainments.

The new year is also considered to be a time for kindness and forgiveness. People try to resolve old quarrels by visiting each other and putting aside their anger. Many make new year's resolutions, just as people do in the United States.

The thirteenth and final day of No-Rooz features another old tradition. The ancient Persians considered 13 an unlucky number. They chose the thirteenth day of the new year as a time to combat bad luck. Today's Iranians still follow this tradition. On *Seezduh-bedar* (sēz′ də bə där′)—which means "Thirteenth Day Out"—Iranian families head for the countryside, park, or courtyard. By going outdoors, they hope to draw bad luck away from their homes.

Along with their picnic baskets, families bring the *sabzee*, or new green plants. Children toss these pots into streams of running water. According to tradition, they are also throwing away bad luck, illness, and quarrels. No-Rooz is now over—until the next year!

How is the tradition of No-Rooz important to Iranian culture?

IMPORTANT EVENTS

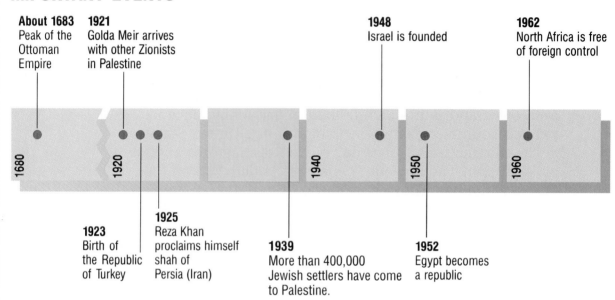

About 1683
Peak of the Ottoman Empire

1921
Golda Meir arrives with other Zionists in Palestine

1948
Israel is founded

1962
North Africa is free of foreign control

1680 | 1920 | 1940 | 1950 | 1960

1923
Birth of the Republic of Turkey

1925
Reza Khan proclaims himself shah of Persia (Iran)

1939
More than 400,000 Jewish settlers have come to Palestine.

1952
Egypt becomes a republic

PEOPLE TO KNOW

Reza Khan
A.D. 1877-1944

Mustafa Kemal Atatürk
A.D. 1881-1938

Golda Meir
A.D. 1898-1978

Gamal Abdel Nasser
A.D. 1918-1970

IDEAS TO REMEMBER

■ The decline of the Ottoman Empire led to the growth of nationalism in the Middle East and North Africa. The modern nations of Turkey and Iran emerged after World War I. At about the same time, Zionism led to the growth of the Jewish population in Palestine and to the creation of Israel in 1948.

■ Nationalism emerged in Egypt and other North African lands after World War II. Many new nations were born in the years that followed.

REVIEWING VOCABULARY

export   terrorism
import   Zionist
sultan

Number a sheet of paper from 1 to 5. Beside each number write the word or term from the above list that best matches each statement.

1. This term refers to acts of violence that are performed against innocent people.
2. This term was applied to people who wanted to create a Jewish state with Jewish laws and customs.
3. These are goods that a nation buys from other countries for its own use.
4. The name for one of many Ottoman rulers who forced people to pay high taxes and observe Muslim law in the lands they controlled.
5. This term refers to goods that one country sells to another, oil being the major example in the Middle East.

REVIEWING FACTS

1. Name three things that Mustafa Kemal Atatürk and Reza Shah had in common. How were they different?
2. Why were Arab countries forced to let foreign oil companies develop their oil resources? Name two things Arab countries did to increase their income from oil.
3. The phrase "conflicting nationalism" is used to describe the dispute between the Palestinians and the Israelis. What does this phrase mean? How has conflicting nationalism contributed to conflict in the Middle East?
4. What does the term *historic legacy* mean when applied to the modern nations of Israel, Iran, and Turkey? What are these legacies?
5. How did Egypt's Gamal Abdel Nasser help bring about the independence of the Arab nations in North Africa?

WRITING ABOUT MAIN IDEAS

1. **Writing a Paragraph:** Write a paragraph that shows the relationship among the following names: *Palestine, Zionism, Golda Meir, Israel, Palestinians, Palestine Liberation Organization.*
2. **Writing a Letter About Life in Israel:** Imagine you are an American student who has been visiting Israel for one week. You are eager to share your experiences with your family and friends at home. Write a letter describing your impressions of life in Israel.
3. **Writing About Perspectives:** Imagine that you are an Israeli or Palestinian representative at a peace conference. Write a speech explaining your position on the disagreements between the two groups. Also give recommendations on how you think peace can be achieved.

BUILDING SKILLS: EVALUATING INFORMATION

1. List three ways in which the accuracy of a fact may be checked.
2. What is a credible source?
3. Why is it important to evaluate information for accuracy?

REVIEWING VOCABULARY

Number a sheet of paper from 1 to 10. Beside each number write whether the following statements are true or false. If the statement is true, write **T**. If it is false, rewrite the sentence using the underlined vocabulary word correctly.

1. A Zionist is a strong believer in Islam who fought to create a Palestinian state of their own.
2. Terrorism is an act of violence against innocent people.
3. A caliph was a leader of Islam after Muhammad who had great religious and political authority.
4. Islam is a polytheistic religion that regards Abraham, Moses, and Jesus as false prophets.
5. Goods that a country buys from another are called exports.
6. The Koran was a sacred building in Mecca where Arabs worshipped the images of many different gods.
7. Wind-blown sand is a major source of erosion in desert regions.
8. A mosque is a palace where caliphs and other Islamic rulers lived.
9. An oasis is a well-watered place in the desert that is often the site of a town or city.
10. A sultan was an Arab warlord at the time of Muhammad.

WRITING ABOUT THE UNIT

1. **Writing a List:** You read that Muslim armies carried Islam far into Europe. You may recall that the Muslims were defeated at the Battle of Tours in France. Imagine that the Muslims had won that battle. List five things that would be different today if the Muslims had conquered Europe.
2. **Writing a Pamphlet:** Imagine that you are the owner of an oil field in a Middle Eastern country. Write a pamphlet for visitors that describes how oil is pumped out of the ground, refined, and shipped to customers around the world. Explain why oil is an important export and what your country does with the money it gets from oil.
3. **Writing About Perspectives:** Imagine that you are a Muslim soldier in the 700s. Record in your journal the events of a single day as you experience them. These events may include battles, meetings with local leaders, new towns or customs you encounter, or other experiences.

ACTIVITIES

1. **Using Newspapers and Magazines to Research an Oral Report:** Gather newspaper and magazine stories about an issue in the Middle East, such as the Arab-Israeli conflict, Lebanon, or OPEC. Write a summary of the issue. Then present your summary in an oral report to the rest of the class.
2. **Working Together on a Population Bar Graph:** Use reference sources such as almanacs and encyclopedias to learn the populations of the five largest countries in the Middle East and North Africa. Using the information you find, draw a bar graph showing their populations.

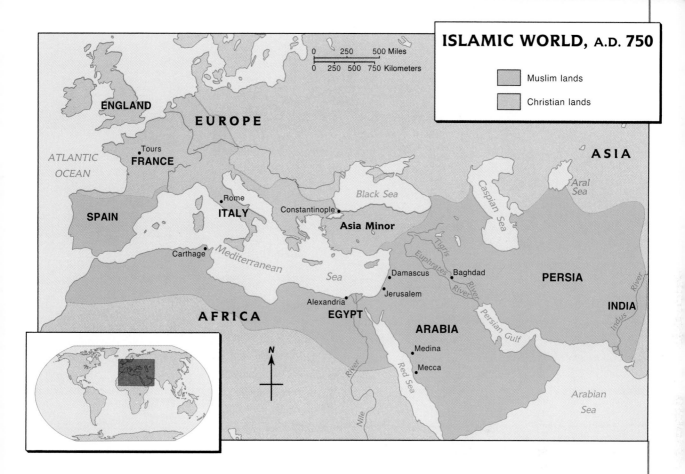

ISLAMIC WORLD, A.D. 750

Muslim lands

Christian lands

0   250   500 Miles
0 250 500 750 Kilometers

ENGLAND

EUROPE

ATLANTIC
OCEAN

Tours
FRANCE

ASIA

Aral
Sea

SPAIN

Rome
ITALY

Constantinople

Black Sea

Caspian Sea

Carthage

Mediterranean

Asia Minor

Sea

Tigris

Euphrates
River

Damascus
Jerusalem

River

Baghdad

PERSIA

Indus
River

INDIA

Alexandria

AFRICA

EGYPT

ARABIA

Persian Gulf

River

Medina

Red Sea

Mecca

Arabian
Sea

Nile

N

BUILDING SKILLS: USING MAPS AT DIFFERENT SCALES

Use the map above to answer the following questions.

1. What is the difference between a large-scale map and a small-scale map?

2. Why is the map above a small-scale map? What does it show?

3. How many miles does the line scale represent on the map? How many kilometers are shown on the scale?

4. How can using maps at different scales be useful?

LINKING PAST, PRESENT, AND FUTURE

Imagine you are a Middle Eastern historian living in the twenty-first century. You have just written a book that covers more than 2,000 years of Arab and Jewish history down to the present day. The last chapter is titled "The End of the Arab-Israeli Conflict." What will you write?

75°N
Arctic Circle
60°N
45°N
30°N
Tropic of Cancer
15°N
0° Equator
15°S
Tropic of Capricorn
30°S
45°S
60°S
Antarctic Circle

45°W 30°W 15°W 0° 15°E 30°E 45°E 60°E

CAPE
VERDE
SENEGAL
GAMBIA
GUINEA-
BISSAU GUINEA
SIERRA LEONE
LIBERIA

MAURITANIA
MALI
NIGER
CHAD
SUDAN
DJIBOUTI Gulf of Ad

BURKINA
FASO
BENIN
NIGERIA
CÔTE
D'IVOIRE
(IVORY
COAST) GHANA TOGO
CENTRAL
AFRICAN
REPUBLIC
ETHIOPIA
SOMALIA

Gulf of Guinea
CAMEROON
EQUATORIAL GUINEA
SÃO TOMÉ AND
AND PRINCIPÉ
CONGO
UGANDA
KENYA
GABON
ZAIRE
RWANDA
BURUNDI
Lake
Victoria
TANZANIA

CABINDA
(ANGOLA)

ATLANTIC

OCEAN

COMOROS
ANGOLA
MALAWI
ZAMBIA
MOZAMBIQUE
MADAGASCA
Mozambique Channel
ZIMBABWE
NAMIBIA
BOTSWANA
SWAZILAND
LESOTHO
SOUTH
AFRICA

Red Sea

UNIT
7

AFRICA SOUTH OF THE SAHARA

WHERE WE ARE

Africa is the second-largest continent. The large part of Africa that extends south of the Sahara is known as *sub-Saharan* Africa. Sub-Saharan means "south of the Sahara."

Sub-Saharan Africa is a region of deserts and highlands, of rain forests and grasslands. Mighty rivers wind from the interior to the coasts, often falling in great waterfalls or rapids. Many great societies have blossomed in this beautiful land. As the map shows, Africa today is a continent of many nations.

SEYCHELLES

INDIAN

OCEAN

AURITIUS

90°E

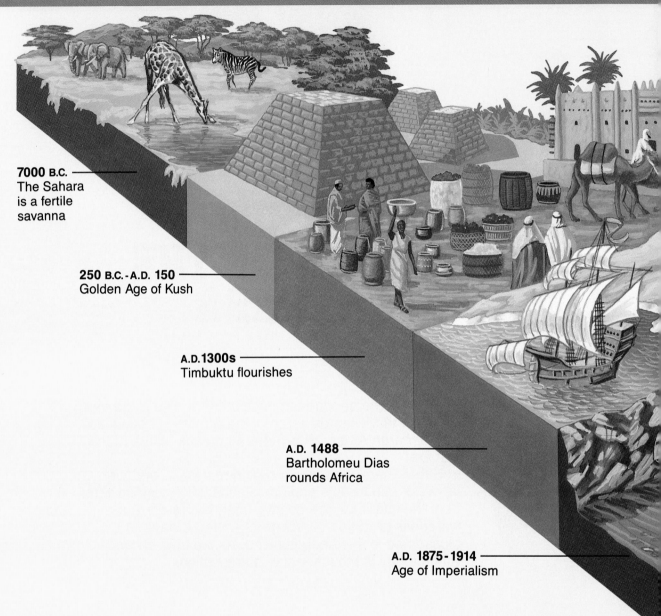

7000 B.C.
The Sahara
is a fertile
savanna

250 B.C.-A.D. 150
Golden Age of Kush

A.D. 1300s
Timbuktu flourishes

A.D. 1488
Bartholomeu Dias
rounds Africa

A.D. 1875-1914
Age of Imperialism

A.D. 1957-Present
African colonies
gain independence

WHAT HAPPENED

Thousands of years ago the
Sahara was a fertile plain overflowing with
wildlife. Later, great kingdoms grew up along
the southern edge of the Sahara. Can you find
the pyramids of Kush on the time line? Hundreds of
years later, Timbuktu was one of the world's busiest
trading centers. Other kingdoms flourished farther south along
the coasts of the Atlantic Ocean and Indian Ocean.

404

AFRICA SOUTH OF THE SAHARA

BURUNDI

Capital ★
Bujumbura

Major languages: Kirundi and French
Population: 5.8 million
Area: 10,745 sq mi; 27,830 sq km
Leading export: coffee

CAMEROON

Capital ★
Yaoundé

Major languages: English and French
Population: 11.4 million
Area: 183,568 sq mi; 475,440 sq km
Leading exports: oil, coffee and cocoa

ANGOLA

Capital ★
Luanda

Major languages: Portuguese and
  Ovimbundo
Population: 8.5 million
Area: 481,352 sq mi; 1,246,700 sq km
Leading exports: oil and coffee

CAPE VERDE

Capital ★
Praia

Major languages: Portuguese and
  Crioulo
Population: 0.4 million
Area: 1,556 sq mi; 4,030 sq km
Leading exports: fish and bananas

BENIN

Capital ★
Porto-Novo

Major languages: French and Fon
Population: 4.8 million
Area: 43,483 sq mi; 112,620 sq km
Leading exports: fuels and coffee

**CENTRAL
AFRICAN
REPUBLIC**

Capital ★
Bangui

Major languages: French and Sango
Population: 3.0 million
Area: 237,362 sq mi; 622,980 sq km
Leading exports: coffee, diamonds,
  and timber

BOTSWANA

Capital ★
Gaborone

Major languages: English and
  Setswana
Population: 1.3 million
Area: 231,803 sq mi; 600,370 sq km
Leading exports: diamonds and cattle

CHAD

Capital ★
N'Djamena

Major languages: French and Arabic
Population: 5.1 million
Area: 495,754 sq mi; 1,284,000 sq km
Leading export: cotton

**BURKINA
FASO**

Capital ★
Ouagadougou

Major language: French
Population: 9.4 million
Area: 105,869 sq mi; 274,200 sq km
Leading exports: cotton and
  manufactured goods

COMOROS

Capital ★
Moroni

Major languages: French, Arabic
  and Comoran
Population: 0.5 million
Area: 838 sq mi; 2,170 sq km
Leading export: vanilla

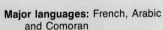

CONGO

Capital ★
Brazzaville

Major language: French
Population: 2.3 million
Area: 132,047 sq mi; 342,000 sq km
Leading export: oil

GAMBIA

Capital ★
Banjul

Major languages: English and Mandinka
Population: 0.9 million
Area: 4,363 sq mi; 11,300 sq km
Leading export: peanut products

CÔTE D'IVOIRE (Ivory Coast)
Capital ★
Abidjan

Major language: French
Population: 12.5 million
Area: 124,502 sq mi; 322,460 sq km
Leading exports: cocoa, coffee, and fuels

GHANA

Capital ★
Accra

Major language: English
Population: 15.5 million
Area: 92,101 sq mi; 238,540 sq km
Leading exports: cocoa and gold

DJIBOUTI

Capital ★
Djibouti

Major languages: Arabic and French
Population: 0.4 million
Area: 8,494 sq mi; 22,000 sq km
Leading exports: hides and skins

GUINEA

Capital ★
Conakry

Major languages: French
Population: 7.5 million
Area: 94,927 sq mi; 245,860 sq km
Leading export: bauxite

EQUATORIAL GUINEA
Capital ★
Malabo

Major language: Spanish
Population: 0.4 million
Area: 10,830 sq mi; 28,050 sq km
Leading exports: cocoa and coffee

GUINEA-BISSAU
Capital ★
Bissau

Major language: Portuguese and Criolo
Population: 1.0 million
Area: 13,946 sq mi; 36,120 sq km
Leading export: peanut products

ETHIOPIA

Capital ★
Addis Ababa

Major language: Amharic
Population: 53.2 million
Area: 471,777 sq mi; 1,221,900 sq km
Leading export: coffee

KENYA

Capital ★
Nairobi

Major languages: English and Kiswahili
Population: 25.2 million
Area: 224,962 sq mi; 582,650 sq km
Leading exports: coffee and tea

GABON

Capital ★
Libreville

Major languages: French and Fang
Population: 1.2 million
Area: 103,348 sq mi; 267,670 sq km
Leading export: oil

LESOTHO

Capital ★
Maseru

Major languages: Sesotho and English
Population: 1.8 million
Area: 11,718 sq mi; 30,350 sq km
Leading exports: manufactured goods and wool

407

LIBERIA

Capital ★
Monrovia

Major language: English
Population: 2.7 million
Area: 43,000 sq mi; 111,370 sq km
Leading exports: iron ore and rubber

MADAGASCAR

Capital ★
Antananarivo

Major languages: French and
   Malagasy
Population: 12.4 million
Area: 226,656 sq mi; 587,040 sq km
Leading exports: coffee, vanilla,
   and sugar

MALAWI

Capital ★
Lilongwe

Major languages: English and
   Chichewa
Population: 9.4 million
Area: 45,745 sq mi; 118,480 sq km
Leading exports: tobacco, sugar,
   and tea

MALI

Capital ★
Bamako

Major languages: Bambara and
   French
Population: 8.3 million
Area: 478,765 sq mi; 1,240,000 sq km
Leading exports: cotton and
   manufactured goods

MAURITANIA

Capital ★
Nouakchott

Major languages: Arabic and French
Population: 2.1 million
Area: 397,954 sq mi; 1,030,700 sq km
Leading exports: iron ore and fish

MAURITIUS

Capital ★
Port Louis

Major languages: English, Creole,
   and Hindi
Population: 1.1 million
Area: 718 sq mi; 1,860 sq km
Leading export: sugar

MOZAMBIQUE

Capital ★
Maputo

Major language: Portuguese
Population: 16.1 million
Area: 309,495 sq mi; 801,590 sq km
Leading exports: shrimp, cashew nuts,
   and sugar

NAMIBIA

Capital ★
Windhoek

Major languages: English, Afrikaans,
   and German
Population: 1.5 million
Area: 318,259 sq mi; 824,290 sq km
Leading exports: diamonds, uranium,
   and livestock

NIGER

Capital ★
Niamey

Major languages: French and Hausa
Population: 8.0 million
Area: 489,190 sq mi; 1,267,000 sq km
Leading export: uranium

NIGERIA

Capital ★
Lagos

Major languages: English, Hausa,
   Yoruba, and Ibo
Population: 122.5 million
Area: 356,669 sq mi; 923,770 sq km
Leading exports: oil, cocoa, and
   rubber

RWANDA

Capital ★
Kigali

Major languages: Kinyarwanda
   and French
Population: 7.5 million
Area: 10,170 sq mi; 26,340 sq km
Leading exports: coffee and tea

**SÃO TOMÉ and
PRINCIPE**
Capital ★
São Tomé

Major language: Portuguese
Population: 0.1 million
Area: 371 sq mi; 960 sq km
Leading export: cocoa

SENEGAL

Capital ★
Dakar

Major languages: French and Wolof
Population: 7.5 million
Area: 75,749 sq mi; 196,190 sq km
Leading exports: fuels, fish, and chemicals

SIERRA LEONE

Capital ★
Freetown

Major languages: English, Mende, and Temne
Population: 4.3 million
Area: 27,699 sq mi; 71,740 sq km
Leading exports: rutile, diamonds, and bauxite

SOMALIA

Capital ★
Mogadishu

Major languages: Somali and Arabic
Population: 7.7 million
Area: 246,201 sq mi; 637,660 sq km
Leading exports: bananas and bauxite

SOUTH AFRICA

Capitals ★
Pretoria, Cape Town and Bloemfontein

Major languages: Afrikaans, English, Zulu, Xhosa, and Sesetho
Population: 40.6 million
Area: 471,445 sq mi; 1,221,040 sq km
Leading exports: gold, coal and minerals

SUDAN

Capital ★
Khartoum

Major language: Arabic
Population: 25.9 million
Area: 967,496 sq mi; 2,505,810 sq km
Leading export: cotton

SWAZILAND

Capital ★
Mbabane

Major languages: siSwati and English
Population: 0.8 million
Area: 6,703 sq mi; 17,360 sq km
Leading exports: food, sugar, and wood products

TANZANIA

Capital ★
Dar es Salaam

Major languages: Swahili and English
Population: 26.9 million
Area: 364,900 sq mi; 945,090 sq km
Leading exports: coffee and cotton

TOGO

Capital ★
Lomé

Major languages: French, Kabiye, and Ewe
Population: 3.8 million
Area: 21,927 sq mi; 56,790 sq km
Leading export: phosphates

UGANDA

Capital ★
Kampala

Major languages: English and Luganda
Population: 18.7 million
Area: 91,135 sq mi; 236,040 sq km
Leading export: coffee

ZAIRE

Capital ★
Kinshasa

Major languages: French, Kiswahili, and Kiluba
Population: 37.8 million
Area: 905,565 sq mi; 2,345,410 sq km
Leading export: copper

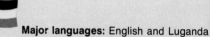

ZAMBIA

Capital ★
Lusaka

Major languages: English, Nyanja, Bemba
Population: 8.4 million
Area: 290,583 sq mi; 752,610 sq km
Leading export: copper

ZIMBABWE

Capital ★
Harare

Major languages: English, Chishona, and Sindebele
Population: 10.0 million
Area: 150,803 sq mi; 390,580 sq km
Leading exports: tobacco and gold

CHAPTER 16

GREAT AFRICAN KINGDOMS

FOCUS

It is the oba [ruler of Benin] that is mighty. Though his attendants wear ivory rings, the oba is decorated with gold.

These words were recorded by an Egyptian visitor to the rich kingdoms of West Africa. In this chapter you will read about the varied geography and history of Africa south of the Sahara.

1 Geography: Africa South of the Sahara

READ TO LEARN

Key Vocabulary

rift valley
equatorial
Sahel
savanna

Key Places

Mount Kilimanjaro
Serengeti Plain
Great Rift Valley
Lake Victoria

Read Aloud

If I know a song of Africa . . . I thought of the elegant giraffe, and of the new African moon lying on her back, and of the many plows in the fields. . . .

Like the African farmer who wrote these words, you will also learn the "song of Africa." In this lesson you will begin a great adventure. You will travel to Africa—the giant continent. Its geography is as varied as the people who live there.

Read for Purpose

1. **WHAT YOU KNOW:** Name two facts that help to unite the people of North Africa and the Middle East.
2. **WHAT YOU WILL LEARN:** What are Africa's important geographical features?

AFRICA THE GIANT

When you have caught the rhythm of Africa, you find that it is the same in all her music.

The Mbuti (em büd′ ē) people sing these words as they gather food in the thick rain forests of central Africa. To the Mbuti, the rain forest is everything— mother, father, giver of life. While in eastern Africa, the words to the song that the Masai (mä sī′) people sing are different. This nomadic group sings of the grasslands:

Without grass there are no cattle, and without cattle there are no Masai.

The words that the two groups of people sing are different, but the rhythm with which each speaks is African. It is a rhythm whose source is the great continent of Africa. For millions of people, life is defined by their connection with the great African landscape.

Africa is a giant continent. It is the second-largest continent in the world, making up more than 20 percent of the world's land area. You will learn that Africa is a continent of great variety. There are, for example, thick rain forests where it rains almost every day.

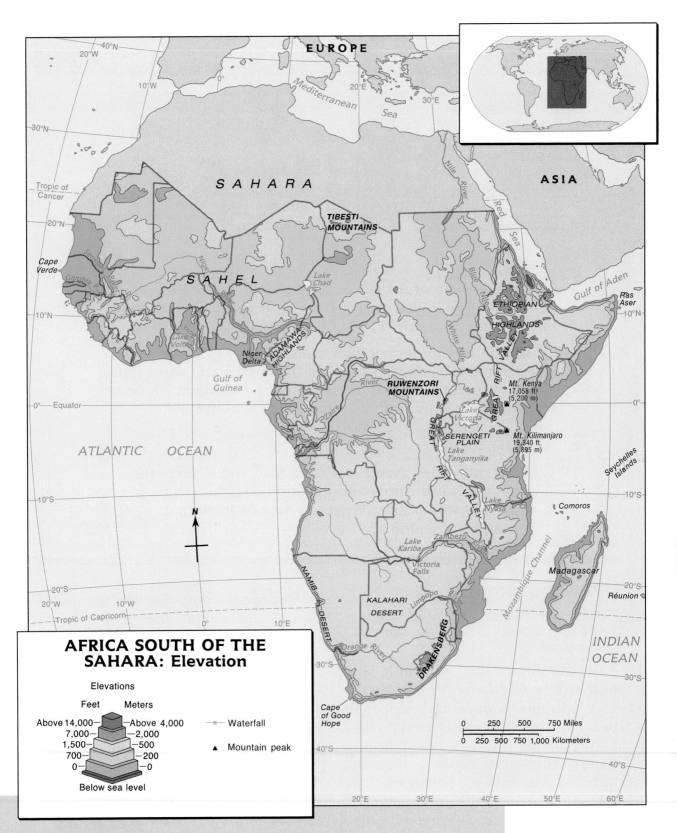

AFRICA SOUTH OF THE SAHARA: Elevation

Elevations

Feet	Meters
Above 14,000	Above 4,000
7,000	2,000
1,500	500
700	200
0	0

Below sea level

⊬ Waterfall

▲ Mountain peak

EUROPE

ASIA

Mediterranean Sea

SAHARA

TIBESTI MOUNTAINS

Tropic of Cancer

Cape Verde

SAHEL

Senegal River

Niger River

Lake Chad

Gambia R.

Lake Volta

ADAMAWA HIGHLANDS

Niger Delta

Gulf of Guinea

Red Sea

Nile River

Blue Nile

White Nile

Gulf of Aden

Ras Aser

ETHIOPIAN HIGHLANDS

RUWENZORI MOUNTAINS

Zaire River

GREAT RIFT VALLEY

Mt. Kenya 17,058 ft. (5,200 m)

Lake Victoria

SERENGETI PLAIN

Mt. Kilimanjaro 19,340 ft. (5,895 m)

Lake Tanganyika

Seychelles Islands

Equator

ATLANTIC OCEAN

GREAT RIFT VALLEY

Lake Nyasa

Comoros

Lake Kariba

Zambezi R.

Victoria Falls

Madagascar

Mozambique Channel

Réunion

NAMIB DESERT

KALAHARI DESERT

Limpopo River

DRAKENSBERG

Orange River

Cape of Good Hope

INDIAN OCEAN

Tropic of Capricorn

N

| 0 | 250 | 500 | 750 Miles |
| 0 | 250 500 750 | 1,000 Kilometers |

MAP SKILL: Africa is a giant continent. Name the large bodies of water that surround the African continent.

412

But you will also find vast and empty deserts where it may not rain for many years.

THE AFRICAN LANDSCAPE

Look at the elevation map on the opposite page. Note that Africa is a vast, flat plateau. Apart from lowlands along the coasts and scattered highlands, the African plateau stretches the length of the continent. This flatness is common to most of Africa. Africa's deserts are flat, its thick rain forests are flat, and its grass-covered lands are flat. As the map shows, however, southern Africa may be flat, but it is not low.

You read about Africa's Atlas Mountains in Unit 6. Do you recall where they are located? They are found in northwestern Africa, along the Mediterranean Sea. Africa's highest mountains, however, are found in the eastern part of the continent. Find Africa's highest mountain peak on the map on page 412. As you can see from the photograph below, Mount Kilimanjaro (kil ə mən jär′ ō) towers over the flat grasslands of the Serengeti Plain. As you can imagine, this mountain attracts many visitors.

A famous American writer named Ernest Hemingway visited Mount Kilimanjaro and wrote:

Kilimanjaro is a snow-covered mountain 19,710 feet high, and is said to be the highest mountain in Africa. Its western summit is called the Masai "Ngàje Ngài," or the House of God. Close to the western summit there is a dried and frozen carcass of a leopard. No one has explained what the leopard was seeking at that altitude.

Herds of wild zebras graze on the Serengeti Plain. Nearby, Africa's tallest mountain—Mount Kilimanjaro—rises majestically.

413

THE GREAT RIFT VALLEY

One of the remarkable things about the African plateau is the series of deep valleys that extend along its eastern coast. Millions of years ago, the continent was broken by a series of faults, or cracks. Between the faults, parts of the plateau's surface dropped down to form valleys. A long, steep-sided valley lying between two parallel faults is called a rift valley.

In Africa you can find one such rift valley, called the Great Rift Valley. This is a series of valleys that extend about 6,000 miles (9,600 km) from the Mozambique (mō zəm bēk') Channel north to the Red Sea.

Most of Africa's lakes have formed in the bottom of its rift valleys. Africa's largest lake, Lake Victoria, lies in a basin between two branches of the Great Rift Valley. Lake Victoria is larger than the state of West Virginia.

When rivers reach the Great Rift Valley, they cascade downward in great waterfalls, like Victoria Falls in Zimbabwe.

All of Africa's major rivers are located south of the Sahara. Most of them descend from the African plateau over waterfalls and rapids. Even the mighty Nile River, Africa's longest river, has its source in sub-Saharan Africa. The Zaire River, formerly known as the Congo River, is Africa's second-largest river.

EQUATORIAL AFRICA

Africa's location has a great effect on its climate. You may have noticed from the map on page 412 that the equator runs across Africa. You will recall that this imaginary line circles the earth halfway between the North and South poles. How does the equator influence Africa's climate?

As you can imagine, temperatures are often very high along the equator. Except for the mountainous regions, most of Africa is warm or hot all year round. There is not much difference between the summer and winter temperatures. There is, however, often a great difference between daytime temperatures and nighttime temperatures, especially in the deserts. The temperature variation, or difference, can be as much as 60°F. (15°C) between day and night.

In the middle of the African continent, along the equator, lie equatorial (ē kwə tôr' ē əl) rain forests. *Equatorial* means "near the equator." These are hot lands that receive at least 50 inches (127 cm) of rain a year. Because there is so much rainfall, vegetation thrives and grows rapidly. Plants, vines, and trees grow so close together that it is impossible to see far into the forest. The tops of gigantic trees form a ceiling overhead and block the sunlight from the ground.

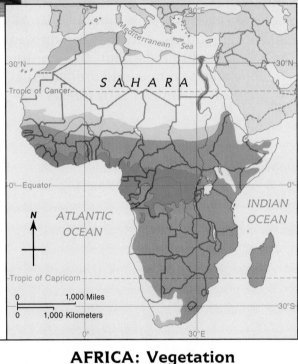

AFRICA: Vegetation

- Equatorial Rain Forest
- Mediterranean
- Savanna
- Sahel
- Desert

SAHEL AND SAVANNA

As the map on this page shows, Africa's rain forests lie near the equator. What other vegetation zones are shown on the map?

The climate and vegetation zones of sub-Saharan Africa gently stretch across the continent in wide bands. In the north, extending from North Africa, lies the Sahara. As you read in Chapter 14, almost no vegetation grows in this desert. The few plants found are those that can survive in high temperatures and require little water. The only parts of the desert that are fertile are the oases, where water comes from underground springs.

Stretching across the African continent is a narrow belt of semiarid grassland known as the Sahel (sa' hil). *Sahel* is an Arabic word meaning "border" or "shore." As you see from the map on this page, the Sahel lies on the edge of desert lands.

The Sahel merges with the desert on one side and with the savanna on the other side. The savanna is a broad, grassy plain that covers more than one fourth of the African continent. Some vistors from the United States to Africa say that the savanna looks like the prairies of North and South Dakota. The African savanna, however, is much warmer.

ANIMAL LIFE IS PART OF GEOGRAPHY

In this lesson you have been learning about the geography of Africa. It is important to remember that animal life is also part of the environment. As you know, Africa is world-famous for its wildlife. From the aardvark to the zebra, animals are one of Africa's greatest natural resources.

Like plants, many groups of animals are better suited to the climate and vegetation of one region than to that of another. In fact, most animals are very selective about where they live. In Africa, there are animals that live only in the desert, animals that live in the Sahel or the savanna, and animals that live in the equatorial rain forests.

Africa's large animals need a lot of food to survive. Wildlife preserves let them roam freely in their natural environment.

THE ANIMALS OF AFRICA

How many different animals that are found in Africa can you name? When people think of African wildlife, they usually think about animals who live in the savanna or rain forests. Zebras, giraffes, lions, leopards, and elephants roam the savanna in huge herds. One visitor to Africa found herself near one such herd.

I had seen a herd of elephants traveling through dense native forest . . . pacing along as if they had an appointment at the end of the world.

There are hundreds of different kinds of animals in the African savanna. A wide variety of animals also lives in the rain forests of equatorial Africa. For example, the chimpanzees and giant gorillas found there are found nowhere else in the world. Some animals, such as buffaloes and wild pigs, live in the rain forests but are hardly ever seen.

Gorillas, monkeys, and snakes live in the dense plant life of equatorial

416

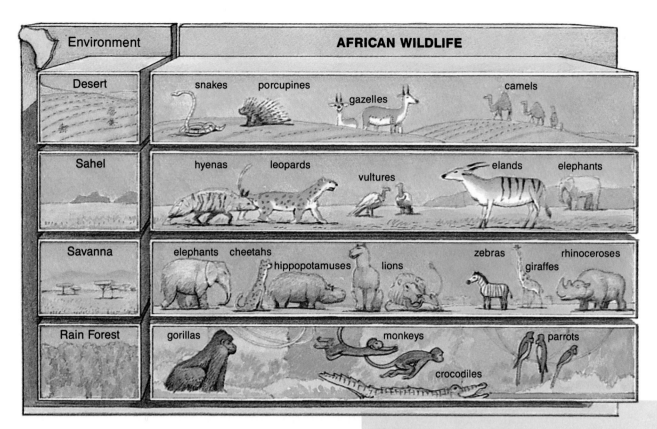

Environment	AFRICAN WILDLIFE
Desert	snakes porcupines gazelles camels
Sahel	hyenas leopards vultures elands elephants
Savanna	elephants cheetahs hippopotamuses lions zebras giraffes rhinoceroses
Rain Forest	gorillas monkeys crocodiles parrots

CHART SKILL: Most of Africa's animals live in just one environment. Which animal is found in two different environments?

Africa. More than 2,300 different kinds of birds are found there. Hippopotamuses and crocodiles swim in its rivers and swamps. The chart on this page lists only a few of the most well-known African animals.

THE AFRICAN LAND

Like all natural resources, wild animals are precious. For many years people came to Africa on safaris to hunt wild animals. But recently the nations of Africa have passed laws to protect the wildlife. Great sections of land have been set aside as wildlife preserves, where hunting is outlawed. These huge wildlife preserves protect the herds of wild animals from becoming extinct, or being wiped out.

As you have read, Africa is a giant continent. Stretching from the South Pole toward the Mediterranean Sea,

it is a region of highlands, deserts, grasslands, and equatorial rain forests. You have also read about Africa's abundant wildlife. In the next lesson you will begin a journey through Africa's rich history. This journey will take you far into Africa's ancient past.

Check Your Reading

1. What is a rift valley?
2. Describe some of Africa's important geographical features.
3. **GEOGRAPHY SKILL:** Which animals live in Africa's savanna?
4. **THINKING SKILL:** What are two sources you could check to determine the accuracy of the information given in this lesson?

417

READ TO LEARN

Key People
Piankhi
Ezana

Key Places
Kush
Meroë
Ethiopia
Axum

Read Aloud

As you know, the lands of North Africa have long been part of the Mediterranean world—the world of the Phoenicians, Greeks, Romans, and the Arabs. You also know that the world's largest desert—the Sahara—lies south of the Mediterranean coast.

The Sahara has been a great dividing zone in African history. In this lesson you will read about the people who were the first to build cities in sub-Saharan Africa.

Read for Purpose

1. **WHAT YOU KNOW:** Who conquered the Egyptian Empire?
2. **WHAT YOU WILL LEARN:** In what ways did Egyptian civilization influence other ancient African kingdoms?

THE GROWTH OF KUSH

You have already read about one of Africa's first civilizations—ancient Egypt. You may recall that it flourished in the Nile River Valley for more than 3,000 years. You may also recall that its mighty empire gradually crumbled because of its powerful neighbors. Who were those neighbors?

In 751 B.C. an African king named Piankhi (pyan' kē) led his army down the Nile and conquered Egypt. This marked the beginning of a great kingdom called Kush.

As the map on the next page shows, the people of Piankhi's kingdom lived south of Egypt. You can see that, like the Egyptians, the Kushites also lived along the Nile River. In Chapter 3 you read that the Egyptians dominated Kush from about 2000 to 1000 B.C. During this time, the Kushites learned a great deal about Egyptian civilization. For example, the Kushites learned to write with Egyptian hieroglyphics.

ANOTHER LAND OF PYRAMIDS

After the fall of Egypt, Kush became Africa's new center of culture. From its grand capital city called Meroë (mer ə wē'), Kush enjoyed a "Golden Age" from about 500 B.C. to A.D. 150.

418

Visitors to Meroë were amazed at the riches they found there. You can see some of the ruins of Meroë in the photograph on this page. Can you find the influence of the Egyptian legacy? As you see, the Kushites also built pyramids. The flat tops, however, were a unique characteristic of the Kushite style.

"A MAGNIFICENT CITY"

Do you remember the famous Greek historian named Herodotus? You may recall that he is called "the father of history." He visited Meroë and recorded the following:

> *I found a magnificent city with gold in great abundance. I found ironworkers capable of creating tools of wonderful strength. And everywhere there are animals called elephants. . . . No larger animals can be found.*

Archaeologists have searched the ruins of Meroë and discovered iron

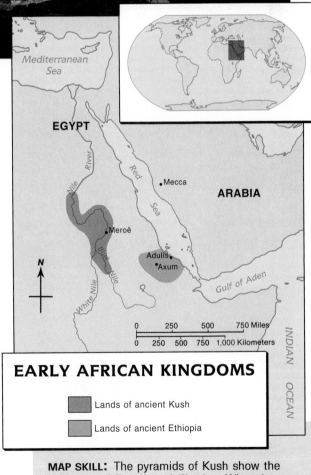

EARLY AFRICAN KINGDOMS

- Lands of ancient Kush
- Lands of ancient Ethiopia

MAP SKILL: The pyramids of Kush show the influence of Egyptian civilization. What river linked Kush with Egypt? What sea did the Ethiopians cross to reach Arabia?

419

tools buried in the earth. Gold objects believed to have been made in Kush have been found in many parts of the Middle East and even as far away as India. Merchants from Meroë took elephant-loads of their golden objects and iron tools to the Red Sea. There the Kushites exchanged their goods for luxuries from Arabia and India, such as jewelry, glass, and fine cotton cloth.

ETHIOPIA INVADES KUSH

I burnt their towns, both those built of brick and those built of straw, and my soldiers carried off their food, iron, and gold; my soldiers raided temples and storehouses and threw what was not of value into the Nile River.

Although much of Axum is in ruins, some tall, decorated columns have survived.

According to legend, a great king from an ancient African land called Ethiopia wrote these words. Like Hammurabi's Code of Laws, these words were carved into the surface of a tall stone column. The words on the column tell how, in about A.D. 325, a powerful kingdom destroyed Meroë.

Meroë's conquerers were from a city called Axum. Axum lay between the Nile River and the Red Sea south of Kush. By the year 300 Axum had grown rich and powerful by controlling trade between the African interior and the Red Sea. Persian and Arab merchants sailed to the Ethiopian port of Adulis. Here they exchanged their goods for African gold, ivory, and spices.

ETHIOPIA AND CHRISTIANITY

In the late fourth century, Greek Christians traded with Axum. They were astonished at the splendor of the court of King Ezana. One Greek described Ezana riding through the streets of his capital in a four-wheeled, golden chariot pulled by four painted elephants.

King Ezana became a Christian in the year 324. Ethiopia's rulers remained Christian through the centuries. When Muslim armies swept through Egypt in the seventh century, Ethiopia was not conquered.

During Europe's Middle Ages, Ethiopia's kings lost contact with Christian lands to the north. Then, in 1520, a Portuguese explorer journeyed to the Ethiopian highlands. He was amazed to find Christians worshiping in beautifully decorated churches.

As the photograph on the next page shows, there is something special about the Ethiopian churches. Built in the thirteenth century, many of them

420

About half of the people in Ethiopia today are Christians. These photographs show people at a church that was carved out of solid rock more than 700 years ago.

had been hollowed out of solid rock. Instead of cathedrals that towered into the sky like those in Europe, the ancient Ethiopians carved their places of worship into the bedrock. Worshipers reached the church door by climbing deep into the earth.

A HISTORIC LAND

Kush and Ethiopia were two of Africa's most ancient kingdoms. They both date as far back as ancient Egypt. In many ways, Kush inherited the legacy of Egypt. Egypt and Kush were neighbors for many years before Kush conquered the Egyptian people. As you read, the people of Kush also used hieroglyphics and built pyramids.

Ethiopia was also a rich and ancient African kingdom. Based on trade, it grew into a powerful, long-lasting Christian kingdom.

Check Your Reading

1. What important things did the Kushites learn from the Egyptians?
2. Name two things that amazed the European visitors to Axum.
3. **GEOGRAPHY SKILL:** How did the Sahara divide Africa?
4. **THINKING SKILL:** Compare and contrast Meroë and Axum.

421

3 Kingdoms of the African Savanna

READ TO LEARN

Key People

al-Bakri
Ibn Battutah
Mansa Musa
Leo Africanus

Key Places

Ghana
Mali
Kanem-Bornu

Timbuktu
Songhai
Zimbabwe

Read Aloud

Their religion is the worship of their kings, for the people believe that kings bring life and death, sickness and health.

These words were recorded by an Egyptian merchant in the tenth century. He had just returned from a remarkable journey deep into the heart of the African continent. In this lesson you will read about the places he visited. It is a journey that will lead you to dazzling, golden courts.

Read for Purpose

1. **WHAT YOU KNOW:** What is the geography of the African savanna?
2. **WHAT YOU WILL LEARN:** What caused trade to develop in West Africa between A.D. 300 and 1600?

THE GOLDEN COURTS OF WEST AFRICA

While the city-states of Meroë and Axum were flourishing in eastern Africa, new kingdoms were beginning to grow in western Africa. Between A.D. 300 and 1600 these kingdoms flourished in the savanna, the sweeping grassland between the Sahara and the equatorial rain forests. According to one visitor to West Africa:

The king is decorated with golden jewels, with glittering necklaces around his neck and bracelets on his forearms. . . . Behind the king stand ten guards holding golden shields.

These words were used by **al-Bakri**, a Spanish Arab, to describe the court of **Ghana** (gän′ ə). *Ghana* means both "warrior king" and "king of the gold." The kingdom described by al-Bakri became known by the title of its ruler.

From 400 to about 1235, Ghana controlled West Africa. As the map on the opposite page shows, other kingdoms existed in West Africa. As the map also shows, the empire of **Mali** emerged after Ghana fell. At about the same time as Mali, **Kanem-Bornu** was thriving to the east. Each of these kingdoms was noted for its abundant wealth.

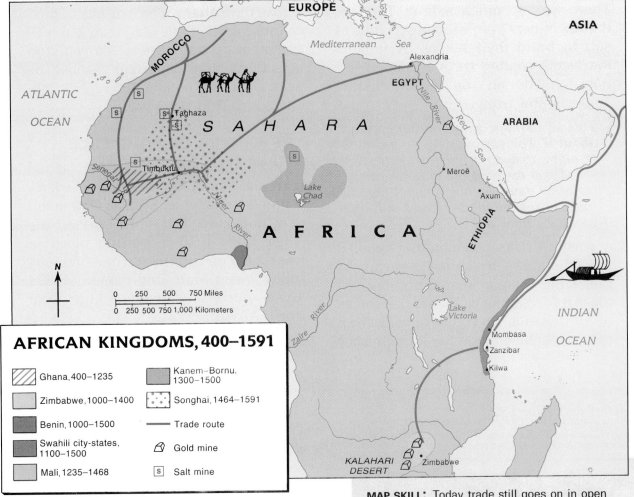

AFRICAN KINGDOMS, 400–1591

- Ghana, 400–1235
- Zimbabwe, 1000–1400
- Benin, 1000–1500
- Swahili city-states, 1100–1500
- Mali, 1235–1468
- Kanem–Bornu, 1300–1500
- Songhai, 1464–1591
- Trade route
- Gold mine
- S Salt mine

MAP SKILL: Today trade still goes on in open marketplaces. What desert did North African traders cross to reach Timbuktu?

TRADE IN WEST AFRICA

The wealth of Ghana, Mali, and Kanem-Bornu was based on two precious substances: gold and salt. The gold came from a forest region south of the savanna between the Niger and Senegal rivers. Miners dug gold from deep in the earth or sifted it from the rivers. Until about 1350 at least two thirds of the world's supply of gold came from the West African forests.

Despite this wealth in gold, the West African savanna was poor in salt. The vast Sahara, on the other hand, was rich in salt. Deep in the desert lay a salt-mining village called Taghaza.

There was so much salt in Taghaza that its miners even used great slabs of salt to build their homes. A famous fourteenth-century traveler named **Ibn Battutah** (ib′ ən bə tüt′ ä) visited Taghaza and wrote:

> This is a village with nothing good about it. The surrounding dunes shift at night, making it impossible to travel. Yet the heat is too fierce to travel by day. The only marvel here is that houses are made of rock salt and roofs of camel skins.

West African merchants traveled long distances by camel caravan for this salt. After a six-month journey, these traders reached the market towns of North Africa. As you have read, Arab merchants also made the long journey across the Sahara. The two sets of merchants met in **Timbuktu** (tim buk tü′) and other trading centers. Many historians think that Timbuktu reached its peak when the people of **Songhai** conquered Mali in the 1400s.

THE CENTER OF COMMERCE

Of all the many crossroads on the savanna, Timbuktu was West Africa's center of commerce. Even as Ghana fell and Mali rose, this village along the Niger River held a leading place in trade. One of Timbuktu's most famous rulers was a Mali king named **Mansa Musa**. According to one visitor from North Africa:

> [Mansa Musa] is the most powerful of the [West African] kings; he is the most able to do good to those around him.

If you could go back in time to visit Timbuktu under Mansa Musa, you would be amazed by the number of people always coming and going. "Caravans come to Timbuktu from all points on the horizon," wrote one merchant. The photograph of an old map on this page shows Mansa Musa and an Arab traveler. As you see, Mansa Musa is tempting a caravan leader with a golden nugget.

Timbuktu was a strong magnet for traders. It even drew famous Muslim scholars who wrote about what they saw. For example, **Leo Africanus** visited the city. He wrote down his view of Timbuktu in about 1512 when he returned to his home in Morocco.

> I myself found a great many doctors, judges, priests, and other learned men, that have bountiful [rich] lives at the king's cost. . . . The rulers and peoples of these lands are most rich and generous.

Tales of the wealth of Timbuktu spread as far as Europe. This ancient Spanish map shows Mansa Musa offering gold for trade.

"THE SILENT TRADE"

Imagine that you are traveling through West Africa with Leo Africanus. You stop to watch West Africa's elaborate trading rituals, called "the silent trade." At a spot along the Niger River near Timbuktu, Arab traders pile their slabs of salt in neat rows. Pounding on drums, they invite the gold merchants to trade. Then the Arabs mount their camels and ride away.

Once the Arabs are out of sight, the gold merchants arrive, look over the piles of salt, leave some of their gold, and withdraw into hiding. Next the Arabs return and decide whether enough gold has been offered for their salt. If so, they take the gold and leave. If not, they beat their drums, suggesting a second round of trading. Thus, the traders swap salt for gold without either group meeting face to face.

SWAHILI CITY-STATES

Trade was also a key part of the lives of the people who lived along the eastern coast of Africa. From 1100 to 1500 there were more than 35 city-states. This new culture came to be known as *Swahili* (swä hē′ lē), which is an Arabic term meaning "people of the coast." At Swahili ports, trading vessels arrived from Arabia, India, and China. In the marketplaces of Kilwa, Mombasa, and Zanzibar, Arab merchants exchanged bowls and vases from China, jewels and cotton from India, and African ivory, gold, and rhinoceros horns.

The African gold and ivory in Swahili markets came from the interior. Gold mines, for example, were found near Zimbabwe (zim bäb′ wē). The ruins of its massive walls still rise over the southern savanna.

The ruins of Zimbabwe tell the glory of an ancient African kingdom. A modern African nation was renamed Zimbabwe in its honor.

A VALUABLE LEGACY

As you have read, the glory of the West African empires is known because many travelers thought to write about their visits. The West Africans themselves had no written language at that time. You have read, however, about how they developed a culture built on trade and trust. Trade was the legacy of the West African empires to the future. In the next chapter you will see this valuable contribution when you read about the later Africans.

Check Your Reading

1. What were the names of West Africa's trading empires?
2. How did West Africa develop as a center of commerce?
3. **GEOGRAPHY SKILL:** Name three ways the Niger and Senegal rivers were important geographic features.
4. **THINKING SKILL:** How did gold and salt cause the growth of the West African empires?

425

Understanding Map Projections

Key Vocabulary

distortion
projection
equal-area projection
mercator projection
polar projection

Maps and globes are both ways of representing the earth. A globe, like the earth, is a sphere. As you know, globes are the most accurate representations of the earth. You will recall having studied that on a globe, sizes, shapes, distances, and directions are shown correctly.

You also know that maps are drawings of the earth or part of the earth, on a flat surface. However, did you know that because the earth is a sphere and maps are flat, no map can show the earth in a way that is completely accurate.

Distortion and Projection

To show what is on a globe on a flat surface, parts of the globe must be cut or stretched. The cutting and stretching result in errors called distortion. All maps have distortion. No map can show all the properties of the earth (size, shape, distance, and direction) without one of them being distorted.

Making a map requires some kind of projection. A projection is a systematic way of transferring places on the earth to a map. No projection is perfect. Different projections are used to show different things. Only a few of the hundreds of different projections are often used. You will read about three types of projections.

Equal-Area Projections

Map A, shown below, is drawn on a projection commonly used for showing the whole earth at a glance. This equal-area projection is useful for comparing sizes. Near the center of this map, shapes are fairly accurate, and distances are shown more or less correctly. At the edges of the map, though, shapes and distances are badly distorted. East and west are constant directions on this kind of map. But only along 0° longitude is north directly toward the top of the map and south directly toward the bottom.

Map B, below, is another equal-area projection. Shapes are shown more correctly here than they are on Map A. To show true shapes of land areas, the oceans have been interrupted, or "cut."

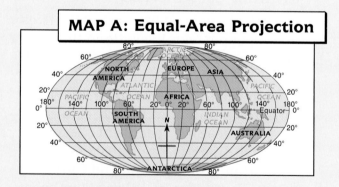

MAP A: Equal-Area Projection

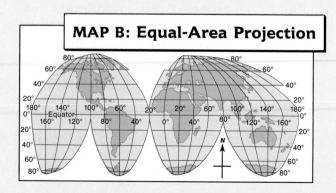

MAP B: Equal-Area Projection

426

Mercator Projections

Map C on this page is a mercator projection. On **Map C** as on **A** and **B**, there is little distortion in areas near the equator. On **Map C**, however, shapes—but not sizes—are shown correctly. Compare Greenland and South America on this map and on your classroom globe. Which appears larger on the map? Which is really larger?

The advantage of **Map C** is that it shows directions correctly. Any straight line on this map is a line of constant compass direction. Thus, as you can understand, navigators of ships use mercator projections to guide them from place to place.

Polar Projections

Polar projections are centered on either the North Pole or South Pole. Most polar projections show only half the earth (a hemisphere) or less. **Map D** is a polar projection centered on the North Pole. Sizes and shapes of places near the pole are accurate, but are distorted at edges.

On **Map D** all lines of longitude are shown as straight lines meeting at the pole. A straight line between any two places on the map that passes through the pole is the shortest distance between them. Distances along these lines are either north or south. Any of these routes that go through the poles are called great-circle routes, which you will learn about on pages 528–529. Because these routes are the shortest, polar projections are used by pilots on polar routes.

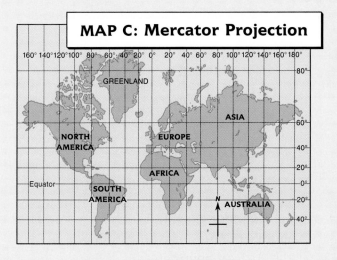

MAP C: Mercator Projection

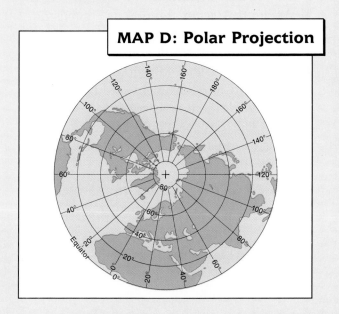

MAP D: Polar Projection

Reviewing the Skill

1. Why are there many different kinds of map projections?
2. Which map, **C** or **D**, would you use to find correct distances? Why?
3. On **Map D** how are lines of latitude shown? Where are east and west?
4. Where is north on **Map D**? In what direction would a plane be flying from the North Pole?
5. Why is it helpful to understand map projections?

427

IMPORTANT EVENTS

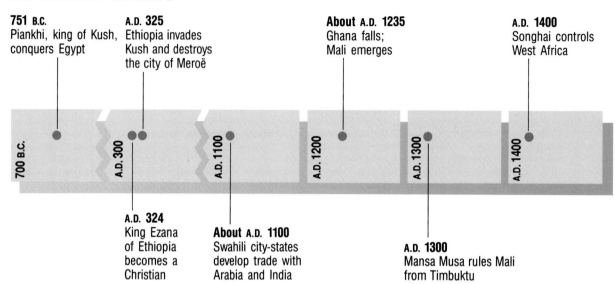

751 B.C.
Piankhi, king of Kush, conquers Egypt

A.D. 325
Ethiopia invades Kush and destroys the city of Meroë

About A.D. 1235
Ghana falls; Mali emerges

A.D. 1400
Songhai controls West Africa

700 B.C.

A.D. 300

A.D. 1100

A.D. 1200

A.D. 1300

A.D. 1400

A.D. 324
King Ezana of Ethiopia becomes a Christian

About A.D. 1100
Swahili city-states develop trade with Arabia and India

A.D. 1300
Mansa Musa rules Mali from Timbuktu

PEOPLE TO KNOW

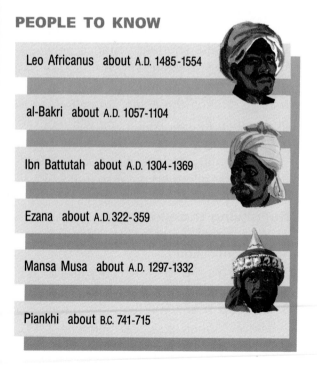

Leo Africanus about A.D. 1485-1554

al-Bakri about A.D. 1057-1104

Ibn Battutah about A.D. 1304-1369

Ezana about A.D. 322-359

Mansa Musa about A.D. 1297-1332

Piankhi about B.C. 741-715

IDEAS TO REMEMBER

■ Africa is a giant continent with great geographic diversity. Deserts, rain forests, and the savanna make up the three main climate and vegetation zones of the African continent.

■ Ancient African kingdoms, such as Kush and Ethiopia, expanded their power through trade and conquest.

■ The West African kingdoms of Ghana, Mali, and Kanem-Bornu owed much of their wealth to a busy trade in gold and salt. The city of Timbuktu was West Africa's most important center of commerce.

REVIEWING VOCABULARY

equatorial   Sahel
rift valleys   savanna

Number a sheet of paper from 1 to 5. Beside each number write the word or term from the list above that best completes each sentence.

1. _____ is an adjective and means "near the equator."
2. The _____ is a belt of semiarid grasslands that borders on the desert.
3. Low-lying areas that extend along ancient fault lines are called _____.
4. Though similar to the American prairie, the African _____ is a good deal warmer.
5. Rain forests are often found in the _____ areas of the world.

REVIEWING FACTS

1. Why does the author call Africa "a continent of incredible diversity"? Which three natural regions make up most of Africa?
2. How did Africa's Great Rift Valley form? How is this different from the formation of other valleys?
3. Many biologists believe that most species of animal life originated in Africa. What feature of modern Africa would seem to support this idea?
4. What was the name of the first African kingdom to conquer Egypt? When did this invasion occur? What did the conquerors borrow from Egypt?
5. How did the city of Axum grow to be rich and powerful? How did the city's location contribute to its wealth and power?

◖◗ WRITING ABOUT MAIN IDEAS

1. **Writing a Newspaper Article:** Imagine that you are a newspaper reporter who is visiting Timbuktu. Write an on-the-scene report for your hometown paper describing "the Silent Trade."
2. **Writing a Comparison of the Kingdoms of Ghana and Mali:** Think about what you have learned about Ghana and Mali. Then write a paragraph in which you describe and compare these two kingdoms.
3. **Writing a Journal Entry:** Imagine you are a European traveling through Ethiopia for the first time. Write a journal entry covering one day of your visit.
4. **Writing About Perspectives:** Write two paragraphs that describe Africa's climate. In the first paragraph tell how a person living in the Sahel would describe Africa's climate. In the second paragraph tell how a person living in the rain forest would describe it.

BUILDING SKILLS: UNDERSTANDING MAP PROJECTIONS

1. How are maps and globes similar? How are they different?
2. Explain the difference between equal-area, mercator, and polar projections.
3. Which kind of map represents the earth more exactly? Explain why.
4. Define the term *distortion* as it relates to the making of maps.
5. Why is it important to know how to compare different map projections?

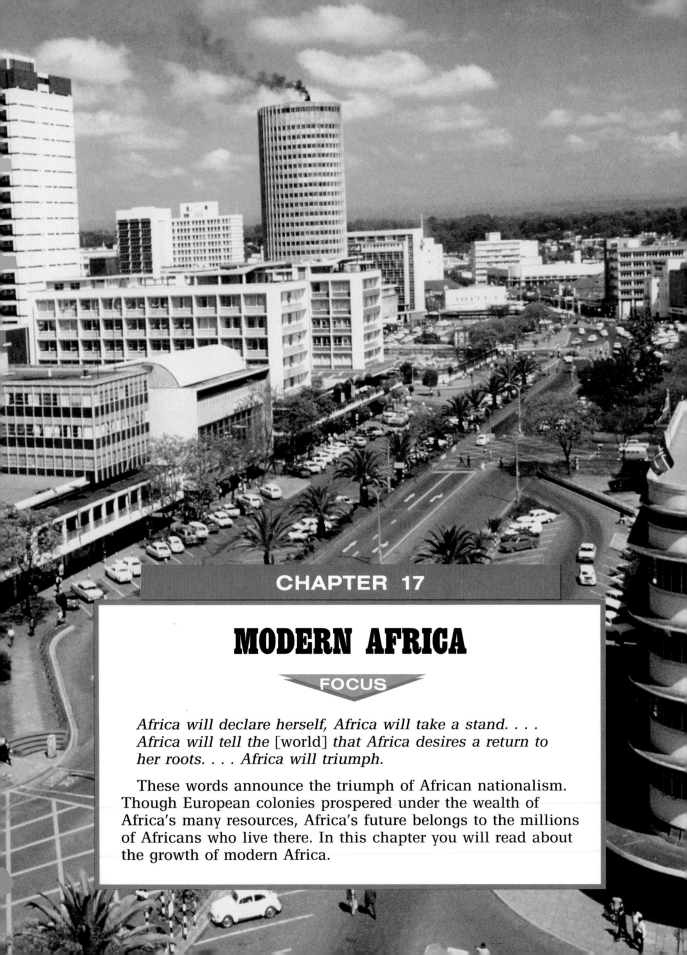

CHAPTER 17

MODERN AFRICA

FOCUS

*Africa will declare herself, Africa will take a stand. . . .
Africa will tell the* [world] *that Africa desires a return to
her roots. . . . Africa will triumph.*

These words announce the triumph of African nationalism.
Though European colonies prospered under the wealth of
Africa's many resources, Africa's future belongs to the millions
of Africans who live there. In this chapter you will read about
the growth of modern Africa.

1 The Age of Imperialism

READx TO LEARN

Key Vocabulary

slave trade
plantation
imperialism
missionary

Key People

Cecil Rhodes
David Livingstone
Henry Stanley

Read Aloud

They raided our city with such might and terror that no one, neither man nor woman, neither the old nor the young, nor even the children, however small, was spared to live.

The sultan of Mombasa used these words to describe the arrival of the first Europeans in Africa. The Portuguese were not friendly visitors. One by one, the Swahili city-states fell to Portuguese attacks. After centuries of independence, Africa began to fall to European guns.

Read for Purpose

1. **WHAT YOU KNOW:** How did the kingdoms of the African savanna differ from the Egyptian Empire?
2. **WHAT YOU WILL LEARN:** How did Africa become a continent of European colonies?

THE PORTUGUESE ARRIVE

The Europeans saw Africa as an obstacle in a very rich trade route. European merchants were far more interested in trade with Persia, India, and China than with the continent of Africa.

Think back to what you read in Chapter 10. You may recall that the Portuguese sailed up and down Africa's western coast during the 1400s. Do you remember that Prince Henry was convinced that there was a water route around Africa to Asia?

You know, of course, that Prince Henry was right. Vasco da Gama successfully sailed his ship around the African continent and reached Asia in 1498. This event was a turning point in African history. As the Europeans discovered new water routes, they also learned more about the riches of Africa. They became determined to obtain these riches. In fact, Portuguese geographers called Africa's west coast the *Gold Coast*. As you know, West Africa deserved that title.

As early as the twelfth century, the **slave trade** was carried on by Arab merchants in East Africa.

THE SLAVE TRADE

Soon after the Portuguese arrived in Africa in the late 1400s, they began to capture African men, women, and children and ship them to Europe as slaves. Over the next 350 years, the main trade carried on between Africa and Europe was trade in humans. The slave trade, as it was called, had been carried on by Arab merchants for hundreds of years in Africa. However, under this system, enslaved people were not treated as harshly and could sometimes gain their freedom after working many years. The practice of slavery changed dramatically when the Europeans became involved.

Portugal and other European nations set up small trading posts and forts along Africa's western and eastern coasts. By the 1600s these outposts had become the center of a trade that forced Africans to cross the Atlantic to North America and South America.

The slave trade had disastrous effects on the people of Africa. Whole communities were destroyed. Families were torn apart. As one Portuguese trader recorded in his journal, "the slave trade is a horror." He also wrote:

We anchored off the mouth of the Senegal River. A few sailors got into a boat and rowed ashore, and hid behind bushes near a village. After waiting a short time, the sailors seized a boy who carried a spear. A small girl wandered nearby and she too was seized. It is possible that the children are from the same family. Delighted, the sailors brought the Africans—like tiny prizes—back to the ship and on to the New World.

UNWILLING COLONISTS

The "New World" to which slave traders took this brother and sister was what the Europeans called the continents of North America and South America. If the Africans survived the difficult voyage across the Atlantic, they were sold to work on sugar or cotton **plantations**, or large farming estates. Plantations required many workers, and the plantation owners wanted to find a steady source of cheap labor. They found that source in the slave markets of Africa.

European slave traders counted on African merchants to bring men, women, and children to trading posts on the coast. The Africans exchanged people for guns, ammunition, and other goods. They used the guns to raid villages and capture more people.

The journal entry you read on this page is only one account of the horrors caused by the slave trade. Before the

slave trade was ended in the 1800s, more than 14 million Africans had been captured and shipped against their will to plantations in the Americas. The greatest number of Africans was taken to Brazil to work on the sugar plantations there. But huge numbers were also brought to the United States.

Countless numbers of African people were forced into dark, filthy ships headed for North America and South America. As the painting on this page shows, they were packed closely together and had no room to move. Many of them died on the ten-week voyage.

THE BIRTH OF IMPERIALISM

The Portuguese were not the only Europeans to bring Africans to the New World as slaves. The English, Spanish, French, Dutch, and Italians all took part in the profitable slave trade. Although the slave trade was outlawed in most nations by the mid-1800s, Europeans continued to control trading posts along Africa's coasts.

By 1850 the European powers had adopted a policy of imperialism. Imperialism is the extension of a country's power over other lands and people by military, political, or economic means. Imperialism is like empire-building. Between 1850 and 1914, European nations divided much of the globe among themselves. This period of time is called the Age of Imperialism.

Imperialist governments proudly displayed world maps with their nation's colonies in bright colors. British colonies, for example, usually appeared in red. The British Empire was the largest empire the world had ever known, covering an area 100 times bigger than the island of Britain. In fact, Britain controlled territory on every continent but Antarctica. About one fourth of the world's land and people were held under British rule.

433

IMPERIALISM IN AFRICA

Africa was the continent that was most affected by imperialism. European colonies were established across the continent. Some colonies were used to provide land for European settlement. Other colonies were used to help provide raw materials that were needed for industry in Europe.

The Industrial Revolution had an important effect on the growth of imperialism. Due to new technology, European imperialists gained not only the weapons needed to win an empire, but also the means to control it. Steamships, railroads, telegraph cables, and other inventions allowed nations to keep in close touch with faraway colonies.

This new technology also caused Europeans to think that they were "superior" to the people of Africa. Moreover, European imperialists believed that they had a right and a duty to conquer other countries. The Europeans may have wanted to bring new technology to Africa, but they also needed Africa's precious minerals for their industries in Europe. Indeed, many Europeans who arrived to live in Africa believed that they were "of the first race in the world." One such European, named Cecil Rhodes, wrote:

I believe that we Britons are of the first race in the world, and the more of the world we inhabit, the better it is. I believe it is my duty to God, my queen, and my country to paint the whole map of Africa red [the color of the British colonies on maps]—red from the Cape of Good Hope to Cairo.

Imperialism led to many changes. While many Europeans in the colonies lived in luxury, Africans often were treated like slaves.

MISSIONARIES IN AFRICA

Imperialism also had religious causes. The push for expansion often came from European missionaries. Missionaries were religious teachers who wanted to spread their beliefs to people in lands beyond Europe. Most missionaries also believed that European rule in Africa was the best way to end the evil practices of slave trading.

One of the most famous missionaries was David Livingstone. A Protestant minister and doctor from Scotland, Livingstone went to Africa in 1841 to "teach religion and heal the sick." He grieved to see East Africans carried off to be sold as slaves in Arabian, Turkish, and Persian lands.

When David Livingstone wrote a book about his work in Africa, thousands of people in Europe and the United States bought copies. People all over the world wanted to learn more about the African continent.

"DOCTOR LIVINGSTONE, I PRESUME?"

Livingstone was not only a missionary and doctor but also an explorer. Between 1851 and 1873, Livingstone traced the route of the Zambezi River, crossed the Kalahari Desert, and located "The Smoke that Thunders," or Victoria Falls.

In the late 1860s Livingstone traveled deep into the heart of the continent for evidence to use against the slave trade. When a few years passed with no word from him, many people feared he was dead. An American newspaper hired a reporter named Henry Stanley to find Livingstone.

David Livingstone was not lost in a remote part of Africa when Stanley found him in 1871. He was going about his work as a missionary, doctor, and explorer in a region where he was known and loved. In fact, Livingstone was looking for the source of the Nile River. Stanley's account of the meeting was published in newspapers around the world. It read:

> After ten months of hard travel in Africa, I found the man. As I drew near to him I noticed he was pale, looked tired, and had a gray beard. . . . Indeed, I would have rushed to him, cheered, and embraced him, but it occurred to me that I was uninvited. So I took off my hat and simply said, "Doctor Livingstone, I presume?"

A PATCHWORK QUILT

Finding Livingstone made Stanley the world's most famous reporter. Stanley's next trip to Africa established him as an explorer. In 1877 he sailed

Magazines all over the world ran stories about Livingstone and Stanley. The drawing at left shows Stanley's journey. Above, you can see the joyful meeting.

around Lake Victoria and proved that it was the source of the Nile River. Later, by tracing the Congo River west to the Atlantic Ocean, he proved it was possible to cross Africa from the Indian Ocean to the Atlantic Ocean.

Stanley returned to the Congo River Valley in 1879. Since this trip was paid for by Belgium, Stanley claimed most of the Congo River Valley for the Belgian king. The scramble for African territory had begun. Soon Britain, Germany, Italy, Portugal, and Spain were also staking claims to parts of Africa.

The competition was so fierce that countries feared it would result in a war. To prevent fighting, representatives from European countries met in Berlin, Germany in 1884 and 1885. Even though this meeting was about

MAP SKILL: By 1914 European countries controlled nearly all of Africa. Who dominated most of northwestern Africa?

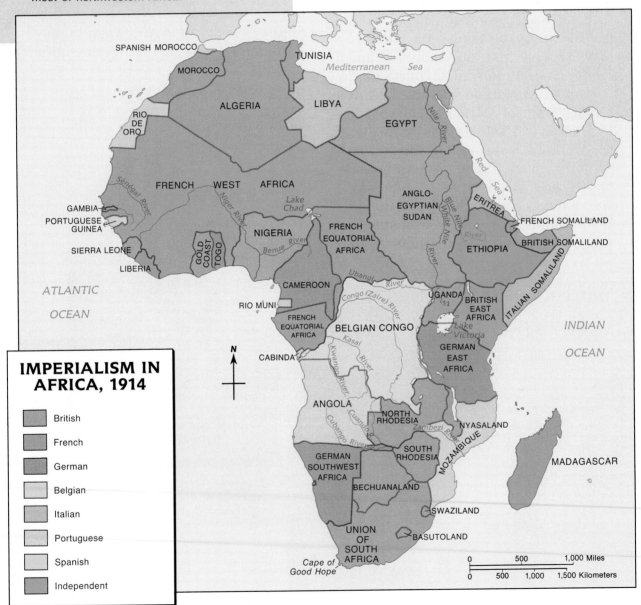

IMPERIALISM IN AFRICA, 1914

- British
- French
- German
- Belgian
- Italian
- Portuguese
- Spanish
- Independent

The British Museum displayed stuffed giraffes. The envelope at right was sent to Africa from Britain.

Africa's future, the imperialist leaders of Europe did not invite any African rulers. The Europeans agreed that any European country could claim land in Africa simply by sending troops. As a result, by 1914, a map of Africa looked like a patchwork quilt of many colors.

THE EFFECTS OF IMPERIALISM

Imperialism had a devastating effect on Africa. The people of Africa often had to change their ways of life under European rule. Local governments often lost their power when Europeans came in and gave orders. European missionaries forced many Africans to abandon their traditional religious beliefs. People took new jobs in order to pay the taxes charged by European rulers. Many young men left their villages to work in mines or on coffee and cocoa plantations. Villages often suffered from this loss of workers and leaders. Many Africans resisted by rebelling against European rule. Others adjusted to imperialism by adopting European customs.

A CONTINENT OF COLONIES

The African people were now second-class citizens in their own land. They could not stand against the guns and technology of the Europeans. But this would not be the case forever. As one leader from Senegal wrote after the French seized his country:

The blacks had slept long; perhaps too long. But beware! Those who have slept long and soundly, when once they wake up, will not easily fall back to sleep again.

Check Your Reading

1. Describe the slave trade.
2. How did the Industrial Revolution encourage European imperialism?
3. **GEOGRAPHY SKILL:** Use the map on page 436 to identify the German and French colonies in Africa.
4. **THINKING SKILL:** Reread the words of Cecil Rhodes on page 434. What is his point of view?

437

Drawing Conclusions

Imagine that your sister ran for the student council last year. She hung campaign posters in the hallways and made speeches every day. She even called up all her friends reminding them to vote. Then she won the election. You might conclude that a lot of campaigning helped your sister win the election.

Drawing a conclusion is pulling together pieces of information so that they mean something. A conclusion is an end point of a process. It is a statement about information that has been presented. But it does not repeat any of that information.

Learning how to draw conclusions will help you learn history. When you study, you should try to use the facts that you find to draw conclusions about the meaning of the facts.

Trying the Skill

Read the following statements. Then draw conclusions about the lives of Africans who had to live under colonial rule. Read these points carefully.

- Africans were punished if they disobeyed their colonial rulers.
- Africans were often forced to work for their rulers without pay.
- Africans rarely had even the smallest amount of political power during the period of colonial rule.

1. What conclusions did you draw?
2. What did you do to draw your conclusions?
3. When is it important to be able to draw conclusions?

HELPING YOURSELF

The steps on the left will help you to draw conclusions. The example on the right shows how you can apply these steps to the statements on page 438.

One Way to Draw Conclusions	Example
1. Identify the topic of all the information given.	The topic is how colonial rule affected people in Africa.
2. Skim, or quickly read through, the information.	Read through the information quickly to get the general picture that the facts create.
3. Find any common features.	You might find that all three statements tell how foreign rulers treated Africans.
4. Write a sentence that tells how the common features are connected to each other and to the subject.	Put the ideas together so that they make sense. Remember not to repeat any of the information given. Here is one example: "The colonial rulers treated the Africans as though they were slaves."

Applying the Skill

Now apply what you have learned by drawing a conclusion from the following statements.

- To escape British rule, Dutch settlers in South Africa, called Boers, moved inland around 1830.
- After the British colonial government abolished slavery in 1833, many Boers left the British-controlled regions of South Africa for the interior.
- When gold was discovered in lands under the control of the Boers, a war broke out between the Boers and Great Britain.

1. What is the topic of the three statements above?
   a. the history of the Boers
   b. the African gold rush
   c. the abolition of slavery

2. What common feature do all of the statements share?
   a. British colonial rule
   b. anti-European feelings by the Boers
   c. the economy of Africa

3. Which of the following might be a conclusion drawn from the information in column one?
   a. The Boers fought to continue owning enslaved people.
   b. The Boers were farmers and cattle ranchers.
   c. The Boers did not feel loyal to any European country.

Reviewing the Skill

1. What is drawing a conclusion?
2. Name some steps you could take to draw conclusions.
3. When is it important to be able to draw conclusions?

READ TO LEARN

Key Vocabulary

boycott
apartheid
sanction

Key People

Kwame Nkrumah
Sékou Touré
Jomo Kenyatta
Nelson Mandela

Key Places

Ghana
Guinea
Kenya
South Africa

Read Aloud

Africa
mother of children
determined
to prescribe [declare] *themselves free.*

Freedom means a great deal to poet Ilva Mackay. She was jailed twice for speaking out against South Africa's unfair laws. In this lesson you will read about Africans like Mackay who have struggled to control their future.

Read for Purpose

1. **WHAT YOU KNOW:** How did colonialism change Africa?
2. **WHAT YOU WILL LEARN:** How have Africans achieved independence?

UHURU! UHURU!

Since 1957 the powerful Swahili slogan *Uhuru! Uhuru!* has been the rallying cry of millions of Africans. These words hold great meaning. If you heard them in English, you would understand the words "Freedom! Freedom!"

At midnight on March 6, 1957, this slogan became a reality in Accra, the capital of the British colony called the Gold Coast. Thousands of Africans and Europeans watched silently as the British flag was lowered. Then, very slowly, a red, green, and gold flag was raised. At that moment the colony of the Gold Coast became the independent nation of Ghana (gä′ nə).

Ghana was the first black African nation to win its independence from colonial rule. But even as the people of the world's newest nation were celebrating, most of Africa was still governed by Europeans. Kwame Nkrumah (kwäm′ ē en krü′ mə), who was Ghana's new prime minister, warned his people about the great challenges that still faced most Africans.

Our independence is meaningless unless it is linked up with the total liberation of the African continent.

FIGHTING COLONIAL RULE

The people of Africa had long fought against colonial rule. During the Age of Imperialism, independence movements had emerged in Egypt, the Gold Coast, and Rhodesia. Not until after World War II, however, did the drive for independence meet with success. Many leaders of the African independence movements were inspired by the strategies that Mohandas Gandhi had developed in the British colony of India. You will read more about this Indian leader in Chapter 18.

To gain support for the independence movement, Nkrumah helped organize **boycotts** against the colonial governments. A boycott is a special kind of protest in which a group of people refuse to buy or use goods that were produced by another group. Many people in the French colony of **Guinea** (gin′ ē) also believed that it was better to do without European goods. A leader from Guinea named **Sékou Touré** (sā′ kü tou rā′) explained this position to the colonial rulers.

We prefer poverty in freedom to riches in slavery. Take your fancy jewels and take your fancy technology away from us and go back to France. At last we shall live freely and with our dignity.

The boycotts that Touré led against French goods helped to bring about the independence of Guinea in 1958.

A STRUGGLE FOR INDEPENDENCE

Leaders in Guinea and Ghana worked largely through peaceful channels to gain independence for their countries. In other African countries, however, people died in violent struggles for independence.

The people of Ghana celebrated their newly won independence on March 6, 1957. A year later, Sékou Touré led Guinea to freedom.

441

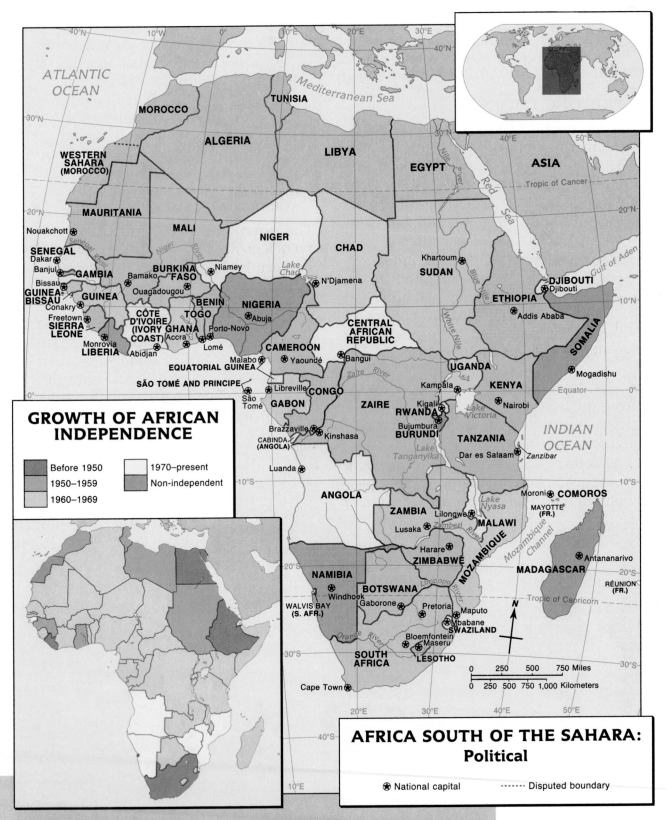

GROWTH OF AFRICAN INDEPENDENCE

Before 1950
1950–1959
1960–1969
1970–present
Non-independent

ATLANTIC OCEAN

Mediterranean Sea

MOROCCO
TUNISIA
ALGERIA
LIBYA
EGYPT
ASIA

Tropic of Cancer

WESTERN SAHARA (MOROCCO)

MAURITANIA
Nouakchott
MALI
NIGER
CHAD
SUDAN
Khartoum

SENEGAL
Dakar
Banjul
GAMBIA
Bissau
GUINEA-BISSAU
Conakry
GUINEA
Freetown
SIERRA LEONE
Monrovia
LIBERIA
BURKINA FASO
Niamey
Bamako
Ouagadougou
CÔTE D'IVOIRE (IVORY COAST)
Abidjan
GHANA
Accra
BENIN
TOGO
Porto-Novo
Lomé
NIGERIA
Abuja
N'Djamena
Lake Chad

DJIBOUTI
Djibouti
ETHIOPIA
Addis Ababa
SOMALIA

CENTRAL AFRICAN REPUBLIC
CAMEROON
Yaoundé
Bangui
Malabo
EQUATORIAL GUINEA
SÃO TOMÉ AND PRINCIPE
São Tomé
Libreville
GABON
CONGO
Brazzaville
CABINDA (ANGOLA)
Kinshasa
ZAIRE
UGANDA
Kampala
Kigali
RWANDA
Bujumbura
BURUNDI
KENYA
Nairobi
Mogadishu
Equator

TANZANIA
Dar es Salaam
Zanzibar
Lake Victoria
Lake Tanganyika

Luanda
ANGOLA
ZAMBIA
Lusaka
Lilongwe
MALAWI
Lake Nyasa
Moroni
COMOROS
MAYOTTE (FR.)
INDIAN OCEAN

Harare
ZIMBABWE
MOZAMBIQUE
Mozambique Channel
Antananarivo
MADAGASCAR
RÉUNION (FR.)

NAMIBIA
Windhoek
WALVIS BAY (S. AFR.)
BOTSWANA
Gaborone
Pretoria
Maputo
Mbabane
SWAZILAND
Bloemfontein
Maseru
LESOTHO
SOUTH AFRICA
Cape Town

Tropic of Capricorn

N

0   250   500   750 Miles
0   250 500 750 1,000 Kilometers

AFRICA SOUTH OF THE SAHARA: Political

⊛ National capital   ······· Disputed boundary

MAP SKILL: Use both maps to identify the countries in Africa that became independent between 1950 and 1959.

British imperialism in Kenya left African people with no power in their own land. Although they only numbered 30,000, Europeans controlled Kenya's government and economy. In the late 1940s, the bitter frustration felt by many Kenyans erupted into violence. A secret movement among black Africans called Mau Mau (mou mou) staged what the British called acts of terrorism. The British held the Mau Mau responsible for the deaths of 40 whites in Kenya.

In an effort to eliminate support for the Mau Mau, British leaders put thousands of nationalist supporters in jail. One of those jailed was Jomo Kenyatta (jō' mō ken yä' tə), the leader of Kenya's nationalist movement. The British accused Kenyatta of leading the Mau Mau, although he had condemned that group's acts of terrorism.

During the eight years that he remained in prison, Kenyatta's popularity among the people grew. When Kenya won its independence in 1963, Kenyatta was elected to be the country's first prime minister. As you can see from the map on page 442, Africa is no longer a continent of colonies.

APARTHEID IN SOUTH AFRICA

The only sub-Saharan nation that is not controlled by black Africans is South Africa. Although South Africa gained its independence from Britain in 1931, it remained under the rule of a white minority. Today whites control virtually all of South Africa's valuable land and mineral resources, including the richest gold and diamond mines in Africa. Black South Africans still have no voice in South Africa's government, even though they make up more than 75 percent of the country's population.

In 1948 the white rulers of South Africa set up a system of laws called apartheid (ə pär' tīd). *Apartheid* means "separateness" in Afrikaans (af ri käns'), the language related to Dutch that is spoken by many white South Africans. Under apartheid it was against the law for whites and people of other races to live in the same area, attend the same schools, or even use the same drinking fountains. The South African government enforced these laws with a powerful army and police force.

People who protested the unfairness of apartheid were put in prison. Many prisoners died from the brutal treatment that they received while in jail.

In South Africa the system of apartheid separated people. Apartheid laws made it illegal for blacks and whites to share public facilities.

Nelson Mandela has been an important leader in the effort to bring equality to all South Africans.

In the 1950s, a young lawyer named Nelson Mandela became a leader in the struggle against apartheid. He, too, was imprisoned in 1964. Before going to jail, Mandela declared:

> I have cherished the idea of a democratic and free society in which all persons live together in harmony. . . . It is an ideal which I hope to live for and to achieve. But if need be, it is an ideal for which I am prepared to die.

SEEKING FREEDOM

Although South African leaders put Mandela in prison, they could not stop his ideals from spreading throughout South Africa and the world. In the 1980s clashes between anti-apartheid groups and the South African army reached a peak. World leaders began to pressure the South African government to end apartheid.

In 1986 the European Community and the United States called for sanctions against South Africa. Sanctions are actions by one or more countries that keep certain benefits from another country. For example, the United States refused to buy South African farm products after 1986, which cost South Africa $400 million in lost trade.

In 1990 President F. W. de Klerk began responding to anti-apartheid pressures inside and outside his country. He released Nelson Mandela from prison and brought an end to many of the apartheid laws. Soon the sanctions against South Africa were dropped. In 1991 Nelson Mandela and other black leaders began to work with the South African government to finally gain voting rights for black South Africans. Although there has been progress, many changes remain to be made before democracy is fully achieved in South Africa.

CHALLENGES AND CHANGES

Their common struggle for independence from colonial rule has united the more than 500 million people who live in Africa south of the Sahara. But in other ways, Africans are very different from one another. People in various parts of Africa look very different and speak different languages. In fact, the people of Africa speak more than 1,000 different languages. Many Africans speak more than one language.

Most Africans today live in the densely populated regions of West Africa, in the lake areas of East Africa, and in coastal areas. Few people live in the desert and rain-forest regions. Although most Africans make their homes in rural areas, about one in every four Africans lives in a city.

Although Africans have won their struggle for independence, other difficult problems remain. Colonial rule left huge problems throughout the

Rural farms in Zambia, market towns in Côte d'Ivoire, and huge cities like Lagos, Nigeria, are all part of modern Africa.

continent. Before Europeans arrived, most of Africa was self-sufficient and its resources were shared by the people. Europeans carved the continent into separate areas and took control of Africa's gold, oil, agriculture, and other valuable resources. The result was poverty for millions of Africans.

Today, Africans are finding different ways to solve these problems. In some urban areas, new industries such as electronics and textiles have provided jobs. In other areas, people have returned to traditional methods of agriculture. Developed over thousands of years, these farming methods often provide more food than the large-scale agriculture that was introduced by Europeans. Traditional farming also helps to protect the environment by limiting erosion and pollution.

LOOKING TO THE FUTURE

People in Africa south of the Sahara have faced many challenges and changes in the twentieth century. Africans won independence for their countries after many years of colonial rule. But even independence could not bring an end to some of Africa's most troubling problems.

Life in Africa today is a blend of the modern and the traditional. Although many new changes have come to Africa, many Africans continue to draw on their rich history in many ways. You will read about one important African tradition on pages 448–451.

Check Your Reading

1. Why was *Uhuru!* such a powerful word in Africa during the 1950s?
2. In what different ways have Africans achieved their independence?
3. Why do black South Africans still not share equally in South African society?
4. **THINKING SKILL:** What are three causes that helped bring an end to apartheid?

445

1960—Should Colonialism Continue in Africa?

In early 1960 British Prime Minister Harold Macmillan visited Britain's African colonies. He was impressed by the strength of African nationalism. He found that the desire of Africans to regain their independence from European rule was widespread.

In different places it may take different forms, but it is happening everywhere. The wind of change is blowing through the continent.

As Macmillan said, the desire for freedom took "different forms." In order to understand the "wind of change," it is very important to realize that many of Europe's African colonies had thousands of white settlers—settlers whose families had lived in Africa for generations. These people believed that Africa was their home. In the British colony of Rhodesia, for example, a powerful white minority wished to set up its new government. Black Africans, however, demanded an equal role.

POINT ☆

Self-Government Over Time

David Hawke was a white Rhodesian whose family had lived in Africa for more than a century. His ideas express the position of many white settlers.

Self-government needs people who will take an active role in society. A great percentage of our black African people must first gain learning, skill, and wealth to take on this role. This education will be better not only for the economy of a new nation, but for the social and political progress of the country. Africans must be trained to play a full part in the life of the country.

I have no quarrel with political progress for all our people. We must move in steady stages—one step at a time. We must protect the unskilled and uneducated. We must allow democracy to unfold over the people, gradually and over time. It may even be that British or American democracy is not suited to the people of this continent. Perhaps Africa must slowly develop its own form of democracy. It will need time.

● Why did David Hawke want democracy to come slowly to Rhodesia?

COUNTERPOINT ☆

Self-Government Now

One of the strongest arguments for the right of black Africans to govern themselves was written by Touba Dewala, a black teacher from Kenya.

Democracy in Africa must be allowed to spread quickly. If not, something else will take its place. Some other form of European imperialism will poison our continent.

Africans must rule themselves like any other people. We are not perfect. But we demand the right to govern ourselves. I do not believe that Africa needs to prove to Europe that it is capable of self-government. Why should we care what Europeans think? Have they forgotten all they have taken from us? Have they forgotten their own history? They forget that there is not a single European nation that has a clean record. Under Europe's leadership, the world saw two devastating world wars. Therefore it is no excuse to deny Africans the right to rule themselves on the grounds that they cannot rule well. We must govern ourselves.

● Why did Touba Dewala believe that freedom should come quickly to Africa?

UNDERSTANDING THE POINT/COUNTERPOINT

1. Who do you think made the stronger argument about whether black Africans should have self-government?
2. What opinions might Americans have expressed about the issue of African self-government?
3. Can you suggest a compromise that might have been acceptable to both David Hawke and Touba Dewala?

KENTE: A TRADITION IN CLOTH

by Herbert M. Cole

What can clothing tell us about a person and a culture? Look at the photograph to the left. It shows the current king of the Asante (ə sän' tē) people, who live in the West African nation of Ghana. The king's beautiful robe and gold jewelry suggest that he is very wealthy and highly respected. The multicolored robe the king is wearing is called a Kente (ken' tā) cloth.

Kente cloth was first woven by people in the ancient kingdoms of West Africa, which you read about in Chapter 16. The people of these kingdoms developed a style of weaving that lives on today. Their descendants, the Asante and the Ewe (ā' vā) of Ghana and Togo, have been making and wearing Kente cloth for centuries. The technique of weaving Kente cloth is passed down from generation to generation. Making and wearing Kente cloth are traditions that go back hundreds of years in West Africa. As you read this lesson, think about why Kente cloth is a source of pride to West Africans and to people of African ancestry all over the world.

A FAMILY OF WEAVERS

Anani peers over his father's shoulder. He watches his father's hands quickly moving orange and blue threads across a narrow loom (lüm). A loom is a machine for weaving thread into cloth, and the narrow cloth strip that Anani's father weaves is made up of beautiful patterns. Anani is twelve years old and he looks forward to the day when he will be able to sit on a stool next to his father, weaving colorful threads into beautiful strips of cloth. He pictures his favorite Kente patterns and imagines them appearing under his own hands on the loom in front of him.

Kente cloth is made only by special families of weavers. Anani and his father belong to a family of Ewe weavers. They live in a city not far from Accra, the

capital of Ghana. Anani's father learned to weave Kente by watching his own father work at his loom. Someday, Anani too will be a master weaver, and he will probably teach his own sons to make Kente cloth. Although Anani's sister and mother wear Kente cloths, they do not weave them. Women in West Africa weave wider cloth bands on different kinds of looms, but only men weave Kente.

Although Anani is eager to work on a loom of his own, he knows there is much to learn first. Kente cloth is made of narrow strips woven together into a single large rectangle that is wrapped around the body. Many times, Anani has watched his father at work. First he weaves the threads into strips many feet long and two to three inches wide. Then he cuts the long strips into shorter lengths and sews them together edge to edge.

THE CLOTHING OF KINGS

Anani has seen the incredibly beautiful Kente cloths worn by the kings and chiefs of the Ewe and Asante peoples. The richest and most spectacular Kente cloths are worn by chiefs and kings to show their wealth and high status. These cloths are very expensive. They are woven of silk threads instead of the usual cotton. It has always been an unwritten rule among the Ewe and the Asante that no one can wear a Kente cloth more beautiful than the one worn by the king.

In the past certain patterns of Kente cloth were reserved for special occasions. Ceremonies in which teenagers passed into adulthood required one pattern. People wore another design to funerals. Special designs were also worn by members of particular professions. One pattern was commonly worn by Kente weavers, while another was worn by priests. When Asante chiefs were called upon to act as judges, they wore Kente cloth bearing an intricate blue-and-white design called a "liar's pattern." It was believed that the presence of this cloth made it impossible for people to lie to the chief.

AN ARTISTIC TRADITION

The making and wearing of Kente cloth are traditions that are very old. In dry caves several hundred miles north of Ghana and Togo, narrow strips of cloth have been found that are nearly 1,000 years old. These strips are considered the earliest known examples of Kente cloth. They are blue and white, simpler in color than Kente worn today.

Over the centuries Ewe and Asante weavers have developed and refined the art of weaving Kente cloth. They have created hundreds of different patterns and designs. Each design or pattern has its own name, and many have special meanings, too. A cloth with a cross-shaped design refers to the saying, "Every man carries his own mark." This means that every person has his or her own personality. A design that is shaped like a hand recalls the saying, "It is with the hand that we work."

A SPREADING TRADITION

Today people outside of West Africa know about the beauty of Kente cloth. Wearing Kente has become popular among African Americans in the United States and among people of African ancestry in other parts of the world. People whose ancestors came from West Africa are particularly proud to wear Kente patterns.

When Kente cloth is imported from Ghana and Togo to the United States, it is often cut and sewn to make hats, shirts, pants, dresses, and even bow ties. The beautiful patterns of Kente cloth woven in West Africa have also been copied and produced in large quantities by factories in the United States. From a distance this machine-made cloth looks very similar to handmade Kente, but up close it is clear that real Kente is much richer and more beautiful.

Because the handmade cloth is so beautiful, the tradition of weaving and wearing Kente cloth remains strong in Ghana and Togo. Families like Anani's continue to teach their sons to weave colorful threads into beautiful strips of cloth. Every year, more people all over the world learn about the beautiful cloth produced by this West African weaving tradition.

Why has the wearing of Kente cloth become popular among people of African ancestry all over the world?

IMPORTANT EVENTS

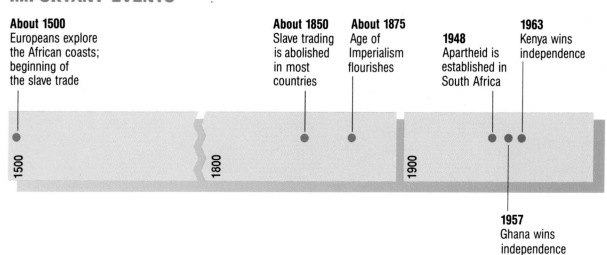

About 1500
Europeans explore
the African coasts;
beginning of
the slave trade

About 1850
Slave trading
is abolished
in most
countries

About 1875
Age of
Imperialism
flourishes

1948
Apartheid is
established in
South Africa

1963
Kenya wins
independence

1500

1800

1900

1957
Ghana wins
independence

PEOPLE TO KNOW

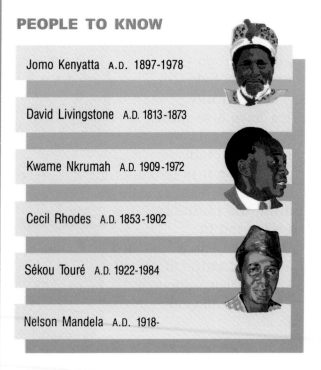

Jomo Kenyatta A.D. 1897-1978

David Livingstone A.D. 1813-1873

Kwame Nkrumah A.D. 1909-1972

Cecil Rhodes A.D. 1853-1902

Sékou Touré A.D. 1922-1984

Nelson Mandela A.D. 1918-

IDEAS TO REMEMBER

■ For 350 years the slave trade was the largest and most profitable type of trade between Europe and Africa. Between 1850 and 1914 European imperialism divided Africa into a patchwork of colonies.

■ African nations struggled for many years to become independent from colonial rule. Ghana became the first black African nation to achieve independence from colonial rule. Today Africa is no longer a continent of colonies.

REVIEWING VOCABULARY

apartheid   sanction
imperialism   slave trade
missionaries

Number a sheet of paper from 1 to 5. Beside each number write the word or term from the list above that best matches each statement.

1. This word means "separateness," and refers to a system of laws in South Africa that creates much inequality.
2. Often used against South Africa, this is an action taken by one country to hurt another country.
3. This action brought millions of Africans to America against their will.
4. This policy of extending national power over other lands brought much of the world under European control by 1900.
5. These people came from Europe and spread their religious beliefs among the people of Africa.

REVIEWING FACTS

1. Why did Europeans at first view Africa as an obstacle to trade with Asia?
2. What European country was first to trade with Africa? What other countries became involved in trade and conquest with African nations?
3. How did the slave trade change in Africa after the Europeans became involved in it?
4. What was the Age of Imperialism?
5. What were the main reasons for imperialism in Africa?
6. Who was David Livingstone? What was he doing in Africa?

7. What was the first black nation to achieve independence from colonial rule after World War II?
8. Describe how Sékou Touré helped Guinea to free itself from French colonial rule.
9. What African group used terrorism to end colonial rule? How did this method differ from the boycott as a means of achieving independence?
10. What methods did the government of South Africa use to maintain apartheid?

WRITING ABOUT MAIN IDEAS

1. **Writing a Letter:** Imagine that you have a pen pal who lives in Lagos, Nigeria. Write to him or her about your community. Ask your pen pal about life in Lagos.
2. **Writing About Perspectives:** Write a paragraph expressing your opinion about whether sanctions were effective in pressuring the government of South Africa to end apartheid.

BUILDING SKILLS: DRAWING CONCLUSIONS

1. Draw a conclusion from the following facts.
   - In 1948, the white rulers of South Africa set up a system of apartheid.
   - In South Africa, it was illegal for whites and other races to live in the same area.
   - Black Africans made up over 75 percent of South Africa's population and had no voice in government.
2. What steps did you use to draw a conclusion?

REVIEWING VOCABULARY

Number a sheet of paper from 1 to 10. Beside each number write whether the following statements are true or false. If a statement is true, write **T**. If it is false, rewrite the sentence using the underlined vocabulary word or term correctly.

1. A rift valley is a valley that forms along a fault, often with steep-sided cliffs that mark the fault's edges.
2. Apartheid means "togetherness" and refers to a government policy that is designed to overcome racial hatred in South Africa.
3. Equatorial is an adjective that means "near the equator."
4. The European slave trade in Africa was established by the Portuguese in the late 1400s and lasted for 350 years.
5. Terrorism is the deliberate use of fear and violence to force a government to meet a group's demands.
6. The savanna is a type of grassland in Africa that is identical to the prairies of North America.
7. Sahel means "border" and refers to a narrow belt of semiarid grassland on the edge of Africa's desert lands.
8. Imperialism is the extension of a country's power beyond its borders by military, political, or economic means.
9. A boycott is a special kind of protest in which people refuse to buy or use certain goods.
10. A sanction is a policy of forming stronger economic, military, or political ties with another nation.

WRITING ABOUT THE UNIT

1. **Writing a Report:** Write a report comparing and contrasting the struggle against apartheid in South Africa with the Civil Rights struggle in the United States in the 1950s and 1960s. How were the movements alike and how were they different?
2. **Writing a Paragraph:** Write a short paragraph about the different natural regions of Africa. For each region, describe its landforms, climate, and vegetation.
3. **Writing About Perspectives:** Imagine that you are a captured African who is crossing the Atlantic on a slave ship. Describe your feelings and the conditions you experience during one day of the crossing.

ACTIVITIES

1. **Researching a Contemporary African Issue:** Widespread drought and famine in the African Sahel have focused world attention on this region in recent years. Gather articles about events in the Sahel from newspapers and magazines, then write a summary of your findings.
2. **Working Together on a Map:** With your classmates draw a map of Africa that shows the countries, major cities, and important geographic features, such as lakes, rivers, and mountain ranges. Collect pictures of places of interest in Africa and connect each picture with colored string to its location on the map. Write a caption for each picture.

THE LEADER OF THE YAO PEOPLE

In 1890 the commander of the German forces in East Africa demanded the surrender of the Yao people. Below is the Yao ruler's reply:

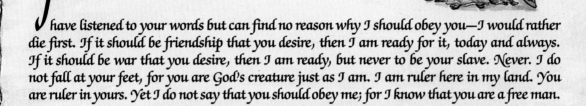

I have listened to your words but can find no reason why I should obey you—I would rather die first. If it should be friendship that you desire, then I am ready for it, today and always. If it should be war that you desire, then I am ready, but never to be your slave. Never. I do not fall at your feet, for you are God's creature just as I am. I am ruler here in my land. You are ruler in yours. Yet I do not say that you should obey me; for I know that you are a free man.

BUILDING SKILLS: DRAWING CONCLUSIONS

Use the information in the box above to answer the following questions.

1. What is meant by drawing conclusions about information?
2. Name some steps you could take to draw conclusions.
3. What is the topic of the information in the box?
4. What can you conclude about the attitude of the German commander?
5. What can you conclude about the attitude of the Yao leader?
6. Why is it important to draw conclusions about the information you read?

 **LINKING PAST, PRESENT, AND FUTURE**

Imagine that you have been elected to be the first president of a new African nation. Your people are looking to you to lead them into the future. In addition to wanting peace, your people want economic growth. They also want to restore the rich African legacy. What kind of government will you set up? How will you restore the rich legacy of the African past?

+North Pole

ARCTIC   OCEAN

Arctic Circle

75°N

60°N

ASIA

AFRICA

MONGOLIA

AFGHANISTAN

NORTH
KOREA

Sea
of
Japan

CHINA

JAPAN

PAKISTAN

SOUTH
KOREA

NEPAL

Arabian
Sea

BHUTAN

East
China
Sea

INDIA

BANGLADESH

Bay
of
Bengal

South
China
Sea

TAIWAN

135°E

45°E

MALDIVES

SRI
LANKA

INDIAN
OCEAN

60°E

75°E

90°E

105°E

120°E

AUSTRALIA

Tropic of Capricorn

30°S

45°S

456

UNIT 8

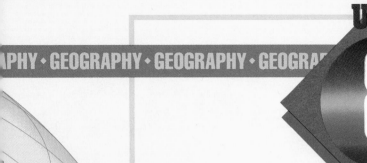

SOUTH ASIA, CHINA, JAPAN, AND KOREA

WHERE WE ARE

As you know, the world around us is a land of many different nations, cultures, religions, and ideas. As the map shows, in Unit 8 you will travel to some of the largest countries of Asia.

You have already met the ancient people of the Indus and Huang river valleys. You may recall that they built the first cities of ancient India and ancient China. In this unit you will learn more about the land and people of South Asia, China, Japan, and Korea.

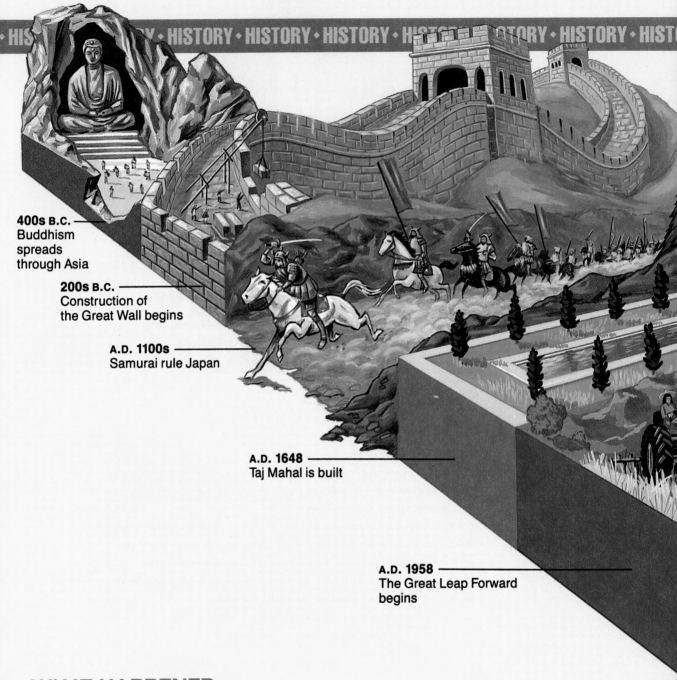

400s B.C.
Buddhism
spreads
through Asia

200s B.C.
Construction of
the Great Wall begins

A.D. 1100s
Samurai rule Japan

A.D. 1648
Taj Mahal is built

A.D. 1958
The Great Leap Forward
begins

A.D. 1980s
Bullet trains speed
across Japan

WHAT HAPPENED

As the time line shows, many
remarkable events influenced the
history of South Asia, China, Japan,
and Korea. You will learn, for example,
that the growth of two major religions played
a central role in the history of the region. You will
also read about the men and women who led their
people to new and wonderful heights.

458

SOUTH ASIA, CHINA, KOREA, AND JAPAN

AFGHANISTAN

Capital ★ Kabul
Major languages: Pushtu and Dari Persian
Population: 16.6 million
Area: 251,773 sq mi; 647,500 sq km
Leading exports: natural gas, fruit, and carpets

CHINA

Capital ★ Beijing (Peking)
Major language: Chinese
Population: 1,151.3 million
Area: 3,705,396 sq mi; 9,596,960 sq km
Leading export: manufactured goods

BANGLADESH

Capital ★ Dhaka
Major language: Bengali
Population: 116.6 million
Area: 55,599 sq mi; 144,000 sq km
Leading exports: textiles and jute

INDIA

Capital ★ New Delhi
Major languages: Hindi and English
Population: 859.2 million
Area: 1,269,342 sq mi; 3,287,590 sq km
Leading export: machinery

BHUTAN

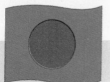

Capital ★ Thimphu
Major language: Dzonkha
Population: 0.7 million
Area: 18,147 sq mi; 47,000 sq km
Leading export: cement

JAPAN

Capital ★ Tokyo
Major language: Japanese
Population: 123.8 million
Area: 143,749 sq mi; 372,310 sq km
Leading export: machinery

KOREA, NORTH

Capital ★ Pyongyang
Major language: Korean
Population: 21.8 million
Area: 46,541 sq mi; 120,540 sq km
Leading export: minerals

NEPAL

Capital ★ Katmandu
Major language: Nepali
Population: 19.6 million
Area: 54,363 sq mi; 140,800 sq km
Leading exports: food products and manufactured goods

KOREA, SOUTH

Capital ★ Seoul
Major language: Korean
Population: 43.2 million
Area: 38,023 sq mi; 98,480 sq km
Leading exports: machinery and manufactured goods

PAKISTAN

Capital ★ Islamabad
Major languages: Urdu, Punjabi, and English
Population: 117.5 million
Area: 310,402 sq mi; 803,940 sq km
Leading exports: cotton products, clothing and rice

MALDIVES

Capital ★ Malé
Major language: Divehi
Population: 0.2 million
Area: 116 sq mi; 300 sq km
Leading exports: fish and clothing

SRI LANKA (Ceylon)

Capital ★ Colombo
Major languages: Sinhala, Tamil and English
Population: 17.4 million
Area: 25,332 sq mi; 65,610 sq km
Leading export: tea

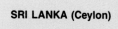

MONGOLIA

Capital ★ Ulaanbaatar
Major language: Khalkha Mongolian
Population: 2.2 million
Area: 604,248 sq mi; 1,565,000 sq km
Leading exports: fuels, minerals, and machinery

TAIWAN (Formosa)

Capital ★ Taipei
Major language: Chinese
Population: 20.5 million
Area: 13,892 sq mi; 35,980 sq km
Leading exports: machinery, plastics, and textiles

461

CHAPTER 18

SOUTH ASIA

FOCUS

This is indeed India! The land of dreams and romance, . . . of splendor and rags, of palaces and hovels. . . . the country of a hundred nations and a hundred tongues, of a thousand religions and two million gods. . . .

The American writer Mark Twain wrote these words about India more than 100 years ago. India is the largest nation in South Asia. As you read this chapter, you will learn that Mark Twain's words are still a good description of the amazing Indian subcontinent.

1 The Geography of South Asia

READ TO LEARN

Key Vocabulary

monsoon

Key Places

Hindu Kush
Himalayas
Mount Everest
Khyber Pass

Indus-Ganges Plain
Deccan Plateau
Cape Comorin

Read Aloud

It is a land of great peaks and deep valleys, of plunging gorges and rushing rivers; a barren beautiful country of intense sunlight and clear sparkling air.

These words were used by an American student named Anne Savery to describe her impression of South Asia's mountains. She went to this "barren, beautiful country" in the early 1980s. In this lesson you will read more about the geography of South Asia. It is an amazing land of many different environments.

Read for Purpose

1. **WHAT YOU KNOW:** What is an environment?
2. **WHAT YOU WILL LEARN:** What are the different environments of South Asia?

SOUTH ASIA

You will recall having read about ancient India in Chapter 5. You read, for example, about the great city of Mohenjo-Daro that grew along the banks of the Indus River. The Indus River is located on the Indian subcontinent. This region is also called South Asia. As you read above, South Asia is a land of many different environments. Its geography, ranging from mountains to deserts, is as varied as the people who live there. Read on. A new journey is about to begin.

"HELLO FROM THE ROOF OF THE WORLD!"

Anne Savery's first postcard home to her family in Virginia began with these words: "Hello from the roof of the world!" She was not joking when she called South Asia's mountains the world's rooftop. Mighty mountain ranges extend along South Asia's northern borders with the Soviet Union and China. The towering Hindu Kush mountains rise in northeast Afghanistan. These mountains rise over the Indus Valley. From here the mighty

Because of its height, Mount Everest was a huge challenge to mountain climbers. No one reached the top of it until 1953.

Afghanistan. You may recall how the invading Aryans passed through the Khyber Pass on their way to the Indus Valley in about 1500 B.C.

THE INDUS-GANGES PLAIN

South of the Himalayas lies a very large flat and fertile plain called the Indus-Ganges Plain. Because the land is flat, easy to irrigate, and very fertile, this plain is the rich center of the Indian subcontinent.

The Indus-Ganges Plain receives its name from the two rivers that flow across it. These rivers have their sources in the Himalayas. As you know, the mighty Indus River and its tributaries flow south from the western Himalayas into the Arabian Sea. The Ganges River and its tributaries drain the central part of the Himalayas.

THE DECCAN PLATEAU

The southern part of the Indian subcontinent is a peninsula that thrusts south into the Indian Ocean. The center of the peninsula is a high plateau cut by twisting rivers. This region is called the Deccan Plateau. A range of mountains called the Western Ghats (gôts) rises along the western edge of the plateau. A lower range of mountains, the Eastern Ghats, extends along the eastern edge of the plateau.

Compared to the Indus-Ganges Plain, the Deccan Plateau is very harsh. It is covered with thick forests or scrubby grasses. Anne Savery called this part of India "a land where the sun bakes the rivers." Indeed, the farmland of the Deccan Plateau bakes rock-hard, and its rivers often dry up. Even so, Indian farmers succeeded hundreds of years ago in growing cotton on the Deccan Plateau.

Himalayas stretch in a vast curve for more than 1,500 miles (2,400 km).

Along the border between Nepal and China is Mount Everest, the world's highest mountain. The crest, or the very top, of the Himalayas is made up of more than 40 peaks that are higher than 24,000 feet (7,300 m). It is no wonder that Anne Savery has called this region "the roof of the world." In fact, the Himalayas are the highest mountains in the world.

Lower mountains run south from both ends of the Himalayas. Passes at each end of the Himalayas have been used for centuries as invasion and trade routes. One of the most famous passes is the Khyber (kī′ bər) Pass on the border between Pakistan and

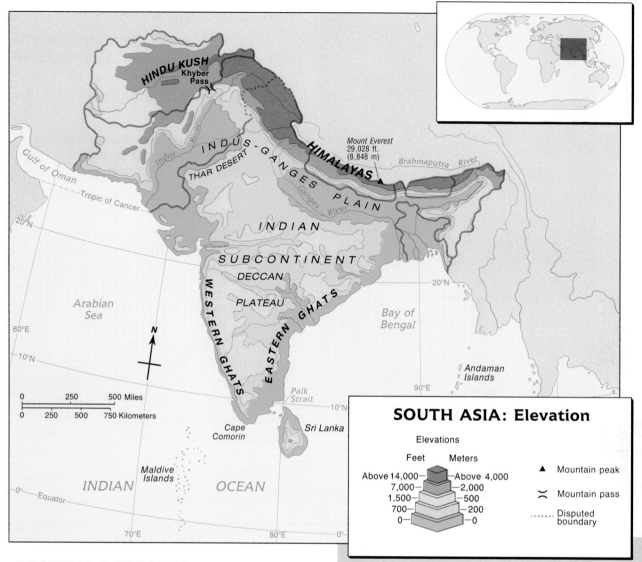

SOUTH ASIA: Elevation

Elevations

Feet	Meters
Above 14,000	Above 4,000
7,000	2,000
1,500	500
700	200
0	0

▲ Mountain peak

✕ Mountain pass

⋯⋯ Disputed boundary

MAP SKILL: South Asia includes the world's highest mountains. In what direction would you go to reach them from Cape Comorin?

TROPICAL LOWLANDS

As you can see on the map above, Cape Comorin lies at the very tip of South Asia. About this beautiful cape, one traveler wrote:

Here the white sand of the Arabian Sea, the black sand of the Bay of Bengal, and the red sand of the Indian Ocean meet.

Throughout history Cape Comorin often has been called "a land apart." A narrow border of lush, tropical land lies along the coasts of southern India. This coastal rim has a wet climate and rich soil.

Like the Deccan Plateau, these tropical lands also provide India with important goods. When the European explorer Vasco da Gama arrived in South Asia in 1498, it was the first time he tasted spices like pepper, cinnamon, and cloves. In addition to spices, India's tropical forests grow valuable teak and sandalwood—highly prized since ancient times.

465

THE MONSOON CLIMATE

In order to understand the different environments of South Asia, there is something else you need to know. Climate is very important in India. As one geographer wrote:

In India the climate sets the pace of people's lives. This fact is clear throughout the subcontinent.

India's climate is dominated by seasonal winds called **monsoons**. As the map below shows, monsoon winds blow from many different directions at different times of the year. This climate pattern has shaped life for South Asia's farmers since prehistoric times.

As the map on this page shows, from October to May, winter monsoons from the northeast blow dry air across the subcontinent. Then, in the middle of June, the winds change their direction. Summer monsoons begin to blow from the southwest, carrying moisture from the Indian Ocean in great rain clouds. According to Anne Savery:

MAP SKILL: Monsoon rains flood the city streets of South Asia. Farmers, however, are generally happy when the monsoons arrive. From what direction do the winter monsoons come? In what direction do the rainy summer monsoons blow?

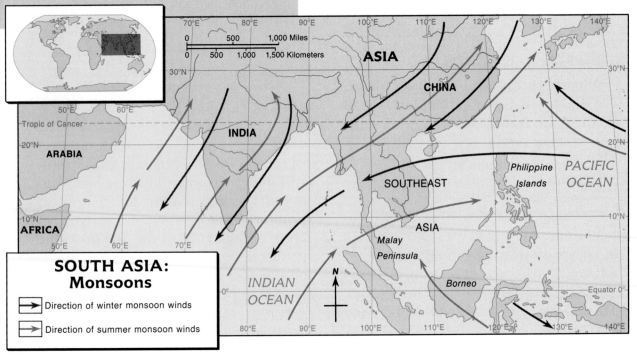

SOUTH ASIA:
Monsoons

→ Direction of winter monsoon winds

→ Direction of summer monsoon winds

The summer monsoon is preceded by several months of working up a thirst . . . . From the end of February, the sun starts getting hotter and spring gives way to summer. Flowers wither [die] . . . . The sun goes on, day after day, until there is a flash of light which outshines the daylight. The winds fill the black sails of the clouds and they billow out across the sun. A great shadow falls on the earth. There is a clap of thunder. Big drops of rain fall and dry in the dust. A fragrant smell rises from the earth. Another flash of lightning and another crack of thunder like the roar of a hungry tiger. It has come! Sheets of water, wave after wave. The people lift their faces to the clouds and let the water cover them. Schools and offices close. All work stops. Men, women, and children run madly about the streets, waving their arms and shouting "Ho, Ho,"—hosannas to the miracle of the monsoon.

The monsoons made a great impression on one visitor to India. This account is from her diary, published in England in 1956.

The summer monsoon is everyone's friend. It makes the crops grow. It cools the air. It feeds the rivers. It fills the wells. It brings new life.

The people of South Asia depend on these monsoons for rain to water their crops of cotton, rice, and wheat. If there is too little rain, plants dry up in the fields and people go hungry. If there is too much rain, floods may sweep away whole villages. As you can read in the box on this page, the monsoons also bring a great burst of happiness to South Asia's farmers.

A MOSAIC OF ENVIRONMENTS

As you have read, South Asia is made up of many different environments. From the "roof of the world" in the north to Cape Comorin in the south, South Asia is like a mosaic, or a design made up of many pieces of colored stone. As you continue to read this chapter you will learn more about South Asia's lands and people. You will also read how a rich civilization grew in this mosaic of environments.

Check Your Reading

1. What are the three chief rivers of South Asia?
2. Give three facts about South Asia's different environments.
3. **GEOGRAPHY SKILL:** What is the name of the world's highest mountain?
4. **THINKING SKILL:** How do monsoons affect India's climate?

2 Hinduism and Buddhism

READ TO LEARN

Key Vocabulary

Hinduism   Buddhism
Vedas   edict
caste

Key People

Siddharta Gautama
Asoka

Read Aloud

No visitor can come to India without learning that religion is very central to its people, its history, and its future.

As this traveler has observed, India is a land where religion is central. He continued, "Everywhere one looks, there are religious scenes taking place and beautifully decorated temples." It is perhaps no wonder that this writer is describing the birthplace of two world religions.

Read for Purpose

1. **WHAT YOU KNOW:** What three religions were born in the Middle East?
2. **WHAT YOU WILL LEARN:** What new religions developed in South Asia?

THE BIRTH OF HINDUISM

Think back to what you read in Chapter 5 about ancient India. You may recall that a powerful group called the Aryans migrated to the Indian subcontinent from Central Asia. When they arrived in about 1500 B.C., they brought a rich collection of myths, or tales about their gods and goddesses. They had gods of thunder, fire, earth, heaven, the moon, and the sun. Priests made special offerings of food and drink to the gods. For the Aryans everything in nature was believed to be in some way holy.

Aryan priests could sing from memory hundreds of long poems about their gods and goddesses. Hinduism (hin′ dü iz əm), one of the world's major religions, grew out of the ancient Aryan myths. Today there are more than 644 million followers of Hinduism on the Indian subcontinent. The beginnings of their religion lie among the poems, rituals, and myths of the Aryans. According to one historian,

Hinduism grew from the mingled beliefs of many groups in India. However, the earliest records of Hinduism grew from Aryan songs.

468

Followers of **Hinduism** often make a pilgrimage to bathe in the Ganges River as part of their religion.

WHAT THE ARYANS BROUGHT

The Aryans wrote beautiful hymns, or religious songs. Some of these hymns date back to about 1500 B.C. Hindu priests gathered the hymns into four groups called **Vedas** (vād' əz). The word *veda* means "knowledge." The most ancient and important of these collections, the *Rig-Veda*, includes more than 1,000 hymns of praise. It is probably the oldest set of religious songs still in use. The Vedas were finally written down in about A.D. 1400.

The Aryans also brought with them their way of dividing society into different classes. Like Egypt's social pyramid and France's three estates before the French Revolution, the Aryans had a very rigid social structure. The class to which a person belonged depended entirely on birth.

According to the *Rig-Veda*, four different classes had been made from the body of a Hindu god. First, the Brahmins (brä' minz) were created from the god's mouth. They were the Hindu priests, the highest class in Hindu society. The second class came from the god's arms. They were the warriors and rulers. The third class came from the god's legs. They were the landowners, merchants, and artisans. The fourth class came from the god's feet. They were the servants and workers.

Below these four classes, at the bottom of this social pyramid, were the Untouchables. This group was not even considered a class. The Untouchables were shunned by others. They had to use separate wells for water or wait for a higher-ranking person to get water for them.

Over time these classes developed into a **caste** (kast) system of many local

469

social groups. Each caste had its own jobs, which were passed down from parent to child. People ate only with members of their own caste and usually married within their caste as well.

INDIA'S NEW RELIGION

The roots of Hinduism and its caste system lay in the coming of the Aryans. The roots of another important world religion lay in Hinduism and in a Hindu prince named Siddharta Gautama (sid där′ tə   gau′ tə mə).

Gautama was born in about 563 B.C. in a kingdom at the foothills of the Himalayas. According to one legend Hindu priests made a prediction at his birth. They told his father that if ever the young prince learned about suffering in the world, he would leave home, never to return. For well over 20 years, the prince's father kept all knowledge of human suffering from him.

Legend says that Gautama's life was shattered one day when he saw proof of human suffering. While riding in his chariot, Gautama saw a man who was terribly sick, another who was old, and a third who had died. He decided that life was a cycle of pain and the only way to escape it was by seeking wisdom.

According to legend, Gautama tried to find wisdom through harsh discipline and suffering for six years. For days at a time, he ate only one grain of rice each day. His stomach became so empty that, by pressing it with his finger, he could touch his backbone.

Sculptors did not make statues of Buddha until several hundred years after his death. The artists tried to capture his inner peace, as in this sleeping Buddha.

The "Four Noble Truths" became clear to Buddha while he was sitting under a tree. Today there are followers of **Buddhism** throughout the Asian continent.

At last, enlightenment, or knowledge, came to him. After thinking for many days in the shade of a tree, Gautama suddenly felt that the truth was clear—that suffering is caused by desire and attachment. He set out to tell his friends what he had learned. From then on, his friends called Gautama the *Buddha*, a title meaning "the Enlightened One."

THE TEACHINGS OF BUDDHISM

Buddhism (bŭd′ iz əm), or the religion that was founded by Buddha, is one of the world's largest religions. There are more than 300 million Buddhists in the world today. The Buddha gave his first sermon, or speech, to his friends. That sermon was a landmark in the history of world religions. Buddha taught the four main ideas that had come to him in his enlightenment, calling them the "Four Noble Truths." These ideas became the foundation of Buddhism. As you can read in the box on this page, the Four Noble Truths taught that suffering was caused by desire and attachment.

471

These lions once stood on top of one of the pillars Asoka built throughout his kingdom. One **edict** proclaimed, "It is good to give, but there is no gift like justice."

INDIA UNDER ASOKA

As you read, Buddha lived in the sixth century B.C. More than 1,000 years had passed since the fall of the Indus valley cities and the coming of the Aryans. In all those years not one ruler was able to unite India's many kingdoms. In Buddha's time 12 families had carved the vast Indus-Ganges Plain into little kingdoms that were often at war. However, a change was coming. Soon India was to have a new kind of government that brought together large territories under one very powerful king.

Asoka (ə sō′ kə) was the greatest of these kings. Crowned in 273 B.C., Asoka was a Hindu general. He gained his power while leading a war against a southern Indian kingdom. His victory there ended in the brutal massacre of more than 100,000 people.

According to legend Asoka felt very sorry for having ordered this killing to take place. After he became king, Asoka decided to rule according to Buddha's teachings of "peace to all living things." His first action as king was to send "his sorrow and his riches" to the people of southern India.

RELIGIOUS TOLERATION

Asoka ruled his kingdom wisely, and he earned the respect of his people. For example, Asoka demanded that all government officials be "officials of righteousness" and look out for the welfare of people of every caste. When anyone was imprisoned unfairly or a family suffered because of flood or drought, King Asoka would tell his officials to give all the help that was necessary. Above all, Asoka stressed religious toleration, or the respect for other religions.

All religions deserve reverence [respect] for one reason or another. Reverence for another person's religion improves one's own faith and at the same time honors the religions of other people.

To spread his ideas, Asoka ordered huge stone pillars to be built throughout his kingdom. Each pillar had a special **edict**, or public notice, written on it. Some edicts were guarantees of fair treatment by Asoka's government. Other edicts explained the teachings of Buddhism. The lions shown in the photograph on this page once stood on top of one of Asoka's pillars. The modern nation of India has made this figure its national symbol.

472

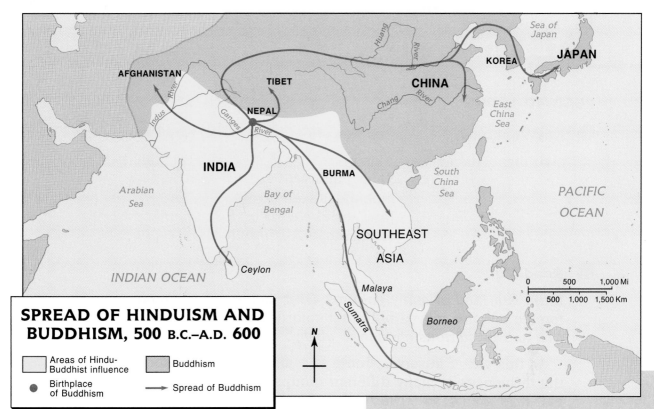

SPREAD OF HINDUISM AND BUDDHISM, 500 B.C.–A.D. 600

- Areas of Hindu-Buddhist influence
- Birthplace of Buddhism
- Buddhism
- → Spread of Buddhism

Buddhism so impressed Asoka that he sent out missionaries to spread its teachings. Buddhist missionaries spread their religion throughout the Indian subcontinent. They also went to the island of Ceylon and even to the distant land of Syria. As the map on this page shows, Buddhism spread eastward throughout Asia. Buddhism temporarily replaced Hinduism as India's major religion, and it influenced many of the beliefs of Hindus.

THE BIRTHPLACE OF TWO RELIGIONS

As you have read, South Asia was the birthplace of Hinduism and Buddhism. Both religions strongly affected Indian civilization. Hinduism gave it a rigid social structure called the caste system. Hinduism demanded that its followers accept their caste and live by its rules.

Buddhism brought the ideas of the "Four Noble Truths" to the Indian subcontinent. Asoka helped spread the new religion in Asia. As you will learn, Hinduism and Buddhism continue to be important parts of life in South Asia and have influenced its history.

Check Your Reading

1. What is the caste system?
2. List two ways in which Buddhism is different from Hinduism.
3. **GEOGRAPHY SKILL:** Use the map above to identify five places to which Buddhism had spread.
4. **THINKING SKILL:** What was the point of view of Asoka regarding religion and religious toleration? Why?

3 The Growth of India

READ TO LEARN

Key Vocabulary

civil disobedience

Key People

Akbar
Shah Jahan
Mohandas Gandhi
Jawaharlal Nehru
Muhammad Ali Jinnah

Key Places

Taj Mahal

Read Aloud

India is a land of many cultures. Over the centuries, many foreign peoples moved onto that colorful land. India was rich and mysterious enough to absorb her newcomers.

As this writer observes, India is a land that has absorbed the influences of many different groups. In this lesson you will read about the powerful peoples who moved in and out of the Indian subcontinent.

Read for Purpose

1. **WHAT YOU KNOW:** Who were the first people to migrate into the Indian subcontinent?
2. **WHAT YOU WILL LEARN:** How did the outside groups that came to South Asia influence Indian civilization?

THE MUSLIMS CONQUER INDIA

Think back to what you learned about the religion of Islam in Chapter 14. As you read, the followers of Islam —the Muslims—believed that they had a duty to spread their religion across the world.

Around the year A.D. 1000, a group of Muslims began to enter India. Moving to the Indus-Ganges Plain, they brought with them the monotheistic religion of Islam. The Muslims did not approve of Hinduism. Remember the central Muslim belief: "There is no god but one God, and Muhammad is his prophet." Imagine how shocked the Muslims were by the Hindu worship of many gods and goddesses.

The Muslims also disliked the caste system. To Muslims all people were equal before God. They could not understand how Hindus could believe that the people of the higher castes were better than those of lower castes, or that anyone could be "untouchable."

The Muslims succeeded in changing some followers of Hinduism to Islam. It is not surprising that many of these new Muslims came from the lower castes and the Untouchables. Nor is it surprising that the Hindus and Muslims frequently fought with one another. In places where the Muslims ruled, they forced Hindus to pay a heavy tax for being "unbelievers."

THE MOGUL EMPIRE

In 1526 another Muslim group conquered India. Called the Moguls, they brought to India many strong and creative leaders. As the map on this page shows, the Mogul Empire spread throughout the Indian subcontinent.

One of the greatest rulers of the mighty Mogul Empire was named **Akbar** (ak′ bər). He came to the throne in 1556. Akbar was not happy just to expand the Mogul Empire. He also wanted to put an end to the hatred and fighting between Muslims and Hindus.

Akbar wisely took steps to unite his Hindu and Muslim subjects. Though a Muslim himself, he brought in Hindus to advise him and help him rule. Akbar's tax system stressed fairness. For example, in years of famine, taxes were dropped. He also ended the hated "unbeliever tax" on Hindus. Following the example of Asoka centuries earlier, he promoted religious toleration, or respect for other religions. He even married a Hindu princess so that his successors to the throne would be both Muslim and Hindu by birth.

But perhaps Akbar's most lasting gift to the Mogul Empire and to India grew out of his love of art. Throughout his nearly 50-year rule, he encouraged Hindu and Muslim poets, painters, and architects to work together.

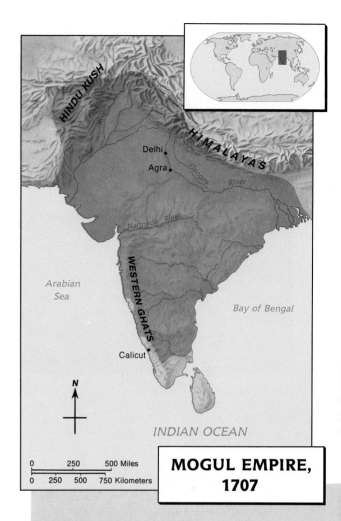

MOGUL EMPIRE, 1707

MAP SKILL: Akbar wanted Mogul art to combine the traditions of Islam and Hinduism. Name his empire's chief cities.

The Taj Mahal, which shimmers across the plain like a palace in a dream, is said to be the world's most beautiful building.

THE TAJ MAHAL

Probably the most famous work of art the Mogul Empire produced was the glorious Taj Mahal. Akbar's grandson, Shah Jahan, ordered it to be built when his new wife died. Deeply grief-stricken, Shah Jahan promised to build a tomb for his wife that would be "as beautiful as she was beautiful."

The Taj Mahal stands in Agra and was finished in 1648. Workers toiled for more than 20 years to build this magnificent building. Its beauty was quickly world famous and earned many glowing descriptions. One writer called it "poetry in stone," and another called it a "miracle of miracles, the final wonder of the world."

Today the Taj Mahal stands as a great landmark of civilization as well as a reminder of the great Mogul Empire. Under Akbar and other Mogul rulers, Hindus and Muslims lived together in peace. Peace did not last, however. Akbar's successors did not support his policy of religious tolerance. Hindu temples were destroyed, and people were forced to accept the Islamic religion.

THE BRITISH IN INDIA

During Akbar's rule a group of British merchants formed the British East India Company. They knew that Europeans wanted many of the goods India produced—fine cotton and silks, precious woods, spices to preserve and flavor food. So the British East India Company set up trading posts in three of India's coastal villages. In time these villages grew into the major cities of Bombay, Madras, and Calcutta.

To protect their trading posts, the British hired armies. They also used these armies to extend British power over much of India. By 1857 the British

East India Company ruled half of India. The next year the British government declared this territory part of the British Empire and seized complete control of its government.

Britain set out to make India "the jewel in the Empire's crown." It unified India under one code of law—British law. Heading the government was the British viceroy, aided by other government officials sent by Britain. The British army was there to enforce British rule.

Think back to what you learned about how European nations used their colonies in Africa. As you may recall, the imperialist powers had two goals. First, to gain the use of their colonies' natural resources and farm products. Second, to turn their distant colonies into markets for their own manufactured goods.

To achieve these goals and to defend its rule, Britain set out to improve India's transportation and communications systems. For example, the British built a network of roads and railroads that linked the vast subcontinent. They stretched telegraph wires across the Indian countryside, linking distant cities. They even founded schools that taught the Indian people the English language, English sports, and English ways of doing things.

At first, the people of India had welcomed the British as traders. They soon grew to resent them as foreign rulers. They wanted to drive the British out and make India self-governing once again. One of the greatest leaders in history emerged to lead the fight for Indian independence.

Many British people lived a life of luxury in India. The merchant riding on an elephant has a servant to protect him from the sun.

"THE GREAT SOUL"

My mission is not merely the brother-hood of Indian humanity. My mission is not merely the freedom of India. . . . But through the realization of the freedom of India, I hope to realize and carry on the mission of the brotherhood of all men and women.

With these bold words **Mohandas Gandhi** (mō han däs' gän' dē) described the aims he worked for all his life. To achieve his goals, this Hindu leader wanted to remove the tensions between Hindus and Muslims in India. Gandhi also wanted to drive the idea of "untouchability" out of India forever.

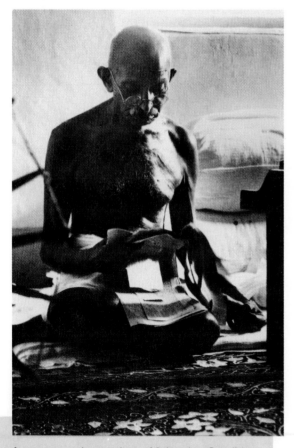

As an example to others, Mohandas Gandhi lived simply, like the poorest Untouchable. His **civil disobedience** movement helped bring about India's independence.

To him, it was completely wrong and "the greatest of all blots on Hinduism." To Gandhi, all men and women were "the children of God."

Indians called Gandhi *Mahatma*, which means "great soul." Gandhi had been educated as a lawyer in Britain, and he knew the British well. He knew that driving them out of India would be very difficult. But he began to work out a plan.

Gandhi looked back to the great emperor Asoka for guidance. As you recall, that Buddhist leader favored nonviolence. Gandhi believed the fight against the British must be a nonviolent one. He said that India would gain its freedom only "by sympathy, patience, and long-suffering."

Gandhi planned a number of protests aimed at forcing the British to give India independence. There were two parts to Gandhi's plan. First, he told Indians to boycott British goods. This would make India less profitable for its colonial rulers. Second, he asked Indians to practice **civil disobedience** toward British rule. Civil disobedience is the refusal to obey a law or laws as a means of protest against something.

Under Gandhi's leadership, civil disobedience spread throughout India. This way of protesting did not need money or skill with weapons. It took only courage. Men and women, young and old, weak and strong—all could join in Gandhi's movement. For example, Gandhi and his followers refused to pay taxes, vote, or hold office. They stopped trains by lying across railroad tracks. Civil disobedience helped to make it hard for Britain to rule India. You can read more about civil disobedience and India in the Point/Counterpoint on pages 480–481.

INDEPENDENCE AT LAST

Gandhi rejoiced as Britain's hold on India loosened. But as independence drew near after World War II, tensions between Hindus and Muslims exploded. India's Muslims feared that the Hindu majority would control the new nation. So they demanded a separate nation of their own. Two areas were carved out of India—one in the northwest and one in the northeast. Separated by Indian territory, they became the Muslim nation of Pakistan. Gandhi was deeply saddened by this division.

On August 15, 1947 India and Pakistan became independent countries. One of Gandhi's followers, named Jawaharlal Nehru (jə wä' hər ä nä' rü), became India's first prime minister. Muhammad Ali Jinnah (ä lē' jin' ä) became Pakistan's first prime minister.

As Gandhi and others feared, however, violence followed. Millions of Hindus in Pakistan tried to get to India, while Muslims in India tried to get to Pakistan. Trainloads of refugees, who had fled from the violence in search of safety, were killed on both sides of the border. More than 2 million refugees left their homes for religious reasons. In all, more than 500,000 people lost their lives. Gandhi himself was the victim of violence between Hindus. In January 1947 he was shot to death by a young Hindu who was against Gandhi's efforts to win equal treatment for Muslims.

One of the first acts of Nehru's government was to abolish untouchability. Years earlier, Mohandas Gandhi had written:

Self-government is deserved by a people who care for all their people. India will achieve self-government when she embraces the Untouchables.

Jawaharlal Nehru founded India's most important political family. His daughter and grandson later became prime ministers, too.

A CHANGED CIVILIZATION

In this chapter you have read about the growth of India. You read about the great influence of the Muslims and Moguls on India. You also read about the British who turned India into one of their colonies. Finally, you also learned about the heroes of Indian independence. In the next lesson you will read about life today on the Indian subcontinent.

Check Your Reading

1. Which outside groups influenced Indian civilization?
2. How did Akbar try to lessen Hindu-Muslim tensions?
3. How did Mohandas Gandhi lead India to independence?
4. **GEOGRAPHY SKILL:** What two modern nations emerged in South Asia after World War II?
5. **THINKING SKILL:** From the facts in this lesson, draw four conclusions about the Indian subcontinent's history.

Is Civil Disobedience a Good Way to Protest?

The independence movement in India was unique. A special philosophy called "nonviolent noncooperation" found many supporters on the Indian subcontinent. This method of protest was also called civil disobedience. Under the leadership of Mohandas Gandhi, civil disobedience spread throughout India. Protesters took part in sit-ins and other nonviolent actions. Though the British could explain why they fired on an armed uprising, it was hard to justify killing people who sat quietly.

Not everyone in India believed that civil disobedience was the best course of action. As you can imagine, this way of protesting did not always change things quickly. Others believed that only a violent revolution would rid India of the colonial British government. Thus many Indians looked to the example of the American, French, and Russian revolutions.

POINT

Organized Nonviolence

In his 1925 letter to the British viceroy of India, Mohandas Gandhi served notice that civil disobedience would begin in nine days. In the letter he expressed his beliefs on nonviolent acts of protest.

> I believe British rule to be a curse. Yet I do not intend harm to a single Englishman or to any interest he may have in India.
>
> Nothing but organized nonviolence can stop the organized violence of the British government. This nonviolence will be expressed through civil disobedience. My ambition is to convert the British people through nonviolence. Thus I hope to make them see the wrong they have done to India. If the people join me, as I expect they will, they will experience sufferings.
>
> It is, I know, possible for you to interfere with my plan by arresting me. I hope that there will be tens of thousands ready, in an orderly manner, to take up the work after me.

● Why did Mohandas Gandhi believe that nonviolent protest would lead to Indian independence?

COUNTERPOINT

Revolution Must Take Place

Manabendra Nath Roy was an Indian who believed that the best way for India was the way of revolution. He wrote these words after the British arrested and imprisoned him in 1929.

> I believe that revolution is necessary. Strong forces in our society have reached a violent outburst. This always happens when old ideas resist the new. The task of the leaders of the revolution is to push the process faster. I have been a pioneer of the Indian revolution, but I did not invent it. The revolution grows out of the terrible conditions in the country.
>
> The revolution must take place in order to open up the Indian people to the road of liberty, progress, and prosperity. The British colonial government has created terrible conditions. To punish me will not stop the revolution. Imperialism has created its own gravedigger; namely the forces of national revolution.

● Why did Manabendra Nath Roy believe that revolution was necessary in India?

UNDERSTANDING THE POINT/COUNTERPOINT

1. Who do you think made a stronger argument about how India should have achieved independence from Great Britain?
2. How do you think that a leader of the American Revolution would have felt about this issue?
3. Can you think of a compromise that might have been acceptable to both Mohandas Gandhi and Manabendra Nath Roy?

4 South Asia Today

READ TO LEARN

Key Vocabulary

literacy

Key Places

Calcutta
Bombay
New Delhi

Read Aloud

Today seven independent nations have emerged out of the richness and variety of Indian civilization. Together and alone they face major challenges. They must adapt their ancient ways to meet the demands of survival in a modern world.

Read for Purpose

1. **WHAT YOU KNOW:** What causes people to organize themselves into separate and independent nations?
2. **WHAT YOU WILL LEARN:** What modern nations have emerged in South Asia?

INDIA AND SRI LANKA

Look at the map on the opposite page. As you can see, the largest nation on the Indian subcontinent is India itself. One sixth of all the world's people alive today live in India. By the early 1990s, the population numbered over 850 million, more than three times the population of the United States. And it was growing at the rate of 1 million a month.

India's major cities teem with life. Calcutta, Bombay, and New Delhi are three of the world's most crowded cities, with close to 10 million people each. Yet most Indians do not live in cities but in small rural villages. There they work the land in order to grow enough food for India's people.

Look at the map again to find Sri Lanka, India's close neighbor to the southeast. As you can see, Sri Lanka is an island nation. Though it is now a republic, for nearly four centuries it was controlled by European traders. They called the island Ceylon and prized its lush beauty and its many different valuable products for trade—spices, tea, rubber, and precious stones.

Today Sri Lanka is one of South Asia's most modern nations. It also has South Asia's highest literacy rate. Literacy is the ability to read and write. Fully 85 percent of the people of Sri Lanka enjoy literacy. It also has a fine transportation system, unlike most of India's neighbors to the north.

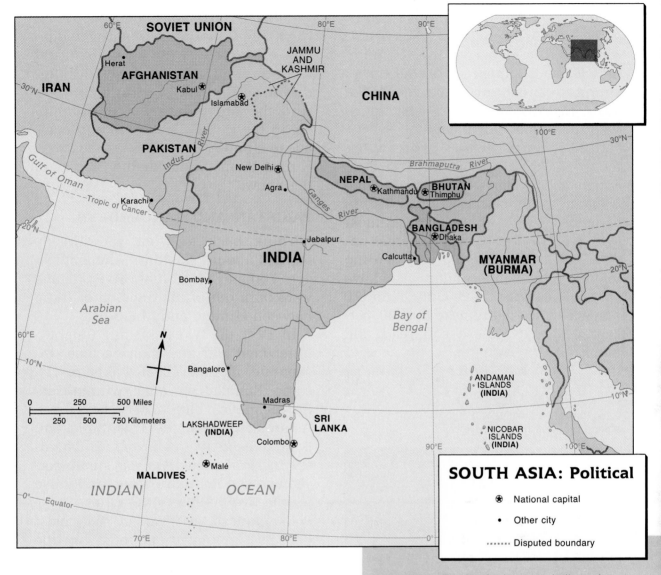

Inset map legend:

SOUTH ASIA: Political

⊛ National capital

• Other city

••••••• Disputed boundary

MAP SKILL: The border between India and Pakistan is still disputed. Which nations of South Asia have no seacoast?

AFGHANISTAN, NEPAL, AND BHUTAN

In contrast to Sri Lanka, Afghanistan is one of the poorest countries in the world. It also has one of the lowest rates of literacy. It is located in the Hindu Kush mountains.

Afghanistan's rugged mountain terrain has isolated its people from the rest of the world and made them fiercely independent. It has also made them very self-sufficient. Afghan families can grow or make just about everything they need.

Almost all Afghans live in rural areas in high mountain valleys. Here they farm the land and herd goats, sheep, and even camels in the high grasslands. When winter comes, mountain snows force them inside their homes. There they spend the winter getting ready for the new year. For example, they weave cloth for clothing and make shoes and tools.

483

Until 1973 Afghanistan was ruled by a king. But in recent years it has been a republic torn by a civil war. Communist leaders, supported by the Soviet Union, took control of the country in 1979. In 1989, however, Soviet troops withdrew from Afghanistan.

Unlike Afghanistan, two other mountain nations of South Asia have remained kingdoms—Nepal and Bhutan. Nepal and Bhutan have a great deal in common with Afghanistan. Almost everyone in these mountainous nations lives in a farming and herding region. Nepal and Bhutan also have very low literacy rates. Only about 10 percent of the Bhutanese and 20 percent of the Nepalese can read and write.

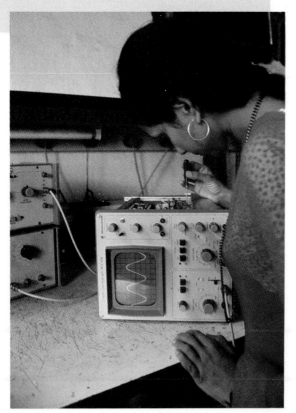

New, growing industries in South Asia can help in the fight against poverty.

Like the Afghans, the people of Nepal and Bhutan are hardy mountaineers. Probably the most famous of them are the Sherpas of Nepal. Since they have Mount Everest in their backyard, they are the best mountain climbers in the world. Their skill and courage in climbing icy mountain faces has earned them the nickname "Tigers of the Snow."

PAKISTAN AND BANGLADESH

Think back to what you already learned about Pakistan in the last lesson. You may recall that two Pakistans were born out of the division of India between Hindus and Muslims.

In 1971 the two Pakistans fought a bitter civil war and then became two separate nations. East Pakistan became Bangladesh after winning its independence. Like most of their South Asian neighbors, the Pakistanis and Bangladeshis live as farmers and herders in rural areas. Only a small percentage can read and write, and those people live mainly in the cities.

Bangladesh is one of the most densely populated nations on the earth. It is about the size of the state of Wisconsin, and 116 million people, or nearly half of the population of the United States, live there. Obviously, overcrowding is one of the major problems in Bangladesh, as it is in much of South Asia.

FIGHTING POVERTY

One of the greatest challenges in all the nations of South Asia today is also an ancient one—widespread poverty. Poverty is not only a lack of money— it is also a lack of food, shelter, and education. India has taken the lead in fighting poverty in South Asia.

Since gaining independence, India has adopted many modern farming methods to increase its food production. In some places, tractors have replaced oxen. Irrigation systems have multiplied, and so have factories that produce fertilizer. Farmers now plant new, more productive seeds.

The result has been a "green revolution." India now grows three times as much food as it did in 1947. It grows enough to feed its own large population, as well as surplus for export. Food exports help India to pay for better housing, medical care, and schools.

India is working to fight poverty by developing its industries. New, successful industries create jobs and pay taxes that the government can spend on programs to improve conditions.

MANY RELIGIONS

At the beginning of this lesson, you were asked to think about a question: What causes people to organize themselves into separate and independent nations? Perhaps you answered that they shared a common language or a common religion.

Look at the map on this page. As you see, the map shows South Asia's many religions. What religions are represented on it? Note that the nations of Pakistan and Bangladesh are Islamic. Hinduism is the chief religion of India. What are the chief religions of Nepal and Sri Lanka?

FACING THE FUTURE

You have read in this lesson that the nations of South Asia share many of the same challenges. You also read that they share the same rich past. South Asia was the birthplace of major world religions and great leaders. As

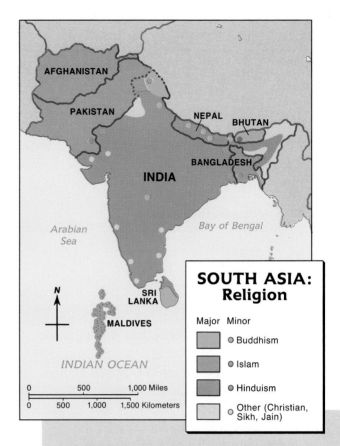

SOUTH ASIA: Religion

Major Minor
- Buddhism
- Islam
- Hinduism
- Other (Christian, Sikh, Jain)

MAP SKILL: South Asia has many different religions. Which nation on Pakistan's border has the same religion as Pakistan?

you know, solving problems is not always an easy job. It will no doubt demand the same qualities that Gandhi said would be needed to win the struggle for independence: "sympathy, patience, and long-suffering."

Check Your Reading

1. What is literacy?
2. What South Asian nation was once part of Pakistan?
3. **GEOGRAPHY SKILL:** What are the eight nations of South Asia?
4. **THINKING SKILL:** Look at the map above. What are three conclusions you can draw about religion in South Asia from the map?

Comparing Circle, Line, and Bar Graphs

Key Vocabulary

graph
circle graph
line graph
axis

horizontal axis
vertical axis
bar graph

As you have read about South Asia, you have learned that India has a population of more than 850 million people and that 83 percent of its people practice Hinduism. Those numbers, or statistics, give information about India. One way of showing statistics that makes them easy to understand is by putting them on graphs A graph is a diagram that shows statistics in a visual way. In this lesson you will compare three different kinds of graphs.

Circle Graphs

A circle graph shows how parts of something are related to each other and to the whole. A circle graph is often called a pie graph because it looks like a pie cut into slices. The circle, or pie, is equal to 100 percent. Each slice, or part, is shown as a percentage of the whole.

Circle graphs have many uses. For example, a circle graph might be used to show how much of a whole school budget is spent on various items. A circle graph, such as **Graph A** on the next page, helps you to make comparisons. For example, **Graph A** shows you which religion has the most followers worldwide. Use the circle graph to name the religion that has the second greatest number of followers.

Line Graphs

A line graph is used to show changes over time. For example, **Graph B** on the next page shows the change in India's population over 20 years. A line graph lets you see *trends*, or general patterns over time. What trend does this graph show? As you can see, **Graph B** shows that the population of India has very much increased over time. How can you read this from the graph?

A line graph is made up of a grid of horizontal and vertical lines. Each line is called an axis. The horizontal axis is the bottom line of the grid. It shows information that changes at a rate that may be determined. For example, the information may be time. You can use seconds, days, years, or whatever is useful to illustrate best the trend of what is changing on the vertical axis. The vertical axis is the outside left line. This information changes in relation to how the information on the horizontal axis changes.

As you can see, dots are placed on the graph to represent the information. A line is then drawn through the dots to show the trend. Use **Graph B** to study the upward trend of India's population.

Bar Graphs

A bar graph is used to compare amounts. Bar graphs can also be used to compare the same item at different times or to compare different items.

Like line graphs, bar graphs have labeled horizontal and vertical axes. In a horizontal bar graph, the bars go to the side. In a vertical bar graph, the bars go up or down.

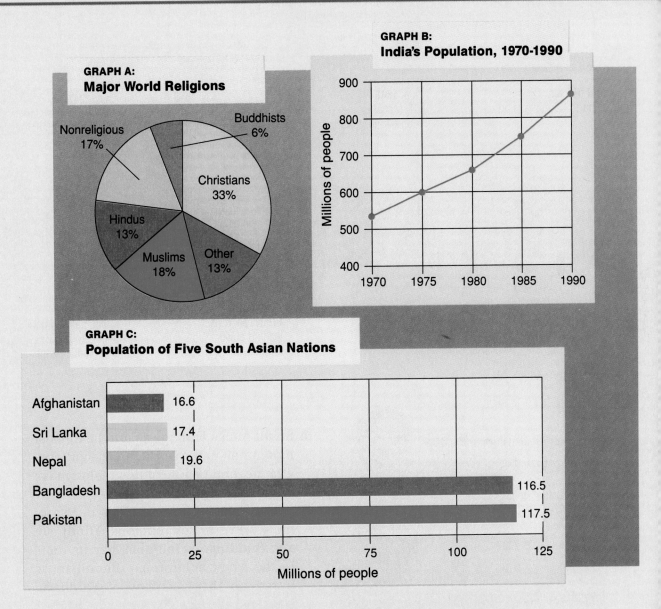

GRAPH A:
Major World Religions

Nonreligious 17%
Buddhists 6%
Christians 33%
Hindus 13%
Muslims 18%
Other 13%

GRAPH B:
India's Population, 1970-1990

Millions of people

900
800
700
600
500
400

1970 1975 1980 1985 1990

GRAPH C:
Population of Five South Asian Nations

Afghanistan 16.6
Sri Lanka 17.4
Nepal 19.6
Bangladesh 116.5
Pakistan 117.5

0   25   50   75   100   125

Millions of people

Bar graphs use solid bars to show the measurement, or extent of something. For example, **Graph C** is a horizontal graph that uses bars to represent the populations of five South Asian nations. It compares the populations of five southern Asian nations. Note that these populations have no relationships to each other. The population of Sri Lanka, for example, is shown separately from the population of Pakistan.

Reviewing the Skill

1. What is the difference between a circle graph and a line graph?
2. According to **Graph B**, during what five-year period was there the greatest increase in population?
3. Would you be able to plot the information in **Graph C** on a line graph? Why or why not?
4. Why is it important to be able to understand how to read graphs?

487

IMPORTANT EVENTS

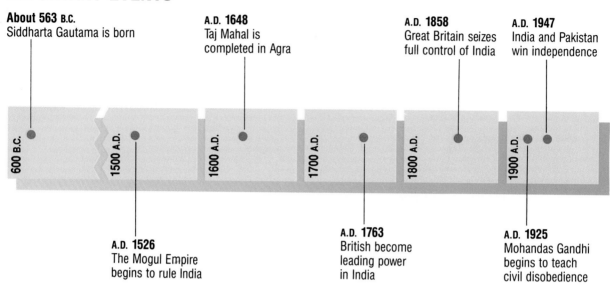

About 563 B.C.
Siddharta Gautama is born

A.D. 1648
Taj Mahal is
completed in Agra

A.D. 1858
Great Britain seizes
full control of India

A.D. 1947
India and Pakistan
win independence

600 B.C.　1500 A.D.　1600 A.D.　1700 A.D.　1800 A.D.　1900 A.D.

A.D. 1526
The Mogul Empire
begins to rule India

A.D. 1763
British become
leading power
in India

A.D. 1925
Mohandas Gandhi
begins to teach
civil disobedience

PEOPLE TO KNOW

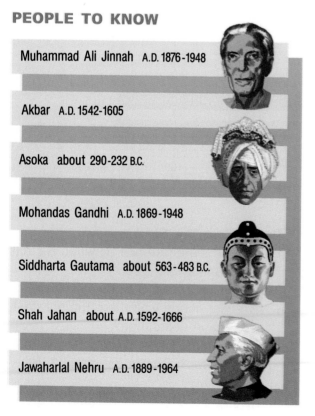

Muhammad Ali Jinnah　A.D. 1876-1948

Akbar　A.D. 1542-1605

Asoka　about 290-232 B.C.

Mohandas Gandhi　A.D. 1869-1948

Siddharta Gautama　about 563-483 B.C.

Shah Jahan　about A.D. 1592-1666

Jawaharlal Nehru　A.D. 1889-1964

IDEAS TO REMEMBER

■ South Asia's Himalayas are the highest
mountains in the world. The geography,
climate, and people of this region make
it a land of incredible variety.

■ South Asia is the birthplace of two of
the world's major religions, Hinduism
and Buddhism. Hinduism has its roots
in the Aryan migrations. Buddhism is
based on the teachings of Siddharta
Gautama.

■ The Muslims and the British were two
outside groups that had great influence
on Indian civilization.

■ Many new nations have emerged from
Indian civilization.

REVIEWING VOCABULARY

Buddhism   monsoon
caste   Vedas
civil disobedience

Number a sheet of paper from 1 to 5. Beside each number write the word or term from the list above that best matches each statement.

1. Gautama used parts of Hinduism and his own teachings to found this important religion.
2. This wind from the northeast and the southwest greatly influences the climate of the Indian subcontinent.
3. Brought to India by the Aryan invaders, this is a rigid, highly structured way of organizing society.
4. These written collections contain thousands of hymns to the gods and goddesses of the Aryan people.
5. Gandhi encouraged this nonviolent form of protest in which people refuse to obey certain laws.

REVIEWING FACTS

1. Why did Anne Savery call the northern boundary of the Indian subcontinent "the roof of the world"?
2. Why is the Indus-Ganges Plain called the heartland of the Indian subcontinent? What are the three largest rivers in this region?
3. What are the two most important monsoons in South Asia? List two characteristics of each.
4. Name two things that the Aryans brought with them to the Indian subcontinent that were to change civilization there forever.
5. Name the four major castes in the Aryan caste system.
6. According to the Four Noble Truths of Buddhism, what is the source of all human suffering?
7. What effect did Buddhism have on life in South Asia?
8. Why did Muslim teachings appeal to the lower castes and the "untouchables" of India?
9. What methods did Mohandas Gandhi use to drive the British from India?
10. Name the different nations that have emerged from Indian civilization.

◖◆▶ WRITING ABOUT MAIN IDEAS

1. **Writing an Outline:** Write an outline of the major geographical regions of the Indian subcontinent. List the important features of each region.
2. **Writing About Perspectives:** Imagine you are Mohandas Gandhi in the last days of India's struggle for independence. Record your hopes and fears for India. You may wish to use encyclopedias and books from the library for research.

BUILDING SKILLS: COMPARING CIRCLE, LINE, AND BAR GRAPHS

1. Why is a graph often used instead of a list?
2. Name one example of a good use for a bar graph.
3. When might a circle graph be used to report numbers?
4. Why is it helpful to be able to read and construct different kinds of graphs?

CHAPTER 19

CHINA

FOCUS

Physical barriers, such as high mountains, deserts, and even the Great Wall have isolated China from other civilizations. But the people of China have created a remarkable culture.

According to the historian who wrote these words, the people of China have created a "remarkable culture." As you will learn, China has a rich past. Today more than 1 billion people live in China—that is more than one out of every five people on the earth.

1 The Geography of China

READhP TO LEARN

Key Vocabulary

terrace
paddy

Key Places

Tibet   North China
Sinkiang   Beijing
Outer China   South China

Read Aloud

As you know, geography is one of the main factors that affect the history and culture of people all over the world. In this chapter you will learn that China is a vast country— almost one fifth of the world's people live inside its borders. China's location, landforms, rivers, and climate have played an important part in its growth.

Read for Purpose

1. **WHAT YOU KNOW:** How does geography affect your daily life?
2. **WHAT YOU WILL LEARN:** What are the geographic regions of China?

A LARGE AND VARIED LAND

Think back to what you learned in Chapter 5 about the growth of civilization in ancient China. Do you remember that it began in the fertile Huang River Valley? You may recall that the Huang River makes its way to the Yellow Sea through northern China. Today this is only a small part of China.

Modern China is a large and varied land. It is the third largest country in the world and has more people than any other country. Geographers often divide this large land into three different regions. Each of these regions has its own geography.

OUTER CHINA

Much of China is enclosed by high mountains. These mountain ranges include the Himalayas that separate China from the nations of South Asia. The Himalayas lie along the southern part of Tibet Tibet is a high, dry plateau surrounded by high mountains. It is the largest region of high elevation in the world. North of Tibet are the deserts and steppes of Sinkiang (shin jē äng'). This region, with its basins and salt lakes, looks like the Great Basin of the United States.

Together, the regions of Tibet and Sinkiang are often called Outer China. If you look at the map on page 492, you

MAP SKILL: Buddhist monasteries stand in the shadow of the world's highest mountains. What are the three parts of China?

will understand why. Outer China lies in western China. The lands of Outer China have sometimes been described as among the least hospitable, or least friendly, in the world. People there call them the lands of the three "too manys" and the three "too littles." One saying goes:

Too many winds and too little rain.
Too much sand and too little grass.
Too many stones and too little soil.

Lands with such characteristics as these do not usually attract much settlement. In fact, only 1 percent of all Chinese people live in Outer China. Yet, as you can see from the map above, Outer China makes up about one third of China's land.

NORTH CHINA

A second region of China is known as North China. As you remember, the Huang [Yellow] River flows across the North China Plain. If you were to look at this great plain from the air, it would appear dusty and yellowish-brown. This color comes from a fine dust, called loess (les), that blows in from deserts far to the west. Like the silt that was carried by the Nile River, loess is very fertile and improves the quality of northern China's soil.

Loess does create a problem, however. Fierce summer winds often stir up so much loess that it blots out the sky. In fact, it is not unusual to see the people of China's capital city, Beijing (bā jing') [Peking], wearing thin cloth masks to help keep out dust. Find Beijing on the map on the next page.

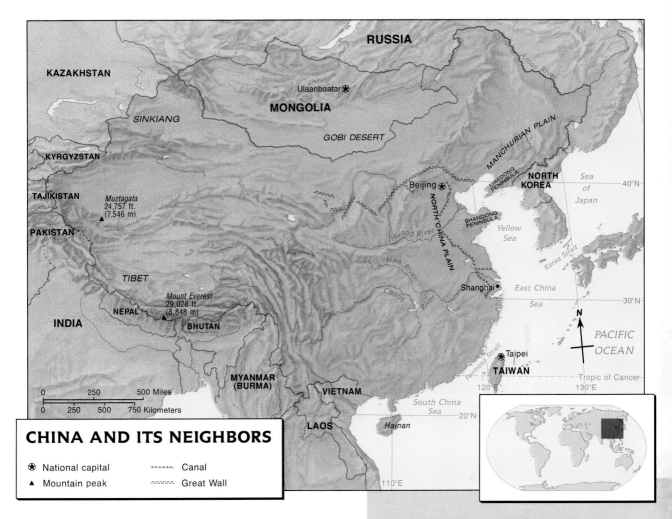

CHINA AND ITS NEIGHBORS

✹ National capital
▲ Mountain peak
⋯⋯⋯ Canal
∿∿∿ Great Wall

MAP SKILL: Pinyin is the system for spelling Chinese names in English. What is the pinyin spelling of China's capital?

Indeed, North China is one of the most fertile regions in all of Asia. In addition to having good soil, it is also one of the richest in mineral resources. Rich deposits of iron ore, coal, and oil have been mined in North China. So it has become the major center of China's industry. Iron and steel mills, oil refineries, shipyards and factories are centered around Beijing and along North China's coastline.

SOUTH CHINA

Most people in China live in the region known as South China. Lush vegetation grows well in this subtropical region. Much of the area is watered by one of the world's longest rivers, the

In this chapter you will notice that the pinyin form of names is followed by a respelling for pronunciation. Then you will often find the older form of names in brackets after the respelling.

Chinese names and places may be spelled in different ways. In the 1950s the Chinese government introduced the pinyin system. It uses letters similar to the Roman alphabet and spells a word the way it really sounds in Chinese. For example, *Peking* is the older form of the spelling for China's capital and is more familiar to many people. *Beijing* is the pinyin spelling and is how the word sounds in Chinese.

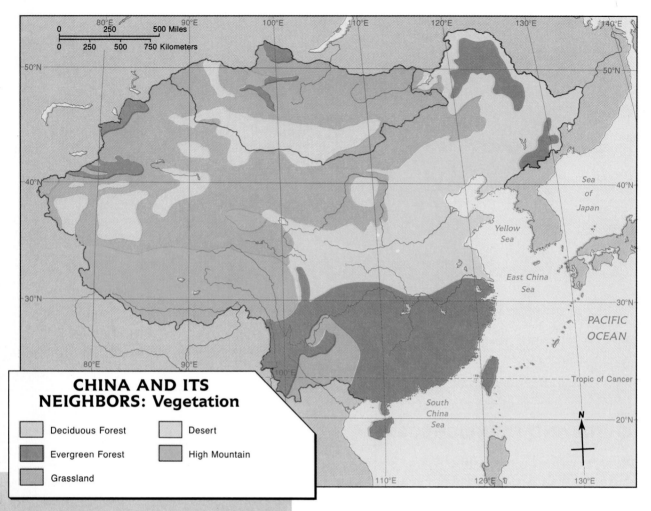

CHINA AND ITS NEIGHBORS: Vegetation

- Deciduous Forest
- Evergreen Forest
- Grassland
- Desert
- High Mountain

MAP SKILL: Vegetation is distributed unevenly throughout China. What part of China is largely grassland? What part has many evergreen forests?

Chang [Yangtze], and its many tributaries. You may recall that the Huang River was often called "China's Sorrow." The Chang River has caused far more happiness for the Chinese people.

Monsoons bring still more moisture to help the growth of South China's vegetation. South Asia is affected by monsoon wind patterns like the ones you read about in Chapter 18. Unlike the Indian subcontinent, however, rain falls year-round in South Asia rather than during only one season.

FARMING IN CHINA

Many geographers think that no people have been so greatly devoted to farming as have the Chinese. Although only about 12 percent of the land is good for farming, the country grows enough food to support the largest population in the world. In fact, China is today the world's largest producer of food grains.

Through the centuries the Chinese have changed their environment through farming. Hills were reshaped, trees torn down, rivers dammed and rechanneled, and canals built to reach more crops around the country. Chinese farmers have invented special ways of farming their land.

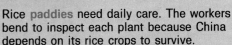

Rice **paddies** need daily care. The workers bend to inspect each plant because China depends on its rice crops to survive.

IRRIGATION, TERRACES, PADDIES

In many places, Chinese farmers use irrigation to make use of greater amounts of land. They dig trenches in the earth to bring water into their fields from nearby lakes and rivers. Where the land is hilly, farmers plant their crops in **terraces** along the sides of hills. Terraces provide more flat land to farm. Rainfall is caught and held in the terraces.

Farming in South China is marked by a long growing season and a stable water supply. This is the great rice-growing area of China. Rice **paddies**, or the shallow flooded fields where rice is grown, fill the countryside. A Chinese proverb says, "If the rice paddies of the South produce a good harvest, no one in China will starve."

As you see from the photograph on this page, the cultivation of rice is backbreaking work. During the growing season, the paddies must be carefully weeded. When rice is ready to be harvested, workers pick the plants by hand and remove the rice kernels.

GEOGRAPHY AND PEOPLE

As you have read, China is a land of vast plateaus, mighty rivers, fertile soil, and mineral resources. You have also read how the people of China invented special ways of farming to feed their many people.

China's vast size and huge population make it one of the most powerful nations on the earth. As you will learn, China's 4,000-year history is marked with many great achievements.

Check Your Reading

1. What are the three main geographic regions of China?
2. How do irrigation, terraces, and paddies help Chinese farmers?
3. **GEOGRAPHY SKILL:** What are China's two chief river systems? Into what body of water do they flow?
4. **THINKING SKILL:** Compare and contrast China's three regions.

BUILDING SKILLS
GEOGRAPHY SKILLS

Reading Time Zone Maps

Key Vocabulary
time zone
International Date Line

Is it the same time everywhere on the earth? The measurement of time is related to the revolution and rotation of the earth. As you know, one year is the time it takes for the earth to make one revolution around the sun. You also know that one day is the time it takes for the earth to make a complete rotation on its axis.

Time Zones
The division of a day into hours is closely related to longitude. The earth has 360° of longitude. In one day, or 24 hours, the earth rotates 360°. In one hour it rotates 15°. One hour is 15° of longitude wide.

In 1884, 24 standard time zones were established. Places within each of the world's time zones were to follow the time of the longitude passing through the center of that zone. The prime meridian was to be the center of the zone to establish noon. The 180° line of longitude became the line for midnight.

International Date Line
The standard time zones have been changed to work with state and national boundaries. The line which determines the date, originally established at 180°, has been redrawn to avoid as many land areas as possible. This line, the International Date Line, makes the boundary between one day and the next.

As the map shows, the time zone lines of longitude do not always follow at 15° intervals. In some places the boundaries of time zones zigzag so that people living in the same region or country can have the same time.

The map on the next page shows the world's standard time zones. The time is shown for each zone when it is 12 noon in the zone centered on the prime meridian. Use the map to follow these examples.

When it is 5:00 A.M. in Denver, it is 7:00 A.M. in New York City and 2:00 A.M. in Honolulu. It is the same day in all three places. In counting the time, neither the time zone where it was midnight, nor the International Date Line was passed. There are, however, always two days in existence throughout the world.

How do you know what date it is in another part of the world? These rules will help.

1. If you cross the time zone where it is midnight, counting eastward, today becomes tomorrow. If you cross the time zone where it is midnight, counting westward, today becomes yesterday.

2. If you cross the International Date Line, counting eastward, today becomes yesterday. If you cross the International Date Line, counting westward, today becomes tomorrow.

3. If you cross both the midnight time zone and the International Date Line, counting either eastward or westward, today remains today. (When the midnight time zone coincides with the zone centered on the International Date Line, rule 2 applies.)

496

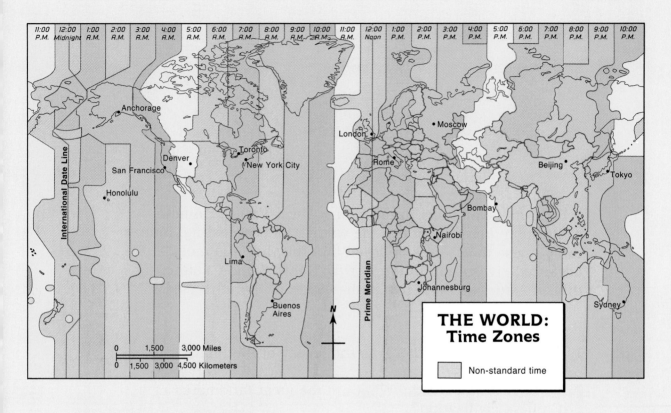

THE WORLD: Time Zones

☐ Non-standard time

Using the Time Zone Map

Study the following examples on the map to understand how these rules work.

A. When it is 10:00 P.M. Thursday in Sydney, it is 2:00 P.M. Thursday in Johannesburg. (As the map above shows, Johannesburg is eight time zones west of Sydney.)

B. When it is 9:00 A.M. Monday in Tokyo, it is 3:00 P.M. Sunday in Anchorage. (As the map above shows, Anchorage is six time zones east of Tokyo, and the International Date Line was passed.)

C. When it is 4:00 A.M. Thursday in San Francisco, it is 10:00 P.M. Thursday in Sydney. (Sydney is six time zones west of San Francisco, and both the midnight time zone and the International Date Line were passed.)

Reviewing the Skill

Use the map on this page to answer the following questions.

1. If it is 1:00 P.M. Friday in Denver, what is the day and time in New York City? In San Francisco?

2. If it is 9:00 P.M. Sunday in New York City, what is the day and time in Rome?

3. If it is 8:00 A.M. Monday in Toronto, what is the day and time in Tokyo?

4. If it is 10:00 P.M. Tuesday in Bombay, what is the day and time in Lima?

5. What day and time will it be when you arrive in Johannesburg, if your five-hour flight left Buenos Aires on Thursday at 10:00 P.M.?

6. Why is it important to be able to read a time zone map? When would you most likely use such a map?

2 Chinese Civilization

READttt

READ TO LEARN

Key Vocabulary

Mandate of Heaven

Key People

Confucius
Shihuangdi
Kublai Khan

Key Places

Gobi Desert
Great Wall
Grand Canal
Forbidden City

Read Aloud

From its beginnings in the Huang River Valley, Chinese civilization grew into one of the world's longest lasting. Indeed, the Chinese themselves believed that they had the most advanced civilization in the world. "Surely," one Chinese thinker said, "we must live at the center of the universe!"

Read for Purpose

1. **WHAT YOU KNOW:** What was the legacy of the Shang dynasty?
2. **WHAT YOU WILL LEARN:** What are the great landmarks of Chinese civilization?

THE DYNASTIES OF CHINA

Dynasty—you first met that word in Chapter 5. There you learned that a dynasty is a line of rulers who belong to the same family and who pass the right to rule from one generation to the next. You also learned that the Shang dynasty set up China's first important government.

As the chart on the opposite page shows, many dynasties followed the Shang. You can see from the chart that China was ruled by ten dynasties over a period of more than 3,500 years. Each dynasty was very different and each dynasty left its own legacy. Use the chart to guide your reading.

Once in power, the ruler of a new dynasty organized his government. He made laws and named officials who would carry them out. For a time he and his dynastic successors ruled with great strength.

But in time—perhaps after a few years or a few centuries—the dynasty's hold on government began to weaken. Sometimes officials became dishonest, and the government became corrupt. Or perhaps the dynasty began producing weak rulers.

At that point the cycle would begin all over again. A new leader would emerge, take power, and found a new dynasty to replace the old one.

THE DYNASTIES OF CHINA

夂人 英 中	**Shang Dynasty** 1766 B.C.-1122 B.C.	Writing on oracle bones tells of events and customs of the period. Wheeled chariots are introduced in warfare. Silk weaving is invented. Chinese writing develops.
	Zhou Dynasty 1122 B.C.-221 B.C.	Iron casting is invented, as are the multiplication tables. Irrigation is introduced on a large scale. The great philosopher Confucius teaches a code of behavior that spreads widely.
	Qin Dynasty 221 B.C.-206 B.C.	A warrior king unites much of China into one empire. A strict law code and tax system is designed. Writing, weights and measures are standardized. Building of the Great Wall begins.
	Han Dynasty 206 B.C.-A.D. 220	Buddhism is brought to China from India. Trade routes to India and Persia are established. Paper is invented. For the next 370 years, warring kingdoms keep China in disorder.
	Sui Dynasty A.D. 589-618	Powerful emperors reunite China. A great transportation network is built, including the Grand Canal linking the Huang and Chang rivers. Gunpowder is invented.
	Tang Dynasty A.D. 618-907	Tang emperors extend China's control to neighboring areas. Height of Silk Road trade. A golden age of art and learning develops. A half-century of disorder follows.
	Song Dynasty A.D. 960-1279	Age of high culture: printing, poetry, calligraphy. Movable type and paper money are developed; invention of compass.
	Yuan Dynasty A.D. 1279-1368	Genghis Khan leads Mongols from the northwest in an attack on China. His grandson Kublai Khan founds the Yuan Dynasty. His elaborate court is visited and described by Marco Polo.
	Ming Dynasty A.D. 1368-1644	European traders arrive. Commerce flourishes. Ming emperors build the Forbidden City in Beijing and extend the Great Wall.
	Qing Dynasty A.D. 1644-1912	Manchu invaders come from the north and set up the Qing Dynasty. Foreign trade and industry grows but nationalist uprisings bring on final collapse.

CHART SKILL: China traces its dynasties back 3,500 years. Which dynasty lasted the longest? When did the last dynasty end?

China's rulers had something else in common, too. They all believed that they were "Sons of Heaven." They believed that they had a special right to rule the people of China. To them it was a command from on high, and they called it their Mandate of Heaven. How does this mandate compare to the divine right claimed by the French kings you read about in Chapter 11?

No matter what dynasty was in power, life went on much the same for the common people of China, most of whom were peasants.

The teachings of Confucius stress the importance of respect and knowledge of one's duty. Why are these important principles?

THE SAYINGS OF CONFUCIUS

- Daily I examine myself on three points: Have I worked hard? Have I been loyal to my friends? Have I shared what I have learned?

- Do not worry about having an important job; worry about doing your job well.

- Have no friends not equal to yourself.

- Things that are done, it is needless to speak too much about...things that are past, it is needless to blame.

- When we see good and kind people, we should think of following their example; when we see criminal and greedy people, we should look at ourselves.

- The good person is satisfied and calm; the mean person is always full of distress.

- Without knowing the force of words, it is impossible to know the world.

THE WISDOM OF CONFUCIUS

At about the same time Buddha was teaching in India, civilization in China had its own great and wise teacher. Born in 551 B.C., he was named Confucius (kən fū′ shəs).

Confucius lived during a time of great unrest. Under the Zhou (jō) dynasty, China was a group of kingdoms whose rulers often made war on one another and often treated their people harshly. Confucius wanted to bring peace and justice to China.

Confucius taught that peace and justice begin in the home. Children should respect and obey their parents, and parents must treat their children well. People should respect and obey their rulers. In turn, rulers should treat people with respect, too. And everyone should respect the emperor, who should be kind.

Confucius wanted to change society by showing rulers how to govern wisely. To govern well, he said, a ruler must be honest and kind. The people would then follow the ruler's example.

If a ruler himself is upright, all will go well without orders. But if he himself is not upright, even though he gives orders they will not be obeyed.

After his death in 479 B.C., Confucius's teachings spread throughout China. His ideas about duty to family and country became part of the fabric of Chinese society. His many sayings became rules for how people should improve themselves and act toward one another. Look at some of Confucius's sayings in the box on this page. You probably know one of them already, although in a different wording: "What you do not want done to yourself, do not do to others."

THE GREAT WALL OF CHINA

The China of Confucius's time was troubled by warfare among its own kingdoms. But then and in following years, China also suffered attacks from outside its borders. Fierce nomads from the harsh north often came south in waves, to rob and kill. Not even the large and harsh Gobi Desert could keep them out.

Beginning in the fifth century B.C. feudal lords built walls along their northern borders to try to hold back the invaders. In the third century B.C., the emperor Shihuangdi (shē' hwäng dē), founder of the Qin (chin) dynasty, decided to unite these walls and strengthen them. He ordered the building of the Great Wall of China "that still stands like a big dragon of stone across the hills of China."

The Great Wall stretches from China's east coast far into Outer China.

Building it was an incredible task. Shihuangdi drafted an army of 300,000 peasants to do the work. The emperor ordered the people to pay high taxes to feed the workers and pay for their tools.

At first the Great Wall ran only 1,500 miles (2,200 km) in length and was made mainly of packed earth. In the centuries that followed, other emperors added to the wall. Great stones were raised to make new walls and watch-towers that overlooked the country-side. Look at the diagram on pages 502–503 to see how the Great Wall was constructed. When it was finished, it was the longest structure ever built.

A moat ran alongside the outer walls. Soldiers' camps lined the inner walls. Once the enemy was spotted from the watchtowers, fires were lighted to alert the soldiers. But for all this effort, the Great Wall was not a perfect barrier. For example, it could not hold back Ghengis Khan (jeng' is kän) and his warriors. These invaders swept into China during the 1200s.

Only a strong, unified nation could carry out such a vast project as building the Great Wall of China. Chinese school children enjoy visiting the wall today.

BUILDING THE GREAT WALL OF CHINA

THE GREAT WALL

——— 221–210 B.C.
——— A.D. 1368–1644

CHINA

Beijing

Huang
River

Chang

River

Under Kublai Khan's direction the Grand Canal became a major inland waterway. Today it remains an important transportation route between north and south.

KUBLAI KHAN

The powerful Mongols did not take long to conquer North China. The grandson of Genghis, Kublai Khan (kü′ blī kän), continued the Mongol conquest southward. They followed and fought the last remnants of the Song (sùn) dynasty. Knowing that defeat was at hand, the Song royal family drowned themselves in the China Sea rather than accept the disgrace. Now Kublai was Grand Khan of all China— North and South. Under the Mongols' Yuan (yū än′) dynasty, China, for the first time, was ruled by an emperor from a foreign land.

Kublai Khan chose Beijing to be his capital. He determined to make it into a dazzling capital city. He laid out straight, wide streets in a grid pattern. Kublai Khan also worked to improve transportation to Beijing. Centuries earlier, emperors had ordered the Grand Canal to be built to form a north-to-south link between the Huang and Chang rivers. Like the Great Wall, the Grand Canal was one of the greatest building feats of all time. Now Kublai Khan ordered 100,000 workers to lengthen the canal to reach Beijing. As the photograph above shows, the Grand Canal is still used today.

Within a few years boats filled with rice from South China were unloading their cargoes at Beijing docks to feed the growing city. The European visitor Marco Polo, marveled at China's riches. He wrote in about 1220:

More precious goods are imported into this city than into any other city in the world. All the treasures from India— precious stones, pearls, and other rarities—are brought here. . . . Every day more than 1,000 cart-loads of silk enter the city.

504

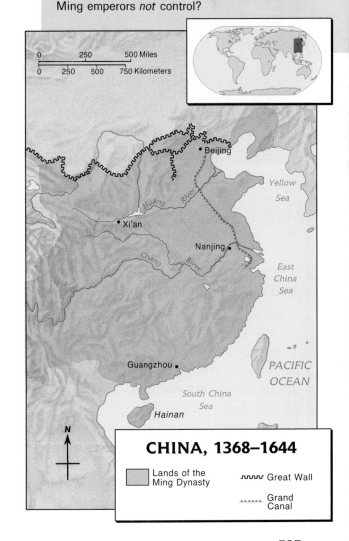

MAP SKILL: The Forbidden City remained the home of Chinese emperors until the twentieth century. What part of today's China did the Ming emperors *not* control?

0   250   500 Miles

0   250   500   750 Kilometers

Beijing

Yellow Sea

Huang River

Xi'an

Nanjing

Chang River

East China Sea

Guangzhou

PACIFIC OCEAN

South China Sea

Hainan

N

CHINA, 1368–1644

Lands of the Ming Dynasty

Great Wall

Grand Canal

THE FORBIDDEN CITY

The Yuan dynasty was replaced in 1368 by the Ming dynasty. Proud of their great history, the Chinese emperors of the Ming ordered new buildings in Beijing to be built. They created the magnificent Forbidden City. It was so named because only the emperor and his family and servants were allowed to live there. All others, except guards and government officials, were forbidden even to set foot in it.

Located in the center of Beijing, the Forbidden City is surrounded by walls. Within these walls lie three stately halls that different emperors used for religious and government ceremonies. They are separated by vast open spaces. Three palaces housed the imperial family. Carved dragons, the symbol of the emperor, appear everywhere, as do peacocks, the symbol of the empress. Streams filled with goldfish flowed among the buildings. Gardens filled with every variety of flower greeted the eye.

Shihuangdi's burial place, found in 1974, contained great numbers of life-size statues of the soldiers and horses in his army.

A DYNASTIC LEGACY

As you have read, the dynasties led China through periods of greatness. They were helped by the wise teachings of Confucius. His ideals of duty, obedience, and respect gave the Chinese people a common code of behavior. Chinese emperors encouraged this code. It helped them to unite their people to build works of a size and scope that still stagger the imagination. As you have read, the Great Wall of China is one of the world's greatest wonders.

As you will read in the Traditions lesson that follows, the people of China continue to build upon this rich cultural legacy.

Check Your Reading

1. Describe the Mandate of Heaven.
2. List three important developments of Chinese civilization.
3. **GEOGRAPHY SKILL:** Use the map on page 505 to name the rivers that flowed through the lands of the Ming dynasty.
4. **THINKING SKILL:** Compare and contrast the teachings of Confucius, Buddha, and Solomon.

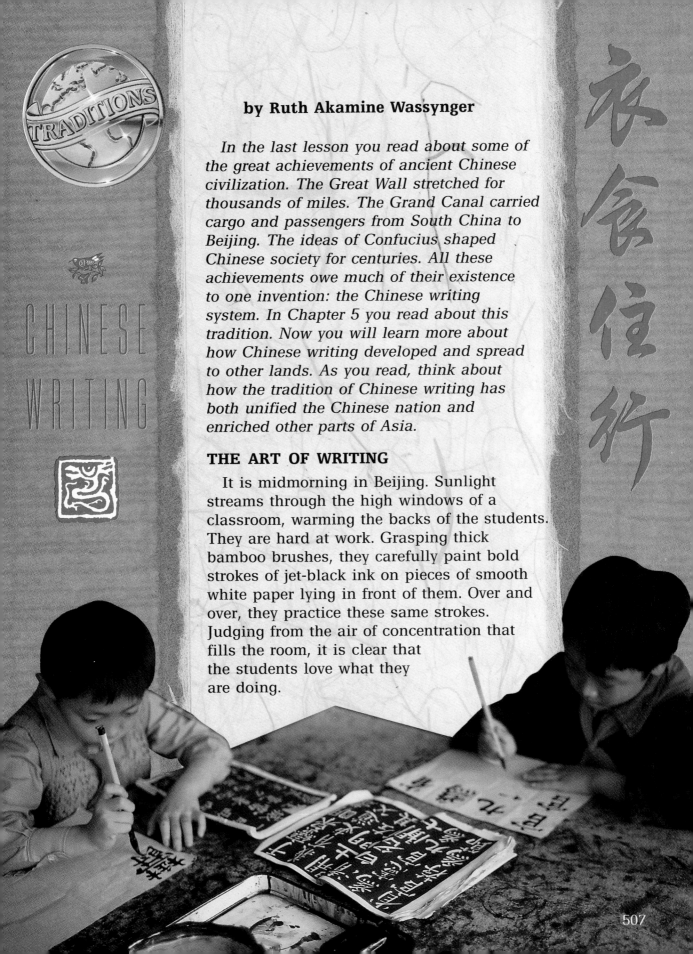

TRADITIONS

CHINESE WRITING

衣食住行

by Ruth Akamine Wassynger

In the last lesson you read about some of the great achievements of ancient Chinese civilization. The Great Wall stretched for thousands of miles. The Grand Canal carried cargo and passengers from South China to Beijing. The ideas of Confucius shaped Chinese society for centuries. All these achievements owe much of their existence to one invention: the Chinese writing system. In Chapter 5 you read about this tradition. Now you will learn more about how Chinese writing developed and spread to other lands. As you read, think about how the tradition of Chinese writing has both unified the Chinese nation and enriched other parts of Asia.

THE ART OF WRITING

It is midmorning in Beijing. Sunlight streams through the high windows of a classroom, warming the backs of the students. They are hard at work. Grasping thick bamboo brushes, they carefully paint bold strokes of jet-black ink on pieces of smooth white paper lying in front of them. Over and over, they practice these same strokes. Judging from the air of concentration that fills the room, it is clear that the students love what they are doing.

507

Is this an art class? A writing class? In fact, it is both. The students are busily practicing one of the oldest skills, as well as one of the oldest traditional arts, in Chinese culture—writing.

THE HEART OF CHINESE CULTURE

Think for a moment about why writing is important in any culture. People use writing to capture their thoughts and turn them into poetry. They depend on the written word to preserve their laws, their history, their religious beliefs, and even such everyday things as recipes. China's writing system has helped the Chinese to do all these things and more.

It also has served as a powerful "glue" in Chinese society. Although all the people in China speak Chinese, they speak hundreds of different dialects, or versions, of the language. These dialects differ from one another so much that they are almost separate languages.

Written Chinese, however, has the same meaning everywhere. For example, a newspaper printed in Beijing can be read and understood by people throughout China who speak different dialects. But if that newspaper were read aloud to these same people by a Beijing resident, many of them would not understand what was being said. In this way, the Chinese writing system has helped to unify a diverse land into a nation with a rich, shared heritage.

CHINA'S GIFT TO ASIA

China's writing system is one of the oldest in the world. It began about 3,500 years ago, during the time the pharaohs were ruling Egypt and the Aryans were migrating into the Indus River Valley. The Chinese writing system uses ideographs (id′ ē ə grafs), or simple pictures, to represent things and ideas. These ideographs are similar to the Egyptian hieroglyphs that you read about in Chapter 3.

China's writing system impressed people in neighboring countries who had none of their own. In the years after A.D. 400—as the Roman Empire was crumbling and Ethiopia was expanding its power throughout Africa—people in Korea, Japan, and what is present-day Vietnam began to adopt China's writing system. They also came to value the ideas and artistic traditions that they encountered in Chinese books. Soon these people were studying the ideas of Confucius as well as the art of writing itself. As a result of its writing system, Chinese culture spread throughout Asia.

A VISUAL LANGUAGE

Today the Chinese writing system is made up of about 50,000 ideographs. Fortunately for students, however, only about 3,000 are used in everyday life. Some Chinese ideographs also are used today in Japan.

Written Chinese is very different from alphabet-based languages such as English. In written English, for example, letters representing sounds are arranged in different combinations to make up words. In written Chinese, by contrast, ideographs "picture" things and ideas. This is why people who speak different Chinese dialects—and even different languages, such as Japanese or Korean—are all able to understand a Chinese ideograph. They might have different ways of pronouncing the ideograph, but its meaning is the same for everyone.

This ancient Chinese scroll combines a painting of a woman with an inscription in ideographs.

Written Chinese is a difficult language to learn. But ideographs can also make learning easier. Since written Chinese is a picture-language, ideographs sometimes look like the things that they are meant to represent. Here are two examples:

KOU: the mouth

MU: tree or wood

A TRADITION CONTINUES

Today China's ancient writing system faces new challenges. As computers become more and more widespread, ideograph-based languages are at a great disadvantage. Imagine trying to design a computer keyboard that could produce 3,000 different ideographs! Until the 1980s, there were no computer programs that made printing of Chinese characters fast and easy. Most documents had to be written by hand, slowing down work considerably. This led some people in China and Japan to call for a change to an alphabet-based writing system.

While this suggestion is practical, it has not gained widespread support. Many Chinese and Japanese feel that their heritage is deeply rooted in China's unique picture-language. It is a tradition that continues to withstand time and technology.

How has the tradition of Chinese writing enriched both China and other parts of Asia?

3 A Changing China

Key Vocabulary

warlord
Long March

Key People

Sun Yat-sen
Chiang Kai-shek
Mao Zedong

Key Places

Manchuria
Mongolia
Guangzhou
Shanghai
Formosa

Read Aloud

After centuries of dynastic life, China has begun to change. China has passed through a new door. It will lead her millions of people into an unknown and unpredictable future.

The author of these words left China for Europe in 1910. His journal records many different hopes and fears that he felt toward his homeland. When he returned home in 1937, China had greatly changed. In this lesson you will read about the events that changed the course of Chinese history.

Read for Purpose

1. **WHAT YOU KNOW:** What dramatic changes took place in Europe after the Industrial Revolution?
2. **WHAT YOU WILL LEARN:** How did China change?

THE MANCHUS

The conquerors of the Ming dynasty were the Manchus. They came south from the fertile plain of Manchuria. Today Manchuria is an important part of North China.

The Manchus boldly claimed that the Mandate of Heaven had passed to them. When they conquered Beijing in 1644, they founded a dynasty called the Qing (ching). The Qing dynasty would rule for nearly 300 years—and it would be China's last dynasty. The Manchus ruled until 1912.

Under the Manchus, China grew and prospered. Qing control spread far beyond China's old borders to areas of today's Outer China, such as Mongolia and Tibet. China's population more than doubled. By 1800 food for more than 300 million people had to be grown.

As China grew, European traders from the West—the British especially—wanted Chinese goods, such as fine silks, porcelain, and tea. But their desire for trade quickly grew into demands that threatened China's future.

511

In this French political cartoon from the late 1800s, Britain, Germany, Russia, France, and Japan carve up China.

CHINA'S TROUBLED FOREIGN TRADE

The Manchu emperors did not trust the Europeans. Thus they allowed foreign merchants to trade in only one Chinese port—Guangzhou (gwäng jō), also called Canton.

Moreover, the Chinese did not really want Europe's manufactured goods. As a result, European traders could get Chinese goods only by paying gold or silver for them. To the Europeans this was too high a price.

Soon, however, the British discovered a new and cheaper way to pay for Chinese goods. They began bringing the drug opium, produced in India and Turkey, to China's shores. Before long Chinese from every walk of life became addicted to the destructive drug.

Chinese goods as well as Chinese gold and silver began pouring out of the country to buy opium.

The effects on China and its people were terrible. One of the emperor's officials warned:

The country will become poorer and poorer and its people weaker and weaker. Eventually not only will there be no adequate funds to support an army, there will be no useful soldiers at all!

The emperor ordered that the opium trade be stopped. In response, the British attacked Chinese ports. Starting in 1839, this "Opium War" went on for three years. Superior British weapons defeated the Chinese military. Not only did the opium trade continue, but the Manchu emperor was forced to open all of China to Western traders. From now on, they, not he, would make the rules for how trade was carried on.

Weakened from the outside, the Qing dynasty was weakening from within, too. High government officials were stealing tax money to build up their own fortunes. One high official was rumored to have stolen over 1 billion dollars. To make up for such losses, the government taxed the peasants even more heavily. Rebellion, overthrow, and the end of a dynasty were again about to take place.

FATHER OF THE REPUBLIC

In their last days the Manchu rulers realized that to rid China of European control, they must make it more modern. They sent thousands of young Chinese students to schools in Europe and the United States to be educated. They hoped these students would bring back Western skills and technology to modernize China.

The flags over Guangzhou's harbor reflect the trading interest placed on China. As you can see, the painting also shows many different European ships and buildings.

But while they were studying, these young people also learned about Western democratic government. One of them was Sun Yat-sen, who had been sent to study in Hawaii. Like many other Chinese students, he returned to China hoping to turn it into a republic.

Sun Yat-sen led a revolt against Manchu rule in 1895, but it failed. He was forced to flee into exile. By 1912, however, another rebellion succeeded. The Manchus were overthrown and China became a republic.

Sun Yat-sen found that trying to unify China under a republican government was a huge task. "The Chinese people have only family and clan solidarity," he complained. "They do not have national spirit. . . . They are just a heap of loose sand."

Even so, Sun Yat-sen and his followers, called the Nationalists, struggled on. Their new government was able to gain control only in some parts of South China. Elsewhere in the country, army generals took control of vast territories, where they named themselves rulers. Called warlords, these generals were very harsh rulers. As always in time of unrest, the peasants suffered the most. The warlords forced some peasants into their armies to battle other warlords. They taxed and robbed the remaining peasants, often to the point of starvation. When Sun Yat-sen died in 1925, China was in chaos. No one knew what the future would bring.

Although they were bitter enemies, Chiang Kai-shek (*left*) and Mao Zedong (*right*) united during World War II to fight the Japanese.

THE NATIONALISTS

In an effort to defeat the warlords, Sun Yat-sen founded a powerful Nationalist army. After his death, a general named Chiang Kai-shek (chäng kī shek), rose to head the army and the government.

During this same time, another political group was forming in China—the Communists. They did not like Chiang Kai-shek, and he did not like them. But like the Nationalists, the Communists wanted to see China unified. So they joined the Nationalists to fight the warlords. One by one, the warlords were defeated. By the late 1920s Chiang had united much of China under Nationalist rule.

Now Chiang made a fateful decision. He decided to destroy the Communists. With this decision, China entered into a civil war—Nationalist against Communist. It would hurt the nation for the next 20 years.

THE LONG MARCH

The Nationalists quickly took the upper hand in the war. Chiang first sent troops to Shanghai, a center of Communist support. There, in a number of raids, the Nationalists killed thousands of Communists. Some survivors went into hiding.

Leading the Communists was a young teacher named Mao Zedong (mou' dzu dùng). The son of peasants, Mao believed that eventual Communist victory depended on winning the support of the peasants. If the peasants were promised freedom from high rents and taxes, they would "rise up like a mighty storm," he said.

Once again, Chiang sent his troops against the Communists. The small army the Communists had raised, called the Red Army, was no match for the Nationalist forces of half a million soldiers. In 1934 the Communists were once again forced to flee. One hundred thousand of them set out on foot to find refuge in Outer China.

Their dangerous journey would turn out to be one of the greatest marches in the history of the world. It was called the Long March. You can find its route on the map on the next page.

Mao Zedong said that the Long March took the Communists "across the longest and deepest and most dangerous rivers in China, across some of the worst mountain passes, through empty grasslands, through cold and through intense heat, through wind and snow and rainstorm." They were pursued by half the Nationalist armies and had to fight their way "past the local armies of nine provinces."

514

THE LONG MARCH 1934–1935

→ Route of the Long March

Huang River

Yan'an

CHINA

Nanjing

Luding

Chogqing

Chang River

East China Sea

Kunming

Rui Jin

0   200   400 Miles
0   200   400   600 Kilometers

MAP SKILL: The Communists' Long March lasted an entire year. What Chinese cities were its starting and ending points?

THE COMMUNIST TRIUMPH

In the midst of the civil war, World War II brought the two sides together for a short time. When Japan invaded China, the Chinese stopped fighting each other and fought the Japanese invaders instead. But when Japan was defeated in 1945, the civil war began once again.

This time the Communists had the upper hand. Mao Zedong had been right. Promises of reform to the peasants won their widespread support. Also, dissatisfaction with the Nationalist government had grown. Many Chinese people thought it was both inefficient and corrupt. They saw government officials growing rich while poor people starved.

By 1949 Mao and his well-trained Red Army routed the last of the Nationalist forces. Chiang and remnants of the Nationalist government fled to Formosa, an island off China's east coast. On October 1 the Chinese mainland became a communist nation—the People's Republic of China.

THREE CENTURIES OF CHANGE

From the Manchu conquest in 1644 to the end of World War II in 1945, the Chinese found their ancient civilization attacked by foreigners. The Manchus had taken the imperial throne, and then the Europeans had forced their influence upon China. Once China freed itself from outside forces, it faced new troubles. Dreams of a fair, democratic republic were torn apart, first by warlords and then by civil war.

Check Your Reading

1. What caused the Opium War?
2. How did China change after the Ming dynasty?
3. **GEOGRAPHY SKILL:** What was the route of the Long March?
4. **THINKING SKILL:** Why do you think Mao Zedong was able to win the support of so many Chinese people?

Evaluating Information

"That's not fair!" How many times have you heard those words? Sometimes they are said to show sympathy. Other times, they are spoken to try to convince you of something.

When you are faced with arguments or descriptions that seek to persuade or convince, you need to evaluate the information. To evaluate means to decide if the information is true and whether or not you should trust it.

You can use many of the thinking skills you have learned in this book to evaluate information you hear or read. One way to begin is to separate the facts from the opinions. Remember, a fact can be proven true, an opinion cannot. Once you do this, you will then be able to identify the writer's or speaker's point of view. The way a person looks at or feels about something can limit or distort the information. Determining point of view will help you decide if the source of the information is credible and can be believed.

Trying the Skill

Following are two reports about the conflict between the Nationalists and the Chinese Communists. **Report A** is from the private diary of a United States general who was in China between 1911 and 1945. **Report B** was written in 1956 by an American whose parents had lived in China from 1930 to 1940. Read both reports and then evaluate the information in **Report A**.

Report A

In 1934, 700,000 Nationalists launched a campaign against 160,000 Communists. Even with many weapons and planes, the Nationalists could not stop the Communists from escaping. The Nationalist forces then tried to kill the local peasants. They burned their houses and drove away their cattle.

Report B

In 1934, the Nationalists tried to drive the Communist rebels out of China. Over the years, the Communists had been growing stronger and stronger. Their plan was to mount a revolt against the government. They wanted to start a revolution. The Nationalists were right to fear the Communists.

1. What is your evaluation of the information in **Report A**?
2. How did you form this opinion?

HELPING YOURSELF

The steps on the left will help you evaluate any information that tries to convince or persuade you. The example on the right shows one way to apply these steps to **Report A**.

One Way to Evaluate Information	Example
1. Identify the subject or topic.	The subject is the conflict in China between the Nationalists and the Communists.
2. Determine if the source can be believed.	The writer is an eyewitness. Since the account is a personal diary, there is no reason why the writer should give wrong or false information.
3. Separate the facts and opinions.	The year and the number of troops on each side are facts. The report states that the Nationalists were armed with weapons and planes. These are factual statements. They can be proven to be true by actual evidence. There are no clue words to tell you that the writer is giving an opinion.
4. Identify the author's point of view.	This report does not mention how the Communists acted. However, the writer described the Nationalists in harsh terms. The writer must be telling the story from the point of view of someone opposed to the Nationalists.
5. State your evaluation of the information. Should you believe it?	One evaluation might be that the author of **Report A** is a credible source, but that his writing is influenced by his opinions.

Applying the Skill

Now reread **Report B**. What is your evaluation of the information?

1. Which of the following pieces of information could you use to determine if this source can be believed?
   a. the writer's background
   b. the length of the account
   c. the main idea of the account
   d. the publication date
2. Which of the statements in the report are facts?

3. What is the point of view of the writer of **Report B**?
   a. procommunist
   b. an objective observer
   c. anticommunist

Reviewing the Skill

1. What are you doing when you evaluate information?
2. What are some steps you could take to help you evaluate information?
3. When is it important to be able to evaluate information?

4 China Today

READ">READ TO LEARN

Key Vocabulary

commune
Cultural Revolution

Key Places

Tian An Men Square

Read Aloud

No matter North, South, East, or West, in ancient times or present, human beings know intuitively [naturally] *to pursue peace, to pursue happiness, to pursue freedom, to pursue a better world.*

With these words, Chinese scientist Fang Lizhi accepted the Nobel Peace Prize in 1989. In this lesson you will read about the ways in which China's people have tried to "pursue a better world" during the last 40 years.

Read for Purpose

1. **WHAT YOU KNOW:** What is communism?
2. **WHAT YOU WILL LEARN:** In what ways has China changed since 1949?

A NEW COMMUNIST NATION

When Mao Zedong took power in 1949, he faced huge challenges. China lay in ruins, shattered by 12 long years of war. It had lost its place among the world's greatest nations. Factories stood silent. Hungry people crowded city streets begging for food. More food had to be grown to feed the country's huge population. More factories had to be built to produce the steel, machines, and energy needed to rebuild China.

Mao and his followers set out to meet these needs by applying the principles of communism. The Communist leaders took large areas of farmland away from wealthy landowners and divided them among peasants. The government also took control of China's businesses and factories.

THE "GREAT LEAP FORWARD"

But Mao was not satisfied with the progress that China was making. In 1957 he announced that it was time for China's people to take a "Great Leap Forward." Mao believed that with much hard work and self-sacrifice, the Chinese people could make their economy grow at a faster pace. The slogan of the Great Leap Forward became "more, faster, better, cheaper."

Mao urged factories to stay open around the clock. In order to increase

Mao thought that communes would make better use of China's farmland. But many Chinese liked their old ways better.

crop production, Mao's government reorganized China's system of agriculture. Peasants were forced to give up their private farms, and their land became part of large farming communities called communes. Farms and villages were joined together into single communes of about 8,000 people. The government assigned each commune certain crops to produce. Men and women in the commune were divided into teams called "production brigades." Each brigade had responsibility for a different chore, such as hoeing fields or running the commune's child-care center.

The Great Leap Forward turned out to be a failure. Factory machines broke down from overuse. Farm production suffered because most political leaders knew very little about farming. Many government leaders realized that reforms, or changes to correct problems, were desperately needed. They began to close down unproductive factories. They gave some peasants their own small plots of land to farm. And they offered farmers and workers rewards

for working harder. However, these reforms angered Mao, who was still China's most powerful leader. Mao said that the reformers' changes were "copying the West." He thought that these new programs wrongly stressed the importance of the individual over that of the group.

THE CULTURAL REVOLUTION

In 1966 Mao removed these reformist leaders from office. Then he called on the people to create a new culture in China based entirely on communist ideas. This drastic new program was called the Cultural Revolution. Millions of young people joined together to form armies called the Red Guards to carry out Mao's Cultural Revolution.

The Red Guards arrested and tortured people who disagreed with Mao's policies. They destroyed ancient temples, books, and paintings that they felt were anticommunist. Teachers,

519

scientists, artists, and other citizens were arrested for holding beliefs that were different from Mao's.

Liang Heng was one of the people whose family was arrested during the Cultural Revolution. His father, a journalist, had angered government officials with his writings. Liang later wrote about the confusion he felt when he and his family were relocated from the city to a commune in the country.

> I reached down and broke a piece of the cold, dry earth in my fingers. . . . Then Father's freshly polished leather shoes caught my attention. He looked bizarre in this place where everything was [tinted] with the color of the land. I suddenly wondered how we were ever going to make it.

Liang and his family worked on a commune for more than a year before they were released. But the harsh practices of the Cultural Revolution continued until 1976, when Mao died and new leaders took control of China.

OPENING DOORS

Although these new leaders were Communists, they had a different plan for helping China. Their plan, called the "Four Modernizations," stressed the development of agriculture, industry, technology, and defense.

The Four Modernizations prompted China to open its doors wide to other countries. Thousands of Chinese students were sent abroad to study science and technology. The new leaders also began improving working conditions in the countryside. Peasants could now sell part of their crops for their own profit.

THE DEMOCRACY MOVEMENT

But many Chinese believed that the government also needed to work

During China's **Cultural Revolution** the teachings of Mao Zedong were very important. In fact, the Red Guards often marched through the streets carrying giant portraits of Mao.

In 1989 Chinese students protested for democratic reforms in Beijing's Tian An Men Square. The government sent in tanks and troops to end the protests.

toward a "Fifth Modernization"— democracy. In May 1989, over 1 million people, mainly university students, camped out in Beijing's Tian An Men (tē an' an men) Square. These demonstrators called for democracy in China. But meanwhile, the Communist government prepared to crush the democracy movement.

On June 3 the demonstrators learned that the army would strike soon. One student who remained in the square made the following observation.

> *At about four o'clock, just before dawn, all the lights on the square suddenly went out. . . . A deep chill went through me. The time had come.*

Early on the morning of June 4, army tanks rolled into the darkened square. As demonstrators ran for safety, soldiers started shooting into the crowd. Hundreds of people were killed, and still more were imprisoned for taking part in the protest. For the moment, the democracy movement in China was silenced.

TOWARD THE FUTURE

China has come a long way since Mao Zedong first took control of the war-torn country in 1949. But many old problems and new challenges face China today. China's ability to feed and clothe its people is strained by its large population of more than 1 billion. And the Communist government itself must deal with the Chinese people's increasing desire for democracy.

 Check Your Reading

1. How did the Communist government rebuild China after 1949?
2. What did Mao Zedong try to accomplish with the Cultural Revolution?
3. GEOGRAPHY SKILL: How did communes change the way in which peasants interacted with their environment?
4. THINKING SKILL: What are two conclusions that you can draw about China since 1949?

IMPORTANT EVENTS

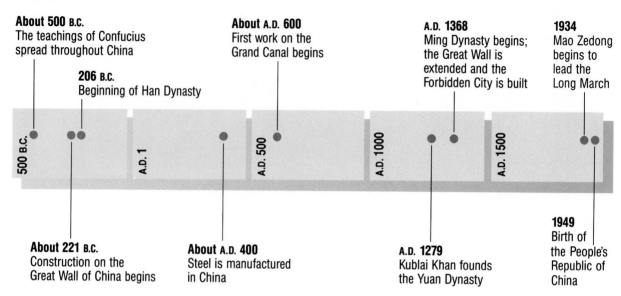

About 500 B.C.
The teachings of Confucius spread throughout China

206 B.C.
Beginning of Han Dynasty

About A.D. 600
First work on the Grand Canal begins

A.D. 1368
Ming Dynasty begins; the Great Wall is extended and the Forbidden City is built

1934
Mao Zedong begins to lead the Long March

About 221 B.C.
Construction on the Great Wall of China begins

About A.D. 400
Steel is manufactured in China

A.D. 1279
Kublai Khan founds the Yuan Dynasty

1949
Birth of the People's Republic of China

500 B.C.   A.D. 1   A.D. 500   A.D. 1000   A.D. 1500

PEOPLE TO KNOW

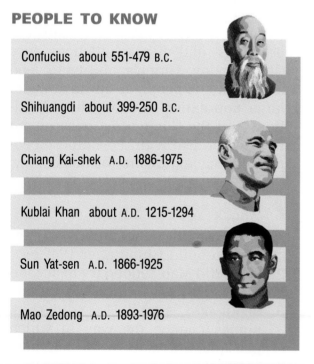

Confucius   about 551-479 B.C.

Shihuangdi   about 399-250 B.C.

Chiang Kai-shek   A.D. 1886-1975

Kublai Khan   about A.D. 1215-1294

Sun Yat-sen   A.D. 1866-1925

Mao Zedong   A.D. 1893-1976

IDEAS TO REMEMBER

- From Tibet to the Pacific Ocean, China is a huge country. About one fifth of all the world's people live within its borders.
- The landmarks of Chinese civilization—a dynastic cycle, the Great Wall, the Forbidden City—represent many years of incredible growth.
- During the Qing dynasty China was influenced by many outside forces.
- Life in China was transformed by communism and the rule of Mao Zedong. For many years China was closed to outside influences. Recently, however, China has opened its doors to the West.

REVIEWING VOCABULARY

commune	paddy
Mandate of Heaven	terrace
	warlord

Number a sheet of paper from 1 to 5. Beside each number write the word or term from the list above that best completes each sentence.

1. China's emperors justified their absolute power by claiming they had a _____ to rule China.
2. By building _____, Chinese farmers have for centuries created more flat land on which to farm.
3. Mao Zedong ordered that all the farms in an area join together in a single unit called a _____.
4. A _____, or a wet field surrounded by earthen walls, is the main method of growing rice in South China.
5. In the first decades of the twentieth century, due to a weak central government, much of China was ruled by generals called _____.

REVIEWING FACTS

1. In which two regions of China do most people live? Where is China's most productive farmland found?
2. Why do people call Outer China the land of "too manys" and "too littles"?
3. How did a terrace help farmers increase food production?
4. Why is the history of China's dynasties called a "cycle?"
5. Why did Confucius want to reform Chinese society?
6. List three changes that Mongol rulers brought to China.

7. How did the Opium War prove the weakness of China's Manchu rulers?
8. Why did Sun Yat-sen call the Chinese people "just a heap of loose sand"?
9. To what class of Chinese did Mao Zedong appeal against the Nationalists? How did this help his cause?
10. Who was responsible for the Great Leap Forward? What were the major reasons for its failure?

WRITING ABOUT MAIN IDEAS

1. **Writing a "Help-Wanted" Ad:** Imagine that you are the "contractor" responsible for the construction of China's Great Wall. Write a "help-wanted" ad for workers. Be sure to describe the type of work, its purpose, working conditions, salary, and benefits.
2. **Writing About Perspectives:** Imagine that you were a student demonstrating in Tian An Men Square. Write a paragraph describing how you felt about the government's actions.

BUILDING SKILLS: EVALUATING INFORMATION

Read the quotation in the Chapter Opener on page 490. Then answer the following questions.

1. What is the subject of the quotation?
2. How could you determine whether the source of this quotation should be believed?
3. Identify the facts and opinions in this quotation.
4. Identify the author's point of view.
5. In what situations is it important to know how to evaluate information?

CHAPTER 20

JAPAN AND KOREA

FOCUS

I have heard that it is a land of beauty and that hundreds of communities rise near the surrounding seas. I have been told that the dwellers of its many islands are charmed with great kindness and culture. . . .

When Marco Polo returned to Europe after many years in Asia, he reported that a remarkable people lived in the lands east of China. He was writing about the Japanese, who lived on a chain of islands on the rim of Asia.

1 The Geography of Japan and Korea

READ TO LEARN

Key Vocabulary

archipelago
typhoon

Key Places

Mount Fuji
Korean Strait

Read Aloud

The people of Wa [Japan] *dwell in the middle of the ocean on the serene* [calm] *mountainous islands. . . .*

As this ancient writer noted, there is a group of islands off the eastern coast of Asia called Japan. Nearby, there is a peninsula that extends from the Asian mainland called Korea. In this lesson you will begin to learn about these neighbors. As you know, in order to understand a group of people, it is helpful to first learn more about the place in which they live.

Read for Purpose

1. **WHAT YOU KNOW:** What is the largest continent?
2. **WHAT YOU WILL LEARN:** How is the geography of Japan and the Korean peninsula similar?

JAPAN IS AN ARCHIPELAGO

Japan lies east of China, in the direction of the sunrise. In fact, the name "Japan" comes from the Chinese word *jih pen*, which means "origin of the sun." The islands of Japan are separated from China by about 500 miles (800 km) of ocean. The part of the Asian mainland nearest to Japan is Korea, 100 miles (170 km) across water. In their early history the Japanese were close enough to feel the civilizing influence of China. Yet they were far enough away to be safe from invasion.

More than 3,000 islands make up the archipelago (är kə pel′ ə gō), or island group, that forms Japan. Many of these islands are very small. The Japanese archipelago was created by volcanoes beneath the sea. Over the ages billions of tons of lava rose from deep within the earth and built up many islands. Most of Japan's people have always lived on the four largest islands.

Much of Japan is covered by hills and mountains. Mount Fuji, the highest peak in Japan, is snow-covered for most of the year. The mountainous landscape means that Japan has limited farmland. But, like the Chinese, the Japanese use terraces to create more farmland. You will also learn that fishing is an important industry in Japan.

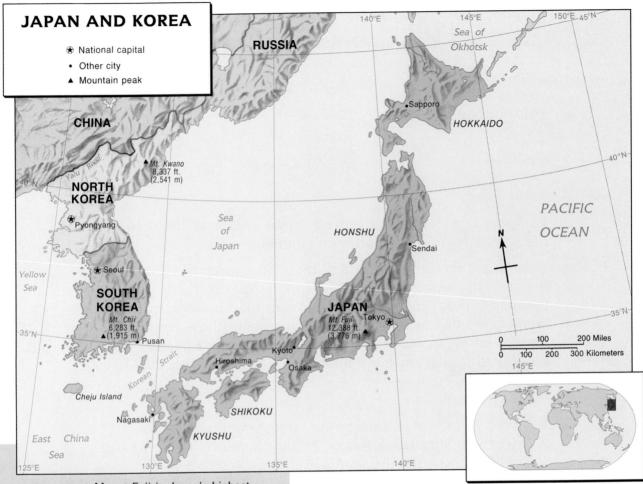

JAPAN AND KOREA

- ⊛ National capital
- • Other city
- ▲ Mountain peak

RUSSIA

CHINA

Sea of Okhotsk

Sapporo

HOKKAIDO

▲ *Mt. Kwano*
8,337 ft.
(2,541 m)

NORTH
KOREA

⊛ Pyongyang

Sea of Japan

HONSHU

Sendai

PACIFIC
OCEAN

⊛ Seoul

SOUTH
KOREA

Mt. Chii
6,283 ft.
▲(1,915 m)   • Pusan

Yellow Sea

JAPAN

Mt. Fuji
12,388 ft.
(3,776 m) ▲   Tokyo ⊛

Kyoto •

Hiroshima •

Osaka •

Korean Strait

Cheju Island

Nagasaki •

SHIKOKU

KYUSHU

East China Sea

N

0   100   200 Miles

0   100   200   300 Kilometers

MAP SKILL: Mount Fuji is Japan's highest mountain. Use the map above to find its elevation.

THE KOREAN PENINSULA

As the map above shows, Korea is a peninsula attached to China. The Korean peninsula is bounded by the Yellow Sea on the west, the East China Sea on the south, and the Sea of Japan on the east. The waters of the Korean Strait separate Korea from Japan.

Mountains and hills cover most of the Korean peninsula, making it a land of great natural beauty. But the mountains and hills take up so much land that most of the people live on narrow plains along the coasts. These coastal plains have much of Korea's best farmland. Like the Chinese and Japanese, the Koreans use terraces to create more farmland.

Though Japan and Korea differ in land shape, their landforms are similar. Mountains also cover about 80 percent of Japan's land. The climates of Japan and Korea are also similar.

A MILD CLIMATE

As you have read, both Korea and Japan lie near large bodies of water. You will remember that ocean currents affect temperature. In fact, southern and eastern Japan are both warmed by the Japan Current. Like the North Atlantic Drift that you read about in Chapter 8, the Japan Current warms the air over Japan.

Monsoons also affect Japan and Korea. During the summer, warm southeast winds bring heavy rains. In the late summer and early fall, fierce storms roar into Japan from the Pacific Ocean. Called **typhoons**, their winds blow up to 150 miles (230 km) an hour. Typhoons batter the coastlines and uproot trees. They flood valleys, causing great damage. Typhoons sweep across the Sea of Japan and hit hard against Korea's coasts.

NATURAL RESOURCES

Neither Japan nor Korea is rich in natural resources. Japan mines less than one per cent of the iron ore it needs. It imports the rest, along with most of the coal and oil that a modern industrial country must have. Korea has large deposits of coal and iron and has used them to develop industry.

A long, jagged coastline is one resource that both Japan and Korea share. The surrounding waters of both countries are abundant with fish. Since ancient times these seas have provided Japan and Korea with their major source of food.

With such long coastlines, the people of Japan and Korea have always used the sea as a resource to supply their food.

NEIGHBORS

As you read this chapter, you will learn more about the archipelago of Japan and the Korean peninsula. You will read that these lands have more in common than just their geography. Both Japan and Korea were greatly influenced by their powerful Chinese neighbor to the west. You will also learn that Japan and Korea borrowed from each other as they grew.

 Check Your Reading

1. What is an archipelago?
2. How do warm currents affect the climate of Japan and Korea?
3. **GEOGRAPHY SKILL:** What bodies of water surround Japan and Korea?
4. **THINKING SKILL:** What are three conclusions you can make about the geography of Japan and Korea?

527

Understanding Great-Circle Routes

Key Vocabulary

great circle
great-circle route

Imagine that you are making a trip to China and Japan. After spending a few weeks in China, you want to fly the shortest route between Hangzhou, China, and Otaru, Japan. Your route would take you over South Korea as shown below on **Map A**. It would follow a special route known as a **great circle**.

A great circle is any circle that divides the earth into equal halves, or hemispheres. It is the largest circle that can be drawn along the earth. The equator is a great circle. The equator divides the earth into the Northern Hemisphere and the Southern Hemisphere. Another great circle is formed by the 0° line of longitude and the 180° line of longitude. It divides the earth into the Eastern Hemisphere and the Western Hemisphere. Every line of longitude and the line of longitude opposite it make up a great circle.

The Shortest Route

Ship and airplane navigators like to know the shortest route from one place to another. They cannot use most ordinary maps for this purpose. Maps, as you know, distort distances between places around the earth. You may recall having read that the easiest way to find true distances is by using a globe.

Remember that the earth can be divided into an almost endless number of hemispheres. You have read, for example, that geographers often divide the earth into the Northern, Southern, Western, or Eastern Hemisphere. There is an almost endless number of great circles around the earth.

Great circles are important. The shortest, most direct route between any two places on the earth lies along a great circle. Such a route is called a **great-circle route**. You can understand why ships and planes can save time and money by traveling these routes.

Some simple exercises with a globe will help you understand great circles and great-circle routes. For example, take a string and wrap it tightly around the globe along the equator. Mark the distance. You have just measured a great circle. Now take the string and wrap it tightly around the globe in any other direction. If the distance is the same as that of the equator, you have found another great circle.

You can find the great-circle route between two places without measuring an entire great circle. When you hold your string tightly between any two places on the globe, you are measuring the shortest distance between them. These are also great-circle routes.

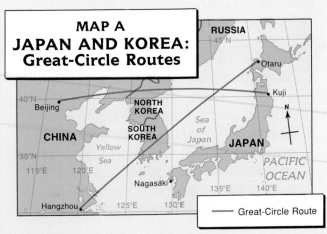

MAP A
JAPAN AND KOREA:
Great-Circle Routes

RUSSIA
45°N
Otaru
Kuji
40°N
Beijing
NORTH KOREA
Sea of Japan
N
CHINA
SOUTH KOREA
JAPAN
Yellow Sea
35°N
115°E   120°E
Nagasaki
PACIFIC OCEAN
135°E   140°E
Hangzhou   125°E   130°E

—— Great-Circle Route

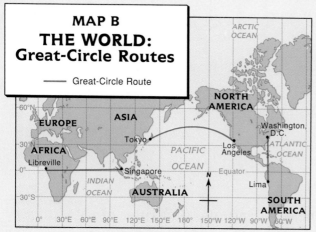

MAP B
THE WORLD:
Great-Circle Routes

—— Great-Circle Route

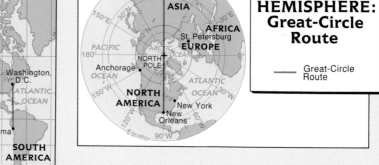

MAP C
NORTHERN HEMISPHERE:
Great-Circle Route

—— Great-Circle Route

Using a Great-circle Route

On most maps a straight line appears to be the shortest distance between two places. A great-circle route may appear as a longer, curved line. On **Map B**, shown on this page, all the lines of latitude and longitude are shown as straight lines. Every line of longitude is part of a great circle. The equator is the only line of latitude that is a great circle. Between places on the equator or on the same line of longitude, a pilot can set a course in a constant compass direction. For example, as the map shows, in flying the great-circle route from Libreville to Singapore, a pilot would fly east.

As you can see on **Map B**, Tokyo and Los Angeles are on approximately the same line of latitude. The shortest distance between them is the great-circle route shown on **Map B**. A plane flying the great-circle route from Los Angeles to Tokyo would travel northwest at the beginning of the trip and southwest at the end of the trip. When flying a great-circle route, a pilot may have to change directions often, especially between cities that are at the same latitude.

Navigators use special maps on which great-circle routes appear as straight lines. On **Map C** great-circle routes are drawn to appear as straight lines, such as the route shown. The great-circle route from New Orleans to Dhaka passes through the North Pole. To fly this route, a pilot would fly directly north along 90°W to the North Pole and then directly south along 90°E to Dhaka.

Reviewing the Skill

1. Which line of latitude is a great circle? Why is no other line of latitude a great circle?
2. What line of longitude, together with 60°W, makes up a great circle?
3. On **Map C** would the great-circle routes between St. Petersburg and New York and between St. Petersburg and Anchorage each appear as a straight line or as a curved line?
4. Look at **Map A.** List the directions for the start and end of the following flights taking the great-circle routes between: Beijing and Kuji, Otaru and Hangzhou, Beijing and Nagasaki.
5. Why are great-circle routes useful? Who would find such routes to be especially important?

529

2 The History of Japan

READ TO LEARN

Key Vocabulary

clan
Shintoism
samurai
shogun

Key People

Shotoku
Murasaki Shikibu
Yoritomo
Meiji

Key Places

Tokyo
Hiroshima
Nagasaki

Read Aloud

According to an ancient Japanese legend, the first ruler of Japan was Amaterasu (äm′ ə ter ä sü), the goddess of the sun. The Japanese have thus called their many islands *Nippon*, meaning "land of the rising sun." Even the flag of modern Japan has a symbol of the rising sun on it. In this lesson you will read about Japan's history. You will learn that its past is filled with fascinating people and events.

Read for Purpose

1. **WHAT YOU KNOW:** What is the geography of Japan?
2. **WHAT YOU WILL LEARN:** How has Japan been influenced by other cultures?

EARLY JAPAN

The first mention of Japan comes from Chinese writings of about A.D. 300. However, artifacts found by archaeologists show that people lived in Japan for many centuries before that. Because the early Japanese had no system of writing, they left no historic records of their own.

In the year 300 Japan was not a united country. Instead, each clan controlled its own territory. A clan was a group of people who believed they came from the same ancestor.

The leading clan in ancient Japan was the Yamato (yä′ mə do). The Yamato emperors claimed the sun goddess was their ancestor. Other clans worshiped their own nature gods and goddesses. In different parts of Japan, people honored thousands of local gods and goddesses. Their different customs and beliefs eventually joined to form Japan's earliest religion. It was called Shintoism (shin′ tō iz əm), meaning "the way of the gods." One Shinto song went like this:

The earth is the Mother of all creatures. She gives them life and they give her songs. Great trees and tiny herbs, stones, sand, and soil, winds and waves—all have a soul.

Japanese actors perform a play about the ancient Yamato **clan**. Japan takes great pride in its history and traditions.

KOREA'S GIFT TO JAPAN

Around the year 500, the Japanese began to have more contact with mainland Asia. Historians think that Korean travelers brought the ideas of China to Japan.

As you know, Korea was close to China and could have known about China first. In fact, for centuries Korea had been in close contact with China. Then, during the sixth century, many Koreans migrated to Japan, bringing Chinese influences with them. One group of Korean travelers brought with them a bronze statue of the Buddha. Within 50 years Buddhism had spread widely throughout the islands of the Japanese archipelago.

The Japanese did not give up their Shinto faith, however. The ideas of Shintoism and Buddhism were comfortable together. Most people in Japan practiced both Buddhist and Shinto rituals. For example, weddings were often Shinto events and funerals were often Buddhist events.

PRINCE SHOTOKU

The ruler of Japan at this time, Prince Shotoku (shō′ tō kü), welcomed Buddhist teachings. Prince Shotoku came to admire many other parts of Chinese civilization—its writing, art, philosophy, and government. In 607 Prince Shotoku sent many Japanese scholars to China. He ordered them to learn all they could about Chinese achievements and bring their knowledge back to Japan.

531

Genji was known as "the shining prince" because of the great art produced in his court. Yet Murasaki Shikibu hints that he was too concerned with art to govern wisely.

TALE OF GENJI

𝓕or Genji life had become an unbroken string of problems. He must consider what to do next. If he went on pretending that all was well, then even worse things might lie ahead.

Genji thought of the Suma coast. People of great value had once lived there, he was told, but now it was deserted, save for the huts of fishermen. According to his attendants, however, Suma was known to be the home of one mysterious resident: a puppet. And the puppet had powers to make human beings a joyful lot.

Genji thought to himself, "Soon, I shall make the journey to Suma. Soon, a wonderful puppet shall rest on my arm. Soon, I shall turn to a puppet and gain the gifts of friendship and joyfulness."

The Japanese embraced many Chinese ideas. For example, the Japanese used the Chinese system of writing. They adopted Chinese styles in painting, literature, and furniture. They even organized their central government to be like China's. In fact, Prince Shotoku drew up a written plan of government based on the teachings of Confucius.

The leading writer in early Japan was Murasaki Shikibu (mùr ä säk′ ē shē′ kē bù). Around the year 1000 she wrote a book called *The Tale of Genji* (gen′ jē). Often called the world's first novel, *The Tale of Genji* tells a long and complex story about a prince named Genji. Shikibu described her hero Genji as a "shining prince." A modern version of this book fills more than 4,000 pages. You can read part of Shikibu's famous book on this page.

FEUDALISM IN JAPAN

What was happening in Europe at about this time? Think back to what you read in Chapter 8. You may recall that this was the time of the Middle Ages. Lords owned and ruled vast manors that were worked by serfs. Knights swore loyalty to their lords and fought to defend their manors and kingdoms. This system, you may recall, was called feudalism.

During the 1100s a similar feudal system developed in Japan. Clan leaders took control of large regions. Each leader built up a strong force of warriors to defend his territory.

The warriors who fought for lords were called samurai (sam' ù rī), meaning "one who serves." Like the knights of Europe, the samurai swore to give their lives for their leader if necessary. One samurai wrote:

The business of the samurai is to serve his master and to be loyal to friends and, above all, to be devoted to duty.

In the late twelfth century, a samurai named Yoritomo rose to power. Like many other generals you have read about—Alexander the Great, Julius Caesar, Kublai Khan—Yoritomo was a shrewd leader. After helping to unite some of Japan's many different clans, he won the support of the common people as well as the friendship of the emperor. In 1192 the emperor gave Yoritomo the title of shogun (shō' gən). *Shogun* means "supreme general of the emperor's army." In effect, however, the shogun had the powers of a dictator. Judges, armies, taxes, and roads were all under his authority.

For the next 700 years, until 1868, Japan lived under the rule of the shoguns. Under the early shoguns, local lords still had power. Later, however, the shoguns ruled as dictators.

Tales of samurai bravery are part of the folklore of Japan. Like European knights, stories were told about samurai slaying dragons. Their armor was made of strips of steel and leather laced together.

Perry arrived in Japan in 1853. His huge warship dwarfed the Japanese boats that went out to meet him. With this show of strength, Perry forced Japan to open its ports to trade.

JAPAN MEETS THE WEST

For several hundred years Japan had little contact with other countries. A small number of traders and missionaries from Portugal, Spain, the Netherlands, and Great Britain settled in Japan starting in the 1500s. Also Chinese and Korean traders continued to cross the Sea of Japan. However, the Japanese government did not allow these outsiders to travel freely or to own land or businesses.

In 1853 four United States ships commanded by Commodore Matthew Perry steamed into Tokyo harbor. Perry came to ask the Japanese to open their country to foreign trade. The Japanese were amazed by the foreigners' black ships made of iron and powered by steam. They were also shocked by the powerful guns and cannons. The Japanese felt that they had no choice but to agree to Perry's request.

After Perry's arrival, Japan underwent many changes. In 1868, the emperor Meiji, who was a descendant of the ancient Yamato rulers, took control from the shogun. Under Meiji, Japan entered a period of rapid modernization. Factories were built, railroads crisscrossed the country, and ports were expanded to handle the bustling foreign trade. In just 20 years, Japan became one of the world's leading industrial nations.

In order to get the natural resources needed to continue this economic growth, Japan began to extend its power throughout Asia. Japan's military strength swelled, and soon Japanese armies were marching into Korea, China, and the Philippines. As the map on page 535 shows, the Japanese controlled much of East Asia by 1942. You may recall that the Japanese also attacked the American naval base at Pearl Harbor in Hawaii, drawing the United States into World War II.

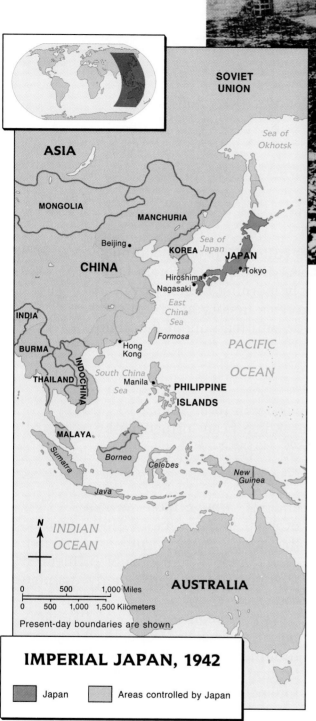

ASIA

SOVIET
UNION

MONGOLIA

MANCHURIA

Sea of
Okhotsk

Beijing

Sea of
Japan

KOREA

JAPAN

CHINA

Hiroshima
Nagasaki

Tokyo

INDIA

East
China
Sea

Formosa

PACIFIC

BURMA

Hong
Kong

OCEAN

THAILAND

South China
Sea

Manila

PHILIPPINE

MALAYA

ISLANDS

Sumatra

Borneo

Celebes

New
Guinea

Java

INDIAN
OCEAN

N

AUSTRALIA

0   500   1,000 Miles
0   500   1,000 1,500 Kilometers
Present-day boundaries are shown.

IMPERIAL JAPAN, 1942

Japan   Areas controlled by Japan

MAP SKILL: One atomic bomb destroyed almost all the buildings in Hiroshima on August 6, 1945. What parts of China were controlled by the Japanese during World War II?

Nagasaki. After both cities were destroyed, Japan was forced to surrender and World War II ended.

THE LEGACY OF THE PAST

In this lesson you have read about Japan's history. You read, for example, how its early people lived in clans and practiced a religion called Shintoism. You also read that the Japanese borrowed many ideas from China, including Buddhism. When Matthew Perry arrived in 1853, he found a Japan that had flourished and built upon the legacy of its past.

 Check Your Reading

1. Describe Shintoism.
2. What foreign countries influenced Japanese history?
3. **GEOGRAPHY SKILL:** Use the map to name four islands that were controlled by the Japanese in 1942.
4. **THINKING SKILL:** State one opinion mentioned on page 533.

By the end of the war in 1945, American and other Allied forces had freed most of East Asia from the Japanese. On August 6 and 9, American planes dropped atomic bombs on the big Japanese cities of Hiroshima and

3 The History of Korea

READING TO LEARN

Key People
Yi Sunsin

Key Places
Seoul
Pyongyang

Read Aloud

Long ago the land of Korea was called *Choson*, meaning "the land of the morning freshness." Serene mists often hang over Korea's mountains in the early morning hours. However, as you will read in this lesson, Korea's history has been complex and stormy. In this lesson you will read about the interesting history of Korea.

Read for Purpose

1. **WHAT YOU KNOW:** What did Japan learn from Korea?
2. **WHAT YOU WILL LEARN:** How has Korea been influenced by its neighbors China and Japan?

EARLY KOREA

According to legend, Korea was founded by a spirit-king named Tangun in 2333 B.C. The dynasty established by Tangun is said to have lasted until 1122 B.C.

Archaeologists think that Korea's first people arrived during the Old Stone Age. These early Korean settlers were nomads who came from the north, from Manchuria and Mongolia. Over the centuries the number of settlers grew. Then, in about 1200 B.C., a new group came to the Korean peninsula. They built settlements near Seoul (sōl) and Pyongyang (pē ong' yäng), the capitals of South Korea and North Korea.

According to legend this new group of people migrated from China at the end of the Shang dynasty. They brought to Korea many skills such as irrigation, weaving, and iron-making. The Koreans were deeply influenced by the Chinese and eagerly adopted their technology.

Early Korean society was like early Japanese society. People lived together in large, independent clans. However, around 100 B.C., the Koreans lost their independence for the first time. The armies of the Han dynasty in China conquered Korea.

Although Chinese control lasted only 50 years, Chinese influence would prove lasting. Koreans adopted Chinese culture quickly. For example, the Koreans used the Chinese writing system as well as Chinese styles of art.

THREE KINGDOMS

In order to protect themselves from outside attack, the Koreans organized their country into three competing kingdoms. As you can see from the map on this page, these three kingdoms covered most of the Korean peninsula. During this time, missionaries from China and India carried the ideas of Buddhism down the Korean peninsula. The period of three kingdoms also marked a high point in the development of Korean culture. Archaeologists have found beautiful wall paintings, ceramics, and gold ornaments that people created during this time.

In 668 the kingdom of Silla formed an alliance with China and conquered the two other kingdoms. Under Silla rule, Buddhism became increasingly popular and Korean traders spread out through Asia.

KOREA'S THREE KINGDOMS, A.D. 500

- Koguryo
- Paekche
- Silla

CHINA

Yalu River

Taedong River

● Pyongyang

Kwangju ●

Yellow Sea

Kongju ●

Naktong River

● Kyongju

KAYA

Sea of Japan

Korean Strait

JAPAN

0   100   200 Miles
0   100   200   300 Kilometers

MAP SKILL: Today more than one out of every five South Koreans live in Seoul. What were the names of the chief cities of Korea's three kingdoms?

537

Buddhism came to Korea through China. Today Buddhist worshipers still come to the ancient Yi palace—now both a religious shrine and a reminder of Korea's past.

THE CHOSON DYNASTY

Beginning in 1392, the Choson dynasty ruled Korea for more than 500 years, over twice as long as any Chinese dynasty. During the first 100 years of this period, there was peace throughout Korea and the arts flourished. The world's first printing press was invented in 1403 and a unique form of poetry, called *sijo*, became popular. Also during this time, Confucianism again became important.

The later centuries of the Choson dynasty were filled with civil unrest and periodic invasions by the Japanese and Chinese. In 1592, the Japanese shogun crossed the Korean Strait and marched his army into Korea. With the help of the Chinese, the Koreans finally drove the Japanese out. Admiral Yi Sunsin commanded the victorious Korean navy from his "turtle ship," the world's first armored vessel.

LIVING UNDER JAPANESE RULE

By the 1800s, the Choson dynasty had been weakened by corrupt officials who disagreed over how Korea should be governed. Meanwhile, the nearby countries of Japan, Russia, and China grew increasingly powerful. In 1910 Japan invaded Korea.

The Japanese were harsh conquerers. In addition to taking over the Korean economy, the Japanese banned the Korean language. Koreans had to learn how to speak Japanese or "speak no language at all." The Japanese also took land away from the Koreans.

Throughout this period, Koreans resisted Japanese rule and longed for the day when they would again achieve independence. In 1945 the dream seemed to be coming true. Japan was about to be defeated in World War II. And the Allies had agreed that Japan would be forced out of Korea.

TWO COUNTRIES

After Japan surrendered to the Allies in 1945, the Soviet Union took control of northern Korea and the United States took control of southern Korea. North Korea became a communist nation. South Korea became a noncommunist nation.

Then, in 1950, North Korean troops invaded South Korea in an effort to reunite the nation by force. The Korean War lasted for about three years and was part of the Cold War struggle between communist and noncommunist nations. In the Korean War, noncommunist nations—chiefly the United States—supported South Korea. China and the Soviet Union, two communist nations, aided North Korea. The war ended in 1953. But neither side won a real victory, and a permanent peace treaty was never signed. Korea continues to be divided into two separate nations. In 1991 the two Koreas met to begin resolving their differences.

A STRUGGLE TO BE FREE

In this lesson you have read about the history of Korea. There is an old Korean proverb that says, "Korea is a land that is like a shrimp caught between two whales." Through much of its history, China and Japan have tried to control Korea. Yet the Koreans have struggled to protect their culture and independence.

South Korea has been the scene of violent demonstrations in recent years. Young Koreans have led the demand for a more democratic government.

Check Your Reading

1. Why did the Koreans organize themselves into three kingdoms?
2. What hardships did the Koreans suffer under Japanese occupation?
3. How has geography affected Chinese and Japanese influence in Korea? Do you think the role of geography has been important?
4. **GEOGRAPHY SKILL:** Use the map on page 537 to name Korea's three kingdoms. What bodies of water surround the Korean peninsula?
5. **THINKING SKILL:** Sequence the major events in this lesson.

4 Japan and Korea Today

READ TO LEARN

Key Vocabulary

gross national product
per capita income

Read Aloud

After World War II Japan lay in ruins. When the Korean War ended in 1953, North Korea and South Korea also lay in ruins. Twenty years later Japan and South Korea had gotten rid of most of the traces of war. North Korea continues to rebuild. The recovery of Japan and South Korea, however, is often called "a modern miracle."

Read for Purpose

1. **WHAT YOU KNOW:** What goods do you own that were made in Japan or Korea?
2. **WHAT YOU WILL LEARN:** How has modernization changed life in Japan and South Korea?

A REMARKABLE RECOVERY

World War II took a tremendous toll on Japan. Entire cities had been leveled by American bombs. Author John Hersey described Hiroshima, one city that had been hit by an atomic bomb.

[There was] range upon range of collapsed city blocks . . . and in the streets a macabre [horrible] traffic—hundreds of crumpled bicycles, shells of streetcars and automobiles, all halted in mid-motion.

After the Korean War, the two Koreas also faced a huge task of rebuilding. More than 1 million people had died during the fighting. Factories and houses had been destroyed.

Today, few traces of these wars remain in Japan and the Koreas. North Korea, which is governed by Communists, remains largely an agricultural country. But South Korea has developed a strong industrial economy. And Japan has become an economic powerhouse, known around the world for its cars, computers, and other products. In fact, the United States is the only country in the world that has a larger gross national product, or GNP, than Japan. Gross national product refers to the total value of all the goods and services a nation produces each year.

What made this remarkable recovery possible? First of all, it is important to remember that Japan and Korea had been strong industrial countries for many years. Japanese and Korean workers were familiar with modern manufacturing. In addition, the United States helped both Japan and South Korea to rebuild their industries by providing money and advice.

Japanese and South Korean companies have become enormously successful. As a result, per capita income in Japan and South Korea has grown in recent years. Per capita income is the amount of money each person would have if the country's total income were divided equally among its people. Use the graph on this page to see the per capita income of Japan, South Korea, and the United States.

DRIVE FOR EDUCATION

South Korean and Japanese workers are among the most educated workers

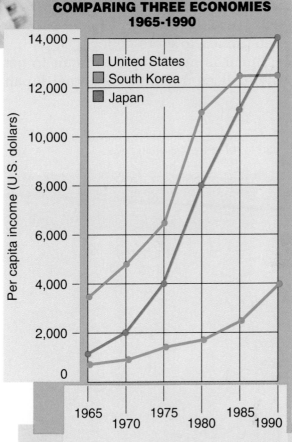

COMPARING THREE ECONOMIES
1965-1990

- United States
- South Korea
- Japan

Per capita income (U.S. dollars)

14,000
12,000
10,000
8,000
6,000
4,000
2,000
0

1965　1970　1975　1980　1985　1990

GRAPH SKILL: The development of high-tech industries has brought prosperity to Japan and South Korea. Does Japan or the United States have a higher per capita income?

541

in the world. In both countries, people believe that education is the key to a person's success. Chung Seong Tae is an 18-year-old university student who lives in South Korea's capital city of Seoul. He says:

> Education [in South Korea] is everything, and going to university means success. It is the only way to improve your social position, so we must study religiously.

Chung's family lives in a tiny "matchbox" house with no running water or electricity. Chung's mother supports her family by working in a factory, sewing labels into 2,000 pairs of running shoes each day. In order to achieve a better life, Chung became determined to go to college.

But it is much more difficult to get into college in South Korea and Japan

These students in Tokyo have worked very hard to reach the university level.

than it is in the United States. First, Chung had to pass a very difficult exam. The year before the test, he attended "cram school" at night to help prepare. These cram schools are in addition to regular school, which begins at 8:30 A.M. and ends at 6:00 P.M., six days a week. Chung's hard work paid off, and he was accepted at the Seoul National University.

DAILY LIFE

Hard-working and determined people like Chung helped bring about the economic recoveries of Japan and South Korea. But in spite of the economic success in these countries, daily life is hardly luxurious for most people.

Like many Japanese, Hiroki Takada and his family live in a tiny three-room apartment outside Tokyo. Sixteen-year-old Hiroki and his brother share a bedroom that is nine feet square. Since land in Japan's urban areas is so expensive, few can afford to live in anything but small apartments. Look at the map on page 543 to find the population density of Tokyo.

Hiroki's father is a car salesman in Tokyo. Like most Japanese workers, he leaves the house early in the morning and returns home late at night. Hiroki commutes every day by subway. The journey from home to school to baseball practice and back home takes him four hours every day. Usually he has to stand the whole way. "I hate the crowded subways," Hiroki sighs, "but that's life in Tokyo. We just accept it." Another thing that Japanese people must accept is high prices. Because their island nation must import much of its food and most of its natural resources, prices for most goods are very high.

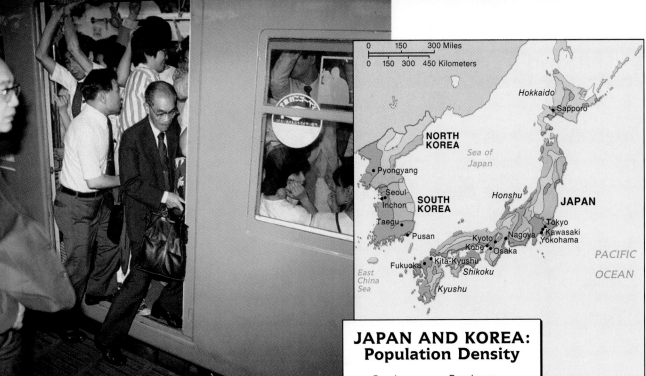

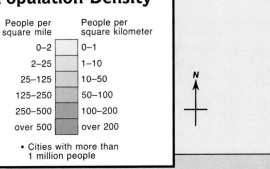

JAPAN AND KOREA: Population Density

People per square mile		People per square kilometer
0–2		0–1
2–25		1–10
25–125		10–50
125–250		50–100
250–500		100–200
over 500		over 200

• Cities with more than 1 million people

MAP SKILL: Japan's dense population is concentrated in cities. Which island of Japan has the lowest population density?

Like Japanese workers, Koreans put in long hours at work. Yet many receive low wages for their efforts. In recent years factory workers have gone on strike for better wages. But the South Korean government has worked with businesses to break those strikes. This has created bitterness among workers and university students.

CHANGING SOCIETIES

After destructive wars, Japan and the Koreas faced the task of rebuilding their economies. Today, different challenges face each country. North Korea is becoming increasingly isolated as communism collapses around the world. South Korean workers are fighting to get higher wages for their work. Japan, which has become one of the world's richest and most powerful nations, is more dependent than ever on foreign resources. Still, the people of this small area of East Asia have created a story of economic success that is a model for the rest of the world.

 Check Your Reading

1. Why is education so important to people in South Korea and Japan?
2. How have people's lives been affected by Japan and South Korea's economic growth?
3. **GEOGRAPHY SKILL:** How does the fact that Japan is an island nation affect people's lives there?
4. **THINKING SKILL:** Compare and contrast Japan after World War II with Japan today.

543

IMPORTANT EVENTS

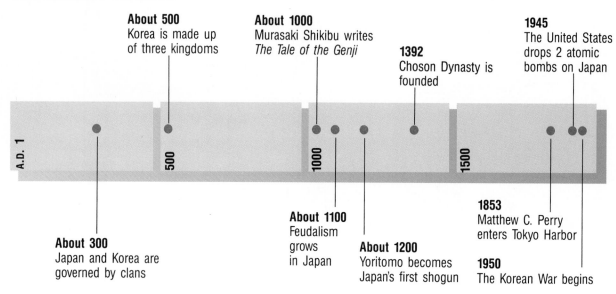

About 500
Korea is made up of three kingdoms

About 1000
Murasaki Shikibu writes *The Tale of the Genji*

1392
Choson Dynasty is founded

1945
The United States drops 2 atomic bombs on Japan

About 300
Japan and Korea are governed by clans

About 1100
Feudalism grows in Japan

About 1200
Yoritomo becomes Japan's first shogun

1853
Matthew C. Perry enters Tokyo Harbor

1950
The Korean War begins

A.D. 1   500   1000   1500

PEOPLE TO KNOW

Emperor Meiji A.D. 1852-1912

Murasaki Shikibu about A.D. 970-1013

Shotoku about A.D. 573-621

Yi Sunsin A.D. 1545-1598

Yoritomo A.D. 1148-1189

IDEAS TO REMEMBER

■ Although they differ in size and shape, Japan and Korea share a number of geographical and cultural similarities.

■ In little more than 100 years, Japan has transformed itself from an isolated farming country into one of the world's great powers.

■ Korea has often had to fight off its neighbors China and Japan. After the Korean War the Korean peninsula was divided into two nations—South Korea and North Korea.

■ Japan and South Korea have built "economic miracles." Both lands have developed into two of the most productive nations in the world.

REVIEWING VOCABULARY

Number a sheet of paper from 1 to 5. Beside each number write whether the following statements are true or false. If the statement is true, write **T**. If it is false, rewrite the sentence using the underlined vocabulary word correctly.

1. A country's gross national product is the largest industrial product made in that country.
2. The samurai were businessmen who built many of the country's first manufacturing industries.
3. Shintoism is the Japanese word for Buddhism.
4. An archipelago is a chain of islands.
5. Shogun means "leading general" and is the name for military dictators who ruled Japan for 700 years.

REVIEWING FACTS

1. What four major islands make up the Japanese archipelago?
2. How do Japan and South Korea deal with a lack of natural resources?
3. List three ways in which feudalism in Japan was similar to feudalism in Europe during the Middle Ages.
4. What event forced Japan to modernize? List four results of Japan's decision to enter the modern world.
5. What single event brought the United States into World War II against Japan?
6. What event caused the Japanese to finally surrender?
7. Why do Koreans refer to their country as "a shrimp caught between two fighting whales"?
8. Why was Korea divided into two nations with two different political systems in the twentieth century?
9. How were the people of Korea and Japan similar in their responses to Chinese civilization?
10. How have Japan and Korea used education to become world economic powers? How does education in these countries differ from that in the United States?

◖◖≡▷ WRITING ABOUT MAIN IDEAS

1. **Writing a Travel Brochure:** Write a brochure describing geographical features in Japan. Choose those features which might interest travelers on their first visit to Japan.
2. **Writing About Perspectives:** Reread the description of life in Japan on page 542. Write a paragraph explaining what you would and would not enjoy about living in Japan.

BUILDING SKILLS: UNDERSTANDING GREAT-CIRCLE ROUTES

1. What is a great circle? Why is the distance around any great circle the same?
2. What is the connection between a great circle and a great-circle route?
3. Charles Lindbergh was the first pilot to fly alone from New York to Paris, France. Why do you think he chose a great-circle route?
4. Why is it important to know how to use the great-circle routes?

REVIEWING VOCABULARY

archipelago	monsoon
Buddhism	samurai
caste	shogun
commune	terrace
gross national product	Vedas

Number a sheet of paper from 1 to 10. Beside each number write the word or term from the list above that best matches each statement.

1. Chinese farmers would build one of these level "steps" into hillsides to increase the amount of flat land.
2. Japan is an example of this geographic feature that is made up of many islands.
3. These seasonal winds have a tremendous influence on the climate of the Indian subcontinent.
4. Like the knights of Europe during the Middle Ages, these warriors served feudal lords in Japan.
5. A rigid social class, established in India by the Aryans.
6. When these military leaders became supreme rulers, the Japanese emperor was powerless.
7. These hymns, first sung by the Aryan peoples to their gods, form the basis of India's main religion, Hinduism.
8. This term means the total value of all goods and services produced in a country in one year.
9. This is a large number of farms brought together in a single unit.
10. This world religion was founded by a Hindu prince who became known as "the enlightened one."

WRITING ABOUT THE UNIT

1. **Writing an Interview:** Imagine that you are a reporter in India at the time of Asoka. This man is about to carry out his many reforms based on Buddhism. Interview Asoka about the new policies he intends to put into effect and the reasons behind them. Write a magazine article based on the interview.
2. **Writing an Essay:** Write an essay and title it: "What Japan and the United States Can Learn from Each Other."
3. **Writing About Perspectives:** Reread the sayings of Confucius on page 500. Write a paragraph explaining whether or not you think these principles would be a useful guide for people today.

ACTIVITIES

1. **Drawing a Historical Map:** Draw a map showing the expansion of China from the earliest days to its present size. Color code, date, and label each phase of China's expansion.
2. **Making a Bar Graph:** Make a bar graph showing the gross national product of five countries you have studied in this unit. Use almanacs to obtain the most recent information.
3. **Working Together on Parallel Time Lines:** Work together to construct parallel time lines of Indian and Chinese history. Use encyclopedias for research. Write the time lines on a long sheet of paper. Record the most important people and events on each line. You may wish to illustrate the time lines.

WORLD POPULATION

POPULATION OF CHINA, 1950-1990

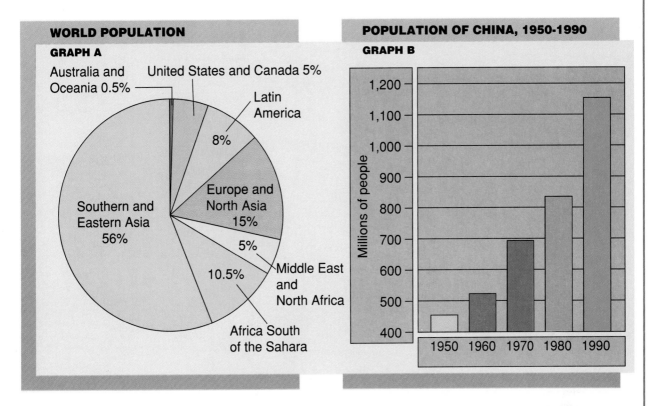

GRAPH A

Australia and Oceania 0.5%

United States and Canada 5%

Latin America 8%

Southern and Eastern Asia 56%

Europe and North Asia 15%

5%

10.5%

Middle East and North Africa

Africa South of the Sahara

GRAPH B

Millions of people

1,200 — 1,100 — 1,000 — 900 — 800 — 700 — 600 — 500 — 400 —

1950 1960 1970 1980 1990

BUILDING SKILLS: READING CIRCLE, LINE, AND BAR GRAPHS

Use the graphs above to answer the following questions.

1. What are the differences between a circle, a line, and a bar graph?

2. According to **Graph A**, which world region has the largest population?

3. According to **Graph A**, which region has the smallest population?

4. According to **Graph B**, how many people lived in China in 1980?

5. Why is it important to be able to understand how to read graphs?

LINKING PAST, PRESENT, AND FUTURE

You have read about the important influence that religion has had on the civilizations of South Asia, China, Japan, and Korea. Some people think that a new world religion is being born in our time. This new religion, they believe, will combine teachings from many of the world's ancient religions. What teachings from the religions you have studied in this book will affect the future?

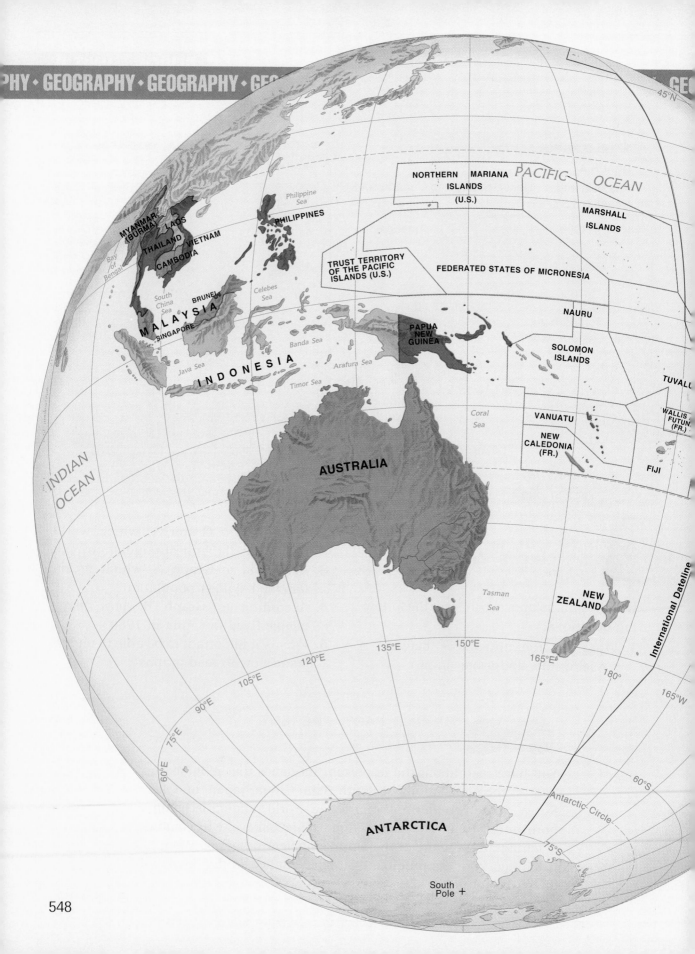

45°N

NORTHERN   MARIANA
ISLANDS
(U.S.)

PACIFIC   OCEAN

MARSHALL
ISLANDS

Philippine
Sea

PHILIPPINES

MYANMAR
(BURMA)   LAOS

THAILAND   VIETNAM

CAMBODIA

TRUST TERRITORY
OF THE PACIFIC
ISLANDS (U.S.)

FEDERATED STATES OF MICRONESIA

Bay
of
Bengal

South
China
Sea

BRUNEI

Celebes
Sea

NAURU

MALAYSIA

SINGAPORE

PAPUA
NEW
GUINEA

SOLOMON
ISLANDS

Banda Sea

TUVALU

INDONESIA

Java Sea

Arafura Sea

Timor Sea

WALLIS
FUTUN
(FR.)

VANUATU

Coral
Sea

NEW
CALEDONIA
(FR.)

FIJI

INDIAN
OCEAN

AUSTRALIA

International Dateline

Tasman
Sea

NEW
ZEALAND

135°E

150°E

120°E

165°E

180°

105°E

165°W

90°E

75°E

60°S

60°E

Antarctic Circle

ANTARCTICA

75°S

South
Pole +

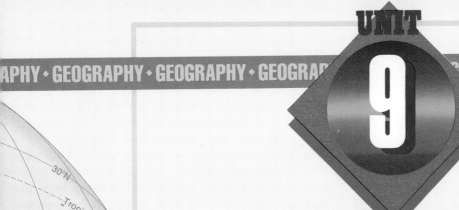

UNIT 9

SOUTHEAST ASIA, OCEANIA, AND AUSTRALIA

WHERE WE ARE

As the map shows, you have reached the region known as Southeast Asia, Oceania, and Australia. Bordering the huge Pacific Ocean, the people of these lands work together to meet the challenges of their environment.

You can see from the map that only Southeast Asia is attached to the continent of Asia. Oceania is made up of thousands of islands and Australia is an island continent.

549

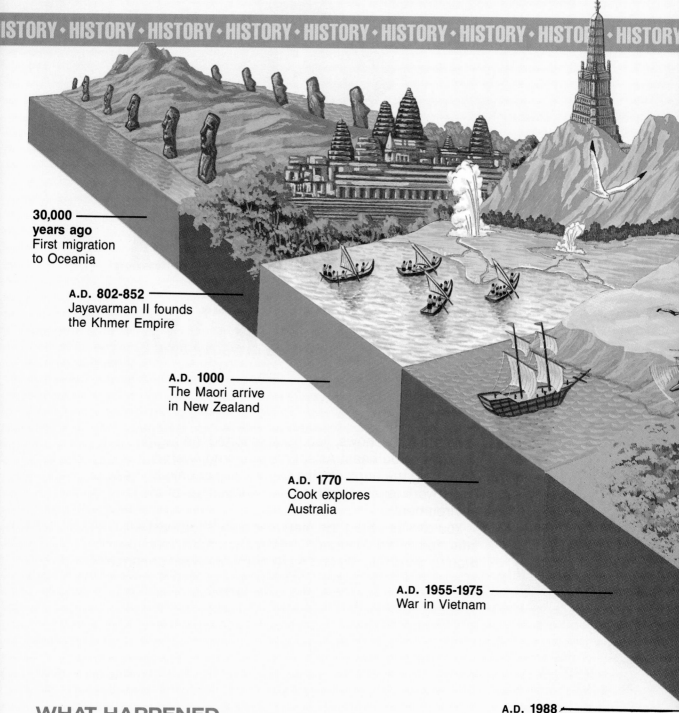

30,000 years ago
First migration
to Oceania

A.D. 802-852
Jayavarman II founds
the Khmer Empire

A.D. 1000
The Maori arrive
in New Zealand

A.D. 1770
Cook explores
Australia

A.D. 1955-1975
War in Vietnam

A.D. 1988
Australia celebrates
bicentennial

WHAT HAPPENED

Settlers came early to Southeast
Asia, Oceania, and Australia. Moving across
the island chains, cultures found a place to grow
and develop. You can see on the time line many of the
events in the history of this vast region.

SOUTHEAST ASIA, AUSTRALIA, AND OCEANIA

FIJI

Capital ★
Suva

Major language: English
Population: 0.7 million
Area: 7,054 sq mi; 18,270 sq km
Leading export: sugar

INDONESIA

Capital ★
Jakarta

Major languages: Bahasa Indonesia and Javanese
Population: 181.4 million
Area: 741,098 sq mi; 1,919,440 sq km
Leading exports: oil and natural gas

KIRIBATI

Capital ★
Bairiki

Major languages: Gilbertese and English
Population: 71,000
Area: 277 sq mi; 717 sq km
Leading export: fish

AUSTRALIA

Capital ★
Canberra

Major language: English
Population: 17.5 million
Area: 2,967,900 sq mi; 7,686,850 sq km
Leading export: wheat

LAOS

Capital ★
Vientiane

Major languages: Lao and French
Population: 4.1 million
Area: 91,429 sq mi; 236,800 sq km
Leading exports: food and timber

BRUNEI

Capital ★
Begawan

Major language: Malay
Population: 0.3 million
Area: 2,228 sq mi; 5,770 sq km
Leading export: oil

MALAYSIA

Capital ★
Kuala Lumpur

Major languages: Bahasa Malaysia, English and Chinese
Population: 18.3 million
Area: 127,317 sq mi; 329,750 sq km
Leading exports: machinery and rubber

CAMBODIA

Capital ★
Phnom Penh

Major language: Khmer
Population: 7.1 million
Area: 69,900 sq mi; 181,040 sq km
Leading export: rubber

MYANMAR

Capital ★
Yangon

Major language: Burmese
Population: 42.1 million
Area: 261,217 sq mi; 676,550 sq km
Leading exports: rice and timber

NAURU

Capital ★
Yaren

Major language: Nauruan
Population: 8,000
Area: 8 sq mi; 20 sq km
Leading export: phosphates

THAILAND

Capitals ★
Bangkok

Major language: Thai
Population: 58.8 million
Area: 198,456 sq mi; 514,000 sq km
Leading exports: food and machinery

NEW ZEALAND

Capital ★
Wellington

Major languages: English and Maori
Population: 3.5 million
Area: 103,738 sq mi; 268,680 sq km
Leading exports: lamb and wool

TONGA

Capital ★
Nukualofa

Major languages: Tongan and English
Population: 0.1 million
Area: 270 sq mi; 700 sq km
Leading exports: copra and bananas

**PAPUA
NEW GUINEA**

Capital ★
Port Moresby

Major languages: English, Pidgin
English and Hiri Motu
Population: 3.9 million
Area: 178,259 sq mi; 461,690 sq km
Leading exports: gold, copper,
and silver

TUVALU

Capital ★
Funafuti Atoll

Major languages: Tuvaluan and
English
Population: 9,000
Area: 10 sq mi; 26 sq km
Leading export: copra

PHILIPPINES

Capital ★
Manila

Major languages: Filipino, Tagolos,
and English
Population: 62.3 million
Area: 115,830 sq mi; 300,000 sq km
Leading exports: food, copra,
and minerals

VANUATU

Capital ★
Port-Vila

Major languages: English, Bislama
and French
Population: 0.2 million
Area: 5,699 sq mi; 14,760 sq km
Leading export: copra

SINGAPORE

Capital ★
Singapore

Major languages: Chinese, English,
Malay, and Tamil
Population: 2.8 million
Area: 224 sq mi; 580 sq km
Leading exports: machinery and
petroleum products

VIETNAM

Capital ★
Hanoi

Major language: Vietnamese
Population: 67.6 million
Area: 127,243 sq mi; 329,560 sq km
Leading exports: coal and agricultural
products

**SOLOMON
ISLANDS**

Capital ★
Honiara

Major language: English
Population: 0.3 million
Area: 10,985 sq mi; 28,450 sq km
Leading exports: copra and copper

**WESTERN
SAMOA**

Capital ★
Apia

Major languages: Samoan and
English
Population: 0.2 million
Area: 1,104 sq mi; 2,860 sq km
Leading exports: copra, cocoa and
bananas

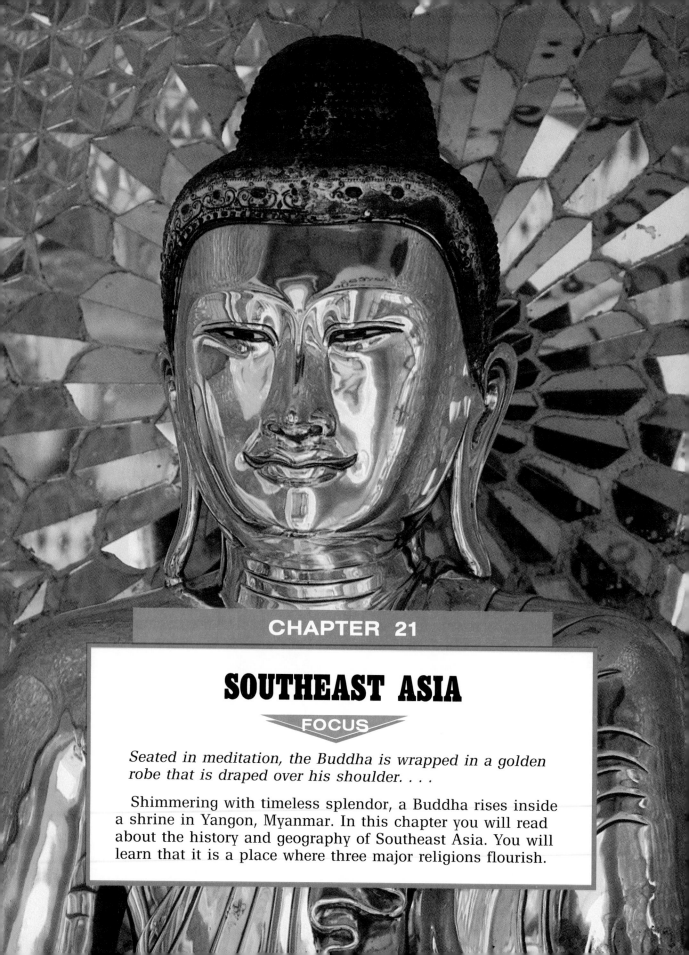

CHAPTER 21

SOUTHEAST ASIA

FOCUS

Seated in meditation, the Buddha is wrapped in a golden robe that is draped over his shoulder. . . .

Shimmering with timeless splendor, a Buddha rises inside a shrine in Yangon, Myanmar. In this chapter you will read about the history and geography of Southeast Asia. You will learn that it is a place where three major religions flourish.

1 The Geography of Southeast Asia

READ TO LEARN

Key Vocabulary

mainland

Key Places

Mainland
  Southeast Asia
Malay peninsula

Malay archipelago
Philippine Islands
Strait of Malacca

Read Aloud

According to one geographer, Southeast Asia is a land that "is anchored between two wide and influential oceans." In the west Southeast Asia borders the Indian Ocean. In the east it borders the Pacific Ocean. Southeast Asia also lies near India and China—two very powerful civilizations. In this lesson you will read more about the geography of Southeast Asia.

Read for Purpose

1. **WHAT YOU KNOW:** How do oceans influence a region's climate?
2. **WHAT YOU WILL LEARN:** What is the geography of Southeast Asia?

A REGION OF PENINSULAS AND ARCHIPELAGOS

The region called Southeast Asia is made up of many islands and peninsulas. Five countries occupy the large peninsula that extends southeast between the Bay of Bengal and the South China Sea. These countries are Vietnam, Cambodia, Thailand, Myanmar, and Laos. They occupy land known as Mainland Southeast Asia. This part of Southeast Asia is part of the mainland, or principal land, of Asia.

In addition to the mainland, Southeast Asia is made up of the long Malay peninsula as well as the vast Malay archipelago. The Malay peninsula extends into the Indian Ocean and makes up part of the country of Malaysia. The Malay archipelago is the largest island group in the world. It extends south and east in a great arc between the Indian Ocean and the Pacific Ocean. It is a chain of more than 13,000 islands, almost half of which are uninhabited. The nations of Malaysia, Indonesia, Brunei, and Singapore make up this archipelago.

Another archipelago called the Philippine Islands can also be found in Southeast Asia. These tropical islands are separated from the mainland by the South China Sea. Look for them on the map on the next page.

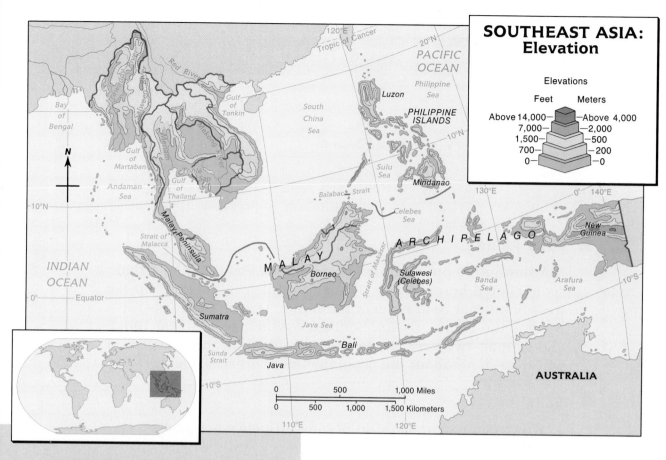

SOUTHEAST ASIA: Elevation

Elevations

Feet	Meters
Above 14,000—	—Above 4,000
7,000—	—2,000
1,500—	—500
700—	—200
0—	—0

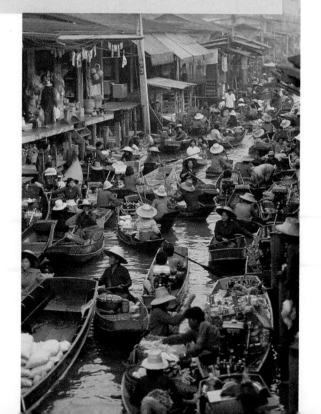

MAP SKILL: In Thailand people use canals and rivers to go to markets. Is Thailand on a peninsula or an island? Where are Southeast Asia's highest mountains?

RIVER AND SEA HIGHWAYS

Think back to what you learned in Chapter 3 about the importance of the Nile River to ancient Egypt. Recall how it served as a river highway through Egypt. Remember that the overflow of the Nile renewed the land each year with a deposit of silt. At its mouth the Nile River built up a rich delta.

Rivers have played a similar role in Southeast Asia's history. Its five most important rivers are found on the mainland. Wide and navigable rivers flow between this region's mountain ranges. Find them on the map above. From the west to the east they are the Irrawaddy (ir wod′ ē), the Salween (sal′ wēn), the Menam (mā nom′), the Mekong, and the Red rivers.

If the rivers are the highways of the mainland, the seas are the major links for the Malay peninsula and the Malay

In Southeast Asia elephants are sometimes used to work in the rain forests. They help carry loads of precious woods to market.

archipelago. Hundreds of straits separate the islands and peninsulas. The Strait of Malacca (mal′ ə kə) between the Malay peninsula and the island of Sumatra forms part of the most direct water route between India and China. Find the Strait of Malacca on the map on page 556.

Like the early Greeks who lived on the peninsulas and islands of the Aegean Sea, the people of Southeast Asia have been greatly influenced by the local seas. Like the ancient Greeks who borrowed an alphabet from their Phoenician trading partners, the people in Southeast Asia have exchanged ideas with each other. In fact, the language of Indonesia, Bahasa Indonesia, began as a mixture of the different languages spoken by traders in this region.

TROPICAL CLIMATE AND VEGETATION

The climate of Southeast Asia is uniformly and lushly tropical. . . . Crops, flowers, and trees grow with little attention. In some places, farmers raise four crops each year. Fruits and vegetables are plentiful all year round.

As this geographer has written, Southeast Asia has a tropical climate. In fact, almost all of Southeast Asia lies in the low latitudes and has a hot, humid climate throughout the year.

Monsoons have a great effect on the climate. These winds, blowing from the ocean to the land, bring heavy rains to most of the region. As in South Asia, the heaviest rains come during the summer monsoon season. As you know, dry seasons occur when the winds blow from the land.

In Chapter 16 you read about Africa's equatorial rain forests. You may recall that these thickly forested regions lie near the equator. Similar rain forests can be found in Southeast Asia. In fact, about 60 percent of the land here is covered by rain forests.

However, Southeast Asia's many rain forests have been rapidly shrinking. The strong demand in industrialized countries for teak and other wood has led to increased logging. If this continues, all of Southeast Asia could be deforested, as parts of Europe were deforested many centuries ago.

Malaysia has vast plantations where rubber trees are grown. Workers cut the bark to drain the sap that is made into rubber.

A TREASURE HOUSE OF RESOURCES

Southeast Asia is the richest area in natural resources in all of Asia. Its lush, tropical growing conditions give this region a great wealth of plant life. For example, it produces so much rice that it is called "the Great Rice Bowl of Asia." Its rubber plantations produce over four fifths of all the world's supply of rubber. Southeast Asia is also a major world producer of spices such as pepper, cinnamon, cloves, and nutmeg.

You may recall that the search for such spices is what first drew European explorers here. Gold and precious stones also attracted Europeans. Today, tin and oil are Southeast Asia's most valuable mineral resources. Half the world's supply of tin is mined in a strip of land that stretches from southern Thailand to eastern Sumatra.

THE SEA'S INFLUENCE

Southeast Asia is a land that is tied to the seas around it. You have read that thousands of islands form the world's largest archipelago here. Wide, navigable rivers serve as water highways deep into this region. Rich in resources, Southeast Asia is a place to which many have come to trade. As you will learn in the next lesson, this geography caused Southeast Asia to become "a crossroads of the world."

 Check Your Reading

1. Describe the geography of Southeast Asia.
2. How does the climate affect vegetation in Southeast Asia?
3. **GEOGRAPHY SKILL:** Use the map on page 556 to name Southeast Asia's five largest islands.
4. **THINKING SKILL:** How has geography affected the way people in Southeast Asia make a living?

2 The History of Southeast Asia

READ TO LEARN

Key People

Jayavarman II

Key Places

Bali
Angkor Wat

Read Aloud

From the earliest recorded history, there is evidence that contact with other cultures helped to shape the history of Southeast Asia.

As this historian has noted, outside influences can affect the history of an entire region. You have read about many lands that have been influenced by other cultures. Ancient Greece was influenced by Phoenicia. Ancient Rome learned from the Greeks and Etruscans. Islamic civilization borrowed from ancient Greece. Indian civilization borrowed from the Aryans. In this lesson you will learn how the history of Southeast Asia was also influenced by other cultures.

Read for Purpose

1. **WHAT YOU KNOW:** What large countries lie near Southeast Asia?
2. **WHAT YOU WILL LEARN:** How did China, India, and Europe influence Southeast Asia?

EARLY SOUTHEAST ASIA

The first Southeast Asians were migrants. Archaeologists and historians agree that they migrated here from China and India about 4,000 years ago. Using the islands of the Malay archipelago like steppingstones, these migrants moved across Southeast Asia.

Not much is known about those first Southeast Asians. Like other early societies, they farmed along major rivers and gradually built cities. The rivers were a source of water for household use and irrigation. They could also be used for transportation.

Historians do know that the Chinese traded with the villages along Mainland Southeast Asia's eastern coast. In about 100 B.C. the rulers of the Han dynasty conquered the northern part of this region and ruled it for 1,000 years.

Indian civilization also influenced Southeast Asia. As early as the sixth century B.C., Indian traders were sailing to Southeast Asia to search for gold and tin. Ancient Indian writings refer

Today Buddhism is the major religion of Southeast Asia. Boys become Buddhist monks at an early age. They devote their lives to prayer and study.

them Southeast Asians took on many Indian ways of life and forms of art. Today Buddhism remains the major faith in much of Mainland Southeast Asia. Hinduism is the main religion on the island of Bali in the Malay archipelago.

THE KHMER EMPIRE

By A.D. 500 Southeast Asia was a land of many kingdoms. Many of these kingdoms were influenced by Hinduism. Others were more closely tied to the teachings of Buddhism and the Buddhist dynasties of China. Of the many kingdoms in Southeast Asia, however, the Khmer (kə mer´) was the most powerful.

Located in Mainland Southeast Asia, the Khmer kingdom emerged as a power in the early ninth century. According to a Chinese scribe, a new leader "rose [among the Khmer] like a fresh lotus." This king was known as Jayavarman (jo yo vor´ mon) II. He came to the throne in 802. In his 50-year rule this mighty conqueror greatly enlarged the Khmer kingdom and turned it into an empire. By 850 the Khmer's rule had reached the boundaries of present-day Cambodia. Six hundred years later the Khmer was still the most powerful empire in all of Southeast Asia.

ANGKOR WAT

The most famous and splendid of the Khmer buildings was Angkor Wat (ang´ kôr wot´), a temple to the Hindu god Vishnu (vish´ nü). Built in the Khmer capital of Angkor in the early twelfth century, this temple is one of the largest religious buildings in the world. In fact, Angkor Wat covers more than a full square mile. The surround-

to Southeast Asia as the "golden peninsula." These early traders carried with them the teachings of Hinduism.

Buddhist missionaries followed the Hindu traders. By A.D. 500 Buddhist missionaries spread the teachings of Buddha throughout Southeast Asia. You may recall how Asoka first sent missionaries to spread the new religion of Buddhism throughout Asia.

Both Hinduism and Buddhism took firm hold in Southeast Asia. Through

ing moat reflected its nine towers, their roofs shining with gold. The towers themselves were built "to look like lotus blossoms in order to please the gods." An American traveler wrote:

If nothing else remained of all their works, Angkor Wat would be enough to mark the Khmers as one of the greats.

Angkor Wat was the chief center of a thriving Khmer community. Irrigation works surrounded the temple and carried water from large reservoirs. The water was used for the crops that provided food for the city of Angkor.

Angkor Wat symbolizes the peak of Khmer power. As Khmer power declined in the fifteenth century, Angkor Wat was abandoned. Thick rain forests quickly covered it. Angkor Wat was not discovered again until the later part of the nineteenth century.

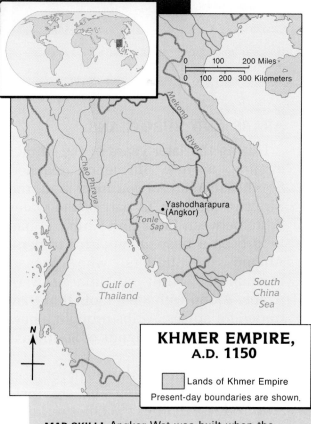

KHMER EMPIRE,
A.D. 1150

☐ Lands of Khmer Empire
Present-day boundaries are shown.

MAP SKILL: Angkor Wat was built when the Khmer Empire was at its height. What rivers flowed through the empire?

561

Dancers in Indonesia perform plays today based on Muslim and Hindu tales. Their costumes show the influence of both cultures.

ARABS AND EUROPEANS

During the later years of the Khmer empire, a new influence reached Southeast Asia. As you have read, the Strait of Malacca is part of the water route between India and China. It has long been a busy channel for traders. Among the traders who passed through the Strait of Malacca were Arabs. Along with steel tools that they traded for spices, Arabs brought a new faith, Islam, to the islands of Southeast Asia.

By 1400 Islam was the major religion of the Malay peninsula and archipelago. Today, Islam is the chief religion of the nations of Malaysia and Indonesia. Find these nations in the Atlas on pages 612–613.

By 1600 the Europeans had arrived in Southeast Asia. British, French, Spanish, Portuguese, and Dutch traders wanted Southeast Asia's silks and spices. By 1800 Britain and France controlled Mainland Southeast Asia. Spain ruled the Philippine Islands. The Dutch and Portuguese set up colonies on the Malay peninsula. Only Siam, now called Thailand, was able to keep its independence.

A CROSSROADS

Southeast Asia has been called "a crossroads of the world." As you have read, this region has been a place where many cultures have come together. Indian traders brought Hinduism. Missionaries brought Buddhism. Arab traders brought Islam. Living under European rule also had strong effects on life in Southeast Asia. For example, under the Spanish, the Roman Catholic religion spread throughout the Philippines.

As you read in Chapter 20, during the early part of World War II, Japanese forces occupied much of Southeast Asia. After Japan's defeat in 1945, the European colonial powers hoped to regain control of this important area. But the people of Southeast Asia had other ideas.

Check Your Reading

1. How did China and India influence Southeast Asia?
2. What is Angkor Wat?
3. GEOGRAPHY SKILL: What major religions are found in Indonesia, the Philippines, and Thailand?
4. THINKING SKILL: What could you do to determine the accuracy of the quotation on page 559?

3 Southeast Asia Today

READ TO LEARN

Key Vocabulary

martial law

Key People

Ho Chi Minh   Benigno Aquino
Pol Pot   Corazon Aquino
Ferdinand Marcos

Read Aloud

The people of Southeast Asia formed independent nations after World War II. The Philippines became independent in 1946. Britain gave up its colonies in Southeast Asia by 1948. A year later Malaysia and Indonesia were the new nations of the Malay archipelago. By 1954 colonialism had ended in Southeast Asia.

Read for Purpose

1. **WHAT YOU KNOW:** What world power controlled Southeast Asia during World War II?
2. **WHAT YOU WILL LEARN:** How do people live in Southeast Asia today?

A BITTER WAR IN VIETNAM

Independence did not come peacefully to Southeast Asia. For example, France left Vietnam in 1954 only after years of fighting. After the French left, Vietnam was divided. North Vietnam had a communist government. South Vietnam set up a noncommunist government.

The Vietnamese fought another war when Ho Chi Minh (hō' chē min), the leader of North Vietnam, led his communist troops against South Vietnam. The Vietnam War lasted for nearly 20 years. Between 1965 and 1973 more than 8 million troops from the United States supported South Vietnamese troops. When the war ended in 1975, all of Vietnam became communist. Communist governments were also set up in Laos and Cambodia.

The governments of Vietnam and Cambodia treated many of their citizens very harshly. Refugees fled their homelands in small, overcrowded vessels. These "boat people" hoped to reach a safe harbor or to be rescued at sea. Thousands drowned, but many reached other countries.

Cambodia suffered greatly. In 1976 a cruel dictator named Pol Pot closed the nation's borders and started a reign of terror. More than 1 million Cambodians—about one of every seven people—died of starvation or in mass killings. In 1991, after many years of conflict, the different warring groups in Cambodia agreed to hold elections.

MAP SKILL: The "boat people" who fled Vietnam were forced into refugee camps in neighboring countries. What countries lie across the South China Sea from Vietnam?

SOUTHEAST ASIA TODAY

Rebuilding the war-torn nations of Southeast Asia has taken many years. People turned to the traditional ways of farming to survive in difficult conditions. Today, many people still work as farmers, raising crops of rice and vegetables. Rice remains the chief crop of this region. But pineapples, corn, tobacco, and sugarcane are also grown and often exported to other countries.

But more and more people in Southeast Asia are moving to cities. The people who live in these urban areas often work in small factories and shops. Factories in bustling cities such as Bangkok, Thailand, and Jakarta, Indonesia, produce goods ranging from textiles to tires. Singapore is one of the busiest port cities in the world, and its

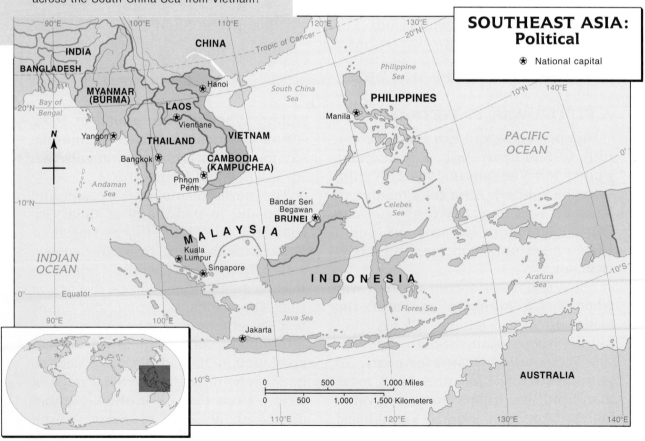

SOUTHEAST ASIA: Political

✹ National capital

factories produce electronics and other modern goods. In recent years, the oil industry has brought great wealth to the Southeast Asian countries of Brunei and Indonesia.

A STRUGGLE FOR DEMOCRACY

When the Philippines became an independent nation in 1946, it declared itself a democratic republic. Getting democracy to work there, however, has been a continuing struggle.

Most of the land in the Philippines was owned by a few very rich people. The peasants who worked on the land were treated poorly by these land-owners. Some peasants supported the communists in an effort to gain more land and power. In 1972, President Ferdinand Marcos declared martial law, or military rule, in the Philippines. Marcos said that he needed more power in order to combat the communist threat. Martial law enabled Marcos to jail his enemies and close newspapers that opposed him.

By 1980 opposition to Marcos's dictatorship grew. In 1983 Benigno Aquino (bä nēg′ nō ä kē′ nō′), a popular leader who opposed Marcos, was killed. Most people suspected that Marcos had ordered the killing.

In November 1985 Marcos gave in to pressure from the United States and agreed to hold elections. Corazon Aquino, widow of the killed leader, ran for president against Marcos. She led a forceful campaign, and most observers believed she had won. But the Marcos government declared that Aquino had lost. Aquino resisted and held her own inauguration in February 1986. Finally, when important military leaders supported Aquino, Marcos and his family fled the country.

Corazon Aquino became president of the Philippines in 1986. Ferdinand Marcos was forced to flee the country.

A PROMISING FUTURE

Southeast Asia is a region with a promising future. After years of colonialism, war, and harsh rule, many of the nations of Southeast Asia are experiencing newfound peace. Rich in natural resources and ideally located as a crossroads of trade, Southeast Asia continues to grow as an important and vibrant area of the world.

Check Your Reading

1. What is life like for people in Southeast Asia today?
2. Describe martial law.
3. **GEOGRAPHY SKILL:** Name five Southeast Asian nations.
4. **THINKING SKILL:** List three questions you could ask to learn more about the Vietnam War.

565

Using Information

Imagine that your teacher has assigned a short research report. You are to write a report and then use puppets to present it to another class. To prepare this report, you can use the skills you learned in this book. Start by choosing a topic and listing questions your report might answer about the topic. Next, look for credible sources that will give you the information you need to know. After you gather the information, try to organize it in a way that will make sense to someone reading your report or seeing your puppet show. Finally, use the information you have collected to draw conclusions about your topic.

Trying the Skill

Use the information in Chapter 21 and in other sources to describe how the United States was involved in the Vietnam War. What questions could you ask to help you find the information you need? What conclusions can you draw? Use the following "question starters" to begin your research.

- *Which* countries was the United States most interested in?
- *When* did this interest begin?
- *Why* did the United States take an interest?

Remember to match your questions with the best sources of information available. Explore your school and town libraries. Books, charts, maps, and time lines will help. Remember, a time line might help answer the question *when*. But a time line never answers the question *why*.

HELPING YOURSELF

The steps on the left will help you collect and use information to write a report. The example on the right shows one way to apply these steps to the report on the Vietnam War.

One Way to Use Information	Example
1. Limit your topic. Brainstorm questions that will get you the information you need to know.	What do you want to know about United State's involvement in Vietnam War? Start fact-finding questions with *who, what, where, when,* and *how.* To learn reasons for U.S. involvement, ask *why.*
2. Look for the answers to your questions in credible sources.	Find answers to fact-finding questions in textbooks and encyclopedias. Refer to magazine articles and books written about Vietnam to find out why Americans became involved or why they left.
3. Evaluate the information you have collected.	Separate facts from opinions. Look for a writer's point of view to determine the credibility of the information presented. Discard inaccurate information.
4. Classify, or group, the information.	Group and label similar information. Maybe your information can be grouped into these categories: How Americans Became Involved; Why They Became Involved; Why They Left.
5. Look for ways the categories of information relate to each other. Draw conclusions about the topic.	Read the information to get the general picture the facts create. Think about how categories connect to each other and to your topic.

Applying the Skill

Now apply what you have learned by using information to describe the economy of Southeast Asia. Do not forget to consult other sources, such as an almanac, to find answers to your questions. What categories did you discover? What sentence did you write?

1. Which of the following might *not* be useful to learn about the topic?
   a. What is the major religion of Southeast Asia?
   b. What is the GNP?
   c. What is life expectancy?
   d. What is the literacy rate?

2. Which of the following categories might serve as labels for the information you collected?
   a. Vital Statistics
   b. Communications
   c. Economic Indicators
   d. all of the above

Reviewing the Skill

1. What are some steps you can follow to find information about a topic?
2. Why is it important to evaluate and organize information before you use it?
3. What are some other times, outside of school, when you might use this skill?

IMPORTANT EVENTS

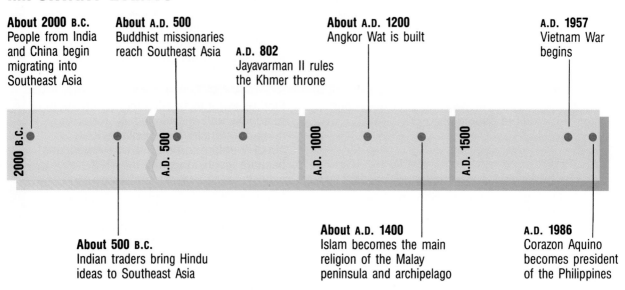

About 2000 B.C.
People from India and China begin migrating into Southeast Asia

About A.D. 500
Buddhist missionaries reach Southeast Asia

A.D. 802
Jayavarman II rules the Khmer throne

About A.D. 1200
Angkor Wat is built

A.D. 1957
Vietnam War begins

2000 B.C.

A.D. 500

A.D. 1000

A.D. 1500

About 500 B.C.
Indian traders bring Hindu ideas to Southeast Asia

About A.D. 1400
Islam becomes the main religion of the Malay peninsula and archipelago

A.D. 1986
Corazon Aquino becomes president of the Philippines

PEOPLE TO KNOW

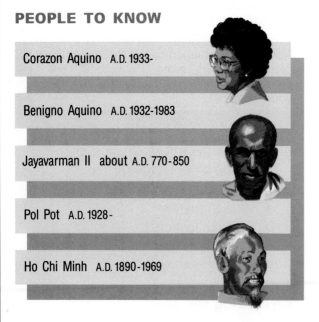

Corazon Aquino A.D. 1933-

Benigno Aquino A.D. 1932-1983

Jayavarman II about A.D. 770-850

Pol Pot A.D. 1928-

Ho Chi Minh A.D. 1890-1969

IDEAS TO REMEMBER

■ Southeast Asia is made up of many peninsulas and archipelagoes. This region also has a tropical climate that is affected by monsoon wind patterns.

■ Southeast Asian religions, languages, and ways of life have been highly influenced by the civilizations of China, India, and Europe.

■ The people of Southeast Asia are rebuilding after decades of war, revolution, and dictatorship.

REVIEWING VOCABULARY

mainland   martial law

Number a sheet of paper from 1 to 5. Beside each number write the word or term from the list above that best completes each sentence.

1. A body of land forming the largest land mass of a region is called a ____.
2. Under ____, government leaders restrict the rights of citizens of a country.
3. The ____ of Southeast Asia includes the countries of Thailand, Cambodia, Myanmar, Laos, and Vietnam.
4. ____ means "military rule," and was the power used by President Ferdinand Marcos to restrict freedoms in the Philippines.
5. The ____ is the principal land of a continent excluding islands and small peninsulas.

REVIEWING FACTS

1. What is the dominant climate of Southeast Asia?
2. What was the most powerful ancient kingdom in Southeast Asia? In what present-day country was it located?
3. What are the three main religions of Southeast Asia?
4. What three Southeast Asian countries became communist following the Vietnam War?
5. List three events that ended the Marcos dictatorship and brought Corazon Aquino to power in the Philippines.

WRITING ABOUT MAIN IDEAS

1. **Writing a Paragraph:** Write a paragraph describing what the existence of a temple like Angkor Wat says about the level of civilization achieved by the Khmer. What does it say about the amount of wealth, the power of the central government, and the importance of religion in that society?

2. **Writing an Interview:** You have read that Southeast Asia has many natural resources. Yet it also contains some of the world's poorest countries. Write an imaginary interview with a Vietnamese farmer, in which the farmer explains this paradox.

3. **Writing About Perspectives:** Many of the "boat people" you read about in this chapter either drowned at sea or were forced to return to their homelands. This was due in part to the refusal by some governments to accept these refugees. Write a letter to your government that makes a case for accepting the "boat people."

BUILDING SKILLS: USING INFORMATION

Imagine that you have been assigned to report on the geography of Southeast Asia.

1. How would you go about finding information on the topic?
2. What steps would you follow to evaluate the information you collected?
3. What are some thinking skills you might use when writing your report?

CHAPTER 22

AUSTRALIA AND OCEANIA

◄ FOCUS ►

They gaze out to sea from whence their creators came. At some time in the past, who can say when, these islands were reached.

An English scientist named Robert Jackson wrote these words in the late 1800s. He was amazed to find huge, carved heads on the uninhabited Pacific island he was visiting. In this chapter you will read about the history and life today of the people of Australia and Oceania.

1 The Geography of Australia and Oceania

READ TO LEARN

Key Vocabulary

outback
coral reef
lagoon
atoll

Key Places

Great Sandy Desert
Great Victoria Desert
Gibson Desert
Great Dividing Range

Australian Alps
Mount Kosciusko
Great Barrier Reef
Mount Cook

Read Aloud

The Pacific Ocean is the largest and deepest body of water in the world. The northern part of the Pacific is nearly an empty stretch of water. Only a few islands are found there.

The South Pacific, though, has more than 10,000 islands. Most of these islands are too small even to appear on maps. But one island—Australia—is large enough to be considered a continent. Australia and the islands of New Zealand make up 90 percent of this region's land.

Read for Purpose

1. **WHAT YOU KNOW:** What important islands have you read about in this book?
2. **WHAT YOU WILL LEARN:** What is the geography of Australia and Oceania?

THE "LAND DOWN UNDER"

If you look at a globe, you can see why the continent of Australia is often called the "land down under." Far away from the land masses of other continents, all of Australia lies in the Southern Hemisphere. In fact the name *Australia* comes from the Latin word meaning "southern land."

Australia is the smallest continent. It is about the same size as the United States without Alaska and Hawaii. It is the only continent that has only one nation—also known as Australia.

Most of Australia is flat. The western two thirds of the land is a plateau. Deserts cover much of this plateau. The people of Australia call this dry region the outback. According to one Australian writer:

The outback lies "out back." You might say it got its name from the fact that most Australians tend to live "up front" in the more fertile lands of the east.

The deserts of Australia's outback have names, of course. As you can see on the map on page 572, in the north the desert is called the Great Sandy Desert, and in the south it is called the Great Victoria Desert. Between these two deserts lies the Gibson Desert. Together, these deserts make up the second largest desert in the world. Only the Sahara is larger. The Gibson Desert has a rocky surface, but the other deserts are areas of high, drifting dunes.

Most Australians live on the eastern coastal plains. Ranges of low mountains border the coastal plains from the outback. Called the Great Dividing Range, these highlands wind their way all the way down the eastern edge of Australia. The highest mountains are the Australian Alps, at the southern end of the Great Dividing Range. Australia's highest peak is Mount Kosciusko (kŏz ē əs' kō). Between the western plateau and the mountains of the east lie the central lowlands. This area covers about one third of the continent, from the Gulf of Carpenteria in the north to the Indian Ocean in the south. This vast region is made up largely of low-lying plains. Most of the land is between 500 and 1,000 feet (150–300 m) above sea level.

The Lake Eyre Basin, in the south-central part of the central lowlands, is the driest place in Australia. The lake itself is usually only a great flat area of salt and mud, and the rivers that flow into it often do not run for many years at a time.

MAP SKILL: Australia's island neighbor is New Zealand. What are the capitals of the two nations? On what coast of Australia is the Great Barrier Reef?

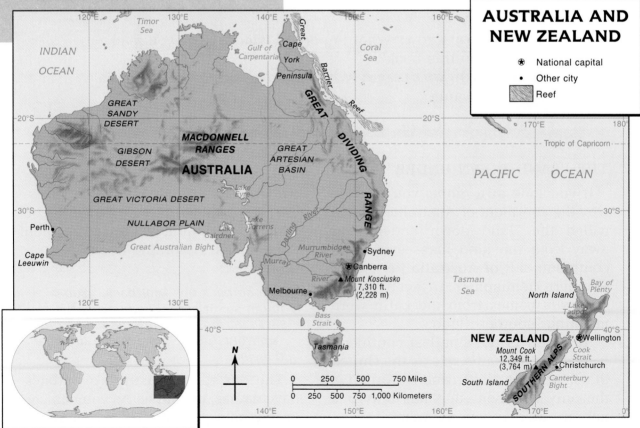

Ayers Rock stands by itself in the middle of Australia's outback. Like the kangaroo, it is a symbol of the country.

AUSTRALIA'S ANIMAL LIFE

One of the most interesting things about Australia's geography is its animal life. It has many animals that are unlike those found in other parts of the world. For example, the best known of Australia's animals is the kangaroo. When the first European explorers arrived in Australia in the eighteenth century, one sailor wrote:

With its body like a greyhound and its head like a rabbit, it has no resemblance to any European animal ever seen.

Perhaps the strangest animal of all is the platypus (plat' ə pəs). Like a duck, it has a bill and webbed feet. Like a snake, it has fangs and can squirt a poisonous venom.

Coral polyps (pol' ips), though not found only in Australia, are another important form of animal life. There are billions of coral animals in the warm, clear water of the Pacific. The skeletons they leave behind build up coral reefs, or long stretches of coral rock. The largest coral reef in the world is the Great Barrier Reef, which stretches for more than 1,250 miles (2,010 km) along Australia's northeastern coast.

In 1979 the government of Australia set aside part of the Great Barrier Reef as a marine park. Every year thousands of people from all over the world visit this natural wonder.

573

THREE ISLAND GROUPS

Coral reefs are common in the southern part of the Pacific Ocean. Oceania is made up of thousands of large and small islands. Divided into three groups—Polynesia, Micronesia, and Melanesia—these groups of islands stretch far across the Pacific Ocean.

The country of New Zealand is made up of the two largest islands of Oceania. The center of North Island is a volcanic plateau. This is a region of many hot springs and geysers, much like Yellowstone Park in the United States. South Island is more mountainous than North Island. Glaciers are found on the mountains of South Island. Mount Cook, New Zealand's highest peak, rises dramatically over the island.

The lava from an undersea volcano hardens into rock. Over time, the rock rises above the sea and becomes an island. Many Pacific islands were created by volcanic eruptions.

Like the islands of New Zealand, most Pacific islands are formed by the tops of mountains rising from the ocean floor. Many of these mountains are active volcanoes. Their flaming eruptions have earned the South Pacific the nickname "Ring of Fire."

Many parts of Oceania lie along the unstable plates of the earth's surface. Thus many of the islands are being slowly raised or lowered. As the diagram on the next page shows, if an island with a coral reef is lowered, the island is separated from the reef by water. The reef continues to grow upward. As the diagram shows, the water lying between an island shore and a reef is called a lagoon.

An island that is surrounded by a barrier reef may continue to sink. Eventually, only a ring-shaped coral island remains above sea. Such an island is called an atoll (at' ôl). Most atolls are

DIAGRAM SKILL: The water inside a coral reef is called a lagoon. What is a ring-shaped reef called?

THE MAKING OF AN ATOLL

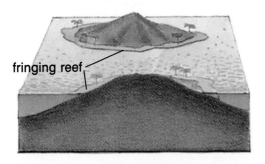

fringing reef

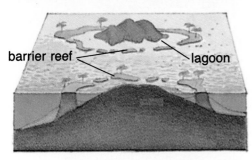

barrier reef

lagoon

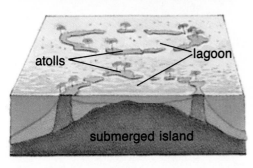

atolls

lagoon

submerged island

shaped like a circle and surround a lagoon. What was once an island lies below the atoll's lagoon. Find the submerged island in the diagram.

"THE LAST PLACES ON EARTH"

Australia and the islands of Oceania have been called "the last places on earth." As you know, they are located far away from Asia, Africa, and Europe. You will learn, however, that people lived in Australia and Oceania long before European explorers and traders arrived. In the next lesson you will read more about "the last places on earth."

Check Your Reading

1. What is the geography of Australia and Oceania?
2. How is an atoll formed?
3. **GEOGRAPHY SKILL:** Into what island groups is Oceania divided?
4. **THINKING SKILL:** What steps could you take to determine the accuracy of the facts in this lesson?

Reading Maps of the Ocean Floor

Earth is sometimes called the water planet. About seventy-one percent of its surface is covered by water.

The ocean is a major factor in the geography of Australia and Oceania. To understand more about their geography, then, it is helpful to be able to read the special photographs and maps showing details of the ocean floor. The ocean floor is the part of the earth's crust that lies below sea level. Have you ever wondered what the ocean floors look like? You will be interested to know that the ocean floor has many different features.

Maps of the earth's land areas are the most common kinds of maps. Less common are maps of the ocean floor. Until about 60 years ago, it was thought that the ocean floor was a nearly flat plain. Scientists have discovered, however, that the ocean's floor is extremely varied.

Ocean Floor Features

The surface of the ocean floor is just as varied as the surface of the earth above sea level. Mountain ranges, basins, plains, ridges, canyons, and valleys are all found there. You can see such features in the special photograph below. Called a Seasat photograph, it shows the roughness of the ocean floor.

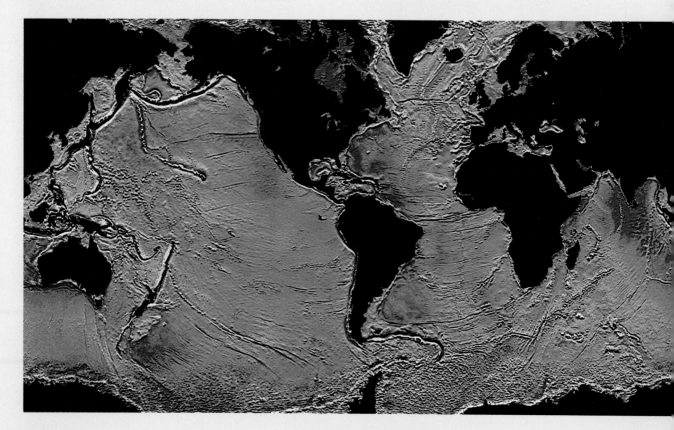

Using Seasat photographs, such as the one on the left page, scientists have been able to make more accurate maps of the ocean floor. The photograph was taken by a satellite in space. If you look closely you can see the deep trenches, or valleys, of the ocean floor. Trenches are the deepest parts of the ocean floor. Use the photograph to find the trenches that run in the Pacific Ocean near Asia and Australia. You can also see the many ranges of hills that lie across the ocean floor.

Contour Maps

Elevation and features of the ocean floor are shown by contour maps. As you read in Chapter 7, contour maps outline landforms with lines or different colors showing different elevations. You may recall that these lines are called contour lines. A contour line on a map connects areas of the same elevation.

As you may recall, contour lines that are drawn close together mean that the land is very steep. Contour lines show height both above and below sea level on land maps and below sea level on sea maps. As shown on **Diagram A** on this page, depth below sea level in meters or feet has a minus sign (−). The minus sign tells you that the figure represents the number of feet or meters below sea level.

Map A and **Map B** also show Fin Island. Note that both maps are contour maps. What is the difference between **Map A** and **Map B**? As you can see, the contour lines shown on **Map A** show land above sea level. The contour lines shown on **Map B** show land below sea level. What is the contour interval on these maps? You may recall that contour intervals are differences in elevation between contour lines. As shown, the contour interval is 20 meters.

Reviewing the Skill

1. What is one difference between a relief map and a contour map?
2. Compare a contour line and a contour interval.
3. Use the Seasat photograph to name the deepest parts of the Pacific.
4. If you wished to have a picnic, a swim, and then take an easy climb to the highest point on Fin Island, using which map and on what basis would you choose the best site? Explain your answer.
5. On maps **A** and **B**, what is the difference in elevation between points **X** and **Y**?
6. How do maps of the ocean floor help you understand the earth's surface?

FIN ISLAND: Contour Lines

DIAGRAM A

MAP A

MAP B

2 The History of Australia and Oceania

READt TO LEARN

Key Vocabulary
boomerang
sovereignty

Key People
Willem Jansz
Abel Tasman
James Cook
William Hobson

Key Places
New Guinea
Tasmania
Botany Bay

Read Aloud

Now we have done these things; you make sure they remain like this for all time. You must not change anything.

With these words a dying hunter in early Australia warned his people to honor their traditions. The land he hunted in is known today as Australia. The first Australians created many rich traditions. When later settlers arrived, they would build a very different society.

Read for Purpose

1. **WHAT YOU KNOW:** What are some of the interesting things about Australia's geography?
2. **WHAT YOU WILL LEARN:** What events caused Australia and the islands of Oceania to emerge as nations?

THE FIRST AUSTRALIANS

The first people to settle Australia and Oceania came there from Southeast Asia about 30,000 years ago. These early inhabitants used canoes to migrate throughout the islands. Most of the islands were settled by the time Europeans began to explore the region in the sixteenth century.

These early people are known as Aborigines (ab ə rij′ ə nēz). The word *aborigines* means "earliest known people to live in a place." The Aborigines were hunters and gatherers. They did not farm the land or build villages. They moved around Australia in small groups of a few families.

The tools and weapons developed by Australia's early people were simple but very effective. For example, they used digging sticks, stone axes, spears, and boomerangs. A boomerang is an elbow-shaped flat piece of wood. When thrown correctly, a boomerang circles and returns to the thrower. The Aborigines used wooden boomerangs to hunt birds and other small animals. You will read more about Australia's Aborigines in the Traditions lesson on pages 582–585.

Many Aborigines have moved to Australia's towns and cities. But some still carry on their ancient way of life in the desert.

OCEANIA'S EARLY PEOPLE

Unlike Australia's first settlers, the early people of Oceania were farmers. In fact, it was the search for new farmland that kept early Oceanians moving across the South Pacific.

These people took long journeys of thousands of miles across the open sea. Their boats were oceangoing canoes, made from hollowed-out tree trunks. All they had to help them navigate were the position of the sun, the way the waves rolled, and the direction the birds flew. Yet that was enough for them to transport many groups of families over great distances.

The first people to settle on the islands of New Zealand were the Maoris (mou' rēz). This group of people came from other Polynesian islands in the eighth century. According to one legend, the Maoris left their homes "across the great sea" in a fleet of canoes. When they reached New Zealand, they called the islands "The Long White Cloud." Perhaps they chose this name because they saw steam rising from geysers.

EUROPEANS ARRIVE

About 700 years after the first Maoris settled New Zealand, the first Europeans reached the South Pacific. The explorers who sailed near Australia were searching for an unknown continent called *Terra Australis Incognito*, meaning "unknown southern land" in Latin. Many believed that an undiscovered continent existed in the Southern Hemisphere.

Spanish and French explorers reached several islands of Oceania. In 1606 a Dutch explorer named Willem Jansz landed in northern Australia. Without knowing it, he was the first European to land in Australia. Jansz thought he had reached the island of New Guinea.

In 1642 Abel Tasman reached the island south of Australia known today as Tasmania. The Dutch also explored the barren areas of western Australia. They decided that the land there was not good enough to farm.

THE JOURNAL OF CAPTAIN COOK

J have sailed the world and beheld many wonders. Here I have found a serene [gentle] people. . .I do not look upon the people of this land to be warlike. On the contrary, I think they belong to a rather shy and inoffensive race, no way inclined to cruelty. . . .

Neither are they numerous. They live in small groups along by the sea coasts, and near the banks of lakes, rivers, or creeks. They move about from place to place in search of food. . . .

From what many sailors have reported, they may appear to be the most wretched [unhappy] people on earth, but they are far happier than we Europeans. . . .

They live peacefully while the earth and the sea of their own accord give all things that are necessary for life. . . .In short, the poeple of this land seem to set no value upon anything Europe can give them, nor would they ever part with the earth's natural gifts. . . .

The Journal of Captain Cook records his views of Australia's first people. After Cook arrived in Australia, many new settlers followed and raised the British flag.

In 1770 a British explorer named James Cook became the first European to explore the fertile eastern coast of Australia. Cook made three voyages there. He made careful charts of Australia and many Pacific islands, and he claimed the land for Britain.

BRITISH SETTLEMENT

At first the British were not interested in faraway Australia. After the loss of their American colonies in 1783, however, they looked at Australia as a place to which they could send prisoners. You may know that, before the American Revolution, the British had sent prisoners to the American colonies.

In January 1788 a fleet of 11 British ships sailed into Botany Bay, on Australia's eastern coast. On board were 775 convicted criminals who had been sentenced to work in Australia as punishment for their crimes.

Convicts kept arriving, more than 160,000 of them over the next 80 years.

So did free settlers. By 1860 colonies had been settled all along eastern Australia and on the west coast.

At first, the colonies were separate and self-governing, though still subject to British rule. In 1901, however, they united into one nation, the Commonwealth of Australia.

NEW ZEALAND BECOMES A NATION

In the late eighteenth century, hunters, whalers, and traders came to New Zealand from Britain and other European countries. These newcomers traded with the Maoris for timber. They hunted for seals and whales off the coasts and islands.

Except for Maori village groups, New Zealand had no government or political organization until 1840. In that year a British officer named William Hobson and a group of 12 Maori chiefs signed a peace treaty. This treaty gave Britain sovereignty (sov' rən tē), or political control, over the islands of New Zealand. The British sovereign, or ruler, would also be the ruler of New Zealand.

The arrival of large numbers of settlers, however, led to tensions between the Maoris, who did not wish to sell their land, and the newcomers, who wanted farmlands. In 1845 tensions erupted into war. Fighting continued off and on until 1872, when Maori resistance ended.

By 1900 even the colonists felt that British sovereignty over New Zealand was unfair. They believed that the time had come for the people of New Zealand to govern themselves. Britain agreed to the colonists' request. In 1907 New Zealand became a self-governing country in the British Empire.

Today's Maoris continue to harvest the riches of the sea, like their ancestors.

A SIMILAR HISTORY

In many ways the history of Australia and Oceania is like the history of the United States. All were settled first by people from Asia. Later, when Europeans arrived in these new lands they set up colonies. As you know, this often led to bloodshed between the colonists and the first settlers. Unlike the United States, however, Australia and New Zealand won their independence peacefully.

Check Your Reading

1. How did Australia and New Zealand become independent nations?
2. What is sovereignty?
3. GEOGRAPHY SKILL: Where did the first settlers of Australia and Oceania come from?
4. THINKING SKILL: Reread page 588. How did Cook view Australians?

581

WALKABOUT

by Carrie Evento

In Lesson 2 you read about the people known as Aborigines, the first people to live in Australia. Although the ways of life of modern Aborigines have changed, Aborigine traditions still survive. One of these traditions is called the Walkabout. As you read, think about how this tradition helps Aborigines today keep alive the beliefs and the knowledge of their ancestors.

A LIVING TRADITION

When Europeans built ranches in Australia in the late 1800s and early 1900s, Australian Aborigines lost lands on which their ancestors had lived for thousands of years. Many Aborigines died from diseases they had never known before. Some Aborigines began to work for European ranchers, while others moved to cities. As their land was taken from them, Aborigines were forced to change some of their ways of life.

But one of the traditions that has remained strong among many Aborigines living on ranches or in the wilderness area called the bush is the Walkabout. From time to time, Aborigines, alone or in a family group, leave the place where they live to go on a Walkabout. Equipped with traditional tools from the old days, such as spears and sticks for starting fires, Aborigines set out on foot into the countryside. Sometimes Aborigines on a Walkabout stay away for a few months or even for a year or longer, but usually a Walkabout is a few weeks long. During this time Aborigines build sleeping shelters and find food in the ways of their ancestors.

Where does a person on a Walkabout go? To an observer it might look as if he or she has no particular destination. But Aborigines speak of the paths they follow as the "footprints" of their ancestors. They say that long ago

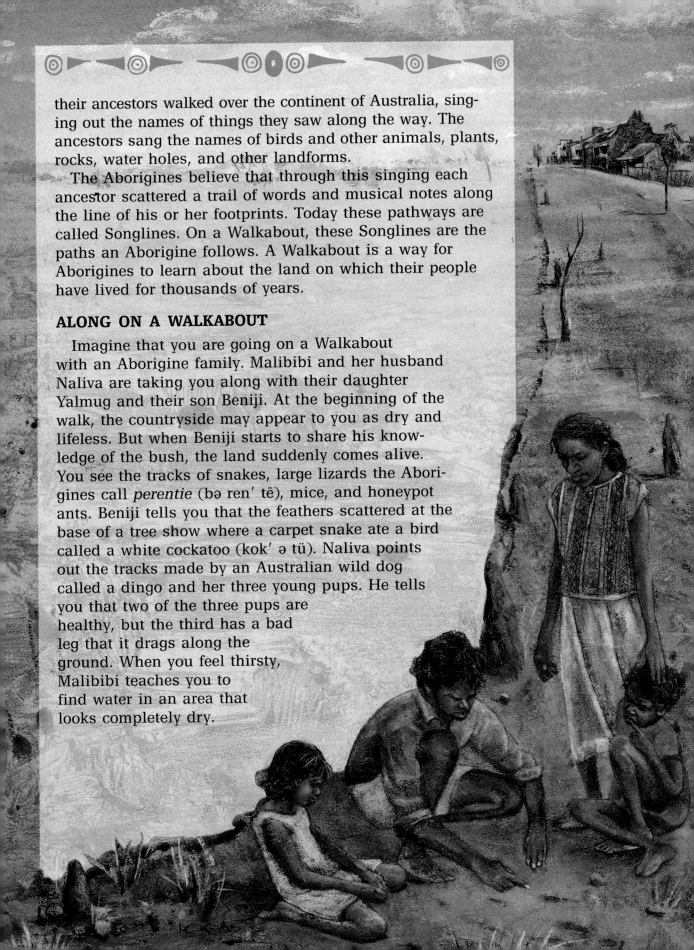

their ancestors walked over the continent of Australia, singing out the names of things they saw along the way. The ancestors sang the names of birds and other animals, plants, rocks, water holes, and other landforms.

The Aborigines believe that through this singing each ancestor scattered a trail of words and musical notes along the line of his or her footprints. Today these pathways are called Songlines. On a Walkabout, these Songlines are the paths an Aborigine follows. A Walkabout is a way for Aborigines to learn about the land on which their people have lived for thousands of years.

ALONG ON A WALKABOUT

Imagine that you are going on a Walkabout with an Aborigine family. Malibibi and her husband Naliva are taking you along with their daughter Yalmug and their son Beniji. At the beginning of the walk, the countryside may appear to you as dry and lifeless. But when Beniji starts to share his knowledge of the bush, the land suddenly comes alive. You see the tracks of snakes, large lizards the Aborigines call *perentie* (bə ren′ tē), mice, and honeypot ants. Beniji tells you that the feathers scattered at the base of a tree show where a carpet snake ate a bird called a white cockatoo (kok′ ə tü). Naliva points out the tracks made by an Australian wild dog called a dingo and her three young pups. He tells you that two of the three pups are healthy, but the third has a bad leg that it drags along the ground. When you feel thirsty, Malibibi teaches you to find water in an area that looks completely dry.

You learn to read messages as you walk—those left by a crushed ant, or a bruised leaf, or tracks in the sand. Naliva reads some sand tracks and tells you a story. "A man went by here yesterday afternoon. One of his camels was lame. But because the man had to cross the mountains by nightfall, he pushed the camel on."

You follow Yalmug's example and learn to pick lily pads in order to eat the green peas at their center. You watch in anticipation as Naliva wades in a river, his spear poised. You hold your breath and scan the riverbank for crocodiles while he walks stealthily through the water.

After a couple of tries, Naliva spears a *barramunda* (bar ə mən′ də) fish to cook for dinner. He shows you how to start a fire using sticks. When you try unsuccessfully to use the fire sticks yourself, Naliva laughs and says, "It's harder than matches." Then he places the large fish in the fire's hot ashes. It is your job to turn the fish over every few minutes. Finally, the large, meaty fish is cooked. Malibibi removes the scales from the cooked barramunda, using a twig, and slices the fish into pieces. She hands you one portion on a piece of bark taken from a paperbark tree. You have never tasted anything quite like it!

After dinner you prepare for sleep. You help to make a shelter without walls, called a *gunyah* (gən′ yə). Malibibi asks you and Yalmug to collect poles of bamboo and large sheets of

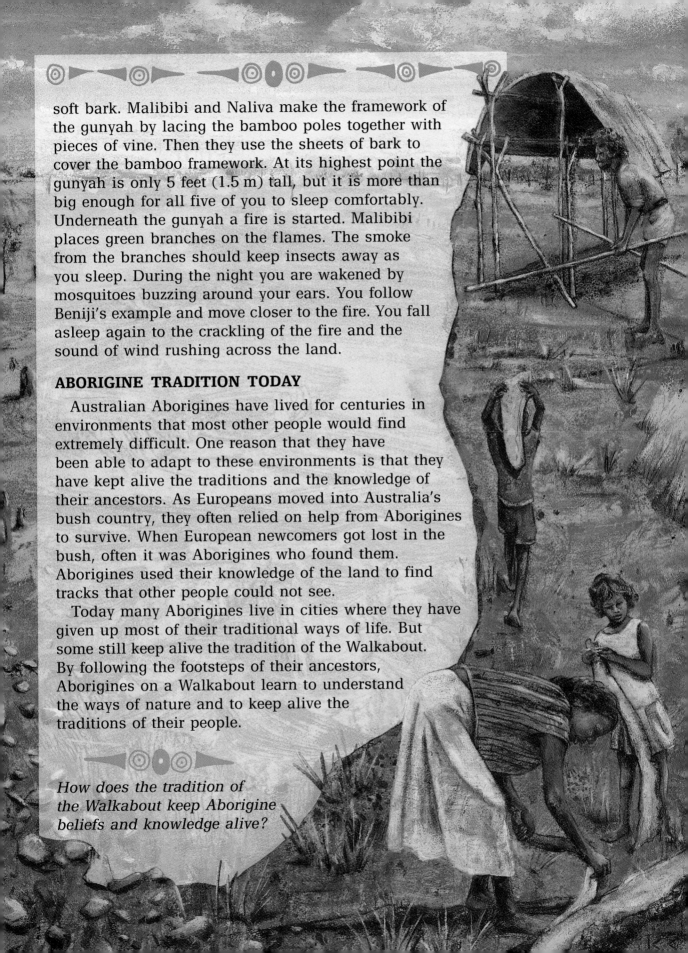

soft bark. Malibibi and Naliva make the framework of the gunyah by lacing the bamboo poles together with pieces of vine. Then they use the sheets of bark to cover the bamboo framework. At its highest point the gunyah is only 5 feet (1.5 m) tall, but it is more than big enough for all five of you to sleep comfortably. Underneath the gunyah a fire is started. Malibibi places green branches on the flames. The smoke from the branches should keep insects away as you sleep. During the night you are wakened by mosquitoes buzzing around your ears. You follow Beniji's example and move closer to the fire. You fall asleep again to the crackling of the fire and the sound of wind rushing across the land.

ABORIGINE TRADITION TODAY

Australian Aborigines have lived for centuries in environments that most other people would find extremely difficult. One reason that they have been able to adapt to these environments is that they have kept alive the traditions and the knowledge of their ancestors. As Europeans moved into Australia's bush country, they often relied on help from Aborigines to survive. When European newcomers got lost in the bush, often it was Aborigines who found them. Aborigines used their knowledge of the land to find tracks that other people could not see.

Today many Aborigines live in cities where they have given up most of their traditional ways of life. But some still keep alive the tradition of the Walkabout. By following the footsteps of their ancestors, Aborigines on a Walkabout learn to understand the ways of nature and to keep alive the traditions of their people.

How does the tradition of the Walkabout keep Aborigine beliefs and knowledge alive?

3 Australia and Oceania Today

READ TO LEARN

Key Vocabulary

station
cash crop

Read Aloud

We are no longer different from the rest of the world. We used to think that we were small, isolated . . . and the ways of the world did not seem to affect us.

These words, spoken by a woman from New Zealand, might reflect the feelings of people all over Australia and Oceania as they face new challenges.

Read for Purpose

1. **WHAT YOU KNOW:** What challenges do people in the United States face today?
2. **WHAT YOU WILL LEARN:** How do people live in Australia and Oceania today?

AUSTRALIA TODAY

Australia today is a modern and diverse country of 16 million people. Large urban areas, such as Sydney and Melbourne, are home to most Australians. These coastal cities have tall skyscrapers, bustling factories, and long sandy beaches.

Part of the reason for Australia's strong economy is that the country is very rich in natural resources. Australia is the world's largest producer of coal and bauxite. You may know that bauxite is used to make aluminum. Australia also produces more than 90 percent of the world's opals and is one of the biggest exporters of iron ore.

Such mineral wealth makes mining

a major industry in Australia. Some minerals are exported to other countries, but many of these resources supply Australia's own manufacturing industries. For example, factories in Sydney produce cars, trucks, trains, and farm machinery.

LIVING IN THE OUTBACK

Sheep and cattle raising is another major business in Australia. In fact, there are ten times as many sheep as people. Nearly one third of the world's wool comes from sheep in Australia. Beef from Australian cattle is exported all over the world.

Much of the ranching in Australia is

586

done in the outback. Here families work huge stations, or ranches. The stations are huge because it takes 40 acres (16 ha) of this dry land to graze one sheep. If you lived in a station, your nearest neighbor might be more than 100 miles (160 km) away. Imagine how difficult it would be to travel to school. It would take a bus hours to travel such distances.

Australians have used modern technology to solve these problems. Many stations now have airstrips. Families use airplanes to visit friends much as Americans might use cars or buses.

The stations also have two-way radios. Each day students use them to tune into their "classroom," called the School of the Air. Students and teachers use two-way radios to communicate with one another because of the great distances that separate them.

Young people who live on Australia's stations go to a "school of the air," and often never see their teachers in person.

HOW GEOTHERMAL ENERGY PRODUCES ELECTRICITY

1 Bore holes release steam from underground
2 Steam and water separated by cyclone separators
3 Steam travels through pipes to power station
4 Steam spins turbines to generate electricity
5 Steam is cooled by water pumped from river

DIAGRAM SKILL: People in New Zealand use geothermal energy to provide power. What is the first step of this process?

NEW ZEALAND TODAY

New Zealand, like Australia, is a dynamic mixture of the traditional and the modern. Many New Zealanders still make a living through farming. Most of these people work raising sheep or cattle. Crops such as potatoes and wheat are grown in the cool climate of the southern island. The warmer climate of the northern island is perfect for raising subtropical crops such as kiwifruit. This green fruit is named after the Kiwi, a bird that is found only in New Zealand. Did you know that people from New Zealand are sometimes called "Kiwis"?

New Zealand is not as rich in natural resources as its large neighbor to the west, Australia. But New Zealanders have developed ingenious ways to use their special resources. Hydroelectric power, or power made by water, makes good use of New Zealand's river resources. In Lesson 1 you read about the hot springs and geysers that spout steam and hot water from underground. New Zealanders have harnessed this unique resource, called geothermal (jē ō thûr′ məl) energy, to provide power for homes and factories. Look at the diagram on this page to see how this process works. Some people even pipe steam from underground and use geothermal energy to heat their houses!

On the Pacific island of Tahiti, people grow coconuts and cacao. These produce a **cash crop**, something that can be exported to bring money to the island.

LIVING IN OCEANIA

The two main islands of New Zealand are just part of the thousands of islands that make up Oceania. These smaller islands are home to about 4 million people. One of the most important of these is Guam.

Both fishing and farming are important jobs in Oceania. Fish in the waters surrounding the islands are a chief source of food. Yams, bananas, coconuts, coffee, and cacao grow well in Oceania's tropical climate. Copra, or ripe coconut meat, is the region's most important cash crop. A cash crop is a plant or plant product raised to make money. Coconut oil is taken from copra and is used to make soap and margarine. Sugarcane and vanilla beans are other important cash crops.

NEW CHALLENGES

To live in modern Australia and Oceania means to learn to adapt to, or learn how to live in, a changing world. As you have read in this lesson, Australia has grown into one of the world's industrial powers. It is also an important exporter of valuable minerals. You have read that the islands of Oceania have valuable cash crops. These crops are bought by nations from all around the world.

Check Your Reading

1. What is a cash crop?
2. What is life like in Australia and Oceania today?
3. **GEOGRAPHY SKILL:** What are Australia's chief minerals?
4. **THINKING SKILL:** What is the point of view of the New Zealander quoted on page 586?

589

Decision Making: Review

Decision making is choosing from among a number of alternatives to achieve a goal. You have read that the goal of the Frenchman who restored the Olympic games was to further international understanding. He chose, or selected, young people's love for sports from among many options, or alternatives, to help him reach his goal.

HELPING YOURSELF
The steps below show one way to make a decision.

One Way to Make a Decision

1. Identify and define clearly the goal to be achieved.

2. Identify alternatives, or options, by which the goal can be achieved.

3. Predict the immediate and long-range outcomes of each option.

4. Evaluate each outcome by determining the cost of each and whether it benefits or harms you and others.

5. Choose the best alternative.

Applying the Skill
Lech Walesa, the Polish leader of Solidarity, once said that one of the world's great challenges is to protect the health of all men and women. Accept this challenge, and decide what you can do now to protect the health of your fellow students. What did you decide to do?

1. The goal is to ____.
   a. protect the health of students
   b. say no to drugs
   c. check medical records
2. Which of the following might not be one of the alternatives for meeting your goal?
   a. antidrug campaign
   b. track-and-field day
   c. antihomework campaign
3. What might be the long-range outcome of sponsoring a track-and-field day?
   a. heat exhaustion
   b. students begin to exercise more
   c. no classes that day

Reviewing the Skill
1. Why is it important to consider as many alternatives as possible?
2. Name the steps you could take to make better decisions.
3. Why should you evaluate the consequences of all possible alternatives before you actually choose one?

BRINGING · GOOD · HEALTH

The people who live in the Marshall Islands of the South Pacific understand the value of windpower. Understandably, this nation of 34 islands has a long tradition of sailing. Myths and songs tell of the skill of their earliest sailors. One of their myths celebrates the ocean winds that blow across the Marshall Islands.

Good health is the reward of those who stand in the path of the Great Breeze.

Today, the ocean winds continue to bring good health to these remote South Pacific islands.

Lonny Higgins and her family depend on the strength of the ocean breezes to sail from island to island. As a doctor, it is her concern that everyone receives good medical attention.

There was a time not long ago, however, when the people of the Marshall Islands could not visit a doctor. Most of the islands lacked medical supplies, as well as doctors and nurses. Lonny knew that with a little effort she and her family could make a difference.

Working with the government of the Marshall Islands, Lonny and her familiy began to bring health care to the outer, remote islands. Lonny developed a system of small clinics, staffed by well-trained doctors. The important link in her chain of clinics was a magnificent "tallship clinic."

Named *Tole Mour*, which means "a gift of life and health," the tallship sails from island clinic to island clinic. *Tole Mour* is equipped with volunteer doctors, dentists, and nurses whose job it is to train new workers and share medical supplies.

People like Dr. Lonny Higgins have made an important difference in the South Pacific. There are now 16 island clinics operating in the Marshall Islands. And the mighty *Tole Mour* carries on an ancient legacy, bringing "good health to those in the path of the Great Breeze."

IMPORTANT EVENTS

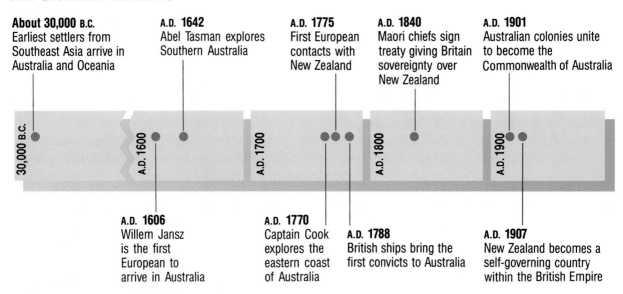

About 30,000 B.C.
Earliest settlers from
Southeast Asia arrive in
Australia and Oceania

A.D. 1642
Abel Tasman explores
Southern Australia

A.D. 1775
First European
contacts with
New Zealand

A.D. 1840
Maori chiefs sign
treaty giving Britain
sovereignty over
New Zealand

A.D. 1901
Australian colonies unite
to become the
Commonwealth of Australia

30,000 B.C.

A.D. 1600

A.D. 1700

A.D. 1800

A.D. 1900

A.D. 1606
Willem Jansz
is the first
European to
arrive in Australia

A.D. 1770
Captain Cook
explores the
eastern coast
of Australia

A.D. 1788
British ships bring the
first convicts to Australia

A.D. 1907
New Zealand becomes a
self-governing country
within the British Empire

PEOPLE TO KNOW

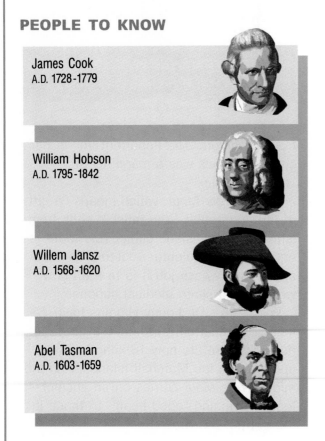

James Cook
A.D. 1728-1779

William Hobson
A.D. 1795-1842

Willem Jansz
A.D. 1568-1620

Abel Tasman
A.D. 1603-1659

IDEAS TO REMEMBER

■ Australia is an "island continent." Oceania is made up of thousands of islands. The geography of these lands range from the dry deserts of Australia's outback to the tropical landscape of the South Pacific.

■ The early people of Australia and Oceania migrated from Southeast Asia. Later, European migrants arrived and set up colonies. Eventually these colonies won their independence.

■ Abundant resources and a tropical climate have brought prosperity to the people of Australia and Oceania.

REVIEWING VOCABULARY

cash crop   outback
coral reef   sovereignty
geothermal energy

Number a sheet of paper from 1 to 5. Beside each number write the word or term from the above list that best matches each statement.

1. These are plant products that are cultivated to make money.
2. These structures in the sea are actually the skeletal remains of billions of tiny sea creatures.
3. This is a kind of heat from underground sources, such as hot springs, that is used to produce power.
4. This is the political control that a government has over a territory.
5. These hot, dry, and thinly populated flatlands make up a large part of the Australian continent.

REVIEWING FACTS

1. Why is Australia sometimes called "the land down under"?
2. What is the name of the geographical feature that separates Australia's east coastal plains from the outback?
3. What kind of economy supported the aborigines of Australia? How was this economy different from that of Oceania? In which of the two regions would you expect to find towns?
4. Who were the original inhabitants of New Zealand?
5. What two things have helped make Australia one of the richest countries in the world?

WRITING ABOUT MAIN IDEAS

1. **Writing a Paragraph:** Write a paragraph to compare the aborigines of Australia and the Indians of North America. You may want to use sources in the library to gather information. Also, compare the effects of European colonization on both groups.
2. **Writing a Paragraph:** You have read that Australia has many animals unique to this "island continent." How can this be explained? Research the animal life of Australia and write a paragraph explaining this fact.
3. **Writing About Perspectives:** Imagine that you are one of the prisoners who has been sent by Britain to Australia during the early period of European settlement. Write a journal entry describing your impressions and experiences after your first week in the new land.

BUILDING SKILLS: READING MAPS OF THE OCEAN FLOOR

1. Does the ocean floor have a varied or flat surface?
2. What is the difference between a relief map and a contour map?
3. Compare a contour line and a contour interval.
4. How are contour lines shown on a map?
5. How are contour intervals shown on a map?
6. What does it mean when contour lines are drawn very close together on a map?
7. How do maps of the ocean floor help you understand the earth's surface?

REVIEWING VOCABULARY

Number a sheet of paper from 1 to 10. Beside each number write whether the following statements are true or false. If the statement is true, write **T**. If it is false, rewrite the sentence using the underlined vocabulary word correctly.

1. Australia's <u>outback</u> is a densely populated fringe of fertile land along the country's eastern coast.
2. New Zealand's rivers are an important source of <u>geothermal energy</u>.
3. The large ranches of Australia, called <u>stations</u>, can be found in the outback.
4. The water lying between an island and a reef is called a <u>boomerang</u>.
5. <u>Sovereignty</u> is political control of a government over a particular territory.
6. <u>Mainland</u> is the principal land of a continent except for islands and small peninsulas.
7. <u>Martial law</u> is a type of democratic rule that allows a large number of personal freedoms.
8. <u>Coral reefs</u> are rocky ridges in the ocean that are made up of the skeletons of billions of tiny sea creatures.
9. A ring-shaped coral island that rises above the ocean is called an <u>atoll</u>.
10. <u>Cash crops</u> are crops that are grown solely for the use of the farmer and his immediate family.

✐ WRITING ABOUT THE UNIT

1. **Writing a Pamphlet:** Imagine that you are organizing a tour of Australia and some of the islands of Oceania. Write a pamphlet describing the places where you will stop.
2. **Writing a List:** List the advantages and disadvantages of attending a "School of Air" in Australia's outback.
3. **Writing About Perspectives:** Imagine that you are a refugee from Cambodia now living in the United States. Write a letter to the government of your homeland. Discuss your country's history as well as its human and natural resources. Explain what policies you think the government should follow in the new era of peace.

ACTIVITIES

1. **Constructing a Time Line:** Refer to encyclopedias and history books to identify the major events of the Vietnam War. Then draw a time line which covers the years from 1945 to the communist victory in 1975.
2. **Using an Almanac to Find Information:** One of the most important indicators of a country's well-being is its level of literacy. Use an almanac to find literacy rates for Thailand, Indonesia, Australia, and New Zealand. Then record the information you find on a chart.
3. **Working Together on a Historical Map:** With a group of classmates, draw a historical map tracing the three great voyages of Captain Cook. Use different colors to show the different routes.

BUDDHISM IN CAMBODIA AND THAILAND

The scholar who wrote the following secondary source
studied Buddhism and the ethnic groups of Southeast Asia.

By A.D. 1300 Southeast Asia was home to two very unique ethnic groups. A variety of Buddhist ethnic groups have lived in Thailand and Cambodia. The most notable are the Khmers (or Cambodians) and the Thai (or Siamese). Buddhism has been widely accepted among these people and probably reached the region from India, possibly as early as the second or third centuries. Our knowledge of the Khmer kingdoms of Cambodia dates from the sixth century. Here Buddhism and Hinduism often within the same period were honored and followed by the rulers. The Thai were rather late arrivals from China.

BUILDING SKILLS: USING INFORMATION

Use the information in the box above to answer the following questions.

1. What are some steps you could take to help you evaluate this information for accuracy?
2. Who is presenting the information?
3. Can the author be considered a reliable source, or does he have a particular bias toward his subject?
4. How accurate is the information in this account?
5. How did you determine this?
6. Why is it important to evaluate information for accuracy?

LINKING PAST, PRESENT, AND FUTURE

In Lesson 2 you read that rain forests once hid Angkor Wat for many centuries. As you may recall, Angkor Wat is the chief landmark of the Khmer people. During the Vietnam War and more recent conflicts, Angkor Wat was badly damaged. What are some of the great landmarks of modern civilization? Do you think a similar fate may await any of them? Why or why not?

CONCLUSION

Working Together Toward a New Century

■ Key Vocabulary

free enterprise	pollution
interdependent	conserve
developing nation	recycle

A CHANGING WORLD

"Our jaws cannot drop any lower," exclaimed one American reporter recently. He was describing the way many people felt about the astonishing events taking place in the world.

In 1989, as the Berlin Wall came down and Eastern European countries formed democratic governments, the Cold War came to an end. Then in 1991 the communist government in the Soviet Union collapsed and its 15 republics became independent countries. In that same year the South African government began to dismantle its system of apartheid. Countries in the Middle East began to work together to find solutions to their region's problems. In 1991 alone, the United Nations welcomed seven new member nations into its ranks.

TECHNOLOGY IN A CHANGING WORLD

Developments in technology have helped to make some of these changes possible. Televisions, telephones, computers, and fax machines have all brought the people of the world closer together. Satellite communication, for

Modern technology has brought people throughout the world closer together. In 1991 television images of Boris Yeltsin's democratic triumph were beamed across the globe.

People in Eastern Europe have quickly developed many forms of free enterprise since the fall of their communist governments.

example, played an important role when anti-democratic leaders tried to take over the government of the Soviet Union in August 1991. As tanks filled the streets of Moscow, Boris Yeltsin, the president of the Russian republic, telephoned leaders around the world to get support for his opposition to the takeover. Television cameras recorded the tense moments when Yeltsin stood on a tank and refused to give in to the anti-democratic forces. Then satellites beamed these images around the globe. As people everywhere watched, Yeltsin's support soared, and the takeover attempt failed.

THE WORLD ECONOMY

Economic developments have also affected the world. In the bustling eastern German city of Cottbus, change is in the air. Work crews are widening the main road outside the city. In a few years the region around Cottbus will be linked with western Germany by a new highway. All over the city new shops and businesses have opened. Free enterprise is taking hold in Cottbus, and in other cities in Eastern Europe. Free enterprise means that peo-

ple can own and run businesses largely free of government control.

One of the new businesses in Cottbus is an automobile dealership owned by a mechanic named Klaus Krause. Krause sells new American cars and his business is booming. In formerly communist East Germany it was very difficult to buy cars. "I had to wait 16 years to buy my own car," Krause recalls. Only one type of car could be bought at that time—a noisy little car called the Trabant. Only a few Trabants were made each year.

Now people who live in Cottbus may choose from a large selection of cars from the United States, Europe, and Japan. Of course, there are still many people in Cottbus who cannot afford a new car. But under a free-enterprise system the government no longer controls the choices they make.

Cottbus and the rest of Eastern Europe have joined a world that is more

597

and more interdependent. This means that people in one region of the world depend on people in other regions to help meet their needs and wants. For example, on any day in the Ukrainian port city of Odessa you might see ships from the United States and Australia unloading their cargoes of wheat, corn, and wool. At the same time, you might see an oil tanker setting sail for India or Cuba.

COMPARING WORLD ECONOMIES

Although the countries of the world are linked by interdependence, not all of them share equally in the world's riches. Some countries have more natural resources or stronger economies than others. Look at the cartogram on this page. A cartogram is a special kind of map that is useful for comparing information about different places. This cartogram shows the gross national products, or GNP, of the countries of the world. The countries that appear larger on this cartogram have stronger economies. Which country has the largest GNP?

By studying the cartogram you will see that the countries in the Northern Hemisphere have stronger economies than the countries in the Southern Hemisphere. Remember that Great Britain, followed by other countries in Europe and North America, led the world's Industrial Revolution in the 1700s. Since then, those countries have always been the first to profit from new developments in technology.

Do you remember how imperialism affected countries in Africa and Asia? The natural resources and labor from those countries helped to build the strong economies of Europe, North America, and Japan.

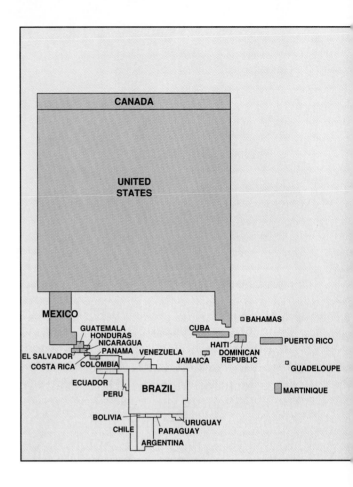

Today the poorer countries of the world are called developing nations because their economies are still developing. Most of the world's nations are developing countries, including many of the new democracies of Eastern Europe. Although many of them are rich in natural resources, they often lack strong industries of their own. These countries are working to develop their own industries and improve the standard of living of their people.

THE UNITED NATIONS

Although there are great differences between the economies of nations, all member nations have a voice in the United Nations. At the United Nations, or UN, all member nations work together to maintain peace and improve

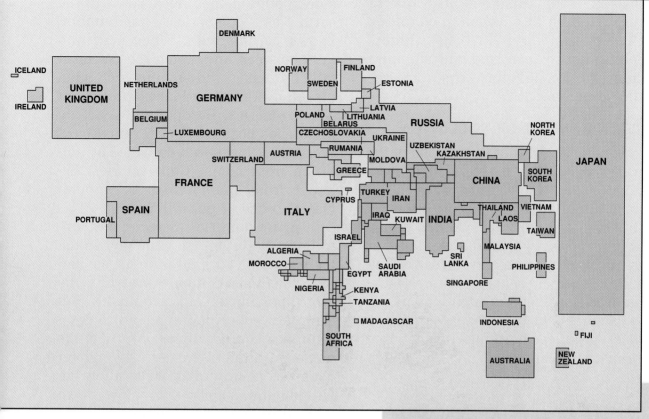

ICELAND
UNITED KINGDOM
NETHERLANDS
IRELAND
BELGIUM
LUXEMBOURG
DENMARK
GERMANY
NORWAY
SWEDEN
FINLAND
ESTONIA
LATVIA
POLAND
LITHUANIA
BELARUS
CZECHOSLOVAKIA
UKRAINE
RUSSIA
NORTH KOREA
JAPAN
SWITZERLAND
AUSTRIA
RUMANIA
MOLDOVA
UZBEKISTAN
KAZAKHSTAN
FRANCE
GREECE
TURKEY
IRAN
CHINA
SOUTH KOREA
SPAIN
PORTUGAL
ITALY
CYPRUS
IRAQ
KUWAIT
INDIA
THAILAND
LAOS
VIETNAM
TAIWAN
ALGERIA
ISRAEL
MALAYSIA
MOROCCO
EGYPT
SAUDI ARABIA
SRI LANKA
PHILIPPINES
NIGERIA
KENYA
SINGAPORE
TANZANIA
MADAGASCAR
INDONESIA
FIJI
SOUTH AFRICA
AUSTRALIA
NEW ZEALAND

living conditions around the world. The UN was founded in 1945 as a "town meeting" for the world, with the goal of preventing future wars. Another goal was to promote "the equal rights of men and women and of nations large and small."

Although the UN has not always been able to prevent wars, it has done much to improve the well-being of people around the globe. Its health agency has rid the world of the deadly disease known as smallpox. Today UN officials are working with doctors and scientists around the world to try to find a cure for AIDS.

Perhaps the most famous UN agency is UNICEF, or the United Nations Children's Fund. When UNICEF was first created in 1946, its goal was to help children in Europe who were suffering

MAP SKILL: The United Nations (*below*) serves as a "town meeting" for the world. Are most of the wealthy countries located in the northern or in the southern part of the world?

from the effects of World War II. UNICEF soon expanded its work to help children in developing countries all over the world. UNICEF workers help to house, feed, and educate more than 1 billion girls and boys from over 100 countries.

THE PROBLEM OF POLLUTION

You have read that the nations of the world are linked by technology, economics, and the UN. But perhaps our most important common concern is for the environment that we all share. Today, pollution of land, water, and air is threatening to destroy the earth. Pollution is the presence of harmful substances that hurt the environment.

Factories that create new products also produce harmful wastes that sometimes pollute our air and water.

What goes up into the atmosphere as smoke often comes back down to the earth as poisonous precipitation known as acid rain. When acid rain falls on trees, they often die. When it falls into lakes and streams, fish often die. Many forests and lakes throughout North America, Europe, and Asia are threatened because of acid rain. Rivers everywhere have been damaged by pollution from homes and factories. Exhaust from automobiles is another major source of pollution.

In many countries there are few controls on pollution. In Bombay, India, for example, air pollution is so bad that scientists compare breathing its air to smoking ten cigarettes a day. But a former leader of India, Indira Gandhi, once charged that "poverty is the greatest polluter." In her view, poorer countries could not afford to allow environmental concerns to slow down their economic development. Today, however, more and more countries are working to reduce pollution.

MAP SKILL: Pollution that falls to earth as acid rain can kill trees. Which parts of the United States and Canada are the most affected by acid rain?

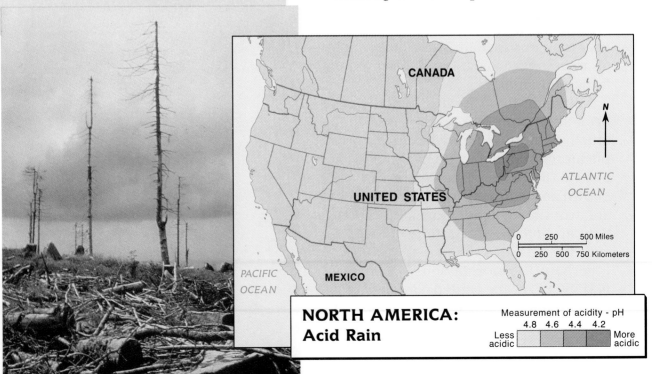

NORTH AMERICA: Acid Rain

Measurement of acidity - pH

4.8 4.6 4.4 4.2

Less acidic — More acidic

Recycling is one way in which people everywhere can help to conserve our natural resources.

PROTECTING OUR ENVIRONMENT

One way to protect our environment is to conserve, or use wisely, our natural resources. Recycling, or using something over and over again, is an effective way to conserve resources. Recycling is a way of life in most developing countries, since many resources are simply too expensive, and too scarce, to throw away. In Moscow, for example, torn stockings often reappear as dish scrubbers, or as stuffing for pillows. Milk cartons are used as pots for tomato plants. "We recycle and save for the very practical sake of survival," says one Moscow woman.

Years ago, recycling was also an important part of life in the United States and other industrial countries. In the 1930s, for example, Americans made clothes out of burlap bags and furniture out of old crates. In recent years, many people have realized that recycling is good for the environment, the nation, and the whole world. What are some ways in which people recycle in your community?

PROTECTING SPACESHIP EARTH

We travel together, passengers on a little spaceship—Earth. We are dependent on its easily damaged supplies of land and soil. We are kept from being wiped out only by the care, the work, and I will say the love we give our fragile craft.

This is how an American leader, Adlai Stevenson, once described our common need to protect our environment. This is only one of the challenges and opportunities that you and your classmates will face as the world moves into the twenty-first century.

YOU CAN MAKE A DIFFERENCE

In your textbook this year you have read about many great men and women who have changed the course of history. Think for a moment of the impressive list. You have also read about people who make a difference in their own communities. For example, you met Sidewalk Sam, the pavement artist. Through his art he has brightened the streets of Boston and involved other people in the process of making art. Ray Proffit makes a difference in his community, too. He tries to prevent pollution of the Delaware River.

You also read about the Association of Space Explorers. These former astronauts encourage the nations of the world to work together to protect the earth. The School for Peace tries to build understanding among people, too. Located in Israel, the school brings together young Arabs and Jews so they can try to know and understand each other better.

Finally, you have read about Dr. Lonnie Higgins and the ship *Tole Mour.* Higgins and many other doctors have brought modern health care to the people of the Marshall Islands.

These are only a few of the many people who make a difference. Perhaps you know someone in your community who saw a problem and worked to solve it. Maybe it was an adult. Maybe it was a student like you.

How can you help to make a difference in your community? You do not have to be an astronaut or a doctor in the South Pacific to help others. Is there a park or a street in your community that needs cleaning up? Are there older neighbors who need help shopping? You might be able to help. There are many ways to help others. The important thing to remember is that *you* can make a difference!

REFERENCE SECTION

ATLAS

The World: Political | 604

The World: Physical | 606

The 50 United States | 608

Europe and North Asia: Political | 610

Europe and North Asia: Physical | 611

South Asia: Political | 612

South Asia: Physical | 613

Africa: Political | 614

Africa: Physical | 615

Australia and New Zealand: Political | 616

Australia and New Zealand: Physical | 617

DICTIONARY OF GEOGRAPHIC TERMS | 618

GAZETTEER | 620

BIOGRAPHICAL DICTIONARY | 628

GLOSSARY | 632

INDEX | 642

CREDITS | 650

ATLAS

THE WORLD
Political

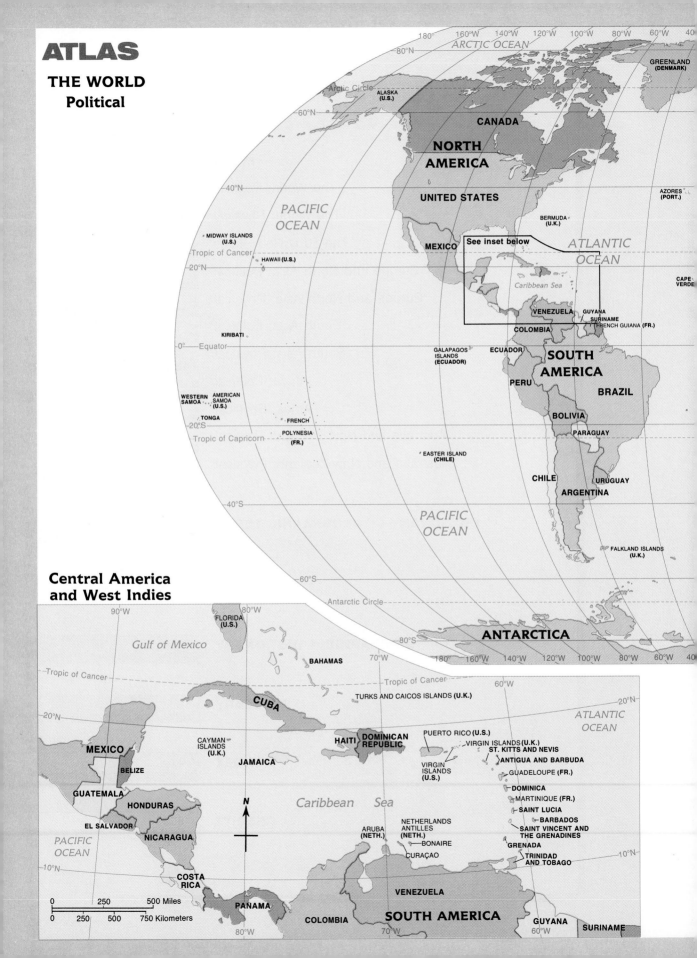

ARCTIC OCEAN

GREENLAND (DENMARK)

Arctic Circle

ALASKA (U.S.)

60°N

CANADA

NORTH AMERICA

40°N

UNITED STATES

AZORES (PORT.)

PACIFIC OCEAN

BERMUDA (U.K.)

MEXICO

See inset below

ATLANTIC OCEAN

MIDWAY ISLANDS (U.S.)

Tropic of Cancer

CAPE VERDE

20°N

HAWAII (U.S.)

Caribbean Sea

VENEZUELA

GUYANA

SURINAME

FRENCH GUIANA (FR.)

COLOMBIA

KIRIBATI

0° Equator

GALAPAGOS ISLANDS (ECUADOR)

ECUADOR

SOUTH AMERICA

PERU

BRAZIL

WESTERN SAMOA

AMERICAN SAMOA (U.S.)

BOLIVIA

TONGA

20°S

FRENCH

PARAGUAY

Tropic of Capricorn

POLYNESIA (FR.)

EASTER ISLAND (CHILE)

CHILE

URUGUAY

ARGENTINA

40°S

PACIFIC OCEAN

FALKLAND ISLANDS (U.K.)

Central America and West Indies

60°S

Antarctic Circle

ANTARCTICA

80°S

180° 160°W 140°W 120°W 100°W 80°W 60°W 40

90°W

80°W

FLORIDA (U.S.)

Gulf of Mexico

70°W

60°W

20°N

ATLANTIC OCEAN

Tropic of Cancer

BAHAMAS

Tropic of Cancer

CUBA

TURKS AND CAICOS ISLANDS (U.K.)

20°N

CAYMAN ISLANDS (U.K.)

HAITI

DOMINICAN REPUBLIC

PUERTO RICO (U.S.)

VIRGIN ISLANDS (U.K.)

ST. KITTS AND NEVIS

MEXICO

JAMAICA

ANTIGUA AND BARBUDA

BELIZE

VIRGIN ISLANDS (U.S.)

GUADELOUPE (FR.)

GUATEMALA

N

Caribbean Sea

DOMINICA

MARTINIQUE (FR.)

HONDURAS

SAINT LUCIA

EL SALVADOR

BARBADOS

NICARAGUA

ARUBA (NETH.)

NETHERLANDS ANTILLES (NETH.)

SAINT VINCENT AND THE GRENADINES

PACIFIC OCEAN

BONAIRE

GRENADA

CURAÇAO

TRINIDAD AND TOBAGO

10°N

10°N

COSTA RICA

VENEZUELA

PANAMA

0 250 500 Miles

COLOMBIA

SOUTH AMERICA

GUYANA

SURINAME

0 250 500 750 Kilometers

80°W

70°W

60°W

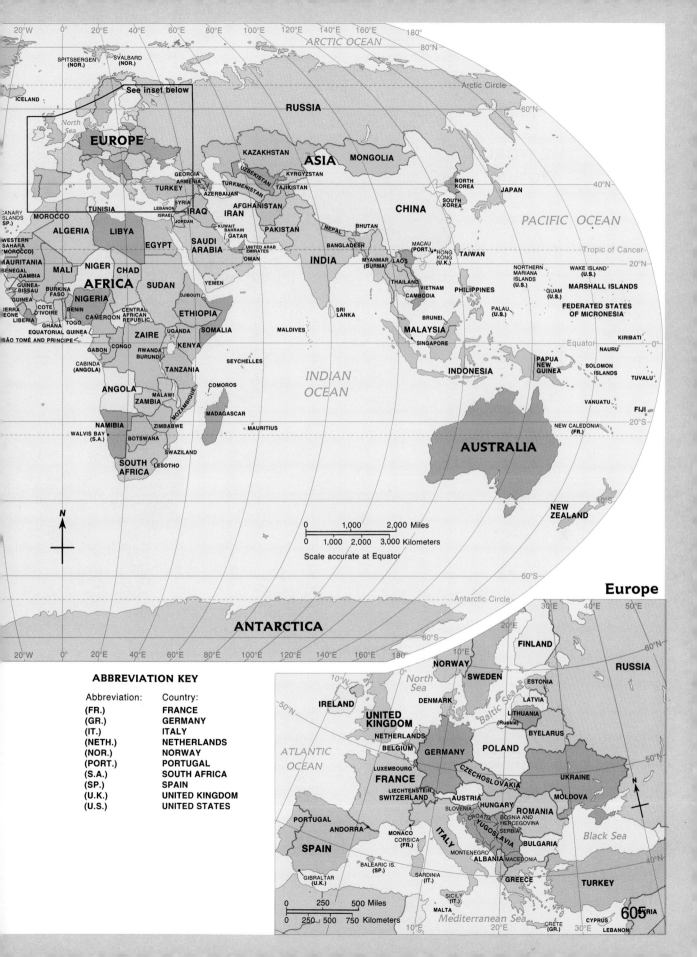

ARCTIC OCEAN

Arctic Circle

60°N

RUSSIA

EUROPE

See inset below

North Sea

ICELAND

SPITSBERGEN (NOR.)

SVALBARD (NOR.)

KAZAKHSTAN

ASIA

MONGOLIA

40°N

GEORGIA
ARMENIA
TURKEY
AZERBAIJAN

UZBEKISTAN
KYRGYZSTAN
TURKMENISTAN
TAJIKISTAN

NORTH KOREA

JAPAN

SOUTH KOREA

CANARY ISLANDS (SP.)

MOROCCO

TUNISIA

SYRIA
LEBANON
ISRAEL
JORDAN
IRAQ

AFGHANISTAN

IRAN

CHINA

PACIFIC OCEAN

WESTERN SAHARA (MOROCCO)

ALGERIA

LIBYA

EGYPT

KUWAIT
BAHRAIN
QATAR

PAKISTAN

NEPAL

BHUTAN

MACAU (PORT.)

HONG KONG (U.K.)

TAIWAN

Tropic of Cancer

20°N

MAURITANIA

MALI

NIGER

CHAD

SAUDI ARABIA

UNITED ARAB EMIRATES

OMAN

INDIA

BANGLADESH

MYANMAR (BURMA)

LAOS

SENEGAL
GAMBIA
GUINEA-BISSAU
GUINEA
SIERRA LEONE
LIBERIA

BURKINA FASO

AFRICA

SUDAN

YEMEN

THAILAND

VIETNAM

CAMBODIA

PHILIPPINES

NORTHERN MARIANA ISLANDS (U.S.)

GUAM (U.S.)

WAKE ISLAND (U.S.)

MARSHALL ISLANDS

BENIN
TOGO
GHANA
COTE D'IVOIRE
CAMEROON

NIGERIA

CENTRAL AFRICAN REPUBLIC

ETHIOPIA

SRI LANKA

PALAU (U.S.)

BRUNEI

FEDERATED STATES OF MICRONESIA

EQUATORIAL GUINEA
SÃO TOMÉ AND PRINCIPE
GABON
CONGO
CABINDA (ANGOLA)

ZAIRE

UGANDA

RWANDA
BURUNDI

SOMALIA

KENYA

MALDIVES

MALAYSIA

SINGAPORE

Equator

KIRIBATI

NAURU

0°

TANZANIA

SEYCHELLES

INDIAN OCEAN

INDONESIA

PAPUA NEW GUINEA

SOLOMON ISLANDS

TUVALU

ANGOLA

MALAWI

ZAMBIA

MOZAMBIQUE

COMOROS

MADAGASCAR

VANUATU

FIJI

20°S

NAMIBIA

WALVIS BAY (S.A.)

BOTSWANA

ZIMBABWE

MAURITIUS

NEW CALEDONIA (FR.)

SWAZILAND

AUSTRALIA

SOUTH AFRICA

LESOTHO

N

0   1,000   2,000 Miles

0   1,000 2,000 3,000 Kilometers

Scale accurate at Equator

60°S

NEW ZEALAND

40°S

Antarctic Circle

ANTARCTICA

80°S

20°W   0°   20°E   40°E   60°E   80°E   100°E   120°E   140°E   160°E   180°

ABBREVIATION KEY

Abbreviation:	Country:
(FR.)	FRANCE
(GR.)	GERMANY
(IT.)	ITALY
(NETH.)	NETHERLANDS
(NOR.)	NORWAY
(PORT.)	PORTUGAL
(S.A.)	SOUTH AFRICA
(SP.)	SPAIN
(U.K.)	UNITED KINGDOM
(U.S.)	UNITED STATES

Europe

FINLAND

NORWAY

SWEDEN

RUSSIA

North Sea

DENMARK

ESTONIA

LATVIA

LITHUANIA

(Russia)

IRELAND

UNITED KINGDOM

Baltic Sea

BYELARUS

NETHERLANDS

BELGIUM

GERMANY

POLAND

ATLANTIC OCEAN

LUXEMBOURG

CZECHOSLOVAKIA

UKRAINE

FRANCE

LIECHTENSTEIN
SWITZERLAND

AUSTRIA

HUNGARY

MOLDOVA

SLOVENIA

ROMANIA

PORTUGAL

ANDORRA

MONACO

CORSICA (FR.)

ITALY

CROATIA

BOSNIA AND HERCEGOVINA

SERBIA

YUGOSLAVIA

BULGARIA

Black Sea

SPAIN

BALEARIC IS. (SP.)

SARDINIA (IT.)

MONTENEGRO

ALBANIA

MACEDONIA

GREECE

TURKEY

GIBRALTAR (U.K.)

SICILY (IT.)

0   250   500 Miles

0   250 500   750 Kilometers

MALTA

Mediterranean Sea

CRETE (GR.)

CYPRUS

LEBANON

THE WORLD
Physical

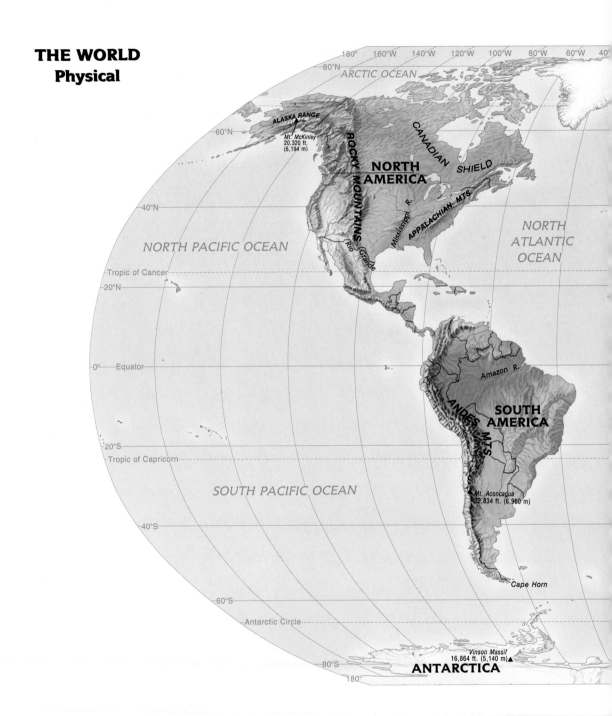

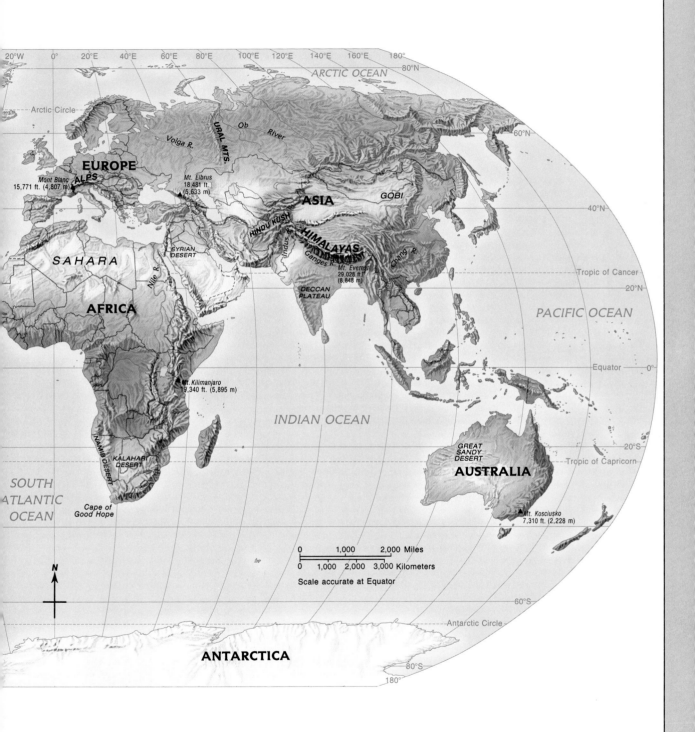

ARCTIC OCEAN

80°N

Arctic Circle

60°N

Ob River

URAL MTS.

Volga R.

EUROPE

ALPS
Mont Blanc
15,771 ft. (4,807 m)

Mt. Elbrus
18,481 ft.
(5,633 m)

ASIA

GOBI

40°N

HINDU KUSH

HIMALAYAS

Indus

Ganges R.

Chang R.

SAHARA

SYRIAN
DESERT

Nile R.

Tropic of Cancer

Mt. Everest
29,028 ft.
(8,848 m)

20°N

AFRICA

DECCAN
PLATEAU

PACIFIC OCEAN

Equator

0°

Mt. Kilimanjaro
19,340 ft. (5,895 m)

INDIAN OCEAN

GREAT
SANDY
DESERT

20°S

NAMIB DESERT

KALAHARI
DESERT

AUSTRALIA

Tropic of Capricorn

SOUTH
ATLANTIC
OCEAN

Cape of
Good Hope

Mt. Kosciusko
7,310 ft. (2,228 m)

N

0   1,000   2,000 Miles

0   1,000 2,000 3,000 Kilometers

Scale accurate at Equator

60°S

Antarctic Circle

ANTARCTICA

80°S

180°

20°W   0°   20°E   40°E   60°E   80°E   100°E   120°E   140°E   160°E   180°

607

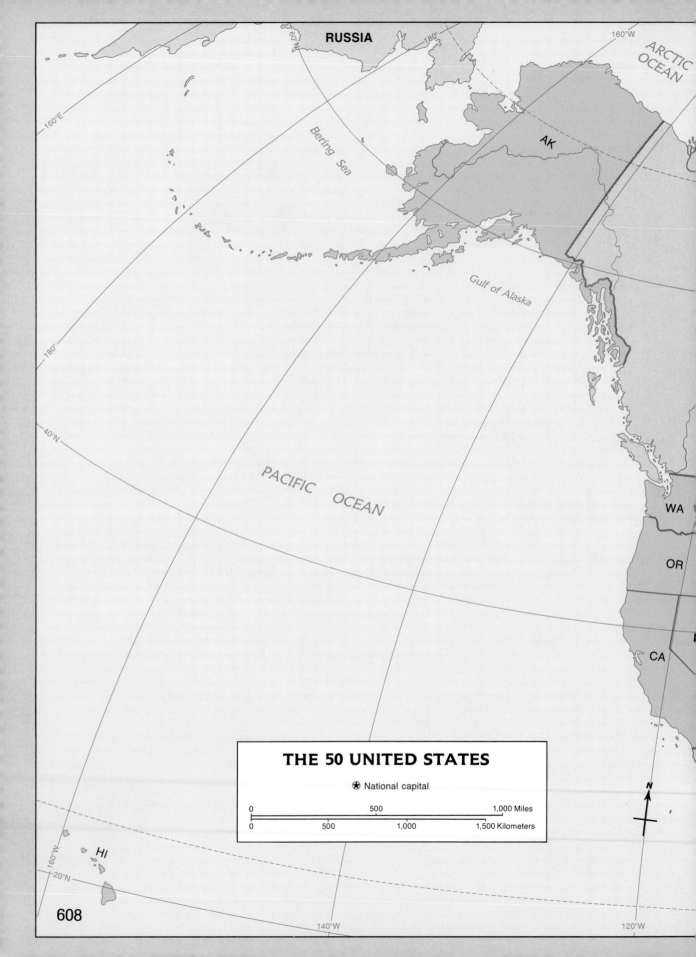

RUSSIA

ARCTIC
OCEAN

160°E

160°W

Bering Sea

AK

Gulf of Alaska

180°

40°N

PACIFIC   OCEAN

WA

OR

CA

THE 50 UNITED STATES

✷ National capital

| 0 | 500 | 1,000 Miles |

| 0 | 500 | 1,000 | 1,500 Kilometers |

N

160°W

HI

20°N

608

140°W

120°W

140°W 120°W 100°W 80°W 60°W 40°W

Greenland
(DENMARK)

60°N

Arctic Circle

Hudson Bay

CANADA

Great Lakes

ME

MT ND MN MI VT
NH
WI NY MA
ID SD MI CT RI
WY 40°N
IA IL IN OH PA NJ
NE Washington, D.C.
UT MD DE
CO KS MO KY WV VA
AR TN NC
AZ NM OK SC
MS AL GA
TX LA

ATLANTIC
OCEAN

FL

MEXICO

Gulf of Mexico

Tropic of Cancer
CUBA 80°W
100°W

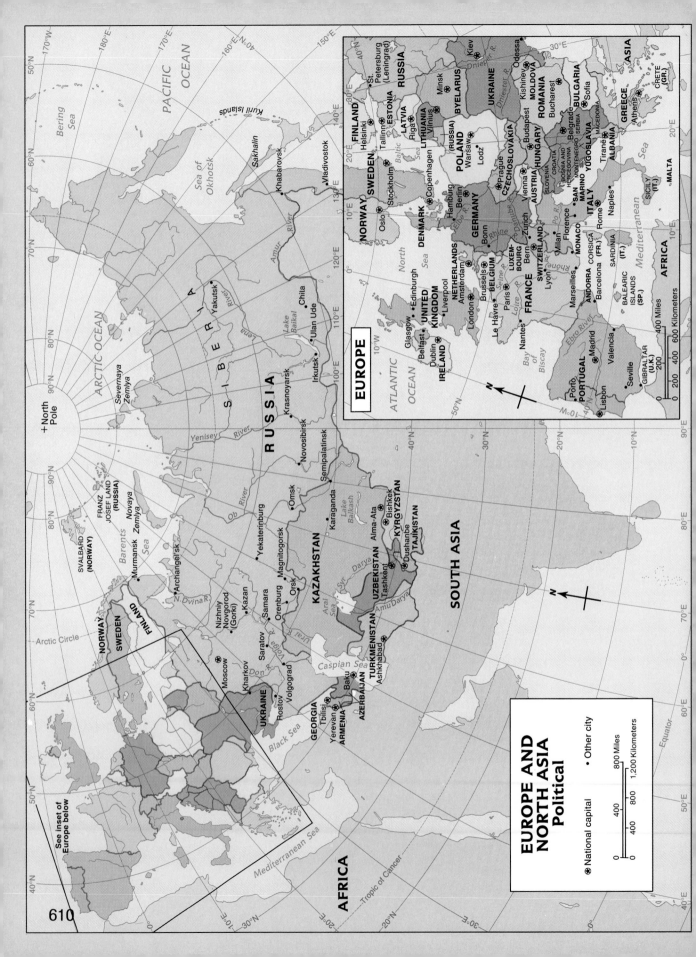

EUROPE

St. Petersburg (Leningrad)

RUSSIA

FINLAND
Helsinki

ESTONIA
Tallinn
LATVIA
Riga
LITHUANIA
Vilnius

NORWAY
SWEDEN
Oslo
Stockholm

Kiev

UKRAINE

BYELARUS
Minsk

Odessa

Kishinev
MOLDOVA

POLAND
Warsaw
Lodz

Bucharest
ROMANIA

BULGARIA
Sofia

Prague
CZECHOSLOVAKIA

Budapest
AUSTRIA HUNGARY
Vienna

SLOVENIA
CROATIA
BOSNIA AND HERCEGOVINA
SAN MARINO
YUGOSLAVIA
MONTENEGRO SERBIA

Belgrade
MACEDONIA

GREECE
Athens

CRETE (GR.)

ASIA

Copenhagen
DENMARK

Hamburg
Berlin

GERMANY
Bonn

Zurich
SWITZERLAND
Bern

Milan

ITALY
Florence
Rome
MONACO
Naples

ALBANIA
Tiranë

MALTA

SICILY (IT.)

North Sea

Baltic Sea

Dnieper R.
Dniester R.
Danube R.
Elbe R.
Rhine
Po R.
Rhône

Mediterranean

NETHERLANDS
Amsterdam

LUXEMBOURG
BELGIUM
Brussels

FRANCE
Paris
Le Havre
Lyon
Marseilles

ANDORRA
CORSICA (FR.)
SARDINIA (IT.)

UNITED KINGDOM
Glasgow
Edinburgh
Liverpool
London

IRELAND
Dublin
Belfast

ATLANTIC OCEAN

Bay of Biscay
Nantes
Loire
Seine

PORTUGAL
Porto
Lisbon

Madrid
Barcelona
BALEARIC ISLANDS (SP.)
Valencia
Seville
GIBRALTAR (U.K.)

Ebro River

AFRICA

N

400 Miles
600 Kilometers
200 400
0

50°N
60°N
40°N

50°N
10°W
0°
10°E
20°E
30°E
40°E

PACIFIC OCEAN

Bering Sea

Kuril Islands

Sea of Okhotsk

Sakhalin

Khabarovsk

Vladivostok

ARCTIC OCEAN

+ North Pole

Severnaya Zemlya

S I B E R I A

Yakutsk
Lena River

Lake Baikal
Chita
Ulan Ude

R U S S I A

Irkutsk

Krasnoyarsk

Yenisey River

Novosibirsk

Ob River

Omsk
Semipalatinsk

Novaya Zemlya

FRANZ JOSEF LAND (RUSSIA)

SVALBARD (NORWAY)

Barents Sea

Murmansk
Archangel'sk
N. Dvina R.

Yekaterinburg

Magnitogorsk

Orsk
Orenburg
Samara
Kazan
Nizhniy Novgorod (Gorki)
Saratov
Ural R.
Volga R.

KAZAKHSTAN

Karaganda
Lake Balkash
Aral Sea

Alma-Ata
Bishkek
KYRGYZSTAN
Dushanbe
TAJIKISTAN

Syr Darya

UZBEKISTAN
Tashkent

TURKMENISTAN
Ashkhabad

AmuDarya

SOUTH ASIA

Caspian Sea

NORWAY
SWEDEN
FINLAND

Arctic Circle

Moscow

Kharkov
UKRAINE
Rostov
Don R.
Volgograd

GEORGIA
Tbilisi
ARMENIA
Yerevan
AZERBAIJAN
Baku

Black Sea

Mediterranean Sea

AFRICA

See inset of Europe below

610

EUROPE AND NORTH ASIA
Political

⊛ National capital   • Other city

800 Miles
1,200 Kilometers
400 800
0 400
0

N

Tropic of Cancer
Equator

AFRICA

80°N 70°N 60°N 50°N 40°N 30°N

10°E 20°E 30°E 40°E 50°E 60°E 70°E 80°E 90°E

170°W 180° 170°E 160°E 150°E 140°E 130°E 120°E 110°E 100°E

EUROPE AND NORTH ASIA
Physical

PACIFIC OCEAN

Bering Sea

Kuril Islands

Kamchatka Peninsula

Sea of Okhotsk

Sakhalin

Sikhote-Alin Mountains

Amur River

Kolyma Range

Cherskiy Mountains

Verkhoyansk Mountains

Stanovoy Mountains

Yablonovy Mountains

LENA PLATEAU

Lena River

Lena River

Lake Baikal

Wrangel Islands

New Siberian Islands

ARCTIC OCEAN

+ North Pole

Severnaya Zemlya

Taymyr Peninsula

Laptev Sea

CENTRAL SIBERIAN PLATEAU

S I B E R I A

Tunguska River

Angara R.

Yenisey River

Franz Joseph Islands

Novaya Zemlya

Barents Sea

Kara Sea

Yamal Peninsula

WEST SIBERIAN PLAIN

Ob River

Irtysh River

Tobol River

KAZAKH UPLANDS

Lake Balkash

Spitzbergen

Kola Peninsula

N. Dvina R.

URAL MOUNTAINS

Ural River

KYRGYZ STEPPE

Aral Sea

Syr Darya

UST'-URT PLATEAU

PLAINS OF TURAN

Amu Darya

Arctic Circle

See inset of Europe below

NORTH EUROPEAN PLAIN

Volga Upland

Volga R.

Don R.

Caspian Depression

Caspian Sea

Sea of Azov

Caucasus Mts.

Black Sea

SOUTH ASIA

AFRICA

Mediterranean Sea

Tropic of Cancer

Equator

EUROPE

ASIA

AFRICA

NORTH EUROPEAN PLAIN

BALTIC PLAIN

Carpathian Mts.

Dniester R.

Danube R.

BALKAN PENINSULA

Rhodes

Crete

Aegean Sea

Ionian Sea

SCANDINAVIAN PENINSULA

Gulf of Bothnia

Baltic Sea

Vistula River

Oder River

Elbe River

Rhine River

A L P S

Mont Blanc 15,771 ft (4,807 m)

Po River

Apennines

ITALIAN PENINSULA

Adriatic Sea

Tyrrhenian Sea

Sicily

North Sea

Shetland Islands

British Isles

English Channel

Seine River

Loire River

Rhône River

Pyrenees

Ebro River

Tagus River

IBERIAN PENINSULA

Corsica

Sardinia

Balearic Islands

Mediterranean Sea

Strait of Gibraltar

Bay of Biscay

ATLANTIC OCEAN

N

0   200   400 Miles
0   200   400   600 Kilometers

N

0   400   800 Miles
0   400   800   1,200 Kilometers

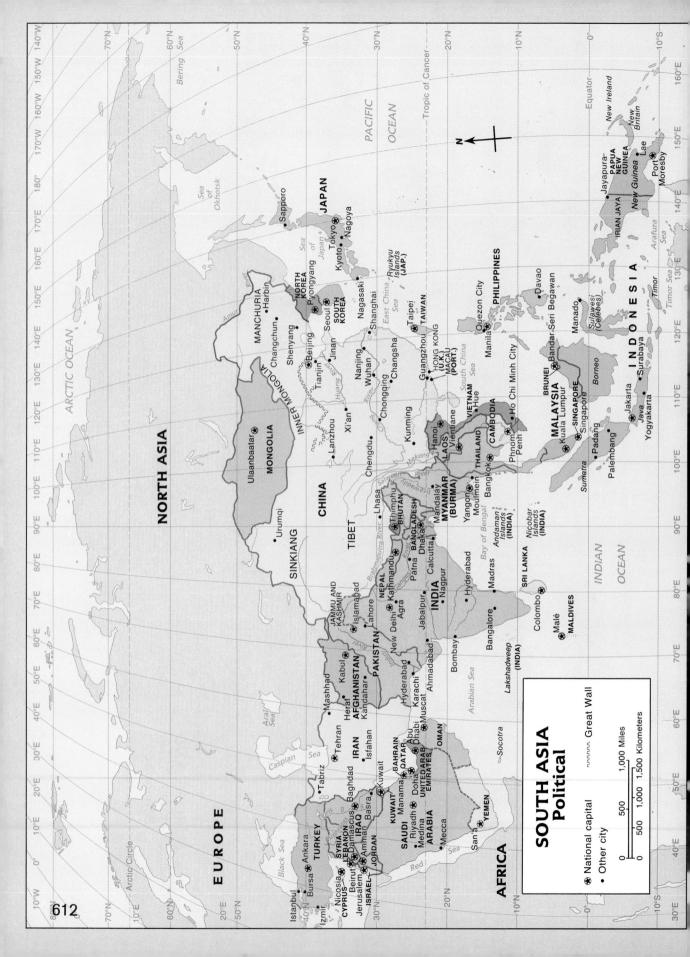

SOUTH ASIA
Political

⊛ National capital
• Other city

ⴖⴖⴖ Great Wall

0   500   1,000 Miles
0   500 1,000 1,500 Kilometers

612

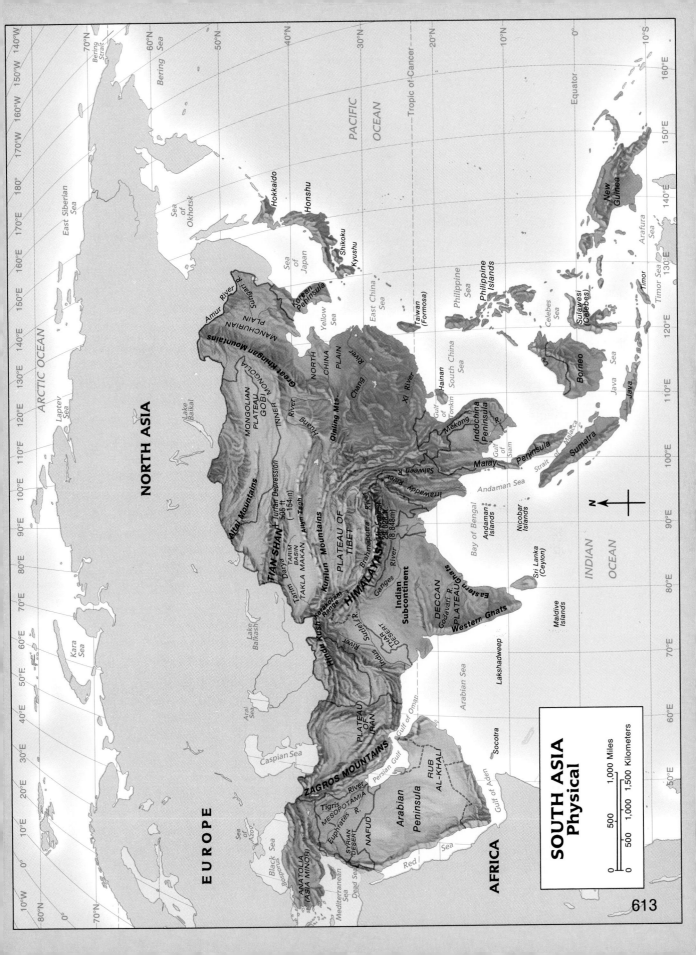

SOUTH ASIA
Physical

ARCTIC OCEAN

Bering Strait

Bering Sea

East Siberian Sea

Laptev Sea

Kara Sea

NORTH ASIA

Lake Baikal

EUROPE

Aral Sea

Lake Balkash

Caspian Sea

Black Sea
Sea of Azov
Bosporus
Mediterranean Sea
Dead Sea

ANATOLIA (ASIA MINOR)

ZAGROS MOUNTAINS

PLATEAU OF IRAN

MESOPOTAMIA
Tigris River
Euphrates R.
SYRIAN DESERT

NAFUD

Arabian Peninsula

RUB AL-KHALI

Red Sea

Gulf of Aden

Socotra

AFRICA

Persian Gulf
Gulf of Oman

Hindu Kush
Karakoram Range

Kunlun Mountains

TIAN SHAN
Turfan Depression 505 ft (−154 m)
TARIM BASIN
TAKLA MAKAN
Dariya
Altyn Tagh

Altai Mountains

MONGOLIAN PLATEAU
GOBI
INNER MONGOLIA

Great Khingan Mountains

MANCHURIAN PLAIN

Amur River
Sungari R.

Korean Peninsula

Sea of Okhotsk

Hokkaido

Honshu
Shikoku
Kyushu

Sea of Japan

PACIFIC OCEAN

Tropic of Cancer

Equator

Yellow River
NORTH CHINA PLAIN
Qinling Mts.
Chang
Yellow Sea
East China Sea

Taiwan (Formosa)

Philippine Sea

Philippine Islands

New Guinea

Arafura Sea

Timor Sea
Timor

Sulawesi (Celebes)

Celebes Sea

Borneo

Java Sea
Java

Xi River
Hainan
Gulf of Tonkin

South China Sea

Indochina Peninsula
Mekong R.

Malay Peninsula
Gulf of Siam
Strait of Malacca
Sumatra

PLATEAU OF TIBET

HIMALAYAS
Mt. Everest (8,848 m)

Brahmaputra River
Ganges
Indian Subcontinent
Sutlej R.
Indus River
THAR DESERT

DECCAN PLATEAU
Godavari R.
Eastern Ghats
Western Ghats

Salween River
Irrawaddy River

Andaman Sea

Bay of Bengal

Andaman Islands
Nicobar Islands

Sri Lanka (Ceylon)

Maldive Islands

INDIAN OCEAN

Arabian Sea

Lakshadweep

N

Scale
0   500   1,000 Miles
0   500   1,000   1,500 Kilometers

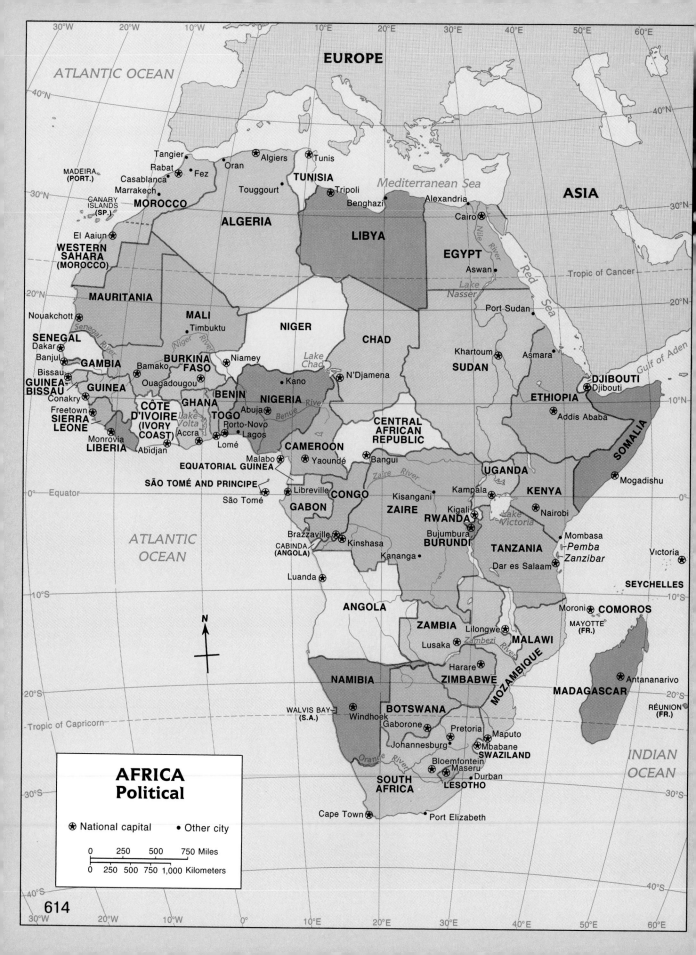

AFRICA
Political

⊛ National capital   • Other city

0   250   500   750 Miles

0 250 500 750 1,000 Kilometers

614

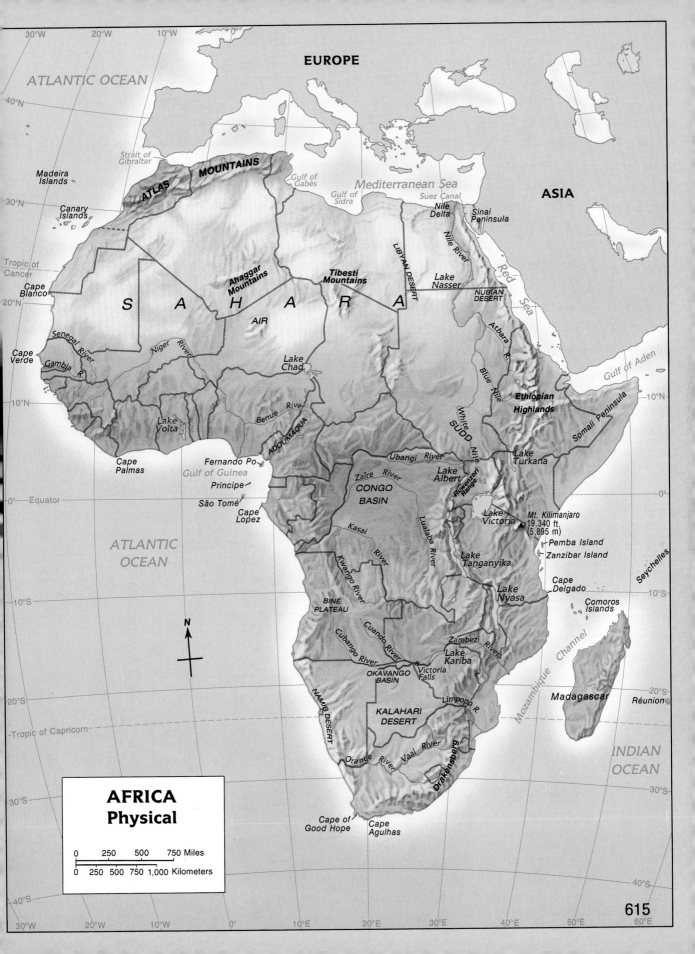

AFRICA
Physical

0	250 500	750 Miles
0	250 500 750	1,000 Kilometers

615

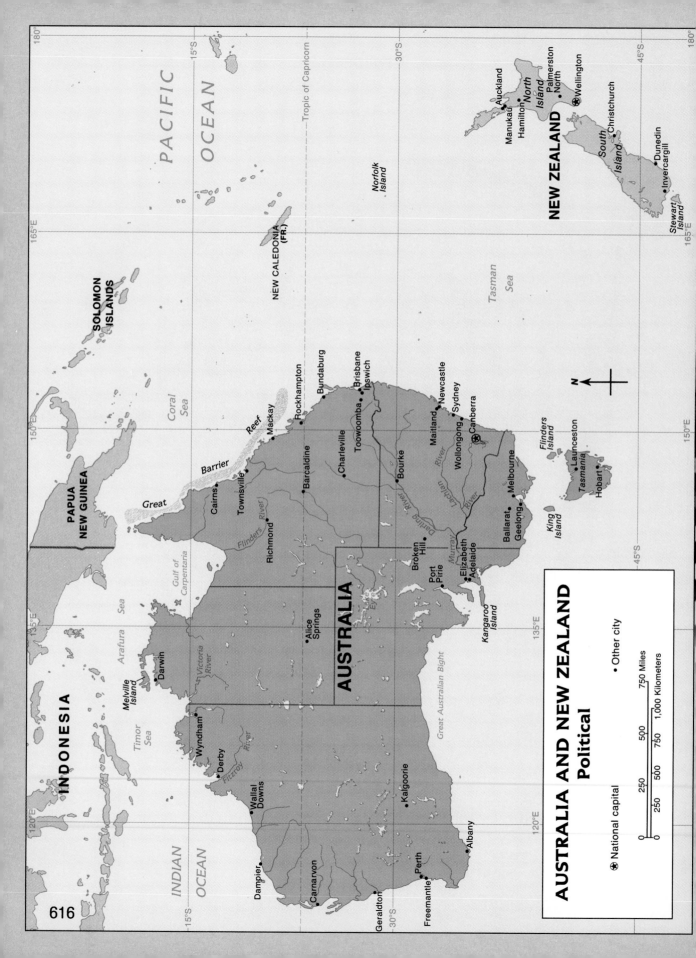

616

INDONESIA

PAPUA NEW GUINEA

SOLOMON ISLANDS

PACIFIC OCEAN

NEW CALEDONIA (FR.)

Norfolk Island

Coral Sea

Tasman Sea

NEW ZEALAND

Auckland
Manukau
Hamilton   *North Island*
Palmerston North
Wellington ✶
Christchurch
South Island
Dunedin
Invercargill
Stewart Island

INDIAN OCEAN

Arafura Sea

Timor Sea

Gulf of Carpentaria

Darwin
Melville Island

Wyndham
Derby
Fitzroy River
Wallal Downs

Dampier
Carnarvon

Geraldton
Perth
Freemantle

Albany

Kalgoorie

AUSTRALIA

Alice Springs
Victoria River

Flinders River

Richmond

Townsville
Cairns

Great
Barrier
Reef

Mackay
Rockhampton
Bundaburg
Brisbane
Ipswich
Toowoomba

Barcaldine

Charleville

Bourke

Broken Hill

Port Pirie
Elizabeth
Adelaide

Kangaroo Island

Great Australian Bight

Lachlan River
Darling River
Murray River

Maitland
Newcastle
Sydney
Wollongong
Canberra ✶

Ballarat
Geelong
Melbourne

King Island

Flinders Island
Launceston
Tasmania
Hobart

N

AUSTRALIA AND NEW ZEALAND
Political

✶ National capital   • Other city

0   250   500   750 Miles
0 250 500 750 1,000 Kilometers

Tropic of Capricorn

180°   15°S   30°S   45°S   180°
165°E   150°E   135°E   120°E
15°S   30°S   45°S

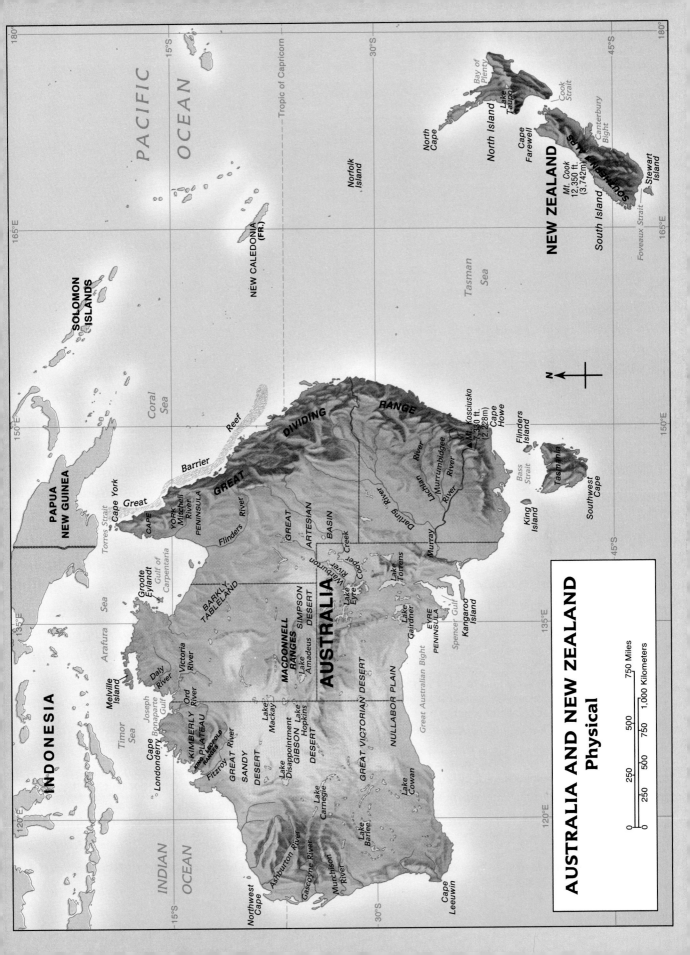

PACIFIC OCEAN

Tropic of Capricorn

INDONESIA

PAPUA NEW GUINEA

SOLOMON ISLANDS

NEW CALEDONIA (FR.)

Norfolk Island

NEW ZEALAND

North Cape

North Island

Bay of Plenty

Lake Taupo

Cook Strait

Cape Farewell

Canterbury Bight

South Island

Southern Alps

Mt. Cook 12,350 ft. (3,742m)

Stewart Island

Foveaux Strait

Tasman Sea

Arafura Sea

Timor Sea

Melville Island

Cape Londonderry

Cape Joseph Bonaparte Gulf

Groote Eylandt

Gulf of Carpentaria

Torres Strait

Cape York

Great Barrier Reef

Coral Sea

GREAT DIVIDING RANGE

YORK PENINSULA

Mitchell River

Flinders River

BARKLY TABLELAND

KIMBERLY PLATEAU

KING LEOPOLD RANGES

Fitzroy River

Ord River

Daly River

Victoria River

GREAT SANDY DESERT

Lake Mackay

Lake Disappointment

GIBSON DESERT

Lake Hopkins

MACDONNELL RANGES

Lake Amadeus

SIMPSON DESERT

GREAT ARTESIAN BASIN

Warburton River

Cooper Creek

Lake Eyre

Lake Gairdner

Lake Torrens

EYRE PENINSULA

Spencer Gulf

Kangaroo Island

Darling River

Murray River

Lachlan River

Murrumbidgee River

Mt. Kosciusko 7,310 ft. (2,228m)

Cape Howe

Flinders Island

Bass Strait

King Island

Tasmania

Southwest Cape

AUSTRALIA

GREAT VICTORIAN DESERT

NULLABOR PLAIN

Great Australian Bight

Lake Carnegie

Lake Barlee

Lake Cowan

Northwest Cape

Ashburton River

Gascoyne River

Murchison River

Cape Leeuwin

INDIAN OCEAN

N

AUSTRALIA AND NEW ZEALAND
Physical

0   250   500   750 Miles
0   250   500   750   1,000 Kilometers

DICTIONARY OF GEOGRAPHIC TERMS

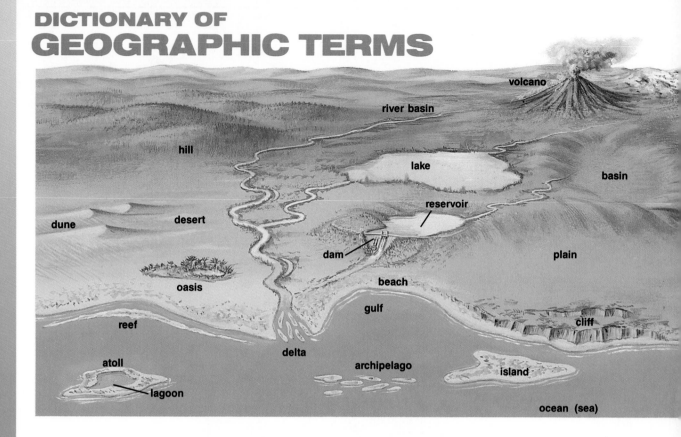

Labels on the illustration: volcano, river basin, hill, lake, basin, reservoir, dune, desert, dam, plain, oasis, beach, cliff, gulf, reef, delta, archipelago, island, atoll, lagoon, ocean (sea)

archipelago (är kə pel′ ə gō) A large group or chain of islands.

atoll (āt′ ôl) A ring-shaped coral island or string of islands, surrounding a lagoon.

basin (bā′ sin) An area of low-lying land surrounded by higher land. *See also* **river basin.**

bay (bā) Part of an ocean, sea, or lake, that extends into the land. A bay is usually smaller than a gulf.

beach (bēch) The gently sloping shore of an ocean or other body of water, especially that part covered by sand or pebbles.

butte (būt) A small, flat-topped hill. A butte is smaller than a plateau or a mesa.

canal (kə nal′) A waterway built to carry water for navigation or irrigation. Navigation canals usually connect two other bodies of water.

canyon (kan′ yən) A deep, narrow valley with steep sides.

cape (kāp) A projecting part of a coastline that extends into an ocean, sea, gulf, bay, or lake.

cliff (klif) A high, steep face of rock or earth.

coast (kōst) Land along an ocean or sea.

dam (dam) A wall built across a river to hold back the flowing water.

delta (del′ tə) Land formed at the mouth of a river by deposits of silt, sand, and pebbles.

desert (dez′ ərt) A very dry area where few plants grow.

dune (dün) A mound, hill, or ridge of sand that is heaped up by the wind.

fjord (fyôrd) A deep, narrow inlet of the sea between high, steep cliffs.

foothills (fut′ hilz) A hilly area at the base of a mountain range.

glacier (glā′ shər) A large sheet of ice that moves slowly over some land surface or down a valley.

gulf (gulf) Part of an ocean or sea that extends into the land. A gulf is usually larger than a bay.

harbor (här′ bər) A protected place along a shore where ships can safely anchor.

hill (hil) A rounded, raised landform, not as high as a mountain.

island (ī′ lənd) A body of land completely surrounded by water.

isthmus (is′ məs) A narrow strip of land bordered by water, that connects two larger bodies of land.

lagoon (lə gün′) A shallow body of water partly or completely enclosed within an atoll; a shallow body of sea water partly cut off from the sea by a narrow strip of land.

lake (lāk) A body of water completely surrounded by land.

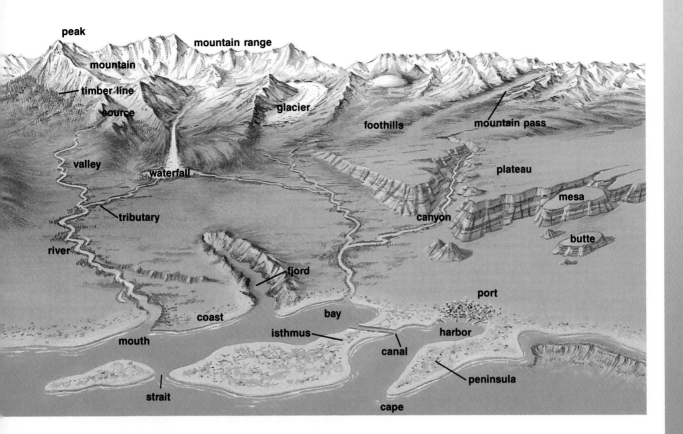

mesa (mā′ sə) A high, flat landform rising steeply above the surrounding land. A mesa is smaller than a plateau and larger than a butte.

mountain (mount′ ən) A high, rounded or pointed landform with steep sides, higher than a hill.

mountain pass (mount′ ən pas) An opening or gap through a mountain range.

mountain range (mount′ ən rānj) A row or chain of mountains.

mouth (mouth) The place where a river empties into another body of water.

oasis (ō ā′ sis) A place in the desert made fertile by a steady supply of water.

ocean (ō′ shən) One of the earth's four largest bodies of water. The four oceans are really a single connected body of salt water that covers about three fourths of the earth's surface.

peak (pēk) The pointed top of a mountain or hill.

peninsula (pə nin′ sə lə) A body of land nearly surrounded by water.

plain (plān) A large area of flat or nearly flat land.

plateau (pla tō′) A high, flat landform that rises steeply above the surrounding land. A plateau is larger than a mesa and a butte.

port (pôrt) A place where ships load and unload goods.

reef (rēf) A ridge of sand, rock, or coral that lies at or near the surface of a sea.

reservoir (rez′ ər vwär) A natural or artificial lake used to store water.

river (riv′ ər) A large stream of water that flows across the land and usually empties into a lake, ocean, or other river.

river basin (riv′ ər bās′ in) All the land drained by a river and its tributaries.

sea (sē) A large body of water partly or entirely surrounded by land; another word for *ocean*.

source (sôrs) The place where a river or stream begins.

strait (strāt) A narrow waterway or channel connecting two larger bodies of water.

timber line (tim′ bər līn) An imaginary line on mountains, above which trees do not grow.

tributary (trib′ yə târ ē) A river or stream that flows into a larger river or stream.

valley (val′ ē) An area of low land between hills or mountains.

volcano (vol kā′ nō) An opening in the earth through which lava, rock, gases, and ash are forced out.

waterfall (wô′ tər fôl) A flow of water falling from a high place to a lower place.

619

GAZETTEER

This Gazetteer is a geographical dictionary that will help you to pronounce and locate the places discussed in this book. Latitude and longitude are given for cities and some other places. The page number tells you where each place appears on a map.

A

Aachen (ä' kən) A city in West Germany. Aachen was the capital of Charlemagne's empire and an important center of learning in the early Middle Ages; 51°N, 6°E. (p. 215)

Adriatic Sea (ā drē at' ik sē) A sea between Italy and Yugoslavia, and an arm of the Mediterranean Sea. (p. 210)

Aegean Sea (i jē' ən sē) A sea between Greece and Turkey, and an arm of the Mediterranean Sea. The Aegean Sea was important to the development of ancient Greek civilization. (p. 140)

Africa (af' ri kə) The world's second-largest continent. Africa lies south of Europe between the Atlantic and Indian oceans. (p. 23)

Agra (a' grə) A city in north-central India and the site of the Taj Mahal; 27°N, 78°E. (p. 475)

Alexandria (al ig zan' drē ə) A city in Eygpt founded by Alexander the Great. Alexandria was also one of the great cities of the Roman Empire and a center of learning; 31°N, 30°E. (p. 167)

Alps (alps) A major European mountain range, extending in an arc from the Mediterranean coast to the Balkan Peninsula. (p. 210)

Anatolia (an ə tō' lē ə) Asia Minor; a peninsula in western Asia. (p. 613)

Antarctica (ant ärk' ti kə) An ice-covered continent surrounding the South Pole and lying mainly within the Antarctic Circle. (p. 23)

Anyang (än' yäng) Ancient city in China, political and cultural center of the Shang dynasty; 36°N, 114°E. (p. 125)

Apennines (ap' ə nīnz) A mountain range that extends down the Italian peninsula. (p. 210)

Arabian Peninsula (ə rā' bē ən pə nin' sə lə) A large peninsula in southwestern Asia. (p. 358)

Arabian Sea (ə rā' bē ən se) The northwestern part of the Indian Ocean, between the Arabian peninsula and India. (p. 483)

Arctic Ocean (ärk' tik ō' shən) The body of water north of the Arctic Circle and surrounding the North Pole. (p. 23)

Asia (ā' zhə) The largest continent, bounded on the west by Europe and Africa, on the south by the Indian Ocean, and on the east by the Pacific Ocean. (p. 23)

Asia Minor (ā' zhə mī' nər) A peninsula in western Asia, bounded by the Aegean, Black, and Mediterranean seas. (p. 613)

Athens (ath' ənz) The capital of Greece, in the eastern part of the country. Athens was for centuries the most important and powerful of the ancient Greek city-states; 38°N, 23°E. (p. 140)

Atlantic Ocean (at lan' tik ō' shən) The body of water separating Europe and Africa from North and South America. (p. 23)

Attica (at' i kə) Peninsula in east-central Greece, on the Aegean Sea. Athens is the most important city in the region. (p. 140)

Australia (ôs trāl' yə) The earth's smallest continent, bounded by the Indian and Pacific oceans. Australia is also a country. (p. 23)

Axum (äk süm') Ancient city in Ethiopia, formerly the capital of the Ethiopian Empire and an important center of Christianity; 15°N, 40°E. (p. 419)

B

Babylon (bab′ ə lon) An ancient city in Mesopotamia and the capital of a vast empire that covered the Fertile Crescent; 32°N, 45°E. (p. 101)

Baghdad (bag′ dad) Cultural and political center of Islam from about A.D. 700 to A.D. 1100; 33°N, 44°E. (p. 369)

Bali (bä′ lē) An island in the Malay archipelago in Southeast Asia and a center of Hinduism. (p. 556)

Balkan Peninsula (bôl′ kən pe nin′ sə lə) A peninsula in southern Europe, bounded by the Black, Aegean, and Adriatic seas. (p. 210)

Baltic Sea (bol′ tik sē) An inland sea in northern Europe. (p. 210)

Barents Sea (bâr′ ənts sē) A part of the Arctic Ocean north of Norway and the Soviet Union. (p. 210)

Bay of Bengal (bā əv beng′ gôl) The northern part of the Indian Ocean, between Myanmar and the Indian subcontinent. (p. 465)

Beijing (bā jing′) [Peking] The capital of China. Beijing became China's capital in the thirteenth century; 40°N, 116°E. (p. 493)

Bering Strait (bâr′ ing strāt) Narrow waterway connecting the Bering Sea with the Arctic Ocean. The Bering Strait separates Russia and the state of Alaska. (p. 300)

Berlin (bər lin′) Capital of Germany; during the Cold War Berlin was divided by the Berlin Wall; 52°N, 13°E. (p. 329)

Bethlehem (beth′ lə hem) A town in Israel where Jesus was born; 31°N, 35°E. (p. 197)

Black Sea (blak sē) An inland sea between Europe and Asia. (p. 210)

Bombay (bom bā′) The largest city and chief port on India's western coast; 19°N, 73°E. (p. 483)

Bosporus (bäs′ prəs) Narrow body of water connecting the Black and Marmara seas. (p. 381)

British Isles (brit′ ish ī elz) A group of islands off the western coast of Europe, made up of Great Britain, Ireland, and some small islands. (p. 210)

C

Cairo (kī′ rō) The capital of modern Eygpt and the largest city in Africa; 30°N, 31°E. (p. 387)

Calcutta (kal kut′ ə) A large port city in northeastern India, on the Arabian Sea; 22°N, 88°E. (p. 483)

Calicut (kal′ ə kut) A port city on the southwestern coast of India. Calicut was visited by Vasco da Gama in 1496; 11°N, 76°E. (p. 190, 260)

Canaan (kā′ nən) A region in the Middle East between the Jordan River and the Mediterranean Sea and homeland of the ancient Hebrews. (p. 111)

Cape Comorin (kāp kô′ mə rin) The southernmost point of the Indian subcontinent. (p. 465)

Cape of Good Hope (kāp əv gud hōp) The southernmost point of Africa. (p. 260)

Carpathian Mountains (kär pā′ thē ən mount′ ənz) A mountain range in eastern Europe. (p. 210)

Carthage (kär′ thij) An ancient city in North Africa. Carthage challenged Rome in a series of wars called the Punic Wars. (p. 184)

Caspian Sea (kas′ pē ən sē) The world's largest totally inland body of water, located in south-central Asia. (p. 300)

Caucasus Mountains (kô′ kə səs mount′ ənz) A mountain range that forms part of the southern boundary between Europe and Asia. (p. 210)

Chang River (chäng riv′ ər) [Yangtze] A major river in southern China. (p. 493)

Clermont (klâr mon′) A city in France where Pope Urban II proclaimed the First Crusade in 1095; 45°N, 3°E. (p. 225)

Commonwealth of Independent States (kom′ ən welth əv in di pen′ dənt stāts) A group of 11 former Soviet republics that joined together to help one another. (p. 341)

Constantinople (kon stan tə nō′ pəl) A former Greek colony that was made a capital of the Roman empire by the emperor Constantine. The city is now called Istanbul; 41°N, 29°E. (p. 204)

Corsica (kôr′ si kə) A French island in the Mediterranean Sea, southeast of France. (p. 210)

Crete (krēt) A Greek island in the eastern Mediterranean Sea, southeast of Greece. (p. 140)

Cyprus (sī′ prəs) An island country in the eastern Mediterranean, south of Turkey. (p. 358)

D

Danube River (dan′ ūb riv′ ər) The second-longest river in Europe. (p. 210)

Dead Sea (ded sē) A body of water between Israel and Jordan, and the lowest point on the earth. (p. 613)

Deccan Plateau (dek′ ən pla to′) A high, rugged plateau in the central region of the Indian peninsula. (p. 465)

Dnieper River (nē′ pər riv′ ər) A river that flows through Europe to the Black Sea. (p. 210)

Don River (don riv′ ər) A river that flows through Europe to the Sea of Azov. (p. 210)

E

Eastern Ghats (ēs′ tərn gôts) A mountain range on the Indian subcontinent that extends along the eastern edge of the Deccan Plateau. (p. 465)

GAZETTEER

Eastern Hemisphere (ēs' tərn hem' is fêr) The half of the earth that is east of the prime meridian, including Europe, Africa, Asia, and Australia. (p. 8)

English Channel (ing' glish chan' əl) Channel between the British Isles and northwestern Europe. (p. 210)

Estonia (es tō' ne ə) A country on the Baltic Sea in northern Europe; until 1991, a republic of the Soviet Union. (p. 341)

Ethiopia (ē thē ō' pē ə) A country in eastern Africa. During the fourth century A.D., Ethiopia was a powerful kingdom. (p. 402, p. 423)

Euphrates River (ū frā' tēz riv' ər) A river in southwestern Asia. (p. 358)

Eurasia (yür ā' zhə) A large landmass that includes the continents of Europe and Asia. (p .23)

Europe (yür' əp) The continent between Asia and the Atlantic Ocean. (p. 23)

F

Fertile Crescent (fûrt' əl kres' ənt) A fertile region in the Middle East. The Fertile Crescent was an important birthplace of civilization. (p. 98)

Florence (flor' əns) A city in north-central Italy that became the center of Renaissance art and ideas; 43°N, 11°E. (p. 243)

G

Ganges River (gan' jēz riv' ər) A river in northern India and Bangladesh that flows from the Himalayas to the Bay of Bengal. (p. 465)

Gaul (gôl) Historical name for region that is part of modern France. (p. 187)

Gaza Strip (gä' zə strip) An area on the southeastern coast of the Mediterranean Sea in the Middle East, occupied by Israel since 1967. (p. 391)

Genoa (jen' ō ə) A port city in northwestern Italy; 44°N, 10°E. (p. 225)

Ghana (gä' nə) A country in western Africa and a powerful kingdom that dominated West Africa between 400 and 1235. (p. 402, p. 423)

Gibson Desert (gib' sən dez' ərt) One of three major deserts in Australia. (p. 572)

Gobi (gō' bē) A large desert in east-central Asia. (p. 493)

Golan Heights (gō' län hīts) A border region between Israel and Syria that has been occupied by Israel since 1967. (p. 391)

Grand Canal (grand kə nal') A giant waterway built by the emperor Kublai Khan to link the Huang and Chang rivers of China. (p. 493)

Great Barrier Reef (grāt bar' ē ər rēf) The largest coral reef in the world, along Australia's north-eastern coast. (p. 572)

Great Dividing Range (grāt di vī' ding rānj) A range of low mountains extending down the eastern edge of Australia. (p. 572)

Great Rift Valley (grāt rift val' ē) A series of valleys in Africa extending 6,000 miles (9,600 km) from the Mozambique Channel north to the Red Sea. (p. 412)

Great Sandy Desert (grāt san' dē dez' ərt) One of the three main deserts of Australia, lying in the northern part of the country. (p. 572)

Great Victoria Desert (grāt vik tôr' ē ə dez' ərt) One of Australia's three main deserts, lying in the southern part of the country. (p. 572)

Great Wall of China (grāt wôl əv chī' nə) A vast defensive wall that extends for more than 1,500 miles (2,415 km) through northern China. (p. 493)

Guangzhou (gwäng' jō') A port city in southeastern China, also called Canton; 23° N, 113°E. (p. 505)

Guinea (gin' ē) A country in western Africa. (p. 441)

H

Harappa (hə rap' ə) One of the two great cities of ancient India. (p. 120)

Himalayas (him ə lā' əz) The world's highest mountain range, forming part of the northern boundary of the Indian subcontinent. (p. 465)

Hindu Kush (hin' dü kùsh) A mountain range in South Asia, forming part of the northern boundary of the Indian subcontinent. (p. 465)

Hiroshima (hêr' ō shē mə) A port city in southern Japan, on the island of Honshu; 34°N, 132°E. (p. 526)

Hokkaido (hä kīd' ō) Northernmost of the four main islands of Japan. (p. 526)

Holy Land (hō' lē land) A name given to Palestine by European Christians. (p. 225)

Honshu (hon' shü) The largest island of the Japanese archipelago. (p. 526)

Huang River (hwäng riv' ər) [Yellow] A major river in North China. (p. 125)

Huang River Valley (hwäng riv' ər val' ē) The valley of the Huang River in China and the region where Chinese civilization was born. (p. 125)

I

Iberian Peninsula (ī bîr' ē ən pə nin' sə lə) A large peninsula of southwestern Europe, between the Atlantic Ocean and the Mediterranean Sea. (p. 210)

Iceland (īs' lənd) A European island country in the North Atlantic. (p. 210)

Indian Ocean (in' dē ən ō' shən) The body of water south of Asia, located between Africa and Australia. (p. 23)

Indian Subcontinent (in' dē ən sub kont' ən ənt) The large land mass that makes up South Asia. (p. 465)

Indus-Ganges Plain (in' dəs gan' jēz plān) A vast fertile plain lying south of the Himalayas on the Indian subcontinent. (p. 465)

Indus River (in' dəs riv' ər) A river that flows from Tibet, through the Hindu Kush, and into the Arabian Sea. (p. 465)

Indus River Valley (in' dəs riv' ər val' ē) A region in present-day Pakistan that was the birthplace of Indian civilization. (p. 120)

Iraq (i rak') An oil-rich country in the Middle East. (p. 387)

Irrawaddy River (êr ə wod' ə riv' ər) An important river in Southeast Asia. (p. 556)

Istanbul (is tan bül') Turkish name for the ancient city of Constantinople; 41°N, 29°E. (p. 387)

Italian Peninsula (i tal' yən pə nin' sə lə) A long peninsula in southern Europe that was the birthplace of Roman civilization. (p. 210)

J

Jerusalem (jə rü' sə ləm) An ancient city in Palestine, now the capital of Israel; 31°N, 35°E. (p. 111)

Jutland Peninsula (jut' lənd pə nin' sə lə) A peninsula in northern Europe located between the North and Baltic seas. (p. 210)

K

Kahtyn (ka tin') A small village in Byelarus that was burned to the ground by Nazi soldiers during World War II. (p. 333)

Kalahari Desert (kä lə här' ē dez' ərt) A desert region in southern Africa. (p. 412)

Kanem-Bornu (kä nēm' bôr' nü) A West African kingdom that flourished between 800 and 1500 in what is now Chad and northern Nigeria. (p. 423)

Kenya (ken' yə) A country in eastern Africa that gained its independence from Great Britain in 1963. (p. 442)

Khmer Empire (kə' mâr em' pīr) An ancient empire in Mainland Southeast Asia. (p. 561)

Khyber Pass (kī' bər pas) A mountain pass in the Hindu Kush; 34°N, 71°E. (p. 110, 465)

Kiev (kē' ev) A port city on the Dnieper River, in Ukraine; 50°N, 30°E. (p. 314)

Kilwa (kēl' wä) A port city in the eastern African country of Tanzania. Kilwa was an important trading center from 1100 to 1500; 8°S, 39°E. (p. 423)

Kola Peninsula (kō' lə pə nin' sə lə) A peninsula in northern Europe bounded by the Barents Sea and White Sea. (p. 210)

Korean Strait (kə rē' ən strāt) A strait separating Korea from Japan and connecting the East China Sea and South China Sea. (p. 526)

Kush (kush) An ancient kingdom in northeastern Africa, which flourished from about 751 B.C. to A.D. 400. (p. 81)

Kuwait (kü wāt') A small, oil-rich country in the Middle East. (p. 387)

Kyushu (kū' shü) Most southern of Japan's four main islands. (p. 526)

L

Lake Baikal (lāk bī käl') A lake in eastern Russia. It is the deepest freshwater lake in the world. (p. 300)

Lake Nasser (lāk nä' sər) A lake in Egypt that was created when the Aswan High Dam was built on the Nile River. (p. 88)

Lake Nyasa (lāk nī as' ə) A large lake in southern Africa, also called Lake Malawi. (p. 412)

Lake Victoria (lāk vik tôr' ē ə) The largest lake in Africa, located in the east-central part of the continent. (p. 412)

Lascaux (las kō') Caves in France that contain some of the most beautiful cave paintings in the world. (p. 51)

Latvia (lat' vē ə) A country on the Baltic Sea in northern Europe; until 1991, a republic of the Soviet Union. (p. 341)

Lithuania (lith ü ā' nē ə) A country on the Baltic Sea in northern Europe; until 1991, a republic of the Soviet Union. (p. 341)

London (lun' dən) The capital of the United Kingdom, located in southeastern England; 52°N, 0° long. (p. 243)

Lower Egypt (lō' er ē' jipt) The northern part of the kingdom of ancient Egypt. (p. 72)

M

Macedonia (mas i dō' nē ə) An ancient empire ruled by Alexander the Great that conquered ancient Greece. (p. 167)

Mainland Southeast Asia (mān' land south' ēst ā' zhə) A large peninsula between the Bay of Bengal and the South China Sea. (p. 556)

a cap; ā cake; ä father; är car; âr dare; ch chain; e hen; ē me; êr clear; hw where; i bib; ī kite; ng song; o top; ō rope; ô saw; oi coin; ôr fork; ou cow; sh show; th thin; <u>th</u> those; u sun; ù book; ü moon; ū cute; ûr term; ə about, taken, pencil, apron, helpful; ər letter, dollar, doctor

Malay Archipelago (mā′ lā är kə pel′ i gō) The largest island group in the world, extending from Southeast Asia into the Pacific Ocean. (p. 556)

Malay Peninsula (mā′ lā pə nin′ sə lə) A long, narrow peninsula extending into the Indian Ocean from the mainland of Southeast Asia. (p. 556)

Mali (mä′ lē) A country in western Africa. Mali was a wealthy kingdom that flourished between the 13th and 15th centuries. (p. 402, p. 423)

Manchurian Plain (man chür′ ē ən plān) A region in northeastern China. (p. 493)

Marathon (mar′ ə thon) A plain in Attica, Greece, where the Athenians defeated the Persians in battle in 490 B.C. (p. 148)

Mecca (mek′ ə) A city in western Saudi Arabia, near the Red Sea. Mecca was the birthplace of Muhammad and is the holiest city of Islam; 21°N, 40°E. (p. 369)

Medina (mə dē′ nə) A holy city to the followers of Islam; 24°N, 40°E. (p. 369)

Mediterranean Sea (med ə tə rā′ nē ən sē) A large, almost landlocked arm of the Atlantic Ocean between Europe, Asia, and Africa. (p. 210)

Mekong River (mā′ kong riv′ ər) An important river in Southeast Asia, flowing southwestward from western China into the South China Sea. (p. 556)

Melanesia (mel ə nē′ zhə) One of three major groups of the Pacific islands. (pp. 548-549)

Memphis (mem′ fis) An ancient Egyptian city on the Nile River; 29°N, 31°E. (p. 72)

Menam River (mā näm′ riv′ ər) A major Southeast Asian river flowing into the Gulf of Thailand. (p. 556)

Meroë (mâr′ ō ē) The capital of the ancient African kingdom of Kush; 18°N, 34°E. (p. 419)

Mesopotamia (mes ə pə tā′ mē ə) The "land between two rivers," referring to the region between the Tigris and Euphrates rivers in the Middle East. Mesopotamia was the birthplace of Sumerian and Babylonian civilization. (p. 98)

Micronesia (mī krə nē′ zhə) One of the three major groups of the Pacific islands. (pp. 548-549)

Middle East (mid′ əl ēst) The region of southwest Asia that stretches from Turkey to Iran. Because of close cultural ties, North Africa is also considered part of the Middle East. (p. 350)

Mogul Empire (mō′ gul em′ pīr) An Islamic empire set up in India in the 16th century. (p. 475)

Mohenjo-Daro (mō hen′ jō där′ ō) One of the two great cities of the Indus Valley civilization in South Asia. The city was abandoned around 1500 B.C., probably in response to the Aryan invasions; 27°N, 68°E. (p. 120)

Mombasa (mom bä′ sə) The main port city of Kenya, on the Indian Ocean. Mombasa was an important Swahili city-state and trading center from 1100 to 1500; 4°N, 39°E. (p. 423)

Mongolia (mong gō′ lē ə) A country in Asia lying between China and Russia. (p. 493)

Moscow (mos′ kou) The capital of Russia; 56°N, 38°E. (p. 300)

Mount Cook (mount kúk) The highest mountain in New Zealand, on the central part of South Island; 43°S, 170°E. (p. 572)

Mount Everest (mount ev′ ər ist) The highest mountain in the world, located in the Himalayas on the border between Nepal and Tibet; 28°N, 87°E. (p. 465)

Mount Fuji (mount fü′ jē) The highest mountain in Japan, located on the island of Honshu; 35°N, 138°E. (p. 526)

Mount Kenya (mount ken′ yə) The highest mountain in Kenya, located in the central part of the country; 1°S, 37°E. (p. 412)

Mount Kilimanjaro (mount kil ə mən jär′ ō) The highest mountain in Africa, located in northern Tanzania; 3°S, 37°E. (p. 412)

Mount Kosciusko (mount kos ē us′ kō) The highest mountain in Australia, in the Great Dividing Range in the southeastern part of the country; 36°S, 148°E. (p. 572)

Mount Olympus (mount ō lim′ pəs) The highest mountain in Greece. The ancient Greeks believed that Mount Olympus was the home of their major gods; 40°N, 22°E. (p. 140)

Mount Sinai (mount sī′ nī) A mountain in Egypt's Sinai Peninsula. According to the Bible, it was on Mount Sinai that Moses received the Ten Commandments from God; 28°N, 35°E. (p. 111)

N

Nagasaki (nä gə sä′ kē) A Japanese city on the island of Kyushu; 33°N, 130°E. (p. 526)

Nairobi (nī rō′ bē) The capital of Kenya, in the southern part of the country; 1°S, 37°E. (p. 442)

Nazareth (naz′ ər əth) A town in Israel where Jesus spent his youth; 32°N, 35°E. (p. 197)

New Delhi (nü del′ ē) The capital of India and one of the largest cities in the world; 29°N, 77°E. (p. 483)

New Guinea (nü′ gin′ ē) An island of the Malay Archipelago in Southeast Asia. (p. 592)

Niger River (nī′ jər riv′ ər) A river flowing from western Africa into the Gulf of Guinea. (p. 412)

Nile Delta (nīl del′ tə) A marshy area in northern Egypt where the Nile River fans out before entering the Mediterranean Sea. (p. 72)

GAZETTEER

Nile River (nīl riv′ ər) The largest river in Africa and the world's longest river. (p. 412)

Nile River Valley (nīl riv′ ər val′ ē) The fertile region watered by the Nile River. The Nile River Valley was the source of Egyptian civilization. (p. 72)

North Africa (nôrth af′ ri kə) The Muslim countries along the Mediterranean coast in northern Africa. (p. 350)

North America (nôrth ə mâr′ i kə) The third-largest continent, located in the northern part of the Western Hemisphere. (p. 23)

North China (nôrth chī′ nə) A large, fertile region in northern China containing most of the country's population. (p. 492)

North China Plain (nôrth chī′ nə plān) A vast, fertile region of flat land that is watered by the Huang River. (p. 493)

Northern Hemisphere (nôr′ thərn hem′ is fêr) The half of the earth north of the equator. (p. 8)

North European Plain (nôrth yür ə pē′ ən plān) A vast region of flat land extending from the Atlantic Ocean in the west to the Ural Mountains in the east. (p. 210)

North Island (nôrth ī′ lənd) One of the two main islands that make up the country of New Zealand. (p. 572)

North Sea (nôrth sē) A large arm of the Atlantic Ocean, between Great Britain and continental Europe. (p. 210)

Novgorod (nôv′ gə rôd) One of Russia's oldest cities, in the northwestern part of the country; 58°N, 31°E. (p. 309)

O

Oceania (ō shē an′ ē ə) The South Pacific islands of Polynesia, Micronesia, Melanesia, and New Zealand. (pp. 548-549)

Olympia (ō lim′ pē ə) A plain in southwestern Greece, the site of the ancient Olympic Games. (p. 162)

Ottoman Empire (ot′ ə mən em′ pīr) An Islamic empire established in the 15th century by the Turks. The empire spread throughout the Middle East and North Africa and lasted almost 500 years. (p. 380)

Outer China (ou′ tər chī′ nə) A vast region in western China made up of the provinces of Sinkiang, Quinghai, and Tibet. (p. 492)

P

Pacific Ocean (pə sif′ ik ō′ shən) The world's largest body of water, bounded by North and South America on the east and Asia and Australia on the west. (p. 23)

Palestine (pal′ is tīn) In ancient times, the land of the Jews and the homeland of Jesus. In recent times, Palestine was a British protectorate that became the country of Israel in 1947. (p. 197)

Paris (par′ is) The capital of France and one of Europe's great cultural centers; 49°N, 2°E. (p. 338)

Peloponnesus (pel ə pə nē′ səs) A peninsula in southern Greece, between the Ionian and Aegean seas. (p. 140)

Persian Gulf (pûr zhən gulf) A body of water between Iran and the Arabian peninsula. (p. 358)

Philippine Islands (fil′ ə pēn i′ ləndz) An archipelago in Southeast Asia, separated from the mainland by the South China Sea. (p. 556)

Phoenicia (fə nē′ shə) An ancient sea power located on the eastern shore of the Mediterranean Sea. (p. 142)

Po Basin (pō bā′ sin) A region in northern Italy drained by the Po River. Etruscan civilization flourished in the Po Basin. (p. 176)

Po River (pō riv′ ər) Italy's largest river. The Po River is located in the northern part of the country and flows into the Adriatic Sea. (p. 210)

Polynesia (pol ə nē′ zhə) One of the three main island groups in Oceania. (pp. 548-549)

Pyongyang (pē ong′ yäng) Capital city of North Korea; 39°N, 125°E. (p. 526)

Pyrenees Mountains (pêr′ ə nēz mount′ ənz) A mountain range in southwestern Europe extending from the Bay of Biscay to the Mediterranean Sea. (p. 210)

R

Red River (red riv′ ər) A river in Southeast Asia that flows from China through northern Vietnam and into the Gulf of Tonkin. (p. 556)

Red Sea (red sē) A narrow sea between the Arabian peninsula and northeastern Africa. (p. 358)

Rhine River (rīn riv′ ər) A European river flowing from the Alps to the North Sea. (p. 210)

Rhodes (rōdz) The second largest of the Greek islands in the Aegean Sea. (p. 140)

---

a cap; ā cake; ä father; är car; âr dare; ch chain; e hen; ē me; êr clear; hw where; i bib; ī kite; ng song; o top; ō rope; ô saw; oi coin; ôr fork; ou cow; sh show; th thin; th those; u sun; ů book; ü moon; ū cute; ûr term; ə about, taken, pencil, apron, helpful; ər letter, dollar, doctor

GAZETTEER

Rhône River (rōn riv′ ər) A European river that flows from the Alps to the Mediterranean Sea. (p. 210)

Roman Empire (rō′ mən em′ pīr) One of the world's greatest empires, it grew from the Italian peninsula to include parts of three continents. (p. 187)

Rome (rōm) The capital of Italy and the former center of the ancient Roman Republic and the Roman Empire; 42°N, 12°E. (p. 176)

Russia (rush′ ə) A country in eastern Europe and northern Asia, it is the largest country in the world; a republic of the Soviet Union from 1922 to 1991. (p. 272)

S

Sahara (sə har′ ə) The largest desert in the world, covering much of northern Africa. (p. 358)

Sahel (sa′ hil) A narrow belt of semiarid grassland in Africa, between the Sahara to the north and the savanna to the south. (p. 415)

St. Petersburg (sānt pē′ tərz bûrg) Russian city on the Baltic Sea built by Peter the Great beginning in 1703. St. Petersburg was called Leningrad from 1924 until 1991; 59°N., 30°E. (p. 309)

Salamis (sal′ ə mis) An island in eastern Greece, west of Athens; site of a decisive Greek naval victory over the Persians in 480 B.C.; 38°N, 23°E. (p. 148)

Scandinavian Peninsula (skan də nā′ vē ən pə nin′ sə lə) A large peninsula in northern Europe. (p. 210)

Sea of Japan (sē əv jə pan′) An arm of the Pacific Ocean separating Japan from the Asian mainland. (p. 526)

Sea of Marmara (sē əv mär′ mə rä) Body of water between Europe and Asia. (p. 381)

Senegal River (sen ə gôl riv′ ər) A river in western Africa. (p. 412)

Seoul (sōl) The capital and largest city of South Korea; 37°N, 127°E. (p. 526)

Serengeti Plain (ser ən′ get ē plān) A vast plain in East Africa, south of Lake Victoria. (p. 412)

Shanghai (shang hī′) The chief port and largest city of China; 31°N, 121°E. (p. 493)

Shikoku (shi kō′ kü) Smallest of the four main islands of Japan. (p. 526)

Siberia (sī bêr′ ē ə) A vast region in the northern part of Russia. (p. 300)

Sicily (sis′ ə lē) An island in the Mediterranean Sea off the southwest tip of the Italian Peninsula. (p. 176)

Sinai Peninsula (sī′ nī pə nin′ sə lə) A desert area in northeastern Egypt between the Mediterranean Sea and the Red Sea. (p. 391)

Sinkiang (sin′ kyang) A vast, dry region in Outer China. (p. 493)

Songhai (sông′ hī) A great West African kingdom that flourished near Timbuktu. (p. 423)

South Africa (south af′ ri kə) A country in sub-Saharan Africa. (p. 442)

South America (south ə mâr′ i kə) The fourth largest continent, in the Western Hemisphere. (p. 23)

South China (south chī′ nə) A fertile region in southern China. (p. 492)

Southeast Asia (south ēst′ ā′ zhə) A region of Asia bounded by the Indian and the Pacific oceans. (p. 556)

Southern Hemisphere (su<u>th</u>′ ərn hem′ is fêr) The half of the earth south of the equator. (p. 8)

South Island (south ī′ lənd) One of the two main islands that make up New Zealand. (p. 572)

Sparta (spär′ tə) An ancient Greek city located on the southern tip of the Peloponessus; 37°N, 22°E. (p. 140)

Strait of Malacca (strāt əv mə läk′ ə) A waterway between the Malay Peninsula and the island of Sumatra in Southeast Asia. (p. 556)

Sub-Saharan Africa (sub sə har′ ən af′ ri kə) Africa south of the Sahara. (pp. 402–403)

Sumatra (sü mä′ trə) The westernmost island of the Malay Archipelago. (p. 556)

Sumer (sü′ mər) An ancient civilization in southern Mesopotamia. (p. 101)

Sydney (sid′ nē) The chief port and largest city of Australia, on the eastern coast of the country; 34°S, 151°E. (p. 572)

Syrian Desert (sêr′ ē ən dez′ ərt) A desert between the cultivated lands along the eastern Mediterranean coast and the fertile lands along the Euphrates River. (p. 358)

T

Tasmania (taz mā′ nē ə) An island south of Australia. Tasmania is named for Abel Tasman, a Dutch explorer who reached the island in 1642. (p. 572)

Tassili Plateau (tas sel′ ē pla tō′) A site in Algeria which contains some of the most beautiful rock paintings in the world. (p. 49)

Thebes (thēbz) An ancient Egyptian city on the Nile River. Thebes became the capital of the Egyptian Empire after the Hyksos period; 26°N, 32°E. (p. 72)

Thermopylae (thər mop′ ə lē) A narrow mountain pass in central Greece where a small group of Spartan soldiers fought the Persian army. (p. 148)

Tian An Men Square (tē an′ an men skwâr) A site in Beijing, China, where government troops killed hundreds of people who were demonstrating for democratic reform in 1989. (p. 521)

Tiber River (tī′ bər riv′ ər) A river flowing southward from north-central Italy, through Rome, and into the Tyrrhenian Sea. (p. 176)

Tibet (tə bet′) A mountainous region in Outer China, formerly an independent country. (p. 493)

Tigris River (tī′ gris riv′ ər) A river in southwestern Asia. The Tigris is one of the two great rivers of ancient Mesopotamia. (p. 98)

Timbuktu (tim buk tü′) A town in western Africa, in the country of Mali. Timbuktu was a major trade and cultural center from the 11th through 15th centuries; 17°N, 3°W. (p. 423)

Tokyo (tō′ kē ō) The capital of Japan, on the island of Honshu; 35°N, 139°E. (p. 526)

Tours (tür) The Frankish king Charles Martel halted the Muslim conquest of Europe in a battle here in 732; 47°N, 4°E. (p. 369)

Trent (trent) A city in northern Italy. The Council of Trent was called by the Catholic Church between 1546 and 1563; 46°N, 11°E. (p. 243)

Tropic of Cancer (trop′ ik əv kan′ sər) An imaginary line at latitude 23.5°N. (p. 23)

Tropic of Capricorn (trop′ ik əv kap′ rə kôrn) An imaginary line at latitude 23.5°S. (p. 23)

U

Upper Egypt (up′ ər ē′ jipt) The southern part of ancient Egypt. (p. 72)

Ur (ûr) A city-state in ancient Sumer, on the Euphrates River. (p. 101)

Ural Mountains (yür′ əl mount′ ənz) A mountain range in central Russia. The Ural Mountains are one of the boundaries between Europe and Asia. (p. 210)

V

Valley of the Kings (val′ e əv thə kingz) An ancient burial place in Egypt near the Nîle River; 25°N, 33°E. (p. 72)

Venice (ven′ is) A port city in northeastern Italy. Venice was a major sea power and center of international trade in the Middle Ages and Renaissance; 45°N, 12°E. (p. 225)

Vladivostok (vlad ə vos′ tok) A port city on the Pacific in Eastern Russia; 43°N, 132°E. (p. 300)

Volga River (vol′ gə riv′ ər) A river in Europe, flowing into the Caspian Sea. It is the longest river in Europe. (p. 210)

W

Warsaw (wôr′ sô) The capital of Poland located on the Vistula River; 52°N, 21°E. (p. 329)

West Bank (west bangk) An area west of the Jordan River in the Middle East that has been occupied by Israel since 1967. (p. 391)

Western Ghats (wes′ tərn gôts) A mountain range on the Indian peninsula that extends along the western edge of the Deccan Plateau. (p. 465)

Western Hemisphere (wes′ tərn hem′ is fêr) The half of the earth that is west of the prime meridian, including North and South America. (p. 8)

Wittenberg (vit′ ən bârg) A city in Germany where Martin Luther nailed his famous 95 statements to a church door in 1517; 52°N, 12°E. (p. 243)

Y

Yalta (yôl′ tə) A city on the Black Sea in Ukraine; the site of a 1945 meeting held by Franklin Roosevelt, Joseph Stalin, and Winston Churchill; 44°N, 34°E. (p. 329)

Yellow Sea (yel′ ō sē) An arm of the Pacific Ocean, between China and Korea. (p. 125)

Z

Zaire River (zä êr′ riv′ ər) The second-longest river in Africa, flowing through the central part of the continent. (p. 412)

Zama (zä′ mə) A city of ancient Carthage in North Africa. (p. 184)

Zambezi River (zam bē′ zē riv′ ər) A river in southern Africa, flowing eastward through Zimbabwe and Mozambique, into the Indian Ocean. (p. 412)

Zanzibar (zan′ zə bär) An island in the Indian Ocean, off the eastern coast of Africa. (p. 423)

Zimbabwe (zim bäb′ wē) A country in southern Africa. Zimbabwe was also the name of an ancient kingdom, rich in gold, that flourished between 1000 and 1400 A.D. (p. 402, p. 423)

---

a cap; ā cake; ä father; är car; âr dare; ch chain; e hen; ē me; êr clear; hw where; i bib; ī kite; ng song; o top; ō rope; ô saw; oi coin; ôr fork; ou cow; sh show; th thin; th those; u sun; u̇ book; ü moon; ū cute; ûr term; ə about, taken, pencil, apron, helpful; ər letter, dollar, doctor

GAZETTEER

BIOGRAPHICAL DICTIONARY

This Biographical Dictionary will help you to pronounce and identify the Key People discussed in this book. The page number tells you where each person first appears in the text.

PRONUNCIATION KEY

a	cap	êr	clear	oi	coin	ü	moon
ā	cake	hw	where	ôr	fork	ū	cute
ä	father	i	bib	ou	cow	ûr	term
är	car	ī	kite	sh	show	ə	about, taken,
âr	dare	ng	song	th	thin		pencil, apron,
ch	chain	o	top	<u>th</u>	those		helpful
e	hen	ō	rope	u	sun	ər	letter, dollar,
ē	me	ô	saw	ù	book		doctor

A

Abraham (ā′ brə ham), 1700s B.C. A great Hebrew leader who lead his people from Sumer to the land of Canaan. (p. 110)

Aeschylus (es′ kə ləs), about 525–456 B.C. One of the writers of tragedies in ancient Greece. (p. 158)

Africanus, Leo (af ri kā′ nəs), about A.D. 1485–1554 Muslim scholar from Morocco. (p. 424)

Akbar (ak′ bər), A.D. 1542–1605 Ruler of the Mogul Empire from 1556 to 1605. (p. 475)

al-Bakri (äl bäk′ rē), about A.D. 1057–1104 Spanish Arab who wrote about his travels in Africa. (p. 422)

Alexander the Great (al ig zan′ dər), about 356–323 B.C. King of Macedonia from 336 to 323 B.C.; conqueror of Greece and Persia. (p. 166)

Alexander II (al ig zan′ dər), A.D. 1818–1888 Tsar of Russia from 1855 to 1881. (p. 310)

Ali Jinnah, Muhammad (ä lē′ jin′ ä), A.D. 1876–1948 First president of Pakistan. (p. 479)

Antoinette, Marie (an twə net′), A.D. 1755–1793 Queen of France from 1774 to 1792; executed by guillotine during the Reign of Terror. (p. 292)

Aquino, Benigno (a kē′ nō, bə nē′ nō), A.D. 1932–1983 Popular Philippine leader who opposed Marcos. (p. 565)

Aquino, Corazon (a kē′ nō, kôr ə zōn), A.D. 1933– Philippine political leader; president since 1986. (p. 565)

Aristophanes (ar is tof′ ə nēz), about 448–385 B.C. One of the most famous writers of comedies in ancient Greece. (p. 159)

Aristotle (ar′ is tot əl), about 384–322 B.C. Ancient Greek philosopher. (p. 166)

Asoka (ə sō′ kə), about 290–232 B.C. Hindu general who became king of India in 273 B.C. (p. 472)

Atatürk, Mustafa Kemal (ä′ tä turk, mus′ tä fä ke mäl′), A.D. 1881–1938 Turkish nationalist leader. (p. 381)

Avicenna (av ə sen′ ə), A.D. 980–1037 Persian philosopher; wrote a medical encyclopedia that was used in Europe. (p. 373)

B

Battutah, Ibn (bə tüt′ ä, ib′ ən), about A.D. 1304–1369 Wrote about salt mines in Taghaza. (p. 424)

Batu Khan (bä′ tü kän), about A.D. 1200–1255 Mongol leader who conquered Russia. (p. 306)

Benedict (ben′ ə dikt), A.D. 480–543 Italian monk; developed rules for monasteries. (p. 220)

Bonaparte, Napoleon (bō′ nə pärt, nə pō′ lē ən), A.D. 1769–1821 French military leader and emperor of France from 1804 to 1815. (p. 292)

C

Caesar, Julius (sē′ zər), about 100–44 B.C. Roman general who became dictator of Rome. (p. 186)

Carter, Howard (kär′ tər), A.D. 1873–1939 An archaeologist famous for discovering the tomb of the Egyptian pharaoh Tutankhamen. (p. 82)

Catherine the Great (kath′ ər in), A.D. 1729–1796 Empress of Russia; expanded Russia's territory; built a museum called the Hermitage. (p. 308)

Chiang Kai-shek (chang′ kī shek′), A.D. 1886–1975 Chinese Nationalist leader. (p. 514)

Charlemagne (shär′ lə män), A.D. 742–814 King of the Franks from 768 to 814. (p. 215)

Churchill, Winston (chûr′ chil), A.D. 1874–1965   British prime minister from 1940 to 1945 and from 1951 to 1955. (p. 328)

Cleopatra (klē ə pa′ tre), 69–30 B.C.   Queen of Egypt during the time of Caesar. (p. 187)

Columbus, Christopher (kə lum′ bəs), A.D. 1446–1506   Italian explorer who arrived in the Americas in 1492. (p. 261)

Confucius (kən fū′ shəs), about 551–479 B.C.   Chinese philosopher. (p. 500)

Constantine (kon′ stən tīn), A.D. 280–337   Roman emperor from A.D. 312 to 337; legalized the Christian religion in A.D. 313. (p. 198)

Cook, James (kùk), A.D. 1728–1779   British explorer; first European to explore the eastern coast of Australia (1770). (p. 580)

Copernicus (kə pûr′ ni kəs), A.D. 1473–1543   Polish astronomer whose observations led him to develop the heliocentric theory. (p. 264)

D

Da Gama, Vasco (də gä′ mə), A.D. 1469–1542   Portuguese navigator who discovered an all-water route to the Indies. (p. 260)

Da Vinci, Leonardo (də vin′ chē), A.D. 1452–1519   Renaissance painter and inventor from Italy; creator of the *Mona Lisa*. (p. 238)

De Coubertin, Baron Pierre (də kü bâr tan), A.D. 1863–1937   Organizer of the first modern Olympic Games. (p. 163)

Dias, Bartholomeu (dē′ əs), about A.D. 1450–1500   The first European to sail around the southern tip of Africa. (p. 260)

Drake, Francis (drāk), A.D. 1540–1596   Englishman who led the defeat of the Spanish Armada. (p. 247)

E

Elizabeth I (i liz′ ə bəth), A.D. 1533–1603   Queen of England from 1558 to 1603. (p. 246)

Ezana (e′ zä nä), about A.D. 322–359   Ancient Ethiopian king who spread Christianity. (p. 420)

F

Ferdinand, Franz (fûrd′ ən and), A.D. 1863–1914   Heir to the throne of Austria-Hungary whose murder triggered World War I. (p. 324)

Francis of Assisi (fran′ sis əv ə sē′ zē), A.D. 1181–1226   A religious teacher. (p. 222)

Frank, Anne (frangk), A.D. 1929–1945   A young Jewish girl killed in a Nazi concentration camp. (p. 330)

G

Galileo (gal ə lā′ ō), A.D. 1563–1642   Italian scientist who used a telescope to prove that the heliocentric theory was correct. (p. 265)

Gandhi, Mohandas (gän′ dē), A.D. 1869–1948   Indian leader who organized acts of civil disobedience to free India from British rule. (p. 478)

Gautauma, Siddharta (gô′ tə mə), about 563–483 B.C.   Called the Buddha; founder of Buddhism. (p. 470)

Gorbachev, Mikhail (gôr bə chôf′), A.D. 1931–   Soviet leader from 1985–1991; supporter of reform. (p. 339)

Gutenberg, Johann (güt′ ən bûrg), A.D. 1400–1468   German printer; probably the first European to use movable type. (p. 242)

H

Hammurabi (hä mù rä′ bē), about 1800–1750 B.C.   Babylonian ruler; recorded the first system of laws, known as the Code of Hammurabi. (p. 105)

Hannibal (han′ ə bəl), about 247–183 B.C.   A general from Carthage who led his people against Rome in the Second Punic War. (p. 184)

Hargreaves, James (här′ grēvz), A.D. 1720–1778   English inventor of the spinning jenny. (p. 282)

Hatshepsut (hat shep′ süt), about 1520–1482 B.C.   A pharaoh who led the Egyptian Empire; the first woman ruler known to history. (p. 81)

Henry the Navigator (hen′ rē thə nav′ i gā tər), A.D. 1394–1460   Prince of Portugal; founded a school for sailors. (p. 259)

Herodotus (hi rod′ ə təs), about 484–425 B.C.   Greek historian; known as the "father of history." (p. 148)

Hitler, Adolf (hit′ lər), A.D. 1889–1945   German dictator, leader of Germany and the Nazi Party from 1933 to 1945. (p. 326)

Hobson, William (hob′ sən), A.D. 1795–1842   Signed a peace treaty with Maori chiefs in 1840 that gave Britain sovereignty over New Zealand. (p. 581)

Ho Chi Minh (hō chē min), A.D. 1890–1969   Leader of North Vietnam. (p. 563)

Homer (hō′ mər), about 950–900 B.C.   Great poet of ancient Greece. (p. 155)

Hussein, Saddam (hü sān′), A.D. 1937–   Iraqi political and military leader. President since 1979. (p. 390)

I

Ivan the Great (ī′ vən thə grāt), A.D. 1440–1505   Ruler of Russia from 1462–1505; freed Russia from Mongol oppression. (p. 307)

J

Jahan, Shah (jə hän′), about A.D. 1592–1666   Grandson of Mogul emperor Akbar; ordered the Taj Mahal built as a tomb for his wife. (p. 476)

Jansz, Willem (jants), A.D. 1568–1620   Dutch explorer; the first European to reach Australia. (p. 579)

BIOGRAPHICAL DICTIONARY

629

Jayavarman II (jä yä vär′ män), about A.D. 770–850 Khmer king of the early ninth century. (p. 560)

Jesus (jē′ zəs), about 4 B.C.–A.D. 29 Founder of Christianity. (p. 195)

John (jon), A.D. 1167–1216 King of England from 1199 to 1216; signed the Magna Carta in 1215. (p. 228)

K

Kay, John (kā), A.D. 1704–1764 English watchmaker who invented the flying shuttle. (p. 282)

Kenyatta, Jomo (ken yät′ ə), about A.D. 1893–1978 Kenya's first prime minister; served from 1964 to 1978. (p. 443)

Khomeini, Ayatollah (kō mā′ nē, ī ə to′ lə), A.D. 1902–1989 Ruler of the Islamic Republic of Iran from 1979 until his death. (p. 382)

Khufu (kü′ fü), about 2650–2600 B.C. Egyptian pharaoh who built the Great Pyramid. (p. 77)

Kublai Khan (kü′ blī kän), about A.D. 1215–1294 Ruler of the Mongol Empire from 1260 to 1294; served by the Italian traveler Marco Polo. (p. 257)

L

Lenin (len′ in), A.D. 1870–1924 Russian communist leader; founder of the Soviet Union. (p. 311)

Livingstone, David (liv′ ing stən), A.D. 1813–1873 Scottish missionary in Africa. (p. 434)

Loues, Spiridon (lü ēz spi rē′ don), A.D. 1868–1940 Greek runner who won the Marathon race at the 1896 Olympics in Athens, Greece. (p. 163)

Louis XVI (lü′ ē), A.D. 1754–1793 King of France from 1774 to 1792; executed by guillotine during the Reign of Terror. (p. 288)

Luther, Martin (lü′ thər), A.D. 1483–1546 German monk and teacher; leader of the Protestant Reformation. (p. 240)

M

Mandela, Nelson (man del′ ə), A.D. 1918– South African lawyer and leader in the struggle against apartheid. (p. 443)

Mansa Musa (män′ sä mü′ sä), about A.D. 1297–1332 Powerful Mali king; Timbuktu became a center of commerce during his rule. (p. 424)

Mao Zedong (mou′ dzu dùng′), A.D. 1893–1976 Chinese Communist leader; founder of the People's Republic of China. (p. 514)

Marcos, Ferdinand (mär′ kōs), A.D. 1917–1986 Philippine leader who declared martial law and became a dictator; forced into exile in 1986. (p. 565)

Martel, Charles (mär tel′), about A.D. 688–741 Defeated the Muslims at Tours in 732. (p. 368)

Marx, Karl (märks), A.D. 1818–1883 German writer whose ideas are called Marxism and formed the basis of communism. (p. 311)

Medici, Lorenzo de' (med′ i chē), A.D. 1449–1492 Renaissance patron of the arts. (p. 236)

Meiji (mā jē), A.D. 1852–1912 Emperor of Japan from 1867 to 1912; he led Japan into a period of rapid modernization. (p. 534)

Meir, Golda (me êr′), A.D. 1898–1978 Prime Minister of Israel from 1969 to 1974. (p. 382)

Menes (mē′ nēz), about 3040–3000 B.C. Ruler who united Upper Egypt and Lower Egypt. (p. 76)

Michelangelo (mī kəl an′ jə lō), A.D. 1475–1564 Italian Renaissance artist; created the *Pietà* and the paintings of the Sistine Chapel. (p. 237)

Moses (mō′ ziz), 1200s B.C. A great leader of the ancient Hebrews; led his people out of captivity in Egypt. (p. 111)

Muhammad (mù ham′ əd), about A.D. 570–632 Founder of Islam. (p. 365)

N

Nasser, Gamal Abdel (nä′ sər), A.D. 1918–1970 Egypt's first president. (p. 387)

Nehru, Jawaharlal (nā′ rü), A.D. 1889–1964 Follower of Mohandas Gandhi; India's first prime minister. (p. 479)

Newton, Isaac (nüt′ ən), A.D. 1642–1727 Englishman who discovered the law of gravity; found final proof of the heliocentric theory. (p. 266)

Nkrumah, Kwame (ən krü′ mə), A.D. 1909–1972 Leader in the African independence movement; President of Ghana from 1960–1966. (p. 440)

O

Octavian (ok tā′ vē ən), about 63 B.C.–A.D. 14 Popular Roman general; ruled the Roman Empire for 41 years. (p. 188)

P

Paul (pôl), about A.D. 11–67 Follower of Jesus who spread the teachings of early Christianity throughout the Roman Empire. (p. 197)

Pericles (pâr′ ə klēz), about 495–429 B.C. Athenian leader; led Athens during the height of its power and influence. (p. 151)

Peter (pē′ tər), about A.D. 5–64 One of the 12 apostles; the first bishop of Rome. (p. 198)

Peter the Great (pē′ tər thə grāt), A.D. 1672–1725 Tsar of Russia from 1682 to 1725; building St. Petersburg was one of his legacies. (p 307)

Petrarch (pē′ trärk), A.D. 1304–1374 Italian poet and scholar whose interest in ancient literature helped spark the Renaissance. (p. 235)

Phillip II (fil′ əp), 382–336 B.C. King of Macedonia; father of Alexander the Great. (p. 166)

BIOGRAPHICAL DICTIONARY

Piankhi (pyan' kē), about 741–715 B.C. Kushite king who conquered Egypt in 721 B.C. (p. 418)

Plato (plā' tō), about 428–347 B.C. Greek philosopher; student of Socrates. (p. 160)

Polo, Marco (pō' lō), A.D. 1254–1324 Italian merchant who journeyed to China. (p. 257)

Pol Pot (pôl pät), A.D. 1928– Former communist dictator of Cambodia. (p. 563)

R

Ramses II (ram' sēz), c. 1326–1237 B.C. Ruler of Egypt from 1304–1237 B.C. (p. 88)

Rhodes, Cecil (rōdz), A.D. 1853–1902 British imperialist leader in southern Africa. (p. 434)

Roosevelt, Franklin (rō' zə velt), A.D. 1882–1945 President of the United States from 1933 to 1945; led the country through World War II. (p. 329)

Rurik (rü' rik), about A.D. 800–879 Viking leader who ruled near Novgorod in Russia. (p. 305)

S

Scipio (sip' ē ō), about 234–183 B.C. Roman general who defeated Hannibal. (p. 185)

Shah, Rezah (shä, ri zä'), A.D. 1878–1944 Persian general who freed his people from European control. He founded Iran. (p. 382)

Shakespeare, William (shāk' spîr), A.D. 1564–1616 Great English writer of poetry and plays. (p. 248)

Shihuangdi (shē' hwäng dē), about 299–250 B.C. Emperor of China and founder of the Qin dynasty; extended the Great Wall of China. (p. 501)

Shikibu, Murasaki (shē' kē bü), about A.D. 970–1013 Early Japanese writer; wrote *Tale of the Genji,* called the world's first novel. (p. 532)

Shotoku (shō' tō kù), about A.D. 573–621 Ruler of Japan who welcomed Buddhist teachings. (p. 531)

Socrates (sok' rə tēz), about 470–399 B.C. Greek philosopher and teacher. (p. 159)

Solomon (sol' ə mən), about 990–933 B.C. King of Israel in the tenth century B.C.; noted for his tremendous wisdom. (p. 113)

Spitz, Mark (spits), A.D. 1950– United States swimmer who won seven gold medals and set seven world records in the 1972 Olympics. (p. 161)

Stalin, Joseph (stä' lin), A.D. 1879–1953 Soviet revolutionary leader and dictator; ruled the Soviet Union from 1924 to 1953. (p. 328)

Stanley, Henry (stan' lē), A.D. 1841–1904 British journalist and explorer in Africa. (p. 435)

Sun Yat-sen (sun yat' sen), A.D. 1866–1925 Leader of the Chinese Nationalists. (p. 513)

T

Tasman, Abel (täs' män), A.D. 1603–1659 Dutch explorer; reached the island south of Australia known today as Tasmania in 1642. (p. 579)

Thucydides (thü sid' ə dēz), about 460 to 400 B.C. Greek historian. (p. 165)

Touré, Sékou (tü rā'), A.D. 1922–1984 African leader; helped Guinea achieve independence in 1958; President of Guinea from 1958 to 1984. (p. 441)

Tutankhamen (tü täng kä' mən), about 1371–1352 B.C. Egyptian pharaoh; began his rule when he was 9 years old; died at 19 in 1352 B.C. (p. 82)

V

Virgil (vûr' jəl), 70–19 B.C. Roman writer; wrote an epic poem called the *Aeneid.* (p. 193)

W

Walesa, Lech (vä len' sə), A.D. 1943– President of Poland since 1990; winner of the Nobel Peace Prize in 1985. (p. 338)

Watt, James (wot), A.D. 1736–1819 Scottish inventor; developed a steam engine that burned coal. (p. 283)

Y

Yeltsin, Boris (yelt' sin), A.D. 1931– Russian political leader and outspoken democrat. President of Russia since 1991. (p. 340)

Yi Sunsin (yē sun sin'), A.D. 1545–1598 Korean admiral who drove the Japanese out of his country in 1592. (p. 538)

Yoritomo (yô rē' tō mō), A.D. 1148–1199 Japanese samurai and first shogun of Japan. (p. 533)

BIOGRAPHICAL DICTIONARY

a cap; ā cake; ä father; är car; âr dare; ch chain; e hen; ē me; êr clear; hw where; i bib; ī kite; ng song; o top; ō rope; ô saw; oi coin; ôr fork; ou cow; sh show; th thin; <u>th</u> those; u sun; ù book; ü moon; ū cute; ûr term; ə about, taken, pencil, apron, helpful; ər letter, dollar, doctor

GLOSSARY

This Glossary will help you to pronounce and understand the meanings of the Key Vocabulary in this book. The page number at the end of the definition tells where the word first appears.

A

abolition (ab ə lish′ ən) The act of doing away with something. (p. 310)

absolute monarchy (ab′ sə lüt mon′ ər kē) Rule by a monarch who has complete power to govern. (p. 249)

acid rain (as′ id rān) A type of pollution caused when rain water mixes with pollutants in the atmosphere. (p. 344)

Acropolis (ə krop′ ə lis) A hilltop fortress in ancient Athens, which included the Parthenon and other famous buildings, where citizens met to discuss affairs of the community. (p. 146)

agora (ag′ ə rə) The central marketplace in ancient Athens and the site of numerous temples and government buildings. (p. 146)

alliance (ə lī′ əns) A formal agreement between two or more nations to work together in war or commerce. (p. 323)

almanac (ôl′ mə nak) A reference book published every year with up-to-date facts on a variety of subjects. (p. 244)

altitude (al′ tə tüd) Height above sea level. (p. 28)

ancestor (an′ ses tər) The people from whom a person is descended. (p. 126)

apartheid (ə pär′ tīd) A policy of the South African government that was designed to keep the races separate and unequal. (p. 443)

apostle (ə pos′ əl) One of the 12 original followers of Jesus of Nazareth. (p. 196)

apprentice (ə pren′ tis) A person who lived and worked, without pay, with a master craftsman in order to learn a trade. (p. 228)

aqueduct (ak′ wə dukt) A large stone structure built by the Romans to carry water from one place to another. (p. 192)

archaeology (är kē ol′ ə jē) The study of the remains of past cultures. (p. 59)

archipelago (är kə pel′ ə gō) A group of islands. (p. 525)

architecture (är′ kə tek chər) The science of building. (p. 190)

arid (ar′ id) Receiving little rainfall; dry. (p. 360)

aristocracy (ar is tok′ rə sē) Members of noble families as a class; the Second Estate in France. (p. 289)

armada (är mä′ də) A fleet of warships. (p. 246)

artifacts (är′ tə fakts) Objects that were made by people long ago, such as tools and pottery. (p. 58)

artisan (är′ tə zən) A person skilled in crafts such as carving or tool-making; craftsworker. (p. 56)

assembly (ə sem′ blē) The basic lawmaking body in a democracy, made up of a group of citizens. (p. 151)

astrolabe (as′ trə lāb) An instrument invented by Muslims to determine the positions of the stars, often used for sea and desert travel. (p. 372)

astronomy (əs tron′ ə mē) The study of the planets, stars, and other heavenly bodies. (p. 259)

atlas (at′ ləs) A book of maps. (p. 244)

atoll (at′ ôl) A ring-shaped coral island that surrounds a lagoon. (p. 574)

axis (ak′ sis) One of the horizontal or vertical lines that make up the grid of a line graph; also an imaginary line that runs from the North Pole and South Pole. (p. 486)

B

bar graph (bär graf) A chart that is used to compare amounts. (p. 486)

barter (bär′ ter) Trade of one kind of product for another without the use of money. (p. 99)

basin (bā′ sin) An area of land drained by a river and its tributaries. (p. 176)

Bill of Rights (bil əv rīts) A political document written by the English Parliament in 1689 that gave certain rights to citizens and limited the powers of the monarchy. (p. 249)

bishop (bish′ əp) A church official who leads a large group of Christians. (p. 198)

blitzkrieg (blits′ krēg) the ''lightning war'' used by the Germans in World War II, which made full use of the weapons of modern war in order to win quick victories. (p. 328)

boomerang (bü′ mə rang) An elbow-shaped flat piece of wood that is used by the Aborigines of Australia for the hunting of birds and small animals, which, when thrown correctly, returns to the thrower. (p. 578)

boundary (boun′ dər ē) An imaginary line dividing one country from another. (p. 92)

boycott (boi′ kot) A special kind of protest in which a group of people refuse to buy or use goods that were produced by another group. (p. 441)

Buddhism (bùd′ iz əm) A world religion founded by Siddharta Guatama (Buddha) in India in the sixth century B.C. (p. 471)

C

caliph (kā′ lif) A term for a leader of Islam who came after Muhammad and who had both political and religious authority. (p. 370)

caravan (kâr′ ə van) A group of travelers, merchants, or pilgrims traveling together for safety and security, especially through desert or dangerous regions. (p. 361)

caravel (kâr′ ə vel) A sailing vessel developed in Europe which, because of its large size and triangular sails, allowed Europeans to safely sail greater distances. (p. 259)

cardinal directions (kärd′ ən əl di rek′ shənz) The directions north, south, east, and west. (p. 9)

cash crop (kash krop) A plant or plant product raised to make money. (p. 589)

caste (kast) One of the rigid social classes into which Hindu society was divided. (p. 469)

cataract (kat′ ə rakt) A waterfall or churning rapids in a river. (p. 93)

cathedral (kə thē′ drəl) A large and elaborate Christian church; many of the greatest cathedrals were built during the Middle Ages in Europe. (p. 222)

cause (kôz) Something that makes something else happen. (p. 230)

charter (chär′ tər) A formal document setting forth the goals and principles of an organization. (p. 228)

Christianity (kris chē an′ ə tē) A world religion founded by Jesus of Nazareth and based on his teachings. (p. 195)

circle graph (sûr kəl graf) A chart showing how parts of something are related to each other and to the whole. (p. 486)

citadel (sit′ ə del) A walled-in area, similar to a fortress, that was built to protect a city. (p. 122)

city-state (sit′ ē stāt) A self-governing city and the lands surrounding it. (p. 101)

civil disobedience (siv′ əl dis ə bē′ dē əns) The act of disobeying certain laws as a means of protesting against something considered to be morally wrong. (p. 478)

civil war (siv′ əl wôr) A conflict in which people within one country fight each other. (p. 188)

civilization (siv ə li zā′ shən) A society that has achieved a high level of culture including the development of systems of government, religion, and learning. (p. 52)

clan (klan) In ancient Japan, a group of people who believed they were descended from the same ancestor. (p. 530)

classics (klas′ iks) The literature of ancient Greece and Rome. (p. 236)

climate (klī′ mit) The pattern of weather that an area has over a long period of time. (p. 26)

Code of Hammurabi (kōd uv hä mü rä′ bē) The world's first system of laws, recorded by Hammurabi, king of Babylonia, around 1780 B.C. (p. 105)

Cold War (kōld wôr) A term used to describe the tensions that developed after World War II between the democratic nations of the West and the Soviet Union. (p. 337)

collective farm (kə lek′ tiv färm) A large farm owned by the government and worked by hundreds of families. (p. 315)

colony (kol′ ə nē) A territory that is under the control of another, usually distant, country. (p. 142)

GLOSSARY

GLOSSARY

Colosseum (kol ə sē′ əm) A large sports arena in ancient Rome. (p. 190)

comedy (kom′ ə dē) A play that is funny and usually has a happy ending. (p. 159)

commerce (kom′ ərs) The buying and selling of goods. (p. 226)

commune (kom′ ūn) A way of producing food in which all the farms of an area are joined together into a single unit. (p. 519)

communism (kom′ yə niz əm) A political and economic system in which land and businesses are controlled by the government. (p. 313)

compass (kum′ pəs) A device showing the direction of the magnetic north that is used to find geographical direction. (p. 259)

concentration camp (kon sen trā′ shən kamp) A type of prison built by the Nazis in which millions of people were murdered. (p. 333)

conserve (kən sûrv′) To use natural resources wisely and with a view toward protecting the environment. (p. 601)

constitutional monarchy (kon stə tü′ shən əl mon′ ər kē) A government headed by a king or queen whose powers are limited by a constitution. (p. 249)

consul (kon′ səl) One of two people elected by the Roman Senate who governed Rome and commanded its army. (p. 181)

continent (kont′ ən ənt) A large body of land. There are seven continents. (p. 7)

contour line (kon′ tùr līn) A line on a contour map that connects areas of the same elevation. (p. 178)

contour map (kon′ tùr map) A map that shows the shape of the land and gives detailed information about the earth's surface. (p. 178)

convent (kon′ vent) A religious community in which nuns lead simple lives of work and prayer. (p. 219)

coral reef (kôr′ əl rēf) A long stretch of coral rock in the sea. (p. 573)

Crusades (krü sādz′) A series of "holy wars" in the Middle Ages in which European Christians attempted to recapture the Holy Land (Palestine) from Muslims. (p. 225)

cultivate (kul′ tə vāt) To prepare and use land for raising crops; cultivation marked the beginning of the New Stone Age. (p. 53)

Cultural Revolution (kul′ chər əl rev ə lü′ shən) A period of chaos in the 1960s in China when the Communist party under Mao Zedong attempted to make sweeping changes in society. (p. 519)

culture (kul′ chər) The way of life of a group of people at a particular time, including their customs, beliefs, and arts. (p. 39)

cuneiform (kū nē′ ə fôrm) A system of writing developed in ancient Sumer that used wedge-shaped symbols. (p. 102)

current (kûr′ ənt) A portion of a body of water or air continuously flowing in approximately the same path. (p. 29)

custom (kus′ təm) A social habit or way of living in a group. (p. 39)

D

degree (di grē′) A unit of measurement indicating the distance between lines of latitude and lines of longitude. (p. 34)

delta (del′ tə) A triangle-shaped area of marshy land made by deposits of silt, sand, and small stones at the mouth of a river. (p. 73)

democracy (di mok′ rə sē) A government run by the people, in which citizens make their own laws. (p. 151)

depression (di presh′ ən) A severe slowdown in business characterized by high unemployment and falling prices. (p. 326)

desert (dez′ ərt) A very dry region that receives less than 10 inches (25 cm) of rain per year. (p. 358)

developing nation (di vel′ ə ping nā′ shən) A poor country that is working to build a strong economy, strong industries, and a higher standard of living for its people. (p. 598)

dictator (dik′ tā tər) A ruler who has absolute power and authority. (p. 187)

dictionary (dik′ shə når ē) A reference book that gives the meanings of words and tells how to pronounce them. (p. 244)

distortion (dis tôr′ shən) The state of being distorted, or twisted, or bent out of shape. (p. 426)

distribution map (dis trə bū′ shən map) A special-purpose map that shows how one particular feature, such as vegetation, is spread over an area. (p. 115)

divine right (di vīn′ rīt) The belief that a monarch received authority to rule from God and could therefore not be questioned. (p. 288)

domesticate (də məs′ tə kāt) To tame in order to make useful to people; animals were domesticated in the New Stone Age. (p. 52)

drought (drout) A long period of dry weather. (p. 98)

dynasty (dī′ nəs tē) A line of rulers who belong to the same family and pass control from one generation to the next. (p. 125)

E

economy (i kon′ ə mē) The use of workers and resources to produce goods and services. (p. 74)

edict (ē′ dikt) A public announcement. (p. 472)

effect (i fekt′) Something that happens as a result of a cause. (p. 230)

empire (em′ pīr) A group of lands and people under one government. (p. 80)

encyclopedia (en sī klə pē′ dē ə) A book or series of books containing articles on many subjects, including important people, places, and events. (p. 244)

environment (en vī′ rən mənt) All the surroundings of a place, such as land, water, weather, plants, and the changes people have made. (p. 21)

epic (ep′ ik) A long poem that celebrates gods, heroes, or events in a people's past. (p. 155)

equal-area projection (ē kwəl âr′ ē ə prə jek′ shən) A map that is useful for showing the whole earth at a glance, on which shapes at the center are fairly accurate but extremely distorted at the edges. (p. 426)

equator (i kwā′ tər) An imaginary line circling the earth halfway between the North and South poles and dividing the earth into Northern and Southern hemispheres. (p. 8)

equatorial (ē kwə tôr′ ē əl) Near the equator. (p. 414)

erosion (i rō′ zhən) The gradual wearing away of land by wind, glaciers, running water, or waves. (p. 359)

estates (e stāts′) The three classes into which the people of France were divided at the time of the French Revolution, including priests, the aristocracy, and common people. (p. 288)

export (eks′ pôrt) A good or product that is sold by one country to another. (p. 388)

F

fact (fakt) A statement that can be proven true. (p. 262)

factory (fak′ tər ē) A building that is used for manufacturing. (p. 282)

famine (fam′ in) A widespread lack of food resulting in hunger and starvation. (p. 98)

feudalism (fūd′ əl iz əm) An economic and political system of Europe in the Middle Ages. (p. 216)

fief (fēf) In the Middle Ages, a large piece of land granted by a king to a lord in exchange for his loyalty. (p. 216)

forum (fôr′ əm) A marketplace in the center of ancient Rome surrounded by public buildings. (p. 192)

free enterprise (frē en′ tər prīz) In a capitalist economy, the freedom to own property and run a business largely free of government control. (p. 597)

G

gazetteer (gaz ə têr′) A list of places of geographical significance, such as countries, cities, rivers, and deserts. (p. 25)

geocentric theory (jē ō sen′ trik thē′ ər ē) The idea that the earth was the center of the universe and that the sun, stars and planets revolved around the earth. (p. 264)

geography (jē og′ rə fē) The study of the earth, how its features affect human life, and how the earth is affected by human activities. (p. 21)

glacier (glā′ shər) A great sheet of slowly moving ice. (p. 43)

gladiator (glad′ ē ā tər) A person, often a slave, prisoner of war, or criminal who fought in the Roman Colosseum or similar arena to entertain the public. (p. 191)

Golden Horde (gōl′ dən hôrd) The Mongol army that conquered large areas of Russia and Central Asia in the thirteenth century. (p. 306)

government (guv′ ərn mənt) The established form of ruling a place. (p. 41)

graph (graf) A chart or diagram that shows statistics in a visual way. (p. 486)

gravity (grav′ ə tē) The force that causes objects to be pulled toward the center of the earth. (p. 266)

great circle (grāt sûr′ kəl) Any circle that divides the earth into equal halves, or hemispheres. (p. 528)

great-circle route (grāt sûr′ kəl rüt) The shortest, most direct route between any two places on the earth, often used by ships and planes. (p. 528)

grid (grid) A pattern of parallels and meridians that cross each other on a map or globe. This pattern makes it possible to pinpoint exact locations. (p. 35)

grid map (grid map) A map that is divided into a series of squares that can be identified by letters and numbers. Grid maps make it easier to find a place. (p. 15)

gross national product (grōs nash′ ən əl prod′ əkt) The total value of all goods and services a nation produces each year. (p. 540)

a cap; ā cake; ä father; är car; âr dare; ch chain; e hen; ē me; êr clear; hw where; i bib; ī kite; ng song; o top; ō rope; ô saw; oi coin; ôr fork; ou cow; sh show; th thin; <u>th</u> those; u sun; u̇ book; ü moon; ū cute; ûr term; ə about, taken, pencil, apron, helpful; ər letter, dollar, doctor

GLOSSARY

635

guild (gild) An organization of people, such as weavers and shoemakers, who practiced the same craft, formed to set standards and promote the interests of the craft. (p. 228)

Gulf Stream (gulf strēm) A warm ocean current, beginning in the Gulf of Mexico, that brings temperate air to Europe. (p. 212)

H

heliocentric theory (hē lē ō sen′ trik thē′ ər ē) Based on Copernicus's ideas, the idea that the earth and other planets moved around the sun. (p. 265)

helot (hel′ ət) A person captured in war by Sparta and forced to live as a slave. (p. 145)

hemisphere (hem′ is fêr) One of the halves of the earth, including the Eastern and Western hemispheres to the east and west of the prime meridian and the Northern and Southern hemispheres to the north and the south of the equator. (p. 7)

hieroglyphics (hī ər ə glif′ iks) A system of writing developed in ancient Egypt that used pictures and signs to stand for objects, sounds, and ideas. (p. 83)

Hinduism (hin′ dü iz əm) A world religion that grew out of the Aryan myths of ancient India. (p. 468)

historical map (his tôr′ i kəl map) A map showing historical information, such as a series of battles or the stages in the growth of an empire. (p. 92)

history (his′ tər ē) The record of what has happened in the past. (p. 58)

Holocaust (hol′ ə kôst) The deliberate killing of millions of Jewish people by the Nazis during World War II. (p. 330)

horizontal axis (hôr ə zont′ əl ak′ sis) The bottom line in the grid of a line graph, showing information, such as days or years, that changes at a given rate. (p. 486)

I

Ice Age (īs āj) A long period in the past that lasted for millions of years; glaciers covered much of the earth during the Ice Age. (p. 43)

imperialism (im per′ ē ə liz əm) The extension of a country's power over other lands by military, political, or economic means. (p. 433)

import (im′ pôrt) A good or product that one nation buys from another nation. (p. 388)

Industrial Revolution (in dus′ trē əl rev ə lü′ shən) A term for sweeping changes in the way goods were produced and the way people lived and worked that began in England and eventually spread throughout Europe and the world. (p. 281)

interdependent (in tər di pen′ dənt) Relying on one another to help satisfy needs and wants. (p. 598)

intermediate directions (in tər mē′ dē it di rek′ shənz) The directions halfway between the cardinal directions; northeast, southeast, southwest, and northwest. (p. 9)

International Date Line (in tər nash′ ən əl dāt′ līn) An imaginary line, mainly in the Pacific Ocean, that marks the boundary between one day and the next. (p. 496)

intifada (in tē fa′ də) The Palestinian uprising against Israeli rule that began in 1987; an Arabic word meaning "stirring" or "uprising." (p. 392)

Iron Curtain (ī′ ərn kûr′ tin) An imaginary border that separated the democratic nations of Western Europe from the nations in Eastern Europe under the control of the Soviet Union. (p. 337)

irrigation (êr ə gā′ shən) The watering of dry land by means of streams, canals, or pipes in order to grow more crops. (p. 75)

Islam (is′ lam) A world religion founded by Muhammad in the eighth century A.D. on the Arabian peninsula. (p. 364)

J

journeyman (jûr′ nē mən) A person in the Middle Ages who had completed his apprenticeship and was paid for his work. (p. 228)

Judaism (jü′ dē iz əm) A world religion founded by the ancient Hebrews. (p. 110)

K

Kaaba (kä′ bə) A religious building in Mecca, now sacred to Muslims, where Arabs worshiped many different gods and goddesses in the days before Muhammad. (p. 366)

kente (ken′ tā) A traditional cloth woven by the Asante and Ewa peoples of West Africa. (p. 448)

knight (nīt) A son of a noble, who was a trained soldier and gave military service in exchange for the right to hold land. (p. 217)

Koran (kô ran′) The sacred book of the Muslims, containing the word of God as revealed to Muhammad. (p. 367)

L

lagoon (lə gün′) A shallow body of water partly or completely surrounded by an atoll. (p. 574)

landform map (land′ fôrm map) A physical map showing how the earth's surface varies from place to place. Landform maps use colors or different shades to show mountains, hills, plains, and other features. (p. 13)

large-scale map (lärj skāl map) A map showing a small part of the earth in a fairly large space, thus showing considerable detail per unit of measurement. (p. 363)

GLOSSARY

latitude (lat′ ə tüd) The distance north or south of the equator, expressed in degrees. (p. 28)

legacy (leg′ ə sē) The traditions and knowledge of a culture that have been handed down to people today. (p. 42)

line graph (līn graf) A chart showing how one kind of information changes continuously in relation to another chart, such as the growth of population in a country over a ten-year period. (p. 486)

literacy (lit′ ər ə sē) The ability to read and write. (p. 482)

Long March (lông märch) A march across China in 1934–1935 by the Communist army led by Mao Zedong; the march was an attempt to find refuge from Nationalist forces. (p. 514)

longitude (lon′ jə tüd) The distance east or west of the prime meridian, expressed in degrees. (p. 34)

lord (lôrd) An important noble in the Middle Ages. (p. 216)

M

Magna Carta (mag′ nə kär′ tə) A document drawn up by English nobles in 1215 that spelled out certain rights and limited the king's power. (p. 229)

mainland (mān′ land) The principal land of a continent not including islands and small peninsulas. (p. 555)

Mandate of Heaven (man′ dāt əv hev′ ən) The belief of Chinese emperors that they had received their right to rule from the god of the sky. (p. 499)

manor (man′ ər) A large self-sufficient farming estate where nobles and serfs lived and worked. (p. 217)

map key (map kē) A list of map symbols with an explanation of what each symbol stands for. (p. 11)

martial law (mär′ shəl lô) Military rule. (p. 565)

mercator projection (mər kā′ tər prə jek′ shən) A map that gives accurate shapes of land masses and correct straight-line directions, but which shows considerable size distortion in the higher latitudes. (p. 427)

meridian (mə rid′ ē ən) Any line of longitude west or east of the prime meridian. (p. 35)

Middle Ages (mid′ əl āj′ əz) The period in European history between the end of the Roman Empire and the beginning of the modern era; the Middle Ages lasted from around A.D. 500 to 1500. (p. 214)

middle class (mid′ əl klas) During the Industrial Revolution, the new class of business people. (p. 284)

migration (mī grā′ shən) The movement of a large group of people from one country or region to another in order to settle there. (p. 123)

mineral (min′ ər əl) A natural substance, such as iron, copper, or salt, that is reached by digging into the earth. (p. 31)

missionary (mish′ ə när′ ē) A person who tries to spread his or her religion to others with different beliefs. (p. 434)

monarchy (mon′ ər kē) A government headed by a king or queen. (p. 150)

monastery (mon′ əs tär ē) A religious community in which monks live simple lives of work and prayer. (p. 219)

monk (mungk) A religious man who lives in a monastery and worships God with other monks. (p. 219)

monotheism (mon′ ə thē iz əm) Belief in one God. (p. 113)

monsoon (mon sün′) A seasonal wind of the Indian Ocean and southern Asia, which blows from the southwest toward the land in summer and from the northeast toward the ocean in winter. (p. 466)

mosque (mosk) A Muslim place of worship. (p. 374)

myth (mith) A story about the gods and goddesses of a particular people. (p. 154)

N

nationalism (nash′ ən əl iz əm) A feeling of intense loyalty and devotion to one's country. (p. 323)

NATO (nā′ tō) The North Atlantic Treaty Organization formed in 1949. (p. 338)

natural resource (nach′ ər əl rē′ sôrs) Something in nature that is useful or essential to humans, such as water, air, soil, or animals. (p. 31)

a cap; ā cake; ä father; är car; âr dare; ch chain; e hen; ē me; êr clear; hw where; i bib; ī kite; ng song; o top; ō rope; ô saw; oi coin; ôr fork; ou cow; sh show; th thin; th those; u sun; ů book; ü moon; ū cute; ûr term; ə about, taken, pencil, apron, helpful; ər letter, dollar, doctor

GLOSSARY

New Stone Age (nü stōn āj) A period in social development that started about 8000 B.C., in which people first domesticated animals, farmed the land, and lived in settled communities. (p. 52)

New Testament (nü tes' tə mənt) The second part of the Bible, containing the life and teachings of Jesus and the story of early Christianity. (p. 195)

nomad (nō' mad) A person without a permanent home who travels from place to place in search of food. (p. 44)

nonrenewable resource (non ri nü' ə bəl rē' sôrs) A natural resource that can never be replaced once it is used, such as coal, oil, or metal. (p. 32)

No Rooz (nō rūz') An Iranian new year's celebration. (p. 394)

North Atlantic Drift (nôrth at lan' tik drift) A warm ocean current in the North Atlantic that flows toward the British Isles; this current helps give northwestern Europe a mild climate. (p. 212)

nun (nun) A religious woman who lives in a convent and worships God with other nuns. (p. 219)

O

oasis (ō ā' sis) A well-watered place in the desert. (p. 364)

Old Stone Age (ōld stōn āj) The earliest period of human culture, beginning about two million years ago and lasting until about 8000 B.C. (p. 43)

oligarchy (ol' ə gär kē) A government that is run by a few people, usually by members of rich, powerful families. (p. 150)

OPEC (ō' pek) An organization formed in 1960 by the oil-producing nations of the world. The OPEC nations work together to control the supply and price of oil on world markets. (p. 389)

opinion (ə pin' yən) A personal view or belief that cannot be proven true. (p. 262)

oppression (ə presh' ən) The act of governing cruelly and unjustly. (p. 306)

oracle (ôr' ə kəl) A special priest in ancient Chinese society who was believed to receive messages from the gods. (p. 127)

outback (out' bak) A vast, dry region that makes up much of Australia. (p. 571)

P

paddy (pad' ē) A shallow flooded field in China where rice is grown. (p. 495)

papyrus (pə pī' rəs) A type of paper made from reeds and used by the ancient Egyptians for writing and keeping records. (p. 84)

parallel (pâr' ə lel) Any line of latitude. Lines that are parallel never meet or cross. (p. 34)

Parliament (pär' lə mənt) The lawmaking body in Great Britain, made up of the House of Commons and the House of the Lords. (p. 248)

patrician (pə trish' ən) A member of a class of wealthy families who held all power in the early Roman Republic. (p. 181)

patron (pā' trən) A person who uses his or her money or influence to support another person, such as an artist or a writer. (p. 236)

Pax Romana (päks rō mä' nə) A period of peace in the Roman Empire that lasted about 200 years, during which trade flourished and the empire reached its greatest extent. (p. 189)

peninsula (pə nin' sə lə) Land that is surrounded by water on three sides. (p. 139)

per capita income (pûr kap' i tə in' kum) The amount of income each person would have if the country's total income were divided equally among all its people. (p. 541)

permafrost (pûr' mə frôst) Permanently frozen earth a few feet below ground level, found in arctic regions. (p. 303)

pharaoh (far' ō) The supreme ruler of ancient Egypt. (p. 76)

philosophy (fə los' ə fē) The study of the basic nature and purpose of life; the search for truth. (p. 159)

physical map (fiz' i kəl map) A map that shows primarily the natural features of the earth, such as lakes, rivers, mountains, and deserts. (p. 13)

pilgrimage (pil' grə mij) A journey to a holy place for a religious purpose. (p. 224)

plantation (plan tā' shən) A large farming estate where mainly one crop is grown; slaves were often used on plantations. (p. 432)

plateau (pla tō') An area of flat land that rises above the surrounding land. (p. 124)

plebeian (pli bē' ən) A member of the common people in ancient Rome. (p. 181)

point of view (point əv vū) The position of an author toward his or her subject; manner of thinking or feeling about something; attitude. (p. 326)

polar climate (pō' lər klī' mit) The climate of the earth's polar regions, characterized by short summers and long winters. (p. 28)

polar projection (pō' lər prə jek' shən) A map projection centered on either the North or South pole. (p. 427)

polis (po' ləs) A city-state in ancient Greece. (p. 144)

political map (pə lit' i kəl map) A map showing primarily political divisions, such as national or state boundaries, important cities, and capitals. (p. 12)

pollution (pə lü' shən) Unwanted or harmful substances in the environment. (p. 600)

polytheism (pol′ ē thē iz əm) Belief in many gods. (p. 113)

pope (pōp) The bishop of Rome and head of the Roman Catholic Church. (p. 198)

population density (pop yə lā′ shən den′ sə tē) The average number of people living in a given space. (p. 316)

precipitation (pri sip ə tā′ shən) Moisture in the form of rain or snow. (p. 26)

prehistory (prē his′ tər ē) The period before events were recorded in writing; the Old and New Stone Age. (p. 58)

primary source (prī′ mâr ē sôrs) A first-hand account of an event, such as an official document, a diary, or a letter. (p. 59)

prime meridian (prīm mə rid′ ē ən) The line of longitude marked 0° on the world map, from which longitude east and west is measured. (p. 8)

projection (prə jek′ shən) A systematic way of transferring locations on the earth to a map. (p. 426)

protectorate (prə tek′ tər it) A weak country that is protected and controlled by a strong country. (p. 386)

Protestant (prot′ is tənt) A Christian who opposed, or protested against, the Roman Catholic Church in the 1500s; today a member of any Protestant church. (p. 242)

pyramid (pêr′ ə mid) A huge stone structure built by the ancient Egyptians as a royal tomb, having a square base and four triangular sides. (p. 77)

R

recycle (rē sī′ kəl) To use something over and over again in order to conserve resources. (p. 601)

reference (ref′ ər əns) Any source of information, such as an almanac, encyclopedia, or atlas. (p. 244)

Reformation (ref ər mā′ shən) A religious movement in sixteenth-century Europe, led by Martin Luther, that began as an attempt to reform the Roman Catholic Church and resulted in the birth of Protestant churches. (p. 240)

refugee (ref ū jē′) A person who has to leave his or her country for safety. (p. 391)

relief (ri lēf′) The variation in elevation of an area of the earth's surface; description of the roughness of land. (p. 179)

religion (ri lij′ ən) The way people worship the God or gods they believe in. (p. 42)

Renaissance (ren ə säns′) A period of cultural and artistic flowering in Europe that began in Italy around 1350 and eventually spread throughout Europe. (p. 235)

renewable resource (ri nü′ ə bəl rē′ sôrs) A natural resource, such as plants or soil, that can be used again and again if used properly. (p. 32)

republic (ri pub′ lik) A government in which citizens have the right to choose their leaders. (p. 181)

revolution (rev ə lü′ shən) The overthrow of an existing political system and its replacement with another; any far-reaching change. (p. 281)

rift valley (rift val′ ē) A long, steep-sided valley lying between two parallel faults. (p. 414)

Roman Catholic (rō′ mən kath′ ə lik) A person who belongs to the branch of Christianity headed by the pope in Rome. (p. 240)

Romance language (ro mans′ lang′ gwij) One of several modern languages, such as French, Spanish, and Italian, that is descended from Latin. (p. 193)

Rosetta Stone (rō zet′ ə stōn) A large inscribed stone discovered in Rosetta, Egypt, in 1799. Because it contained carvings in three languages—hieroglyphics, late Egyptian, and Greek—the Rosetta Stone enabled scholars to learn the meaning of hieroglyphics. (p. 85)

S

Sahel (sa′ hil) A narrow belt of semiarid grassland extending across the African continent and bordering on desert lands. (p. 415)

saint (sānt) According to Roman Catholic teachings, a man or woman believed to be especially holy. (p. 222)

samurai (sam′ ù rī) A class of warriors in feudal Japan who fought for lords and swore loyalty to them. (p. 533)

sanctions (sangk′ shənz) Actions, such as boycotts or trade restrictions, taken by one or more countries to keep certain benefits from another country. (p. 444)

savanna (sə van′ ə) A broad, grassy plain covering more than one third of the African continent. (p. 415)

a cap; ā cake; ä father; är car; âr dare; ch chain; e hen; ē me; êr clear; hw where; i bib; ī kite; ng song; o top; ō rope; ô saw; oi coin; ôr fork; ou cow; sh show; th thin; <u>th</u> those; u sun; ù book; ü moon; ū cute; ûr term; ə about, taken, pencil, apron, helpful; ər letter, dollar, doctor

GLOSSARY

scale (skāl) Relative size as shown on a map, such as 1 inch = 100 miles (161 kilometers). (p. 9)

scribe (skrīb) A person whose profession was writing down or copying letters, contracts, and other documents. (p. 84)

secondary source (sek′ ən dâr ē sôrs) A written record of the past, such as a book by a historian, that is based on information from a primary source or sources. (p. 60)

Senate (sen′ it) The lawmaking body of ancient Rome. (p. 181)

serf (sûrf) A person who was bound to live and work on the land of a noble. (p. 216)

shah (shä) The former hereditary ruler of Iran. (p. 382)

sheik (shēk) A leader of a nomadic group or town in the Middle East. (p. 365)

Shintoism (shin′ tō iz əm) A religion based in Japan, marked by worship of nature and reverence for ancestors. (p. 530)

shogun (shō′ gən) The supreme ruler of feudal Japan, whose power was based on his control of the emperor's army. (p. 533)

silt (silt) Bits of black soil, sand, and clay laid down by flowing water. (p. 72)

slavery (slā′ və rē) The practice of owning people as property. (p. 86)

slave trade (slāv trād) A form of commerce that involved the buying and selling of Africans as slaves. (p. 432)

small-scale map (smôl skāl map) A map on which a small measurement, such as an inch or centimeter, stands for hundreds or thousands of miles. (p. 362)

socialism (sō′ shə liz əm) An economic system in which the government controls all natural resources and industry; also a political philosophy based on the writings of Karl Marx. (p. 312)

society (sə sī′ ə te) A group of people bound together by the same culture. (p. 40)

sovereignty (sov′ rən tē) Political control over a country or other community. (p. 581)

specialize (spesh′ ə līz) To be trained to do a particular kind of work. (p. 55)

station (stā′ shən) A hugh ranch in the outback of Australia where sheep and cattle are raised. (p. 587)

steppe (step) A grassy, fertile plain that covers a large region of Russia and Eastern Europe. (p. 304)

strait (strāt) A narrow waterway connecting two larger bodies of water. (p. 300)

subcontinent (sub kon′ tə nənt) A large landmass that is connected to a continent. (p. 119)

sultan (sult′ ən) A Turkish ruler in the Ottoman Empire. (p. 380)

summary (sum′ ər ē) A short account of the main ideas contained in a piece of writing (p. 129)

surplus (sûr′ plus) An extra supply of something, such as food. (p. 98)

symbol (sim′ bəl) Anything that stands for something else, such as a blue line standing for a highway on a map. (p. 11)

T

taiga (tī gə) A broad belt of forests that stretches along the Arctic Ocean from the Baltic Sea to the Pacific Ocean. (p. 303)

technology (tek nol′ ə jē) The use of skills and tools to serve human needs. (p. 56)

telescope (tel′ ə skōp) An instrument for making distant objects, such as heavenly bodies, appear nearer and larger. (p. 265)

temperate climate (tem′ pər it klī′ mit) Climate characterized by a lack of extremes in temperature. (p. 28)

Ten Commandments (ten kə mand′ mənts) According to the Bible, the ten laws God gave Moses on Mount Sinai. (p. 112)

terrace (târ′ is) A level platform of earth built into hillsides in China to increase the amount of flat land for farming. (p. 495)

territory (târ ə tôr′ ē) Any large area of land; region. (p. 186)

terrorism (târ ə riz əm) The use of violence and fear to make a government meet a group's demands. (p. 391)

textile (teks′ tīl) A fabric made by weaving or knitting; cloth. (p. 281)

time line (tīm līn) A line on which selected dates and events are written; time lines are used to show the order in which events occurred and how much time passed between events. (p. 61)

time zone (tīm zōn) A geographic region where the same standard time is used. (p. 496)

topic sentence (top′ ik sen′ təns) The sentence that contains the main idea in a paragraph. (p. 129)

totalitarian (tō tal ə târ′ ē ən) A government that controls all aspects of people's lives; totalitarian governments are led by a dictator or small group of people. (p. 314)

tradition (trə dish′ ən) A custom or belief handed down from generation to generation. (p. 48)

tragedy (traj′ ə dē) A type of play developed by the ancient Greeks, in which life is treated seriously and which usually has a sad ending. (p. 158)

GLOSSARY

tribune (trib′ ūn) An elected official in ancient Rome who represented the interests of the plebeians, or common people. (p. 182)

tributary (trib′ yə târ ē) A small river or stream that flows into a large river. (p. 120)

tropical climate (trop′ i kəl klī′ mit) The climate of the tropics, characterized by intense heat, much rain, and a lack of seasons. (p. 28)

tsar (zär) The supreme ruler of Russia until the Russian Revolution. (p. 307)

tundra (tun′ drə) A vast, treeless plain in the northern parts of Asia, Europe, and North America, having an arctic or subarctic climate and a layer of permafrost below ground. (p. 303)

Twelve Tables (twelv tā′ bəlz) A group of laws, written down in 451 B.C. and carved on 12 bronze tablets, that became the foundation of Roman law. (p. 182)

typhoon (tī fün′) A fierce storm from the Pacific Ocean that strikes Japan in the late summer and early fall. (p. 527)

tyranny (têr′ ə nē) A type of government in which all power is held in the hands of one ruler, usually a military leader. (p. 150)

U

United Nations (ū nī′ tid nā′ shənz) An organization founded in 1945 whose members include most of the nations of the world. The United Nations serves as an international forum to settle disputes and encourage cooperation among nations. (p. 336)

V

values (val′ ūz) The beliefs or ideals that guide the way people live. (p. 41)

vassal (vas′ əl) A person who, during the Middle Ages, promised to fight when needed by his lord in exchange for land. (p. 216)

Vedas (vā′ dəz) Religious songs composed by the ancient Aryans of India and written down later by Hindu priests. (p. 469)

vegetation (vej ə tā′ shən) Plant life. (p. 24)

vertical axis (vûr′ ti kəl ak′ sis) The outside left line on the grid of a line graph, on which specific information is arranged in progression. (p. 486)

W

walkabout (wôk′ ə bout) An Australian aborigine tradition. (p. 582)

warlord (wôr′ lôrd) Any of a number of army generals who seized control of large parts of China in the early twentieth century when central authority was weak. (p. 513)

Warsaw Pact (wôr′ sô pakt) An alliance of the Soviet Union and seven Eastern European nations. (p. 338)

working class (wûr′ king klas) People who work for wages. (p. 284)

Z

ziggurat (zig′ u̇ rat) A large temple built by the ancient Sumerians to honor their gods and goddesses. (p. 102)

Zionist (zī′ ə nist) A Jewish nationalist favoring the establishment of the country of Israel. (p. 382)

---

a cap; ā cake; ä father; är car; âr dare; ch chain; e hen; ē me; êr clear; hw where; i bib; ī kite; ng song; o top; ō rope; ô saw; oi coin; ôr fork; ou cow; sh show; th thin; th those; u sun; u̇ book; ü moon; ū cute; ûr term; ə about, taken, pencil, apron, helpful; ər letter, dollar, doctor

GLOSSARY

INDEX

Page references in italic type that follow an *m* indicate maps. Those following a *p* indicate photographs, artwork, or charts.

A

Aachen, 215
Abolition, 310
Aborigines, 578, *p579*
Abraham, 110
Absolute monarchy, 249, 288
Abu Simbel, 88–91
Accra, 440
Accuracy of statements, 384–385
Acid rain, 344–345, 600
Acropolis, 146, *p147*
A.D., 61
Aegean islands, 139
Aegean Sea, 358
Aegean World. *See* Greece, ancient
Aeneid, The, 193
Aeschylus, 158
Afghanistan, 483–484, *p487*
Africa, *See also* North Africa; Sub-Saharan Africa
  animals in, 416–417, *p413, p416, p417*
  Egypt, ancient, 71
  geography of, 411, 413–417, *m412*
  imperialism in, 434–437, *m436, p434*
  kingdoms in, *m419, m423*
  Kush in, 418–420
  legacy of, 425
  location of, 403, *m402*
  missionaries in, 434–435
  modern, 440–445, *m442*
  slavery in, 432–433, *p432, p433*
  Taghaza, 423–424
  Timbuktu, 424–425
Age of Exploration
  science in, 264–266
  traders and explorers during, 257–261, *m260*
Age of Faith, 222–223
Age of Pericles, 151–152
Age of the Pyramids, 77
Agora, 146, 192, *p147*
Agriculture
  in Australia, 589
  cash crops and, 589, *p589*
  in China, 494–495, 519, *p519*
  in Egypt, ancient, 74–75
  in Greece, ancient, 140
  in India, 485
  in Indus River Valley, 120
  in Mesopotamia, 98
  in Middle East, 361
  in New Zealand, 588, 589
  in North Africa, 361
  in Russia, 304
  in South Asia, 485
  in Southeast Asia, 564
  in Soviet Union, 314, *p314*
Air pollution, 599–600
Akbar, 475, 476, *p476*
al-Aqsa, 374

al-Bakri, 422
Alexander II, Tsar, 310
Alexander the Great, 166–167, *m167, p166*
Alexandria, 167, 183
Algebra, 372
Allah, 366
Alliances, 321, 327
Allied powers, 322, 329–331
Almanacs, 244
Alphabets, 128, 143, 242, *p143*
Alps, 176, 211
Altitude, 28, 178, *m29*
Anatolia, 358
Ancestors, 126
Angkor Wat, 560–561, *p561*
Animals,
  in Africa, 416–417, *p413, p416, p417*
  in Australia, 573, *p573*
  domestication of, 52–53, *p53*
  Egyptian worship of, 85
Antarctica, 26
Anyang, 125
Apartheid, 443–444
Apennines, 176
Apostles, 196
Apprentices, 228
Aqueducts, 192
Aquino, Benigno, 565
Aquino, Corazon, 565, *p565*
Arabian peninsula, 358, 360, 364
Arabian Sea, 120
Arabian Nights, The, 374, *p374*
Arabic numbers, 372
Arabs, 364–366
  Islam and, 364–365
  Palestine and, 383, 393
  in Southeast Asia, 562
Archaeology, 58–59, *p59*
Archipelagos, 525, 555
Architecture, 190, 374
Arctic Ocean, 299, 302, *m300*
Arid climate, 360
Aristocracy, 289, 292
Aristophanes, 159
Aristotle, 166, 371
Armada, 246
Armstrong, Neil, 21
Art
  Babylonian, *p106*
  Islamic, *p367, p373*
  Mogul Empire and, 475
  Renaissance, 235–239
Artifacts, 58, 59, 121, *p121, p122, p127, p216*
Artisans, 56, 226
Aryans, 123, 464, 468–469
Asia, 17, 209, *m16, m612–613.*
  See also South Asia; Southeast Asia
Asia Minor, 358
Asoka, 472–473, 478
Assembly, 151

Association of Space Explorers, 267
Astrolabe, 372, *p372*
Astronomy, 259, 372
Atatürk, Mustafa Kemal, 381
Athens, 145–146, 149, 158, 165
Atlantic Ocean, 29
Atlas, 604–617
Atlas Mountains, 413
Atolls, 574–575, *p575*
Atomic bomb, 535, *p535*
Attica, 139
Australia
  agriculture in, 589
  animals in, 573, *p573*
  as continent, 17, *m16*
  deserts in, 571–572
  geography of, 571–573, *m572*
  history of, 578–581
  minerals in, 586
  natural resources of, 586
  outback in, 571, 586–587
  people of, 578, *p579*
  ranching in, 586–587, *p587*
Australian Alps, 572
Austria, 328
Austria-Hungary, 322
Avicenna, 373
Axis, 486
Axis powers, 327–328, 329
Axum, 420, *p420*
Ayers Rock, *p573*

B

Babylon, 104, *m101*
Babylonians, 104–106, *m101, p104, p106*
Baghdad, 370
Bali, 560
Baltic Sea, 210, 211, 300, 301, 306, *m300*
Bangkok, Thailand, 564
Bangladesh, 484, *p460, p487*
Barents Sea, 300, *m300*
Bar graphs, 486–487, *p487*
Bar mitzvah, *p114*
Barter, 99
Basins, 176
Bastille, 291
Batu Khan, 306, *p306*
Bauxite, 586
B.C., 61
Bean, Alan, 393
Bedouins, 364
Beijing, China, 492, 504, 505, 521
Belgian Congo, 436
Belgium, 436
Benedict, 220
Bering Strait, 300–301
Berlin Wall, 596
Bethlehem, 194–195
Bhutan, 484
Bible, 110, 111, 195–196, *p196*

Bill of Rights (1689), 248–249, *p249*
Biographical dictionary, 628–631
Bishops, 198
Black Sea, 300, *m300*
Blitzkrieg, 328
"Boat people," 563, *p564*
Bombay, India, 482
Boomerangs, 578
Botany Bay, 580
Boundaries, 92
Boycotts, 441
Brahmins, 469
British East India Company, 476–477
British Isles, 29, 211. *See also* Great Britain
Brunei, 565
Brutus, 188
Buddhism
  in India, 470–473, *m473*
  in Japan, 531
  in Korea, 537, *p538*
  monasteries, *p492*
  in Southeast Asia, 560, *p560*

C

Caesar, Julius, 186–188, *p188*
Calcutta, India, 482
Calicut, India, 260
Caliphs, 370, *p371*
Cambodia, 563, 596
Camels, 360–361, 364, *p361, p365*
Canaan, 111
Canada, 338
Canals, 556, *p556*
Cape Comorin, 465
Cape of Good Hope, 260
Caravans, camel, 361, 364, 365, *p365*
Caravel, 259
Card catalog, 244–245
Cardinal directions, 9
Carpathian Mountains, 211, 305–306
Carter, Howard, 70, 82, *p82*
Carthage, 183, 184–185
Cartograms, 599
Cash crops, 589, *p589*
Caspian Sea, 300, *m300*
Caste system, 469–470
Catal Hüyük, 55–56, 59, 358, *p54, p55*
Cataract, 93
Cathedrals, 208, 222–223, *p208, p223*
Catherine the Great, 308
Caucasus Mountains, 209
Cause, 230–231
Cave paintings, 46, *p46*
Central Powers, 322, 380
Ceylon. *See* Sri Lanka
Chad, *p406*
Chang River, 493–494

Charlemagne, 215, 240, 368, *p215*
Charles Martel, 368
Charter, 228
Chartres Cathedral, 223,*p223*
Chiang Kai-shek, 514, *p514*
Child labor, 283, *p283*
China. *See also* Huang River Valley
    agriculture in, 494–495, 519, *p519*
    civilization of, 498–501, 504–506, *p499, m505*
    Communism in, 514–515
    confucius and, 500, *p500*
    Cultural Revolution in, 519–520
    democracy movement in, 521, *p521*
    dynasties in, 498–499, 506, *p499*
    Forbidden City in, 505, *p505*
    Four Modernizations and, 520
    geography of, 491–495, *m493, m494, m505*
    Great Wall in, 501, *p501, p502–503*
    Kublai Khan and, 257–258, 504, *p504*
    Manchus in, 511–512
    Nationalists and, 514
    Polo's travel to, 257–258
    regions of, 491–494
    Southeast Asia trade and, 559
    Sun Yat-sen and, 513
    trade in, 512
    vegetation of, *m494*
    writing, 507–510
Choson dynasty, 538
Christianity. *See also* Roman Catholic Church
    birth of, 194–195
    Constantine and, 198–199
    in Ethiopia, 420–421, *p421*
    Jesus of Nazareth and, 195–197, *p195, p196*
    in Middle Ages, 219–223
    modern, *p199*
    in Palestine, 194–195
    persecution of followers of, 198
    Reformation and, 240–243
    in Rome, ancient, 198–199, *m197*
    spread of, 197–198, *m197*
    values of, 42
Churchill, Winston, 320, 326, 328, 336–343, *p330*
Circle graphs, 486, *p487*
Citadel, 122
City-states, 101, 144–146, 425
Civil disobedience, 478, 480–481
Civilization
    beginning of, 52

    of China, 498–501, 504–506, *m505, p499*
    definition of, 52
    of Egypt, 83–87
    of Indus River Valley, 120–121
    of Mesopotamia, 100–106
Civil war
    in Afghanistan, 44
    in Pakistan, 484
    in Rome, ancient, 188
    in United States, 310
    in Yugoslavia, 341
Clans, 530, 532, *p530*
Classics, 235–236, 371, 373
Cleopatra, 187
Climate
    altitude and, 28, *m29*
    arid, 360
    currents and, 29–30, *m30*
    definition of, 26
    of earth, 26–30, *m27*
    of Europe, 212, *m213*
    influence of, 30
    of Japan, 527
    of Korea, 527
    latitude and, 28
    of Middle East, 359–360
    of North Africa, 359–360
    polar, 28
    precipitation and, 26
    of Russia, 302–303
    of South Asia, 466–467, *m466*
    temperate, 28
    tropical, 28, 557
    zones, 28, *m27*
Code of Hammurabi, 105, 152, 182, 420, *p105*
Cold War, 337, 539, 596
Collective farms, 314, *p314*
Colonialism. *See* Imperialism
Colonies, 141–143, *m142*
Colosseum, 190–191, *p191*
Columbus, Christopher, 261, *m260, p261*
Comedies, 159
Commerce, 226, 228, 365, 424. *See also* Trade
Commonwealth of Independent States, 299, 304, 341. *See also* Russia; Soviet Union
Commonwealths, 299
Communes, 519, *p519*
Communism
    in China, 514–515
    definition of, 313
    in Soviet Union, 313–314, 340–341
    spread of, 337
    uprising against, 338
    in Vietnam, 563
Compass, 259
Concentration camps, 331, *p331*
Conclusions, drawing, 438–439
Confucianism, 538
Confucius, 500, *p500*

Congo River. *See* Zaire River
Congo River Valley, 436
Conserve, 600–601
Constantine, 198–199, 379, *p198*
Constantinople, *m204*
Constitutional monarchy, 249
Constitution of the United States, 153, *p153*
Consuls, 181
Continents, 7, 17, *m7, m23*. *See also* specific names
Contour lines, 178
Contour maps, 178–179, *m178, m179*
Convents, 219–221, *p220*
Cook, James, 580, *p580*
Copernicus, 264–265, *p265*
Coral reefs, 573, 574, *p575*
Coroebus of Elis, 156
Council of Trent, 243
Credibility, 384–385
Crete, 139
Crocodiles, 417
Crusades, 224–226, *m225*
Cultivate, 53, *p53*
Cultural Revolution, 519–520
Culture
    beginning of, 46
    of Catal Hüyük, 55–56
    definition of, 39, *p40*
    of early people, 39–42
    of Etruscans, *p177*
    features of, *p40*
    government and, 41–42
    of Greece, ancient, 235–236
    of Islam, 370–375
    language and, 46
    legacy of different, 42
    of Muslims, 370–375
    religion and, 42
    of Rome, ancient, 235–236
    values and, 41
Cuneiform, 102–103, *p103*
Currents, 29–30, *m30*
Czechoslovakia, 328, 337

D

Da Gama, Vasco, 260, 465, *m260*
Danube River, 211, *p211*
Dark Ages. *See* Middle Ages
Da Vinci, Leonardo, 237–238
D-Day, 330
Dead Sea, 358
Deccan Plateau, 464
Deciduous forest, 304
Decision making, 108–109, 590
Declaration of Independence, U.S., 291
Declaration of the Rights of Man and of the Citizen, 291
Degrees, 34
De Klerk, F. W., 444
Delaware River, 107
Deltas, 73

De'Medici, Lorenzo, 236, 237
Democracy
    in China, 521, *p521*
    definition of, 151
    in Eastern Europe, 340
    in Greece, ancient, 150–153
    in Philippine Islands, 565
    in Southeast Asia, 565
    in United States, 152
Depression, 326
Deserts
    of Australia, 571–572
    Bedouin's in, 364–365
    in China, 501
    in Middle East, 358–359, *p359, p365*
    Nile River and, 72
    in North Africa, 358–359, *p359, p365*
    oases in, 50, 364, *p365*
    in sub-Saharan Africa, 415, *m415*
Developing nations, 598–599
Dias, Bartholomeu, 260, *m260*
Dictators, 187, 565
Dictionaries
    biographical, 628–631
    of geographic terms, 618–619
    using, 244
Dionysus, 157
Directions, 9
Distortions, 426
Distribution maps, 15, 316–317
Dive bombers, 328, *p328*
Divine right, 288
Dnieper River, 306
Don River, 306, 307
Dragons, 127
Drake, Francis, 247
Droughts, 98
Dunes, 358
Dynasties, 125

E

Earth
    climate of, 26–30, *m27*
    early people of, 43–46
    environments of, 21–22, *p22*
    geography of, 21–25, *m25*
    natural resources of, 31–33
    regions of, 17, *p16*
    time lines of, *p18–19, p68–69*
    vegetation of, 24, *m25*
East Germany, 336–343. *See also* Germany
Eastern Europe, 212, 337–340, 596–597
Eastern Ghats mountain range, 464
Eastern Hemisphere, 6, 8, 17, *m8, m16*
Economy. *See also* specific types

definition of, 74
of Egypt, ancient, 74, p74
of Indus River Valley, 120
of Mesopotamia, 98–99
world, 597–599
Edicts, 472
Education
in Israel, 393
in Japan, 541–542, p542
in Korea, 541–542
in Middle Ages, 220–221
in Sri Lanka, 482
on stations in Australia, 587, p587
Effect, 230–231
Egypt, ancient
agriculture in, 74–75
civilization of, 83–87
economy of, 74, p74
geography of, 71–75, m72
growth of, m93
Hebrew captivity in, 111–112
history of, 76–77, 80–82, m93, p78–79, p92
legacy of, 87
religion in, 85–86
slavery in, 86, 111
trade in, 81
women in, 87
Egypt, modern, 387
Elevation. See Altitude
Elgin Marbles, 170–171
Elizabethan England, 246–249
Elizabeth I, 246–249, p247
Empire, 80–81. See also specific names
Encyclopedias, 244
England. See Great Britain
English Channel, 247
Environments
definition of, 21
on earth, 21–22, p22
of Mesopotamia, 98
protecting, 107, 600–601
of South Asia, 467
Epics, 155–156, 193
Equal-area projections, 426, m426
Equality, 41–42
Equator, 8, 414, m8
Equatorial Africa, 414–417
Equatorial rain forests, 414
Erosion, 359, p359
Estates, 288–289, p289
Estonia, 299, 340
Ethiopia, 420–421
Etruscans, 177
Euphrates River, 97, 98, m98
Eurasia, 209
Europe. See also specific countries in
acid rain in, 344–345
climate, 212, m213
commerce in, 226–229
as continent, 17, m16
countries in, 209, p276–279
Crusades and, 224–226

Eastern, 212, 337, 596–597
European Community and, 342
geography of, 209–213, m210
Industrial Revolution in, 281–285
Islam and, 373
location of, 17
Middle Ages, life in, 214–218
NATO and, 336–343
Reformation in, 240–243
religion in, in 1500s, m243
Renaissance art in, 235–239
Roman Catholic Church and, 219–223
science in, 264–266
traders and explorers from, 257–261, m260
World War I and, 321–323
World War II and, 326–331, m329
European Community (EC), 342
Evaluating information, 516–517
Exploration, 257–261, m260
Exports, 389
Ezana, 420

F

Factories, 282, 564
Facts, 262–263
Families, 126, p126
Famines, 98
Farming. See Agriculture
Faruk, King, 386
Ferdinand, Franz (Archduke), 322, p322
Fertile Crescent. See also Mesopotamia
geography of, 97–98, m98
Judaism's birth in, 110–115
legacy of, 96
Fertile soil, 71, 72–73, 120
Feudalism, 216–217, 309, 532–533
Fief, 216
Fiji, p552
First Estate, 288, p289
Floods, 72, 467, 527
Florence, Italy, 236, p236
Flying machines, 238, p238
Folktales, 374
Forbidden City, 505, p505
Forests, 304, 344–345. See also Rain forests
Formosa, 515
Forum, 192
France
and Africa, 437
Napoleon's rule of, 292–293, p293
national anthem of, 290
Ottoman Empire and, 380
before revolution, 288–289, p289

revolution in, 288–292
World War I and, 322
Francis of Assisi, 222
Frank, Anne, 330–331, p331
Franks, 214–215, m215
Freedom, 444. See also Independence
Free enterprise, 597

G

Galileo, 265
Gandhi, Mohandas, 441, 476–479, p478
Ganges River, 464
Gaul, 177
Gautama, Siddharta, 470–471
Gaza Strip, 391
Gazetteer, 24–25, 620–627
Genghis Khan, 501, 504
Geocentric theory, 264
Geography
of Australia, 571–573, m572
of China, 491–495, m493, m494, m505
definition of, 21, p22
of earth, 21–25, m25
of Egypt, ancient, 71–75, m72
of Europe, 209–213, m210
of Fertile Crescent, 97–98, m98
of Greece, ancient, 139–143, m140
of Huang River Valley, 124, m125
of Indus River Valley, 119–120
of Japan, 525, 527, m526
of Korea, 526–527, m526
of Mesopotamia, 97–98, m98
of Middle East, 358–359, m358
Muslims and, 372
of North Africa, 358–359, m358
of Oceania, 574–575, m572
of Rome, ancient, 175–176, m176
of Russia, 299–304, m300
of Southeast Asia, 555–558, m556
of sub-Saharan Africa, 411, 413–417, m412
terms, dictionary of, 618–619
Geothermal energy, 588, p588
Germany
acid rain in, 344–345
depression in, 326
forests in, 344–345
World War I and, 322
World War II and, 327–331
Ghana, 422, 440–441
Gibson Desert, 572
Glaciers, 43, 211, 574
Gladiators, 191, p191

Glasnost, 339
Global grid, 35, m35, m65
Globe Theatre, 250–253
Globes, 6, p6
Glossary, 632–641
Gobi Desert, 501
Gods and goddesses, Greek, 154, p155
Golan Heights, 391
Gold, 32, 423–425, 558
Golden Horde, 306
Gorbachev, Mikhail, 339
Government
culture and, 41–42
definition of, 41
in Greece, ancient, 150–151
of pharaohs, 77
in Rome, ancient, 180–182
in United States, 41–42
values and, 41–42
Grand Canal, 504, p504
Graphs, 486–487, p487
Gravity, 266
Great Barrier Reef, 573
Great Britain
and Africa, 437
Australia and, 580–581
Elgin Marbles and, 170–171
Elizabeth I and, 246–249
India and, 476–477
industrial growth in, 286–287
Industrial Revolution in, 281–285
Kenya and, 441, 443
New Zealand and, 581
Ottoman Empire and, 380
Spain and, 246–247
temperature in, 212, p212
World War I and, 322
World War II and, 328–329
Great-circle routes, 528–529, m528, m529
Great Dividing Range, 572
Great Lakes, m24, p24
"Great Leap Forward," 518
Great Pyramid, 77, 80
Great Rift Valley, 416
Great Sandy Desert, 572
Great Victoria Desert, 572
Great Wall of China, 501, p502–503
Greece, ancient
Acropolis in, 146, p147
agora in, 146, p147
agriculture in, 140
Alexander the Great and, 166–167, m167, p166
art of, 170–171
city-states of, 144–146
colonies of, 141–143, m142
culture of, 235–236
democracy in, 150–153
geography of, 139–143, m140
government in, 150–151
legacy of, 154–160, p160
literature in, 155–156, p156

Parthenon in, 146, *p147*, *p149*, *p151*
philosophy in, 159–160, *p159*
religion in, 154, *p155*
slavery in, 145, 152
sports in, 145, 156–157, *p145*
theater in, 157–159, *p158*
transportation in, 141, *p141*
Greek alphabet, 143, *p143*
Grid maps, 15, 35, *m14, m35*
Gross National Product (GNP), 540, 598–599
Guam, 589, *m604*
Guangzhou, China, 512, *p513*
Guilds, 228, *p228*
Guillemin, Bob, 47, *p47*
Guillotine, 292
Guinea, 441
Gulf of Carpeneria, 572
Gulf Stream, 212
Gutenberg, Johann, 242

H

Hammurabi, 105
Han dynasty, 559
Hanging Gardens of Babylon, 104, 387, *p104*
Hannibal, 184–185, 211, *p185*
Harappa, 120, 122, *m120*
Hargreaves, James, 282
Hatshepsut, 81, *p81*
Hebrews, 110, 111–112, 115. *See also* Jews
Hegira, 366, *p367*
Heliocentric theory, 265
Helots, 145
Hemingway, Ernest, 413
Hemispheres, 7–8, *m8. See also* specific names
Henry the Navigator, 259, 260, 431, *p259*
Hermitage, 308
Herodotus, 80, 148, 419
Hersey, John, 540
Hieroglyphics, 83–84, *p84*
Higgins, Lonny, 591, *p591*
Himalayas, 119–120, 258, 464, 491
Hinduism, 468–470, 473, *m473. See also* Hindus
Hindu Kush Mountains, 119 120, 463
Hindus, 476, 479. *See also* Hinduism
Hiroshima, Japan, 535, 540, *p535*
Historians. *See also* History craft of, 59–60
Etruscans and, 177
and Southeast Asia's first people, 559
Historical maps, 92–93, *m93*
History. *See also* Historians
archaeology and, 58–59
definition of, 58

influence of, 60
primary sources of, 59–60, 294, *p60*
secondary sources of, 60, 294–295
Hitler, Adolf, 326–329, 330, *p327*
Hobson, William, 581
Ho Chi Minh, 563
Holocaust, 330–331
Holy Land. *See* Palestine
Holy wars. *See* Crusades
Homer, 155–156
Horizontal axis, 486
Huang River, 124, 491, 494, *m125, p125*
Huang River Valley, 124–128, 491, *m125*
Hugo, Victor, 280
Hungary, 338, 340
Hunting, 44–45
Hussein, Saddam, 390, *p390*
Hyksos, 80, 142

I

Ibn Battutah, 424
Ice Age, 43, 52, *m44*
Iceland, 211
Iliad, The, 155–156, *p156*
Imperialism
in Africa, 434–437, *p434, m436*
birth of, 433
competition and, 436–437
debate of, 446–447
effects of, 437
in India, 476–478
Imports, 389
Independence
of Australia, 581
of Ghana, 440–441, *p441*
of Guinea, 441
of India, 479
of Kenya, 441, 443
of Korea, 539
of New Zealand, 581
of Pakistan, 479
India. *See also* Indus River Valley
agriculture in, 485
Buddhism in, 470–473, *m473*
cities in, 482
da Gama in, 260
Gandhi and, 478–479, *p478*
Great Britain and, 476–477
Hinduism in, 468–470, 473, *m473*
imperialism in, 476–478
independence of, 479
Mogul Empire in, 475–476, *m475*
Muslims in, 474–475
population of, 482, *m15, p487*
Indonesia, 564, 565
Indus-Ganges Plain, 464

Indus River, 120, 463, 464, *m120*
Indus River Valley, 119–123, *m120*
Industrial Revolution
Catherine the Great and, 308
in Great Britain, 281–285
imperialism and, 434
of Japan, 534, *m535*
missionaries and, 434–435
Ottoman Empire and, 380
slavery and, 432–433, *p432, p433*
spread of, 380
Industry
growth of, 284–285, 286–287
Information
evaluating, 516–517
using, 566–567
Interdependence, 598
Intermediate directions, 9
International Date Line, 496
Intifada, 392
Inventions, 238, *p238*
Iran, 381–382, *p354*
Iraq, 370, 389–391, *p354*
"Iron Curtain," 337
Iron ore, 586
Irrawaddy River, 556, *m556*
Irrigation, 74–75, 98, 361, 495, *p75*
Isis, 85, *p85*
Islam. *See also* Muslims
Arabs and, 364–365
architecture and, 374–375
art and, *p367, p373*
culture of, 370–375
emergence of, 366–367
empire of, 369, 370–371, *m369, m401*
Europe and, 373
Koran and, 367
legacy of, 375
literature and, 373–374
Muhammad and, 365–366
science and, 372–373
in Southeast Asia, 562
spread of, 368
teachings of, 367–368, *p368*
Islands, 139, 211, 525. *See also* specific names
Israel
birth of, 382–383
Palestinian conflict in, 391–392, 393
religious beliefs of, 115
Istanbul, 379, 381
Italian peninsula, 175–176
Italy
and imperialism in sub-Saharan Africa, 437
in Middle Ages, 226
Ottoman Empire and, 380
Renaissance in, 235, 236
World War I and, 322
World War II and, 327
Ivan the Great, 307

J

Jansz, Willem, 579
Japan
Buddhism in, 531
climate of, 527
daily life in, 542–543
economy of, 540–541, *p541*
education in, 541–542, *p542*
feudalism in, 532–533
geography of, 525, 527, *m526*
history of, 530–535, *m535*
Korea and, 531, 538–539
modern, 540–543
natural resources of, 527, *p527*
population density in, *m543*
World War II and, 327, 329, 331, 534
Jayavarman II, King, 560
Jerusalem, 114, *p113*
Jesus of Nazareth, 195–197, *p195, p196*
Jews. *See also* Hebrews; Judaism
Holocaust and, 330–331
Nazis and, 327
Palestine and, 382–383, 391, 393
Jinnah, Mohammad Ali, 479
John I, King of England, 228–229, 248, *p229*
Jordan, *p354*
Joseph (father of Jesus), 194, 195
Journeyman, 228
Judaism. *See also* Jews; Hebrews
Egyptian captivity and, 111–112
legacy of, 114
monotheism and, 113
origins of, 110–111, *m111, m133*
Solomon and, 113–114
Ten Commandments and, 112–113, *p112*
values of, 42
writings of, *p115*
Jutland Peninsula, 210, *m210*

K

Kaaba, 366, *p366*
Kanem-Bornu, 422
Kay, John, 282
Kente cloth, 448–451
Kenya, 441, 443, *m11, p407*
Kenyatta, Jomo, 443
Khanbalik, China, 257
Khmer Empire, 560–561, *m561*
Khomeini, Ayatollah, 382, *p382*
Khufu, 77, 80
Khyber Pass, 464

Kiev, Ukraine, 306
Kiribati, p552
Knights, 217–218, p218
Kola peninsula, 210, m210
Koran, 367–368
Korea
    Buddhism in, 537, p538
    climate of, 527
    dynasties in, 538
    education in, 541–542
    geography of, 526–527,
        m526
    history of, 536–539
    independence of, 539
    Japan and, 531, 538–539
    kingdoms in, 537, m537
    modern, 540–543
    natural resources of, 527,
        p527
Korean peninsula, 526, m526
Korean Strait, 526, m526
Kublai Khan, 257–258, 306,
    504, p504
Kush, 81, 418–420
Kuwait, 386, 390–391

L

Labor, child, 283, p283
Lagoons, 574–575, p575
Lake Eyre Basin, 572
Lake Baikal, 302
Lake Geneva, 211
Lake Victoria, 414
Landforms, 23, 211, 358. See
    also Geography; specific
    types
Language, 46, 127–128, 193,
    p193
Laos, 565
Latins, 177
Latitude, 28, 34–35, m29,
    m34, m37
Latvia, 299, 340
Laws, 105
Lenin, 309, 312, 313, p313,
    p315
Leningrad. See St.
    Petersburg
Leo Africanus, 424–425
Leo III, Pope, 215
Leo X, Pope, 241
Lesotho, p407
Liang Heng, 520
Liberia, p408
Library, using the, 244–245
Line graphs, 486, p487
Lions, 416, p416
Literacy, 482
Literature, 155–156, 248,
    373–374, p156
Lithuania, 299, 340
Liverpool-Manchester
    Railroad, 284–285
Livingstone, David, 434–435,
    436, p435
Loess, 492
London, England, 212, 248,
    326, m14, p212
Longitude, 34–35, m34, m37

Long March, 514, m515, p515
Lords, 216, 217, 228–229
Lotus flower, 73, p73
Louis XVI, King of France,
    288, 290, 291–292
Lower Egypt, 72, 76
Luther, Martin, 240–241, 242,
    243, p241

M

Macedonia, 166
Mackay, Ilva, 440
Madagascar, m11
Madison, James, 153
Magna Carta, 229, 248–249,
    p229
Mainland, 555
Mainland Southeast Asia,
    555, 562
Malay archipelago, 555,
    556–557
Malay peninsula, 555, 562
Malaysia, 565
Mali, 422
Manchuria, 511
Manchus, 511–512
Mandate of Heaven, 499
Mandela, Nelson, 443–444,
    p444
Manors, 217, p217
Mansa Musa, 424, p424
Maoris, 579, 581, p581
Mao Zedong, 514, 518–519,
    520, p514, p520
Maps
    cartogram, 599
    contour, 178–179, m178,
        m179
    distribution, 15, 316–317,
        m15, m316, m317
    global grid, 35, m35
    great-circle routes,
        528–529, m528,
        m529
    grid, 15, m14
    historical, 92–93, m93
    landform, 13, m13
    latitude and longitude,
        34–35, m34, m37
    ocean floor, 576–577,
        m576, m577
    physical, 13, m13
    political, 12–13, m12
    projections, 426–427,
        m426, m427
    relief, 179, m179
    scale, 9–11, 362–363, m10,
        m362, m363
    symbols, 11, m11
    time zone, 496–497, p497
Marathon, 148
Marcos, Ferdinand, 565
Marie Antoinette, 292, p292
Marshall Islands, 591
"La Marseillaise," 290
Martial law, 565
Marx, Karl, 311, 313, p312
Mary (mother of Jesus), 194,
    195

Masai, 411
Mathematics, 372
Mau Mau, 443
Mbuti, 411
Mecca, 364–365, 366
Medicine, 591
Medina, 366–367
Mediterranean Sea, 71, 97,
    139, 141
Meiji, Emperor, 534
Meir, Golda, 379, 382, 391
Mekong River, 556, m556
Melanesia, 574
Melbourne, Australia, 586
Memphis, Egypt, 76
Menam River, 556, m556
Menes, 76, 77
Mercator projections, 427,
    m427
Merchants, 226
Meridians, 35, m35
Meroë, 418–419, p419
Mesopotamia
    agriculture in, 98
    Babylonians in, 104–105,
        106, p104, p106
    civilization of, 100–106
    economy of, 98–99
    environment of, 98
    geography of, 97–98, m98
    legacy of, 106
    Sumerians in, 100–103,
        106
    trade in, 99, p99
Michelangelo, 237, p237
Micronesia, 574
Middle Ages
    cathedrals in, 208, 222,
        223, p208, p223
    Charlemagne in, 215
    Crusades in, 224–226,
        m225
    education in, 220–221
    feudalism in, 216–217, 309
    Franks in, 214–215
    Italy in, 226
    Knights in, 217–218, p218
    legacy of, 229
    manor life in, 217, p217
    marketplaces in, 226, p226
    Roman Catholic Church
        and, 219–223
    time period of, 214
    Vikings in, 215–216
Middle class, 284
Middle East
    agriculture in, 361
    climate of, 359–360
    conflict in, 391–392
    countries in, p354–355
    deserts in, 358–359, p359,
        p365
    geography of, 358–359,
        m358
    history of, 357
    Iran, 381–382
    Israel, 382–383
    modern, 386–392, m387
    nationalism in, 381
    oil in, 387–389, p388

Ottoman Empire in,
    374–380, m380
Persian Gulf War and,
    389–391, p390
political map of, m12
precipitation in, 360,
    m360
religions in, major, m363
Turkey, 380–381
World War I and, 380
Migration, 123
Minerals, 31–32, 493, 586.
    See also specific types
Ming dynasty, 505
Missionaries, 434–435, 473,
    562
Mogul Empire, 475–476,
    m475
Mohenjo-Daro, 120–121,
    121–122, m120, p122,
    p123
Mona Lisa, 238–239, p238
Monarchies, 150, 249, 288
Monasteries, 219–221, p220,
    p492
Mongolia, 511, p461
Mongols, 306
Monks, 219
Monotheism, 113, 115, 369
Monsoons, 466–467, 494,
    m466, p466, p467
Moscow, Russia, 301, 306
Moses, 111–112, p112
Mosques, 374
Mountains
    in Australia, 572
    in China, 463–464
    in Europe, 209, 211
    Indus River Valley and,
        119–120
    in Japan, 525, p526
    in New Zealand, 574
    in Rome, ancient, 176
    in South Asia, 119–120
    in sub-Saharan Africa, 413
Mount Cook, 574
Mount Everest, 464, p464
Mount Fuji, 525, p526
Mount Kilimanjaro, 413
Mount Kosciusko, 572
Mount Olympus, 140, m140
Mount Sinai, 112
Mozambique, p408
Mozambique Channel, 414
Muhammad, 365–366, 369,
    370
Mummies, 86, p86
Murasaki Shikibu, 532
Muslims. See also Islam
    Crusades and, 224–225,
        m225
    culture of, 370–375
    definition of, 224, 367
    geography and, 372
    Hindus and, 476, 479
    in India, 474–475
    Palestine and, 224–225
    in Southeast Asia, 562
Myanmar, 565
Myths, 154, p155

N

Nagasaki, Japan, 535
Najjar, Abdel El-Salam, 393
Napoleon Bonaparte, 292–293, 321, *p293*
Nasser, Gamal Abdel, 386
National Assembly, 291
Nationalism, 321, 381
Nationalists, 514
Natural gas, 32
Natural resources
 of Australia, 586
 definition of, 31
 of earth, 31–33
 of Japan, 527, *p527*
 of Korea, 527, *p527*
 nonrenewable, 32–33, 388
 in North China, 493
 renewable, 32, *p33*
 of Southeast Asia, 558, *p557, p558*
Navigable rivers, 211, 556
Navigation, 259
Nazareth, 195
Nazis, 327, 328–329, *p327*
Needs, 39–40
Nehru, Jawaharlal, 479
Nepal, 484
Neve Shalom/Wahat al Salam (NS/WAS), 393
New Delhi, India, 482
Newfoundland, 29
New Guinea, 579
New Stone Age, 52–57, 71
New Testament, 195–196, *p196*
Newton, Isaac, 266, *p266*
New Zealand
 agriculture in, 588, 589
 history of, 578–581
 independence of, 581
 Maoris in, 579, 581
 modern, 588–589
 mountains in, 574
 people of, 579, 581, *p581*
"Next World," 86
Nicholas II, Tsar, 311
Nile Delta, 73
Nile River
 dams along, 361
 desert and, 72
 Egyptian life and, 71–74
 importance of, 556
 source of, 414, *m72, p73*
Nile River Valley, 71–74, *m72, p73. See also* Egypt, ancient
Nkrumah, Kwame, 440, 441
Nobel Peace Prize, 518
Nomads, 44, 80, 411
Nonrenewable resources, 32–33, 388
No-Rooz, 394–397
North Africa. *See also* Africa
 agriculture in, 361
 climate of, 359–360
 countries in, *p354–355*
 deserts in, 358–359, *p359, p365*

Egypt, ancient, 71
 geography of, 358–359, *m358*
 history of, 357
 modern, 386–392, *m387*
 oil in, 387–389, *p388*
 precipitation in, 360, *p360*
North America, 17
North-Atlantic Drift, 212
North Atlantic Treaty Organization (NATO), 338
North China, 492–493
Northern Hemisphere, 8, *m8, m529*
North European Plain, 211
North Island, 574
North Korea, 536, 539, 543, *p461. See also* Korea
North Pole, 8, 28, *m8*
North Sea, 210
North Vietnam, 563
Novogorod, Russia, 305, 306
Nuns, 219

O

Oases, 364–365, *p365*
Ocean-floor maps, 576–577, *m576, m577*
Oceania
 countries in, *p552–553*
 geography of, 574–575, *m572*
 history of, 578–581
 islands of, 574–575, *m575*
 people of, 579
Oceans, 7, *m7, m23*
Octavian Augustus, 188–189
Odyssey, The, 155–156
Oil
 in Middle East, 387–389, *p388*
 as natural resource, 387–388
 in North Africa, 387–389, *p388*
 OPEC and, 389
 production in various countries, *p32, p388*
 refining, *p389*
 in Saudi Arabia, 32, *p32*
 in Southeast Asia, 558
Old Stone Age, 43–46, 52
Oligarchy, 150–151
Olympic Games, 156–157, 161–164, *p157*
Omar, 374
Opals, 586
Opinions, 262–263
Opium War, 512
Oppression, 306
Oracle bones, 127
Organization of Petroleum Exporting Countries (OPEC), 389
Osiris, 85, *p85*
Ottoman Empire, 379–380, *m380*

Outback, 571, 586–587
Outer China, 491–492

P

Pacific Ocean, 571
Paddies, rice, 495, *p495*
Pages, 218
Pakistan, 479, 484, *p487*
Palestine
 Arabs and, 383, 393
 Christianity's birth in, 194–195
 conflict over, 391–392, 393
 Crusades and, 224–226, *m225*
 Jews and, 382–383, 391, 393
 Muslims and, 224–225
Palestine Liberation Organization (PLO), 391
Palestinians, 383, 391–392, 393
Papyrus, 84
Parallels, 34
Parliament, 248–249
Parthenon, 146, *p147, p149, p151*
Patricians, 181–182, 289
Patrons, 236
Paul (apostle of Jesus), 197–198, *m197*
Pax Romana, 189
Pearl Harbor, Hawaii, 329
Peking. *See* Beijing
Peloponnesian Wars, 165
Peloponnesus, 139
Peninsulas, 139, 210, 555
Per capita income, 541
Pericles, 151–152, *p152*
Permafrost, 303
Perry, Commodore Matthew, 534
Persian Empire, 148–149, 381
Persian Gulf War, 389–391, *p390*
Persian Wars, 146, 148–149, *m148*
Peter (apostle of Jesus), 198
Peter the Great, 307–308, *p308*
Petrarch, 235, 236
Petroleum, 387. *See also* Oil
Pharaohs, 76–77, 86
Philip II, 166
Philippine Islands, 555, 562, 565
Philosophy, 159–160, *p159*
Phoenicia, 141–143, *m142*
Physical maps, 13
Piankhi, 418
Pietà, 237, *p237*
Pilgrimage, 224
Pinyin system, *p493*
Plains, 120, 176, 211, 302
Planets, 265
Plantations, 432
Plateaus, 124, 358
Plato, 160
Plebeians, 181–182

Po Basin, 176
Point of view, 324–325
Poland, 212, 328, 338, *p212*
Polar climates, 28
Polar projections, 427, *m427*
Polis, 144
Political maps, 12–13
Pollution, 107, 344–345, 600–601
Polo, Marco, 257–258, 504, 524
Pol Pot, 563–564
Polynesia, 574
Polytheism, 113
Pope, 198
Population, 209, 482, 484, *m15, p487*
Population density, *m316, m317, m543*
Po River, 176, *m176*
Portugal, 431–432, 437
Poverty, 484
Precipitation, 26, 360, 414, *m360*
Prehistory, 58
Primary sources, 59–60, 294, *p60*
Prime meridian, 8, 35, *m8, m35*
Printing, 241–242, *p242*
Proffitt, Ray, 107, *p107*
Projections, 426–427, *m426, m427*
Protectorate, 386
Protestants, 242
Proverbs of Solomon, 114, *p114*
Punic Wars, 184–185, *m184*
Pyongyang, North Korea, 536
Pyramids, 77, 418–419, *p77, p78–79, p419*
Pyrenees, 211

Q

Qin dynasty, 501
Qing dynasty, 511–512
Questions, asking, 168–169

R

Railroads, 284–285, 301–302
Rainfall. *See* Precipitation
Rain forests, 411, 414, 557, *p557*
Recycling, 600–601
Red Guards, 519–520
Red River, 556, *m556*
Reference section of library, 244
Reformation, 240–243
Refugees, 391, 392, 563, *p564*
Reign of Terror, 292
Relief maps, 179, *m179*
Religion. *See also* Buddhism; Christianity; Hinduism; Shintoism; Islam; Judaism

INDEX

culture and, 42
definition of, 42
in Egypt, ancient, 85–86
in Europe, in 1500s, m243
in Greece, ancient, 154,
    p155
in Middle East, m363
in Old Stone Age, 46
in South Asia, 485, m485
of Sumerians, 101–102
toleration of, 472, 475
in world, m362, p487
Remus, 180
Renaissance
art of, 235–239
beginning of, 235, 236
da Vinci and, 238–239
Elizabethan England and,
    246–249
in Italy, 235, 236
Michelangelo and, 237,
    p237
patrons and, 236
Reformation and, 240–243
spread of, 239
Renewable resources, 32,
    p33
Republic, Roman, 180–182,
    p181
Resources. See Natural
    resources
Reza Khan, 372, 382
Rhine River, 211
Rhodes, 139
Rhodes, Cecil, 434
Rhone River, 211
Rift valley, 416
Rivers
in Egypt, ancient, 71–74,
    m72, p73
in Europe, 211
floods of, 72
Indus River Valley and,
    119–123, m120
in Russia, 301
in Southeast Asia, 556
in sub-Saharan Africa, 416
Roads, Roman, 192, 226,
    p192
Roman Catholic Church. See
    also Christianity
Council of Trent and, 243
Europe and, 219–223
First Estate and, 288
Middle Ages and, 219–223
in Philippine Islands, 562
Reformation and, 240–241,
    242–243
Romance languages, 193,
    p193
Romania, 340
Rome, ancient
aqueducts in, 192
architecture in, 190
Christianity in, 198–199,
    m197
civil war in, 188
Colosseum in, 190–191,
    p191
culture of, 235–236

empire of, 186–189, m187
fall of, 199
forum in, 192
geography of, 175–176,
    m176
growth of, 177, 183
legacy of, 190–193
legend of, 180
people of, 176–177
Punic Wars and, 184–185,
    m184
republic in, 181–182, p181
roads in, 192, 226, p192
Romulus, 180
Roosevelt, Franklin, 329,
    336–343, p330
Rosetta Stone, 84–85, p85
Rurik, 305, 306
Rus, 305–306
Russia. See also
    Commonwealth of
    Independent States;
    Soviet Union
agriculture in, 304
Alexander II and, 310
Catherine the Great and, 308
climate of, 302–303
Commonwealth of
    Independent States
    and, 299, 304
Communism in, 313–314
geography of, 299–304,
    m300
growth of, 305–310, m309
independence of,
Ivan the Great and, 307
Mongols in, 306–307
Peter the Great and,
    307–308, p308
revolution in, 310, 311–313,
    322
serfdom in, 309–310
Slavs in, 305–306
Trans-Siberian Railroad in,
    301–302
vegetation of, 302–303,
    m303, m349
Vikings in, 305–306
World War I and, 322

s

Sahara Desert, 26, 358–359,
    418
Sahel, 415, p415
Said, William, 356
St. Petersburg, 301, 302,
    308, p308
Saints, 222
Salt, 423–425
Salween River, 556, m556
Samurai, 533, p533
Sanctions, 444
Satellite communication,
    596
Saudi Arabia, p32
Savanna, 415
Scale maps, 9–10, 362–363,
    m10, m362, m363
Scandinavia, 212, m13

Scandinavian peninsula, 210,
    m210
"Scarborough Fair," 226, 227
Schweickart, Rusty, 267
Science
in Age of Exploration,
    264–266
Copernicus and, 264–265
da Vinci and, 238
Galileo and, 265
geocentric theory and, 264
heliocentric theory and,
    265
Islamic, 372–373
Newton and, 266
Scientific method, 266
Scipio, 185
Scrapbook, 60, p60
Scribes
Chinese, 127–128, p128
church, 221, p221
definition of, 84
Egyptian, 84
Mesopotamian, 100
Scriptorium, 221, p221
Seas, 140–141
Secondary sources, 60,
    294–295
Second Estate, 289, p289
Seoul, South Korea, 536
Serbia, 322
Serengeti Plain, 413, p413
Serfdom, 309–310
Serfs, 216–217, 309–310
Sermon on the Mount, 196,
    p196
Shah Jahan, 476
Shahs, 382
Shakespeare, William, 248
Shamash, 105
Shang dynasty, 125
Shanghai, China, 514
Sheiks, 365
Shelter, 39–40
Shihuangdi, 501, p506
Shintoism, 530, 531
Shogun, 533, 538
Shotoku, Prince, 531–532
Siberia, 299, 302, m300
Sicily, 175
Silent trade, 425
Silla, kingdom of, 537
Silt, 72–73, 120, 304
Singapore, 565, p553
Sinkiang, 491
Sistine Chapel, 237, p234
Six Day War, 391
Slavery
definition of, 86
in Egypt, ancient, 86, 111
in Greece, ancient, 145,
    152
imperialism and, 432–433,
    p432, p433
in sub-Saharan Africa,
    432–433, p432, p433
in United States, 310
Slavs, 305–306
Small-scale maps, 362–363,
    m362

Socialism, 312
Social pyramids, 86–87, p87
Society, 40
Socrates, 159–160, 371
Solidarity, 339
Solomon, King, 113–114
Song dynasty, 504
Songhai, 424
Sources
credibility of, 384–385
primary, 59–60, 294, p60
secondary, 60, 294–295
South Africa, 32, 443– 444,
    596, p409
South America, 17
South Asia. See also specific
    countries
agriculture in, 485
Buddhism in, 471–473,
    m472, m473
climate of, 466–467, m466
countries in, p460–461
da Gama in, 465
environments of, 467
future of, 485
geography of, 463–466,
    m465, m483
Hinduism in, 470–471, 473,
    m425, m473
India, 474–478, 482, m475
religion in, 485, m485
South China, 493–494
Southeast Asia. See also
    specific countries
agriculture in, 564
Buddhism in, 560, p560
climate of, 557
geography of, 555–558,
    m556
history of, 559–562, m561
Islam in, 562
Khmer empire in, 560–561,
    m561
modern, 563–565, m564
natural resources of, 558,
    p557, p558
vegetation of, 557, p557,
    p558
Southern Hemisphere, 8, m8
South Korea, 536, 539, 543.
    See also Korea
South Pole, 8, 28, m8
South Vietnam, 563
Sovereignty, 581
Soviet Union. See also
    Commonwealth of
    Independent States;
    Russia
Afghanistan and, 484
agriculture in, 314, p314
birth of, 313
collapse of, 304, 336–343
communism in, 313–314,
    336–343
glasnost in, 336–343
Warsaw Pact and, 336–343
World War II and, 328–329
Spain, 246–247, 437, 579,
    p279
Spanish Armada, 246–247

INDEX

Sparta, 144–145, 165
Specialize, 55–56
Sphinx, 80, *p80*
Spices, 558
Spinning jenny, 282
Sports, 145, 156–157, *p145*
Squires, 218
Sri Lanka, 482, *p487*
Stalin, Joseph, 314, 328,
     336–343, *p314, p330*
Stanley, Henry, 435–436,
     p435
Stations, 587, *p587*
Steam engine, 282–283
Steppes, 304, 491
Stevenson, Adlai, 601
Stone seals, 121, *p121*
Strait of Malacca, 557, 562
Straits, 300, 557
Subcontinent, 119, 463
Sub-Saharan Africa. *See also*
     Africa
     countries in, *p406–409*
     deserts in, 415, *m415*
     equatorial, 414–417
     Swahili city-states, 425
     vegetation in, 415, *m415*
     West Africa, 422–425,
        m423
Sultans, 380, 381
Sumer, 101, *m101*
Sumerians, 100–103, 106,
     m101
Summary, writing a, 129
Sun Yat-sen, 513
Surplus, 98
Swahili city-states, 425
Symbols, map, 11, *m11*

T

Taghaza, 423–424
Taiga, 303–304
Taj Mahal, 476, *p476*
The Tale of the Genji, 532,
     p532
Tasman, Abel, 579
Tasmania, 579
Technology, 56–57, 80, 259,
     282, 596, *p57*
Telescope, 265, *p265*
Temperate climates, 28
Temperature
     altitude and, 28
     in Antarctica, 26
     in equatorial Africa, 414
     in London, England, 212,
        p212
     in Pikes Peak, Colorado,
        p28

in Sahara Desert, 26
in Warsaw, Poland, 212,
     p212
in Washington, D.C., *p28*
Ten Commandments,
     112–113, 196, *p112*
Terraces, 495
Territories, 186
Terrorism, 391, 443
Textile industry, 281–282,
     p282
Thailand, 564, 565
Theater, 157–159, 248, *p158*
Thebes, 81
Thermopylae, 148
Third Estate, 289, 291, 292,
     p289
Thoth, 85, *p85*
Thucydides, 165
Tian An Men Square, 521,
     p521
Tiber River, 177, 180
Tibet, 491
Tigris River, 97, 98, 370, *m98*
Timbuktu, 424–425
Time lines, 61
Time zone maps, 496–497,
     p497
Tin, 558
Title cards, 244–245
Tokyo, Japan, 534
Tools, 45, 419–420
Topic sentences, 129
Torah, *p115*
Touré, Sékou, 441, *p441*
Tournaments, *p218*
Trade. *See also* Commerce
     in Baghdad, 371
     in China, 512
     Crusades and, 226
     in Egypt, ancient, 81
     in Mesopotamia, 99, *p99*
     routes, in Age of
        Exploration, 258–259
     silent, 425
     slave, 432–433, *p432,
        p433*
     in Southeast Asia, 559
     in West Africa, 423–425
Tragedies, 158–159
Transportation
     in deserts, 360–361, *p361*
     in Greece, ancient, 141,
        p141
     Industrial Revolution and,
        284–285, *p284*
     railroads, 301–302
     Roman roads, 192, *p192*
Trans-Siberian Railroad,
     301–302

Treaties, 323, 326
Treaty of Versailles, 323,
     326
Trench warfare, 322–323,
     p323
Trent, Italy, 243
Tribunes, 182, *p182*
Tributaries, 120, 124
Trireme, 141, *p141*
Tropical climates, 28, 557
Tropic of Cancer, 28
Tropic of Capricorn, 28
Tsars, 307
Tundra, 303
Turkey, 380–381, 382
Tutankhamen, 82
Twelve Tables, 182
Typhoons, 527
Tyranny, 150

U

Ukraine, 306
United Nations (UN), 337,
     391, 599
United Nations Children's
     Fund (UNICEF), 599
United States
     Constitution of, 153, *p153*
     democracy in, 152
     government in, 41–42
     jury system in, 152, *p152*
     latitude of, *m29*
     NATO and, 338
     recycling in, 601
     sanctions against South
        Africa and, 444
     slavery in, 310
     World War I and, 322–323
     World War II and, 329–330
Untouchables, 469
Upper Egypt, 72, 76
Ural Mountains, 209, 211,
     299, 301, *m300*
Urban II, Pope, 225

V

Valley of the Kings, 81–82,
     p82
Values, 41–42, 126
Vassals, 216
Vatican City, 209, *p279*
Vedas, 469
Vegetation, 24
Venice, Italy, 226, 258
Versailles, 289
Versailles, Treaty of, 323, 326

Vertical axis, 486
Vietnam, 563–564, 565,
     p553
Vietnam War, 563
Vikings, 215–216, 305–306
Virgil, 193
Volcanoes, 574, *p574*
Volga River, 211, 301, 306,
     p302

W

Walesa, Lech, 338
Warlords, 513
Warsaw Pact, 338
Water, bodies of, 23–24, 32
Water mills, 282
Watt, James, 283
West Africa, 422–425
West Bank, 391
West Germany, 337, 340. *See
     also* Germany
Western Ghats mountain
     range, 464
Western Hemisphere, 8, 17,
     m8, p16
Women, 87, 156–157,
     312–313
Working class, 284
World War I, 321–323, 380
World War II, 326–331,
     534–535, *m329*
Writings
     ancient, 100
     Chinese, 127–128, 507–510,
        p128
     Egyptian, 83–84, *p84*
     of Indus people, 121
     of Judaism, *p115*
     Sumerian, 102–103, *p103*

Y

Yalta, 336
Yamato clan, 530, *p531*
Yeltsin, Boris, 340, 596
Yi Sunsin, 538
Yoritomo, 533
Yuan dynasty, 504
Yugoslavia, 341

Z

Zaire River, 414
Zama, Battle of, 185
Ziggurats, 102, 122, *p102*
Zimbabwe, 425, *p414, p425*
Zionists, 382–383

CREDITS